Intelligence and the War against Japan offers the first comprehensive scholarly history of the development of the British secret service and its relations with its American intelligence counterparts during the war against Japan. Richard J. Aldrich makes extensive use of recently declassified files in order to examine the politics of secret service during the Far Eastern War, analysing the development of organisations such as Bletchley Park, the Special Operations Executive and the Office of Strategic Services in Asia. He argues that, from the Battle of Midway in June 1942, the Allies focused increasingly on each other's future ambitions, rather than the common enemy. Central to this theme are Churchill, Roosevelt and their rivalry over the future of empire in Asia. Richard J. Aldrich's cogent, fluent analysis of the role of intelligence in Far Eastern developments is the most thorough and penetrating account of this latterday 'Great Game' yet produced.

RICHARD J. ALDRICH is a senior lecturer in the School of Politics at the University of Nottingham and is Director of the Institute of Asia-Pacific Studies. He was previously a Fulbright Fellow at Georgetown University, Washington. Co-editor of the journal *Intelligence and National Security*, he has produced several books, including *The Key to the South: Britain, the United States and Thailand during the Approach of the Pacific War* (Oxford, 1993).

Intelligence and the War against Japan

Intelligence and the War against Japan

Britain, America and the Politics of Secret Service

Richard J. Aldrich

CAMBRIDGE
UNIVERSITY PRESS

PUBLISHED BY THE PRESS SYNDICATE OF THE UNIVERSITY OF CAMBRIDGE
The Pitt Building, Trumpington Street, Cambridge, United Kingdom

CAMBRIDGE UNIVERSITY PRESS
The Edinburgh Building, Cambridge CB2 2RU, UK   http: // www.cup.cam.ac.uk
40 West 20th Street, New York NY 1011–4211, USA   http: // www.cup.org
10 Stamford Road, Oakleigh, Melbourne 3166, Australia

First published 2000

Printed in the United Kingdom at the University Press, Cambridge

Typeset in Times 10/12pt [wv]

A catalogue record for this book is available from the British Library

Library of Congress cataloguing in publication data
Aldrich, Richard J. (Richard James), 1961–
Intelligence and the War against Japan: Britain, America and the politics of secret
service / Richard J. Aldrich.
     p.   cm.
Includes bibliographical references and index.
ISBN C 521 64186 1 (hardbound)
1. World War, 1939–1945 – Secret service – Great Britain. 2. World War, 1939–
1945 – Secret service – United States. 3. World War, 1939–1945 – Asia.
I. Title.
D810.S7A482 2000
940.54′ 8641 – dc21   99–29697 CIP

ISBN 0 521 64186 1   (hardback)

For Libby
(when even a badger is asleep)

Contents

x   Contents

Plates

Photographs denoted IWM or SUL are reproduced with permission of the Imperial War Museum and Southampton University Library respectively. All other photographs are drawn from the United States National Archives.

Maps

Maps 1–4 are reproduced by permission of *The New York Times* Company. Other maps and charts are from the United States National Archives.

Preface

When V-J Day occurred on 2 September 1945 it marked the unexpected end to a long and bitter struggle against the forces of Imperial Japan. In Allied countries across the world, crowds celebrated in their millions. In London this appeared to be Britain's 'finest hour'. The wartime objectives that Roosevelt and Churchill had framed even before Pearl Harbor, during their famous mid-Atlantic meeting of August 1941, at last seemed to have been attained. The Axis powers had now surrendered unconditionally, with all the good things that most believed would surely flow from this momentous achievement.

But at the highest levels of Government, matters appeared very different. Gazing down upon the crowds celebrating V-J Day from his office in Whitehall, Sir Alexander Cadogan, one of Britain's most senior officials, recorded bitterly: 'London not at its best, with scores of thousands of morons wandering about and doing not much more than obstruct the traffic.' He hoped for a downpour to damp their celebratory fervour. Cadogan had justifiable reason to be downcast for he had just read a paper on Britain's financial outlook. 'It is certainly grim reading! . . . there are terrible times ahead'. Britain was now exhausted and bankrupt as a result of her exertions.[1]

In Whitehall, Westminster and also in Washington, politicians and policymakers had been privately thinking about the end of the war from its very beginning. How would the post-war world be ordered, and what would be the place of the European colonial empires within it? Would the real cost of American assistance against the Axis be the subordination – indeed the eventual dissolution – of empire, as some in the British Cabinet had predicted as early as 1939? In June 1942, the Battle of Midway turned the tide in the Pacific and the sporadic bombing of Tokyo began soon afterwards. The defeat of Japan, though still far distant, was nevertheless only a matter of time and thus attention increasingly turned to the issue of who would control the resources of the vast Asia–Pacific region after V-J Day. 'Secret service' – a term employed herein to denote all forms of clandestine activity – had a central and hitherto little understood role to play in these long-range issues.

This book examines the politics of secret service during the Far Eastern

War, focusing upon Churchill, Roosevelt and their discordant visions of the future of post-war Asia. It also examines the development of British secret service and its institutional relations with its American intelligence counterparts during the Far Eastern War. In the context of the European War, secret service has helped to explain the strategic victory over the Axis. But in the Far Eastern War, where the conflict was truncated by the atomic bomb, the role of secret service was more evenly balanced between the military and the political. Here it is equally significant in offering a 'hidden hand' explanation of the bitter rivalry between London and Washington, as well as Paris and Chungking, over the nature of the post-war settlement. Secret service was an essential catalyst in what proved to be the most acrimonious inter-Allied disputes of the Second World War.

Secret services quickly became key players in the struggle between Churchill and Roosevelt over post-war Asia. Their initial task was to report on the rival plans and ambitions of Allied governments, headquarters and civil affairs staffs. By 1944 this had translated into a barely disguised 'Great Game' to achieve the upper hand in clandestine pre-occupational activities across South East Asia. At times the war against Japan appeared relegated to a sideshow. Senior British and American secret service officers in Asia, many of whom had past commercial associations with the region, needed little encouragement. Informed by an over-optimistic view of how clandestine struggle might influence the future, they sometimes indulged in injudicious activities.

Admiral Lord Louis Mountbatten and his South East Asia Command became the storm centre. Tasked by Churchill with recovering British colonies and rebuilding imperial prestige in Asia, Mountbatten's new headquarters at Kandy in Ceylon hosted at least twelve Allied secret services, each attempting to make their mark. Despite Mountbatten's own boyish enthusiasm for secret service, and his considerable efforts to create effective 'umpire' mechanisms, relations deteriorated. In January 1945, the American 14th Air Force suggested that they might have shot down two British Liberator aircraft carrying intelligence operatives into French Indochina, in circumstances that still remain unclear.

Events on the ground were merely symptoms of wider pathologies. In both Britain and the United States no-one had resolved the issue of secret service control. Viewed as key instruments of national purpose, in a manner that distinguished them from armed forces, London and Washington refused to submit them to proper local control by theatre commanders. Yet secret service was the Second World War's growth industry, with new clandestine departments created almost on a monthly basis. Being neither strictly political, economic or military in nature, they occupied a 'grey area', characterised by perennial disputation over ministerial authority. The longer-term outcomes were also significant, shaping attitudes towards secret service in subsequent decades.

It should be stressed that this is not intended as a study of the detailed impact of intelligence upon Allied strategy and military operations. Some key documentation for that larger subject remains closed to public inspection and when these materials are eventually released, the task awaiting the required team of historians will be very substantial. More emphasis is given to British than American organisations partly because of the relative absence of American secret service in this region before 1942. Widespread American secret service activities after 1942 have been more fully investigated by others, underlining the commendably early development of the study of intelligence history in the United States.

Acknowledgements

It is a pleasure for me to express my deep appreciation to those who have offered kind assistance during the preparation of this book. Many have expended time and energy helping me to understand the work-a-day life of secret service. Sadly not all those who shared their experiences have survived to see the completion of this project. Seminars in which academic historians and past practitioners exchange views have been an especially welcome development. Such groups have the capability to deliver an especially withering type of historical crossfire, combining modern scholarship and vast personal experience, and I am grateful for their special contribution. I am also indebted to the many institutions which have invited me to give papers in particular, Professor Ralph Smith of the School of Oriental and African Studies, London, and all the members of his seminar on the recent history of South East Asia, who provided special encouragement at an early stage.

I have benefitted greatly from the observations of many scholars working in adjoining fields, not least the readers who evaluated the book. I would particularly like to thank Catherine Baxter, Antony Best, John Chapman, Michael Coleman, Alex Danchev, Peter Dennis, David Dilks, Ralph Erskine, John Ferris, M. R. D. Foot, Anthony Gorst, Michael Handel, E. D. R. Harrison, Michael Herman, Andrew Mackay-Johnston, Sheila Kerr, Scott Lucas, Kate Morris, Tim Naftali, Ian Nish, Richard Popplewell, Tilman Remme, David Reynolds, E. Bruce Reynolds, Anthony Short, D. C. S. Sissons, Bradley F. Smith, Michael Smith, David Stafford, Tracy Steele, Anthony Stockwell, Judy Stowe, Philip Taylor, Martin Thomas, Stein Tonnesson, Wesley K. Wark, Donald Cameron Watt, John W. Young and Yu Maochun. At Cambridge University Press, Richard Fisher and his colleagues were remarkably patient and offered well-considered advice. Responsibility for interpretation and errors, however, remains with the author.

An army of archivists, librarians and record officers have been more than helpful and I cannot name them all here. I owe a special thanks to Sally Marks, Dane Hartgrove of the Diplomatic Branch of the United States National Archives, and also to the staff of the Public Record Office at Kew. Nicholas B. Scheetz and Marti Berman at the Lauinger Library provided a fantastic bibliographic resource. Richard Bone and Duncan Stewart at the Foreign Office proved tireless in their efforts. But above all I must thank the legendary John E. Taylor who presides over records that originate with the CIA. This study could not have been completed without his patient guidance.

Colleagues at the University of Nottingham provided a most stimulating atmosphere during the five years over which this study was written. Georgetown University offered a happy home for a visiting research fellow and I would like to thank Rosamund Llewellyn, David Painter, Nancy Berkoff Tucker and Aviel Roschwald for all their kindness. Anthony Cave Brown took enormous pains to encourage me at the very outset of this project, and allowed early inspection of the Donovan papers. E. Bruce Reynolds provided expert and friendly guidance amongst the labyrinthian archives and libraries of the West Coast together with huge encouragement.

Transcripts and maps from Crown-copyright records appear by permission of the Controller of Her Majesty's Stationery Office. Permission to quote from private papers was given by the Liddell Hart Centre for Military Archives and by Lady Avon. Sections of chapters 9 and 13 appeared in an earlier form in the journals *Intelligence and National Security and Modern Asian Studies* respectively and I acknowledge their permission here. This research arose out of an earlier programme of study on Thailand supported by the British Academy. The American dimension would not have been possible without the generous support of a Fulbright Research Fellowship awarded in 1992 presided over by the American Council of Learned Societies and the British American Studies Association. Further help also came from Corpus Christi College, Cambridge, the Franklin D. Roosevelt Library and the Harry S. Truman Library.

There are a few individuals to whom I owe a particularly heavy debt of gratitude. I should like to thank Peter Lowe and Arthur Mawby for awakening my historical interests at the outset. With infinite patience, Anthony Low persuaded me to diversify beyond an interest in Thailand and to consider the virtues of a wider canvas. Christopher Andrew has helped me immeasurably in my efforts to understand the significance of secret service. Friends and family are the victims of academic writing as the hours spent in front of a screen are not spent in their company. Accordingly, I should like to thank my wife Libby, for both fabulous and unfailing support, and Nicholas and Harriet, for many happy and unscheduled distractions.

Abbreviations

A-2	US Air Force Intelligence
ABDA	American–British–Dutch–Australian Command
AFO	Anti-Fascist Organisations [Burmese]
AFHQ	Allied Forces Headquarters
AFPFL	Anti-Fascist People's Freedom League [Burmese]
AGAS	Air–Ground Aid Section [American]
AGFRTS	Air and Ground Forces Resource and Technical Staff [American]
AIR	Air Ministry [British]
AJUF	Anti-Japanese United Front
ALFPMO	Allied Land Forces Para-Military Operations [British]
ALFSEA	Allied Land Forces South East Asia
BAAG	British Army Aid Group, China
BBC	British Broadcasting Corporation
BEW	Board of Economic Warfare [American]
BIA	Burma Independence Army [Burmese]
BIS	Bureau of Investigation and Statistics
BJ	British-Japanese intercepts (colloquially 'Black Jumbos')
BJSM	British Joint Services Mission (Washington)
BNA	Burmese National Army [Burmese]
BP	Bletchley Park
BPF	Burma Patriotic Front
BRUSA	Britain–USA
BSC	British Security Co-ordination, New York [British]
C	Chief of the British Secret Intelligence Service (MI6)
CAS (B)	Civil Affairs Service (Burma)
CBI	China–Burma–India Theater
CD	Chief of the Special Operations Executive
CIA	Central Intelligence Agency [American]
CIBHK	Combined Intelligence Bureau, Hong Kong [British]
CIBM	Combined Intelligence Bureau, Malaya
C. in C.	Commander in Chief

CIC	Counter Intelligence Corps [American]
CICB	Counter-Intelligence Combined Board
CIGS	Chief of the Imperial General Staff [British]
CLI	Corps Léger d'Intervention [French]
CO	Colonial Office [British]
COI	Co-ordinator of Information (predecessor of OSS)
COIS	Commanding Officer Intelligence Staff, Singapore
COS	Chiefs of Staff [British]
COSSEA	Chiefs of Staff to South East Asia
CPA	Chiefs Political Adviser
CSDIC	Combined Services Detailed Interrogation Centre [India]
CT	China Theatre
CX	Prefix for a report originating with SIS
D/F	Direction finding
DGER	Direction générale des études et reserches [French]
DIB	Director of the Intelligence Bureau [India]
DMI	Director of Military Intelligence [British]
DMO	Directorate of Military Operations [British]
DNI	Director of Naval Intelligence [British]
D of I	Director of Intelligence
DSO	Defence Security Officer
ENIGMA	German rotor cryptograph
ESD 44	Economic Survey Detachment/Group 44
FBI	Federal Bureau of Investigation [American]
FDR	Franklin D. Roosevelt
FE	Far East
FEB	Far Eastern Bureau, the PWE mission in India [British]
FECB	Far Eastern Combined Bureau, Singapore [British]
FESS	Far Eastern Security Service, Singapore [British]
FETO	Far Eastern Theater of Operations
FO	Foreign Office [British]
Force 136	SOE in the Far East [British]
G-2	Military Intelligence [American]
GBT	Gordon–Bernard–Tan network in Indochina
GC&CS	Government Code and Cipher School (later GCHQ) [British]
GCHQ	Government Communications Headquarters [British]
GHQ	General Headquarters
GOC	General Officer Commanding
GOI	Government of India
GSOI	General Staff Officer Intelligence
HF/DF	High frequency/Direction finding

IB	Intelligence Bureau [India]
IBT	India–Burma Theater
ICP	Indian Communist Party
IIS	Institute for International Studies
IJA	Imperial Japanese Army
IMFTE	International Military Tribunal for the Far East
INA	Indian National Army
IPI	Indian Political Intelligence
ISLD	SIS/MI6 in the Middle East and the Far East [British]
ISUM	Intelligence Summary
JCS	Joint Chiefs of Staff [American]
JIC	Joint Intelligence Committee
JICPOA	Joint Intelligence Committee Pacific Ocean Area
JIFs	Japanese Inspired Fifth-Columnists
JN-25	Japanese Naval Operational Code
JPS	Joint Planning Staff [British]
JSM	Joint Services Mission, Washington [British]
KMT	Koumintang, Chinese nationalist party
Magic	Decrypts of Japanese diplomatic material
MCP	Malayan Communist Party
MEW	Ministry of Economic Warfare [British]
MI1c	Military section of SIS
MI2c	London military intelligence section dealing with Asia
MI5	Security Service [British]
MI6	Secret Intelligence Service (SIS) [British]
MI8	Army Y interception
MI9	Escape and Evasion [British]
MID	Military Intelligence Division [American]
MI(R)	Military Intelligence, Research
MIS	Military Intelligence Service [American]
MO	Morale Operations Branch, OSS [American]
MOI	Ministry of Information [British]
MPAJA	Malayan People's Anti-Japanese Army
MU	Maritime Unit Branch, OSS [American]
NEI	Netherlands East Indies
NKVD	People's Commissariat for Internal Affairs, predecessor of KGB [Soviet]
NID	Naval Intelligence Division [British]
NSA	National Security Agency
O of B	Order of Battle
ONI	Office of Naval Intelligence [American]
Op-20-G	American naval codebreaking organisation

ORI	Office of Research and Intelligence (post war R&A)
OSS	Office of Strategic Services [American]
OTP	One-time pad cipher system
OWI	Office of War Information [American]
PHPS	Post Hostilities Planning Staff [British]
POA	Pacific Ocean Area
'Purple'	American name for the Japanese Type B cryptograph
PWE	Political Warfare Executive [British]
R&A	Research and Analysis Branch, OSS [American]
RII	Resources Investigation Institute
RSS	Radio Security Service
SA	Service d'action [French]
SAC	Supreme Allied Commander
SACEUR	Supreme Allied Command Europe
SACO	Sino-American Cooperative Organisation
SACSEA	Supreme Allied Commander South East Asia
SAS	Special Air Service [British]
SCIU	Special Counter Intelligence Unit
SD	State Department
SEAC	South East Asia Command
SEATIC	South East Asia Translation and Interrogation Centre, SEAC
SHAEF	Supreme Headquarters Allied Expeditionary Force
SHAPE	Supreme Headquarters Allied Powers Europe
SI	Secret Intelligence Branch, OSS [American]
SIFE	Security Intelligence Far East (MI5/SIS V) [British]
sigint	Signals intelligence
SIS	Secret Intelligence Service (SIS) [British]
SLFEO	Service Liaison Français d'Extrême Orient [French]
SO	Special Operations Branch, OSS (American)
SO1	SOE Propaganda [British]
SO2	SOE Special Operations [British]
SOE	Special Operations Executive [British]
SoS	Secretary of State
SR	Service de reseignements [French]
SRH	Special Research History [American]
SSU	Strategic Services Unit [post-war OSS]
SWPA	South West Pacific Area
Ultra	British classification for signals intelligence
WEC	Wireless Experimental Centre, India [British]
WO	War Office [British]
W/T	Wireless Telegraphy

| X-2 | Counter-intelligence Branch, OSS [American] |
| Y | Wireless interception, usually of a low-level variety |

ADDITIONAL ABBREVIATIONS USED IN REFERENCES

BDEE	Ashton and Stockwell, *British Documents on the End of Empire*
BE	Bank of England
BL	British Library
BLPES	British Library of Political and Economic Science
BRO	Brotherton Library, University of Leeds
BUL	Birmingham University Library
CCC	Churchill College, Cambridge
CMH	Center for Military History, US Army War College
CUL	Cambridge University Library
DAFP	*Documents on Australian Foreign Policy*
DP	Donovan Papers
FDRL	Franklin D. Roosevelt Library, Hyde Park, New York
FRC	Federal Record Centre, Suitland, Maryland
FRUS	*Foreign Relations of the United States*
HIWRP	Hoover Institute on War Revolution and Peace, Stanford
HSTL	Harry S. Truman Library, Independence, Missouri
INS	*Intelligence and National Security*
IOLR	India Office Library and Records, Blackfriars, London
IWM	Imperial War Museum
JRL	John Rylands Library, University of Manchester
LC	Library of Congress
LHCMA	Liddell Hart Centre for Military Archives, Kings College, London
LL	Special Collections, Lauinger Library, Georgetown University
MML	MacArthur Memorial Library, Norfolk, Virginia
NA	National Archives, Washington DC
NAM	National Army Museum, London
NY	New York
PRO	Public Record Office, Kew Gardens, Surrey
PWTM	*Principal War Telegrams and Memoranda*
RG	US Record Group
PSF	President's Secretaries Files
SFI	H. Tinker (ed.), *The Struggle for Independence*
SUL	Southampton University Library

TOP	N. Mansergh (ed.), *The Transfer of Power*
UP	University Press
USNA	US National Archives

1 Introduction: intelligence and empire

> Foreign Secretary. What do you say? I am lukewarm and therefore looking for guidance. On the whole I incline against another S.O.E.–O.S.S. duel, on ground too favourable for that dirty Donovan.
>
> Winston Churchill to Anthony Eden, April 1945.[1]

In early April 1945, Winston Churchill requested guidance from his Foreign Secretary, Anthony Eden. The subject of his enquiry, 'dirty Donovan', was none other General William J. Donovan, the Director of the America's new wartime secret service, the Office of Strategic Services (OSS). Donovan was the 'founding father' of OSS and also of its direct successor, the Central Intelligence Agency (CIA), where his statue now dominates the entrance to the headquarters building at Langley, Virginia. Donovan had proved himself a most sincere and valuable friend to Britain from the very outset of the Second World War, championing American intervention against the Axis in the inner circles of Roosevelt's Cabinet in 1940 and 1941.[2] Moreover, the wartime years are viewed by most historians as a period during which an increasingly close and co-operative relationship was constructed between the intelligence communities of Britain and the United States.[3] Prominent diplomatic historians have identified these links as being 'at the heart of what made the Anglo-American tie so different from other alliances'.[4] Donovan was central to this process, so it is curious to find Churchill referring to Donovan in 1945 with such unequivocal distaste.

Churchill's outburst was provoked by clandestine rivalry over the future of China. In microcosm, this matter illustrates the complex wartime connections between the politics of secret service and the politics of empire, explored at length in this book. A vigorous dispute over secret service activity had arisen in the area around Hong Kong. Churchill had first sought the advice of Lord Selborne, the minister responsible for Britain's wartime sabotage organisation, the Special Operations Executive (SOE). Selborne had explained that the American-controlled China Theater was attempting to exclude the British SOE mission in China. Selborne's resources were stretched elsewhere, and he saw no military reason for SOE to intrude 'where we are not wanted'.

1

However he conceded the political aspect, noting that if SOE were present in the region 'our recovery of Hong Kong and British Borneo might well be facilitated'.[5]

Churchill also consulted Oliver Stanley, the Secretary of State for Colonial Affairs. His attitude was very different, declaring 'a major interest' in the continued activities of Britain's SOE in China, and insisting that SOE's presence close to Hong Kong was of the 'greatest importance'.[6] SOE, Stanley explained, could play a crucial role in facilitating the smooth recovery of the Crown Colony of Hong Kong into British, rather than Chinese or American hands, at the end of the war. For Stanley, SOE constituted a body of shock-troops which would physically begin the recovery of British imperial territories throughout the Far East, even before the moment of Japan's surrender. Churchill therefore decided to defend the presence of Britain's SOE in the American-dominated China Theater. Accordingly, Churchill's outburst was provoked by two related subjects, both of which concerned him passionately throughout his life: intelligence and empire.[7]

This study explores the interconnection between these two themes during the Far Eastern War, focusing particularly on Anglo-American colonial controversies.[8] Accordingly, it deals with the high politics of British and American secret services in Asia, rather than cataloguing the low-level complexities of individual operations. It suggests that the intelligence failures of 1937 to 1941 owed much to a colonial *mentalité,* which prompted the West to focus on internal colonial stability rather than external threats, and also encouraged the underestimation of Japan. Thereafter, it suggests that the course of the Far Eastern War witnessed the development of separate and divergent 'foreign policies' by numerous secret services, some poorly controlled. Their directors, whether British, American, Chinese, French or Dutch, were increasingly preoccupied, not with the war against Japan, but with mutual competition to advance national interest in the fluid situation created by Japan's dramatic southward expansion of December 1941.

The important role of secret service within the wider framework of American wartime anti-colonialism has often been alluded to. Donald Cameron Watt has noted how Roosevelt was receiving regular American intelligence reports about a European colonial conspiracy in South East Asia: 'Nothing could have been more calculated to make Roosevelt's flesh creep', observing that the roots of this lay in 'an inter-intelligence agency intrigue . . . within the British led South East Asia Command Area'. Bradley F. Smith, in his path-breaking study of OSS, has noted the survival of a 'huge' SOE organisation in Asia beyond V-J Day, explaining 'that London used the Southeast Asian SOE contingent as a catchall organisation for those who would do the work of reestablishing British authority in the area'. William Roger Louis has also remarked in his discussions of decolonisation that intelligence 'is a topic worth pursuing'.[9] But despite these invaluable pointers, the links between intelligence and empire have not been substantially explored.[10]

Important recent studies have not demonstrated a consensus about the significance of secret service matters. Xiaoyuan Liu's detailed study of Sino-American wartime relations makes not a single reference to clandestine organisations, in contrast to earlier work by Michael Schaller.[11] Equally, recent accounts of relations between Churchill and Roosevelt have chosen to ignore secret service, despite the fact that Roosevelt shared some of Churchill's extreme enthusiasm for the subject; indeed many modern studies of the wartime 'special relationship' disregard this sphere altogether.[12] Others, by contrast, regard it as highly important, but these differences of approach are rarely articulated or explained.[13]

Accordingly, this book moves between two large but barely connected bodies of literature: one on Allied diplomacy during the Far Eastern War, the other dealing with Allied intelligence. The wider framework, developed by the late Christopher Thorne, is especially important.[14] This book also seeks to provide an antidote to the official history of SOE in the Far East, which presented a misleadingly anodyne interpretation of its central purposes. This official study focused narrowly on SOE's military activities, neglecting the political dimensions, which arguably became the dominant concern of its senior officers.[15]

Official history has greatly advanced our knowledge of wartime secret service. As early as 1966 M. R. D. Foot's official history, *SOE in France*, demonstrated how the history of special operations should be done. In the 1980s, the complex challenge of explaining the impact of secret intelligence upon wartime strategy and operations was met by Sir Harry Hinsley and his collaborators in a magisterial series.[16] But the regrettable decision not to extend this series to cover the Far Eastern War has left us with a vast lacuna. This anomaly inevitably prompted speculation about the motives underpinning that decision.[17] Whatever the reason, it has denied many a place in history.[18]

In contrast, the treatment of the American secret service activities during the Far Eastern War has been much more satisfactory. American secret service records were declassified in the 1980s, ten years before equivalent British papers, allowing American historians to combine consideration of the written records with interviews with surviving practitioners. Indeed, the work on MacArthur's South West Pacific Area, and Nimitz's Pacific Ocean Area has been very comprehensive and accordingly this book restricts itself to the war in Asia, and does not attempt to stray into the Pacific.[19] Nevertheless, the corpus of American work also contains distortions. For understandable reasons, disproportionate attention has been devoted to Indochina. The assistance given to Ho Chi Minh by the OSS, though a natural extension of Roosevelt's anti-French and anti-colonial policies, is a beguiling subject for a country that suffered more casualties in Vietnam than in the First World War.[20] But this can only be properly understood when it is placed in the context of a vigorous and broadly consistent OSS anti-colonial policy across all of Asia.[21] Meanwhile, the work of the French and Dutch secret services remains largely a cipher.[22]

The politics of empire

Wartime conflict between British and American secret services in Asia mirrored political disagreement at the highest level between Roosevelt and Churchill. While Churchill envisaged restored European colonial control in post-war Asia, Roosevelt desired rapid independence for colonies, in some cases under temporary United Nations tutelage, and the end of the British Empire system of preferential trade. Yet neither Churchill nor Roosevelt was prepared to allow their disagreements over Asian issues to frustrate their friendship, or their shared sense that the European War should take priority. The result was silence at the highest level on many sensitive questions. Both found it convenient to postpone the moment when they would have to confront the full scale of their disagreements.

Churchill was the worst offender. He repeatedly frustrated attempts by the Foreign Office to tackle Roosevelt on the question of the post-war status of French Indochina, a Rooseveltian obsession. 'Do not raise this before the presidential election, the war will go on for a long time', minuted Churchill in March 1944, in response to an urgent plea from the Foreign Office.[23] Roosevelt later complained to Eden that he had discussed Indochina twenty-five times with Churchill, adding, 'Perhaps discussed is the wrong word. I have spoken about it twenty-five times. But the Prime Minister has never said anything.' In March 1944 Churchill explicitly instructed his officials to 'adopt a negative and dilatory attitude' on these questions.[24] A similar silence was preserved on Thailand, due to Churchill's secret territorial designs on Thailand's southern peninsula, the Kra Isthmus. Roosevelt became equally cautious about raising the matter of Indian independence, which he felt should flow naturally from the provisions on self-determination in the Atlantic Charter, the Allied declaration of war aims, agreed in August 1941. But by 1942, he understood that attempts to discuss India simply made Churchill angry and intractable. Thereafter, silence prevailed, and in the meantime each leader attempted to inch ahead within their own areas of strategic control.

Consequently, the wartime management of these awkward questions was often passed to reluctant subordinates in the Foreign Office and the State Department, who were equally loath to articulate the full extent of their discord on Asia. Meanwhile they watched each other and waited. Allied intelligence organisations, instead of being briefed upon agreed joint post-war planning, were required to fill the silence by reporting things that might be indicative of each other's future intentions in Asia. Therefore, the American OSS, and the British SOE and its sister service, the British Secret Intelligence Service (SIS) – three key agent-based secret services operating in Asia – and even signals intelligence, were increasingly directed towards political and economic targets of an inter-Allied nature.[25] Their activities in turn exacerbated tensions at higher levels.

Secret services were rapidly drawn into the arena of foreign policy-making because, as they discovered, no military action was without political consequences. Moreover in the absence of agreed joint long-term planning, British and American commanders, their political advisers, propaganda bureaux and intelligence agencies gained an exaggerated impression of the extent to which their wartime military control would determine the post-war settlement. Operational pressures also required the rapid settlement of post-war Asian questions. The inseparability of immediate military questions from long-term political issues is nowhere more clearly underlined than in the wartime despatches of John Paton Davies.

Davies was Chief Political Adviser to General Stilwell, Commander of the American China–Burma–India (CBI) Theater and a central figure in the politics of secret service in CBI. In December 1943, soon after the formation of Mountbatten's neighbouring South East Asia Command (SEAC), he prepared a commentary on 'Anglo-American Cooperation in East Asia' which went to both Stilwell and OSS in Washington.[26] It explored, with remarkable prescience, the potential for Anglo-American political wrangling as the Japanese were driven back across Asia. Davies asserted that to push Japan out of Burma and Malaya was, at the same time, unavoidably to assist in the restoration of British colonial rule, adding: 'Why should American boys die to repossess colonies for the British and their French and Dutch satellites?' Moreover, Britain was secure in the knowledge that the Soviet Union was bearing the brunt of the war in Europe and the United States was taking the strain in the Pacific. This left Britain free to concentrate on the recovery of its empire in the Mediterranean, South and South East Asia. He continued:

The re-acquisition and perhaps expansion of the British Empire is an essential undertaking if Britain is to be fully restored to the position of a first class power. Therefore reconquest of the Empire is the paramount task in British eyes. The raising of the Union Jack over Singapore is more important to the British than any victory parade through Tokyo . . . This interpretation does not impute heroic qualities to the British Government; it does imply that it has lost none of its political acumen.

The display of American military strength in India and South East Asia was a problem for an empire whose façade, as British officers frankly admitted, was visibly crumbling. He noted: 'We embarrass them by our very presence, for the fact that it is necessary for us to be here reflects on British prestige.' The presence of Americans working in the fields of propaganda or civil affairs in India made the British 'acutely apprehensive lest there occur some ingenuous American outburst on the subject of liberty for colonial peoples'.

OSS was influenced by Davies' prescient analysis of the Mountbatten approach to limiting the damage inflicted by the American presence. British tactics were to accept American assistance 'for they have no alternative', but subsequently to consolidate with the United States on grounds of efficient co-operation and then, 'by dominating the integrated partnership, bring us into line with their policy and action'. Britain repeatedly tried to apply these techniques to OSS and to American propaganda bureaux, but in vain. Instead Washington followed Davies, who urged the maintenance of 'a purely American identity' in all things.

A 'purely American identity' was of even greater importance, Davies argued, in areas which had not previously been under the formal control of European empires. A highly visible commitment to anti-imperialism was essential to American credibility in the independent countries of post-war Asia such as China and Thailand, where the United States cherished her own ambitions. Therefore the danger of being associated with the British was a problem with the *widest possible* ramifications for the future of the American position in all of post-war Asia. Davies put it succinctly: 'The Chinese and later the Thais, will feel – as many Chinese already do – that we have aligned ourselves with the British in a ''whiteocracy'' to reimpose western imperialism in Asia.'[27] To many, including Davies, the new secret services, including OSS and its sister propaganda organisation, the Office of War Information (OWI), were the ideal instruments to deal with these awkward politico-military questions and to help maintain the crucially separate American identity.

There were more specific reasons why secret services were quickly drawn into political controversies. First, from the outset, the wily nationalist and communist resistance movements in Japanese-occupied areas demanded political assurances about the future in return for co-operation with Allied intelligence. British and American secret services found themselves bidding against each other with policy statements, often extempore in nature, in order to obtain indigenous agents and influence. Such policy statements confronted sensitive political issues on which the diplomats had contrived to remain silent. Secondly, contact with senior resistance figures, in some cases clearly the embryonic political leaders of post-war Asia, offered irresistible opportunities.

Thirdly, and arguably most importantly, rivalry was exacerbated by the nature of the personnel recruited during the rapid wartime expansion of secret service. The urgent need for regional expertise and personnel fluent in obscure languages led them to recruit predominantly from the businessmen, financiers, traders, colonial officials and policemen active in Asia before 1941. Many of these men were keenly interested in the post-war survival or, alternatively, the demise of the European colonial economic system in Asia, along with its tariffs and preferential trade agreements. This influx of new personnel occurred at all levels. The first overall Far Eastern Director of SIS, Godfrey Denham, was a director and later Chairman of Anglo-Dutch Plantations Ltd, while the Far Eastern director of SOE appointed in 1942, Colin Mackenzie, was a Director of J. & P. Coats Limited, with extensive regional textile interests. Until Mackenzie's arrival, the most senior SOE figure had been John Keswick, a Director of the China trading conglomerate Jardine Matheson Limited. As the war progressed, SOE began to resemble empire trade in khaki. Equally, many American OSS officers had previously worked for Texaco or Westinghouse.[28]

Empire interest within OSS, SIS and SOE met with different reactions from officials in London and Washington. In London, Anthony Eden and the Foreign Office had entertained reservations about the sabotage organisation, SOE, even from its formation in 1940.[29] They had found requests for political declarations to assist SOE in their contact with various resistance groups, such as the Free Siamese (Thais), awkward and tiresome. In August 1944, Sir Maurice Peterson, a senior official overseeing Far East policy confronted Mackenzie, the Head of SOE in the Far East. Peterson was not a sympathetic figure and was known to Foreign Office juniors as 'Uncle Beastly'. But he had also worked closely with both SOE and the Political Warfare Executive (PWE), and was well placed to fire penetrating questions at Mackenzie.[30] Peterson saw limited military value in SOE operations, and asked what the real motives were. Peterson recorded:

I had a long conversation last night with Mr Mackenzie (in private life director of J. and P. Coats) who is, I understand, head of SOE in SEAC . . . I dealt faithfully with the Free Siamese Movement and said I hoped we had heard the last of it. Mr Mackenzie was reduced to defending it on grounds of post-war trade.[31]

The re-establishment of British influence in post-war Asia was also top priority for SOE's Director of Overseas Operations, the Australian Colonel (later Brigadier) George F. Taylor, based at the SOE London headquarters in Baker Street. From mid-1943, the energetic Taylor was effectively Chief of Staff of SOE, superintending all its operations outside Europe. Passionately concerned with empire, he travelled constantly to Cairo and the Far East.[32] When the British clandestine presence in China and Indochina became major issues in the London Joint Intelligence Committee towards the end of the war, it was Taylor who was determined 'to hold the floor and do all the talking'.[33]

In September 1944, Taylor visited the Foreign Office for conversations with John Sterndale Bennett, Head of the Far Eastern Department, regarding a bitter Anglo–American–French dispute over operating boundaries for clandestine operations in Asia. Taylor advocated a tough line, explaining that SOE's permissions in Asian theatres related directly to attempts to restore British influence throughout the region.[34] Taylor interpreted this dispute

as being part of an American plan to squeeze us altogether out of Indochina and Siam . . . and to relegate us to a comparatively minor role in the whole Far Eastern war. He felt that the Chiefs of Staff might look at it from a purely military point of view without giving full weight to the disastrous political results which could ensue if such intentions on the part of the United States succeeded . . . He hoped that the Foreign Office would take up the political point strongly.

Taylor then explained that SOE could compensate for the fact that Britain did not have large conventional forces in places such as China. He asked Sterndale Bennett, 'whether, with a view to counteracting this American plan, if it existed, it would not be a good thing to intensify SOE activities in Siam, Indochina and even on the South China coast [Hong Kong]'. Taylor's argument was that even if Britain was relegated to a minor role, 'our share in the freeing of these territories would at least be realised locally'. The Foreign Office had traditionally been unhappy about clandestine operations of any kind, especially as a device to steal a march on Washington, and Sterndale Bennett became evasive. He suggested that this was a military matter and a question for the Chiefs of Staff alone. Taylor, however insisted that it was a political question and, to Sterndale Bennett's alarm, proposed approaching the strategic planning teams to have his ideas inserted into a brief for a forthcoming Churchill–Roosevelt summit at Quebec in mid-September 1944. Alarmed, Sterndale Bennett told Taylor bluntly that the Foreign Office, 'did not favour the intensification of SOE activities in Indochina, Siam and South China if this was purely intended to forestall the Americans. The friction which might be created might not be worthwhile.'

But fundamentally the Foreign Office shared Taylor's deep concerns about Roosevelt's future plans and accepted that all might not go well at Quebec. They were also increasingly aware of the activities of the American OSS. So Sterndale Bennett added that, after very careful consideration, they might support SOE activities 'to mitigate the effects locally of any decision which might be taken adversely to our general interests at the forthcoming meeting with the President'. Plausible deniability for any such activity was the key. If plans could be presented as military in purpose then 'naturally' the Foreign Office would 'be inclined to consider them favourably'. This whole conversation 'was very tentative . . . and we left it at that for the moment'.[35]

Such discussions on the underlying purpose of SOE activities in Asia were extremely rare. Taylor was not inclined to suffer restraint, while the Foreign Office was uncomfortable with Taylor's pronounced interest in political matters. In contrast, SOE received strong encouragement from the Colonial Office, who shared SOE's view of the political importance of pre-occupational activities and regarded Eden as unduly deferential to American anti-colonial sentiments. The Colonial Office repeatedly encouraged SOE and made available many of its personnel to facilitate operations in Asia. Equally, SOE enjoyed good relations with the British imperial network in Africa.[36]

The politics of secret service

Insoluble political differences over the future of empire, in which the actors were sometimes personally interested, constitute the most powerful explanation of political antagonism between Allied secret services during the Far Eastern War. But the situation was vastly complicated by cross-cutting national and inter-allied disputes over the organisation and control of expanding secret services. Each country began the war with several long-established secret services and continued to launch new ones with alarming frequency throughout the war. Inevitably, in London and Washington, and later in regional centres such as Algiers, Cairo and Delhi, there ensued unseemly internal struggles over empires of a different type: the new and uncharted areas of burgeoning secret service bureaucracy.

It cannot be pretended that contests for bureaucratic power were the sole preserve of wartime government, or of secret services. Throughout the twentieth century, in both Whitehall and Washington, ministries and departments were in constant competition for resources and for control of policy. As a former Cabinet Secretary once observed, the first thing to remember about a central government is that it is 'merely a federation of departments'.[37] But the advent of war had transformed the bureaucratic landscape completely. In the past there had been incremental, sometimes almost imperceptible, shifts of power, with disputes tending to focus on particular issues that engaged the remit of more than one department. But now the scale of change was entirely different, with the complete re-allocation of functions, and the overnight creation of whole new ministries with ill-defined rights and permissions. Government now dealt with subjects in which, hitherto, it had not concerned itself. Established departments met these problems by launching new sub-sections. The British Foreign Office had twelve departments in 1940 and twenty-seven departments by 1942. In capital cities and regional centres, hotels, schools and prisons were appropriated to accommodate new organisations and temporary buildings disfigured open spaces.[38]

In the United States, Donovan's new OSS organisation outgrew its initial building in Washington within months and the nearby National Health Institute was evicted from their offices to make room for it. The previous occupants expressed their annoyance by bequeathing them a laboratory full of virus-laden animals on the top floor. OSS continued to grow, expanding into vast temporary wooden buildings as its personnel mushroomed from a few hundred in 1942 to 13,000 by 1944. Plywood was the ubiquitous material that characterised bureaucratic growth. Graham Greene captures this well in his description of the Ministry of Information, based in the requisitioned Senate House at the University of London:

He opened the door of his dark room. It had been built of plywood in a passage, for as the huge staff of the Ministry accumulated like a kind of fungoid life – old divisions sprouting daily new sections which then broke away and became divisions and spawned in turn – the five hundred rooms of the great university block became inadequate: corners of passages were turned into rooms, and corridors disappeared overnight.[39]

Meanwhile, outside Oxford, at Bletchley Park, workmen were busy erecting what would become perhaps the most famous temporary structures of the war, the numbered huts for the greatly increased staff required by the Government Code and Cypher School (GC&CS).

The politics of expanding wartime secret service quickly became notorious. Many organisations competed over new and ill-defined responsibilities. By 1939, secret and semi-secret service encompassed a broad interrelated spectrum of activities including propaganda, deception, escape and evasion, and economic warfare, as well as the more traditional forms of sabotage and espionage. In London, the ministries that had traditionally owned overseas policy, such as the Foreign Office and the Board of Trade, now found themselves rudely jostled by the new ministries, such as Economic Warfare, with vague responsibilities for everything from trading with the enemy to radio broadcasts. These disputes were difficult to ignore, for many new protagonists enjoyed direct access to Churchill or Roosevelt, and used this to press their case. Donovan's entrée to key members of Roosevelt's inner circle, such as Henry Stimson, Frank Knox and Henry Morgenthau, was especially alarming to officials in wartime Washington.

Senior figures resented the time spent adjudicating between these new shadow organisations with their ill-defined remits. The diary of Sir Alexander Cadogan, Eden's Permanent Under-Secretary at the Foreign Office, perhaps the most lucid account of wartime Whitehall, reveals the nature of these problems, which had begun to dog him even in 1939:

R. A. B. [Rab Butler] about administrative questions. I can't stand these. I am suddenly told that a Department in the Ministry of Obfuscation has to be reorganised: it must come back 'under control' of the Ministry of Circumlocution. But there is a great difficulty, as the Head of the Department – Colonel Shufflebottom – ought not to be there, and I ought to substitute Mr Piffkins. (Other people tell me this is a ramp, and that the real man is Nuffkins.) I don't know S., or P., (or even N.). I can't grasp what they are supposed to be doing. I have no data to go upon: how the Hell can I decide? But I was at it all day – and work accumulating.[40]

As this extract makes clear, matters were not helped by the fact that these new areas of unconventional warfare were not widely understood. The arcane terminology was baffling and was sometimes employed to deliberately confuse.

Yet Cadogan's diary is also eloquent on the genuine need for new secret service organisations at the outset of the war. In Britain this was due to alarming inadequacies of the traditional overseas service, SIS. The extended bureaucratic turmoil that accompanied the expansion of British secret and semi-secret activities in the period 1938-42 can be explained in two ways. Firstly, by the long-term neglect and chronic underfunding of SIS in the inter-war years, necessitating rapid expansion and repeated reform of secret service activities from 1938. SIS had encountered some catastrophic failures during 1938 and 1939 and minsters were looking elsewhere to locate new initiatives. Cadogan noted as late as 25 May 1940: 'We agree to overhaul SIS, which wants it BADLY!'[41] Secondly, and just as important, was the response of Sir Stewart Menzies, the new Head of SIS, to these attempts at reform. By deflecting attempts at a thorough recasting of SIS in 1939–40, he missed the opportunity of creating a centralised and well-organised body, dealing with a full range of secret activities, under direct Foreign Office control. Indeed, as an intelligence officer of the old school, he initially even refused to serve as a member of the Joint Intelligence Committee (JIC), preferring SIS's traditional aloofness from the rest of Whitehall.[42] Churchill, not yet Prime Minster when Menzies took up his post in late 1939, was right to be uneasy about the appointment.[43]

In Washington too, various functions, such as propaganda and economic warfare, escaped Donovan's initial conception of a single centralised secret service at a fairly early stage. The result was diaspora, and the bureaucratic equivalent of a bar-room brawl of five years' duration. But Donovan was more intelligent than either of his British counterparts and had the sense to place himself under the wing of the US Joint Chiefs of Staff by 1943, reducing frictions somewhat, enhancing his power and eventually ensuring some longevity for field clements of OSS, who passed to War Department control in 1945.[44]

Brawls occurred on the ground as well as at the policy level. In late 1941, Nigel Clive, a young SIS officer, arrived at his first posting in Baghdad for his first taste of 'the jungle of the intelligence world'. He made a point of enquiring how all these rival organisations had come into existence:

If I was at first puzzled, I soon became cynical about the time spent on fierce interdepartmental warfare. It became a commonplace to say that if fifty per cent of the day

1 Sir Alexander Cadogan, senior official at the Foreign Office

could be devoted to trying to defeat Hitler, we were doing well and might win the war. The SOE team was unquestionably the best in my view and I collaborated with them closely. This did not always please the head of my office (SIS), who preferred to believe what he was told by his own sources of information, and had restricted his contacts with the rest of the intelligence community to an irreducible minimum.

This state of affairs had developed even before rival American and Free French organisations had arrived in the region.[45]

The established literature on intelligence during the Second World War has tended to emphasise signals intelligence. The organising and exploiting of the invaluable 'real time' information derived from cryptanalysis (signals intelligence), in a manner that allowed it to effectively inform strategy and operations, was indeed remarkable. Much attention has been given to the Joint Intelligence Committee system in London and Washington which, by the latter phases of the war, provided an increasingly refined mechanism for overseeing this. Undoubtedly, this experience compared well with Germany, where Hitler deliberately pitted one secret service against another with disastrous results, and *a fortiori* with Japan.[46] Yet it remains a mystery why Allied governments, capable of producing this system for co-ordinating intelligence, failed to co-ordinate the human agencies that conducted a broader range of activities from espionage and sabotage to propaganda. This book, which has but a regional focus, can only shed tangential light upon this troublesome question.

Anthony Eden certainly resented the fact that SOE, which for a while also controlled 'black' propaganda, was under the new Ministry of Economic Warfare, headed by its notably abrasive minister, Hugh Dalton. There were frequent and bitter confrontations. SOE caused Eden multiple embarrassments in neutral countries as far apart as Portugal, Turkey, Iran and Thailand. British ambassadors felt persecuted by SOE personnel, whom they did not control, but who nevertheless made use of the diplomatic immunity offered by their embassies. In April 1942 Eden complained to Churchill that he had recently been confronted about SOE activities in Istanbul by the Ambassador of neutral Turkey, who had observed:

They seem to have too much money to spend. We know they are employing men of very disreputable character who are well used to all forms of international sharp practice. Some of these men are also being paid by the Germans ... he would have taken this matter up with the [British] Ambassador some time ago, but he knew that these men were not under his control, but under the control of a man called 'Dawson' [Dalton] or some such name in London.[47]

Eden responded in the short term by demanding a Foreign Office veto over Dalton's SOE operations in neutral countries. His long-term reaction was a campaign to place SOE under the authority of either the Chiefs of Staff or the Foreign Office. But this latter ambition was not realised until early 1946.

Events in Washington during the emergence of Donovan's OSS organisation, together with its sister organisations, such as the OWI and the Board of Economic Warfare (BEW) mirrored the London pattern almost exactly. Although the organisational culture of Washington was more tolerant of uncoordinated action, the radical nature of the resulting changes, combined with the personality of Donovan, a man supremely intolerant of proper administrative procedure, drove senior officials to distraction. Breckinridge Long, a senior figure in the State Department, lamented that Donovan 'is into everybody's business – knows no bounds of jurisdiction – tries to fill the shoes of each agency charged with responsibility for a war activity'. He added that Donovan 'has had almost unlimited money and a regular army at work and agents all over the world'. Donovan's greatest achievement was to have recognised, perhaps more than officials in London, the need for secret service to be centrally organised, but in wartime Washington this was a dangerous mission.[48]

After 1942 these national problems were multiplied by their increasingly inter-allied nature. Although history is littered with examples of secret service co-operation between states, often termed 'liaison', the Second World War marked a qualitative change. The presence of large numbers of organisations operating on a global scale resulted in what was effectively a new form of diplomacy, characterised by the negotiation of elaborate secret service treaties, defining rights, permissions and spheres of interest. Liaison was valued not only because of the very real cost-efficiencies of information sharing, but also because it could be used to track, or even to restrict, allied activities. 'Co-ordination' and 'integration' were words which came to be regarded with justified caution by all concerned.[49]

A key dimension of the developing politics of secret service was the tension between nationally directed secret services and the dictatorial tendencies of regional commanders with 'Allied' authority. No suitable wartime formula was ever found to resolve this problem. OSS, SOE and, *a fortiori*, SIS considered themselves to be global organisations, taking orders from their respective executive chiefs in Washington and London. They were reluctant to concede more than the loosest 'co-ordination' to theatre commanders and departed at will from formal agreements. Theatre commanders demanded the right of veto over their operations, if not complete control. This problem had repercussions in every wartime theatre. General MacArthur, who operated his South West Pacific Area (SWPA), like a private fiefdom, was a prime example. OSS did not set foot inside it, while conversely MacArthur complained that he 'had to bargain like a rug merchant throughout the war' to obtain intelligence from the US Navy. Mountbatten tackled this issue more successfully in South East Asia Command, based in Ceylon, developing an apparatus, known as Priorities (P) Division, for co-ordinating the twelve separate secret services, but its edicts were often ignored. This problem remained unresolved in the post-war period. A considerable section of the 'treaty' concluded by SIS with the newly formed CIA in the late 1940s tried to address this complex matter. But this did not preclude endless argument about how these matters were to be arranged under entities such as NATO and SHAPE (Supreme Headquarters Allied Powers Europe) and SACEUR (Supreme Allied Command Europe). The Korean War was marked by real difficulties between MacArthur and the CIA.[50]

Finally, tensions were exacerbated by the inner culture of secret service organisations. That their activities depended upon secrecy offered a strong inducement to avoid consultation or collaboration. Operations were inevitably less secure if they had been discussed in detail by five interested departments in three different countries. Moreover, it was argued, if security was tight then the operation would remain invisible and other interested departments could not be offended. Indeed, it seemed only a natural extension to apply the techniques of their own service to bureaucratic competition, described by one senior OSS officer as using the 'rubber dagger'.[51] But while the use of the 'rubber dagger' delivered some tactical successes, in the long term its effects were deleterious. By the end of the Second World War the very mention of secret service induced a neuralgic twinge in senior officials, who wanted it curtailed or abolished. It was its contribution to bureaucratic warfare, rather than real warfare, that coloured the views of many in Whitehall and Washington on secret service for decades to come.

Part 1

Before Pearl Harbor, 1937–1941

2 Wing Commander Wigglesworth flies east: the lamentable state of intelligence, 1937–1939

> According to a recent recce appreciation written by HQ Far East, it would be difficult, if not impossible, to provide complete security from [Japanese] air attack and enemy carriers should be able to launch a morning raid without warning.
>
> Deputy Director of Air Intelligence, London, 30 June 1938.[1]

On 8 December 1941, Japan launched her remarkably successful attacks on the Americans at Pearl Harbor and the Philippines, and also upon the British in Malaya and Singapore. Almost from that moment there erupted a series of claims and counter-claims, focusing on the absence of warning, or 'intelligence disasters'. Over time there has developed a stream of speculation about 'secrets' that might explain Japan's dramatic success and, indeed, the underlying nature of the Far Eastern War in general. For over half a century, investigative journalists and academic historians alike have lavished particular attention upon Pearl Harbor. The weight of this body of material is now so great that, like a small planet, it exercises its own gravitational pull, forever drawing in new historians. Yet we are no closer to a consensus explanation of the events of 1941. Indeed, as Saki Dockrill has observed, half a century on, historians do not agree on very much about the Far Eastern War, not even what this conflict should be called or when it began.[2]

In one sense the obsession with Pearl Harbor is understandable. During late 1941 both Roosevelt and Churchill were searching for a route by which the United States could join the war against the Axis. The idea that one, or both of them, knew of the Japanese attack in advance, but conveniently chose to ignore it, has sometimes proved too tempting to allow sound historical methodology to get in the way. Indeed the mistaken idea that Churchill knew in advance and 'betrayed' Roosevelt has become quite pervasive in the public mind.[3] But there was neither Allied conspiracy nor a 'betrayal' at Pearl Harbor. Instead, the real lesson is a familiar but powerful one: that confusion has more explanatory power than conspiracy.

Concentration on Pearl Harbor has distracted attention from other issues

19

of importance. More has been written on Pearl Harbor than on all other aspects of intelligence in the Far Eastern War put together. Accordingly, this study deals only fleetingly with Pearl Harbor and the Pacific. Its main focus is upon India, South East Asia and China.[4]

Several puzzling questions predominate in any consideration of the period preceding the cataclysmic events of 1941. Firstly, why was British and American secret service in Asia and the Pacific in such a lamentable state? Secondly, why, in spite of these deficiencies, did it manage to perform relatively well? Thirdly, why, despite providing forewarning of Japanese intentions and capabilities, did this intelligence appear to make little difference? The British experience at Singapore was the opposite of Pearl Harbor, with ample warning. Yet good intelligence did nothing to avert the single greatest disaster in British military history, which left over 166,500 Allied troops killed or captured. The answers to these questions lie largely in the politics and organisational problems of intelligence in that region.[5]

The imperial dimension is central to any attempt to understand the impoverished nature of British, and indeed to some degree even American, intelligence before 1941. British intelligence in this region was primarily an *imperial* service concerned with colonial security issues. The colonial governments in India and Malaya had developed, over many decades, proficient, but narrowly focused, security intelligence services, designed to address internal threats from nationalists, communists and 'agitators'. Their undoubted success in penetrating and manipulating these groups contributed to an atmosphere of complacency. Meanwhile, little in the way of resources or first-class personnel was devoted to assessing external foreign threats, such as Japan, China and the Soviet Union.

The British Raj typified this approach. It had long operated a sophisticated system of domestic surveillance based upon police intelligence operations of the Special Branch type. At a provincial level such activities were under the auspices of the local police chiefs. However, at a higher level, the direction across the whole of the Indian subcontinent was centralised under the Intelligence Bureau (IB) in Delhi, part of the Government of India's Home Department. There was also a liaison office in London called Indian Political Intelligence (IPI), which was closely integrated with the British Security Service (MI5).[6] IB was effective and enjoyed agents at a high level in most Indian 'subversive' organisations, including the Indian Communist Party (ICP). The Indian Government had also developed an overseas capability against its enemies based outside India, typically Sikh nationalists in Canada. In the wake of recent declassifications, one historian of the Raj has concluded that Delhi relied very heavily upon surveillance and covertly obtained information to retain its supremacy. But despite its global reach, it remained centrally concerned with domestic threats to colonial rule.[7]

The same observation could be made about the colonial administration in Malaya and Singapore. During the inter-war years they paid limited attention to the problem of Japan and focused on the Malayan Communist Party (MCP) and its possible links with larger communist parties in China and the Soviet Union. The Special Branch of the Straits Settlements (Singapore) Police ran effective operations to intercept MCP correspondence and placed its own agents at a high level.[8] Operations in Malaya led directly to the capture of the entire Comintern archive in the Far East and the British arrest of Ho Chi Minh in Hong Kong in 1931–2.[9] In the early 1930s the War Office still pressed SIS to give the problem of 'Reds' in Asia the top priority.[10] By 1935 the main communist network in the Far East, based at Shanghai, was attempting to rebuild itself and to re-establish its links with the national parties in South East Asia. However, as one British diplomat drily observed, the principal communist emissary engaged on this task, travelling from Singapore on to Thailand, then Indochina and Shanghai, was 'unfortunately for his Communist employers, a British police agent'.[11] By 1939, one such British agent, Lai Tek, had risen to the rank of General Secretary of the Malayan Communist Party, reflecting the judicious arrest of those who stood in the path of his promotion.[12]

Those who had constructed this system of imperial surveillance, perhaps the only international clandestine entity that then rivalled the Comintern, were lifelong secret servants and were justly proud of their achievements. In 1947, Sir Phillip Vickery, Head of IPI in London, noted in his retiring missive that he had been its chief since 1926.[13] In London many of his colleagues in the Special Branch, MI5 and SIS, began their careers in India.[14] In 1940, Sir Eric Holt-Wilson, the Deputy Head of MI5, retired by the reforming hand of Churchill, described the British secret services as 'the Imperial Security Services'. MI5, he explained, did not so much conduct security operations, as preside over a vast empire web of police, civil and military organisations. The result was a 'consolidated Imperial Security Service with one Central Record Office and Registry for the whole Empire'. Its central index of suspicious persons, he insisted, ran to 4.5 million anti-British names worldwide. In 1940, disillusioned, he tried to market himself and this system to the American Federal Bureau of Investigation (FBI).[15]

Holt-Wilson's overture to the Americans was not surprising. The inter-war period was characterised by a continuous stream of British–Commonwealth–European–American security intelligence co-operation against 'agitators' and 'radicals' which has hitherto received little attention. Special Branch officers from Singapore regularly visited Bangkok and Hanoi to facilitate co-operation with the Thai and French secret services.[16] They also co-operated with the intelligence branches of the American forces, who watched the political activities of American private citizens, and later with the FBI.[17] The origins of the modern Western intelligence community is often traced to the Second World War. However, the remarkable volume of European security intelligence material in American archives demonstrates that the most important antecedent lies in extensive domestic security collaboration, originating before 1914, but accelerating after the Bolshevik Revolution.[18] The State Department was a key conduit, working with the SIS station in New York, and circulating materials to a burgeoning FBI.[19]

By contrast British *external* or foreign intelligence in Asia and the Pacific was a picture of complacency, while American foreign intelligence in the region was very small. From 1933, British intelligence priorities slowly began to shift towards Japan, under pressure from the War Office and the Admiralty.[20] But there was also ambivalence, for many saw the growing Japanese presence on the mainland as a bulwark against communist influence. Only with the Sino-Japanese War of 1937 did Japan attract concerted attention. Even in 1940, intelligence chiefs in India complained that they could not persuade their officers to stop thinking about an attack by the Russians from the north and instead to take Japan seriously.

Wing Commander Wigglesworth flies east

During the approach of the Far Eastern War, British secret service activity fell naturally into at least four different categories: the domestic activities of security intelligence, special operations designed to achieve sabotage or subversion, the discreet use of human agents to collect overseas intelligence and the increasingly technical field of ciphers, codebreaking and signals intelligence. These functions were presided over by a variety of authorities, colonial, diplomatic and military, many of whom were inclined to maintain their own separate departments for such work. The result was a complex network of rather parochial secret services, often poorly co-ordinated. Some *tour d'horizon* of British secret service organisations east of the Suez Canal is essential at the outset, and each is best considered in its setting. In 1938, one individual, Wing Commander H. E. P. Wigglesworth, the Deputy Director of Intelligence at the Air Ministry, was asked to explore the ramshackle system east of Suez. In March, Wigglesworth flew east across the Mediterranean towards India, to begin a broad-ranging investigation that lasted three months.[21]

Wigglesworth's journey had been delayed by the outbreak of the Sino-Japanese War. Now, with an increasing Japanese presence on the Chinese coast, the major British inter-service intelligence centre in Asia, situated at Hong Kong, appeared vulnerable. Talk of relocation to Singapore had exacerbated local rivalries. This, together with serious MI5 problems, rendered Wigglesworth's tour an urgent priority. Travelling by Imperial Airways flying boat, Wigglesworth flew east via Marseilles, Corfu, India and Bangkok. Even before setting foot in Asia he was given cause for real concern. The flying boats, he noted, also carried British diplomatic and secret mail in an on-board 'safe' with an unlockable door, concealed beneath the carpet of the longest compartment. But the real weakness was the lack of secure locations for mail during stop-overs. At Marseilles, diplomatic mail was stored overnight in a simple unattended locker, while in Bangkok nothing was available, so someone 'literally sleeps on the diplomatic and secret mail'. This inauspicious beginning prefigured insights into serious security problems in the region prior to 1942.[22]

The largest of the three British intelligence centres in Asia was the Combined Intelligence Bureau, Hong Kong (CIBHK), formed in 1935, and which covered all of China south of Foochow, Formosa and the Philippines. CIBHK was also referred to as the 'Far East Combined Bureau' and constituted a compromise location. The Army had wanted Shanghai, close to Japanese land fighting, while the Navy had wanted the main naval base of Singapore. Hong Kong was chosen as a compromise and also because signals intelligence activities were being expanded there.[23] CIBHK was located at the main naval dockyard at Victoria Island, with the local office of SIS close by. In theory an inter-service organisation, CIBHK was in practice dominated by naval intelligence, in common with Singapore. Wigglesworth complained that the Navy appeared to believe that 'intelligence is gained solely for the benefit of their service'. RAF intelligence was literally the poor relation, enjoying an annual budget for secret service work of only £100, in comparison to the Army's lavish £1,700. The thin representation of air intelligence was significant, given the damage inflicted by Japanese air power in 1941.

Military operations during the Sino-Japanese War forced the Japanese to reveal their capabilities. However, CIBHK was small and divided, preventing the full exploitation of this new window. SIS saw fit to keep only two full-time representatives in the Far East, one in Hong Kong and one at Shanghai. The SIS officer in Hong Kong, Commander Charles Drage, had enjoyed some success in recruiting Chinese harbour pilots who had worked in Japanese ports and returned to Hong Kong 'on sick leave' to make their reports. But reliable high-grade agents in Japan were few and far between.[24] Developments in China were easier to follow using agents working under a British commercial cover. SIS recruited a senior military officer in the puppet government of Wang Ching-wei, offering them insights into the growing effectiveness of the Chinese Communist guerrilla forces in Japanese-occupied China. There were also contacts with German military advisers and with Europeans working for Koumintang (KMT) intelligence.[25]

Internal security was a problem in Hong Kong with its vast transient population. Hitherto, security had been in the hands of the small and overworked

1 Japan and East Asia to December 1941

local police Special Branch and it was only recently that MI5 had seen fit to despatch a Defence Security Officer (DSO) to the colony. Only the Navy bothered to check on the background of its local employees with the Special Branch. The Governor of Hong Kong confessed that he was anxiously awaiting a long-delayed visit from Sir Eric Holt-Wilson, the Deputy Head of

MI5 in London, to advise on improvements, but they did not know where to begin.[26]

One crucial factor offset the generally chronic state of British intelligence and security: the relative success of signals intelligence operations. At Hong Kong, an Asian outstation of Britain's GC&CS (later GCHQ) worked on the secret enciphered communications of Japan, China and the Soviet Union. Signals intelligence work on Japanese communications had begun on a somewhat amateur basis as early as 1924, under Paymaster-Lieutenant Eric Nave and one assistant, with interception being carried out from the ships of the China Squadron. GC&CS also saw all the material sent by major British commercial cable companies. After Nave's departure in 1927 there was no continuity in staff and results were mixed. Nevertheless, in 1931, intercepts clearly revealed to the British the pre-meditated nature of the 'incident' at Mudken that triggered Japan's incursion into Manchuria.[27]

Finally, in November 1934, responding to Service pressure for more information on Japan, Alastair Denniston, the Head of GC&CS, who chaired the Coordination of Interception Committee in London, proposed the formation of a proper cryptographic bureau at Hong Kong. By June 1935, this had been formed under Commander H. L. Shaw and was located alongside CIBHK in the Victoria Island dockyard, while the physical interception of radio messages was carried out nearly one hour's journey away on Stonecutter's Island in Hong Kong harbour. There were numerous practical problems, reception aerials had to be dismantled whenever a typhoon threatened and nothing could be intercepted when an adjacent naval transmitter was in operation. Despite awkward conditions, and staff shortages, they were reading most Japanese naval material in 1935.[28] With the surge in Japanese radio traffic in 1937 resulting from the Sino-Japanese War, this had become 'the most valuable and reliable of all sources of information available in the Far East'.[29]

By the time of Wigglesworth's visit in 1938, the main intercept station was located in a flimsy wooden building on top of Stonecutter's Island, dominated by a long aerial array. Other technical facilities and generators were located in more substantial barrack-like accommodation. Twenty-nine personnel worked there, with a further seventeen on a nearby ship, HMS *Tamar*. The Navy dominated, for all but nine were naval personnel and they considered their primary duty to be to give an accurate day-to-day picture of the disposition of the Japanese fleet. There were no RAF personnel at all.[30] In 1936 the Army despatched additional personnel to Hong Kong, partly because the Navy were sharing little material, arguing that they did the work of collection. By 1937, four Army cryptographers supported by twenty-four signallers worked on Japanese Army codes from out-stations at Tientsin and Shanghai. Co-operation was gradually improved, with a deliberate attempt to get officers and their families to mix socially.[31]

Interception was carried out at Stonecutter's Island twenty-four hours a day, with the raw intercepts being laid out on prepared 'cages'. This material was taken by safe hand on a launch to CIBHK, where the messages were broken. Until early 1938, the Commanding Officer Intelligence Staff at Hong Kong had control of distribution, but thereafter, to prevent arguments over access, everything was sent to GC&CS in Britain by Army mail. The hard-pressed staff were rightly proud of their achievements. They claimed to have offered advanced warning of the outbreak of the Sino-Japanese War and to be providing detailed information on relations between Japan and her allies. But the whole operation, observed Wigglesworth, was precarious:

Any eulogy on the intercept service must, however, be tempered by the fact that at present only the [Japanese] naval messages can be read – the high grade army code, and until quite recently the Military Attaches' code, have not been broken in spite of intensive examination, both in England and Hong Kong over a period of many months.[32]

In short, regarding Japan, most of Britain's intelligence eggs were in one or two cryptographic baskets, the Japanese naval codes and also Japanese diplomatic material (which Wigglesworth failed to mention).[33] To Britain's horror, Italian diplomatic personnel in Hong Kong, who were very alert to the possibilities offered by intercepts, had warned the Japanese about interception. But the Japanese were over-confident about the security of their cipher systems, and the only result was a routine warning to Japanese army units.

Even so, the Japanese Navy modified their code from time to time, resulting in breaks in the flow of intelligence. Moreover, Wigglesworth noted, if the Japanese Navy ever shifted to an impenetrable army-type code, the consequences would be 'terrible'.[34] In 1939 this occurred when the Japanese Navy shifted to the more secure JN-25 cipher, which was then continually upgraded. Contemporaneously, the Japanese Foreign Office introduced a new machine encryption system known to the West as 'Purple' which rendered high-grade diplomatic messages secure, although the Japanese often sent important material in low-grade consular ciphers.[35]

Given the extraordinary value of intercepts, Wigglesworth was stunned by the physical dilapidation at Stonecutter's Island. The intercept building was totally inadequate, 'even a washing place is being used as an operating room' and personnel were being worked literally round the clock. One operative complained that since arriving three years ago he had not enjoyed a single weekend of leave. This paucity of staff meant that while Japanese high policy material was decrypted immediately, operational material was backed up and all tactical intelligence was simply discarded. The lack of physical security was remarkable: 'Chinese cooks . . . for the operators mess work within a few feet of the operation rooms.' The expansion of

2 The primitive GC&CS intercept station at Stonecutter's Island, Hong Kong

interception at Stonecutter's Island had been halted while consideration was given to moving to Singapore. The possibility of a surprise attack on Hong Kong launched by Japanese forces located in Formosa, or on Hainan Island, preyed constantly on the minds of the military staff and, despite protests from the Navy, the British Chiefs of Staff increasingly viewed Hong Kong as indefensible. The intercept station, located at the highest point on Stonecutter's Island, was very vulnerable to both air attack and gunfire.[36]

The Co-ordination of Interception Committee, under Denniston, had already met in London to discuss the problem on 8 July 1936. They had not considered Hong Kong since November 1934 and the situation had clearly worsened. Denniston accepted that the arguments for and against moving the intercept station were evenly balanced. To stay at Hong Kong 'might be risking its dispersal or destruction at a time when it was most required', yet he was reluctant to interrupt fine work on Japanese ciphers. Japanese high-grade naval codes were still being read satisfactorily in 1936 and there was progress with military and consular traffic. Service politics were also evident, with the Navy wishing to move to the safety of the Singapore Naval Base while the Army thought that Hong Kong intercepts could be invaluable under siege. Both the Army and William F. Clarke from GC&CS also pointed out that the sort of traffic that could be intercepted from Singapore might be quite different. No firm decision was reached, other than to conduct technical research at alternative sites at Singapore and to increase staff at Hong Kong.[37]

The outbreak of the Sino-Japanese War in 1937 had resolved the debate, and by the time of Wigglesworth's visit relocation to Singapore was well advanced. Ten GC&CS staff at a naval radio station at Kranji, near Singapore, were investigating the new intercept site. Four months of further trials were required, but it was already clear that most Japanese traffic could be intercepted from Singapore, partly because much of it went through Formosa. There was good coverage of the strategically important French colony of Indochina. Wigglesworth also reported that Soviet traffic between Moscow and the Far East could be intercepted from Singapore because Soviet landlines regularly broke down, forcing them to rely on radio transmissions. There was no-one at Singapore who could presently read this Soviet material, but it represented a bonus to 'be tapped at a favourable opportunity'. Cryptanalysis was now developing from an obscure handcraft to an activity on an industrial scale: Japanese Army messages were transmitted so fast that they would need new automatic recording equipment. Modern direction-finding aerials were also a high priority. A large well-equipped Singapore station was planned for 1939 with fifty-seven operators.[38]

From Hong Kong on the south China coast, Wigglesworth travelled north to the cosmopolitan international treaty port of Shanghai. This marked the low point of a worrying tour. With most of the fighting taking place in the north, Shanghai was theoretically well placed, and was tasked with watching all of China north of Foochow, Japan, Korea, Manchuria and Soviet Siberia. Here information could be gathered on such critical subjects as Soviet foreign policy, on foreign assistance to China and on the capabilities of Japanese forces.

Shanghai was home to another inter-service Combined Intelligence Bureau, subordinate to Hong Kong. There was poor organisation here with the different service components scattered about in disparate embassy, consulate and municipal buildings. Their geographical separation underlined vigorous inter-service rivalry – the Navy had ordered its senior intelligence officer in Shanghai to have nothing to do with SIS. The Army had long dominated here, and the RAF representative was isolated. Security was weak, so no intercept material had ever been circulated to Shanghai.[39] Wigglesworth was aware that his main brief concerned service intelligence and he was wary of poking his nose into SIS business. Notwithstanding this, he could not let the SIS situation at Shanghai pass without comment:

Both at Hong Kong and at Shanghai I was asked by civilians if I knew 'Steptoe'. No, who was he? Oh, he's the head of the secret service organisation at Shanghai – he's the arch-spy – everyone in China knows who and what 'Steptoe' is!

Harry Steptoe's cover was that of a vice-consul and his office was in the British consular buildings. But he made 'little or no pretence at being a Consul' and his real work aroused 'curiosity'. Surely, he asked, SIS could do better than this? As early as December 1933, the American military attaché in Shanghai had deduced Steptoe as the 'British intelligence agent', since his name did not appear in the list of the British Consulate's personnel and his peculiar movements suggested a secretive 'roving commission'.[40] Steptoe was indeed a remarkably colourful character with an odd gait that gave an air of ostentatious subterfuge to everything that he did. This was complemented by an exotic taste in foreign uniforms. At one diplomatic reception he appeared in an unorthodox lovat green outfit, dripping with gold braid. A foreign diplomat had greeted him and expressed admiration for what, he presumed, was the splendid ceremonial dress of the British secret service.[41]

Steptoe later made striking impressions on two of his SIS colleagues. Malcolm Muggeridge recalls meeting this 'purely Wodehousean figure' after he was released following an exchange of captured diplomatic personnel in early 1942. A 'little cock-sparrow of a man, with a bristling moustache, a high voice and a monocle'. His exaggerated sense of secrecy, 'every encounter, however innocent, was clandestine', had paid off in the end. The invading Japanese had refused to take him seriously, but instead turned their suspicions on a blameless British Council representative who got 'the full treatment'.[42] Kim Philby was less impressed and recalled the 'near-mental case' who covered the Far East for SIS between the wars: 'I found it difficult to believe that he could hold any job for a week.'[43]

The intelligence gathered by Shanghai was meagre. Reliable Chinese agents were, as ever, elusive, and they found it increasingly hard to travel freely in what was now a war zone. The Yangtze River had been closed to traffic and informers had to travel slowly by land routes. Accordingly, the information from the missionaries and traders employed by SIS was often dated. Although there were many white Russian exiles in Shanghai, successful penetration into Soviet Siberia was all but impossible and two SIS agents were already on trial there. 'There are not many Russians who are prepared to enter Siberia', noted Wigglesworth, as 'they know that suspicion means ''liquidation'''.[44]

Japan, increasingly gripped by ultra-nationalism and by spy-mania, was also a tough target for human espionage. SIS operated a number of harbour-watchers. Wigglesworth had only a brief uninformative meeting with the British consul from Nagasaki, who reported that intelligence from Japan was 'negligible'.[45] In theory, the British military attachés in Japan offered an alternative means of obtaining intelligence, but there were two obstacles. Firstly, the British Military Attaché in Tokyo, Major General F. S. G. Piggott, was an extreme Japanophile, having served a previous tour of duty there in the 1920s, when Anglo-Japanese relations had been good. In June 1936, when the British Director of Military Intelligence in London asked Piggott to set up a covert intelligence network, he refused point blank, arguing that any skulduggery would destroy his position with the Japanese.[46] Secondly, there was growing Japanese public paranoia which ensured that all foreigners were subjected to a formidable level of surveillance.[47]

Piggott's intransigence over secret work reflected a realistic appreciation of the dangers. In the late 1930s, the Japanese Navy nursed an obsession about SIS activity. Although British officials seem to have limited themselves to open and legitimate observation, harassment gradually turned to brutality. In October 1938, Lieutenant T. A. Peacocke vanished without trace in Japan. In July 1940, fifteen Britons were arrested on spying charges. One of them, Melville Cox, was the Reuters correspondent, whose predecessor, Malcolm Kennedy, had certainly been working for SIS. Three days later Cox died under interrogation. The Japanese police alleged that he had committed suicide by jumping from a window, but the Foreign Office official who investigated, Patrick Dean (later chairman of the JIC), concluded that the facts did not fit, he had been killed elsewhere. Other reports suggested Cox's body had twenty injection marks in the arm.[48]

Wigglesworth now flew south to inspect Singapore and Malaya. GHQ Fort Canning in Singapore contained the third British inter-service intelligence centre, the Combined Intelligence Bureau, Malaya (CIBM), which covered

Siam, French Indochina, the Netherlands East Indies and Australasia. Here, CIBM intelligence officers from all the three services and MI5 pooled and exchanged intelligence on developments across South East Asia. Co-operation was uncommonly good, but sources were poor.[49]

Remarkably, in all of mainland South East Asia, an area of growing strategic importance, there was no permanent British intelligence representation of any kind. There were certainly no SIS officers stationed there, nor even a single permanent service attaché. Instead overworked officers from Singapore occasionally undertook roving tours through Bangkok, Saigon and Hanoi. In contrast the numbers of Japanese attachés was growing fast. British diplomats in the region were not entirely devoid of secret information. On economic issues they could turn to the private clandestine apparatus run by large firms in the area, such as Armstrong Vickers or Asiatic Petroleum, the local subsidiary of Royal Dutch-Shell. In December 1938, Sir Josiah Crosby, the British Minister in Bangkok, noted wistfully,

the intelligence service of the local branch of the Asiatic Petroleum Company is such an efficient one, there is no information which I can myself usefully impart ... It is they, indeed, who keep the [British] Legation up to date and to whom I myself have to resort for what is afoot.[50]

But British officials were uneasy about companies which might select what they decided to pass on.

In Singapore, Wigglesworth was most struck by the under-resourcing of air intelligence. He noted that 'much midnight oil is burned' by the dreadfully understaffed RAF intelligence. Singapore itself was gathering little material on the Japanese in 1938, with the only first-class intelligence coming from intercepts. There was an atmosphere of unreality and officers at CIBM spent much of their time summarising British diplomatic reports from Bangkok and Tokyo. The most alarming problem at Singapore was security. London had long been aware of this, and had just despatched Holt-Wilson of MI5 in London on a parallel mission to investigate. Wigglesworth called for 'drastic and energetic action' and agreed with Holt-Wilson that the major problem was Lt Colonel Hailey-Bell, the local MI5 representative. He was variously described as 'incompetent' and lacking 'in energy and tact'. There was poor co-operation between MI5, the police and service intelligence on security matters and no conception of what was meant by modern security work. Singapore needed a 'live wire', preferably a staff-college graduate.

But the problems were broader than poor quality staff and were rooted in the narrowly colonial focus of British secret service in Asia. Security in Singapore and Malaya still meant countering nationalist or communist sedition. This area, reported Wigglesworth, was well in hand: 'Communism presents no difficulties and is well under control. The Police here have agents in every known cell, and the policy is not to take action unless information is available from other sources which could be used in open court without incriminating the agents themselves.' But as Anglo-Japanese relations deteriorated, the colonial government had gradually become more aware of the large immigrant Japanese community in Malaya and Singapore. Three thousand Japanese lived on Singapore island alone and, although the authorities claimed a draconian policy of 'banishment of undesirables even on the flimsiest excuse', in reality security organisations lacked the resources to keep track of the vast Japanese population. The Japanese exploited the huge army of native employees drawn from the Malay, Javanese, Chinese and Tamil communities, who provided manual and clerical support in every avenue of Singapore's official life.[51]

In December 1937, the Governor of Singapore, Sir Shenton Thomas, had treated the Colonial Office in London to an excitable warning of the dangers posed by the thousands of Japanese under his jurisdiction. Japanese officials, he insisted, could not only organise them to carry out espionage but also sabotage, offering a lurid account of the possibility of attack with various improvised weapons, including a local speciality, 'incendiary coconuts'. In February 1938 the Foreign Office and the Colonial Office met with the Director of MI5, Sir Vernon Kell, and R. T. Parkin of SIS, to consider a response, but resources were simply too thin and no action was taken.[52] Europe and the Middle East increasingly took priority for defence resources of all types.

American intelligence and Japan

Although Western powers had long exchanged security intelligence relating to the Far East and, although attachés co-operated, Wigglesworth made no reference to Anglo-American 'liaison'. In London the first formal Anglo-American exchange had just taken place during the highly secret visit of the US Navy's Captain Ingersoll.[53] British officers were dismissive of American intelligence capabilities in Asia and the Pacific. Historians have been equally dismissive of pre-war American assessments of Japan, asserting that there was effectively no organised intelligence effort and in its place stood racially driven underestimates of Japanese capabilities. But this was not the whole story.[54]

American intelligence in the inter-war years was also weak, but in a different way. It shared the British problem of under-resourcing, but also suffered from an incomplete structure. The United States lacked a real secret service. Overseas, American diplomats and service attachés were the main source of intelligence, but were largely forbidden from conducting covert operations.

This was sometimes disregarded, but they lacked the established 'secret service funds' enjoyed by their British counterparts. Instead, attachés combed open sources such as the naval press and gleaned what they could on official tours and from personal contacts. They also made use of commercial contacts, especially oil companies and shipping lines. But the value of open sources was declining. In 1937 the advent of the war in China triggered a creeping spy-mania in Japan, and a veil was thrown over previously open subjects, sometimes literally. One historian has noted how Mitsubishi's Nagasaki shipyard erected entire new buildings and then surrounded the slipway with enormous hemp curtains, simply to hide its construction of the massive battleship *Musashi*. After 1939 the Japanese ended visits to naval installations and American officers resorted to surreptitious photography from passenger vessels.[55]

Although the British had the largest attaché staff, a legacy of the Anglo-Japanese alliance, the Americans regarded the Soviets as having the best network in Japan, run through the Communist Party. They all met at the Tokyo Attachés Club, an informal gathering to swap gossip and speculate about the latest Japanese technological developments. Despite the American self-denying ordinance against covert operations, Japanese suspicions were limitless and their counter-surveillance was less than subtle. This included parking a 'broken down' limousine outside the American embassy which remained stationery for two years and was known to all as the 'spy-wagon'. Japanese secret police were inside, hidden by curtains and stripped down to their underwear against the heat.[56]

Although the United States had a record of great achievement in signals intelligence, this lacked a centralised authority. During the Washington Treaty negotiations of 1921–2, which set the naval ratios for Pacific naval powers for more than a decade, their cryptanalysts deciphered no less than 5,000 foreign communications. The American negotiators were exceedingly well informed, although the cryptanalysts 'were wrecks from nervous exhaustion'.[57] Despite this remarkable dividend, the State Department had abandoned cryptanalysis in the 1920s, while the two services had maintained small independent programmes. An effective group of Navy cryptographers, the Fleet Intelligence Unit, was attached to the 4th Marines in Shanghai in 1935. In late 1940, like FECB at Hong Kong, they were moved for security reasons, and relocated in the Philippines and Guam, at the cost of poorer reception.[58] By 1939 the small American naval cryptographic section, Op-20-G, had barely commanded 100 staff at all its locations.[59] American Army cryptographers were equally constrained by minute budgets and very limited personnel, to the point where they could only attack one Japanese cipher at a time. Although this team did crack the Japanese Purple code, a staggering achievement, it required them to abandon all work on Japanese Army ciphers and cost their senior cryptographer a nervous breakdown. Even in 1940 and 1941 they were struggling to put right years of neglect.[60]

Accordingly, intelligence problems could not be much offset by London or Washington through liaison with allies or potential allies. Indeed, emerging co-operation probably served to reinforce certain defects. The very different types of intelligence system deployed by London and Washington slowed their integration. As late as 1941, the American General Lee recorded his amusement at British disbelief when they 'discovered that the Military Attaché remains the most important cog in all the [American] Intelligence machinery', but thereafter British invitations began 'to blow in from unexpected quarters'.[61] Britain enjoyed good relations with the Dutch in the East Indies. The French in Indochina were more guarded, concluding a written agreement that precluded British or French operations into or against each other's colonial territories. But prior to 1940, these were essentially security intelligence relationships.[62]

Conclusions

A year after the outbreak of the Sino-Japanese War, and despite the increasing pace of regional events, intelligence in Asia and the Pacific was under-resourced and labouring against serious impediments. But Wigglesworth neglected to mention one of the few major assets enjoyed by British and American intelligence in this region: long-term regional specialists with excellent language ability, assured by the system of 'language officer' attachments. This guaranteed that while information was sometimes thin, the quality of analysis was often high.[63] Partly for this reason, an under-resourced intelligence system functioned surprisingly well prior to 1942. While the flow of detailed intelligence on the Japanese Naval Air Service, which the British had themselves originally created and trained, was often poor, nevertheless, local analysts were clear about its effectiveness and about the potential for a devastating surprise. A small number of dedicated analysts enjoyed great insights into the Japanese approach to warfare, not least the penchant for surprise attack. They specifically warned Wigglesworth of the danger posed by growing Japanese naval air power, noting that enemy carriers could 'launch a morning raid without warning.'[64] This observation was not the last of a number of startlingly accurate predictions, made by under-resourced but perceptive intelligence officers prior to 1941. For reasons that must now be explored, such warnings went largely unheeded.

3   Insecurity and the fall of Singapore

> Much of the Japanese success has been due to the very large sums they
> have spent on an absolutely first class intelligence organisation. And
> it is rather tragic to know that in spite of every kind of warning of what
> was going on, for example in Malaya, none of the local government
> officials would believe it or take any steps to keep the Japs under proper
> control.
>
> Colonel Grimsdale, Deputy Head of FECB, 8 March 1942.[1]

Japanese intelligence, although seemingly amateurish in its methods to Western eyes, achieved a remarkably detailed picture of British dispositions at
Singapore prior to 1942. Mainstream accounts of the Malayan Campaign
have ascribed the fall of Singapore, in part, to poor British intelligence, but
these observations largely constituted a smokescreen laid down by senior
commanders attempting to obscure responsibility. The greatest problem in
this period was instead internal security. Faced with a desperate situation in
Europe and the Middle East, London gave security at Singapore almost no
priority, while Japan enjoyed a near free hand in the field of espionage and
subversion.

Intelligence and security work at Singapore were connected in unexpected ways. Although Japan's vast programme of clandestine activities, building to a crescendo in late 1941, was not impeded by Britain's meagre
security organisation, its broad progress was followed by British cryptanalysts. Because these Japanese clandestine activities were co-ordinated with
overall Japanese strategic planning in the latter stages of 1941, they
provided an important window upon Japanese intentions. As a result, *both
British and Japanese intelligence* had a relatively clear picture of each
other's strategic thinking. However, in the event, the Japanese proved not
only to be superior practitioners of jungle warfare, but also better at
exploiting intelligence. In contrast, the British high command was impermeable to intelligence warnings, especially about the capability of Japanese
forces. Notwithstanding this, intelligence could not have made a substantial
military difference at Singapore. No amount of advanced warning could
deal with superior forces.

Moving to Singapore: the Far Eastern Combined Bureau

During 1938 and 1939 British intelligence in the Far East was heavily reorganised but only marginally improved. These changes reflected a shift in British strategic thinking. The Admiralty had accepted that they could not fight the German, Italian and Japanese Navies simultaneously. The defence of Hong Kong and French Indochina looked increasingly impossible, and even Singapore would receive no relief for many months. This pessimistic outlook dictated the removal of the main British intelligence centre from Hong Kong, replaced by a new inter-service intelligence organisation at Singapore in August 1939 entitled the 'Far Eastern Combined Bureau' (FECB).

While FECB Singapore, like its predecessor in Hong Kong, remained under naval dominance, some of the problems of inter-service antagonism were eliminated. This owed much to a new FECB chief, Captain K. L. Harkness, a young and amiable naval officer who later recalled that 'we never saw ourselves as other than three services of equal standing'. FECB was located at the Singapore naval base and consisted of three service sections, each in daily contact with its own service intelligence division in London. Air Vice-Marshal Sir Robert Brooke-Popham, the British Commander in Chief Far East, wanted it close by: 'I must be able to ring a bell and summon my Intelligence Staff, namely FECB.' But moving to the naval base did not help the continuing imbalance between the services. As late as February 1941 Brooke-Popham conceded:

Another problem which I have not got solved satisfactorily is that of Intelligence generally and the organisation of F.E.C.B. It is supposed to be a combined bureau in which the Navy, Army and Air Force have equal status. At present it is about 90% Navy . . . We are able out here to strengthen up the Army representation but the RAF side is much too weak.

Brooke-Popham pleaded for a really good RAF intelligence officer, but this request was ignored by London. He had even toyed with the idea of moving FECB away from the naval base, but had concluded that the disruption to their work would be too great at a time when international tension was already high.[2] In late 1941, the head of the air intelligence section of FECB, Group Captain Chappell, was still doubling up as a travelling air attaché, farcically trying to 'cover' all of mainland South East Asia.[3]

The best intelligence continued to be derived from the interception of Japanese signals. Since August 1939, the main intercept location had been the naval radio station at Kranji which now retained almost a hundred operators, a mixture of WRENS and civilians. Only a skeleton organisation remained in Hong Kong. The signals interception effort in the Far East was now reinforced by the work of Australian naval bases and ships, and by new sites operating at Naura Island, Esquimault and Bombay. With a worldwide shortage of trained signals personnel the contribution of Australia was especially important. Originally, the cryptanalysis section was co-located with FECB; however, the Commander of the East Indies Fleet took a fancy to their accommodation so they were banished to Selatar Bahru in Singapore city, far from FECB and Kranji. Before teleprinters arrived, everything had to be sent for processing by despatch riders.[4]

Some of the best signals intelligence came not from cryptanalysis, but from using radio direction finding (D/F) and radio traffic analysis to keep track of Japanese shipping movements. The advantage of D/F was that it relied on the volume and direction of radio activity for its information, and was therefore immune to Japanese attempts to improve cipher security. An eventual chain of seventeen D/F stations allowed FECB to keep a very effective track of the Japanese Navy by taking cross-bearings. An ultra-secret technique, called Radio-Finger-Printing, using high-speed cine cameras to capture oscilloscope pictures of each unique signal pattern, allowed the British to identify individual ships.[5]

In the new FECB organisation, only the signals intelligence centre was operating efficiently, while its other facets remained wanting. The inadequacies of SIS in the Far East were a particularly sore point for Brooke-Popham, who felt that the newly appointed Chief of SIS in London, Sir Stewart Menzies, was deliberately neglecting Asia in favour of Europe. On 6 January 1941, Brooke-Popham completed a tour of intelligence organisations in the Far East, not unlike that undertaken by Wigglesworth three years before. Dismay at what he uncovered prompted him to fire off an immediate complaint to London:

Weakest link undoubtedly is S.I.S. organisation in Far East. At present little or no reliance is placed upon S.I.S. information by any authorities here and little valuable information in fact appears to be obtained. I am satisfied that the identity of principal officer at Shanghai, Hong Kong and Singapore is known to many. Their chief subordinates are in general local amateurs with no training in Intelligence duties nor adequate knowledge of military, naval, air or political affairs. Agents are chiefly uneducated Chinese and up till now in Thailand and Indo China reliance has been placed entirely upon French sources of information.

SIS had repeatedly promised to send an officer out from London to review the situation but nothing had happened. Brooke-Popham now demanded a regional head for SIS 'with power to make changes in personnel without delay'.[6]

London had long been familiar with these problems, but a representative from the SIS London headquarters in Broadway Buildings was only despatched in May 1941. This was Geoffrey Denham, a businessman with extensive interests in Java. Denham and Brooke-Popham agreed that an overall regional controller was needed and worried about the complete lack of any SIS organisation in Burma which 'will become a principal centre in war'. Brooke-Popham was impressed by Denham and SIS approved his request that Denham stay as regional controller, adding that 'his business activities would provide good cover for his work'.[7] Denham was to reside at FECB, but remained only 'responsible to "C"' ', the Chief of SIS in London.[8]

SIS problems were underlined again in August 1941 when FECB was confronted with dramatic events in Vichy French Indochina. Japan already enjoyed bases in northern Indochina, conceded the previous year. Japan now pushed southwards to secure a number of airbases near Saigon and the Thai border, within range of Malaya. Brooke-Popham ordered both SIS and FECB to 'spare neither time, nor trouble, nor expense in obtaining up-to-date information about the state of preparedness of these aerodromes'. But little information was forthcoming.[9] Even in mid-1941, SIS reports still contained a great deal of material from the French, whose own service was thought to exaggerate wildly.[10] In some cases SIS circulated French reports around Whitehall without bothering to translate them, which their Whitehall customers dismissed as 'valueless'.[11]

Denham set more adventurous programmes in train. In the last months of 1941, SIS and SOE began to develop relations with the MCP, despite the reservations of the colonial government in Malaya. The MCP supplied several Chinese agents who received wireless training as a stay behind network which would report on the main Japanese lines of advance during an invasion, and who were controlled by Major Rosher of SIS in Singapore. However, as Brooke-Popham himself observed, a clandestine network could not be created overnight and this, in practice, was what Denham was now asked to do.[12]

Liaison by all services with their regional counterparts was slow to develop. On 5 September 1940 Roosevelt had ordered an expansion of exchanges by British and American naval intelligence in London and Washington. An American naval observer was assigned to Singapore in 1940, and a British officer was attached to the US Navy in Manila, but comprehensive regional liaison was not established until early 1941. At the end of February 1941 an Anglo-American signals intelligence conference was held at Singapore, and thereafter there were regular exchanges of information with American codebreakers in the Philippines.[13] Thereafter a large volume of British material from FECB began to arrive on the desk of the G-2 officers in Washington responsible for South East Asia, which was presumably reciprocated in London.[14]

Subversion from below

While British signals intelligence at Singapore continued to read some Japanese traffic, the uneven performance of other parts of FECB in gathering intelligence was not a serious handicap. Poor security was more problematic. Despite the arrival of a new MI5 representative as Singapore's Defence Security Officer (DSO), and the creation of a Local Intelligence Section in FECB to watch Japanese residents, the sheer scale of the problem proved insurmountable. As early as 1938 it was clear that a major Japanese secret service effort was under way throughout South East Asia, employing the large Japanese expatriate community. Yet it was diffuse and, short of mass internment, it was hard to counter.

Throughout South East Asia and India, assertions that resident Japanese constituted a huge informal spy network had become commonplace, even over-familiar. Sir Josiah Crosby, the British Minister in Bangkok, complained, 'I am growing weary of the tale, to which I have been listening for over thirty years now, that every Japanese doctor, dentist, barber or photographer . . . is either an Admiral or a Field Marshal in disguise'.[15] But these rumours eventually proved to have some substance, when President Quezon of the Philippines discovered in 1942 that two of his domestic staff of some years standing had really been captains in the Japanese Army.[16]

But even the phlegmatic Crosby, while trying to resist the growing spy-mania, accepted that the problem was real. As early as November 1935 he had held private discussions with the neutral government of Thailand on the purpose of the ever-expanding staff of the Japanese Legation in Bangkok. All participants agreed that the only possible purpose was espionage. This was dramatically confirmed the following year by a Japanese 'goodwill aircraft flight' from Tokyo to Bangkok. *En route* to Bangkok it lingered over Thailand's military aerodrome in a suspicious manner. With the Japanese crew absent, this supposedly civilian aircraft was found to be a repainted bomber, 'with mapping camera cleverly concealed in the fuselage'. Righteous indignation followed, but the Japanese continued to expand their programme.[17] Bangkok became the centre for the Japanese intelligence service in the region and by 1941 over fifty diplomatic personnel were active, with new consulates being opened in the sensitive strategic area to the south, on the Kra Isthmus near the border with Malaya.[18]

British successes in the field of signals intelligence at least allowed them to monitor the flow of agent information passing back to Tokyo, since agents gave their information to Japanese attachés and consuls in South East Asia for radio transmission to Japan. In 1935, the Singapore authorities were able to follow Japanese reactions to 'the Nishamura Case', in which a senior member of the Japanese community in Singapore had been arrested for espionage and had then died in police custody. The Singapore authorities believed he had committed suicide using a capsule of prussic acid.[19] Merely keeping a record of the vast scope and scale of activities revealed by signals intelligence stretched British resources. In 1938, Sir Eric Holt-Wilson, the Deputy Director of MI5, had recommended the development of a large specialist

Defence Police Force to deal with this security problem, but this idea was never implemented.[20] Meanwhile local relations between MI5 and the head of the Japanese section of the Special Branch, Major Morgan, were at an all-time low.[21]

From September 1939 the politics of intelligence was dominated by resource, with Europe and the Middle East taking priority. In December, London despatched a single officer, Captain Tyrwhitt, to join FECB specifically to create a card index of security material 'from "Y" sources' (meaning intercepted from consular and attaché traffic) at Singapore and Hong Kong: in other words a list of Japanese agents. But these increments of one or two extra staff officers made no impact.[22]

The spring of 1941 was characterised by a war scare in Asia. GC&CS were finally moved to enhance Singapore's capacity to analyse the growing Japanese consular traffic, sending out an additional team of cryptanalysts led by Captain P. Marr Johnston and his deputy, Captain G. C. Stevens.[23] This increased volume of special intelligence was now handed to the Far Eastern Security Service or FESS. But the grandly named 'FESS' organisation was laughably small and consisted of only two officers and five clerical staff. FESS complained that simply recording the deluge of information on espionage from intercepts was 'straining capacity'.[24]

In reality 'FESS' was merely a small sub-section of FECB. Yet their official responsibilities laid out in the FESS charter were vast. They included the 'safeguarding of the armed forces and property of the crown from injury by sabotage, espionage, betrayal of information, seditious or subversive propaganda and from other hostile or "secret service" activities'. They were required to collate reports of anti-British activities not only throughout Asia and the Pacific, but also in Australasia, South America, the United States and the West Indies.[25] During the spring of 1941, Brooke-Popham continued to battle with London for more FECB security staff. However in August 1941 several vacant posts at FECB involving 'purely MI5' work had still not been filled, while Europe and the Middle East had priority.[26]

In the summer of 1941 the colonial government in Singapore contemplated a radically different approach. Painfully conscious of the growing stream of intelligence being radioed back to Tokyo, they toyed with the idea of withdrawing cipher privileges from Japanese diplomats, thus shutting off the main conduit by which the information was passed back to Tokyo. Perhaps wisely, they decided against this, concluding that this might merely serve to expose a key intelligence source, while failing to deal with the underlying problem.[27] Instead, FECB pressed for limited internment. But these unpalatable measures were resisted locally by the Malayan Government, the Colonial Office and the Foreign Office in London, not least because of the impact upon the imperial economy.[28] In retrospect, Brooke-Popham singled out the Malayan Government as establishing 'procrastination as a fine art'. They countered, rightly, that the haughty personnel of FECB and FESS had refused to co-operate with the lowly police Special Branch.[29] In fact much of the resistance to internment and other action had occurred higher up at Cabinet level.[30]

Intercepted Japanese consular signals revealed subversion as well as espionage, for Japanese agents had been carrying out propaganda activities among Indian troops since 1939.[31] In January 1941 an intercepted telegram from Tokyo to the Japanese Consul-General in Singapore, explained that Japan's propaganda and intelligence efforts would increasingly be directed southward, into South East Asia, with the ultimate objective of obtaining the raw materials, such as oil, that Japan required for her war effort. Achieving this economic 'New Order' in Asia required an acceleration of 'agitation, political plots, propaganda and intelligence'.[32] Equally alarming was an intercepted Japanese Consular Special Intelligence Report, dated 17 May 1941, from the Japanese Minister of Foreign Affairs to the Japanese Consul-General in Singapore, explaining that, because he feared the imminent entry of the United States into the war, he was urging the rapid expansion of clandestine networks in the Indian Ocean area. There was a new focus on the subversion of British colonial populations and native troops, hence intelligence was now requested on specific subjects:

(i) Machinations of England, USA and Russia and native reactions thereto.
(ii) Native sponsored anti-British, anti-rebel and anti-Russian movements.
(iii) Religious and social problems that can be used as channels for (ii).
(iv) Forecast of war operations in the Mediterranean and Indian Oceans
(v) All other matters of military intelligence including morale of native troops.

This telegram was repeated to Japanese personnel in Bangkok, Melbourne, Sydney, Simla, Capetown, Mombasa, Colombo, Bombay and Karachi.[33] In November 1941 further intercepts revealed meetings between influential Malay nationalist leaders and Japanese officers based in Thailand.[34]

The problems of FECB were exacerbated by the presence of Thailand on Malaya's northern border. Thailand was a weak neutral state with a significant minority population of Indians. In April 1941, Japan despatched Major Iwachai Fujiwara, a graduate of the Nakano School of Military Intelligence in Tokyo, and Lieutenant Yamaguchi, to Thailand to investigate the full potential for increased subversion directed against British Indian troops in Malaya and Burma. The rich possibilities were quickly apparent. On 18 September the Japanese Army General Staff set up a subversion mission in Bangkok, where the local Japanese intelligence chief, Colonel Tamura, introduced him to Pritam Singh of the Indian Independence League.[35] GC&CS had intercepted Fujiwara's initial instructions and in early October informed Singapore of what was afoot. Major Fujiwara would later become famous as the organiser of 'Fujiwara Kikan' an organisation subverting British Indian troops in the Burma campaign.[36]

Fujiwara in Bangkok, and his counterpart in Burma, Colonel Keiji Suzuki, were all the more effective for their unorthodox views, for these two officers desired an equal Pan-Asian partnership with the various nationalist movements. On the last day of December 1941 Fujiwara's organisation, along with recently captured Indian officers and Pritam Singh's Indian Independence League, agreed to create the Indian National Army (INA), a pro-Japanese force drawing on the 55,000 Indian troops captured in the Malayan Campaign. The INA problem would loom large for British security in Asia from this date until 1947.[37]

Remarkable evidence of the extent of the disaffection of Indian troops in Malaya in 1941 only came to light in the 1990s. Early studies of the Malayan Campaign rarely pause to consider that Indian troops constituted more than half the defending forces. It is hard to discern to whether disaffected Indian troops had reached their frame of mind independently, or as the result of Japanese persuasion. Units in Malaya were certainly subjected to intense Pan-Asian propaganda, especially by Japanese radio, during 1941. During 1940 and 1941 there were several outbreaks of disaffection amongst new regiments arriving from India, which were hushed up with difficulty. Unrest in the 19th Hyderabad Regiment in May 1940 was so bad that a neighbouring regiment, the Argyll and Sutherland Highlanders, were put on stand-by in case of a full mutiny.

Once the Japanese attacked in December 1941 some units quickly disintegrated. Lt Colonel C. A. Hendricks, Commander of the 1st Battalion of the Hyderabads, had to be given an escort for his own protection. But he was soon shot by his own troops, along with the battalion's Adjutant. The Hyderabads were eventually disarmed by a special provost unit on 14 December 1941 and turned into an unarmed labour battalion. Brooke-Popham was severely shaken and commanders in the entire 3rd Indian Army Corps were instructed that fifth columnists were on no account to be arrested, and were instead to be 'summarily liquidated'.[38] In after-action reports the embarrassing extent of the insurrections amongst Indian troops in Malaya was disguised with vague phrases. Reports generated in 1942 discussing the 'Causes of Failure' in Malaya, spoke only loosely of 'Eastern races less able to withstand the strain of modern war'.[39]

Intelligence chiefs in London were in no doubt about what had happened. The Directorate of Naval Intelligence in London secured the following illuminating account from the editor of *The Straits Times*, G. W. Seabridge. Some Indian troops fought well, but others 'gave themselves up to the enemy distressingly readily'. He continued:

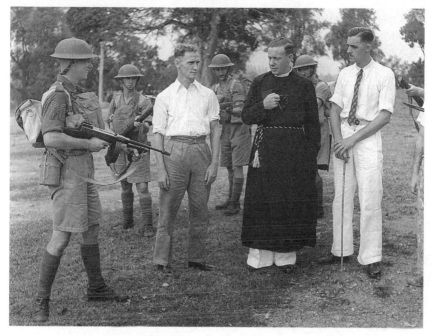

3 A counter-subversion exercise at Singapore, 1941 (IWM)

Here the Japanese propagandists were at their most brilliant. By means of radio and pamphlets dropped by aircraft, they flogged the point that they were fighting only the white man; that the British were putting Asiatic troops in the front line as cannon fodder, while the white soldiers remained skulking in the background. They promised that any Asiatic soldier who gave himself up would go unharmed, and there is evidence the promise was kept, at least in the first instance . . . Singapore fell so rapidly because the fight for it was less than half-hearted.[40]

Japan had not only launched a massive intelligence-gathering programme, but also an effective subversion programme which employed anti-colonial nationalism. With British forces falling back on India in late 1941 this internal security issue could not have been of greater concern.

Espionage from above

The traditional picture of Japanese secret service is one of amateur activities at the tactical level that succeeded only by virtue of the immense scale on which they were conducted. This is misleading, for Japan was also engaged in effective high-level espionage. From the late 1930s, Japan had access to sensitive British documentation, partly due to full Axis co-operation on the ground. A good example is the Japanese penetration of the Anglo-French regional strategic conference held in Singapore in June 1939.[41]

Anglo-French strategic talks in Paris had accelerated due to a deteriorating situation in Europe; they also opted for parallel defence talks at Singapore. Chaired by Admiral Sir Percy Noble, the senior British naval commander in the region, it focused upon their grave problems of military over-stretch. It was reluctantly conceded that both Hong Kong and French Indochina were all but indefensible, and that all forces should be concentrated to defend Singapore as the keystone of their strategy. Lengthy discussions, rather belli-cose in tone, were also held on how to handle the awkward problem of neutral Thailand.[42]

It was with the utmost dismay that the British learned that the Japanese had secured a detailed picture of the conference proceedings. This informa-tion was provided by signals intelligence from HMS *Tamar* at Hong Kong, which was conducting some of the last intercept work at this location before transfer to Kranji at Singapore. On 29 June, only two days after the confer-ence, they intercepted Japanese consular traffic carrying a detailed agent's report. It conveyed the essence of the pessimistic Anglo-French conversations and captured British thinking that

in the event of war with Japan, Hong Kong could not be held and that the Anglo-French fleet would concentrate on Singapore. This would mean however the abandon-ment of French rights and interests in the Far East and for this reason it was decided that a frontal clash with Japan must be avoided at all costs.

The source was given as 'a friend of Liu Wen Te' who worked in the Hong Kong Government's Information Bureau. This spy appeared to be run by the Italian secret service in Hong Kong, which was passing intelligence to the neighbouring Japanese Consulate. The Director of Naval Intelligence in London now faced the embarrassing task of informing the French.[43] MI5 and the Foreign Office considered expelling the Italian diplomats involved, but it remains unclear whether the agent, almost certainly a clerk in the Hong Kong Government, was identified or caught.[44]

Although the British were shocked by this episode, they learned little from it, and were destined to repeat the experience during the summer of 1940. The fall of metropolitan France in May 1940 had resulted in a Vichy govern-ment in French Indochina, which was then forced to cede bases to the Japanese, initially in the north of the colony. French weakness also caught the attention of the neutral Thai government, and in late 1940 the Thais decided to recover disputed border provinces in Cambodia and Laos, resulting in border fighting with the Vichy French in late 1940 and early 1941. In this nasty local dispute, the main concern of the British was to avoid Japanese arbitration, something which might bring Japanese forces yet closer to Malaya. Sir Shenton Thomas, the British Governor at Singapore, decided that Britain must intervene first, offering her services as a secret arbitrator and achieving a quick settlement that would shut the Japanese out.[45]

The Vichy French regime in Hanoi, which also feared Japan, was anxious to secure a British-sponsored settlement, and sent Admiral Jouan to talks in Singapore in December 1940. Sir Shenton Thomas pressed on with these arbitration efforts during January 1941, until the Japanese suddenly imposed their own mediation upon the dispute by means of threats.[46] Initially it seemed that the Thais, who were less amenable to British mediation, had tipped the Japanese off. However, in February 1941, the British learned that the main Japanese source on the supposedly 'secret' arbitration effort was not the troublesome Thais, but material secured by the Japanese espionage service at Singapore.[47]

Remarkably, Japan even recruited British officers as agents who continued to serve them even as the Malayan Campaign developed. The prime example is Captain Patrick Heenan. Serving in 300 Air Intelligence Liaison Section, Heenan was able to offer the Japanese espionage service detailed information on RAF dispositions in the months leading up to the Malayan campaign. His unit was responsible for collating air reconnaissance material and for intelligence liaison between the Army and the RAF. His contacts with the Japanese were initially facilitated by secret trips into nearby Thailand. As the Malayan Campaign began, he provided operational details about the movement and dispersal of the weak RAF presence by means of a hidden transmitter. The RAF in the Far East were already in a perilous position, outnumbered two to one and operating obsolete aircraft that were no match for the Japanese Zero aircraft.

Air power was undoubtedly a deciding factor in the campaign and Heenan gave Japan an intimate understanding of the air dimension. Born in New Zealand in 1910, and brought up in Burma and England, he suffered from multiple discrimination on grounds of illegitimacy, being of mixed race and inheriting Irish Republican sympathies from his father. The circumstances of his recruitment by the Japanese remain unclear, but a long leave taken in late 1938 and early 1939 which, unusually, he chose to spend in Japan, appears to have been instrumental. Senior officers only became suspicious in the weeks before the invasion because of his inquisitive behaviour and his continual visits to Thailand. A search of his room revealed incriminating items, including encoding materials, and during an evacuation a concealed two-way radio set was discovered in Heenan's baggage. Arrested and moved to Singapore, there was barely time for a court martial. Days before the surrender of Singapore he appears to have been marched down the harbour wall, whereupon there was a dispute amongst his captors as to who should have the privilege of executing him.[48]

Japan's detailed picture of the defence limitations of Malaya and Singapore was reinforced by active Axis intelligence co-operation, formalised by a treaty in October 1940. This revealed its potential the following month.[49] Japanese suspicions about the vulnerability of Singapore to both land and air attack was now dramatically confirmed by captured documents from a British merchant ship. Its cargo included quantities of British highly classified mail for Singapore, including detailed assessments of the parlous state of British defences at Singapore. The SS *Automedon* was initially located by Italian signals intelligence units in Africa who passed the information on to a German merchant raider, the *Atlantis*, sailing the Indian Ocean disguised as a Dutch merchant vessel. The Atlantis sunk her quarry on 11 November 1940. The most sensitive papers were carried in special weighted canvas bags on the bridge to be thrown overboard at the first sign of trouble. Twenty-eight rounds were fired at the Automedon and, by a stroke of extreme ill-fortune, one of the first shells killed or disabled everyone on the bridge, allowing the most sensitive materials to be recovered before she sank. The main safe contained six million 'Straits Dollars' of new currency that had been printed for Singapore. But far more valuable was an envelope retrieved from the bridge addressed to Brooke-Popham, containing a War Cabinet report dated 5 August 1940. This detailed the deficiencies of Singapore and emphasised the deep consternation of British military planners. They confided that, nevertheless, the demands of the war in Europe and the Middle East ensured that this problem would not be remedied.

The *Atlantis* arrived in Japan with its captured haul on 5 December 1940 and the report was selected for immediate transfer to Berlin. It was later passed on to the Japanese by the German Naval Attaché, who was thanked profusely.[50] There seems little doubt about the impact of this material in Tokyo. Japanese naval historians have argued that this document not only convinced the Japanese that they could deal with Singapore, it encouraged them to consider risking the simultaneous attack on Pearl Harbor, which was incorporated into Japanese planning at about this time. As John Chapman observes: 'Only in his wildest fantasises could a top commander imagine being privy to the calculations of his opponents.'[51] After the war, British Special Counter-Intelligence Units, combing the rubble of Berlin for surviving archives, found the original copy of the missing report. Scrawled across the front, in what they believed to be Hitler's own handwriting, was the observation 'This is a document of first importance and should be sent to NA [German Naval Attaché] Tokyo.'[52]

Serious security problems were apparent even in Britain itself. Since early 1941, as a result of help from American codebreakers, the British had been reading high-level diplomatic messages from the Japanese Embassy in London to the Japanese Foreign Ministry in Tokyo; they had also been tapping the telephones. Churchill himself was in the habit of insisting on perusing raw intercept material, in addition to the summaries prepared for him by GC&CS. This was an unusual practice for a premier, revealing not only Churchill's extreme fascination with intelligence, but also his penchant for interfering in detail. In the autumn of 1941, Churchill received a particularly unpleasant shock when reading an intercepted telegram from the Japanese Chargé d'Affaires in London to Tokyo dated 13 September. This message contained detailed information on Churchill's immediate political circle. Churchill was troubled by this, and at once asked Eden to 'get some information about his contacts'. Eden responded that five Englishmen had close contacts with the Japanese Embassy in London and acted as informants including Sir Edward Grigg MP, 'who has already been warned' and Lloyd George's research assistant, Mr Gerothowl, described as a 'sinister figure' of German origin.

Amongst the names of the other three informants supplied by Eden was that of Admiral Sempill, who was 'suspected of receiving a subvention from Japanese funds'. This caught Churchill's eye. Sempill was a trusted member of Churchill's political circle and a Commander in the Naval Air Service employed at the Admiralty. Commander McGrath, also personally known to Churchill, constituted a fourth name.[53] Churchill was astounded that Sempill and McGrath were so close to the Japanese and viewed the whole business as 'most serious'. On 20 September he told Eden:

At any moment we may be at war with Japan, and here are all these Englishmen, many of them respectable, two of whom I know personally, moving around collecting information and sending it to the Japanese Embassy. I cannot believe that the Master of Sempill, and Commander McGrath have any idea what their position would be on the moment of a Japanese declaration of war. Immediate internment would be the least of their troubles.

Churchill, also worried about the likely political repercussions, instructed Eden to act immediately to close down 'the activities of this English nebula'.[54]

By 3 October the net was tightening around Sempill. Eden sent Churchill the transcript of a tap placed by MI5 on Sempill's telephone detailing a conversation discussing contacts between Sempill and Captain Kondo at the Japanese Embassy. Sempill warned the Japanese that on no account must they ring him while he was at the Admiralty. Eden now discussed with the Admiralty whether he should be sacked. Instead he was quietly retired.[55] But Churchill should not have been so surprised at the existence of a pro-Japanese 'English nebula'. When the Anglo-Japanese alliance was at its height Sempill had led the British Aviation Mission to Japan which, over a three-year period and in great secrecy, had established the Japanese Naval Air Service. One of the key Japanese figures engaged in this project was Yamamato Isokuru who, as Admiral in 1941, planned the attack on Pearl Harbor.[56] Older British naval officers still regarded the Japanese Navy as a protégé. Indeed, prior to June 1941, when it appeared that Britain might also face a belligerent Soviet Union allied to Germany, some in Whitehall pondered reviving the Anglo-Japanese relationship on an anti-Soviet basis.[57]

But Sempill was not only pro-Japanese. He also belonged to a motley group of right-wing peers and MPs who believed that Britain should be fighting the Soviet Union rather than Germany. Prior to opening a debate in the Lords in May 1940, Lord Hankey complained to one of Churchill's secretaries that he 'would be addressing most of the members of the Fifth Column'.[58] An ardent admirer of Hitler, Sempill had lectured to the German Aeronautical Society in Berlin during the 1930s. He was a close associate of Captain Archibald Ramsay, MP for Peebles, one of the principal organisers of the pro-fascist Right Club who had been arrested and interned under Defence Regulation 18b in 1940. Sempill was also a member of The Link, another pro-fascist organisation which sought to co-ordinate British pro-fascist and anti-Semitic movements. Like the Right Club and The Nordic League, The Link was under MI5 surveillance and, in 1940, a surprised MI5 had noted the presence of disguised Japanese intelligence officers at these gatherings.[59] Such men were curious company for the British Premier to keep in the summer of 1941.

Conclusions

In April 1944, the Joint Intelligence Staff, using material from captured documents and POW interrogations, completed a retrospective study of Japanese operations against Malaya in 1941. Churchill was informed by Hastings Ismay, the Military Secretary to the War Cabinet that the conclusions were unmistakable. The 'most important single factor in the Japanese success was their intimate knowledge of the area of operations gained by years of intensive study'.[60] This was embarrassing, and perhaps helps to explain Churchill's decision not to proceed with his promised post-war enquiry into the Singapore disaster. Japanese intelligence, although amateurish in its methods, had achieved a great deal. This was painfully obvious even during the last stages of the fighting at Singapore. On 12 January 1942, FECB sent a worried message to London explaining that a document obtained from a crashed Japanese aircraft in China showed the Japanese estimate of the RAF strength in the Far East to be 336 aircraft at the end of 1941, adding 'this is the exact figure agreed by the COS' in early 1941. They concluded that this indicated either a serious leakage, or real success on the part of Japanese signals intelligence. Japanese signals intelligence was poor and this information almost certainly came from human agents. Indeed their relative success with agents helps to explain why Japan did not feel a pressing need for more cryptanalysis.[61]

Accounts of the fall of Singapore written by surviving British commanders criticised the British secret services for providing poor intelligence. But the major area of difficulty was security. The supply of information on Japanese espionage from intercepts was very good, perhaps as good as the window that 'Ultra' provided on the wartime German secret service in Europe, the Abwehr. But Abwehr activity in Britain was modest, and resources were made available to counter it, indeed to exploit it in a sophisticated way. By contrast, in Asia the scale of Axis espionage and subversion was immense and the resources to counter it were not forthcoming.[62]

What was the impact of Japan's relatively unhindered and effective espionage upon decision-making in Tokyo? The Japanese decision-making process, which was highly fragmented, and in any case attached as much significance to national resolve, or 'spirit strength' as to material advantage, is not an easy thing to read. The catastrophic destruction of Japanese documentation in 1945 has rendered this question yet more difficult to resolve. Nevertheless, there is persuasive evidence that such intelligence emboldened a cautious Japanese military, already stretched in China. Conversely, this helps to explain Britain's misperception of Japan as a perennially cautious power. In September 1941, Eden had advised Churchill that he considered Japan to be an 'overvalued' military power with many potential enemies now ranged against her. But Japan's clear understanding of Britain's weakness suggested a gamble worth taking.[63]

Security problems cannot be considered in isolation: the themes of intelligence, counter-intelligence, security and subversion formed a complex pattern. This is reflected at Singapore where the problems of security contained an ironic twist. The clandestine activities of Japan, increasing their pace dramatically during the autumn of 1941, offered FECB one of its clearest windows upon Japanese strategic intentions: the timing, direction and nature of Japan's southward expansion. FECB did not deliberately leave Japan's myriad underground networks in South East Asia unmolested. Nevertheless, their consequent free hand enhanced Britain's ability to forecast the approach of war. It is to these accurate forecasts and the fall of Singapore – an intriguing example of 'surprise despite warning' – that we must now turn.

4   Surprise despite warning: intelligence and the fall of Singapore

> We were not taken by surprise by the Japanese, as the Americans were in Pearl Harbor. Nevertheless things did not go well.
>
> Lt. General Sir Henry Pownall, Singapore, December 1941.[1]

Intelligence and reputation

Structurally, British intelligence during the years before the outbreak of the Far Eastern War was weak, and accordingly many have presumed that its estimates of Japanese intentions and capabilities must have been wide of the mark. Senior commanders, including Brooke-Popham, certainly asserted this in the aftermath of the disaster at Singapore. But recently declassified documentation strongly suggests the contrary: intelligence forecasts were timely and accurate. Instead, the politics of relations between intelligence and command, together with a broadly unfavourable strategic situation, neutralised the value of accurate and timely warnings.

Brooke-Popham's after-action report typifies the orthodox view, conveying an unflattering picture of FECB. Echoing Wigglesworth's observations five years earlier, he concluded that FECB was 'unbalanced' and 'mostly concentrated on Naval Intelligence while Army and Air Intelligence took a minor place, the latter especially being inadequate'. SIS 'improved considerably', he conceded, with the arrival of Denham in mid-1941, but there was too much ground to make up. SIS never provided the information on what was happening at Japanese naval bases, such as Camranh Bay, which Brooke-Popham had continually pressed for. He also stressed that London had denied his requests for a high-altitude photo-reconnaissance. Despairingly, he had asked General MacArthur in the Philippines to undertake this task with American aircraft but Washington had vetoed this.[2] This sort of analysis has received broad support from historians who have suggested that Japan's southward advance was accompanied by an 'intelligence disaster' on Britain's part.[3]

Yet there are incongruous aspects to this orthodox picture. British signals intelligence at Kranji was still providing a stream of reliable material on Japanese activities in the region. Moreover, from early 1941, GC&CS in Britain had begun to produce a great deal of high-grade Japanese diplomatic material, some of which was circulated to Singapore. Given the rich dividends from cryptanalysis, it is puzzling that Brooke-Popham was so concerned to secure improvements to SIS and to aerial reconnaissance. Two separate but complementary explanations for this suggest themselves.

The first answer lies in FECB's own fascinating discussion of the issue of 'Warning of Attack by Japan' produced in December 1940. FECB reviewed the various types of intelligence indicators that might be expected to provide reliable warning of a Japanese attack, ranging from highly secret signals intelligence to openly available material culled from the daily press. FECB were clearly concerned that intercepts were vulnerable. Japan, they warned, might change her transmission methods or ciphers, 'possibly under German influence', at short notice, rendering Singapore blind. They had seen examples of this in 1939 when key Japanese naval and diplomatic codes had been upgraded. Moreover, without confirmation from other sources, signals might conceivably be used as conduits of deception or 'bluffs' by the Japanese. Interception, they insisted, 'cannot be relied upon to give notice of intended operations'. Instead, what FECB wanted was confirmed visual sightings by human spies of three main intelligence targets: troop and transport concentrations, unusual naval movements and concentrations of shore-based aircraft. Thus FECB had rather old-fashioned views of what constituted justification for an attack warning and had not yet embraced the new age of machine cryptanalysis, providing real-time intelligence on an industrial scale.[4]

But there was a second reason for Brooke-Popham's criticisms. Like so many of his operational staff, he was temperamentally disposed to believe that the Japanese simply would not dare attack Malaya. As a result he was inclined to discount FECB reports of increasing Japanese preparations and FECB's largely accurate estimation of the effectiveness of Japanese forces. After the catastrophic defeat of February 1942, Brooke-Popham attempted to use the under-resourcing of intelligence to distract from the fact that he had chosen to ignore what were nevertheless prescient warnings, until shortly before the outbreak of war.[5]

Recognising that FECB were badly starved of staff by wartime theatres in Europe and the Middle East, their performance now looks more impressive than their defeated commanders allowed. On the issue of the probable timing and direction of Japanese strategy in South East Asia, both the FECB at Singapore and the JIC in London offered fairly accurate long-range forecasts.

This in turn reflected the tendency of the Japanese to send some high-grade information in low-grade consular traffic, and was reinforced by the availability of 'Purple' diplomatic traffic to the British from early 1941.

The transparency of Japanese intentions in South East Asia also reflected the extraordinary expansion of Japanese intelligence and subversion effort, which reached a peak in November 1941. The British regretted their obvious inability to counter these activities, but paradoxically, they helped to make Japan's own detailed intentions very clear. Japanese agents had been measuring the width of every road and bridge from Indochina through Thailand to Singapore. British reinforcements, exercising on the Thai–Malayan border in late 1941, came to accept that they were to be followed everywhere by local Japanese equipped with bicycles, pencils and notepads.[6] FECB recognised the warning signs, but they were not believed. There was no intelligence disaster at Singapore; instead there was a stubborn failure of command at several levels to accept warnings.

Japanese intentions

The most important assessments produced by the British during the 1940s were those of the JIC in London. The JIC system was a linchpin in a rapidly evolving British intelligence community. Enduring an uncertain beginning in 1936, nevertheless its responsibilities grew because of the clear need for a central body to conduct a timely and rigorous assessment of the value of incoming intelligence, and to manage the secret services effectively. Thoroughly reorganised in June and July 1939, the JIC grew in complexity and status throughout the war. Thereafter its duties included: the assessment of incoming intelligence, especially for future operations; servicing the Chiefs of Staff and their subordinates the Joint Planners; and to 'improve the efficient working of the intelligence organisation of the country as a whole'. On 17 May 1940 it was given the additional duty of preparing 'urgent intelligence reports' on any critical new situation.

The JIC drew upon all sources and used a high proportion of signals intelligence. Key papers were prepared by the supporting Joint Intelligence Staff and were discussed at JIC meetings chaired by Victor Cavendish-Bentinck of the Foreign Office and attended by the heads or deputies of the three service intelligence organisations, of SIS, MI5 and others whose views might be relevant. But this was only the tip of the iceberg, for other sub-committees were meeting regularly within the JIC machine at a lower level. JIC papers carried growing authority and were circulated to senior decision-makers across Whitehall. Together with the Joint Planning Staff (JPS), the JIC formed the engine-room of British strategic thinking. Key papers were also sent to appropriate theatre commanders, such as Brooke-Popham.[7]

The JIC reports on Japanese intentions during 1941 were strikingly prescient. As early as January 1941, the JIC had begun to give detailed attention to the possibility of a landward attack on Malaya. Their major blunder of that year was to participate in a false war scare in February 1941. But on 17 April they were back on track, examining 'Future Japanese Strategy' and concluding that the most likely move was infiltration into Indochina, Thailand and the Netherlands East Indies, followed by an attack on Dutch Borneo and Singapore. This was, in their own retrospective judgement, 'a remarkably good forecast'. A few days later they elaborated, again accurately, that Japan would not attack Malaya in the near future, for she would first need bases in southern Indochina and Thailand, including Camranh Bay.[8] The main brunt of the criticism levelled at the performance of the JIC has focused on their belief that Japan would move into Thailand before attacking Malaya. Nevertheless, as early as October 1940, the JIC had also warned that once Japan acquired bases as close as Camranh Bay, the move in to Thailand would be a short precursor, and warning time for an attack on Malaya might be as little as three days.[9] Moreover, in April 1941, the JIC's subordinate Axis Planning Section considered Japan's future strategy and pointed out that Japan was *already* infiltrating into Thailand, that is, that this pre-condition was now fulfilled. Accordingly her next move might be an attack on Malaya, Burma or the Netherlands East Indies (NEI).[10]

On 1 May 1941, the JIC produced an almost exact forecast of events in December of that year. They suggested that Japan's most likely moves were the penetration of Thailand, Indochina and the NEI and, when Britain seemed most pre-occupied in other theatres, active operations against Singapore and the oil of Borneo. The likely method of attack was identified as a landing near the frontier of Malaya, and on the east coast of the Kra Peninsula together with landings on the East coast of Malaya.[11] By 2 August 1941, with Japan completing her occupation of bases in the south of what was now Vichy French Indochina, the JIC hedged their bets as they tried to forecast 'Japan's Next Move'. In part this reflected the ongoing turmoil in Tokyo where the next move remained at the mercy of faction fighting. The JIC predicted a Japanese southward advance into South East Asia, with Thailand as the most likely next objective; yet they also noted the lesser possibility of attacks on Eastern Siberia, or the Burma Road. Nevertheless, a full four months before the outbreak of war they forecast:

A MOVE AGAINST THAILAND

. . .

2. Most indications show that the Japan's next move will be to force the Thai government to accept Japanese 'protection' as part of the New Order in Asia, mainly by threats and also with promises of the [Northern Malayan] territories and Laos and Cambodia, which now form part of Indo-China.

3. It is probable that the Japanese will attempt a sudden occupation of the Kra Peninsula [in southern Thailand] as part of the 'protection' of Thailand, because the occupation of Thailand would be of little use to them for an attack on Singapore unless they also occupied the Kra Peninsula. Furthermore, they would wish to anticipate any move on our part to occupy the Peninsula.
4. This occupation might be by a sea-borne expedition, with a landing on the beaches; it is likely that we should have only very short notice of such an expedition.[12]

This important paper was also circulated to Singapore where FECB recorded their agreement.[13] A few days later the JIC came off the fence on the issue of a northward advance into Siberia, asserting that this option was unlikely while Soviet armies in the Far East remained strong.[14] The Cabinet Defence Committee was being given a clear picture of Japanese intentions, for while discussing what they would do if Japan moved into Thailand first, they observed that in reality: 'The probability is that they will go straight by sea to the Isthmus of Kra'.[15]

Throughout 1941 the JIC achieved a strikingly accurate forecast of Japanese strategy in South East Asia at the outbreak of war on 7 December 1941. Nevertheless, to convince operational planners and commanders was quite another thing. Brooke-Popham dissented and in August 1941 remained convinced that Japan would go north and join with Germany in dissecting the Soviet Union. Brooke-Popham could not accept that the Japanese viewed South East Asia as a soft target. Between August and October, while Japan prepared for some major offensive, Brooke-Popham argued that the huge task of subduing China, combined with the threat of the Soviet Union, would obviate any Japanese push into South East Asia, unless specifically aimed against the Burma Road supply route into China.[16]

In mid-October 1941 the pace in Tokyo shifted ominously. General Tojo Hideki, previously the War Minister, took over as Prime Minister giving the extremists more leverage. In London the Cabinet registered the importance of this, and Oliver Harvey, Eden's Private Secretary, noted:

Bad news again this evening. Resignation of moderate Konoye Cabinet in Tokyo, following on Russian difficulties, seems to portend a forward movement by Japanese extremists . . . But where? North against Vladivostok or south against Siam [Thailand]?[17]

By October, the scale of Japanese espionage activity in Thailand was so fantastic that Japanese southward preferences were increasingly transparent. Intercepts of Japanese consular communications revealed that the numbers of Japanese, Formosan and Korean residents had doubled there in the last six months, reaching 966. They had been joined by approximately 1,000 Japanese 'tourists', mostly military personnel from the Japanese Army Intelligence School 'Nakano Gakko'. Travelling in civilian clothes, they were confident and barely troubled to disguise the nature of their activities. There was considerable reinforcement of Japanese garrisons in Vichy French Indochina and high priority extensions to four airbases in the south. By the end of October both the War Office in London and the British Ambassador in Tokyo were convinced that Japan would push into South East Asia very soon.[18]

Diplomatic reports from Bangkok, Saigon and Tokyo during November pointed to a campaign in South East Asia, exploiting the dry season beginning in December 1941. The moment of realisation that such a campaign was imminent was probably 13 November 1941. A simple report from a lowly consul, William Meiklereid in Saigon, convinced FECB of the coming deluge. He calculated that 50,000 troops had landed in the last month and long trains containing every sort of military equipment now left for Cambodia and the Thai border by day and night.[19] Geoffrey Denham's slowly improving SIS verified this. On 15 November 1941 FECB informed London that SIS operatives noted accelerating military activity in Cambodia, indicating an imminent move against Thailand and possibly Malaya.[20] The JIC in London agreed that an invasion of Malaya was approaching. In September, the JIC had doubted whether Japan had sufficient spare forces, but by 18 November this opinion had changed. They now warned that Japan was attempting last-ditch efforts for a diplomatic agreement with the United States. If this failed, Japan would move into Thailand and the Kra Isthmus as a preliminary to an attack on Malaya or the Dutch.[21]

The performance of the JIC against Japan in 1941 was broadly excellent. The complicating issue remained the assertion that a move into Thailand was a precursor to the invasion of Malaya, and retrospective reviews of the JIC certainly attempted to cloud this issue. But in any case for most of 1941 the JIC was wholly accurate in this assertion, since Japan's eventual decision to attack Malaya simultaneously with its move into Thailand was only settled Tokyo in late 1941.[23] In early 1941 Tokyo had been in flux. There had been a decision to move into southern Indochina and Thailand, but the Army had agreed only because the resources from these areas would prove useful whatever Japan's course of action. Later, at the 11 June 1941 liaison meeting, the view of the Navy Chief of Staff, Admiral Nagano, was that: 'We must build bases in French Indochina and Thailand in order to launch military operations', a view mirrored exactly in the reports of the JIC.[23] Uncertainty continued in October with the collapse of the Konoye government. Disagreement continued after the arrival of the new Premier, Tojo Hideki. Even in December 1941, Japan was still undecided what the exact pattern of her advance into South East Asia would be. Japan's military had intended a full invasion of Thailand, but this was vetoed by the Emperor at the last minute.[24]

Intelligence practitioners draw a useful analytical distinction between 'secrets' and 'mysteries'. The former are identified as the discovery of things secret but potentially knowable, and the latter as future outcomes known to no-one.[25] In 1941, the precise pattern of Japan's strategy in South East Asia was in the category of 'mysteries' as this was still unresolved in Tokyo because of the extraordinary dissonance between the Japanese services. Arthur Marder has captured the situation, describing the Japanese Army and Navy as living 'in two separate worlds'. The German Naval Attaché in Tokyo found this especially disturbing and recalled that the Army and Navy were 'constantly suspicious and jealous of each other . . . the disunity was quite amazing to me'.[26] In the face of this mystery the JIC did exceedingly well, giving ample warning in November that Japan was moving south into Thailand, with her eyes on a rapid further advance into Malaya.[27]

In November 1941 London was sure that an invasion was approaching. But in Singapore there remained a crucial difference of opinion between intelligence officers and operational commanders. Brooke-Popham's GHQ continued to maintain that the Japanese might not be bold enough to extend their attack to Malaya. This was an extraordinary contention in the face of the growing evidence that was available from signals intelligence. On 28 October the Japanese Consul-General in Singapore had been ordered by Tokyo to send fishermen with a knowledge of surf conditions on the East Coast of Malaya, where Japan's first wave would land, to Bangkok. A week later he himself left for Bangkok and was not replaced.[28] On 20 November 1941, FECB received the text of a locally intercepted message from the Japanese Consulate in Singapore to Tokyo discussing the planned activities of 'Kame' (tortoise), a Japanese fifth column in Malaya, on the outbreak of war, including its Singapore Group. This organisation, which included both Japanese and Malays, was to create panic and to conduct widespread sabotage. As a result, at the end of November, internment of some members of 'Kame' and also members of legal Malay nationalist organisations such as Kesatuan Melayu Muda, which was secretly linked to 'Kame', began. These were working under the direction of Major Fujiwara Iwaichi in Thailand.[29] As British codebreakers later recorded: 'In November 1941 signs of Japan's belligerent intentions were unmistakable in Japanese diplomatic messages; e.g. arrangements were organised for getting espionage intelligence out of Malaya after the outbreak of war.'[30]

Concentrations of shore-based aircraft offered the clearest short-term indicator of imminent attack. On 28 November, Singapore estimated that there were 245 Japanese aircraft in Indochina, many of them heavy bombers. On 2 December this estimate had risen to 300, by 4 December to 450 and by 6 December to 500. This force was more than was required for a push into neutral Thailand and could have only one meaning. Given that GHQ Singapore had been at the forefront of those proclaiming that neutral Thailand had already gone over to the Japanese, this should have been especially apparent to them.[31]

During the last ten days, warnings poured in from all sources, including Washington. Brooke-Popham was one of many who had been warned by London on 28 November that Japanese–American negotiations were breaking down, and that an attack against Thailand, the Netherlands East Indies or the Philippines was expected. At this point all forces in Malaya were put on a general warning of attack. The JIC now expected an attack very soon, to exploit the cool dry period prior to the monsoons of spring 1942.[32] The next day the American Navy passed to British Naval Intelligence a deciphered Japanese telegram from Tsubokami, the Japanese Ambassador in Bangkok to Tokyo. It advised Tokyo on how to draw neutral Thailand into the war on Japan's side through an amphibious landing in the area of the Thai–Malaya border, known as the Kra Isthmus. Roosevelt felt this matter was important and warned the British Ambassador in Washington immediately and personally on 29 November.[33]

On 3 December the Japanese officials in Bangkok were discussing the passage of troops through Thailand to the Malay border with Field Marshal Phibul, the equivocating Premier of neutral Thailand. Thailand did not formally join the war against the Allies until early 1942 and at this late hour he still chose to convey the substance of these discussions to the British. Finally, at 1400 hours on 6 December 1941 the Australian crew of a Hudson aircraft from No. 1 Squadron RAAF, based at Khota Baru in northern Malaya, and operating at the very limit of its range, spotted Japanese convoys heading for the Gulf of Thailand.[34] British intelligence, for all its weakness, had forecast the approach of war with remarkable precision.

Brooke-Popham received ample warning of the timing of the attack. Moreover, he had been given literally years of warning about the form that it would take. During February 1935, the Thai Ministry of Defence confided to the British that, through recent Japanese espionage cases in Bangkok, they had come:

into the possession of a Japanese plan for attacking the Naval Base at Singapore in the event of war. According to this plan Bangkok and Singora [on the Kra Isthmus near the border with Malaya] were to be seized as bases of operation and suitable sites for aerodromes had already been selected at other spots, whilst the Japanese counted upon uprisings in India to help them in the attainment of their objective.

The British Minister in Bangkok was confident that the Thais had indeed 'got wind of the main lines of Japan's plan of attack'. These ideas were subsequently repeated *ad nauseam* in the press and frequently discussed by defence staffs in Malaya after 1935. In the same year, Ishimaru Tota's influential study, *Japan Must Fight Britain*, was published, emphasising the strategic importance of Siam and of seizing the Kra Isthmus. Japan mounted just this sort of operation: a vanguard attack with amphibious forces with further

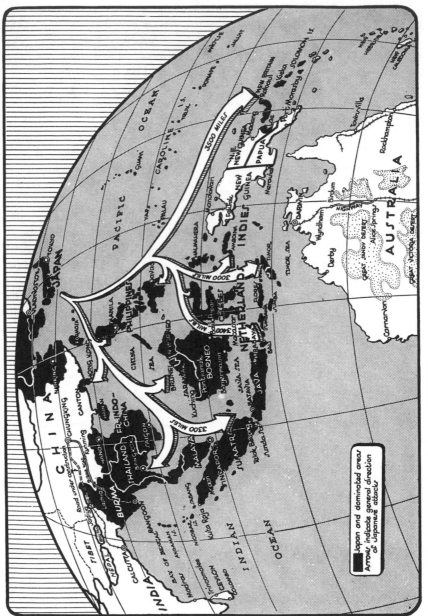

2 The Japanese southward advance, 1941–1942

troops travelling down the peninsula. Japan's landward attack on Malaya, far from being an intelligence disaster, ranks as one of the most widely predicted operations of the Second World War.[35]

But warnings were ignored not only in Singapore. In London the principal culprit was Churchill. The understanding of Churchill's approach to Japan has not been helped by the tendency of historians to focus upon regions, while in contrast Churchill's direction of the war was global in nature. Churchill's blasé approach to the vulnerability of Singapore during 1941 was determined by three global factors: the Soviet Union, the Middle East and the United States. Although Churchill had doubted Hitler's intention to launch an invasion of England from as early as March 1940, firm confirmation that Hitler's attention was turning eastwards towards the Soviet Union came almost exactly a year later, when Ultra intelligence revealed the transfer of many divisions to the Balkans. This, Churchill later wrote, illuminated the scene 'like a lightning flash'. Now confident of home defence, he became increasingly obsessed with the Middle East as the decisive area and desired every available resource for that theatre. Thus he condoned the refusal of the RAF and the Navy to reinforce Singapore. He consistently fought pressure to use fresh Indian units to bolster Singapore.[36]

Reverses in Greece, Syria and Iraq during April had infuriated Churchill and the discovery that Wavell, the Middle East commander, had a contingency plan for the evacuation of Egypt produced one of the most infamous Churchillian explosions. 'Wavell has 400,000 men. If they lose Egypt, blood will flow. I will have firing parties to shoot the generals', screamed Churchill in a vitriolic exchange with the Director of Military Operations. Churchill now judged Wavell and also the CIGS in London, Field Marshal Dill, to be weak and began moves to sack both of them. Meanwhile he ordered the destruction of any evacuation plans and directed Wavell's forces to fight 'with no thought of retreat or withdrawal'. Generals and Staff officers surprised by the enemy were not to surrender but to 'use their pistols in self defence'.

This outburst was not only an indication of Churchill's conviction of the centrality of the Middle East to the survival of the Empire, but also of extreme political pressure for a victory. His iron determination to win against Rommel, whom he knew from Ultra to be badly over-stretched, prompted him to down-grade the Japanese threat. He counselled:

It is very unlikely . . . that Japan will enter the war either if the United States have come in or if Japan thinks they would come in consequent upon a Japanese declaration of war . . . There is no need at present to make any further dispositions for the defence of Malaya and Singapore, beyond the modest arrangements which are in progress.[37]

All this was further underpinned by Churchill's underestimation of Japan's military capability, a tendency he shared with Brooke-Popham.

Japanese capabilities

Superficially, British forecasts of Japanese capabilities and of scales of attack against Malaya seem to have been accurate. The work of JIC in London, the highest level of intelligence appreciation, provides ample confirmation of this. Yet the questions that the JIC confronted were deceptively slippery. Japan was fighting in China while attempting to deter substantial Russian forces in Siberia. The issue of available Japanese forces partly turned upon how far Japan was prepared to risk stripping other theatres in order to press southward. Nevertheless, in the first days of 1942, Whitehall rightly concluded that the JIC's 'estimate of sequence of events and scales of attack were on the whole good'.[38]

In January 1941, a full year before the attack, the JIC offered a remarkably good forecast of the 'Scale of Attack on Malaya', predicting only slightly greater land and sea power than Japan later deployed. The air scale was perfect and estimated at between 336 and 432 land-based aircraft, correctly presuming that Japan would acquire air bases in the Kra Isthmus, along with a further 290 aircraft launched from carriers.[39] In August and September 1941, for some unknown reason, the JIC temporarily changed its mind, asserting that Japan did not quite have sufficient forces for a full-scale attack on Malaya, and could only deploy 160 shore-based and 155 carrier aircraft.[40] In November this assertion was reversed again and scales were revised upwards once more, but Brooke-Popham clung to the aberrant forecasts of the late summer.[41] More important than this, and rarely addressed by the JIC, was the elusive question of the *quality* of Japanese forces. This debate was played out in an inconclusive way at a lower level.

Brooke-Popham and his planners were not only very slow to accept the idea that Japan might have the temerity to attack Malaya while preoccupied with China and the Soviet Union. They also rejected accurate estimates of Japanese fighting capability provided by Military Intelligence in London and, to a lesser extent, by FECB in Singapore. The British dispute over Japanese quality was sharply delineated in terms of the politics of function and responsibility. Professional Army intelligence officers, often with considerable language skills, understood the strengths of the Japanese Army and admired it. These officers were concentrated in MI2c, the specialist military intelligence section responsible for Asia. But their opposite numbers in the Directorate of Military Operations (DMO) in the War Office, had immense faith in their own troops and rejected any notion that the Japan could be qualitatively their equal. Ethnic stereotyping and cultural misunderstanding exacerbated this. Colonel Scott, the senior DMO staff officer with responsibility for Asia, rejected the views of MI2c and, with touching simplicity, asserted that the Japanese were physically very small and therefore any British soldier could easily deal with three at once.[42] The minds of Brooke-Popham's staff were cast in similar way.

The interaction of estimates with strategy and operations against Japan is a complex subject requiring an entire study in itself. Nevertheless, the broad politics of the subject are clear and had a strong bearing upon the subsequent pattern of secret service during the Far Eastern War; recent studies by Antony Best and John Ferris have underlined how politicised the thorny issue of Japanese capabilities was. After the fall of Singapore, Brooke-Popham made bitter retrospective complaints about underestimation of both the Japanese Army and the Japanese Airforce, which he blamed on naval dominance at FECB. Percival, Brooke-Popham's Chief of Staff, was also anxious to cover himself by making the same points. However, when official historians came to test these defensive claims, they found them to be groundless. To avoid controversy, their vindication of intelligence, and their sharp criticisms of Brooke-Popham and Percival, found little place in the final draft of the official histories of the war against Japan.[43] Unsurprisingly, Brooke-Popham and Percival had already adopted a very defensive mentality even prior to 7 December 1941. During 1941 pressure was mounting for the replacement of Brooke-Popham, who was now sixty-three years of age. Duff Cooper, the Chancellor of the Duchy of Lancaster, had been sent out by Churchill to investigate Singapore, earning himself the local nickname 'Tough Snooper'. Brooke-Popham was 'damn near gaga', reported Cooper. By early November Brooke-Popham became aware of Churchill's clumsy attempts to replace him with a younger officer, and this made him irascible and unsympathetic.[44]

Although small in number, Japanese-speaking officers who had served as attachés or language officers in Tokyo, and who could speak knowledgeably about Japanese forces, were on hand in both FECB and also MI2c in London. While perhaps underestimating the extent to which the Japanese had moved to incorporate lessons about technology and firepower since the Sino-Japanese War in 1937, nevertheless their overall opinion was that the Japanese Army was an efficient and superbly motivated fighting force.[45] One important factor clouded the issue. British observers in China, watching the initial mediocre Japanese performance against what was undoubtedly a poor opponent, the Chinese Army, tended to write Japan off. This tendency was reinforced by the drubbing which Japan received in border clashes with the Soviets in 1938–9. Senior British commanders at Hong Kong bought this alternative view, as did a few 'China-hands' who began to appear at FECB by 1941. Nevertheless, throughout 1937 to 1941, it was Japanophile officers who continued to dominate the MI2c section of the War Office in London, producing accurate appreciations of the Japanese Army's strengths and arguing that Japan had not deployed first-class formations in China.

But accurate appreciation was not the final stage of the intelligence cycle. For intelligence to be effective it must be disseminated appropriately and acted upon, and this certainly did not occur at Singapore. While FECB had plenty of material that indicated that the Japanese Army was a formidable opponent, along with detailed studies of the tactics of infiltration that so disconcerted the inexperienced British troops in December 1941, this was not digested by senior commanders or units in the field. FECB held formal responsibility for 'dissemination', but this was undermined by under-staffing and the distractions of an immense security problem. More importantly, when FECB officers did attempt to challenge the low regard for the Japanese during briefings, they were dismissed as 'defeatist' by staff officers.[46] Colonel Gordon Grimsdale, Deputy Head of FECB, captured the situation precisely:

[After mid-1941] GHQ staff never believed us and always called us 'alarmists' when we told them how many divisions or aeroplanes the Japs could use. As it happens our estimates were more accurate than even we had suggested they were. On the day before the war started one of the GHQ staff said publicly that he couldn't understand why the Governor had got the wind up and mobilised the volunteers! If that was the attitude of GHQ you can understand why people lower down adopted a complacent attitude.[47]

Effective intelligence chiefs must be the unhesitating bearers of unwelcome news. But in 1941 the new and youthful head of FECB, Captain K. L. Harkness, had no previous experience in intelligence and was not sufficiently abrasive for this task. Indeed, Harkness had been deliberately appointed by Brooke-Popham for his amiability, with a view to smoothing over the inter-service tensions in FECB.[48]

FECB nevertheless worked hard at a lower level to get its message across. As Peter Elphick has shown, they found the mental construct of an inferior enemy firmly established among British field officers and their troops. The 1941 FECB pamphlet on Japanese forces for issue to British officers left the reader in no doubt about their effectiveness. It highlighted many of the Japanese facets that proved crucial in the Malayan Campaign, including proficiency in night operations, combined operations and opposed amphibious landings, and stressed infiltration and superior air-power. At least 1,500 of these FECB pamphlets were produced but the Army in Malaya persisted in its ignorantly low opinion of the Japanese adversary.[49]

Meanwhile, in London, the Japanophile MI2c were also encountering problems of source credibility. The longest-serving British Military Attaché in Tokyo, F. S. G. Piggott, who had been closely associated with Japan since 1904, although enjoying excellent entrée with the Japanese, was considered to have 'gone native'. During the 1930s his reports were dismissed as 'Piggotry' in Whitehall. Indeed, when he retired to Britain in 1941 he joined Admiral Sempill's 'English nebula'. On 13 September 1941, Eden warned

Churchill that surveillance showed that Piggott was now one of 'the Japanese Embassy's principal sources of information'.[50] Upbeat forecasts of Japanese capabilities from this quarter were bound to be greeted with scepticism.

Japanese naval strength had proved harder to gauge, for it was not deployed significantly in the Sino-Japanese War. Japanese naval building had been followed with some accuracy from open sources up until 1937, but thereafter Japan introduced ferocious domestic security measures. With budgets hidden, the movements of foreign naval attachés in Japan highly restricted and Japanese reluctant even to be seen talking to Westerners, Japan's naval and industrial capabilities became increasingly a matter of guesswork. As a result Britain had not begun to contemplate the sort of serious force projection that Japan achieved in her powerful attack on Ceylon in April 1942.[51] Moreover, without clear indicators there was a tendency to extrapolate from general factors. In February 1940 Churchill lectured the Director of Naval Intelligence that it was 'of the greatest importance to form a true opinion about present and prospective Japanese building'. But then he went on to insist that the financial condition of Japan has lamentably deteriorated due to 'a most ruinous war with China' and was 'extremely sceptical' of the Japanese matching the British or American fleets.[52]

Brooke-Popham made voluble retrospective complaints about the inadequate intelligence picture of the Japanese Air Force, which have been supported by official historians. But these look increasingly suspect. This controversy centres on the Zero fighter, the best aircraft of the Far Eastern War, which accounted for so many Allied pilots in 1941–2. Detailed information of its startling performance was obtained from China in May and again in September 1941. Some have suggested that FECB had not disseminated this, charging FECB with responsibility for 'a disastrous surprise causing many casualties to pilots'. Others have suggested that senior RAF officers were given the information, but refused to believe it, and so did not pass it on to their pilots.[53]

New documentation supports the latter view. The senior RAF officer at GHQ Far East, the optimistic Group Captain Lawrence Darvall, rejected FECB projections about the strength of Japanese air power in southern Indochina, as 'alarmist and defeatist'.[54] Equally Admiral Tom Phillips did not bother with an FECB briefing before leading Force Z against the Japanese. Yet, privately, most senior RAF officers knew how obsolete their aircraft were. In the 1930s they had even declined friendly 'air exchanges' with the Thai Air Force to the north, as they would have been embarrassed by their own poor machines.[55] Air intelligence was indeed small and could not cope with the pressures of war. A few days into the Malayan Campaign, FECB confessed to London that its picture of the Japanese Air Force was 'very confused'.[56]

Ethnic stereotyping, racism and cultural misperception were particularly important in warping the consumption of intelligence by policy-makers at a high level. Churchill, atop the command pyramid, entertained some fantastically picturesque views on what he supposed to be the poor performance of the Japanese, deeming them to be 'the Wops of the East'. Sir Alexander Cadogan, the Permanent Under-Secretary at the Foreign Office, preferred the term 'little yellow dwarf slaves', while the Italians were the 'dirty ice-creamers'.[57] A racial hierarchy was emerging. In May 1941 the Chiefs of Staff declared they had 'no reason to believe that Japanese standards are even comparable with those of the Italians'. This was echoed in the same month by the JIC. Reflecting on the large numbers of shore and carrier-based aircraft at Japan's disposal, the JIC remarked dismissively that 'the operational value of the Japanese Air Force is probably akin to that of the Italians'.[58]

Racial views were not the preserve of senior officials and warped appreciations at every level. In 1935 Captain Vivian famously reported from Tokyo that he could not conceive that 'these people' were capable of springing a technical surprise in war, and offered in support the view that the Japanese have 'peculiarly slow brains'.[59] The historian Arthur Marder, who took especial pains to investigate the real opinions of operational naval officers, discovered the commonly held view that 'because of their slit eyes . . . the Japanese fighter pilots could not shoot straight, and Japanese naval officers could not see in the dark'.[60] The persistence of the idea of the Japanese as incapable of exploiting technological methods of war found its ultimate expression in reports on the performance of the Japanese Airforce over Hong Kong during the first days of the war. Unable to accept that Japanese pilots could outfly the RAF, it was concluded that the Japanese must have borrowed German pilots.[61]

Similar misperceptions dogged the Americans. For example, in 1940, in a rare occurrence, a volunteer agent brought the American Naval Attaché in Tokyo detailed information about the Type 93 Torpedo. This torpedo was a remarkable advance which, by using oxygen, could carry an enormous warhead and travel at 'phenomenal speed', while leaving almost no wake. Japanese naval tactics were altered to exploit this weapon by day and night, reaping the benefits at the Battles of the Java Sea and of Savo Island in 1942. But in 1940, when the American Office of Naval Intelligence (ONI) offered this information to its customers, insisting that it came from an 'impeccable' source, the Navy's Bureau of Ordinance declared such a weapon to be impossible. Neither the British nor the Americans had yet mastered oxygen technology, so it was inconceivable that the Japanese had done so. This was not so much the crude application of racial views, but of a persistent image, or construct, of Japan as technologically weak.[62]

The story was repeated with the Japanese Zero. When the American Naval

Attaché, Stephen Jurika, attended an air show outside Tokyo he had an extra-ordinary stroke of luck. There he encountered, on a static display, a new fighter, which turned out to be the Japanese Zero, developed in great secrecy. He was able to inspect everything in great detail, to sit in the cockpit and read essential details such as weight and horsepower. When this was reported, Washington replied that the United States had no aircraft of comparable per-formance, and so Jurika must be wrong. He was cautioned to be more discern-ing in future reporting. The achievements of attachés were remarkable, but the picture they painted was not acceptable to their superiors.[63]

It has often been observed that power is not a static possession, but a relationship.[64] Accordingly, the greatest misconception entertained by British operational commanders in the period prior to December 1941 was about Japan *relative to themselves*. Japan's ambitions in the region were transpar-ent, but senior policy-makers in London and Singapore did not believe that Japan was capable, or indeed would dare, to take on a first-class power, while still engaged elsewhere. Aware of the reverses that the Japanese had suffered in border clashes with Soviet forces under General Zhukov during 1938–9, they had rightly concluded that the Japanese were no match for a first-class enemy. But a first-class opposition did not await the Japanese in Malaya. Britain had garrisoned Malaya with inexperienced troops and the partly disaf-fected remnants of an already over-stretched Empire.[65]

Conclusions

Throughout the half-century following the outbreak of the Far Eastern War, historians and practitioners of intelligence alike have declared themselves anxious to glean lessons from this experience. Indeed, the multiple surprise attacks inflicted by the Axis in 1941 were directly employed as justification for the post-war development of modern intelligence communities.[66] Yet the intelligence dimension of 1941 remains poorly understood, reflecting the manner in which Pearl Harbor has loomed very large, with correspondingly little attention given to the rest of Asia.

The official accounts of the fall of Singapore, and the politically motivated narrative of Brooke-Popham himself, are misleading, perhaps even deliber-ately so. There was no 'intelligence disaster'. Instead the JIC and MI2 in London, and also the under-resourced FECB, performed surprisingly well. As elsewhere, a moribund SIS was compensated for by the modern methods of signals intelligence. Thereafter, the transparent superiority of signals inter-ception would have profound impact upon the politics of intelligence for the duration of this conflict. But FECB did not have the strength to disseminate widely or to forcefully present material to field commanders who were reluct-ant to listen. Brooke-Popham's staff flatly rejected some FECB appreciations.

This was more a failure of command than of intelligence, and its result was technological and doctrinal surprise. Singapore was told when, where and how the Japanese were coming, but their arrival still represented a shock.[67]

The major shortcoming of British secret service in the Far East was not in the area of intelligence, but of security. Yet since the mid-1930s, the interception of Japanese consular and attaché wireless traffic had allowed the small Far Eastern Security Service the most detailed insight into vast Japanese espionage and subversion. Small British security organisations fought amongst themselves while lacking the resources to exploit what the intercepts were providing. As a result, a well-informed Japanese enemy advanced on a British force nurturing within it a significant fifth-column element.

Yet, in contrast to Pearl Harbor, it is highly unlikely that better British intelligence or security could have averted the single largest defeat in British military history at Singapore in early 1942. Japanese forces were better equipped, more experienced and better motivated. There was not a single British tank or a single modern aircraft allocated to the defence of Malaya. No amount of warning could have conjured forces of better quality into existence. However, better British security, and intelligence, properly disseminated and accepted, would have allowed British forces to hold out longer, permitting a more orderly evacuation, instead of the ignominious surrender of 100,000 Allied troops that occurred in February 1942.

Singapore also highlights interesting links between sabotage and subversion on the one hand, and warning on the other. Some states will always precede surprise attacks by elaborate attempts to steal extra advantage through pre-emptive clandestine operations. The Japanese had made elaborate preparations of this sort in South East Asia during 1941. But such clandestine operations of the 'action' variety conducted on any scale are usually insecure. These activities, often linked to strategic planning at a high level, are a useful but oft-neglected indicator of intentions. The same was true of Pearl Harbor. Although the Japanese carrier fleet maintained radio silence, Japanese human agent activity continued on Hawaii.

Singapore cast its weighty shadow in the secret service politics of the wartime period in ways which are explored in the remainder of this study. Signals intelligence had proved to be the cutting edge and by 1942 was providing the war-winning intelligence. This only accelerated the decline of an already moribund traditional human agent based service, SIS. The way was now paved for something of a *bouleversement* amongst the British secret services in Asia. Even before Singapore fell, SIS was already being displaced by a relative parvenu, SOE, a new sabotage organisation formed in 1940 with its own minister. By the time Mountbatten had arrived in Asia late in 1943, the eager amateurs of SOE, with their promise of action, had overtaken SIS, generating intense political friction.

More broadly, across all of Asia and the Pacific, the rise of technical sources of intelligence – signals and photographic reconnaissance – as the medium which informed strategy and operations, had a further profound impact on all human agent based agencies, both old and new. The major burden of providing the work-a-day intelligence for winning the war against Japan lay now elsewhere. This permitted Washington and Whitehall the luxury of deploying some human-based secret services on longer-range tasks of a more political nature, related not to the winning of the war but the winning of the peace.

5   Conspiracy or confusion? Churchill, Roosevelt and Pearl Harbor

We knew that they changed course. I remember ... asking 'Have we informed our transatlantic brethren?' and receiving an affirmative reply.
Victor Cavendish-Bentinck, British JIC Chairman, 1941.[1]

'Betrayal' at Pearl Harbor?

The Japanese surprise attack on Pearl Harbor in December 1941 is amongst a small number of dramatic events in the twentieth century that have exercised a peculiar grip upon the public imagination. Each new study, and there have been many, promises fresh interpretations, yet the cumulative process is disappointing. With each passing year, historical consensus regarding this subject seems to diminish, while confusion grows. Moreover, it is often the books with implausible interpretations that are most readily available in the high-street book stores and the negative impact of this phenomenon upon the wider understanding of contemporary history is a growing problem.

Conspiratorial explanations of Pearl Harbor began to emerge even in the week following 7 December 1941. In some ways this was to be expected for, by November 1941, and perhaps as early as the previous summer, Roosevelt was looking for an opportunity to join the war against the Axis powers. Roosevelt's increasingly interventionist outlook has formed a compelling context for American suspicions that Roosevelt enjoyed forewarning of Pearl Harbor, but chose not to act.[2] For some this offered a plausible alternative school to rival the orthodox ideas that either scandalous incompetence by a few, or general bureaucratic dysfunctionality, had allowed the Japanese to achieve a genuine surprise attack.[3]

In 1991 a new 'school' of thought on Pearl Harbor appeared. This was a British 'betrayal' theory advanced by James Rusbridger and Eric Nave in the book *Betrayal at Pearl Harbor* which attracted considerable public attention. This thesis suggests that it was in fact Churchill who received a clear intelligence warning of the attack on Pearl Harbor, which he then deliberately chose to withhold from Roosevelt, knowing that a Japanese surprise attack would propel America into the war.[3] This British conspiracy theory, denoted here as the *Betrayal* thesis, is potentially of some importance. Firstly, if correct, it would substantially revise our picture of the Anglo-American relationship during a critical period in the formation of the alliance, a period which most historians see as characterised by genuine friendship between Churchill and Roosevelt. Secondly, it is also of importance for the many scholars who have attempted a generic explanation of the phenomena of surprise attacks and related intelligence failures. Herein, Pearl Harbor has been deployed as a key case study. If correct, the *Betrayal* thesis would undermine some of their findings. Accordingly, the *Betrayal* thesis deserves critical assessment.

Like all plausible conspiracy theories, there is some significant underlying strength in the *Betrayal* thesis. In reality, Britain did 'predict' a Japanese attack on Pearl Harbor a few days beforehand, and this was discussed at a high level in London, but there was no 'betrayal' of Washington. Quite the contrary, it is likely that a warning telegram voicing these worries was sent to Washington. But this British 'warning' lacked the hard evidence required to attract appropriate attention, or to overturn firm presumptions about the 'logical' course of Japanese strategy. Anglo-American betrayal, or deception, in the context of Pearl Harbor in 1941 is unlikely.

Yet several factors enhance the plausibility of the *Betrayal* thesis. One is the curious decision by the British government not to extend the authoritative five-volume official history of British intelligence during the Second World War to include the struggle against Japan. This series covers the war in the Atlantic, in Europe and the Middle East, but not the war in the Far East. Indeed it contains more material on the Soviet–German contest on the Eastern Front, than the war against Japan. The official explanation, that Anglo-American intelligence co-operation in this region renders a separate 'British' history an awkward exercise, is unconvincing.[5] The Far Eastern conflict has not been neglected in previous series of official histories, either military or diplomatic, despite the existence of integrated 'Allied' commands.[6] Respected historians have suggested that, even fifty years on, the authorities still have things to hide. The late Patrick Beesly speculated that this might relate to British prior knowledge of Japan's attack on Pearl Harbor, adding that government behaviour on the matter was 'indefensible'.[7]

Betrayal at Pearl Harbor was published in 1991, although the first intimations of this controversial thesis began to appear as early as 1982.[8] *Betrayal* is part-autobiography and part-historical study, with all the confusions inherent in this sort of approach. The memoir material was supplied by the late Eric Nave, a veteran Australian codebreaker who was in his late eighties when the book was published. He had served with GC&CS at its various Far Eastern outstations, including Stonecutter's Island on Hong Kong, during the 1930s and 1940s. Subsequently, he became a Director of Australia's equivalent of MI5, the Australian Security Intelligence Organisation. Most of the historical research was conducted by his co-author, James Rusbridger, who claims to have worked in a minor capacity for SIS in Eastern Europe in the 1950s.[9]

Central to the *Betrayal* thesis is the contention that before 1941 both Britain and the United States were not only reading the Japanese diplomatic cipher, 'Purple', but also the Japanese naval operational cipher, JN-25, which carried communications to and from the fleet that attacked Pearl Harbor. Furthermore, it is argued that Britain was ahead on JN-25 and chose not to share this achievement with its *de facto* ally. The numerous public enquiries and books written on this subject, have focused upon the 'Purple' diplomatic traffic, rather than the more important naval cipher. Certainly, British code-breakers were not permitted to attend the retrospective American Congressional investigations into Pearl Harbor in 1946. The lacuna in the official history of intelligence regarding the Far East is interpreted as being of a piece with this. Finally, and most remarkably, the *Betrayal* thesis suggests that, because of the breaking of the JN-25 cipher, Churchill enjoyed significant forewarning but chose not to inform Roosevelt. Instead, Churchill welcomed the news, which arrived during a dinner with Averell Harriman, Roosevelt's special envoy, and John Winant, the American Ambassador in London. Reportedly, his American guests were then amazed that Churchill appeared to be willing to act on the news without awaiting confirmation.[10]

Britain and the United States had indeed begun to break the JN-25 Japanese Naval Operational Code before Pearl Harbor, but this does not go far to substantiate arguments about conspiratorial behaviour. In the American case, while some of the decrypts from JN-25 produced before 1942 appear to have been destroyed, several declassified internal narratives, known as Special Research Histories (SRH), written during the 1940s and 1950s by American codebreaking organisations, discuss this success. Initially Japanese naval cyphers were penetrated with relative ease. Codebooks were photographed by means of the burglary of Japanese diplomatic premises, known colloquially as 'black-bag jobs'. Later the insecure procedures of Japanese wireless operators were exploited, including sending the same messages, with elaborate and easily recognised formal opening passages, in both high and low-grade ciphers. The low-grade cipher was quickly broken, offering a key into the high-grade material. Nevertheless, American government policy on releasing archival material relating to JN-25 has been uneven and contradictory, raising unwarranted suspicions that something important is being hidden.

The evidence deployed to suggest that Britain had made at least some breaks into JN-25 as early as 1939 is also persuasive. The personal testimony of Eric Nave is alarmingly adrift on some basic facts and subsequent to publication he withdrew some statements. Nave muddles key facts, for example, William Mortimer, one of the authors' star witnesses, is assigned to the wrong unit and given the wrong rank.[11] Instead, the persuasive evidence is extant copies of British decrypts of JN-25. Some of these are of questionable provenance, since naval matters were often discussed by the Japanese in low-grade cipher systems that were less secure. Notwithstanding these problems, there is enough to indicate that some high-grade Japanese naval operational material was being read by December. This British material discusses recently intercepted Japanese messages, including the telling phrase: 'the majority of signals originating from the C-in-C Combined Fleet (Yamamoto)'.[12]

But how important are British breaks into JN-25? Two fatal flaws undermine the assertion that this is important. First, JN-25 was superseded by an improved Japanese naval code system, JN-25b, as early as December 1940. Subsequently, during 1941, the Japanese introduced JN-25B7 and, on the eve of Pearl Harbor, JN-25B8, two forms of elaborate super-encipherment that greatly complicated the task of allied cryptanalysts and resulted in lengthy breaks in the flow of intelligence.[13] Secondly, the fact of British reading of some JN-25 has been in the public domain for many years, and this fatally undermines repeated assertions about government efforts to hide duplicity on the part of Churchill.

It is essential to appreciate that, as in so many conspiracy theories, contentions about missing records and 'cover-ups' are the main driving force of the argument. Documentary evidence for conspiracy in late 1941 is very thin, forcing the *Betrayal* thesis to fall back on inference. Obfuscation on the part of the various signals intelligence agencies over historical documents has taken place, but is no greater in this area than in many others. Moreover, on the supposedly ultra-sensitive subject of JN-25, we find that the British authorities have long admitted to considerable success in breaking the Japanese naval operational or 'fleet' cipher and tracking naval movements before 1942. In 1979 the first volume of Hinsley's official history of British intelligence asserted:

By 1935 GC and CS had broken the chief army and naval cyphers of Japan.

... from 1937 the naval cryptanalysts at GC and CS worked almost entirely on non-naval Japanese cyphers, leaving the naval cyphers to be worked on at Hong Kong, while in 1939 some of the Army cryptanalysts were engaged on breaking the new Japanese naval cyphers.[14]

Hinsley notes, correctly, that Japan revised its ciphers in the late 1930s, presenting new problems for GC&CS but adds, significantly, that in September 1939, '*beginning with the fleet cypher*, the new cyphers began to yield to GC&CS's attack'. He adds: 'It remained possible for example, to keep track of her main naval movements'.[15] The so-called British policy of 'official disinformation and censorship' outlined in *Betrayal* cannot be squared with this official candour.[16]

Without a 'cover up', the limited evidence for the central assertion about calculated betrayal by Churchill, melts away. Nowhere is any material evidence presented suggesting that Churchill enjoyed forewarning of Pearl Harbor. It is merely asserted, quite improbably, that every Japanese operational naval message was collected and broken without exception. Moreover, they assert this 'must have' been forwarded to Churchill and read in person. But the volume of material produced by GC&CS by late 1941 makes this implausible.[17] In 1993 the British government saw fit to release the selected decrypt material or 'edited highlights' that were chosen for Churchill to view personally. Churchill's decrypt files suggest he saw nothing on Pearl Harbor and indeed very little on any aspect of Asia and the Pacific during all of 1940 and 1941.[18]

American signals intelligence

The overwhelming balance of the evidence suggests orthodoxy, namely that both Roosevelt and Churchill were surprised by Pearl Harbor. But beyond this broad generalisation there is little consensus. Many respected historians are at odds with each other, often unconsciously, over the basic facts of British and American signals intelligence and Japan prior to 1942. On the one hand, official historians, unofficial historians and some FECB witnesses agree that Britain was reading some Japanese operational material at Singapore in 1941. But on the other hand, it has been shown convincingly that the Admiralty signals intelligence centre in London was receiving almost nothing on the Japanese fleet in 1941. David Kahn, the doyen of American codebreaking historians, and the National Security Agency (NSA), independently assert that Americans were reading only a small amount of JN-25 and that there is 'no reason to believe that the British exceeded these accomplishments'. Moreover, Kahn and Prados have also suggested that Japanese fleets observed such good radio silence in December 1941, that there was little to intercept. In short, fifty years after the event, historians even disagree over whether Pearl Harbor was in any sense a 'warnable' event.[19]

It is important to establish at the outset what sorts of signals the British and Americans were gathering, reading and exchanging with each other. American intelligence efforts were, above all, characterised by the bitter division between the two armed services. The US Army codebreaking effort had suffered badly in 1929, when the new Secretary of State, Henry Stimson, had decided to cut off funding from this 'unethical' activity. Shortly thereafter, the publication of a sensational account of American codebreaking by Herbert O. Yardley advertised this activity to other states. The efforts of the Axis powers to create very secure cryptographic systems can be attributed in part to these revelations. Against this background, the success of the small, resource-starved US Army team against 'Purple' was a startling achievement. By contrast the US Navy only started its cryptanalytic effort in the inter-war period and had less experience. Nevertheless by the late 1930s the Navy organisation had outstripped the Army and was several times larger, reaching 147 personnel in 1940.[20]

The American codebreaking achievements were all the more impressive given that these were single services working largely in isolation, indeed at times even in active hostility to each other. As Christopher Andrew has shown, in 1940, the Army and Navy cryptographers reached a stupefying agreement regarding 'Purple': the Army would work on messages sent on an even date, and the Navy on messages with an odd date. A system better designed to create confusion and dispersal of effort is hard to imagine. This even extended to the critical interface with the White House, where the Army and the Navy took turns, month by month, to present such material to the President, with the Army system in some disarray, resulting in breaks in the supply of this material, even in November 1941. This extraordinary service rivalry continued through the war. It was only in 1952, when this state of affairs had threatened progress during the Korean War, that Truman enforced centralisation upon the still reluctant service chiefs. Inevitably, this state of affairs complicated co-operation with London.[21]

Attempts by American naval signals intelligence to look at Japanese naval operations encountered the problem of radical change. By 1940, the US Navy had achieved a very clear picture of Japanese strategy, including their preference for night action, and this was fully incorporated into war games at the US Naval War College in Newport, Rhode Island. Until the eve of the war, Japan viewed carrier operations *only* as a support arm, a way of weakening an enemy before a surface engagement, not as an offensive arm in its own right. But in April 1941, possibly influenced by the course of the war in the Mediterranean, Japan formed the First Air Fleet, giving the Allies little time to appreciate its future significance.[22]

Two complementary explanations have dominated orthodox interpretation of American intelligence and Pearl Harbor. Firstly, the idea that precise details of the attack were simply unobtainable: even if advanced Japanese naval codes such as JN-25b had been fully penetrated, the fleet's radio silence was essentially perfect, with fuses removed from radios. Secondly, the idea of bureaucratic inertia focused upon the Chief of Naval Operations, who was unresponsive to warning. The fact that the officer serving as the Director of Naval Intelligence was the third incumbent in 1941 did not improve its power relative to Operations. Dysfunction between intelligence and operations branches was apparent everywhere. Japanese orders for the mass destruction

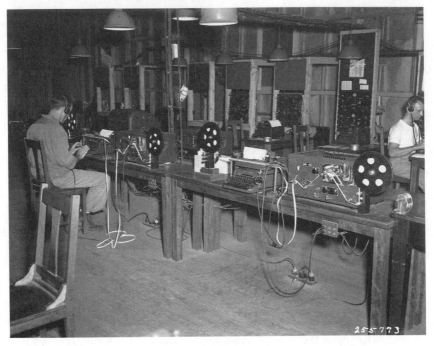

4 A signal interception centre in operation

of codes in London, Manila, Singapore and Hong Kong, on 1 December, and in Washington the following day, rang bells for US Army intelligence, but US Army operations staff were unimpressed.[23]

More recent evidence has emphasised the long-term strategic problems in the deployment of the American signals intelligence effort. It is crucial to understand how badly resourced this was prior to 1942. As General Miles of the Military Intelligence Division (MID) remarked: 'The astonishing thing, gentlemen, is not that these messages were delayed, but that they were able to do it at all.'[24] Only limited material was available and this was given very limited circulation. In September 1944, Brigadier General Hayes W. Kroner, Head of MID's Intelligence Branch, testified before an Army enquiry into Pearl Harbor that he had not been privy to signals intelligence. Although aware that this material existed, he had accepted the 'long custom' of limited circulation and had not sought to question it.[25]

A study by the American post-war sigint agency, the NSA, has concluded that Pearl Harbor was a warnable event and that ample material existed to allow anticipation of a sneak attack on Pearl Harbor on the basis of naval traffic sent in the preceding six months.[26] This study still remains classified, but its findings, released in summary, suggest that the answer to the question of the 'warnability' of Pearl Harbor is 'Most emphatically yes'.[27] These messages were sent in JN-25b, which was yielding even as the Japanese attacked Pearl Harbor and Singapore. But hitherto American emphasis had been placed on diplomatic 'Purple' traffic, while a mere five cryptanalysts worked on naval material, rising to eight in late 1941. The revealing JN-25b messages were recorded in 1941 but only broken retrospectively, some as late as 1945. Although JN-25b was the main target for FECB with as many as forty personnel engaged on this task, they were still too late. Lack of warning was essentially a resource problem.[28]

British signals intelligence and Allied co-operation

Remarkably, some of the most important British signals intelligence concerning Japan did not depend on breaking Japanese ciphers. Skilled radio operators had long understood how much could be derived from simple direction finding work (D/F). By 1941, as we have seen, the British had a chain of fourteen D/F stations around Singapore, allowing them to follow the movements of the Japanese fleet by taking triangulated bearings. Individual Japanese vessel movements in and out of ports on the coast of China and Japan could be followed at a range of over 1,000 miles, due to distinctive transmission patterns. Much could also be learnt from the volume of traffic sent in a particular cipher or addressed to particular units. These methods were immune to improvements in enemy communications security, other than complete radio silence.[29]

Britain also derived a surprising amount from the interception of low-level Japanese 'Consular Y' which often carried sensitive information. It was this sort of material that made it very clear how far the 'neutral' Thais were prepared to accommodate Tokyo during 1940 and 1941. The Thais continually assured British diplomats in Bangkok that they were resisting severe pressure from Tokyo. But as early as August 1940, Y intercepts revealed that in fact the Thais were pressing the Japanese for a deal that would give Thailand coveted parts of neighbouring French Indochina.[30] In December 1940 London informed their diplomatic representative in Bangkok, Sir Josiah Crosby, of this. Material giving him details of discussions between the Japanese and the Thai Prime Minister was accompanied by the firm instruction: 'This telegram should be burned after perusal.'[31]

Britain was also working on high-grade Japanese diplomatic ciphers and, as late as 1939, reading much of this material. In Whitehall this was denoted by the term 'BJ'. BJ probably meant Blue Jacket, a file with a blue strip denoting its sensitivity, but this quickly became rendered more colloquially as 'British-Japanese', 'Black Jumbos' or 'Bloody Japanese'.[32] Antony Best has convincingly demonstrated that during late 1938 and early 1939 Britain was able to follow the negotiation of the Tripartite Pact between Germany, Italy and Japan in detail. It was clear from this material that Germany was pressing Japan unsuccessfully for a more anti-British format to the treaties. However, later in 1939 this invaluable source was lost, due to the introduction of the new 97-Shiki O-bun Injiki cipher machine on the Berlin, Rome and London to Tokyo circuits, which defeated the British codebreakers. This machine was known as 'Purple'.[33]

Intercepted material was not always advantageous. Under wartime pressure to provide enormous volumes of material, and with influxes of inexperienced staff, mistranslation was a serious problem. In London, some insights into Japanese diplomacy were available by tapping the telephones of the Japanese Embassy in London. But this 'tap' was by no means a perfect window upon Tokyo's policy and in February 1941 misunderstandings about this material led directly to a war scare in Whitehall.[34] This episode is highly instructive about the impact of 'raw' intercept material upon senior policy-makers. Cadogan, for example, noted in his diary on 6 February 1941:

Some more very bad-looking Jap telephone conversations, from which it appears that they have decided to attack us. A. [Anthony Eden] was seeing Hopkins and I went in and guardedly gave them the news. We then went over to see the P.M., about 6.50 . . . Instructed H. [Lord Halifax] to pass on to the U.S. Government our information about the machinations of these beastly little monkeys.[35]

It was only in May 1941 that professional Japan-watchers of MI2 came to the conclusion that the person responsible for transcribing the intercepted calls had only weak colloquial Japanese and seemed to be exaggerating the contents of the messages. They then attempted to claim that the taps had not markedly affected policy, but this was not the case.[36] Such false alarms became less likely by March 1941. Thereafter, the main British diplomatic codebreaking centre at Berkeley Street in London began to produce some of the first decrypts of high-grade Japanese 'Purple' diplomatic traffic, with the product being known as 'Magic'. This capability was a gift from the Americans who had made extraordinary progress on 'Purple'.[37]

But the sophisticated American operation against 'Purple' was vulnerable to the same sorts of errors, with perhaps even graver results. This is clear from important, yet somewhat neglected, work on intelligence, mistranslation and the outbreak of the Pacific War by scholars such as Keiichiro Komatsu. Their work underlines how badly the shortage of Japanese-speaking personnel affected the quality of the American cryptanalytical operation. It demonstrates convincingly how ambiguous passages in Japanese diplomatic messages were rendered more aggressive by poor translation during the final negotiations between Tokyo and Washington in 1941. This helped to convey to Roosevelt and Hull the sense that all actors in Tokyo were insincere and bent on pre-meditated aggression, at a time when in fact Tokyo was highly factionalised and without consensus.[38]

The initial American offer to Britain of the solution to 'Purple', made on 31 August 1940, was a remarkably early and open-handed example of Allied cryptanalytic co-operation. The US Army's reconstruction of the Japanese cryptograph (with some naval assistance), which Americans had never seen, must constitute one of the most astonishing technical feats of the war.[39] The specific offer was made by Brigadier General George Strong of the US Military Observer Mission, to the surprise of the British Chiefs of Staff, even before the system had been entirely perfected.[40] Commander Laurence F. Safford, Head of Op-20-G, the naval codebreaking centre, had opposed the offer to the British when consulted, but General George Marshall had overruled him.[41]

The British had been more reticent about cryptographic exchange in 1940, with Menzies voicing uncertainty to Churchill about American security procedures, believing that material they had already given the American Embassy had sometimes been leaked.[42] Nevertheless, Strong's dramatic offer led to a preliminary agreement on co-operation against Axis ciphers concluded in December 1940. Contrary to most orthodox accounts, it seems likely that Britain did reveal to the Americans their own remarkable successes against the German Enigma, including Luftwaffe codes, in late 1940 and early 1941. This, together with the means by which this had been done, using primitive computers or 'Bombes', probably constituted the most closely guarded British secret of the war.[43]

The United States supplied selected decrypts to London in late 1940 and then, in February 1941, donated to the British one of their precious machines for reading 'Purple'. This machine was brought to Britain by Dr Abraham Sinkov of the US Army Signals Intelligence Service, who led a four-man team of Army and Navy cryptanalysts. The machine had originally been destined for an American codebreaking centre at Pearl Harbor, known as Station Hypo. Commander Safford, the senior naval cryptanalyst, who was not present on the visit, later speculated that the machine given to the British might have prevented the attack on Pearl Harbor (which seems unlikely), and also that the British did not reciprocate with Enigma material. However, it now transpires that the British donated the limited naval Enigma information that they then had. The British did not yet have all the answers the Americans desired; nevertheless, Menzies explicitly sought Churchill's permission to show them the 'Bombes'. American visitors toured Bletchley Park's famous Hut 6, where advanced work was being done on the German Army and

Airforce Enigma. The Sinkov mission reported that 'no doors were closed to us' and the result of this early exchange was 'a saving of several years of labor on the part of a fairly large staff'.[44]

Anglo-American exchange was not entirely smooth. As the historian Ralph Erskine has revealed, in 1941 the United States gave Britain not one precious 'Purple' machine, *but two*. In a truly remarkable episode this machine was sent by GC&CS to Singapore in late 1941 and was then 'lost'. The American donation of a 'Purple' machine had triggered a widening and deepening of the Anglo-American signals intelligence partnership. Then, in the summer of 1941 FECB at Singapore asked GC&CS for their own machine, to which the Americans agreed. This was sent from England on a warship but, against instructions, had been transferred to a freighter at Durban. This freighter had delivered the crate into the hands of naval stores at Singapore during late December 1941, but the stores denied knowledge of the delivery. GC&CS could only hope that it had been destroyed or dumped in the seas by a demolition party, but equally it could have been captured by the Japanese and not recognised for what it was. The fate of this extraordinary cargo remains unknown.

If the Japanese had captured this 'Purple' machine and realised what they had obtained, it is likely that the most valuable source of Allied intelligence would have been lost for the duration of the war. Japan would have improved her security, denying the Allies the sort of intelligence that contributed so vitally to battles such as Midway in 1942. There would also have been an impact in Europe. Throughout the war, the messages of the Japanese Ambassador in Berlin, Baron Oshima, relaying his conversations with Hitler, constituted the single most valuable Allied window upon thinking in Germany. Moreover, Japan would probably have alerted the Germans, leading to an improvement in their Enigma, which rendered it vulnerable.[45] Counterfactual history is a notorious area. But it is striking to note that the official historian of British intelligence has consistently argued that signals intelligence may have shortened the war in Europe by three years. The loss of Magic and Ultra at an early stage in the war would undoubtedly have been very grave.[46]

Notwithstanding this dangerous episode, the new flow of high-grade Japanese 'Purple' material, facilitated by the United States, had an important bearing on British decision-making. Although only two members of the Foreign Office were officially indoctrinated into these secrets (one being Victor Cavendish-Bentinck of the JIC), many saw this valuable material without knowing its source.[47] The American donation of 'Purple' persuaded the British to be more open about their intense efforts against the Japanese naval code JN-25, and its successors.[48] 'Purple' allowed MI2 to prepare a detailed summary on Japanese–German conversations in February 1941 and to follow

Japanese–German–Italian collaboration throughout the rest of 1941. The material derived from the Berlin–Tokyo circuit included many exchanges between Matsuoka and Hitler and also Ribbentrop's briefing of Oshima two days after the launching of Operation *Barbarossa*.[49]

Such material also warned the British well in advance of the Japanese decision of late June 1941 to seize strategic bases in the south of Vichy French Indochina. This confirmed their picture of a Japan turning south, emboldened by news of Germany's attack on the Soviet Union on 22 June 1941. On 25 June 1941, the British Chief of the Imperial General Staff, Field Marshal Dill, was informed that the JIC knew from 'unimpeachable sources' that Japan was about to acquire two harbours and eight airbases in Southern Indochina, if necessary by force. The Chiefs of Staff met on that same day to decide on their response. On 7 July the British Cabinet was also considering its response to events which had not yet taken place.[50] This foreknowledge of Japan's intention to seize key points in southern Indochina appeared a full week *before* the decision had even been confirmed by a high level Japanese Imperial Conference in Tokyo on 2 July 1941, and a full month before Japan executed this operation. This reflected Japanese attempts to square their planning with Berlin.[51]

Nevertheless, this episode also indicates that Anglo-American patterns of dissemination for this material were still unstructured and amateurish. On 10 July 1941, more than two weeks after the JIC's warning to the Chiefs of Staff, a surprised American Under-Secretary of State, Sumner Welles, showed the British Ambassador in Washington material indicating the same thing. Only on 14 July did Cadogan, the senior Foreign Office official receive the news. Remarkably, on 21 July 1941, it seems Roosevelt had still not been informed. Eden was amazed and complained that 'President Roosevelt still holds the idea that the Japanese are unlikely to do anything drastic in Indochina and that we can afford to wait and deal with them later.'[52] The politics of the circulation of this very high-grade material, more freely available to the military than to civilians on both sides of the Atlantic, were fraught and complex.

When British Naval Intelligence reviewed their successes and failures at the end of the war they identified two decrypted diplomatic message circuits as being of primary importance. Firstly, that between the Japanese Minister of Foreign Affairs and the Japanese Ambassador in Moscow. His interviews with Molotov, the Soviet Foreign Minister, revealed the depth of anxiety in Tokyo about the Soviet threat. Secondly, the messages between Tokyo and Baron Oshima, the Japanese Ambassador in Berlin. Although Hitler exaggerated, he regarded Oshima as something of a confidant and often outlined his thinking about every theatre of the war.[53] It was intelligence from this circuit on 4 June 1941 that finally convinced the British that Germany was certain to take the momentous step of attacking the Soviet Union.[54]

By contrast, British efforts against high-grade Japanese naval communications such as JN-25 and its successors, were more frustrating. FECB held a signals intelligence conference with Americans from the Cast station on the Philippines in February 1941 with a hand-over of material on JN-25, and by May 1941 they were exchanging material by a special radio link. But this did not take them much further against Japanese Naval ciphers. In late 1941 Singapore received long-awaited new 'Hollerith' punched-card machinery from GC&CS at Bletchley Park to assist with JN-25, but it had not been fully utilised by the time of the Japanese invasion. Reading of JN-25 and its successors remained fragmentary and problematic, and so the most valuable naval signals intelligence at Singapore remained D/F and radio finger-printing work.[55]

The evolving pattern of co-operation and distribution of British and American signals intelligence was now increasingly important, but also appallingly complex. In late May 1941, Brigadier Raymond Lee conveyed a US Army request for comprehensive intelligence exchange in the Far East. There followed painfully slow and complex discussions about who would get what and levels of security: 'The whole thing has been so tangled up', he complained.[56] On 6 June 1941, the British JIC had met to consider a proper structure for co-operation in the Far East.[57] They noted that Americans had been at FECB for some time; however, exchange had been limited to intelligence directly related to army planning, and this was now replaced by comprehensive exchange. The characteristic American single-service approach to intelligence matters struck the JIC as odd. Britain now suggested that co-operation be extended to naval matters, with the Admiralty reportedly 'very anxious to co-operate'. Eventually FECB was instructed that 'there should be a full exchange of intelligence between British and American officials in the Far East', including signals intelligence, though the latter required the approval of the local SIS chief. Firm instructions for 'the fullest co-operation' were also issued to all British personnel in Shanghai, Hong Kong, Tokyo, Chungking, Bangkok, Manila and Peking. The JIC explicitly decided that local liaison and a multiplicity of Anglo-American channels for exchange were the 'best solution'.[58] SIS information on the Far East was now to be exchanged with the Americans at FECB, rather than in London.[59]

As these windows opened, Britain was surprised to find that, unlike Britain's GC&CS, American signals intelligence was less centrally organised, resulting in greater inter-service rivalry. FECB discovered that in the Philippines Japanese Army traffic was not even being intercepted. Washington refused a request from General Short, the Commander at Hawaii, that he be sent an Army cryptanalytical unit to work alongside the naval cryptanalytical centre, Station Hypo, at Pearl Harbor. War was the eventual antidote to bureaucratic stupidity and only in February 1942 did the US Army in Hawaii finally establish links with naval cryptanalysts.[60]

Expanded co-operation also allowed GC&CS to shed burdens. High-grade Japanese Army cyphers had proved impenetrable for a decade. By 1941, FECB, struggling to cope with the mass of security-related material derived from 'Consular Y' intercepts, had all but abandoned this target. On 22 August 1941 Anglo-American co-operation lifted this task from their shoulders. During talks in Washington, Alastair Denniston, the head of GC&CS, persuaded the US Army that they should 'take over investigation of Japanese main army cipher soon as priority commitment'. Shortly afterwards, Captain G. C. Stevens from FECB at Singapore travelled to Washington carrying all their material on the Japanese main Army cipher.[61] In 1945 approximately 2,500 people would still be working on this one cipher to no avail.

By late 1941 the networks of Anglo-American intelligence exchange were growing fast. In October, Colonel Greenwell, the US Assistant Military Attaché in London, was visiting the office of the British Deputy Director of Military Intelligence 'every morning' to collect the latest material on the Far East.[62] The *multiplicity* of links between British and American intelligence developing throughout the Far East and in London was highly significant. It renders it improbable that Churchill, or any single individual, could exercise detailed control over the exchange of specific pieces of information. Notwithstanding this, Churchill was still *trying* to achieve this during 1941, at least regarding major documents going to Washington. In July, Brigadier Vivian Dykes of the War Cabinet secretariat had complained to the American Military Attaché that it was impossible to give him an estimate of the situation 'without having Winston Churchill's own "chop" on it'. Churchill, he added, 'insists on anything going to the United States being vetted by himself'. But the new agreements on comprehensive exchange involving many centres eroded this central control. This development alone, far advanced by October 1941, renders the *Betrayal* thesis highly improbable.[63]

The politics of signals intelligence co-operation was also multilateral and included the efforts of smaller units, such as the Dutch in the East Indies. Their co-operation in the 1920s and 1930s had been mostly focused on work against communists, nationalists and 'agitators'. The JIC now entertained fears about Dutch security.[64] In January 1941, the head of Dutch signals intelligence at Bandung arrived in Singapore and revealed an impressive array of work against Japanese communications. However, London remained cautious, refusing a request from Singapore to be allowed to improve Dutch decryption and instead favouring the passing of selective information only to the Dutch.[65] By August 1941, the Dutch were gradually being drawn into the picture. Colonel Leonard Field, with extensive knowledge of interception in the Far East, was despatched

on a regional co-operation tour, visiting San Francisco, Honolulu, Manila, Sourabaya, Batavia and Singapore.[66] The Dutch, like the British, were working on
allied and neutral, as well as Axis communications and were sharing KMT
(nationalist) Chinese material with the British.[67]

All parties withheld or 'selected' material to influence their allies. As
Antony Best has convincingly shown, during the February 1941 war scare
Britain used material from the telephone tapping of the Japanese and Thai
embassies in London in an attempt to generate a sense of crisis. When Hitler
expressed anti-American sentiments to Baron Oshima in Berlin, this was
always passed on to Washington with priority on Churchill's express orders.[68]
Indeed by 1941, Churchill, who had his own series of specially selected
signals intelligence highlights, habitually scribbled in the margin of some
decrypts, 'Make sure the President sees this', especially on Japanese material.[69] Britain also withheld material which might have influenced the Americans in an undesirable direction. In late 1940, Britain had secured information which revealed that the Thais were co-operating closely with Japan, but
did not want further American pressure on Bangkok. So this was deliberately
withheld on the grounds that Washington was 'already sufficiently stiff-
necked with the Thais'.[70]

One further intriguing facet of the politics of Anglo-American cryptanalytical relations requires explanation. Amongst the series of decrypts selected
for the personal perusal of Winston Churchill (released in 1995) were not
only the traffic of many neutral countries, but also allies such as the Free
French. GC&CS was also clearly working successfully on the American diplomatic code GREY until December 1941. Indeed reliable GC&CS witnesses
have recalled staff working on the traffic of American consuls and commercial attachés throughout the war.[71] All sides seemed to have been quite phlegmatic in this regard. In June 1941, when agreements about the comprehensive
sharing of Far East intelligence were negotiated, London JIC staff asked the
US Military Attaché, General Lee, for his opinion on the security of American cyphers. He replied tartly that the GC&CS already knew a great deal
about this matter!

Importantly, this underlines one of the hidden benefits of Allied cryptanalytical co-operation. Once the Allies began to share their most precious assets,
Ultra and Magic, then absolute communications security by all parties
became paramount. For the first time London and Washington had a vested
interest in the complete impenetrability of each other's systems. Quite simply,
if GC&CS could break American codes then so, perhaps, could the Germans,
and vice versa. Lee's excellent diary of talks with the British brings out this
facet of the politics of intelligence very well:

The talk then turned again on the question of security. They wanted to know whether my despatches went by radio or cable and were relieved to hear that they went by cable, and were further relieved to hear that we have a direct wire straight into the War Department. However, I pointed out that this wire was subject to interception by their people here in England [GC&CS] and I had no doubt they had taken our messages and attempted to decipher them. Saw a wonderful opportunity, too good to miss, and said, 'If you are worried about this, why don't you let me give you two or three messages in our cipher and you can put it up to your cryptographic crowd to crack it, and if you do succeed in cracking it, then you can let me know and also cease giving me vital information to transmit to Washington.' This has them where I want them. Under any other circumstances I might ask them to crack the cipher and if they succeeded in doing it, they might tell me that they had not done so, in order to take off the stuff I am sending. But it is now in their interest to assure me as to its security or not, because the stuff that is going over it is more vital to them than to us.[72]

Equally, in August 1940, when the initial American offer of cryptanalytical co-operation had been made, the US Army and the US Navy had been clear that nothing should be passed to the British about American cryptographic procedures, such as the US Army's high level Sigaba machine. General Marshall specifically forbade such exchange in September 1940.[73]

The importance of preconception

Major breakthroughs, especially by the Americans, together with rapidly growing co-operation had greatly increased the quality and quantity of intelligence about Japan. But there were also serious impediments to its correct interpretation. During 1941 a firm matrix of preconceptions about the most likely Japanese target developed in London and Washington, focused upon South East Asia. These presumptions ensured that at the many levels of intelligence analysis in Washington and Whitehall, deductions about less probable targets such as Hawaii were filtered out of the material selected for the attention of senior policy-makers. Moreover, primary attention was focused on theatres of active war.

In London, it is clear that had information about an attack on Pearl Harbor reached Churchill, or those around him, they would not have believed it. Churchill's mind, although vacillating, was set against the possibility of *any* sort of Japanese attack in late 1941. As late as 2 December 1941, in a Top Secret personal minute to Anthony Eden, he outlined his firm belief that Japan would attack neither Britain nor the United States before the spring of 1942. Instead Churchill presumed continued Japanese 'nibbling', perhaps into neutral Thailand. This was reinforced by Churchill's opinion of the martial abilities of all Asian peoples, which was singularly low.[74]

Across London and Washington in 1941, there was a developing consensus that the Japanese would attack South East Asia – either Thailand, the Philippines or one of the European colonies. In late 1941, Roosevelt held lengthy discussions of current intelligence with his 'Cabinet'; they spoke of Japanese forces on the move, with a range of possible destinations, including American bases in the Philippines. Henry L. Stimson, the American Secretary of State for War, records a Cabinet meeting on 25 November in which Roosevelt assured them 'we were likely to be attacked next Monday for the Japan are notorious for making an attack without warning'. But the focus remained firmly fixed on South East Asia. On 27 November, Stimson recorded another 'tense' White House meeting:

The [intelligence] paper . . . pointed out that it might develop into an attack on the Philippines, or a landing of further troops in Indochina, or an attack on the Dutch Netherlands [sic] or on Singapore. After the President had read these aloud, he pointed out that there was one more, it might . . . develop into an attack on Rangoon . . . This, I think, was a very good suggestion on his part and a very likely one.[75]

Equally, Roosevelt's frequent discussions with Lord Halifax, Britain's Ambassador in Washington, focused on an attack on South East Asia in the first week of December 1941.[76]

This picture accords with the broader findings of those considering the general nature of surprise attack. The key barriers to effective warning are often these sorts of fixed ideas that hinder clear analysis and also hinder the acceptance of material to policy-makers.[77] Above all, leaders tend to reject information that does not fit an already established pattern of presumptions about likely enemy behaviour. Stalin ignored more than eighty separate indicators of the German attack on Russia on 22 June 1941, because a German attack, deliberately opening a war for Hitler on two fronts, seemed to him illogical.[78] London and Washington shared Stalin's presumptions for a long time. Even with the benefit of Ultra, it took the JIC until March 1941 to predict Operation *Barbarossa*, with the Chiefs of Staff resisting the idea until May 1941. Even at this late hour Cadogan noted dismissively: 'I should love to see Germany expending her energy there, But they're not such fools (as *our* general Staff).' Like Stalin, Cadogan expected Hitler to present Moscow with a limited ultimatum for some concessions.[79] *A fortiori*, London could not conceive of a simultaneous attack on Britain and the United States by a Japan with its limited industrial capacity already stretched by war in China.

No material suggesting an attack on Pearl Harbor seems to have reached Churchill during 1941. At the end of the war, NID 12, the signals intelligence staff at the Directorate of Naval Intelligence in London, produced a summary of the warning indicators of the approach of the Far Eastern War. All this pointed to South East Asia, including the possibility of an attack on the Philippines. The material seemed to indicate a clear pattern. Before the end of 1940 the Japanese Consul-General in North Borneo was told that offensive action would extend to his location 'after Manila'. In February 1941, Japanese officials were told to be ready to quit London at short notice. In late June 1941, as we have seen, the Japanese acquisition of bases in southern Indochina was clearly foretold. More importantly, the Japanese were planning to evacuate their nationals from British Commonwealth territories such as South Africa as early as 24 July 1941. But the clearest indication of Japanese southward intentions against European colonial territories was offered by two messages from Tokyo to the Japanese Consul-General in Singapore. On 7 November he was informed that the last Japanese ship to call there would leave on the 16th of that month. A few days later, on 11 November 1941, he was told to return to Japan without relief. These indicators seemed unambiguous.[80]

A similar picture, emphasising presumptions about South East Asia, emerges from the diaries of senior figures who saw the highly secret flow of signals intelligence. Oliver Harvey, Eden's private secretary, noted after Pearl Harbor: 'We're all astounded over Japan. We never thought she would attack us and America at once. She must have gone mad.'[81] Field Marshal Alan Brooke, who had replaced Dill as Chief of the Imperial General Staff, was in continual receipt of high-grade signals intelligence and considered that the most likely target for the Japanese forces massing in early December 1941 was exclusively the weak European colonial territories in South East Asia. His diary records that the British Chiefs of Staff spent much of 5 and 6 December 1941 debating how they might contrive to draw the United States into a resulting war between Britain and Japan only. Brooke was clearly shocked by Pearl Harbor and consequently, on 7 December 1941, greeted the attack on the United States with the ungrateful words: 'All our work of the last 48 hours wasted.'[82]

Those concerned with the processing of British signals intelligence tell much the same story. In 1941 Malcolm Kennedy occupied the Japan desk of the GC&CS Diplomatic Section at Berkeley Street, London. He also maintained close contact with MI2c, the military intelligence section dealing with Asia. Kennedy's diary notes that by 6 December, Churchill was aware that Japanese forces were really on the move, but was unsure as to their destination and telephoned frequently, asking for more information. Significantly, he adds 'the news of the 9 p.m. wireless, that Japan had opened hostilities with an air raid on Pearl Harbor, more than 3,000 miles away out in the Pacific, came as a complete surprise'.[83] If the British had received any significant information about Pearl Harbor, then numerous diaries and documents would have to have been deliberately falsified to disguise it. This seems quite implausible. Moreover, Naval Intelligence digests of the salient achievements of signals intelligence during the war state quite explicitly that the British received no specific warning of the attack on Pearl Harbor.[84]

The British 'warning' of Pearl Harbor

Yet, it is equally clear that in November and December 1941 some British officials came surprisingly and frustratingly close to a prediction of the attack on Pearl Harbor. Indeed, their concerns were probably voiced directly to Washington. But the British lacked *hard* evidence to support what was a speculative warning, so it carried no weight. Nevertheless, for heuristic reasons alone, it is worth considering how some senior British intelligence officials managed to surmise future Japanese intentions.

The first element in British guesswork was the famous 'Winds' message. Despatched by Tokyo on 19 November 1941, it informed Japanese diplomatic and military personnel of the codewords that would be openly broadcast on Japanese civilian radio, during weather reports, when diplomatic relations were about to be severed. With impressive finality, Japanese officials were told that on hearing this warning they were to burn their codes and ciphers. The pre-arranged codewords were as follows:

(1) With the USA. The words – HIGASHI NO KAZE AME (easterly winds rain)
(2) With the SOVIET UNION. The words – KITA NO KAZE KUMORI (north winds cloudy)
(3) With BRITAIN, including invasion of THAILAND.
 Words NISHI NO KAZE HARE (westerly winds fine).

'Easterly winds rain' was decrypted by the British as it was sent to the Japanese Chargé d'Affaires in London, some time before 25 November 1941. This increased fears of an imminent conflagration in Whitehall. London had already concluded that the Hull–Nomura talks were unlikely to produce compromise and this confirmed that war was close.[85]

Australian, British and American codebreakers all intercepted and decrypted the 'easterly winds rain' broadcast in the days before Pearl Harbor, but it gave them few specifics. 'easterly winds rain' was a warning of relatively low security status which was sent in a wide variety of Japanese ciphers. Equally, on 2 December 1941, the Japanese Foreign Minister warned Japanese representatives in Berlin and Rome that Japanese–American negotiations were expected to 'breakdown'. On 3 and 4 December, Japanese cipher machines in London *and Washington* were reported destroyed. Although these messages gave no indication of when or where hostilities would start, they were bound to prompt intense speculation about an attack on the United States, focused on American forces in the Philippines.[86]

Accordingly, in late November and early December the Japanese fleet was a matter of extreme interest. Although the British had broken JN-25 and its successors only intermittently, radio direction finding had always allowed them to follow the Japanese fleet precisely. Now it had changed course before adopting an ominous radio silence. This was sufficient to merit high-level discussion at the London JIC. In 1975, Victor Cavendish-Bentinck, the JIC chairman, informed his close friend, the author Constantine Fitzgibbon, that the prospect of a Japanese attack on Hawaii was discussed at a meeting of the JIC on Friday, 5 December, two days prior to Pearl Harbor. He asserted:

We knew that they changed course. I remember presiding over a J.I.C. meeting and being told that a Japanese fleet was sailing in the direction of Hawaii, asking 'Have we informed our transatlantic brethren?' and receiving an affirmative reply.[87]

In a similar, overlooked passage, William Casey, one of Eisenhower's senior intelligence officers in Europe, and later Director of the CIA, has noted: 'The British had sent word that a Japanese fleet was steaming east towards Hawaii.'[88] How plausible are these remarkable passages? Uncorroborated by other sources, they have passed almost unnoticed over the years. Moreover, at first glance they appear to be contradicted by the recently released JIC minutes for the fateful week prior to Pearl Harbor. These reveal that the JIC did not even meet on 5 December. It met on 3 and 9 December and did not mention Pearl Harbor at either meeting.[89]

But the statements of authoritative figures such as Cavendish-Bentinck and Casey should not be dismissed lightly. The formal minutes and memoranda of the JIC are very thin, capturing only a small percentage of the work-a-day discussions and meetings of the JIC and its subordinate staff, which took place at many levels. Moreover these statements have recently received confirmation from Captain Julian E. Ridsdale (subsequently the MP Sir Julian Ridsdale). In 1940, Ridsdale had been one of the last British language officers serving in Japan and had narrowly avoided arrest by the Kempei Tai, the Japanese Secret Police, during a wave of retaliatory arrests that followed the British ejection of Colonel Suzuki, a Japanese intelligence officer, from Hong Kong. By 1941, Ridsdale was serving in Whitehall with MI2c, liaising with both Cavendish-Bentinck's JIC and with Lt Colonel Leo Steveni, the SIS officer responsible for the Far East.[90] Ridsdale recalls a JIC meeting at which the radio silence adopted by the Japanese fleet was discussed and its possible destinations reviewed. Pearl Harbor was one of the targets thought most likely and as a result a warning telegram was despatched to Washington. Years later, Ridsdale met Cavendish-Bentinck again and enquired whether the telegram really had been sent; Cavendish-Bentinck confirmed that it had.[91] It is unlikely that a copy of this telegram still survives.[92]

These recollections are impressive because they stress speculation based on tracking the Japanese fleet, and are congruent with the fact that the best material was coming from direction finding. This had allowed the Operational Intelligence Centre at Singapore to follow the initial Japanese naval mobilisation before radio silence was adopted on the eve of war. Captain Hillgarth, Admiral Mountbatten's naval intelligence chief, noted in his internal narrative, written in 1946, that they 'had a fair idea of the fleet's composition, organisation and movements, and were aware of the formation of five divisions of aircraft carriers and of a special task force. We did not know its purpose, against Pearl Harbor . . .'[93] But someone made an educated guess about possible targets for this special task force and decided it was worth a warning. All this is consistent with the recollections of codebreakers working under the auspices of the FECB, who asserted that they had suspected a Japanese attack on Pearl Harbor and had conveyed this speculation to London.[94] But for all this, the talk of Pearl Harbor in both Singapore and London amounted to little more than intelligent guesswork.

In 1942, Major General Francis Davidson, the British Director of Military Intelligence in London, outlined clearly the matrix of preconceptions that ensured that these speculations would be ignored. Britain had 'generally credited Japan with conservative conceptions'. 'Where they were badly wrong was failure to realise that Japan could and would attack America and Britain simultaneously.' Moreover, they had always worked against the background presumption that Japan hoped to attack Britain 'without rousing America'.[95] Policy-makers were necessarily prisoners of sensible preconceptions. As one official with lifelong experience of intelligence in Asia has observed: 'Intelligence is like cheese, you buy the sort you like, or the sort you bought last week.'[96]

Conclusion

The whole question of intelligence estimates and the coming of the Far Eastern War has focused upon Japan. Nicholas Tarling eloquently summarises this scholarship, observing: 'The US, and indeed the UK, did not believe that the Japanese would go to war with both of them. A remembrance of Japanese caution, a mistaken impression of the fragility of their economy and an absurd underestimation of their determination led to a quite unfounded optimism.'[97] A complex and well-informed debate is now developing as to the nature of Britain's intelligence assessments of Japan. Were they an 'intelligence disaster', combining chronic underestimation of capability with a misunderstanding of intention, or was the problem rooted in a lack of receptivity by policy-makers?

What is clear is that Japanese intentions during much of 1941 were largely unknowable. Certainly in the autumn of 1941 Japanese service ministers were increasingly of the opinion that Japan was being gradually crushed, and that war was the only chance of escape. But equally Tokyo was still in the grip of 'remarkable indecisiveness in policy-making', underlined by the collapse of the Konoye government.[98] The arrival of the new Tojo government did not help initially. On 23 October Admiral Nagano complained: 'We were to have reached a decision in October, and yet here we are.'[99] At the operational planning level, fist fights broke out amongst senior Admirals as the details of the various future scenarios were discussed.[100] Only from early November 1941 was there a gradually emerging decision to go to war in early December. The Tojo Cabinet, neatly characterised by Butow as 'the unpredictable Manchurian Gang', at last resolved for war if a settlement had not materialised by the end of the month. Only then had Japanese intentions ceased to be a moving target.[101]

Britain's key intelligence failure probably lay elsewhere. Eden, Churchill and Brooke-Popham did not expect Japan to go to war in 1941 because, as Eden had noted in September 1941, the range of deterrent power confronting Japan was formidable. The Soviet Union was at war with Japan's allies, whilst American determination to support Britain was increasingly visible. With Germany engaged in Russia, Britain too looked stronger. But the critical miscalculation here was not about Japanese intentions, but about Roosevelt's intentions. London, and indeed many American intelligence analysts in Washington, failed to recognise that, certainly from October 1941, Roosevelt was less engaged in an applying deterrent power, and increasingly embarked on a path of confrontation. Roosevelt had made clear to Tokyo that the price of a settlement was withdrawal from China, a price which most obviously, after five long years of war and a third of a million Japanese casualties, no Japanese government could countenance. Contemporaneously, the rapidly tightening screws of economic warfare and the shifting military balance left Japan with limited options. This is not to suggest a crude Rooseveltian 'back door to war' but certainly American foreign policy towards Japan hardened notably in late 1941. London was insufficiently aware of this.[102]

Intelligence analysts on both sides of the Atlantic were only dimly aware of the sea change in Roosevelt's foreign policy in the last months of 1941. Eden had deliberately left the business of negotiating with Japan to the United States, and so the British 'were told little of these talks' and 'wanted more information'. In November, when Roosevelt and Churchill discussed these matters, the latter's presumption was about deterrence, urging: 'The firmer your attitude and ours the less chance of their taking the plunge.' But this was not the case. The Australians were more astute. Shrewd diplomats such as Richard Casey had already warned the Americans about a policy of 'pinpricks and provocation' and Canberra had asked whether Washington properly appreciated the 'consequences of tactics of irritation'.[103] Roosevelt, although keeping his inner foreign policy from the majority of his own administration, certainly gave London some clear hints. On 24 November 1941 he confided to Churchill 'we must all be prepared for real trouble, possibly soon'.[104] But on 2 December, Churchill, with his attention firmly focused on the Middle East, was asserting that Japan would not attack for a long time. London did not understand Roosevelt, who was increasingly in the driving seat in late 1941. This was reflected in Churchill's irritation at the famous Final Report of Sir Robert Craigie, the British Ambassador in Tokyo, which was suppressed with vigour. It was not so much that Craigie's report appeared pro-Japanese (although it had this attribute), but more that as early as June 1941 Craigie had warned Eden explicitly that extending sanctions on any scale, would 'produce those very actions which we wish to avoid'.[105]

Britain's principal intelligence failure in 1941 was probably misjudging her ally not her enemy. This is not easy to explain, given the effort that Britain had expended in developing contacts in Washington. By 1941 Roosevelt's speech writer, Robert Sherwood, a confirmed Anglophile who had served in the Canadian Army and spent half his life in England, regularly showed drafts of speeches to the Canadian William Stephenson, the SIS chief in New York.[106] Moreover the records of the Joint Intelligence Committee and its cognate bodies suggest that they were aware, in principle, of the importance of watching American policy towards Japan. On 15 April 1941, the Axis Planning Section, a special group set up in London to emulate the thinking of the Axis military, considered the 'Future Strategy of Japan' and asserted quite clearly:

The U.S.A. is the uncertain factor . . . Owing to the present British and United States economic pressure, which is likely to increase, Japan's economic capacity to wage war will progressively deteriorate . . . If Japan feels it necessary to take measures involving the risk of war there must be a tendency for her to do so sooner rather than later.

But in London, as in Singapore, policy-makers at the highest level were inclined to subordinate such prescient warnings to their own subjective notions and they continued to view United States policy as a deterrent rather than a provocation.[107]

The wider debate over Pearl Harbor is unlikely to be resolved, underlining the problematic nature of conspiracy theories in contemporary history and the qualities that perpetuate them. First, it remains logically impossible to prove the negative case conclusively: that Churchill did not enjoy forewarning of Pearl Harbor. Second, there is a symbiotic relationship between conspiracy theory and archives destroyed or else closed for long periods of time. Imaginative authors will always find it convenient to suggest that they must contain any number of secrets, for why else would they be unavailable? Meanwhile, sensationalised accounts seem to underline the official wisdom of keeping 'sensitive' documents closed. The relationship between conspiracy theorists and government archivists is often portrayed as adversarial, but in reality it contains elements of mutual dependency. Third, conspiracy theory offers us a reassuring vision of decision-makers as people who control events; this is more attractive than the idea of governments as victims of surprise.

Yet within the context of the Far Eastern War, conspiracy theory has an important counterpart in reality and has an important contribution to make to understanding the politics of intelligence. A disturbingly large proportion of leaders in 1941 displayed a simplistic belief in the value of secret service in providing a 'hidden hand' solution to awkward problems. Churchill, Roosevelt and indeed Stalin could all be placed in this category. Churchill adored Buchanesque secret service exploits, displaying this tendency even in his last years of office when he delighted in a CIA–SIS coup d'état which restored the Shah of Iran to the Persian throne.[108] Equally, Roosevelt's enthusiasm for the construction of a new American wartime secret service under General William J. Donovan owed much to a picaresque and exaggerated view of an omnipotent British secret service in the First World War. Indeed Roosevelt's entire approach to foreign policy could be described as conspiratorial. It is to this shared enthusiasm of Churchill and Roosevelt for secret service, setting in train a vast expansion and duplication of these organisms in the early years of the war, that we must now turn.

6

'Imperial Security Services': the emergence of
      OSS and SOE

> Security Co-ordination is the counterpart in the . . . Western Hemisphere of
> Imperial Security Services, London.
>> British Security Co-ordination, New York, 1 October 1941.[1]

SOE in London

On 6 June 1941, six months before Pearl Harbor, the JIC in London firmly
instructed Singapore to initiate 'a full exchange of intelligence' with the
United States, including signals intelligence. This was symptomatic of a
global Anglo-American–Commonwealth intelligence relationship developing
during 1940 and 1941. Simultaneously, the JIC instructed Singapore to keep
one activity from American liaison officers: the work of the local British
SOE station at Singapore. SOE was a new British secret service formed in
1940 tasked with sabotage and subversion.[2] Anthony Eden was particularly
anxious that SOE in the Far East remain unknown to Washington. The British
Ambassador in Washington was told that, as regards SOE at Singapore, for
the time being 'we should not (repeat not) disclose any future operations' to
the United States. Closing off aspects of SOE operations from the Americans
was not easy to achieve, for British and American officials were simultaneously working together to create what would become the OSS. OSS was a
new American secret service that would perform the roles of both the British
SOE and SIS, and initially held responsibility for propaganda.[3] Six months
before the United States joined the war against the Axis, the ambiguous
nature of the Anglo-American wartime intelligence relationship was already
becoming clear, with the agent-based human services often engaged on
national tasks of some political sensitivity.

  The idea of a new British sabotage organisation to meet the challenge of
imminent war had arisen as early as 1938, and was developed simultaneously
in two different government departments. SIS founded a covert warfare
department in March 1938, codenamed Section D (D for Destruction).

Headed by the energetic Major Laurence Grand, it was not permitted to undertake any operations before the outbreak of war and confined its activities to research. Meanwhile the War Office was conducting experiments with irregular warfare under the guise of special unit that became known as Military Intelligence, Research (MI(R)). Led by Major J. C. F. Holland and his assistant, Major (later Major-General) Colin Gubbins, MI(R) concentrated its thoughts on partisan-type operations, exploiting Army experience in irregular warfare derived from campaigns in Ireland and Palestine. Meanwhile Grand's Section D favoured schemes of a decidedly unmilitary nature. Their divergent styles ensured that these two departments mostly kept their distance. At the outbreak of war in September 1939 they were joined by a further body, the Ministry of Economic Warfare (MEW). Together they began to look at the possibility of sabotaging vulnerable sections of Germany's war economy, particularly oil from Romania and iron ore from Sweden, but they achieved little.[4]

In May 1940 Germany swept across mainland Europe in a Blitzkrieg campaign, defeating France in six weeks. For some, this startling success could only be explained by a substantial German fifth-column effort and this served to further increase interest in sabotage. Between the summer of 1939 and the summer of 1940, Britain was swept with repeated waves of panic about the fifth-column menace, culminating in 'near-hysteria' in May 1940 when, with the fall of France, more than 27,000 people were in detention in Britain under Defence Regulation 18B.[5] Sir John Anderson, the minister responsible, had pleaded for a reasonable policy but had given in 'owing to popular clamour and fear of Fifth Columnists'.[6] Thereafter, in the period while Britain's conventional forces were rebuilt following Dunkirk, military planners also looked to unconventional warfare, as well as bombing and blockade, to fill the gap. Churchill decided that Britain's sabotage efforts now had to be more professional.

This decision reflected bureaucratic as well as strategic imperatives. There was a growing consensus among senior Foreign Office and Cabinet Office officials that SIS was weak. On 4 November 1939 they had been greatly relieved to hear of the death of Admiral Sir Hugh Sinclair, the ineffective inter-war chief of SIS, a post whose incumbents were known as C.[7] A fierce battle then ensued for the post of C. Lobbying from within SIS helped to secure the position for Stewart Menzies, an experienced SIS officer heading its military section. On the day after Sinclair's death, Menzies had boldly walked into the office of the senior official at the Foreign Office, Sir Alexander Cadogan, bearing 'a sealed letter' from the deceased Sinclair, nominating Menzies, but Cadogan mused: 'I am not sure Menzies is the man.'[8] The fortunes of SIS continued to decline over the next six months, with many of its networks in mainland Europe being 'wound up' by the German security service. In May 1940, Cadogan and Eden had 'agreed to try and overhaul SIS' but only marginal improvements were made. By 1941 Cadogan had assessed the new C as second-rate, complaining that he 'babbles and wanders' and gave the impression he was 'putting up a smokescreen of words and trying to pull his questioners off the track'.[9] But Menzies excelled at bureaucratic manoeuvre and managed to escape a root-and-branch reform of SIS which it needed, partly by hiding behind the achievements of Bletchley Park and Ultra.

The malaise which afflicted SIS throughout the war, largely the result of inter-war neglect and under-funding, prompted Churchill and others to place the responsibility for sabotage and subversion elsewhere. In an ideal world SIS would have been reformed and expanded to create a centralised organisation under the Chiefs of Staff or the Foreign Office, responsible for clandestine propaganda, deception, sabotage and intelligence, and indeed this idea was mooted several times during the war. But instead Churchill opted to create a new organisation, the SOE, under the Minister for Economic Warfare, Hugh Dalton, which absorbed Section D and MI(R). Menzies and SIS were not even consulted, and the resulting enmity between SIS and SOE would cast a shadow for a decade. SIS and SOE, together with additional MEW agencies responsible for propaganda and economic warfare, found themselves working in overlapping fields and competing for the same resources.[10] Operational rivalry was present from the outset; indeed Churchill actively encouraged Dalton's MEW to intrude into the SIS preserve of intelligence gathering. In July 1940 Churchill wrote to Eden:

It is of course urgent and indispensable that every effort should be made to obtain secretly the best possible information about German forces in the various countries overrun, and to establish intimate contacts with local people, and to plant agents. This I hope is being done on the largest scale as opportunity serves, by the new organisation [SOE] under M.E.W.[11]

This hasty minute implicitly recognised that underground networks for sabotage purposes would need, and would also produce, a great deal of intelligence. This ensured that the work of SOE and SIS would overlap. Accordingly, as early as the first week of April 1942, Churchill found it necessary to personally instruct Dalton 'to see Menzies [C] and put an end to the friction between the two branches'.[12]

SOE created political as well as operational rivalry. The Chiefs of Staff and the Foreign Office were dismayed to find that the expanding fields of sabotage and subversion were removed from their control and given to Hugh Dalton. Dalton had been anxious to secure control of this area and undeniably there were connections with economic warfare. For a short while Dalton also controlled Britain's clandestine or 'black' propaganda, before it was hived off in early 1942 to form part of yet another new organisation, the PWE or 'Peewee', also characterised by bitter rivalry.[13] Dalton ruefully observed that his new organisations had been tasked by Churchill with 'setting Europe ablaze', but by 1942 the only things that had been set on fire were the corridors of Whitehall.[14] Cadogan recognised the dangers at the outset. To smooth relations he had his own private secretary, Gladwyn Jebb, seconded to Dalton as the new SOE senior official, but matters did not improve.[15]

New York and Washington

The United States did not enjoy a centralised intelligence service before 1941. Only in June 1941 did Roosevelt approve the creation of the post of Co-ordinator of Information which, the following year, developed into Donovan's OSS. Throughout the war, the burgeoning OSS organisation fulfilled both the secret intelligence role of the British SIS and the special operations role of SOE, as well as conducting analysis, counter-intelligence and propaganda work. Although formally abolished in 1945, some its remnants survived long enough to be incorporated into the new Central Intelligence Agency (CIA) in 1947.

Yet during the first forty years of the twentieth century the United States had boasted significant intelligence organisations, albeit operating largely in isolation. The FBI under J. Edgar Hoover, a police-style organisation, maintained an elaborate surveillance of subversives and foreign agents, akin to Britain's MI5. Substantial Army and Navy intelligence organisations controlled large numbers of attachés overseas and periodically engaged in 'secret service' activities. Both services had devoted substantial resources to 'negative intelligence' or the watching domestic subversives.[16] There were also several intelligence-type organisations within the Treasury. Most importantly, the Army and the Navy had both maintained small signals intelligence organisations. However, there was no centralised system for pooling and analysing intelligence, nor even for the proper co-ordination of signals intelligence. The most significant espionage case in the pre-war United States, a German spy-net run by Guenther Rumrich, was uncovered as the result of information supplied by MI5 in London. When Roosevelt was asked by the press which of the many intelligence services was in charge, he offered the disconcerting reply: 'They all are, within limits.'[17]

The United States also lacked sabotage, propaganda or economic warfare organisations of the sort that Britain gathered under Hugh Dalton in 1940. The individual who recognised this problem and addressed it was General William J. Donovan. Donovan was America's most highly decorated soldier of the First World War, earning the nickname 'Wild Bill'. His service in New York's 69th Regiment, 'the Fighting Irish', reflected the Irish ancestry of his grandparents, but rather than evincing an interest in the conflicts of the old country, he was an Anglophile and a long-term anti-isolationist. A New York corporate lawyer who moved in well-connected Republican circles, he attended Columbia Law School contemporaneously with Franklin D. Roosevelt, although they were not well acquainted. Instead, Donovan enjoyed important Republican political contacts in Roosevelt's immediate circle, including Henry Stimson and also Frank Knox, the Secretary of State for the Navy. As early as 1935 he had begun to undertake private reconnaissance missions to Europe on behalf of this circle.[18]

In 1937, influenced by the deteriorating world situation, Donovan pressed Roosevelt to set up an office that would co-ordinate existing intelligence and develop a fuller range of secret service capabilities. But Roosevelt expressed only a passing interest. Still pre-occupied with the domestic economy, he preferred in any case a multiplicity of intelligence organisations that could be played off against each other, in much the same way as he handled government departments in Washington.[19] The crucial moment came in July 1940, when Roosevelt asked Donovan to undertake a secret mission to Britain to assess the progress of the European War. Distrustful of the State Department, Roosevelt retained a growing army of such 'special envoys'. Through contacts established with Britain from the summer of 1940, the eventual establishment of Donovan's new intelligence agency became increasingly an Anglo-American effort.

American assistance to Britain was the centrepiece of Churchill's grand strategy, lending special importance to Anglo-American intelligence co-operation. At the end of 1939, Sir James Paget, the head of the SIS station in New York, had begun to supply material to Roosevelt's inner circle at their request.[20] In the early summer of 1940, at Churchill's personal instigation, SIS appointed a new Head of station in New York, the diminutive William 'Little Bill' Stephenson, a wealthy Canadian businessman and First World War aviator. His steel business had supplied SIS with industrial intelligence on Germany before the war and now, accompanied by Colonel Dick Ellis, a career SIS officer, he headed for New York.[21] Stephenson took over two floors of the International Building in the Rockefeller Center on Fifth Avenue, New York, and entitled his organisation British Security Co-ordination (BSC). During the period 1940–2, BSC was indeed much concerned with security, working with the FBI to prevent the sabotage of American assistance to Britain, shipped from New York, by a suspected huge German–American fifth column.[22] But BSC also grew into a 'department store' with representatives of all the secret services in London.

The exact nature of BSC assistance to Donovan's embryonic OSS organisation has proved controversial.[23] Some writers, not least Stephenson himself, have been anxious to promote the view that Donovan was a suggestible creature. After the war, Stephenson even hired one of his subordinates, H. Montgomery Hyde, to write his biography, entitled *The Quiet Canadian*, which promoted this view, describing SIS and BSC as the 'parent' of OSS and its post-war successor, the CIA. Some senior American officials have actively bolstered this view. Ray Cline, Deputy Director of the CIA in the 1960s, remarked that OSS 'might never have come into existence had it not been urged upon the United States by the British'.[24] Similar arguments have been advanced about British influence over American intelligence in the First World War.[25]

Other writers have been simultaneously anxious to resist such claims. Instead they have sought to explain the success of OSS in terms of Donovan's personal qualities, his excellent political judgement, combined with good timing and high-level connections. R. Harris Smith, one of the first serious historians of OSS, asserts: 'In every respect, OSS was Donovan's child' and stresses the continuation of his interventionist spirit in the CIA. Thomas F. Troy, the CIA official historian of this period, views the early history of OSS as one of bureaucratic survival against American competitors, who wished to strangle it at birth, rather than as a period of Anglophile dependency. Corey Ford similarly emphasises Donovan winning in the 'dog-eat-dog struggle' in Washington.[26]

The reality is complex. The idea that the robust Donovan was in any way a suggestible individual is hardly plausible. But it is equally clear that, until 1942, Donovan was dependent upon practical British assistance in establishing his credentials in the largely hostile political environment of wartime Washington. Intelligence organisations cannot be created overnight; meanwhile a precious stream of intelligence borrowed from SIS was central to establishing his credibility. Above all, it was at the work-a-day level of operational tradecraft, transferred by instructors on secondment from organisations such as SOE, that Britain appears to have made a lasting mark on OSS and the early CIA. It was these two elements that Donovan himself identified as crucial when describing the work of Stephenson to the US Joint Chiefs of Staff in June 1944.[27]

In the summer of 1940, at Roosevelt's request, Donovan visited London to assess British potential to resist an Axis onslaught. The American Ambassador in London was pessimistic and Roosevelt had no wish to send war supplies to Britain if they were likely to fall into Axis hands within a matter of weeks. During a three-week tour Donovan spoke to Churchill and most of Britain's intelligence chiefs, developing a good relationship with the head of Naval Intelligence, Admiral John H. Godfrey. He had also been told to look at 'fifth column' issues and was briefed on the new SOE organisation, on propaganda and also the importance that the British attached to deception. He returned to Washington with a favourable view of Britain's prospects and advocated urgent and large-scale assistance. The 'Destroyers for Bases Deal' followed shortly afterwards and the British Ambassador was in no doubt about the critical nature of Donovan's contribution.[28]

In December 1940, as Roosevelt prepared the Lend-Lease act, Donovan made a second visit to London. This was also a crucial moment in the relations between GC&CS and their American partners, prompting a debate about how secure American officials might be with Ultra, with Churchill cast in the role of sceptic. This led to some initial anxiety about what Donovan could be told, but across Whitehall Donovan was already perceived as a firm friend who could be spoken to with candour. Cadogan wrote a revealing note for the Foreign Secretary, Lord Halifax:

'C' [Menzies] tells me that Mr. Stephenson, who travelled over with Colonel Donovan, has impressed upon him that the latter really exercises a vast degree of influence in the administration. He has Colonel Knox in his pocket and, as Mr. Stephenson puts it, has more influence with the President than Colonel House had with Mr. Wilson.

Stephenson had perhaps exaggerated Donovan's relationship with the President, but official London was clearly respectful, rather than patronising or manipulative.[29]

Donovan's visit lasted until March 1941, during which he toured the length of the Mediterranean, making extended forays into a dozen countries in the Balkans and the Middle East. His appetite for work was formidable, gathering not only current intelligence in the world situation from a bewildering array of leaders, but also visiting British secret service centres. He held a remarkably prescient discussion with Yugoslav commanders about a future German attack on the Soviet Union.[30] Donovan was exactly the sort of person likely to make an impression upon Churchill, who wrote personally to thank Roosevelt for Donovan's 'magnificent work', describing him as carrying an 'animating, heart-warming flame'.[31] Donovan also toured the large British intelligence outposts in Bermuda and the Caribbean run by BSC, from which Stephenson was by now running operations into South America. Donovan's interventionist views were now swimming with a broader official tide in Washington during 1941, which expected the European civil war of 1939 to become a global war that threatened the United States.[32]

Donovan's visits to Britain served an additional purpose. During the fall of France in May 1940 the American press had, like the British, emphasised the dangers of the German fifth column. Frank Knox had been particularly anxious about this and Donovan's visits to Europe allowed him to become something of an expert, returning to publish *Fifth Column Lessons for America* and syndicated articles for the press.[33] London was not slow to play up the idea of a German fifth column and in June 1941 the British Chiefs of Staff were warning their allies that:

We wish to draw your particular attention to the existence of a highly organised world wide organisation of the Italian and Germans for the prosecution of para-military and fifth column activities. Experience gained from recent German activities of this nature show this organisation to be one of great efficiency which has largely contributed to the recent German military successes . . . German activities are far more advanced and their plans more deeply laid than is commonly suspected.[34]

The fifth column was largely a myth. There was almost no German underground work in America and MI5 gradually realised that there were few German secret service (Abwehr) agents in Britain. Nevertheless, the *idea* of a fifth column now gripped the mind of the American public as it had done in Britain. In April 1940, in a melodramatic radio speech, Roosevelt announced: 'We know of new methods of attack. The Trojan Horse. The 5th Column that betrays a nation unprepared for treachery. Spies, saboteurs and traitors are the actors in this new tragedy.' The American public could hardly fail to respond to this excitable language and on one day alone in 1941 there were 2,981 separate telephone reports to the FBI of suspected German sabotage. In such a climate, the argument that the United States needed her own clandestine services was irresistible.[35]

On 10 June 1941, twelve days before Germany conducted her surprise invasion of the Soviet Union, Roosevelt approved a memorandum by Donovan calling for the central collation of intelligence and appointing him 'Co-ordinator of Information'. With the accelerating pace of world events, Roosevelt could no longer afford a divided intelligence community, and had been toying with a number of alternative solutions. Donovan's proposal was carefully crafted, emphasising the least controversial aspects of his organisation.[36] Donovan had approached Morgenthau, the Secretary of the Treasury, even before speaking to Roosevelt and, together with the support of his friends Stimson and Knox, the ground was well prepared. The establishment of the COI, then OSS, clearly owed much to Donovan's acute political sensibilities, while its credibility during its crucial first year owed much to support from Britain.[37]

During 1941, Donovan and BSC carried out combined operations in South America and in the Far East. Working with the FBI and with American banking contacts, the American John Dickey led a BSC operation to blacklist commercial operations in South America that were helpful to Germany. In July 1941, this campaign became overt when Roosevelt announced an official blacklist, and John Dickey became head of the new State Department section of World Trade Intelligence.[38] In a remarkable coup, British propaganda organisations were allowed to secure control of some commercial broadcasting facilities on the east and west coasts. Picking up on the profitable 'fifth column' theme, Donovan used his excellent press contacts to place articles on anti-Japanese activity by a Nazi fifth column in Asia, which had a detrimental effect on Axis relations.[39] Relations between Stephenson's BSC and American officials were increasingly close.[40]

Yet simultaneously BSC was required to take remarkable risks. It collected intelligence on United States citizens and also undertook inadmissible activities designed to draw the United States into the war. BSC planted forged documents and maps, purporting to show Nazi ambitions in South America, which Roosevelt himself later displayed publicly during an anti-Nazi speech. To lend credence to this, in the autumn of 1941 British intelligence 'framed' Ernst Wendler, the German Ambassador in Bolivia, persuading the Bolivian Government that he was about to carry out a pro-Nazi coup d'état. Wendler's expulsion convinced Washington that the German fifth column was on the march in the Western Hemisphere.[41] This was but one of the products emerging from BSC's 'forgery factory', know as Station M, run under the cover of the Canadian Broadcasting Company in Toronto.[42]

While BSC probably duped the President, Roosevelt and his administration were not their main target. As Susan Brewer, Nicholas Cull and Thomas Mahl show in their path-breaking studies, there was increasingly a sense of working with the American administration and the Eastern internationalist establishment, in a well-organised programme of covert harassment against isolationists.[43] By July 1941, the propaganda branch of BSC was funding and directing many of the 'American' interventionist lobby groups in the USA. Their work included vociferous attacks upon prominent isolationists such as Charles Lindbergh and what they termed 'other conscious or unconscious native Fascists'. They undertook complex 'black' propaganda operations, setting up spurious 'isolationist' attacks on prominent interventionists, such John Ford, in exaggeratedly pro-Nazi terms, designed to discredit the isolationists.[44] There is also evidence that poll results from organisations such as Gallup were manipulated.[45]

BSC recruited Americans to keep isolationist groups such as America First under surveillance for signs of secret Axis support. Donald Downes was one such American who had already undertaken missions for the British in the Middle East. BSC asked him straightforwardly: 'Do you feel strongly enough on these matters to work for us in your own country? To spy on your fellow Americans and report to us?' Downes and others like him, were used to harass and discredit leading isolationist figures such as Congressman Hamilton Fish. But by 1941, Downes found himself increasingly in step with a wave of anti-Axis activity by the American government. He was often in danger of bumping into the FBI, who were conducting surveillance on the same targets and a year later Downes found himself in OSS.[46]

But if a major deception was perpetrated on the United States it concerned the nature of British intelligence itself. During the inter-war period British intelligence was under-resourced and had deteriorated badly, but this was carefully hidden from Washington. In May 1941, in a conversation with Admiral Godfrey, Britain's Director of Naval Intelligence, Roosevelt revealed quite fantastic views about the feats achieved by British agents in the First World War. These were in fact stories concocted to cover the fact that Britain was breaking German (and indeed American) codes. Godfrey certainly made no attempts to disillusion him and lent Washington the services of a young British naval intelligence officer (later novelist), Ian Fleming, as an adviser.[47]

A golden opportunity for London to advance the myth of an omnipotent British secret service occurred in late 1941 when Donovan requested the loan of experienced British personnel to train his rapidly growing staff.[48] Stephenson sent his deputy, Dick Ellis, down to Washington to open a sub-station to facilitate daily liaison with Donovan, who reciprocated by sending Allen Welsh Dulles to liaise with BSC in the Rockefeller Center.[49] Just before Pearl Harbor, the British established a secret service training centre in Canada, ST 103 or 'Camp X'. Staffed by SOE and SIS, it had processed more than 400 American trainees by 1944, including the assassin of Admiral Darlan in North Africa in 1942. The chief of Camp X was Bill Brooker, formerly the senior instructor at the SOE advanced training centre at Beaulieu in the New Forest.[50] The purpose of Camp X was not only to accelerate OSS, it was also 'to impress the Americans'. Many of the seconded British 'professional' training staff had in fact been recruited from civilian life only months before, as Britain scrambled to mobilise. Characteristically, Brooker himself was an ex-travelling salesman and 'had never lived an underground life'. But, after a little research, he could talk to trainees 'as if he had never lived otherwise'. Some were effective and amongst their number was Captain William Fairbairn of the Municipal Shanghai Police Force, who was responsible for introducing the martial arts of the East into Western special forces training.[51]

American trainees passing through Camp X became senior CIA officials after the war. Richard Helms, Director of the CIA in the 1970s, vividly recalled his tuition under Major Fairbairn. In the 1970s, a Congressional enquiry into the CIA concluded that: 'In real terms the British provided American intelligence with the essence of its tradecraft – the techniques required to carry out its intelligence activities.' Others have remarked less enthusiastically on 'the Anglomania' that 'disfigured the young face' of the early CIA intelligence branch.[52] Either way this marked a determined British effort to establish themselves as the senior partners in the growing Anglo-American intelligence relationship.

BSC's covert efforts against American isolationism were unsurprising, given Britain's dire predicament in 1941. But Stephenson was also watching a surprisingly wide range of sensitive issues and undertaking some very risky operations. Some of these were directed against opponents of BSC within

American government. In an infamous incident in 1941 a BSC official was expelled after attempting to gather 'the dirt' on Adolf Berle, a senior State Department official whose duties included liaising with the various intelligence agencies in Washington.[53] It was no coincidence that Berle had been a strong opponent of the BSC presence, complaining that Stephenson pretended to run a small shipping security office, but hid 'a full size secret police and intelligence service' which regularly employed 'secret agents and a much larger number of informers' engaged in illegal activities. In January 1942, Berle observed that a British secret service officer had:

showed up with a plan to organise a revolution in Argentina – about the most disastrous thing anybody could have thought of at the moment – the State Department has a healthy fear of anyone who goes off on adventure in those parts . . . Bill Donovan gets a good many of his ideas from the British.[54]

By March he had had enough and was resolved to take action.[55] Taking up these matters up with Lord Halifax, the British Ambassador, he insisted that Stephenson be replaced.[56] But Berle was too late, for by 1942 Donovan had urged Roosevelt to veto any legislation that might restrict the activities of BSC.[57]

BSC was reporting on prominent British, as well as American citizens. Remarkably, the Foreign Secretary, Anthony Eden, was using BSC to monitor Lord Halifax, his predecessor as Foreign Secretary, who had reluctantly taken up the post of Ambassador to the United States in March 1941. Eden viewed Halifax as an arch-appeaser who had urged the Cabinet to investigate Hitler's peace terms during the Dunkirk evacuation.[58] Cadogan recorded a private meeting with Eden on the evening of Tuesday 6 May 1941: 'Went up to A[nthony Eden]'s flat about 7 . . . Showed him a report from C's men in US to effect that Edward [Lord Halifax] hasn't "clicked". Can't do much about it.'[59] All this recalled the mutual surveillance maintained by the antipathetical Lord Curzon and Lloyd George in the 1920s, and by Churchill and his opponents in the 1930s.[60]

BSC was also watching American economic plans and commercial interests. As early as 1942 they had obtained American documents on British Malaya which they were not supposed to be privy to.[61] This reflected strong undercurrents of British suspicion about the motivation of both isolationists *and* interventionists in the United States. The economic repercussions of American assistance in the First World War, and the extended controversy over war debts, had not been forgotten. Some of the War Cabinet asked whether America would join the war only to confirm her economic ascendancy. Lend-Lease in 1941 prompted the British Chancellor of the Exchequer, Kingsley Wood, to observe that the Americans would 'strip us of everything we possess in payment for what we are about to receive'. Churchill also entertained barely disguised worries about the long-term ascendancy of the dollar. In January 1941, during a dinner with Roosevelt's Special Envoy, Harry Hopkins, the respective economic anxieties in each country surfaced in uneasy humour. Churchill asked 'what the Americans would do when they had accumulated all the gold in the world'. Hopkins shot back 'we shall be able to make use of our unemployed in guarding it'.[62]

As early as 1942 BSC had begun to identify its protégé, OSS, with an American expansionist impulse that offered a potential threat to British economic interests. That Donovan was an interventionist was to Britain's advantage, but this was accompanied by a general desire to see the United States play a larger role in world affairs. Interventionists were, by definition those who envisaged an expanded American world role. In the short term this would be Britain's salvation, but in the long term it was problematic. Even at this early stage, Donovan had begun to submit proposals to Roosevelt for increasing the pattern of American influence in the Middle East, a region of traditional British dominance.[63] Conversely, BSC envisaged their role as securing the broader interests of the British Empire, describing themselves as the North American branch of 'Imperial Security Services, London'.[64] All this pointed to future trouble.

The Oriental Mission: SOE Begins work in Asia

The creation of both SOE and BSC was a response to Britain's reverses in Europe during 1939–40. But those appointed to run them were mostly drawn from the City, empire trade and commerce and did not suffer from a narrowly European vision. Instead they were accustomed to considering British interests in a global context. The background of SOE's first Director or 'CD', Sir Frank Nelson, was rooted in Bombay, the commercial and industrial heart of India, where he had served as President of the Associated Chambers of Commerce during the 1920s, before working informally for SIS in Switzerland. His successor, Colonel Sir Charles Hambro, who ran SOE in 1942 and 1943, was a merchant banker. Both Nelson and Hambro understood that the war was a defence of the British Empire as a world-wide financial and commercial entity.[65]

Accordingly, within months of SOE's formation, Colonel A. G. Warren, a veteran of MI(R), was despatched to assess Far Eastern possibilities. This was followed by a decision to create an SOE Oriental Mission at Singapore under MEW cover. In January 1941, two other emissaries from SOE in London, A. E. Jones and F. H. B. Nixon, passed through Delhi and Singapore and agreed that there were significant opportunities, notably in neutral Thailand.[66] Valentine St Killery, the man finally chosen to head the SOE Oriental Mission at Singapore, was a manager with ICI in China, as was his deputy,

5 Sir Charles Hambro of Hambros Bank, Head of the Special Operations
Executive, 1942–1943

Basil Goodfellow.[67] Arriving on 7 May 1941, Killery concluded that, with
appropriate assistance from the authorities, the Oriental Mission could be
operational within a year. But Killery did not have a year's grace, nor were
the local authorities sympathetic.[68]

Killery quickly encountered one of the central problems of wartime secret
services politics: that of centre and region. He failed to consult either Brooke-
Popham, or the GOC Malaya, Lt General Percival, about his plans for 'stay-
behind parties' after a Japanese invasion, and thus became involved in a
bureaucratic row over the control of para-military operations. MEW, SIS and
SOE in Singapore all saw themselves as answerable only to their head office
in London and were loath to subordinate themselves to the local military
command structure. Yet, unsurprisingly, the local chiefs demanded some
system of co-ordinating overall plans. General Percival's system of co-
ordination was quite simple: he demanded absolute control.

Administrative wrangling ensured that the Oriental Mission's first Malayan recruits did not arrive until a few weeks before the outbreak of war. Only in January 1942, as the Japanese closed on Singapore, did SOE have eight parties of trainees, totalling forty-five men, ready for operations behind enemy lines. The composition of these parties reflected the manner in which the colonial mentality cast a shadow over all types of secret service activities. The forty-five operatives were almost entirely colonial police officers, planters and tin miners of European extraction, accompanied by only two Chinese and one Malay. They could not merge with the indigenous population of occupied Malaya. Yet the Colonial Office and the Malayan Civil Service resisted the arming of the colony's subject population.[69]

An anti-Japanese underground organisation of many years' standing already existed in the MCP, consisting mostly of ethnic Chinese. The MCP had organised a series of strikes which did not endear it to the authorities in the years preceding June 1941 and was heavily infiltrated by the Special Branch. However, after Germany's attack on the Soviet Union, all communist parties received directions from Moscow to join a united front against the Axis. At this point Lai Tek, the Secretary of the MCP, approached the Governor, Sir Shenton Thomas, to offer their services. Lai Tek was rebuffed and it was only on 19 December 1941, after the Japanese invasion had begun, that an uneasy alliance was concluded. A policeman, John Davis, and a senior civil servant, Richard Broome, superintended the matter of arming and training the communists.[70] This was especially delicate because in China itself both Britain and the United States were supporting the Nationalists under Chiang Kai-shek against Japan, who were opposed to the Chinese communists.[71] In the event, most long-term SOE operations in Malaya were conducted with the MCP, who also provided recruits for SIS.[72]

In late 1941, in a similar vein, London was encouraging the Oriental Mission to develop closer relations with the NKVD, the Soviet intelligence organisation. The NKVD had been supplying London with valuable intelligence on Axis schemes in central Asia since the summer.[73] In September 1941, London asked Killery and also Geoffrey Denham of SIS to jointly receive an NKVD liaison mission of five officers.[74] By early December 1941 the final details were under discussion at Kuibyshev, east of a besieged Moscow. With a Soviet capitulation predicted for 1942, they hoped to inherit NKVD assets. London explained to Singapore that in the 'event of a collapse of the present regime in Russia there would be sufficient senior NKVD officials at key points in British territory who could continue to control and direct, for our purposes, NKVD agents in various parts of the world'.[75] Ironically, it was Singapore that was soon to fall, while Moscow repelled its besiegers. On 25 December 1941, the NKVD liaison mission was redirected to Rangoon, but this too was soon overrun.[76]

The official history of SOE in the Far East has suggested that the main objectives of the Oriental Mission were military and that the major impediment was the command structure in Malaya. In reality the main thrust of SOE's operations was political and most opposition came from diplomats, partly because of potentially awkward consequences for Anglo-American relations. The Anglo-American political problems that dogged British special operations in South East Asia in 1940 and 1941 arose out of Britain's anxiety to avoid war with Japan. After the spring of 1940, when Germany conquered continental Europe, the European colonies in South East Asia were weak and therefore an attractive area for Japan to acquire. Nationalists in Japan urged military action with slogans such as 'don't miss the bus'. An over-stretched Britain was in no mood to contemplate the extension of the war to a third front in the Far East; indeed, what London feared most during 1940 was an unholy alliance that embraced not only all the Axis powers, but also the Soviet Union. Accordingly, in the short term, it was essential for Britain to avoid war with Japan, and some even favoured a rapprochement with Japan.[77]

This had direct repercussions for Anglo-American co-operation in the Far East during 1940 and 1941. While Britain was glad of any American pressure on Japan, there was an undercurrent of unease. Firmer measures, such as economic pressure, might push Japan towards an attack on the weak European states only, to seize their resource-rich colonies in South East Asia. This would result in the worst of all possible worlds: one in which Britain would then find herself at war with Germany, Italy *and Japan*, perhaps also the Soviet Union, while the United States remained neutral. As a result, during 1940 and 1941, Britain publicly appeared to resist Japan stalwartly, in the hope of retaining American goodwill, but privately she shied away from confrontation.[78]

Intelligence exchange had its part to play in these matters. During the spring and early summer of 1940, both the Foreign Secretary, Lord Halifax, and his Under-Secretary, R. A. Butler, who dealt with Far Eastern affairs, briefly entertained hopes that Japanese attention might be re-focused on the Soviet Union, with whom Tokyo had recently fought an undeclared border war. In March 1940, Sir Robert Craigie, the British Ambassador in Tokyo, made the suggestion that one possible route to an Anglo-Japanese rapprochement was the limited revival of Anglo-Japanese intelligence co-operation against the communists and the Soviet Union that had flourished in the periods 1926–9 and 1936–8. Craigie had been approached regarding the revival of intelligence exchange by a General Yanagawa, an Army figure with responsibilities in China. General Yanagawa suggested that signing some agreement to exchange intelligence on Comintern activities in the Far East would 'not only provide the answer to those in Japan, who favour rapprochement with the USSR [i.e. the Navy], but also do much to increase

Japanese sympathies with the Allied cause'. Halifax, saw 'advantage' in pursuing the suggestion for work against Comintern activities, although MI5 expected no useful intelligence to be forthcoming.[79]

These ideas were controversial. There was certainly support in the War Office which prepared a paper on the possibilities of an Anglo-Japanese alliance against the Soviet Union.[80] But these ideas also had powerful opponents. Cadogan and other senior officials in the Foreign Office saw Halifax and Butler as appeasers of both Japan and Germany.[81] Cadogan could not abide Butler, confiding in his diary, 'the most baleful man, a craven pacifist, a muddle headed appeaser and a nit-wit, he talks defeatism to the press-men. I'm on his tracks.' Hopes of a deal with Japan continued to circulate until Eden replaced Halifax as Foreign Secretary later in the Spring of 1940. Nevertheless, Eden had no choice but to continue avoiding the provocation of Japan.[82]

Britain's anxiety not to provoke Japan also determined the approach to clandestine work in French Indochina, supervised by the Cabinet Far Eastern Committee under by Butler. In mid-1940 a Vichy administration arrived in Indochina and began to stamp its identity on the colony, attempting to root out pro-British sympathisers. The last British diplomats in Indochina felt the heat, and one of them reported:

two police motor cars are detailed expressly, but not for my protection. They have a blacklist of French anglophiles, and Gestapo methods have commenced. Microphones in rooms and spies from several departments in the hotel, also German agents. Two friends, M. Cozaux, Inspector General of Colonies and Director of Finance, and his representative in Saigon are in military prisons, full charges are not known but one is communication with the British.[83]

In the south of the country a vigorous, if somewhat insecure, Gaullist resistance movement appeared to be developing. This offered SOE the prospect of disrupting Vichy rule and also opposing the Japanese, who were pressing for bases in the north of the country in mid-1940.

But in June 1940 London officials shrunk from action as more fighting might encourage further Japanese intervention. Instead they hoped to exploit the poor relations between Vichy in Indochina and the Japanese. The remarkable upshot was that London ignored the pleas for help from the Gaullist resistance, led by General Martin, and instead hoped that resistance be extinguished by the Vichy security police as soon as possible. MI2c put this bluntly. Resistance would only provoke the Japanese into taking control of Saigon; thus 'the conclusion, however distasteful it may be, is that General Martin should, if he is determined to oppose the Japanese, be left to fight his battle alone'. SIS dismissed the quality of Martin's forces as 'poor'.[84] This was politically embarrassing, since only weeks before, during the fall of France,

Britain had publicly promised to assist all French colonial populations who fought on against Vichy. Halifax now gave instructions for this to be quietly disregarded.[85]

SOE were also reticent on security grounds. During the fall of France in May 1940 the Germans had captured many French ciphers. The pro-Gaullist elements in Indochina continued to use them until the Japanese confronted the French with the texts of their own telegrams.[86] The possibility of SOE support for the Free French in the Far East was looked at again in the autumn of 1940. But Britain still feared that any resistance would appear to be controlled from Singapore and might spark an Anglo-Japanese confrontation. The JIC in London also dismissed any chance of effective resistance, concluding that the indigenous population was highly disaffected under French colonial rule. The War Cabinet decided on no action.[87]

By January 1941, the British had begun an uneasy episode in collaboration with Vichy in the Far East, even signing a regional agreement which guaranteed no naval hostilities and no subversive activities.[88] Meanwhile the Free French in the Far East continued to look unreliable and in February 1941, General de Gaulle removed its leader, de Schompre, accusing him of 'notorious incompetence'. He was replaced by the more effective figure of Baron de Langlade, who was also Head of a large French rubber firm SOCFIN.[89] Nevertheless, SOE plans to conduct demolitions at the Japanese-occupied French naval base of Camranh Bay were suspended, despite the fact that SIS developed the scheme with former Governor-General George Catroux, who had himself provided an elaborate sketch map, detailing vulnerable facilities.[90]

The political circumstances prevailing in nearby Thailand were equally sensitive. Although under strong British influence in the 1920s, the increasingly autocratic military government of Thailand now toyed with the idea of throwing in her lot with Japan. Her foreign policy of uneasy neutrality after 1939 was accurately summarised by the Premier, Field Marshal Phibul, as one of 'watchful waiting'. Thailand had already observed the fate of small pro-British nations such as Norway and Belgium in Europe and had no intention of following their example. Instead they hoped to side with the winner in any future Far Eastern conflict, seizing the opportunity to recover large areas of disputed territory on their borders from French Indochina and also from the British in Malaya and Burma.

The presence of a large and potentially pro-Japanese country so close to Malaya presented acute problems for British defence planners. The inclination of the British diplomats in Bangkok was to try and prolong Thai neutrality by means of a policy of 'bribe' in the form of oil-shipments. However, both SOE and the military planners at Singapore advocated taking coercive action against Thailand. Sir Josiah Crosby, the British representative in

Bangkok, was the main obstruction.[91] SOE infiltration into Thailand was first approved at ministerial level in London at a meeting chaired by Butler in the Foreign Office on 8 May 1941. Victor Cavendish-Bentinck, the chairman of the JIC, was present and argued that it would be unwise for SOE to attempt 'anything too grandiose' in the Far East, and so they should target Thailand. He outlined a range of possible activities, including political infiltration to support neutral Thais against a Japanese coup d'état, military infiltration to offer fifth-column support to a British invasion, and finally sabotage duties. A few weeks later the JIC adopted a general resolution to pursue a 'more aggressive' secret service policy in the Far East.[92] SOE London decided that all this was to be co-ordinated locally by Killery with the authorities in Bangkok and Singapore, to 'stop the Foreign Office getting too windy' when the time came for action. But it was at the local level that SOE met with obstruction.[93]

This more aggressive policy gathered momentum in the summer of 1941. Rumours of a possible Japanese coup d'état in Thailand had been circulating, prompting SOE to prepare a counter-coup. Killery travelled to Bangkok to discuss with Crosby the possibility 'of assisting establishment of a government other than the present one and more willing to resist Japanese pressure'. Crosby was reluctant to work with Killery's amateur saboteurs and would only help if the new Thai government was offered concrete British guarantees of military support.[94] Crosby knew he had imposed impossible conditions on SOE. Killery remained convinced that he could carry out a coup d'état in Thailand without provoking a Japanese invasion and now sought final approval from SOE headquarters in London. Gladwyn Jebb, the senior SOE official in London approached the Foreign Office in the hope of securing the names of Thai figures most disposed to resist the Japanese. But the Foreign Office developed cold feet and ruled: 'the idea of a coup d'état is off and is unlikely to be revived'.[95]

Animosity erupted again in October 1941 when Crosby accused SOE agents of covertly distributing inflammatory propaganda in Bangkok. He complained to London of the 'reckless and irresponsible amateurs serving under Killery', precipitating a row between Eden, Dalton and Brendan Bracken, the Minister for Information.[96] This constituted one of a growing stream of embarrassing SOE incidents in neutral countries, prompting an angry Eden to begin his frequent demands that he should be given control of SOE. But Eden's desire for Foreign Office control would not be realised until January 1946.[97]

By this point Japan had begun a massive clandestine programme as a prelude to overt invasion in early December. SIS reported that in Bangkok 'the influx of Japanese in recent weeks is serious and no doubt includes a large influx of spies, propagandists and potential fifth columnists', speculating that

Tokyo would soon manufacture a political crisis to justify Japanese intervention.[98] Killery now decided to that the situation was so serious that he should operate against the wishes of the diplomats. George Windred, an Australian, posing as a reporter, was despatched to Bangkok on political work in early December 1941, but this was too late and he was overtaken by events.[99]

Prior to December 1941 the main difficulty presented by Thailand's dubious neutrality was geo-strategic, namely the possibility of Japan using Thailand as a stepping-stone in any attack on Malaya. The answer provided by the British military was a controversial plan for a pre-emptive strike from Malaya, driving some hundreds of miles up the peninsula known as the Kra Isthmus into Thailand. Here, where the peninsula reached its narrowest point, the military believed that a Japanese advance could be more successfully resisted. Codenamed Operation *Matador*, these plans were drawn up as early as December 1940.[100] Singapore planners noted that the operation's importance in denying to Japan the nearest possible aerodromes 'cannot be overestimated'.[101] The idea of Britain annexing part of a neutral country seemed politically dubious to many in London, and there were particular worries about how Washington might react. But Brooke-Popham's planners countered that it was 'absurdly squeamish to refrain from doing it'. From July 1941 its merits and demerits were frequently debated in London by Eden and the Chiefs of Staff and it was thought best to wait until Japan had begun to make a move, seeking cover in the general disturbance caused by the outbreak of war.[102]

SOE formed an integral part of plans for Operation *Matador*. Their role was twofold. Prior to the British invasion, SOE were to conduct detailed reconnaissance by infiltrating the area in force. When *Matador* was implemented, infiltrated SOE parties were to capture key strategic facilities such as airstrips and Phuket Island on the west coast of Thailand, and would also conduct demolitions against ports and harbours. SOE groups surveying the Kra Isthmus were accompanied on visits by officers in plain clothes from the 11th Indian Division who were tasked with the main thrust into Thailand.[103] The Thai Prime Minister had stated that he was powerless to stop the build-up of Japanese secret service officers in southern Thailand, so he would turn a blind eye to similar visits by British officers in plain clothes. In the last months of 1941 the sensitive area of the Kra Isthmus was flooded with obvious military figures masquerading as 'tourists'. By October, thirty-six British officers had made visits to southern Thailand, in parties of three and four. Most were SOE personnel, but they also included Brooke-Popham, who insisted on seeing the lie of the land for himself. The indispensable element of farce was added when parties of British and Japanese 'tourists' found themselves staying in the same hotels.[104]

The significance of this British influx in southern Thailand was not lost on

Japan and as early as 16 August 1941 Brooke-Popham warned London of obvious difficulties. *Matador*, with its heavy SOE support, drew on the exaggerated British impressions of German fifth-column pre-invasion activities in France and the Low Countries in 1940. But while Germans could easily blend in amongst other Europeans, his disguised officers could not merge with the rural Thai population.[105] Here Brooke-Popham had identified one of the major impediments to the work of SIS and SOE in wartime Asia. SOE's recruits, mostly British and Australian, were drawn from the mining operations in southern Thailand and briefly trained in Malaya. The rather nervous trainees were then returned, with explosives and weapons hidden in their cars. Radio equipment was in short supply, so they were to be activated by coded broadcasts made by Radio Malaya received by ordinary civilian radio sets.[106]

Although *Matador* was an exercise in strategic denial, it was also politically attractive to colonial officials, as southern Thailand contained a mixed Thai and Malay population. In the 1930s the Thais had carried out a policy of enforced cultural and religious assimilation directed at the Malay Muslims in this area, many of whom desired incorporation into British Malaya. The British annexation of the Kra Isthmus also promised a shared border between Burma and Malaya, with all the attendant benefits for imperial communications. In 1941 Singapore designated Edward Day, a senior Malayan Civil Service official, to accompany Operation *Matador* as the civil administrator for southern Thailand, in expectation of this longed-for acquisition.[107]

The United States, not Japan, was the main inhibitor for *Matador* in December 1941. The Roosevelt administration had attempted to occupy the high moral ground, berating the Axis for the forcible acquisition of weak and neutral states. This found its most concrete expression in the Atlantic Charter, a statement of war aims agreed by Roosevelt and Churchill at their mid-Atlantic meeting in August 1941. The Atlantic Charter declared that the Allies had no intentions of territorial aggrandisement. On 29 November 1941, Eden and Churchill discussed the awkward question of *Matador* once again, and two days later Churchill explained their fundamental reservations to the Australians, who were pressing for its launch. He explained that 'to anticipate the Japanese on the [Kra] Peninsula, if the Japanese had not attacked Thailand elsewhere, would give a handle to the isolationists in the United States to maintain that we were the aggressors thus weakening our claim to support'. The British Chiefs of Staff agreed.[108] Accordingly, *Matador* was only launched once the Japanese had begun to arrive near the Thai–Malaya border. SOE agents inside Thailand did not begin work until 8 December 1941, by which time they were under close surveillance and little was achieved for the cost of ten operatives killed. While SOE managed to seize their objectives in southern Thailand, the main force intended to relieve them, composed of Indian troops from 3 Corps, was repelled by armed Thai border police.[109]

Later the Thais put Operation *Matador* into reverse. Bangkok, impressed by Japan's rapid advance to Singapore, formally joined the war against the Allies in May 1942. In return Japan allowed Thailand to acquire four states in northern Malaya, as well as territory in Burma and Indochina.

Conclusions

In early 1942, the SOE Oriental Mission at Singapore came to an end. In common with the attempts to improve SIS in mid-1941, these efforts had come too late. The acrimonious nature of the politics of secret service, especially that concerning special operations at the theatre level, were already clear. Killery was attempting to run what were essentially para-military operations while being regarded by GHQ Far East as a 'purely civilian outfit'. This had not endeared him to the Army, but his main opponents were in fact civilians who regarded special operations as intrinsically unattractive. In March 1942, Colonel Gordon Grimsdale of FECB asked why it was that so far Killery had 'not got one single thing to show for a year's work and the expenditure of a very large sum of money'. He pointed to opposition from civilian figures:

Neither the Governor of Malaya nor Crosby would allow Killery to make the smallest effort to organise anything in their territories. After the war started Shenton Thomas asked Killery to try and do something, but by then it was naturally far too late. About a week before the war Brokham [Brooke-Popham] sent me to Bangkok to try and persuade that dreadful old man Crosby to do something to help win the war by allowing Killery to start work in Siam. It was quite hopeless however, and he categorically refused to play. The dreadful thing seemed to me that there was no-one who could order him to do so.[110]

As a 'quasi-military' and 'quasi-political' body under Dalton, SOE lacked established military or diplomatic advocates, yet needed the acquiescence of both to function effectively. Looming in the background were the strange impediments of alliance. Britain had sought intelligence co-operation with Japan, favoured Vichy over the Gaullist resistance in Indochina and planned aggrandisement against neutral Thailand. All these activities would have inflamed American opinion, and isolationists would have seized upon them to underline their case against assistance to the British Empire.

Part 2

India and spheres of influence, 1941–1944

7

'Do-gooders' and 'bad men': Churchill,
        Roosevelt and rivalry over empire

We have not bled enough for the liking of the Russians, or the British
or the Chinese . . . With political considerations looming so large in their
calculations, they are each fighting not only the common enemies but also,
in a negative fashion, their allies.
            John Paton Davies, US Political Adviser to Stilwell, 9 March 1943.[1]

Churchill's imperial vision

Hitler's attack on the Soviet Union on 22 June 1941 transformed what was
hitherto another European civil war into a global war. Japan's attack on the
United States, along with British and Dutch territories, followed, on 7
December 1941. Hitler completed this shift to a new level of conflict, declaring war on the United States a few days later.[2] The character of the war had
now fundamentally changed. With the United States in the war, and the
Soviet Union holding on against Germany, Axis defeat appeared increasingly
certain. By June 1942 the tide began to turn, with a dramatic American success at Midway Island, and Montgomery's victory at Alamein, both underpinned by the effective use of signals intelligence. This trend was confirmed
by the Battle of Stalingrad during the winter of 1942/3. Accordingly, 1942
saw the first flurries of serious post-war planning.

The wartime command arrangements also suggested long-term political
implications. In March 1942, at Roosevelt's suggestion, Churchill had agreed
that their activities should be divided into three zones of strategic responsibility. The Pacific, controlled by the Americans; the area from the Mediterranean to Singapore, controlled by the British; and the Atlantic and Western
Europe, which was to be shared responsibility. Allied grand strategy was
nevertheless problematic in 1942. Roosevelt wished to involve Americans
quickly in the war against Germany and the US Joint Chiefs of Staff wished
specifically for a rapid and, they hoped, decisive return to the continent via
France. By contrast Britain was bruised by her continental experiences and
preferred the indirect approach, first weakening Germany through bombing,

blockade and subversion. Churchill persuaded Roosevelt to commit the United States to the invasion of North Africa, Operation *Torch*, despite the clear implication that a return to the continent would be delayed.[3]

Churchill won partly because Washington was divided against itself, with the pugnacious Admiral King and the US Navy demanding a 'Pacific First' policy.[4] Unlike London, Washington had not yet adjusted to the rigours of wartime planning. At the Casablanca conference of 1942 the American General Al Wedemeyer found himself bewildered by efficient London staff officers and cabled back to Washington: 'The British descended on me like locusts . . . We came, we saw, we were conquered.' Agreement on *Torch* ushered in the need for civil affairs planning, with its political context and implications for future settlements. Byzantine dealings with the various Free French and Vichy factions in Africa that followed foreshadowed the problems that returning civil governments brought in their wake.[5]

For Churchill a vast job of work lay ahead. The surrender at Singapore, with the loss of over 100,000 troops at one stroke was, in Churchill's own words, the 'greatest disaster in our history'. This had constituted a political and psychological defeat on a gargantuan scale. The superiority of white rule in Asia had been revealed as a myth and the weakness, even decadence, of the colonial system of rule publicly exposed. The transparent inability of the British to defend themselves was bad, but the refusal of most subject peoples to resist Japan underlined a yet more worrying dissonance. Nevertheless, Churchill conceived of himself primarily as an imperial leader embarked on the process of imperial recovery.[6]

Allied war aims had been spelt out in the Atlantic Charter, the product of a dramatic meeting between Roosevelt and Churchill on the coast of Newfoundland in August 1941, a full four months before the United States entered the war. Churchill had signed this document, which enshrined the principle of self-determination, but at the same time indulged in sleight of hand, claiming its focus to be Europe. When asked about India, he informed Roosevelt that there would have to be 'much thought' before he could assent to its 'application to Africa and Asia'.[7] In contrast, Washington was clear about its global remit.

In 1942 Churchill was still dominant in Allied war councils. American industry had not yet properly mobilised and American policy-makers were unprepared for the war ahead, never mind the peace that would follow. By contrast the British Chiefs of Staff knew what they wanted from the crucial *Arcadia* Allied strategic conference of January 1942. Within a year the American contribution had vastly overtaken that of Britain, producing twice the quantity of munitions and six times the quantity of shipping. American air and ground forces more than doubled during 1943 and Churchill was conscious that his relative position was slipping.[8] Yet London also sensed advantages. The Americans were taking the brunt of the war against Japan and the Soviets were heavily engaged with Germany, giving the British some leeway to recover empire in the Mediterranean, the Middle East and Asia.

There were now contradictory concerns in London about the post-war United States. Some worried about an American return to isolationism, others about the rise of American internationalism and the danger of a new world order as a cloak for American informal imperialism. Churchill's vision was more optimistic than that of some of his xenophobic Cabinet colleagues and he maintained that, eventually, the United States *would* come to appreciate the value of the Empire–Commonwealth, bolstering it in some sort of alliance of English-speaking peoples. Churchill therefore envisaged himself engaged in a holding operation against Roosevelt's internationalist ideas. This was not a mere empty Macawberism, and revealed an acute appreciation that a constantly changing balance in world forces, together with shifting concerns in Washington, would offer opportunities.

In 1942, the American journalist Walter Lippman wrote to Maynard Keynes offering the perceptive, and positive, criticism that London had developed a detailed policy on almost every issue, but lacked an overarching vision of the future.[9] Britain was attempting to project an idealistic vision of a progressive colonial future within the United States, but with only partial success.[10] The absence of a single coherent vision betrayed the overcrowded nature of British overseas policy-making, with any broad strategy requiring the assent of a dozen ministers. It also reflected the nature of domestic political coalition. For the duration of the war it was Churchill's views on colonies that prevailed, while he periodically treated the Cabinet to 'a most fervid harangue against giving away the empire'.[11] Churchill's views on empire sometimes bordered on the perverse, combining a love of colonies with a suspicion, even distaste, for colonial peoples. Churchill's private secretary captured this well, recording a conversation about India on the eve of the formation of the Churchill government:

Winston rejoiced in the quarrel which had broken out afresh between Hindus and Moslems, said he hoped it would remain bitter and bloody and was glad that we had made the suggestion of Dominion status which was acting as a cat among the pigeons . . . this was not the moment to give anything away in India: we must remain firm as a rock, because British rule was today essential in India.[12]

Had the Cabinet been allowed to debate these issues freely, complete fragmentation would have revealed itself. Churchill enjoyed unconditional support from only a minority such as Lord Simon, the Lord Chancellor, James Grigg at the War Office and Lord Linlithgow, the Viceroy of India. Leo Amery and Oliver Stanley, the Secretaries for India and for the Colonies, advocated limited change and could be flexible. Anthony Eden, had he been allowed to control wartime foreign policy, might have seized the opportunity to remodel the empire significantly, compromising with the Americans and drawing on their financial assistance to dispose of numerous areas that were, at best, a dubious drain on the Exchequer. Clement Attlee, the Deputy Prime Minister, was perhaps more anti-colonial and internationalist than even Roosevelt, but his radical views were not shared by all his Labour colleagues.

Attlee, perhaps the most under-rated figure of the wartime years, was busy behind the scenes. In September 1942, he chaired an important meeting of ministers and senior officials looking broadly at future colonial developments in the Far East. The purpose was to respond to American requests for a 'joint declaration' of policy on colonial areas. Key figures attending included Eden, Amery and the Dominions Secretary Lord Cranborne, together with their most senior officials.[13] Attlee offered characteristic fresh-mindedness, objecting to the proposed papers in front of them on several grounds:

firstly . . . it appeared to propose a reversion to pre-war ideas, including a balance of power and uncontrolled free trade. Secondly, the people of this country would not wish to have the exclusive privilege of paying for the defence of all these territories at the expense of their own standard of living and the benefit of certain privileged classes. Thirdly, instead of national armaments he favoured an international force and a general sharing of the burden of defending these colonial areas. This could best be achieved by international control and administration of these territories.

These views were so iconoclastic that Foreign Office officials dismissed them as a 'red herring'. But they would have done well to give them serious consideration, for Attlee's premiership was less than three years away. Eden took a more pragmatic line, simply arguing that American co-operation was essential to win the war. It was therefore necessary to 'adapt' the British position 'to take account of certain essential American requirements', for example free access to rubber and tin at a reasonable price. The India Office and Colonial Office representatives took away the impression that Eden was content to lose areas of British territory.[14]

By 1942 the Colonial Office had concluded that the diplomats were 'supine' and 'spineless', refusing to confront the Americans with the possibility of a progressive colonial system. In 1943, Oliver Stanley, the new Colonial Secretary, accused Eden and his officials of 'treating bits of the Colonial Empire as cheap and convenient gratuities', and viewed plans for UN international trusteeships as a Foreign Office trick to allow the appeasement of the Americans.[15] Yet there was no positive desire to accommodate American views on colonies within the Foreign Office, where, in June 1942, the Head of the North American Department noted that in a recent meeting with Eden they had 'discussed America almost as an enemy'.[16] Accordingly, the task of agreeing a joint declaration on the future of the colonies with the Americans proved impossible during the war, for a Whitehall consensus was elusive. Heel-dragging allowed British representatives to delay until the Spring of 1945, when the 'Big Three' Conference at Yalta and the UN Security Conference at San Francisco required decisions. By then the long-feared American approach to colonies had become toothless and was further nullified by Roosevelt's death in April 1945.[17]

Yet the British Cabinet did enjoy near consensus on its general approach to international politics, based upon power and spheres of influence. This was never more plainly stated than in Churchill's proposal to Stalin for a 'Percentages Deal' to divide up the Balkans in October 1944. Churchill boldly conveyed the inner spirit of this proposal to Stalin, explaining 'that the Americans would be shocked if they saw how crudely he had put it'. However, those present were all experienced in the realities of politics, as Churchill put it: 'Marshal Stalin was a realist. He himself was not sentimental while Mr Eden was a bad man.'[18]

By contrast, in Churchill's wartime Cabinet, probably only Attlee fully shared the radical internationalist ideas outlined by Roosevelt. This difference was so fundamental that it was not frequently articulated in policy documents, instead it surfaced in the exasperated diaries of senior officials like Cadogan, who complained about 'do-gooders' and 'useless pontificating Americans'. Junior British officials in Washington echoed their superiors, complaining of 'a nation of gas-bags'. Such fulminations were symptomatic not only of a clash between imperialists and anti-colonialists, but also between realists and idealists. Many in London were convinced that American internationalism and idealism arose out of naivety, and that in time an opportunity to 'educate' the Americans would put things straight.[19]

Existing accounts of British policy have, however, tended to portray the British as essentially defensive. This view stands in need of some revision. In a number of areas British plans were marked by hopes not of 'what we have we hold' but thoughts of expansion. Thailand, often referred to during the war as Siam, captures this phenomenon neatly. An area of intense 'colonial' disagreement, it was nevertheless a non-colonial territory, which had never endured formal foreign rule at any time in its history. The United States concluded that Thailand was a victim of Japanese aggression and had not reciprocated Bangkok's declaration of war upon the Allies, made in March 1942. But Britain had endured attacks by Thai forces fighting alongside the Japanese in Burma in 1942. Subsequently, Thailand annexed sizeable portions of northern Malaya and Eastern Burma. Therefore Britain gleefully identified Thailand as an enemy who would be punished at the end of the war, perhaps through the annexing of some of southern Thailand, allowing the geographical linking of Burma and Malaya. This idea, recalling the ill-

fated Operation *Matador*, received endorsement at the highest level. Churchill informed Eden in June 1942 that it would be 'necessary after the war to
consider some sort of protectorate over the Kra Peninsula area, including
Singora, in the interests of the future security of Singapore'.[20] In November
1943, as the Cairo Conference approached, Britain conspicuously failed to
follow the Americans and the Chinese in declaring that they had no ambitions
against post-war Thailand. The Foreign Office noted that: 'Our reasons for
not following suit were that the Prime Minister feared that it would tie our
hands as regards the Kra Isthmus.'[21]

Although Churchill took a personal interest in this issue, the main driving
force of British ambitions to annex southern Thailand came from former
senior Malayan civil servants such as Sir George Maxwell, who had served
as Chief Secretary to the Government of the Federated Malay States in the
1920s. For these officials, who had long hoped for the northward expansion
of Malaya, the Japanese invasion was a blessing in disguise. The reports of
the Thai administration of four states in British Malaya, annexed by Bangkok
in 1943 had made the blood of London administrators boil. Moreover, the
manner of the Japanese arrival in the region, by means of the Songkhla
(Singora) the main port on the southerly Kra Isthmus, gave them new strategic arguments which strengthened their case for annexation.[22] Perhaps
Phibul, Thailand's wartime Premier, sensed that the tide was already turning.
In 1943, when he attended a ceremony to celebrate the handover of the four
northern states from Malaya to Thailand, the Japanese noted that he 'showed
little joyful countenance'.[23]

Accordingly, when Maxwell put his argument to Edward Gent, Head of
the Eastern Department of the Colonial Office, in March 1943 he couched it
in strategic terms, claiming, with not a little hyperbole, that events had proved
that Thai possession of the Kra Isthmus was nothing less than '"the Heel of
Achilles" of the whole British Empire'.[24] Maxwell was preaching to the
converted, for Gent's colleagues had already agreed that: 'As regards
PATANI [on the Kra Isthmus] I think it is generally agreed that the future
Malaya must include all the Malay States, which I believe largely by accident
were not transferred to British protection with Kedah, Kelantan etc. in
1910.'[25] William Doll, the inter-war British Financial Adviser to the Thai
Government, urged that the Kra was a 'natural' part of Malaya. He advised
the Bank of England that post-war rubber and tin production could be
restarted here more easily as there had been no scorched earth policy, adding
'if it were to become Malayan territory, I think this is the first point to which
to direct the stockpile'.[26]

In the Colonial Office, Gent's successor, John Paskin, took up the refrain,
and set out a detailed plan for acquiring what he called the 'Siamese

appendix'. No sound arguments could be made on the basis of racial affinity, for much of the Kra Isthmus enjoyed the same population of mixed race and religion as the states of Kedah and Kelantan. In any case Britain had made repeated statements of no territorial ambition in the war and so acquisition on political grounds would 'invite serious criticism'. However, Paskin noted: 'The establishment of British bases down the Kra Isthmus on the analogy of the US bases in the West Indies might prove a less embarrassing solution.' In practice this would require control of the land communication from Malaya to the bases 'on the hypothesis that it will be in the common post war interest of the United Nations'. United Nations global security arrangements thus became a stalking horse for British hopes to tidy up the Kra Isthmus and to fulfil long-nurtured ambitions.[27]

With the approval of his superiors, Edward Gent and Sir George Gayter, Paskins then began to sell the scheme around Whitehall.[28] Ashley Clarke at the Foreign Office responded enthusiastically, saying that Paskins had 'put the matter very well and we entirely agree'. The key to success was clearly 'that our claim should be based not on the ground of racial affinity' but presented as a scheme 'to preserve the strategic security of the UN'. Together they put proposals to the post-war military planners, ensuring this was integrated into future thinking on regional security.[29] Churchill's views were in the back of the minds of senior officials, for Sir Maurice Petersen warned them that the last time they had mentioned Thailand's territorial integrity they 'drew the fire of the Prime Minister'.[30]

By January 1944 these arguments for expansion had secured ministerial support. Leo Amery was the foremost advocate. Writing to Deputy Prime Minister Attlee, who now superintended some of the key post-war planning committees, he noted:

there are certain air bases or other points of defensive advantage which we ought to insist upon in any settlement. Our American friends have made it more than plain that they mean to do so, and certainly Russia has no intention of being behindhand in that respect!

. . . ought we not to insist on the transfer to Malaya of the little Malay States hitherto under Siamese suzerainty which occupy the Kra peninsula and separate Malaya from Burma?[31]

By July 1945 the Cabinet Far Eastern Committee had reformulated this as a broader British demand for 'the right to deploy and maintain armed forces in Siam, including complete freedom of movement for them, and to take such defence measures in Siamese territory as may be necessary'.[32] Similar ideas were being advanced with regard to former Italian colonies in the Mediterranean, such as Tripolitania (later Libya). As in the latter phases of the First

World War, there were some in Whitehall who believed that, far from suffering strategic over-stretch, the empire needed to be larger, if it was to
become safer.[33]

Roosevelt's internationalist vision

In 1941 the world of American foreign policy that confronted British officials
was relatively simple: it was made up of interventionists and isolationists.
But once the United States had entered the war, matters became more complex, with the greatest threat to future British influence in the world potentially emanating from those very interventionist elements in the United States
whom they had viewed as close allies. By 1943, British information officers
in Washington identified no less than three problematic groups within American foreign policy-making: firstly, their old and familiar enemies the 'professional isolationist Anglophobes' such as Randolph Hearst, the press baron,
who continued to oppose measures such as Lend-Lease. These were now
joined by a second group, the 'Professional Liberals and the Left wing', such
as the pro-Indian journalist Louis Fischer who attacked the record of the
British Empire; and finally a third group, the 'New Internationalist-
Imperialists' whose global ambitions represented a rival power bloc which,
they feared, would dismantle the European influence, substituting American
'big business' in its place.[34]

   Although anti-colonialism was in no sense a purely Rooseveltian phenomenon, the priority that the President gave to it was a deciding factor; Roosevelt set the tone. His ideas were more sophisticated than his *ad hoc* statements
on colonial areas sometimes suggested. They were fundamentally underpinned by the idea of trusteeship, a concept which extended to the whole
post-war world, whose freedoms would be preserved by 'Four World Policemen', the United States, China, Britain and the Soviet Union, working within
a United Nations structure. Roosevelt, an idealist whose *modus operandi* was
notably pragmatic, saw that the concept of trusteeship afforded the flexibility
required to overcome key obstacles. He hoped to apply trusteeship not only
to the British Empire, but also to the colonies of the French, the Dutch and
the possessions of the defeated Axis states.[35]

   At least three main reasons for Roosevelt's firm commitment to anti-
colonialism can be identified. First, like President Woodrow Wilson, Roosevelt clearly believed that colonialism bore much of the blame for plunging the
world into a global war, and for the ability of the Axis to move with relative
ease into large geographical areas, such as South East Asia. Moreover, unless
eradicated it would lead to future wars. The war against Japan seemed the
clearest example, with its origins in the imperial contest over the Chinese
seaboard from 1931.[36] Colonial areas had proved staggeringly weak in the

face of the revisionist powers. The collapse of Singapore, 'the City of Blimps' as one American CBS correspondent christened it, seemed to have imperilled the whole Pacific. Stilwell's Political Adviser took the same line on Burma, blaming the collapse there on 'the worst type of colonial bureaucracy . . . cumbersome and inefficient . . . decadent and unintelligent'. European colonial control over commodities such as tin and rubber, and the high prices established by associated cartels were partly blamed for American unpreparedness for war in 1941. It was the failure of France to defend Indochina against the Japanese which, according to the State Department, 'clouded' the possibility of French return after the war.[37] Roosevelt pointed out that it was the downtrodden nature of the Indochinese population that had made the territory so easy for the Japanese to conquer in 1941.[38]

This question of international stability shaded over into a second area of American thinking on colonies: the ideological. The nature of French rule in Indochina, combined with Vichy collaboration, raised in the minds of those like Sumner Welles, the American Under-Secretary of State, 'a great moral question'.[39] Roosevelt emphasised to the press that the ideas of the Atlantic Charter applied to all humanity, and that the broader idea of four freedoms was inseparable from trusteeship and the United Nations. The American treatment of the Philippines was held up as an example of how dependent peoples should be managed.

The third aspect of Roosevelt's anti-imperialism was related to American interest in free trade, together with the European use of colonial cartels to increase the price of commodities in the inter-war period. This was given a heightened profile by the sudden arrival of numerous Americans in regions such as South and South East Asia where, prior to the outbreak of war, the American presence had been relatively small.[40] The course of the war awakened Washington to the commercial importance of a region with raw materials and with a large population which constituted actual or potential markets of great value. Inevitably, London suspected that UN trusteeship was merely a thin cloak for American interests. Eden complained: 'The American attitude to the Pacific, if correctly reported . . . is to give away other people's property . . . to an international committee on which America will be one of three or more.'[41]

The ability of the United States to present these initiatives as modern, progressive and idealistic, in contrast to the 'outdated' and undemocratic system of colonial empires offered an immense advantage. But alongside these Anglo-American differences there were some remarkable similarities. In the inter-war years, many British officials had been groping towards what they hoped would be a more efficient form of empire, a 'stripped down' version of colonialism, variously characterised as 'indirect rule' or 'informal empire'. Indeed, by the 1940s most of Britain's empire in the Middle East consisted of condominium, commercial agreement and treaty permissions, not direct rule.[42] This transformation had proved difficult, for not only was the outline of this new model uncertain, but more fundamentally, it required a strong metropolitan economy to maintain it. Nevertheless, on *both* sides of the Atlantic, there was a conviction that formal rule was not the most efficient vehicle of domination.[43] The United States, like Britain, was beginning to confront the choices between influence, ownership and rulership. By November 1943, for example, Roosevelt and the US Joint Chiefs of Staff were discussing in detail a veritable network of interlocking islands, ports and airbases which the United States required control of to ensure her future security.[44]

While London perceived American internationalism to be on the offensive, Washington often perceived itself as being on the defensive. First, there was a widespread fear that the combination of American assistance and general world turbulence would be exploited by London to shore up the British Empire. Against the background of the planned operations in French North Africa, the State Department warned, as early as March 1942, of British desires to extend its control over former French areas such as Tunisia. Britain certainly had some ambitions to increase its influence in French areas such as Syria and the Lebanon.[45]

Second, Washington feared that European behaviour might trigger a racially derived Pan-Asianism. The Japanese were promoting indigenous nationalism, not only in an anti-European, but also a more dangerous anti-white context. This strengthened American determination to distance herself from the activities of her European allies, fearing for its own relations with China and a future independent India.[46] American fears about a Pan-Asianism that lumped in the Americans with other 'colonial enemies' was heightened by the offensive anti-Western writings of their own partner, Chiang Kai-shek, which had to be suppressed within the United States for the duration of the war. Pan-Asianism offered a profound threat to the ambitions which the United States nurtured for post-war Asia: free trade and the space for cultural-moral expansion.[47]

By the end of 1942, following a furore over India, Roosevelt and Churchill were attempting to avoid direct personal confrontation over colonies. But the President was diverted rather than deterred. If anything, Roosevelt's ideas hardened in early 1943 following a trip to West Africa for the Casablanca Conference, offering him the opportunity to see conditions in the Gambia at first hand.[48] His attention now shifted away to the territories of other European states, especially France. The decision in 1942 to place Indochina in Chiang Kai-shek's command area, to bolster his prestige, had clear implications for its future.[49] On 4 March 1942 a report by OSS concluded that the population of Indochina disliked the French as much as the Japanese and that this population was wholly capable of self-government. Moreover, Roosevelt nurtured a personal loathing for de Gaulle, whom he considered a Fascist and enjoyed informing him personally that, since 1940, France had been unable to assert her sovereignty and was 'in the position of a small child'.[50] By contrast the Dutch approached the issue with more flair, convincing Roosevelt at an early stage that they planned progressive and sweeping reforms in the Netherlands East Indies.[51]

Roosevelt was responsible for the broad style, but not always the detail, of American policy on colonial areas. Much of the detail depended upon the complexities of inter-departmental arrangements, not least because the relationship between the State Department and organisations such as OSS and its sister propaganda agency, the OWI, was ambiguous. Cordell Hull was clearly disquieted by the evinced enthusiasm of the latter two bodies for radical ideas. As early as 1942 he expressed the view that Elmer Davis, Head of OWI, together with Milo Perkins, who looked after Economic Warfare, were more interested in creating a worldwide social revolution than in winning the war. Sumner Welles, the Assistant Secretary of State, a convinced Wilsonian, was more sympathetic. At an operational level matters were also uneven: European sections of the State Department trod warily on these issues for fear of offending their allies. In contrast those concerned solely with Asia made less allowances for the sensibilities of European governments and worked more closely with OSS and OWI.[52] In the words of R. Harris Smith, the pioneering historian of OSS: 'At least on the colonial issue, the OSS was in full accord with State Department officers in the Far East, and Donovan's organisation became the "faithful secular arm" of the diplomats' "anti-colonial fundamentalism".'[53]

Watchful waiting

Donovan undoubtedly encouraged Roosevelt's anti-colonial nostrums and in the first months of the war a high proportion of the reports on empire issues reaching the White House hailed from OSS sources. As early as 19 December 1941, Donovan sent a report on the Burmese and their attitudes to the war, prepared by his Far East Section, warning that the colonial context was critical and inclined the population to be 'anti-British, anti-Indian, and anti-Chinese'. If promised autonomy by Tokyo they could become 'pro-Japanese'. This reflected recent talks between Donovan's staff and the Burmese leader, U Saw, who warned that the Burmese might well sabotage the Burma Road carrying vital supplies into China.[54] As early as April 1942, returning from a tour of the Middle East, Donovan assured Roosevelt that while the small nations of the world viewed Churchill as their great defender, 'they look upon you as the great liberator'.[55] Donovan worked hard to service the White

6 General William J. Donovan, Head of OSS

House and by October 1942, Roosevelt's assistant, Lauchlin Currie, was sending Donovan material that allowed him to keep abreast of Roosevelt's current interests.[56]

Such reports on imperial issues framed the context for Roosevelt and he often responded directly to such information. The quantity of this material was substantial and the surviving files of the State Department and the White House teem with reports by the university professors, turned intelligence officers, of the OSS Research and Analysis (R&A) Branch. As Roger Louis has observed:

Division of Special Research (as well as studies by the Office of Strategic Services) formed a vast pool of accumulating information and advice. When it came to actual territorial decisions, for example, the American representatives at international conferences tapped this reservoir of knowledge . . . In this way there was a continuity of official thought; it might even be said that the officials and academic advisers who spent endless hours toiling on reports about such questions . . . ultimately exerted a great deal of influence indeed.[57]

The OSS Research and Analysis Branch sported a British Empire Section under Dr Conyers Read which tracked prevailing attitudes in London and

Washington. Its subjects included the contrasting British and American views of the applicability of the Atlantic Charter to territories outside Europe.[58]

OSS officers in the field, working ahead of the main forces, were often well placed to evaluate the attitudes and expectations of indigenous national-ists.[59] For the State Department, OSS was the major source of information regarding day-to-day developments in the parts of Asia without Foreign Ser-vice representatives.[60] Accordingly, relations between OSS and American diplomats working on South East Asia were especially close and co-operative. Typically, Kenneth Landon, the Thai desk officer in the State Department, had worked under Donovan until mid-1942 and liaised closely with the OSS Thai Committee in Washington.[61] However, relations between senior American diplomats and OSS were more problematic, especially over China.[62]

SIS and SOE were collecting similar material on American policy for Whitehall customers. The nature of the information desired by London, the level which it addressed, and the somewhat informal manner in which it was circulated – often by means of verbal briefings – can be glimpsed through the work of Lt Colonel Gerald Wilkinson, an SIS officer, who maintained a unique diary.[63] Wilkinson began his wartime career as Churchill's personal representative in MacArthur's South West Pacific Area Command. He briefed Churchill and the Chiefs of Staff, reporting on such subjects as MacArthur's presidential ambitions and his likely prospects for success, and also those who advocated a strategy of 'Pacific First'.[64] Characteristically, the invita-tions to conduct a briefing at No. 10 could come by telephone around mid-night.[65] Wilkinson did his best to capture MacArthur's complex personality, describing him as 'ruthless, vain, unscrupulous and self-conscious . . . but . . . a man of real calibre, with a vivid imagination, a capacity to learn rapidly from the past, a leader of men'.[66] Wilkinson's observations were valued in London and Churchill set such store by his reports that when his term with MacArthur finished in mid-1943 he took it upon himself, rather clumsily, to try to arrange his return for a second term. There followed an 'emergency session' with Menzies, the head of SIS, because Churchill's blundering mess-age to MacArthur was 'quite unsuitable'. Wilkinson and Menzies sub-sequently worked on successive drafts of a suitably urbane telegram, but Wilkinson did not secure a return to SWPA.[67]

Instead Wilkinson remained in London for some time and was used by SIS to brief senior figures on the future prospects for Anglo-American relations in Asia and the Pacific. The circle of people whom he briefed constituted a fascinating mixture of public and private individuals. Neville Butler, Head of the American Department of the Foreign Office, was high on his list. In this meeting Wilkinson 'emphasized as vehemently as possible' the prospects for rapid social and economic development throughout the region 'which, owing

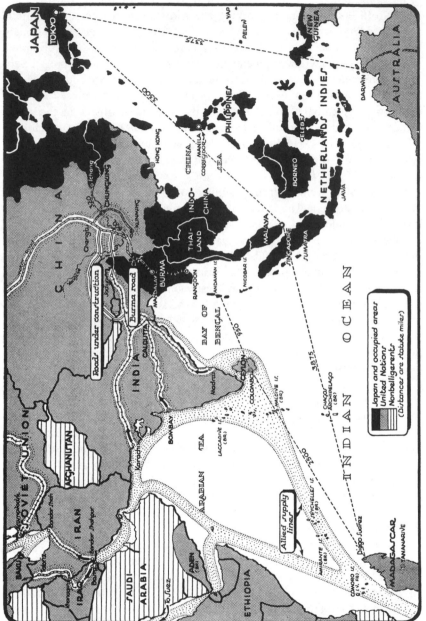

3 Ceylon and the Indian Ocean, 1943

to their vast population, would furnish an enormous market'. But he added the warning that 'Wall Street imperialists were causing America to look far more interestedly already at these Eastern prospects than ourselves.' Butler was impressed and arranged for him to make a return visit to brief Cadogan.[68] Wilkinson also spent time briefing non-governmental figures as varied as Wilfred Anson, the Secretary of Imperial Tobacco, and Barrington-Ward, Editor of *The Times*. The message was unvarying and Wilkinson sketched out 'the danger of an inferior post-war position for British interests as a whole that might result if the defeat of Japan was received by Pan-American successes, during the final stages'. Further meetings followed with the Head of the ICI, the General Manager of Reuters and senior staff from Anglo-Iranian Oil.

Meeting with Sir James Grigg, Secretary for War, on 26 March, Wilkinson complained of 'British apathy' regarding Far Eastern opportunities compared with the 'Wall Street Imperialists'. Grigg wanted him to brief Eden, but in his absence he was received by Ernest Bevin, Minister of Labour, on 8 April. There was only one future destination for this avid watcher of Americans and by the summer of 1943 he had been transferred to William Stephenson's BSC in the United States where, on the suggestion of Ian Fleming, he was given Far Eastern responsibilities.[69] After undertaking a short technical course in London he arrived at BSC in September 1943.[70]

Once in Washington much of his time was spent liaising on Far Eastern intelligence matters with senior OSS figures such as Whitney Shepardson and Colonel Buxton.[71] One of his principal roles was co-ordination of the Canadian 'Oyster Project'. This involved the use of Dr Konrad Hsu, a radio expert and graduate of Columbia University whose company had supplied radio equipment to SOE in India and China and who was also head of the Hsu clan in northern China. The objective was to obtain high-level intelligence on Japan from his clan contacts in the Chinese puppet administration. OSS funded the operation, but Wilkinson was the only figure in contact with Hsu.[72] Wilkinson's strong interest in economic and commercial intelligence also allowed him to warn of plans by Chinese business in the United States to move large amounts of capital to South America in late 1944.[73]

Wilkinson's instructions covered more than intelligence co-operation liaison with OSS. He had been given specific orders to collect from North and South America and from American Commands 'all secret intelligence of Imperial interest relating to Far Eastern matters that is not available to Her Majesty's government through official channels, or other existing S.I.S. representatives'.[74] In other words his duties included obtaining information that related to the future of British interests in Asia, rather than the current war, especially American and Chinese commercial plans. As Sir William Stephenson noted, this work was 'somewhat outside the charter of British Security Coordination's activities'.[75]

Wilkinson's work was typified by his comprehensive review of the 'Post War China Trade' completed on 28 December 1944.[76] It analysed the post-war commercial shipping market in Asia and identified those firms that posed the 'greatest potential threat' to British post-war maritime companies in Asia. It contained detailed advice to Holts Ltd (Butterfield and Swire Ltd) and to Jardine Matheson Ltd and other British companies on countering the problems posed by post-war Chinese economic nationalism and Sino-American economic co-operation. It also dealt with plans for post-war manufacturing in China, particularly in connection with rubber, and offered a detailed review of the membership of Sino-American trade federations.[77] Wilkinson was alarmed by what he saw and warned:

America's ability to manufacture and ship capital goods and heavy machinery with rapidity after hostilities cease should enable her, if she handles her overseas merchandising, financing and servicing properly, to steal a march on British manufactures.

Nevertheless, he counselled that, provided Britain organised herself well, she could defend her areas of traditional commercial strength: 'In financing, insurance, ship operation, general merchandising and distribution, we can still top the list in the Far East if we go at it properly.'[78] Wilkinson's reports for early 1945 examined subjects such as a large hydro-electric power scheme for the Yangtze River near Chungking and various Sino-American Trade meetings.

Wilkinson was anxious that this information be distributed fairly among British companies. He presumed that Jardine Matheson Ltd were already receiving his material because John Keswick, a senior SOE adviser on the Far East in London, was also a director of Jardines. He argued that this information should also be supplied to Jardines' major British rivals in China, Butterfield and Swire Ltd. Wilkinson assured his superiors that they could give this material 'whatever distribution you think fit' as long as company security was tight. Here Wilkinson was, rather presciently, addressing one of the problems confronting any pluralistic state gathering commercial intelligence, namely how to distribute it fairly without jeopardising its source.[79]

Wilkinson's focus on such long-range issues was not untypical of senior secret service officers. John Keswick, SOE's leading figure in China, was the principal informant for the Department of Overseas Trade when they warned the Cabinet Far Eastern Committee about the state of British commerce in China in November 1943:

According to a report by Mr John Keswick . . . the balance of British representation in Free China after the Japanese occupation of the coastal areas could only be described as pathetic. He states that apart from Jardine-Matheson, the Asiatic Petroleum Company, Butterfield and Swire, Barry and Dodwell, the British-American Tobacco and a few others who maintain one man and a boy each, nothing remained.

The various clandestine agencies saw it as their duty to raise the consciousness of government and industry about Britain's seeming lack of preparedness for the potentially booming markets of post-war Asia.[80]

By 1943, OSS, SIS and SOE had all begun to move beyond the field of information gathering and into action. In Whitehall this was marked by deteriorating relations between SOE and the Foreign Office. On the rare occasions when staff officers from SOE Headquarters at Baker Street liaised with the Foreign Office, they made their approaches discreetly, lest they be discovered by their superiors. Major Guise of SOE visited the Foreign Office Far Eastern department in December 1943, but was 'apprehensive' lest his superior, George Taylor, 'should reprove him for what is apparently regarded as reprehensibly close collaboration with the Foreign Office'. Care was taken to ensure that news of his visit 'should not get back' to Taylor.[81]

Because the Foreign Office were not in control of SOE's activities they were increasingly aware of the potential for conflict with OSS in Asia. In January 1944, Sir George Sansom, a senior British diplomat in Washington, raised the matter with Stanley Hornbeck of the State Department and encountered parallel misgivings. Hornbeck, he reported 'does not much like the OSS personnel – to whom he refers as "the gumshoe boys"'. But Sansom was discomforted to learn that Hornbeck believed that the Foreign Office had control over SOE. Nonetheless, Hornbeck believed these low matters were not of great consequence, since 'in the long run consultation between State Department and Foreign Office will prevent differences of opinion or method "on gumshoe level" from having any consequence'.[82] But in fact many in Washington were inclined to take SOE activities in the field as indicators of higher British policy. Sir Maurice Peterson, the senior official superintending British policy in Asia, foresaw problems and noted: 'I hope Dr Hornbeck *can* control OSS.'[83]

Conclusion

Although Roosevelt and Churchill were deeply concerned about colonialism, perhaps more than any other wartime issue, they were not in control of, or even always aware of, detailed confrontations on this subject. The work of the growing number of secret and semi-secret services exacerbated this. Characteristically, at an early stage of the war, Hull warned Roosevelt that the representation of the country was beginning to show signs of disintegration because of the multiplicity of new agencies speaking for government. Intense disagreement, combined with the postponement of delicate questions and constantly changing multiple chains of command, allowed vast scope for independent action by 'the man on the spot', in a way that had perhaps not been seen since the previous century. This had an impact on the texture of

Anglo-American relations at the theatre level, where matters were heavily politicised.

This book employs the term 'the Far Eastern War', others refer to the 'War Against Japan'. But in reality, across the vastness of Asia and the Pacific, there were several separate wars, beginning at different times and not well connected. The geographical pattern of conflict further separated them. Japan's occupation of South East Asia, the crossroads of Asia, along with the Chinese seaboard, ensured that the Americans fighting in the Pacific were cut off from their allies in mainland Asia. China, engaged in its four-way struggle between the Japanese, the puppet regime of Wang Ching-wei, the Communists and the KMT, was but precariously connected to the outside world by a vast air-supply programme over 'the hump' of the Himalayas. South East Asia Command seemed an artificial extension of colonial India, while MacArthur in the South West Pacific was the epitome of self-imposed isolation. To a far greater degree than in Europe and the Middle East, these multiple Far Eastern Wars eluded co-ordinated Allied strategy and were increasingly difficult to synchronise. In 1942 and 1943, the human secret services, OSS, SIS and SOE were increasingly aware that important political developments were occurring in these far-flung localities. They were anxious to develop liaison missions there and to exploit opportunities for local action.[84]

8

American intelligence and the British Raj: OSS
and OWI in India, 1941–1944

> In Bombay I saw the great Gandhi himself come to visit his British dentist
> in a green Rolls-Royce on which was mounted a sign in five languages
> saying 'Boycott British Goods' . . . it was obvious the British Rajh was
> dead. India's foreign rulers had already abandoned hope, and the Indians
> seemed incapable of it.
>
> Donald Downes, OSS, 1942–5.[1]

OSS, India and Roosevelt in 1942

The activities of OSS in India illuminate the intricacies of the inter-allied
diplomacy of intelligence during the Far Eastern War, not only because of
the centrality of India to the British and American perceptions of empire, but
also because of the volatile political developments within India throughout
the war.[2] Although OSS recommended to Washington an anti-colonial programme that was more strident than Roosevelt's, the ultimate impact of OSS
upon United States policy towards India policy was limited. Even before OSS
had received its charter, Roosevelt and Churchill had agreed to disagree on
India, with Roosevelt reluctantly noting that his silence on the subject was
the price to be paid for smooth Anglo-American co-operation on other aspects
of the war.

Instead the significance of the work of OSS in British India lies elsewhere.
India and Burma were the first British imperial territories east of Suez to
receive an OSS mission and the agreements that accompanied this arrival
largely determined relations between OSS and British organisations in Asia
for the rest of the war. The scale and scope of OSS reporting on India's
economic and political condition is striking and undoubtedly encouraged a
conviction in the State Department that these issues were inseparable from
the military conduct of the war against Japan. Propaganda, and the relationship between OSS and its sister organisation, OWI, would prove especially
important on Indian issues, for the battle was fought out not so much in Delhi
as in the American domestic media.

OSS in India provides an excellent case study of 'knowing one's friends'.[3] Notwithstanding the common struggle against Japan, OSS officers experiencing the last years of the Raj, found themselves in a country dominated by a vast and unfriendly British security apparatus which strongly resented the American presence. From 1942, Gandhi's 'Quit India' movement had left the British in the awkward position of attempting to fight a war in Asia from a base which was itself, to all intents and purposes, occupied territory. Attempts to encourage the Indian nationalists from any quarter, whether by British socialists, American officials, or by the Japanese, were viewed as more or less the same thing by the Government of India. The diplomacy of intelligence or 'liaison' here was also multilateral. Matters were further complicated by the close association of Indians, British and Americans with Chinese intelligence organisations whose security was dubious. The British responded by trying to exploit the intense factionalism amongst the numerous American and Chinese intelligence organisations, a strategy that was only partly successful.

The Indian case also underlines the way in which OSS, from an early stage, perceived itself as providing long-term strategic intelligence of benefit to American commercial and political interests, well beyond the war's end. Because of the focus from 1942 upon a post-war transfer of power, it was in the Indian context that OSS first began thinking about its post-war role in both the Middle East and Asia. These early thoughts on intelligence in post-colonial successor states with strong Islamic influence are particularly interesting. Accordingly, it was in the Indian context that OSS offered some of the most perceptive observations on the complexities of nationalisms that had the potential to be not only anti-British, but also neutralist and anti-Western.

OSS and its predecessors were required to produce intelligence on British India from the very outset of the Far Eastern War, for two reasons. First, as noted earlier, it presented an awkward political problem for the British and American governments. The Japanese naval foray into the Indian Ocean in 1942 had helped to raise the temperature of Indian politics markedly. There was immense American popular interest in the volatile Indian political scene and the Indian Congress Party became expert in communicating its views to American political groups. Gandhi appealed personally to Roosevelt to intervene during 1942, although Gandhi did not improve his case by referring in the same breath to the 'negro problem' in the United States. Second, India was of overwhelming importance to the Allied war effort, constituting a seemingly inexhaustible supply of military manpower. Six of the fourteen divisions under British command in the Middle East in 1942 were Indian. India also formed the crucial link for American supplies in transit to China, and the rear area for what became Mountbatten's South East Asia Command in November 1943.[4]

These developments only increased Churchill's determination to reject constitutional concessions. In April 1942 Churchill, under pressure from Attlee and others within his own Cabinet, and from Washington, had been forced to initiate the Cripps Mission to India to explore such possibilities. But once the Cripps Mission failed to secure agreement, Churchill used this as a justification for entertaining no more proposals for the duration of the war. Congress was equally intransigent. In August 1942 it launched 'Quit India', a campaign of civil disobedience which resulted in imprisonment of Gandhi and other Congress leaders. Thereafter India became a major internal security problem.[5]

Donovan's first reports to Roosevelt concerning India appeared in April 1942 and examined the strategic situation as revealed through the work of the first intelligence mission he had sent to Asia, which had escaped capture at Singapore. Donovan offered a detailed military analysis of that campaign, but the broader political implications to be drawn from all this were inescapable. Clearly there had been major problems with fifth-column activity and native desertion in Malaya, while in Burma there were reports of entire units going over to the enemy and the formation of some sort of 'Free Burmese Army' to aid the Japanese. Some of those returning from Malaya suggested that Japan would capture Burma within a month, bringing her to the gates of India and placing China in jeopardy. Donovan assured Roosevelt that the fundamental lesson to be learned from these campaigns was the total bankruptcy of colonialism : 'You can't win a war with slaves.' The British were now 'beaten and groggy' and the 'only hope for both Burma and India . . . is American power and particularly air power'.[6]

One month later Donovan wrote to Cordell Hull, setting out his plans for obtaining intelligence in the Far East, including a station at Calcutta. He expressly stated that this was for gathering 'information from combat and occupied areas not information about India'. But such assurances were quickly rendered obsolete. The onset of the 'Quit India' movement in the summer of 1942 ensured that the political stability of India was central to any OSS analysis on the war effort against Japan. In any case, Indian domestic developments were now of increasing *political* interest to Washington.[7] This was underlined as early as March 1942, when Sumner Welles, Assistant Secretary of State, had forwarded to Donovan copies of correspondence from the prominent Indian nationalist and poet Rabindranath Tagore to the leading Japanese writer, Yone Naguchi, criticising Japanese treatment of the Chinese and arguing that the Japanese conception of Asia rested on 'a tower of skulls'. Tagore was perhaps the best-known Indian figure in the United States between the wars and Welles believed this material should be given a high profile in America's political warfare in Asia.[8]

The relative coherence of opinion on India across official Washington in 1942 might be explained in terms of the wide circulation of gloomy OSS R&

A reports. In the spring of 1942, even before Donovan's organisation had formally become OSS, and before any of his representatives had been despatched to India, his British Empire Section in Washington was preparing detailed political reports on subjects such as Muslim hostility towards a self-governing India and also on the prospects of the Cripps Mission. This material reached key officials such as Adolf Berle and Dean Acheson. The excellence of the academic staff that Donovan had assembled for research and analysis work reveals itself in the quality of these early reports. Their assessment of the Cripps Mission, for example, was penetrating and accurate, suggesting that it was useful in countering Japanese Pan-Asian propaganda, but that it was highly unlikely to resolve the long-term differences between Muslims, Hindus, the princely states and numerous other Indian factions.[9] On 14 May 1942, OSS warned that 'most Indians feel that Britain is the first and most immediate enemy' and urged those responsible for psychological warfare not to identify the American cause with British policies in India.[10]

Donovan was ever-sensitive to the whimsies of presidential interest and this OSS effort on India partly reflected the fact that it was during the first half of 1942 that Roosevelt's desire to intervene was greatest.[11] After some deliberation, Roosevelt wrote to Churchill on 10 March and again on 11 April setting out various schemes that he felt might assist in breaking the deadlock with Congress. Churchill regarded this as an internal British matter and his response was volcanic. In London, the unfortunate Harry Hopkins, Roosevelt's special envoy, received the full force of the eruption and reported that 'the string of cuss words lasted for two hours in the middle of the night'. Churchill drafted a long reply to Roosevelt arguing that it was madness to throw the sub-continent into political confusion at a moment when the Japanese appeared poised to invade, adding that he would rather resign. Although this draft, which spoke of Churchill 'retiring into private life', was not sent, Hopkins verbally relayed the threat of resignation to Roosevelt. The President was now fully aware of the dangerous consequences of overt American incursions on India and increasingly turned his attention elsewhere.[12]

The timing of this crucial Churchill–Roosevelt exchange over the Cripps Mission of April 1942 was highly fortuitous from the British point of view. It ensured that when confronted with the disturbances of Gandhi's 'Quit India' movement later that year, Roosevelt had already set his face firmly against supporting political unrest in India for the duration of the war. Mualana Abul Kalam Azad, the President of Congress, was arrested on the morning of 9 August in the middle of drafting a letter to Roosevelt. Azad was but one of 100,000 nationalists arrested and interned for the duration of the war during August 1942. But Roosevelt ignored urgent petitions by Indians and indeed by Chiang Kai-shek for his intervention. Instead he wrote to Churchill assuring him that he would not now pursue any course which undermined the authority of the Government of India 'at this critical time'.[13]

OSS and its sister service responsible for propaganda, the OWI, together with a stream of high-level American visitors, including Laughlin Currie and the Republican Presidential candidate Wendell Wilkie, were central to the implementation of the new American policy that developed after mid-1942. American official interest in India did not decline at this point; instead the emphasis now shifted away towards the pursuit of several alternative objectives. The volatile Indian scene had to be watched closely in order to identify future opportunities for both discreet political encouragement and commercial advantage. More importantly, the United States could at least ensure that Indian nationalists did not confuse the British and American positions.[14]

In the short term, the political disturbances unleashed by 'Quit India' from the summer of 1942 massively increased the demand in Washington for detailed intelligence on developments in India. The War Department became seriously concerned about the safety of the 5,000 American troops in India, since only a small number of them could be flown out in the event of a general collapse of law and order. Blood-curdling stories began to reach the ears of military intelligence in Washington. The Inspector General of Police in Bengal had privately conceded that: 'if the Japanese attempted an invasion of Calcutta they would be received with garlands by a large proportion of the population and that many of the police themselves would join in the welcome . . . a massacre of Europeans might then ensue'.[15] By early 1943 military intelligence and OSS R&A were regularly preparing reports on 'American Troops and Civil Disobedience in India'.[16]

Working alongside OSS in Washington was OWI. By late 1942 OWI also perceived India as an alarming problem which would reverberate upon American foreign policy not only throughout Asia, but also in the Middle East. OWI warned that the 'eyes of the Moslem world are turned towards India', adding that events there helped to explain the current Iranian attitude towards Britain which was 'bitterly hostile'. Even strongly pro-British Iranians and Arabs who were writing broadcast scripts for OWI programmes had searched in vain for something good to say about the current situation. The wide nature of these reverberations identified India as a general Allied concern. OWI warned that: 'This is not England's war alone, but ours as well, – and China's', adding that 'British intransigence toward Indian nationalist leaders places our control of the Middle East in greater jeopardy each day.' With Germany knocking on the door of the Caucasus, they continued, the British 'hazard their own future and ours'. OSS and OWI could not therefore accept that India was merely a British domestic matter.

OSS and OWI were puzzled by British insensitivity to the wider reverberations of the Indian question. OWI observed that while the 'British Intelligence

Service in the East has been amazingly diligent and efficient in the collection of information' nevertheless it 'misappraised' this critical issue. British intelligence, they argued, had not understood the 'nationalist aspect' of Islam, nor the fact that the Muslim world was as interested in the progress of the Indian Congress Party as Jinnah's Moslem League. This was especially puzzling to them given that the British had plenty of historic experience of Pan-Islamic hostility arising out of the post First World War settlement with Turkey. Surprisingly, it was OSS and OWI, rather than the British services, who were giving sustained attention to the idea of a wider Islamic world.[17]

British intelligence may have missed international currents such as Pan-Islam, but they were taking a profound interest in the international impact of Indian nationalism, for example within the United States, and especially upon OSS and OWI. In March 1942 Stephenson's BSC submitted a lengthy report on Indian nationalists in the United States and their influence upon the machinery of government in Washington. It mapped the network of co-operation between Indians with 'extreme Congress views', certain American journalists, the Indian section of the US Library of Congress and members of the US Congress. BSC were alarmed at the influence that Indians were already having with the embryonic OWI.[18] BSC had succeeded in obtaining American propaganda planning documents and used them to support their general contention that the war in Asia was being 'exploited by those elements in America who consider the British Empire a spent force and who wish America to take over the commercial, industrial and financial leadership of India and the Far Eastern countries'.[19]

BSC's insights into the efforts of Indian nationalists to influence the United States Government were accurate. In the spring of 1942, OSS R&A in Washington was receiving material from Indian nationalists in the United States, from the Indian Congress Movement and even from Gandhi himself. Donovan singled out for Roosevelt's attention reports prepared by Dr Krishnal Shridharani, a prominent Indian nationalist and writer resident in America, a member of the Indian Congress Party and 'associated with Gandhi'. Donovan urged Roosevelt that, with the final collapse of Singapore, India and the attitude of its population to the Allies was 'no longer merely a British domestic question', but a general strategic question. He exhorted Roosevelt to discuss with Churchill measures that would ensure that the Indians offered resistance to Japan. Shridharani's moderate submission to Roosevelt concluded that 'only free men can win this war, and not mercenaries or vassals'.[20]

Shridharani's activities were a matter of increasing concern to London. In 1941 the British Minister of Information, Duff Cooper, who was touring Washington, witnessed the impact of the publication of his book appealing for American support of Indian nationalism, *My India, My America*. Cooper countered this by arranging for T. A. Raman, the London Editor of the United

Press of India, to tour the United States, establishing himself as one of the most outspoken Indian critics of Gandhi. London also published a book-length reply, defending British policy in India written by a PWE official, Guy Wint, with Sir George Schuster, a former member of the Viceroy's Executive Council. By 1942 there was a vast British information effort in Washington with a torrent of books, articles and pamphlets pouring forth in defence of British rule. Halifax, the British Ambassador, worked hard to convert prominent Americans and scored a notable triumph with the prominent journalist, Walter Lippmann, whose articles were effectively an apologia for British rule.

This campaign was effective. In late 1942, Louis Fischer, a prominent American journalist and campaigner for Indian independence, took part in the well-known radio debate programme, 'Forum of the Air', in Washington. He joined the author Pearl Buck in discussing India against two defenders of the British government position namely, Bertrand Russell and the indefatigable T. A. Raman. Later, in a report to OWI, with whom he worked closely, Fischer lamented that Raman had been recommended to the programme's producer by British information units in Washington and was 'intent on doing a job on US listeners'. Fischer thought that they were losing these public 'cockfights'.[21] By 1943, opinion polls indicated that Britain was indeed winning the propaganda battle in America against radical Indian nationalism, with the majority favouring no political change for the duration of the war.[22]

'Quit India' during August 1942 provided opportunities for deliberate Anglo-American tail-twisting. A week into the disturbances, Archibald MacLeish, the Assistant Director of OWI in Washington, wrote to Harold Butler at the British Embassy asking for details about riot control and particular for more information on the Indian Whipping Acts passed in 1933 and 1941. Harold Butler enjoyed composing a blood-curdling reply:

It is felt in London that whipping is a very much less severe punishment than shooting ... Already there has been some major interference with railway lines around Patna ... it may be necessary to resort to the most drastic measures to prevent the interference of military communications, including the machine gunning of saboteurs from the air.

All this, he added, was for his 'private information' and not for quotation.[23]

By the end of 1942, OSS and OWI shared a similar outlook on India. Yet there remained one important distinction: OWI enjoyed a formal presence in Delhi and OSS did not. The British Empire Section of what had now become OSS R&A in Washington was feeling the lack of an OSS station in India keenly. They had to resort to sending detailed questionnaires to the American diplomatic mission in Delhi for information on political subjects. However all this was about to change.[24]

Secret service treaties and liaison missions

By the end of 1942, OSS had expanded beyond all recognition. Its most-established branch was R&A, with a board of ten officials presiding over the work of over a hundred academics recruited mostly from the east-coast academic establishment. Its primary duty was to produce eye-catching material destined for the Oval Office. But there were now other departments. The surprise attack upon Pearl Harbor in December 1941 not only shocked Washington, it also offered Donovan an auspicious moment to expand his organisation. It was shortly after this that Donovan proposed to Roosevelt that he should now incorporate a greater range of intelligence, sabotage and other clandestine operations.[25] Meanwhile Donovan lost control of a his propagandists, who split away to become the OWI. Nevertheless, it was symptomatic of the bureaucratic competition in Whitehall and Washington at that time that Donovan quickly formed a new propaganda section within OSS entitled Morale Operations (MO).[26] In early 1942, Britain's PWE despatched a high-level mission to Washington to discover more about the structure of the American political warfare system. They found that the burgeoning American clandestine organisations, 'which deliberately encroached on each others territories', precisely reflected the British experience. But in the United States: 'The only common factor in this tangled skein of organisation was the President himself.'[27]

By the end of 1942, Stephenson's sprawling BSC empire included an element of the political warfare organisation, PWE.[28] This element became increasingly concerned by the momentum of American propaganda activities towards Asia. They reported that American agencies 'are now going ahead with plans on a gigantic scale for Far Eastern political warfare operations directed from overseas bases in Australia, Hawaii, Alaska and China and for the penetration of occupied territories'. These extensive operations, some from British territory, were 'a new and revolutionary development which was not anticipated'. BSC tried to control these activities by proposing an integrated Allied planning team to guard against 'divergent' policies, but OWI were not taken in.[29]

But in 1943 the primary issue for the Viceroy in India was not OWI but OSS. OSS was not only expanding their range of activities but also their geographical range of operations, with strong interests in India, Burma and China. The principal reasons for OSS establishing stations within India and later, within Mountbatten's newly formed SEAC theatre, was to satisfy the demand for intelligence on British political and economic intentions. As Colonel John G. Coughlin, who directed OSS within India and then SEAC, explained later to Donovan, OSS operations were 'not only important in defeating the Japs but may also be considered in part as cover for an opportunity to serve as a listening post for American interests in Asia'. He was also able to 'provide information as to the activities of British intelligence agencies'.[30] Equally, Britain continually strove to expand its SOE and SIS stations in China for the same purposes. Accordingly, the size and function of intelligence liaison missions were at the epicentre of inter-Allied intelligence controversies in Asia. This is illustrated by the animated discussions surrounding the establishment of OSS missions in British India during 1942 and early 1943. The resulting agreements were important, since they would subsequently frame a wide range of OSS and SOE activities in Asia.

From the outset both British and American intelligence were keenly aware of the potential of each other's 'observation posts'. One counter-measure that could be taken was to ensure the security of sensitive documents, and so the Second World War saw not only the adoption in Britain of the American classification 'Top Secret' instead of 'Most Secret', to provide for standardised inter-Allied levels of security, but also the adoption of two less well known classes, entitled 'Control' and 'Guard'. 'Control' was employed on American documents that were not for circulation to the British, while 'Guard' was employed for the same purposes upon sensitive British documents to be kept from the Americans. There were substantial numbers of these documents and the nightmare of keeping them out of the central inter-Allied registry system in command headquarters such as Allied Forces Headquarters (AFHQ), Supreme Headquarters Allied Expeditionary Force (SHAEF) and SEAC may be readily imagined.[31] John Colville, one of Churchill's private secretaries, endured this nightmare when the word 'Guard' was left off one of Churchill's more intemperate telegrams about the controversial situation in Greece. Once in American hands at Eisenhower's AFHQ in Italy, it was passed quickly to the State Department and then into the hands of Drew Pearson, a leading columnist on the *Washington Post* and the reverberations were considerable.[32]

OSS had in fact enjoyed a technical presence in India within months of the start of the Far Eastern War. In April 1942, Donovan despatched the famous Detachment 101, an OSS special operations unit to the American China–Burma–India Theater. But Stilwell, the irascible American Commander in Burma, would not initially permit an incursion into China, so they were based in Assam in Eastern India, whence they operated against the Japanese in Burma. Donovan was aware of British sensitivity over India and Burma and in April 1942 he warned all OSS personnel arriving in China to 'do nothing concerning India or Burma' without clearance from the British SIS representative in Chungking.[33]

However, by June 1942 the rapid expansion of both British and American clandestine activities in all areas of the world necessitated a series of OSS–SOE conferences to resolve the increasingly tangled web of overlapping activities.[34] Donovan, his deputy Colonel Goodfellow and a team of officers headed for London armed with a presidential order outlining the remit of the new OSS organisation. They sought not only a comprehensive 'turf agreement', but also better co-operation in areas such as field liaison, clandestine weapon development and financial issues. The latter subjects presented no problems but a 'turf agreement' proved more difficult. In principle both OSS and SOE recognised the value of geographical separation from the outset, asserting firmly:

It is essential to avoid the situation where there will be two completely independent organisations working in the field, with all the consequent dangers of crossing of lines, competition for agents and materials etc., and inviting attempts by foreign governments, or groups with whom both organisations would be dealing, to play one off against the other.

In an ideal world this would be dealt with 'by assigning the given region exclusively to the American or British organisation'. However, they were forced to take account of the fact that, in practice, both countries would have 'some interests' in most areas. A compromise solution emerged whereby they would designate a region as a 'predominantly British or American sphere of influence'. Areas of American predominance would have an American controller overseeing and approving all Allied clandestine operations with a small British liaison mission attached, or *vice versa*. Accordingly, while OSS and SOE could operate anywhere, for the purposes of policy and operational control: 'Each area should be defined as being either a British or American area.'[35]

Dividing up the world into areas of operational pre-eminence, or even exclusivity proved awkward. In 1942 Britain granted OSS only a 'secondary role' in most areas of Europe and the Middle East. Equal rights were agreed only in areas under Axis occupation or in neutral areas such as Switzerland, Spain and Portugal.[36] India, most of Africa and relations with the Soviet Union were especially sensitive and the British insisted on dealing with these areas alone. OSS might conduct operations in India or Sub-Saharan Africa, but only under the eye of a British controller. China, however, including Japanese-occupied China, Manchuria and Korea, constituted 'an American sphere of influence'. Quite different arrangements were made for South East Asia:

It was agreed that Burma, Siam, Indo-china, Malaya and Sumatra should be regarded as a no-man's land which could be worked into as convenient by the British S.O.E mission in India, the American S.O. mission in China and [MacArthur's] I.S.D., in Australia.

OSS and SOE recognised that: 'Line crossing inside of this area would have to be avoided by close liaison between these three missions', but they neglected to develop any machinery for the purpose, or to set out any mandatory rules for clearing operations. In 1943 South East Asia was not an area of primary interest and no-one foresaw that this problem would become hopelessly entangled with the related problem of theatre-command boundaries. Indeed, from the outset, both OSS and SOE showed little regard for relations with Theatre Commanders. They simply declared that there would be an SOE mission in India 'with control being exercised from London', and no thought was given to the relationship with Field Marshal Sir Archibald Wavell and GHQ India. Equally the OSS mission at Chungking 'would be controlled from Washington', without any comment on American regional authorities.[37] Only when discussing the Middle East did they concede that plans must 'conform to C-in-C's operation requirements' and required his 'concurrence'.[38]

Geographically, OSS did not secure a generous deal from London in the summer of 1942. But, as Bradley Smith has pointed out, OSS was still an embryonic organisation, albeit growing rapidly. By early 1943 OSS had grown considerably, and had been armed with a new 'mandate' by the US Joint Chiefs of Staff that strengthened its position considerably. In the spring of 1943, OSS also persuaded the British to provide full access to the highly prized decrypts of German secret service (*Abwehr*) radio traffic produced by Ultra, a sure sign of growing status.[39] Accordingly, by the spring of 1943 OSS was ready to push into sensitive areas which the British had previously declared off-limits.[40]

An opportunity arose in India in early 1943 when Roosevelt appointed William Phillips as the new high-level Presidential Representative to India. Phillips had been American Ambassador in Italy and was a personal friend of both Franklin and Eleanor Roosevelt. More importantly he had been Head of the OSS station in London during 1942, a post which offered him an education in the politics of secret service. He had presided over the move into the large new OSS premises in Grovesnor Square and refereed disputes between OSS and its sister services, OWI and the BEW. He also encountered SIS and SOE for the first time, resisting the 'British eagerness to absorb our functions' and 'gobble us up'.[41] Meanwhile he corresponded personally with Roosevelt about a wide range of developments in Britain.[42]

Although no longer strictly a member of OSS, he maintained close OSS links and even took Major Richard Heppner of OSS London to India as his personal assistant. Donovan seized the opportunity to use Phillips for high-level representations to Wavell, and to Viceroy Lord Linlithgow, for permission to open an OSS station in Delhi. The Viceroy was deeply suspicious of OSS and pointed out that the American War Department had already established a liaison group in India eighteen months ago, under Colonel Osmun which had access to all intelligence including 'S.I.S. channels', so OSS seemed 'intent on conducting secret operations of gathering information' within India.[43] Phillips had already upset the Viceroy by seeking an interview with Gandhi and his new request provoked much discussion in London.[44]

Throughout March 1943 the Viceroy cautioned London that OSS intentions were 'all part of the American anxiety to dig in this country with a view to the post-war period'. He added that such purposes were 'increasingly favoured by highly important elements in the machinery of Government in Washington, by a growing body of high military opinion, and also by important commercial interests'.[45] OWI, he claimed, had already 'displayed an eagerness to establish contacts with so-called nationalist elements in this country and with those industrialists who provide their main support'. He also suspected American naval intelligence at Bombay of preparing for 'post-war commercial penetration by the US'.[46] On 2 April 1943, as a direct result of the Viceroy's protestations, London refused permission for an OSS mission in Delhi.[47]

OSS were not easily thwarted. In Washington, Donovan approached Lord Halifax, the British Ambassador, and offered personal assurances that the proposed OSS mission in Delhi would not 'engage in any activities relating to the internal affairs of India'.[48] The question was re-opened at a high-level meeting in London on 13 May attended by Brigadier Walter Cawthorn, the Director of Intelligence from India Command, Brigadier E. H. L. Beddington for SIS, Colonel George Taylor for SOE and Colonel Wren of MI2.[49] Cawthorn was the main protagonist and he deplored the 'sympathy with Congress' evinced by OWI, and their gathering of commercial intelligence as 'of no possible value for the war effort'. He persuaded the representatives of SIS and SOE London to accept the Viceroy's own radical solution whereby all intelligence and clandestine activities in India should be integrated, bringing OSS effectively within the ranks of SIS and SOE and therefore under British 'unified control'. Beddington of SIS was uneasy but Taylor of SOE welcomed it more readily, greeting it as an opportunity to enforce the 1942 global agreement, which would put OSS in India under SOE control.[50]

Therefore, at the end of May 1943, a hopelessly optimistic Cawthorn headed for Washington, armed with agreed British proposals for the amalgamation of Anglo-American intelligence and special operations in India under British control. In Washington Cawthorn secured the assent of Army Intelligence (G-2), the State Department and BEW. Donovan and OWI, however, fully alive to the implications, rejected the Viceroy's idea of 'integration'.[51] Field Marshal Dill's British Joint Staff Mission (JSM) in Washington were permitted to see 'off the record' a telegram from John Paton Davies to Stilwell. This was 'uncompromising in the extreme' and showed that any combined activity would be quite unacceptable. Dill rightly concluded: 'This seems serious . . . and points to future trouble.'[52]

At this point discussions in London over the OSS–SOE relationship in India became intermingled with complex negotiations during which new regional and global agreements were negotiated and old ones adjusted. Throughout April 1943, Colonel David Bruce, who had replaced William Phillips as head of OSS in London, had been talking to SOE about operations in Europe. General Donovan joined Bruce at the end of July 1943 and negotiated further draft agreements governing the Middle East, India and the Far East including Mountbatten's proposed new SEAC theatre.[53] On 12 August the terms were outlined to the Chiefs of Staff. These were:

(i) Hard and fast delineation of spheres [of control] as in present 1942 agreement undesirable.
(ii) SOE would remain the predominant partner for all operations based on India. OSS would, however, establish such organisations in India as are necessary for their work.
(iii) OSS would remain the predominant partner for all operations in and based on China. SOE would, however, establish in China such organisations as are necessary for their work.
(iv) OSS in India and SOE in China will not operate without the full knowledge and consent of the other partner or without the approval of the Commander in Chief or Theatre Commander.

This was a most liberal charter, effectively permitting liaison establishments of any size with only the most general direction from the host theatre commander. It also permitted OSS and SOE to operate into Japanese-occupied South East Asia from two different theatres wholly without co-ordination, which, as SOE later admitted, was quite ludicrous.[54] This charter reflected London's taste for dealing with awkward questions by the simple expedient of delegation.[55]

This draft SOE–OSS agreement was circulated in its final form as a Chiefs of Staff document across Whitehall, so why was the obvious potential for trouble implicit in this agreement not identified? One answer is indicated by the diary of Cadogan, who had endured interminable meetings dealing with the proliferating irregular organisations since 1939. In August 1943 he was sent a lengthy brief entitled 'Co-ordination of Anglo-American Intelligence, Quasi-Military and Political Warfare Agencies in South East Asia Command'. But it remained unread and instead he scribbled on it: 'I just haven't got time to study this now.'[56] By September his patience with arcane discussions over secret service spheres of influence was clearly exhausted:

Meeting of Ministers at No.10, under P.M. to consider SOE Middle East worry. A decision was more or less taken which I hope was the right one, though I cannot understand these hierarchical–theological discussions of 'liaison', integration and the rest. These words mean nothing to me.

A few months later, on a similar secret service jurisdiction issue, Cadogan again noted, 'wrangles must be investigated . . . battle gets us nowhere and no-one has the time to go into the matter and sift it'. After four years of bureaucratic struggle, senior officials in London and Washington increasingly left the secret services to their own devices.[57]

OSS were delighted with this new agreement on Asia, and they expanded their missions as the theatre boundaries shifted. What had been simply the embryonic OSS Far Eastern Theater of Operations in 1942 was now divided up into several centres. OSS was properly established as OSS Detachment 202 in China. William Phillip's assistant, Major Heppner opened an OSS office in New Delhi in July 1943 and then took over OSS Detachment 404 within Mountbatten's new SEAC which was preparing to move to Ceylon. Colonel John G. Coughlin was brought in to head OSS activities in CBI, including eleven new sub-stations in India and OSS Detachment 101. OSS in India was designated Detachment 303 with its main headquarters in one of the grander neighbourhoods of Delhi at 32 Ferozshah Road. The sign outside read implausibly 'Dr L. L. Smith, American Dentist'.[58]

OSS, OWI and India 1943–1944

Paradoxically, by mid-1943, when OSS began to arrive in India in force, the volatile domestic scene which had created a demand for better political reporting had become more stable, partly because of a fierce crackdown involving widespread imprisonment. Gandhi's hunger-strike offered a possible focus for an upsurge of violence, but the hunger-strike was called off in March 1943. The prospects of a Japanese incursion into eastern India had also faded away by 1943. The decision to replace the implacable figure of Linlithgow with the avuncular Wavell, hitherto C. in C. India, also eased the situation, since Wavell as Viceroy went out of his way to communicate with Americans in India.[59]

OSS would continue to play an important role in informing American policy, but for the time being OWI took the limelight. OWI had arrived in India during May 1942, establishing a main office in New Delhi and branches in Bombay, Calcutta and Karachi. OWI had a key role in advertising the distinctive nature of American policy towards colonial areas. As John Paton Davies observed in November 1943, any American presence in India posed several problems for the British. It was not that Americans might make embarrassing remarks about democracy and freedom for dependent peoples, it was the fact that the British needed American assistance to defend their empire. The presence of American soldiers in India – visibly better paid and better equipped – reflected badly on British prestige. As Davies put it:

Yet they have to bear with us. Because they need our men and material – and our

7 The Viceroy, Lord Wavell, talking to Americans at Simla (IWM)

lend-lease – they cannot afford to put us out of India, as they would like to do. The least unsatisfactory escape from their dilemma would seem to be: accept us (for they have no alternative), consolidate us with themselves for ''efficient'' cooperation and then, by dominating the integrated partnership, bring us into line with their policy and action.[60]

This prediction proved accurate. The British again tried to neutralise OWI India using the over-familiar 'integration' formula. Mountbatten, arriving in late 1943, quickly suggested that all the psychological warfare apparatus of the region be combined. But as Ralph Block, the OWI chief in India, later recalled: 'Well, we couldn't be integrated, because that meant we would be backing British policy in Asia. So we didn't integrate.'[61]

OWI had to be protected. John Paton Davies hailed OWI as the key instrument for addressing the American imperial dilemma. He recognised that the Anglo-American partnership in India not only embarrassed the British, but also threatened the Americans with guilt through colonial association. However, he understood that neither could extricate themselves: 'To accomplish our mission we have as much need of the British as they have of us.' Inescapably then, the partnership could not be dissolved. But America's problems could be reduced through organisations such as OWI:

We are still able to exercise a considerable degree of control over our course . . . so long as we retain OWI as an independent American mouthpiece of psychological warfare we can attempt to rationalise our policy to East Asia on our own terms . . . We can hope thereby to mitigate such hostility to us as will develop among colonial peoples and can perhaps even win a larger degree of co-operation than might otherwise be forthcoming. This can be accomplished only if our psychological warfare program preserves a purely American identity.[62]

Highlighting the differences between the American and British positions on the future of India was a top OWI priority. OWI took out newspaper advertisements, explaining American policy in the Philippines, due to receive full independence in 1946, and drawing a contrast with India.[63] In the area of radio broadcasting OWI were limited by an agreement not to broadcast 'uncensored American propaganda' from India. So they awaited the reconquest of the Philippines to facilitate true broadcasting freedom to India; meanwhile they circumnavigated by discreet use of the Indian facilities of OSS Morale Operations Branch.[64]

In 1943, Indian developments unfolded for OSS and OWI in Washington as well as Delhi. Roosevelt's dealings with Phillips, his personal representative in India, underlined his decision not to confront Churchill again over India. Phillips had been on leave in Washington from April 1943 and had spent an unproductive spring and summer trying to persuade Roosevelt to act. Roosevelt signalled indifference by attaching him to Eisenhower's headquarters in London. This was a blow to the OSS mission in India who lost an irreplaceable sponsor. Roosevelt and Hull were determined that there should not be a break with Churchill on India and hoped to damp down discussions of the subject in Washington.[65]

Not every member of Roosevelt's administration was prepared to accept this. The personal commitment of some officials in OSS, OWI and the State Department to anti-colonial policies exceeded that of Roosevelt himself. This was underlined by the leak to the press of Phillips' classified and outspoken final report to Roosevelt, written in May 1943, which urged the White House to press London for concessions on India. On 24 July 1944, this was published extensively in the *Washington Post* by Drew Pearson, probably the most widely read political commentator in the United States. Pearson quoted at length Phillips' strident attack on British intransigence and his forecast of only 'token assistance' from a 'mercenary army' of Indian troops, leaving Americans to carry the brunt of the war against Japan. A furore followed in Washington. Urged on by London, Sir Ronald Campbell, the British Minister, repeatedly pressed Hull for a public repudiation of the offending statements. It also became a *cause célèbre* within the State Department, with Roosevelt and Hull suspecting the recently displaced Sumner Welles of perpetrating the leak.[66]

Campbell complained forcefully to the Editor of the *Washington Post*. With delightful mischievousness, Drew Pearson reproduced Campbell's complaints in his column a few days later.[67] All this was followed by the resignation of Phillips from Eisenhower's staff, giving the impression that Phillips had been dismissed because of his principled line on India. The matter escalated and was taken up by the American Congress. By early September, Halifax had joined the fray, pressing for a presidential refutation of Phillips's 'mercenary' charge. At the Second Quebec Conference, Roosevelt finally agreed to join with Churchill in stating that all Asian nations were, of their own accord, 'ardent' to engage in the war with Japan. Hull was relieved at the resolution of what had become a 'serious' issue.[68]

Significantly, the 'flap' created by this leak in Washington did not extend to Delhi or London. American diplomats in India reported that while the story had reached the Indian papers surprisingly quickly it had 'not . . . made much impression', for the great mass of Indian nationalists had lost any hopes of American intervention on their behalf.[69] In London, Churchill had remained confident that the leak would not prompt Roosevelt to raise the India question again and assured Eden confidently that William Phillips was nothing more than 'a well-meaning ass'.[70]

What was the source of the Phillips leak? The historian Marshal Windmiller has uncovered that the report was leaked by Robert Crane, then in the process of transferring to OSS R&A from the State Department, having been recruited by W. Norman Brown, an eminent Professor of Sanskrit who held a senior position in OSS R&A. Crane passed the report to two Indian friends in Washington and they in turn passed it to Pearson.[71] Remarkably, Pearson was in the enviable position of receiving leaked material from several quarters. In August 1944 Pearson astounded British officials by also quoting telegrams from Eden and from the Government of India. Such material was also freely quoted by American Senators in Congress. Major Altaf Qadir, Third Secretary on the staff of the Indian Agent General section of the British Embassy in Washington, and an ardent nationalist, had smuggled this material to Pearson.

London assigned Stephenson's BSC to find the culprit. BSC routinely watched Indian nationalists who were in close contact with prominent Americans and this allowed them to identify Qadir and also the Indian nationalist, Chamal Lal, who had handed the Phillips report to Pearson. BSC did not identify Crane, but they were close when they suggested that the leaked copy of the Phillips report might have come from OSS rather than from the State Department. Britain toyed with asking the FBI to investigate the original source of the Phillips report, but Halifax warned London that FBI activity would just give Pearson more ammunition.[72] Halifax was right, for a garbled account of BSC's activities soon found its way into Pearson's *Washington Post* column:

British Intelligence, after first blaming Henry Wallace, claims to have traced the leak to the White House, hinting FDR wanted the Phillips letter published, for a better bargaining position with Churchill . . . [Following the further leaks] the British went frantic. Six British Secret Service men and two burglar alarm experts arrived at the British India Office here. They combed files, took finger prints from documents, examined locks, windows . . .

The BSC investigation was now halted.[73] Lal was expelled from the United States and Major Altaf Qadir was quietly transferred to the fighting front in Burma. Earlier plans to move the Indian Agent General's Office out of the British Embassy in Washington and to set it up as a separate Indian Legation, initially favoured by the liberal-minded Halifax, were now dropped.[74]

Compared to these colourful events, mainstream OSS reporting on India was less dramatic. OSS continued to provide the most substantial intelligence reports on Indian internal conditions circulating in Washington during 1943 and 1944. The political scene was quiescent, so OSS attention turned to what many thought to be India's impending economic collapse under the strains of war. Following a visit by Donovan himself to India in early December 1943, his report effectively conveyed the sense of crisis felt by many economic advisers within the Indian Government, who urged a reduction of the demands being made on India, where inflation was rampant. Donovan proved to be a powerful and consistent critic of the colonial system, arguing that it was the inflexibility of officials in Delhi and 'vested interests in London' that prevented any improvement in the Indian situation.[75]

Washington continued to request detailed and accurate reporting on the political scene. Yet OSS had to be cautious: direct contact with Gandhi or other Congress leaders would have angered the British. As early as 1942 the American Mission in Delhi had been explicitly forbidden to pass messages from Roosevelt to Gandhi.[76] However, in June 1944 Hull explained to Roosevelt that this problem had been overcome by devising a method of communication with Indian leaders which evaded the ubiquitous British surveillance. But concern remained about the possibility that it would be uncovered.[77]

OSS and British surveillance in India

In wartime India, a huge British security and counter-intelligence apparatus was developed to confront a miasma of threats and conspiracies, some very real, some the products of the over-active imagination of Churchill and his immediate entourage. Their main business was three separate but related problems. Firstly, the resistance offered by Congress and the 'Quit India' movement which led to considerable violence in 1942. Secondly the Japanese organisations which sent a steady stream of rather ineffective Japanese Inspired Fifth-Columnists (JIFs) westwards towards India. Thirdly, German and Italian-inspired attempts at subversion, based primarily in Afghanistan, but also focused on the creation of an Indian Legion of the Wehrmacht, recruited from 3,000 Indian troops captured in the Middle East. All these threats became less alarming towards the end of 1942, as it appeared that an Axis invasion of India was less likely.

The very extensive British security apparatus also ensured it was easy to follow the activities of American and Chinese allies within India. American officials, especially those in OSS and OWI, were conscious of constant, albeit low-key, surveillance. In August 1944 the American Consul at Bombay warned in unambiguous terms: 'Representatives of the United States Government in India should bear in mind at all times that they are functioning in a police state.'[78]

The responsibility for political surveillance in India rested principally with Sir Denys Pilditch, Director of the Intelligence Bureau (IB) in Delhi. This was a police security intelligence department working under the auspices of the Viceroy and the Home Department of the Government of India. Little is known of these IB activities for, in 1946, as independence approached, the Director of IB informed Wavell that he was disposing of 'certain dangerous . . . records, in anticipation of a [nationalist] Ministry coming into office'.[79] Security work relating to the Indian Army was undertaken by the large intelligence element of GHQ India under Cawthorn, the DMI India, whose duties almost exclusively concerned internal security.[80]

The British derived their best information about the Americans directly. Because OSS and OWI were interested in Indian politics they sometimes recruited Indian 'nationalists' who were already in the pay of the British. The scale of British penetration of Indian nationalist organisations was such that there was probably little need to 'plant' indigenous agents on OSS or OWI. However, this was the impression given. One OSS officer arriving in southern India recalled: 'We had been warned in Delhi that the British were past masters at intrigue and had planted spies in all American agencies to piece together information.' She added that this 'undercurrent of distrust distressed me more than any good healthy sub-rosa political manoeuvring'.[81] This became more apparent from February 1944 when OSS established its own counter-espionage element (X-2 Branch) in India.[82]

American military personnel were routinely watched by Indian Army intelligence and warned off any political activity. Foreign diplomats were watched by IB and the local CID who, it was claimed, 'kept extensive dossiers' on everyone.[83] A crucial source on the American presence in India was British postal interception and censorship. As early as March 1943 the Chief Censor in India completed a report on Bombay in which 'the activities of the

American press and the U.S. Office of War Information have been analysed in detail'. Particular attention had been given to the views of three members of OWI who were considered 'anti-British'.[84] In early 1943 the British decided to begin interception of all mail addressed to American consulates in India.[85]

The Government of India also created a special unit called 'The Chinese Intelligence Wing'. This began as an organisation under Cawthorn, the DMI India, designed to look after the Chinese aspect of Indian internal security, reflecting the influx of Chinese troops for the war in Burma from 1942. But its scope grew quickly to include the ambitions towards India of American organisations based in China. Its targets included subjects as diverse as Sino-Tibetan relations, Chinese Banks, the Chinese Defense Supplies Corporation and large-scale Chinese smuggling. Its chief was Lt Colonel George Fox-Holmes, who had been a medical missionary in Sinkiang in the 1930s. This unit was based at 209 Lower Circular Road, Calcutta and also had offices in China itself. The few extant records show clearly that much of its information was derived from the interception of air mail passing between the United States and China which had to pass via India in order to go 'over the hump'. Nevertheless, by judicious sharing of information on the Chinese, it also enjoyed good relations with its American subjects.[86]

This climate of surveillance affected senior American officials. Ralph Block, the Chief of OWI in India during late 1943, recalled a visit to the Delhi office of General Albert C. Wedemeyer, the newly arrived American Deputy COS to Mountbatten. Here Block found himself sitting next to Wedemeyer during a fraught telephone call to Stilwell's headquarters concerning the war in Burma. Block recounts: 'I took an envelope from my pocket and wrote on it, "Your telephone is tapped" ... Wedemeyer replied, "If that's true, then my position here is untenable".' Worries of this nature seem to have governed their behaviour throughout the headquarters building. Block recalls a subsequent conversation with Wedemeyer:

BLOCK: When I started to say something, he pointed to a big oil portrait on the wall. So, I shut up.
INTERVIEWER: Why, was there a microphone behind the painting?
BLOCK: Probably ...

There is certainly no firm evidence that the British had placed Wedemeyer under technical surveillance. But some American officials working in India clearly believed that they were under technical surveillance and this inevitably influenced their outlook.[87]

OSS in India seemed determined to provide British security with a subject worth watching. The large OSS structure in India had been assembled hastily during mid-1943, without any security and counter-intelligence (X-2) element. In 1944, when OSS X-2 finally arrived in India, they were shocked by conditions in some locations. British security officials, US Army intelligence officers and the US Provost Marshal in India were all ill-disposed to OSS and were quick to provide newly arrived OSS X-2 officers with material on past OSS misdemeanours. These problems allowed the opponents of OSS, both American and British, to exploit the natural tensions between different branches of OSS. During February 1944, Donovan despatched Lt Colonel Sidney S. Rubenstein, the Deputy Head of OSS X-2 in Washington, to India, to establish a comprehensive X-2 branch.[88] His most immediate task was to negotiate a formal agreement with the local security chiefs, Pilditch of IB and Cawthorn, the DMI India, permitting the conduct of X-2 activities, for this was the first suggestion of a full American counter-espionage section in India.

The British again offered 'considerable resistance' to the idea of OSS counter-espionage within India itself. Cawthorn put his case bluntly: 'How would you like it if we came to your country to establish a CE system throughout the United States?' But Cawthorn had met his match. Rubenstein, was not only a trained lawyer with a sharp mind, but also he had previously served as an FBI special agent working in close collaboration with BSC in New York on 'espionage and sabotage matters'. Rubenstein therefore retorted: 'That is exactly what you did', and then proceeded to regale the surprised Cawthorn with a history of Stephenson's activities in the United States. Cawthorn's resistance now melted away and generous agreement was forthcoming.[89] Rubenstein spent the next four months touring India and Ceylon before handing over to the new Head of X-2 India, Major John M. McDonough, on 8 June 1944.[90]

Rubenstein's visit also bore the hallmark of an internal affairs investigation. Colonel Heppner of OSS in Mountbatten's SEAC theatre took the opportunity to ask Rubenstein to probe several worrying OSS issues in India in collaboration with CID personnel from the American Provost Marshal's Office in New Delhi. Indeed, it seems likely that Heppner had pressed Donovan to launch the whole X-2 initiative on this account. The results were explosive and news quickly found its way to OSS in Washington.

The worst problems encountered by X-2 in India were at the OSS Calcutta office. The headquarters building here, located at 140 Regent Estate, Tollygonge, served not only as liaison with regular formations fighting in Burma, but also as the rear headquarters of OSS Detachment 101 which was fighting in Burma. On Rubenstein's arrival in Delhi, the US Provost Marshal opened up his very considerable files on the OSS Calcutta office. The first problem identified was a straightforward procurement scandal involving both OSS and British officers. The US Provost Marshal had launched an investigation but was 'afraid to go too far because the thing was just loaded with dynamite'.

The British had been quietly investigating the same group of individuals, who had also been selling to the British Army, and arrests were imminent. Second, the same members of OSS belonged to a group which regularly held parties on the top floor of the main OSS Calcutta building in which the registry was located. Those in attendance included suspected enemy agents from local 'beauty parlours'.[91] Subsequently, arrangements were made to keep sensitive information from certain OSS staff while surveillance was mounted with the help of the Calcutta police.[92]

X-2 concerns also extended to the recruiting process for Detachment 101 in Burma which was conducted openly, with dozens of individuals queuing outside for interview on any given afternoon. 'No real check is made . . . we have enlisted deserters from the British and Indian Armies.' Rubenstein added that British military intelligence officers and the Calcutta police officers, whom he had worked with, 'have confidentially told me that the security of our establishment is the cause for ridicule on the part of everyone in Calcutta . . . there isn't much they can do about it as they feel the Americans run their own affairs'. Washington was confronted with these findings and was urged that the Calcutta headquarters be 'cleaned out from top to bottom'.[93] OSS in Washington managed to contain this episode during 1944. But in 1945, during the animated debate over the future of OSS, the opponents of OSS used lurid descriptions of occurrences in Calcutta and Bombay to support their case for abolition. Roosevelt commissioned one of his staff, Colonel Richard Park, to prepare a report on OSS. Park's report, which included descriptions of 'a real orgy' in India, was handed to Truman in April 1945. It painted a picture of waste, personal ambition and the prospect of a post-war 'Gestapo scheme', contributing to Truman's decision to wind up OSS at the end of the war.[94]

Relations between OSS, OWI and the British in India were rendered yet more complex by the presence of a new third party, the Chinese nationalists and their secret service. Before the war, foreign diplomatic representation had not been permitted on Indian soil. But now, with a growing volume of allied wartime business, both American and Chinese diplomatic representation had become unavoidable. Delhi still shied away from foreign embassies, but American and Chinese 'commissioners' had arrived. The Chinese Commissioner's Office in New Delhi was a centre of KMT (nationalist) espionage, as was the Chinese Consulate General in Calcutta and a Chinese Consulate at Bombay, permitted after May 1942, because of the Chinese troops training in India for the Burma war. IB quickly concluded that the Chinese were 'familiar with the Axis technique of using consulates as nerve centres for the collection of intelligence' and interpreted diplomatic privileges 'in the widest sense'. Consul General Pao at Calcutta employed a number of agents, including one 'Mr Nyi'. IB in turn planted sub-agents on Mr Nyi and Indians were soon arrested for passing over information on the RAF in India. The British adopted the same approach to the Chinese Commissioner's Office in New Delhi which employed a number of Indians recommended to them by members of Congress. In turn, some of these Indian employees kept IB well informed. One such Indian employee found himself seconded to the Chinese nationalist intelligence organisation, and was specifically tasked by the Chinese with investigating the Delhi Branch of the Ministry of Information. The Chinese were 'willing to pay highly' for any information.[95]

Robert Tharp was one of the British individuals involved in these sensitive operations against Chinese intelligence in India. A prime concern, he recalls, was to track their work in 'secretly supporting Gandhi's nationalist movement'. Tharp recruited a deserter from the Chinese Army in Burma called Chen and furnished him with a new identity. He was then moved into Chinese diplomatic circles in Delhi and provided 'a remarkable amount of information'. Soon he was being given 'suitable disinformation' by his British controllers 'to confuse the opposition'. Chen then heard that documents involving Chinese aid to the Indian nationalists were being sent to Chungking next day in the Chinese diplomatic pouch, which was carried by British aircraft but not accompanied. Late the following day the British announced that the plane had 'crashed' en route to China and the pouch was 'lost'.[96]

Both the British and OSS X-2 regarded the Chinese missions in Calcutta and Delhi as penetrated by Japan. Even where Japanese penetration was not suspected, OSS relations with the Chinese secret service were tense because Chiang Kai-shek was trying to squeeze OSS out of the China theatre. Former OSS officers in Delhi have claimed that OSS did not hesitate 'to eliminate' Chinese thought to be working for Japan, but lived in constant fear of retaliation. In one 'tit for tat' incident an OSS officer was fatally injured when hit by a Chinese embassy car. The Head of OSS in Calcutta, the energetic George H. White, allegedly shot and killed a Chinese bookmaker thought to be working for the Japanese.[97]

The politics of secret service in India were therefore far from straightforward for OSS. Imbued with anti-colonial sentiments at the outset, matters became more complex as IB and the US Army succeeded in accelerating internal OSS tensions. OSS were increasingly uncertain of their natural collaborators. Immersion in the factionalised Indian political scene was an educating, but not an uplifting, process. OSS was also decreasingly enthusiastic about nationalist China. But it was not only American secret services who had their basic assumptions about friends and enemies challenged by the exigencies of wartime Asia. British security organisations in India also found themselves working with strange allies.

9 Strange allies: British intelligence and security in India, 1941-1944

> ... it was essential for the Indian government to have intelligence of under-
> ground political intrigues and conspiracies, to recognize the currents of
> public opinion before they became tidal waves. To do this it was necessary
> to employ spies. The Indian government employed a very large number of
> spies – one Indian estimate I saw placed at thirty thousand the number of
> native police spies maintained by the Raj.
>
> Lt Commander Edmond Taylor, OSS[1]

The British retreat into India, 1941–1942

In the wake of Singapore, British intelligence and security staffs, and the
growing numbers of American liaison officers, had suffered a diaspora. The
precious codebreaking staff focused around Kranji were now despatched to
Ceylon, the headquarters of Admiral Layton, Commander in Chief East
Indies Fleet. Most SIS and SOE elements were evacuated to India. Other
components of FECB and SOE moved to the Netherlands East Indies to
join Field Marshal Wavell's short-lived American–British–Dutch–Australian
Command (ABDA).[2] Wavell's ABDA Command had very limited staff, initially no secure communications and was overrun within months.[3]

'Never before', remarked Pownall, the ABDA Chief of Staff, 'has an H.Q.
been set up under these conditions, nor so many bricks expected from so
little straw'. Wavell, supposedly the commander, had recently fallen six feet
off the pierhead at Singapore onto rocks and barbed wire, sustaining injuries
that had confined him to bed.[4] Brigadier Leonard Field ran the inter-service
intelligence bureau at Wavell's headquarters, rudely fashioned from FECB's
Singapore remnants.[5] In these hostile conditions, inter-service wrangling now
returned with a vengeance. The RAF insisted on the creation of an additional
organisation, the 'Combined Operational Intelligence Centre', presided over
by Captain F. B. Stamp of the US Navy. The Army wanted this located
near Wavell's ABDA Command Headquarters at Lambang, alongside Field's

bureau, but the Air Force located it at a former military academy on the east side of Bandoeng, a full twenty minutes drive away from Wavell, but conveniently close to the Air Staff HQ. There were thus two competing intelligence centres. The Navy was unhappy with either site and wanted everything on the coast. But Japan settled the argument when ABDA was overrun. Most intelligence elements retreated to India, while SOE officers literally washed up in Australia.[6]

In March 1942, the Head of SOE in London, Frank Nelson, advised the British Chiefs of Staff that what had once been a fairly centralised operation in Asia was now split between India, Burma, China and the Netherlands East Indies, with some developing interests in Australia. Commands were being re-organised and the style of operations was changing. Stay-behind parties and economic sabotage were finished, while ahead lay preparation for large-scale guerrilla activity of a more para-military character. With Burma in the process of being occupied, Nelson proposed an expansion of activities in China, while the main SOE centre would be attached to GHQ India at the Viceroy's request.[7]

SOE had despatched a small 'India Mission' to Delhi in early 1941. Prior to Germany's attack on the Soviet Union it had concentrated on possible German or Soviet advances from Iran or the Caucasus into western India and the writ of SOE India ran as far as Iraq and Persia.[8] Such thinking was wholly in keeping with the time-honoured efforts of British security in India to counter the efforts of Czarist, then Soviet, intrigues from central Asia and the traditions of the 'Great Game'. But in the space of a year, between June 1941 and April 1942, this centuries-old pattern of thinking suffered a *bouleversement*. In early 1942, fear of a Soviet collapse in the Trans-Caspian region kept British eyes trained on Persia, Afghanistan and the North-West Frontier. But the Soviets were now allies and SOE made plans to train stragglers from retreating Soviet formations as guerrillas.[9]

In April 1942, a successful foray into the Indian Ocean by a Japanese cruiser squadron finally turned British attention away from the North-West Frontier towards a possible Japanese invasion of the eastern seaboard of India. SOE were tasked with the strategic demolition of the power stations and docks in Calcutta in the event of a Japanese invasion and once more began to train stay-behind parties. All of SOE's work in India during 1941 and 1942 involved preparations for dire emergencies which, in the event, did not materialise. Yet these emergencies were of great political significance, requiring SOE to acquire strange friends: the communists, whom the IB had viewed as a principal threat to Imperial rule in Asia for two decades. Moreover, the relationship that SOE and the NKVD had begun to strike up in late 1941, now bore fruit. As the Axis powers sought to further destabilise an unstable India using groups based in Afghanistan, it was first-rate counter-intelligence supplied by the NKVD that gave imperial security in India the edge.[10]

The SOE India Mission was led by Colin Mackenzie, a formidable figure with the intellectual calibre to take such bewildering changes in his stride. A fine classical scholar, he had won the Chancellor's medal for English verse at Cambridge, before taking a first in economics. He had lost a leg in the First World War and his limp added character, some of his underlings referring to him as 'Moriarty'. Uniquely, he was the only Head of SOE's many overseas missions who lasted the entire duration of the war.[11] Like his chief, Frank Nelson, he had extensive prior experience in Asia, as a Director of J. & P. Coats. He was also a personal friend of Viceroy Lord Linlithgow, sharing a common Scottish background and a deeply conservative outlook, but not the same mental pace. Jawaharlal Nehru's caricature of Linlithgow is widely regarded as accurate: 'Heavy of body and slow of mind, solid as a rock with almost a rock's lack of awareness.'[12] Linlithgow was also a Director of J. & P. Coats, hence the Viceroy had requested that Mackenzie be given the post.[13] In March 1942, when SOE wanted to expand in India, the Viceroy's reception in Delhi was enthusiastic, in stark contrast to the one afforded Killery at Singapore. Linlithgow helped to secure high quality staff and approved *risqué* SOE operations over the heads of the security authorities.[14]

The IB and Gandhi

Throughout the war, Indian security was continually poised to confront a miasma of threats and conspiracies. In 1942 the main problem was the combination of the threat of overt Japanese invasion from April, followed by the launch of the 'Quit India' movement by Congress in August, leading to considerable violence. This led to worries about the reliability of the Indian Army. Although Axis efforts at subversion had encountered minimum success, Churchill had clearly been unnerved by the behaviour of Indian troops in the Malayan campaign and feared the behaviour of the Indian Army if Japan arrived on Indian soil. But as early as 1940, the perceptive officers of MI2, dealing with Asia, had recognised that in reality the main threat came from a civil disobedience movement led by Congress. This would turn India into a strategic liability instead of an asset. Accordingly, MI2 advocated liberal British concessions to Congress, but the War Office chose to ignore this and gave the opposite advice to Cabinet. Arguably, by 1942 MI2 was used to having its prescient advice ignored.[15]

In his wilder moments Churchill viewed the entire Indian Army of two and a half million men as one huge security problem. In 1942, Leo Amery, the Secretary of State for India and Burma, noted: 'Winston at the moment has got one of his fits of panic and talks about the drastic reduction of an army that might shoot us in the back.' Churchill was also disturbed by the enormous Sterling balances that India was accruing as a result of her supply role. Although he wished to preserve this jewel of empire, he simultaneously distrusted it, and was prone to outbursts about 'the gross, dirty and corrupt . . . baboos' of India. These proved to be unwarranted slurs upon the Indian Army in Burma which fought ferociously and upon a country whose war economy bore a terrible burden, coming close to breaking point in 1943.[16]

Contrary to some British assertions, there were no links between Congress and the Axis, other than some strange letters written by Gandhi to Hitler politely requesting that he stop the war. On the contrary, Congress lined up firmly against Japan, partly due to their growing links with Chiang Kai-shek and nationalist China.[17] But Churchill's wild fears persisted and in June 1943 Amery again noted: 'Winston has a curious hatred of India . . . and is convinced that the Indian Army is only waiting to shoot us in the back.'[18] By February 1945, and despite the Indian Army's incomparable war record, at least in Burma, Churchill's attitude had not improved. His private secretary recorded: 'The P.M. said the Hindus were a foul race "protected by their mere pullulation from the doom that is their due" and he wished Bert [Bomber] Harris could send some of his surplus bombers to destroy them.'[19]

This attitude was reflected by security intelligence arrangements on the ground. By 1943, Cawthorn, the Director of Intelligence at GHQ India, was almost exclusively concerned with internal security.[20] When the PWE Mission arrived from London it discovered that Wavell had a whole separate department to deal with the Japanese-sponsored INA, a target he regarded as being of the 'utmost importance'.[21] INA was dealt with by the psychological warfare section of India Command known as GSI(q) under Lt Colonel Hunt, working with Cawthorn, who tried to blunt Japanese subversion through radio counter-propaganda.[22]

The advent of the 'Quit India' movement underlined the effectiveness of British large-scale surveillance of the nationalists in India. On 8 August 1942, in the wake of the failure of the Cripps Mission, Congress passed the 'Quit India' Resolution calling for an immediate transfer of power to an Indian administration and initiating a mass campaign of civil disobedience. But before this could be organised it was declared unlawful and prominent Congress organisers in every state were arrested, eventually numbering over 100,000. The British anticipated Congress plans almost a month before they were launched.[23] Nevertheless, there followed a wave of serious attacks against communications, the populace and government buildings, accompanied by a wave of strikes. Before the end of the year over a thousand people had died and machine gunning from the air had been authorised on six occasions. In the same way that the resistance imposed a drain on German forces in France, so in India approximately 35,000 troops were engaged on internal security duties.

In April 1942, Allied intelligence concluded that if Japan attempted an invasion, a complete collapse of India would ensue. The JIC in London suspected that Admiral Nagumo's naval raid on Ceylon had whetted the appetite of the Japanese for further conquest and that, moreover, the Japanese were aware of India's vulnerability. In Whitehall some military planners had come to accept the fall of India as a foregone conclusion.[24] Cawthorn, reviewing the early stages of the disturbances at the end of August 1942, was anxious to blame the disturbances on the hidden hand of either the Axis or of communists disobeying the Moscow line. However, he could not explain why those most likely to work under foreign direction, namely the frontier tribes and the Sikhs, were silent. The reality was very different. By the end of 1942 only forty-five Axis-inspired agents had been caught in India, mostly poorly trained INA personnel engaged on intelligence gathering and sabotage rather than subversion. Many surrendered quickly to the authorities and were 'played back' to their controllers by deception planners in India.[25] OSS also confused Indian nationalist and Axis activity, asserting that: 'Japanese and Nazi agents have become literally brazen and almost open in their activity.'[26] By March 1943 there was a tacit agreement in London to consider India 'an occupied and hostile country' for military planning purposes.[27]

The wider impact of all this security activity, and particularly of omnipresent surveillance, upon wartime Indian politics has only rarely been given extended consideration by historians.[28] Edmond Taylor, a perceptive OSS officer serving in India during the war, came to the conclusion that its effects, although unmeasurable, were nevertheless profound. Employing thousands of Indians to spy on other Indians created rampant 'spy-phobia'. There seemed to him a very direct connection between this and the 'paranoid suspiciousness that was so characteristic of Indian politics'. All groups came to suspect that they were constantly being plotted against, making the reasonable settlement of political differences more difficult. The refusal of Congress to deal with Jinnah owed something to widespread suspicions amongst some Hindus that he was working for the British. These effects were probably not intentional. Psychological warfare, as Taylor observed, consists of 'filling the minds of enemies with delusions that will cause them to fight among themselves'. This, he considered, also extended to the decision to co-operate with the Indian Communist Party for the duration of the war.[29]

SOE and the Indian Communist Party

It was against this background of near-panic about Japanese invasion that SOE proposed a programme of training Indian communist students in sabot-

age techniques.[30] This reflected their experience in Malaya where communists
had proved the most resilient of those guerrilla groups belatedly set in motion
before the surrender of Singapore in March 1942. SOE concluded, quite
rightly, that in India the communists would again provide ideal 'stay-
behinds', because of their semi-secret infrastructure. Moreover, Moscow's
'United Front' line, which emphasised subjugating nationalist ambitions to
the defeat of the Axis powers, rendered them uniquely co-operative. Understandably, despite Viceregal approval, IB and the local police in Bengal,
Orissa and Madras were uneasy.

SOE began a limited scheme in Madras, negotiating with P. C. Joshi, Secretary General of the Indian Communist Party and recruiting through its student federation. In August 1942 the first group of 150 communists began a
seven-month period of para-military training.[31] Mackenzie had discussed the
precise purpose of these stay-behind parties with Joshi and they had agreed
that they would best be used to liquidate Fifth Columnists actively collaborating with the Japanese during the invasion. This idea was 'welcomed by Joshi'
because he felt that as soon as the Japanese landed, such collaborators would
help the Japanese Kempei Tai in rounding up the communists. Therefore
Joshi argued that 'in taking action against Fifth Columnists they would be
protecting their own lives'. With this vigorous counter-security role in mind
SOE devised a training programme that emphasised 'selected bits of silent
killing'.[32]

The local Madras police, unnerved by the nature of this curriculum, were
not easy to reassure, so SOE agreed to test the controllability of its new
allies. SOE decided that the communists should be informed of the location
of a number of secret weapons' dumps containing both arms and explosives
on condition that they did not approach these locations until the Japanese had
invaded. Two weeks later the communists descended on these secret
weapons' dumps and removed their contents, only to discover that they were
dummies. As a result of this, and taking account of the declining Japanese
threat to the east coast of India, the programme shut down in April 1943.[33]
This episode did not, however, deter SOE from 'bargaining' with Joshi for
the services of particular communists for operations outside India for the rest
of the war.[34]

The Japanese-Inspired Fifth Column

Japanese efforts at subversion in India were hampered from the start by the
transparently 'puppet' status of their Indian independence activities. Until
mid-1943 political efforts were led by Rash Behari Bose, a credible Bengali
terrorist in the 1920s, but now a naturalised Japanese citizen and regarded by
Indian nationalists as Japanese. They were also impeded by strong Congress

support for China in the face of undeniable Japanese aggression, and indeed the barbarism perpetrated in cities such as Nanking, that no protestations about 'Pan-Asian Co-Prosperity' could disguise.[35]

It was Rash Behari Bose who suggested that the Japanese Army could exploit the large numbers of Indian troops based in the Far East by sending two intelligence officers, Colonels Suzuki and Fujiwara, to Bangkok in late 1941. As we have seen, this led to an initial agreement with the Indian Independence League and effective subversion against some Indian troops in Malaya. In late 1941, Fujiwara also linked up with Captain Mohan Singh, a captured officer of the 14th Punjab Regiment who offered to organise an anti-British Indian liberation army. The capture of 45,000 Indian troops at Singapore facilitated the creation of what then became the INA. All awaited the arrival of Subhas Chandra Bose, their so called 'man of destiny', then in Germany. Along with Nehru, Chandra Bose had been one of the young rising stars of the Congress Party during the 1930s. But early 1942 marked the high tide of Japanese efforts and, once the invasion of India became impractical, the INA ceased to have any serious function. Relations between the INA and the Japanese now deteriorated, as responsibility transferred from the sympathetic Fujiwara to the less than enthusiastic Colonel Iwakuro, founder of Japan's super-tough Nakano School for Army Intelligence, from which Fujiwara had graduated.[36]

Accordingly, Japan had no idea how to exploit the 'Quit India' Movement of August 1942; meanwhile the only plausible anti-British leader, Chandra Bose, was still absent in Berlin. His journey was painfully slow. In January 1941 he had escaped from a British prison in Calcutta and began a remarkable and circuitous journey. Fleeing first to the Soviets through Afghanistan, he was passed on to the Germans where he assisted in the formation of an anti-British legion from 3,000 Indian troops, captured in the Middle East, who were to spearhead a German drive from the Caucasus to the western gates of India. But by February 1943 the German drive eastwards had stalled and Chandra Bose concluded that he would be more effective in the Far East. Accordingly, he embarked on U-Boat U-180 at Kiel, transferred to a Japanese submarine at Madagascar, and arrived in Japan three months later. During this epic journey, special messages keeping him informed in detail of the activities of the various pro-Axis Indian movements were intercepted and read by the Allies.[37]

Signals interception more generally was a key weapon for the British in dealing with Axis subversion in India. In July 1941 India asked London to despatch an expert from the Radio Security Service (RSS) to work closely with IB and IPI on internal security. RSS was a highly secret organisation which detected illicit enemy transmitters used by agents in British territory.[38] By March 1943 London had seen fit to expand the RSS organisation in India to no less than 450 personnel. This organisation went under the title of 'No.1 Radio Security Company, India' and was co-located with Special Communications Unit 3 (SCU 3) which delivered Ultra material from Bletchley Park to Wavell.[39] It was decided 'for security reasons that the personnel should be European'.[40]

Aside from the INA, smaller groups of Indians were undergoing Japanese training for secret service. Captain Mohan Singh approved a Special Service Group of 800 at Singapore preparing for deep penetration raids. A further 400 attended spy schools in Penang and Rangoon. But deteriorating relations with Iwakuro, and lack of co-operation from the Japanese submarine fleet who preferred trying to sink Allied shipping to acting as a taxi service for agents (a preference also shared by Allied submarine commanders), meant that few parties were sent. Those despatched by Japan were poorly trained and had no radios; they therefore quickly gave themselves up. The more senior Indian officers captured stated that they saw the operations as a pretext to escape back to India.[41]

From 1942, growing numbers of captured Japanese, INA troops and a smaller number of hapless infiltrators found themselves in the hands of the Combined Services Detailed Interrogation Centre (CSDIC), co-located with the IB at the Red Fort in Old Delhi. Here interrogators attempted to build up a detailed picture of Japanese and INA formations. Later in the war, Mountbatten visited CSDIC to watch interrogations at first hand:

To begin with, it is astounding the way in which they readily, and indeed willingly, and almost enthusiastically, give away information on any point about which they are asked . . . It appears that they can in no circumstances bear solitary confinement. 24 hours is enough to reduce the strongest Jap to tears.

Unfortunately, some of the testimonies included confessions of large-scale severe maltreatment of Allied POWs. Partly for this reason, POW recovery was assuming a very high priority for Mountbatten.[42]

The high proportion of Indian POWs initially attracted to the INA caused Delhi to over-rate the threat. By 1943 GHQ India's Psychological Warfare Section was entirely devoted to broadcasting anti-JIF propaganda with the grudging co-operation of the local PWE station, the Far Eastern Bureau. But even as this gathered pace, INA leaders, including Mohan Singh, were withdrawing co-operation and found themselves incarcerated by the Japanese for the rest of the war. By the time Chandra Bose finally arrived in Asia in mid-1943, both the INA and the Indian Independence League were in an advanced state of dissolution. Their 'man of destiny' had missed his moment.[43]

Japan's final, and most professional, effort was launched in early 1944. Japanese intelligence had been taking an increasing interest in Islam, and now began a late experiment with a group of Muslim POWs, led by Lt Colonel Galena, late of the 1 Bahawalpur Infantry. From seventy initially selected and trained for clandestine duties, only twenty were chosen for the rigours of deep penetration. In December 1944 they were given further training in sabotage, disguises, swimming, handling of boats, propaganda and W/T, and further reduced to twelve. After a final landing practice they were armed with revolvers and grenades and given a large sum of money in currency, notes and small diamonds:

The twelve were divided into 2 groups of 6, namely a W/T group and a propaganda, espionage and sabotage group. The former equipped with wireless sets cleverly concealed in the false bottom of a pail and in the bowl of an ornate hookah . . . The party embarked in a Japanese submarine on the morning of the 27th Feb. On the night of 24/25 Mar. they were landed near Pasni on the Baluchistan coast and immediately surrendered themselves to the local authorities.[44]

The immediate capitulation of this crack squad marked the end of Japanese efforts to subvert British rule in India. By 1944 it was clear even to the Red Fort that the JIF effort was on the wane, although it was convenient to put a pro-Japanese spin on extreme nationalist agitation. Nevertheless, INA presented Britain with lingering political and security problems. Army Intelligence, IB and SIS officers were still chasing the remnants of the INA command across Asia in 1946. Having caught many of them, Delhi had to decide what to do with these 'traitors' on the eve of independence.

Soviet assistance

Although Bose's sojourn in Berlin had encouraged German efforts to undermine British rule in India, two factors conspired to hobble this activity. At the highest level, matters were impeded by Hitler's underlying admiration for British rule in India. At the operational level, the NKVD worked closely with British intelligence against German schemes and provided a remarkable stream of timely information. Hitler nurtured an ideological–racist contempt for anti-colonial movements in general and for non-violent movements in particular, even to the extent of impeding German–Japanese co-operation. Hitler's admiration for empire was almost Churchillian. He longed for an alliance with the British Empire and was appalled by the scale of the Japanese success at Singapore, reportedly complaining that he would 'gladly send the British twenty divisions to help throw back the yellow men'. Within Hitler's racist world-view, a small number of Englishmen ruling over 400 million Indians provided him with a model for German rule over the Slavs who inhabited his planned Eastern *lebensraum*. Hitler was famously inspired by his favourite film, *Lives of the Bengal Lancer* starring Gary Cooper, which he repeatedly inflicted on his entourage at the Berchtesgaden.[45]

During the war, German subversion had very limited practical links with mainstream Indian nationalism.[46] But prior to 1943 it had a profound impact upon British security officials, reflecting a tradition of such activity by Germany stretching back to their links with the Indian Gadr party during the First World War.[47] It was actively encouraged by Ribbentrop, whose practical geopolitical vision recognised the possibilities of Indian political instability. Moreover, after June 1941, the threat to the west of India was boosted by Germany's spectacular drive towards the Caucasus. Initial German hopes had centred on the support or restoration of the exiled ex-King Amanullah of Afghanistan. Amanullah was an ineffectual individual whom IPI had marked down as 'cowardly', but was nevertheless an ideal unifying figurehead. But German exploits were doomed to failure from the start, due to the elaborate British intelligence network in the region. Military networks concerned with tribal matters were run from Peshawar and Quetta on the Indian border, while within Afghanistan the Military Attaché employed a wide circle of informers and IB ran penetration agents from India. IPI, with a centre in Switzerland, watched pro-Amanullah activities in Europe.[48] Matters were further smoothed by the fact that IPI had also arranged 'a present of £250,000' for the Afghan Premier, which was 'secret matter between us'.[49] The overall result was an astonishingly accurate picture of German activities.

Germany also planned guerrilla raids from Afghanistan into India with the assistance of a rebel tribal leader, the Faqir of Ipi. However, Abwehr attempts to render assistance to him were clumsy, bordering on farce. In July 1941 two German agents, Professor Oberdorffer and Dr Brandt, working under the improbable cover of academics and lepidopterists, accompanied by twelve tribesmen, tried to deliver munitions and money to the Faqir. As their plans were known in advance they were intercepted and Professor Oberdorffer was killed. The guide hired by the Abwehr was a British *agent provocateur* who would, in any case, have delivered them into the hands of the British had they reached India. Subsequently, the Afghan Premier warned the German Minister in Kabul that such escapades were bound to fail because of the vast British network in the region. However, IB agents inside the Italian Legation in Kabul discovered that Rome had successfully sent the Faqir 300,000 rupees, two machine guns, a large amount of ammunition and a wireless set.[50]

The foiling of Axis plots ultimately depended upon close co-operation between British security and the Soviet NKVD. During 1941 and 1942 the key German fifth-column figure in Kabul was Dr Brinkman, an SS officer maintaining cover as a dentist. His activities were closely followed through letters intercepted by the Soviet NKVD and speedily delivered to London by air.[51] The British Ambassador in Moscow, Sir Stafford Cripps had negotiated this arrangement personally with Andrei Vyshinksy, the Soviet Deputy Foreign Minister. The first batch of material alone contained 125 German telegrams. IPI in London were delighted with this result and pressed for more assistance. In 1942 the NKVD responded more fulsomely than IPI could have thought possible.[52] Remarkably, Rahmat Khan, Subhas Chandra Bose's key agent in Kabul, was in fact a double-agent working for the NKVD. Rahmat Khan was the chief liaison officer between the Axis legations in Afghanistan and Bose's supporters in India. Himself a former communist sympathiser, he was recruited through a Moscow-trained member of the Punjabi Communist Party, and thereafter reported regularly to the Soviet Embassy in Kabul. During 1942, the intelligence material on India that he supplied to the Germans was seen first, then doctored, by the Soviets. This included reports which vastly exaggerated the scale of Bose's organisation in India, including details of an entirely fictitious 'Revolutionary Central Committee'. This operation was so good that IB and IPI opposed Allied pressure for a reduction in staff in the Axis legations, lest this disturb the smooth relationships enjoyed by Rahmat Khan. It was the Soviets who took the initiative over this co-operation, informing Rahmat Khan that they had discussed his case with the British in Moscow in October 1942. They instructed him that if he was arrested when travelling in India, he should insist on GHQ India at Delhi being informed. This was precisely what happened in late November 1942 when he was arrested then quietly released by British security in Lahore. In 1943 his activities continued to be jointly planned by the British Embassy in Moscow and the NKVD. IB helped to prepare his reports and so Berlin's view of internal dissension in India was thus manipulated.[53]

The NKVD's decision to voluntarily share the invaluable Rahmat Khan material left a deep impression on the British. In November 1943, General Hastings Ismay, Secretary to the British Chiefs of Staff, returned from a visit to Moscow and declared the whole episode to be 'most unexpected and amazing', adding that 'it can be said without exaggeration that a complete new vista of Allied co-operation has been opened up'.[54] The day-to-day contacts with the NKVD were run by SOE's Moscow station under Colonel Hill, and the India operation probably represents one of its most spectacular achievements.[55]

By the end of 1943 serious German attempts at subversion in India had faded away. This left Berlin with the problem of what to do with the 3,000 strong Indian Legion of the Wehrmacht, formed at the behest of Chandra Bose. Having been promised the opportunity of fighting against the British on Indian soil, they were notably disappointed to be find themselves on coastal defence duties in Holland. Wild rumours that the Germans had imprisoned Bose circulated and some of the Indians mutinied. They were then transferred to occupied France and absorbed into the Waffen SS. An especially ill-disciplined element of the occupational forces, they inflicted extreme misery on the local French population as they retreated across France

8 The Red Fort in Delhi, headquarters of IB and CSDIC (IWM)

in the autumn of 1944. Indian SS Legionnaires who were taken prisoner by the Allies in 1945 were sent out to the Red Fort in Delhi to await trial.[56]

Conclusion

The Second World War ruthlessly exposed the inconsistencies of ideologies and ideologues. The stark reality of 3,000 Indians serving in the SS at the European heart of Hitler's state was a delightful affront to its nature. Yet these strange allies were not mere opportunists or momentary collaborators, their relationship was underpinned by curious affinities. In Burma, Ba Maw's memoirs, and in Thailand, the writings of Vachit Vadhakarn, give testimony to the intellectual impact of National Socialist ideas upon Asian nationalists, far beyond anything that Tokyo had to offer.[57]

The Allies also suffered political contradictions. For the stalwarts of British rule in India, including the IB in Delhi, who had laboured for two decades to keep India free from 'the menace of Bolshevism', new co-operation between the communists and the NKVD to defend British imperial rule must have stretched their mental flexibility. The policemen of Madras did not enjoy watching SOE instructing communists in the use of timers and detonators, but nor did Joshi enjoy being lectured by Stalin on how desires for independence must be subjugated to the 'United Front' against fascism for the duration of the war. These contradictions were visible right across Asia. SOE's work with communists in India was paralleled by its strong dependence upon MCP networks in Malaya from 1942, and also by its close relation with more vaguely Marxist groups in Burma. By 1948, the Malayan government would be hunting MCP leaders like Chin Peng, whom Mountbatten personally decorated in 1946.[58]

SOE, at once the vanguard of militant resistance and also of imperial resurgence, encapsulated these contradictions to a peculiar degree. Although its higher echelons were drawn from merchant banks and major businesses, including Lord Hambro and John Keswick, much of its thinking betrayed a Bolshevist tinge. It was for this reason that Hugh Dalton had fought with great vigour to become its chief in 1940 and to bring it within the remit of his Ministry of Economic Warfare. Clement Attlee had pressed his case because, like Dalton, he understood subversion to be a natural job for the left. Although Dalton's vision of a resistance by socialists and trade unionists was gradually occluded by the 'secret armies' concept developed under Sir Colin Gubbins, nevertheless, these organisations remained subversive. As M. R. D Foot has observed, Churchill, SOE's first weighty promoter, was 'best known to that time as a resolute opponent of what he once called "the foul baboonery of bolshevism" ... Yet SOE's subversive purpose was revolutionary.'[59] British and American clandestine organisations could not claim to have orchestrated most of the resistance in Japanese-occupied South East Asia during the war. Nevertheless, they contributed to the corrosive effect on civil order that flowed from the militarising and revolutionising large civil populations that would become apparent in the closing stages of the war. This was nowhere more apparent than in South East Asia.

Part 3

Mountbatten's South East Asia Command,
1943–1945

10   Secret service and Mountbatten's South East Asia Command

I have yet to meet the senior officer who can bear with equanimity the trials
and tribulations inflicted on a suffering world by the clandestine organisations. The trouble is that they are not (repeat not) commanded locally. They
are only controlled locally.

Lt General 'Boy' Browning, COS SEAC, 23 February 1945.[1]

The origins of SEAC

Mountbatten's South East Asia Command was conceived in 1942. The
reverses of that difficult year did not divert the Allies from their policy of
'Germany first'. But fears were voiced that Japan might soon assume a position so strong that her defeat would constitute an alarming task. Accordingly,
at the Casablanca Conference of January 1943, Roosevelt and Churchill
agreed that the proportion of their resources directed against Japan would
now rise from 15 per cent to 30 per cent, ensuring a smooth transition to a
full offensive once Germany had fallen.[2]

Although Roosevelt and Churchill finalised the details of SEAC at the First
Quebec Conference of 1943, the exact command boundaries, a matter of
some importance, were confused. In March 1942 both Thailand and Indochina had been allocated to the unhappy partnership of Chiang Kai-shek and
Stilwell in China–Burma–India Command. In June 1943 Roosevelt had
agreed to transfer them to Mountbatten's SEAC. However, two months later,
at the Quebec Conference of August 1943, Indochina was returned to Chiang
'for face-saving purposes'.[3] Mountbatten addressed this immediately on his
arrival in SEAC, travelling to Chungking for discussions in November 1943.[4]
He sought agreement from Chiang Kai-shek that SOE and SIS should operate
into both Thailand and Indochina. It remained an awkward issue of 'face',
and reportedly it was finally agreed that both could quietly operate into Thailand and Indochina, but no formal changes would be announced. This verbal
'Gentleman's Agreement' would lead to future difficulties.[5]

Although the shape of SEAC remained unclear, there was nevertheless enormous relief in some quarters that a British Commander had been secured. In June 1943 Linlithgow urged Amery that it was 'of the first importance' that SEAC should be 'primarily a British and not an American show'.[6] In London, Brooke, who was alert to the Viceroy's fears about OWI and OSS in Delhi, saw SEAC as an opportunity to assert more British control over them. He saw it as 'imperative that, instead of remaining uncontrolled, they should be taken into the orbit of the supreme commander'.[7] Churchill had similar feelings, strengthened by Roosevelt's tendency to bypass him and to deal with Stalin at the Teheran Conference.[8]

Arriving on 6 October 1943, Mountbatten noted: 'I could not help getting a certain thrill at the moment when we crossed the coast of India, to feel that it had fallen to me to be the outward and visible sign of the British Empire's intention to return to the attack in Asia and regain our lost Empire.'[9] Originally working out of temporary locations in India, by early 1944 SEAC had moved to Ceylon, situating itself a few miles outside Kandy at the botanical gardens of Peridrinia. The innumerable neat green wooden huts spread out across the once green lawns and were dotted amongst the pepper, nutmeg, cinnamon, clove, the flowering trees and the pools of great water lilies. A large brick cinema was constructed in a hollow for the daily intelligence briefings.[10]

Mountbatten was disliked by many of SEAC's senior officers. Some considered that he had been over-promoted on account of his royal connections and lacked command experience. But it was primarily his command *style* that irritated. Mountbatten required an ever-growing body of advisers and special staff for every conceivable task, sparking complaints about the 'crystal gazers and brains trust' types that thronged the corridors of SEAC.[11] The secret services constituted a large part of this unwelcome growth. Certainly the outline plans for his new headquarters had drawn outbursts on all sides. Admiral Somerville, the new C. in C. East Indies Fleet, declared the proposed SEAC intelligence organisation to be a 'fantastic' duplication of what already existed at GHQ India.[12] The original staff ceiling of 4,000 was abandoned and by February 1944 numbers had exceeded 7,000.[13] Mountbatten was unabashed, replying that when Eisenhower moved his headquarters staff to Rome it numbered 26,000.[14]

Despite his vast staff, Mountbatten found it difficult to delegate, adored detail and could not resist what Somerville called the 'urge to have a finger in every pie'.[15] Pownall, SEAC's initial Chief of Staff, was equally vexed by this quality:

To him, to meddle in detail is a relaxation of the mind. He is never so happy as when designing a badge, arranging the seating for a conference, or worrying over some question of flying a flag . . . relieved of detail he will invent other detail for himself and fuss everybody about unnecessarily on some stupid ploy.[16]

But, added another, his tremendous charm of manner made it 'extremely difficult to establish a cast iron case where he has been really naughty'.[17] Similar sentiments were expressed by Mountbatten's superiors. Brooke was clearly exasperated by him at the end of a London meeting about SEAC. He claimed that Mountbatten 'was as usual quite impossible' and had wasted a lot of time by fastening onto irrelevant points: 'Seldom has a Supreme Commander been more deficient of the main attributes of a Supreme Commander than Dickie Mountbatten.'[18]

Mountbatten has been subjected to repeated attacks for his lack of strategic vision, but his political instincts were superb. These attacks have failed to recognise that he was deliberately appointed to a theatre which had a low military priority, and where major operations were unlikely, but which was politically sensitive.[19] Mountbatten was the perfect figure to inject a new sense of energy and vitality into a region where morale had been dangerously low. In November 1943, John Paton Davies, Stilwell's Political Adviser, observed that he appeared to be wholly untypical of British 'indolence' towards the Far Eastern War, combining, 'all of the qualities calculated to appeal most to Americans – forthrightness, vigour and glamour.'[20] Like Churchill, he was attracted to the daring, the innovative, and did not hesitate to champion such initiatives at the highest level.[21]

Political reporting in SEAC

Mountbatten's openness to the unconventional rendered him attractive to the heads of the many secret services to which SEAC was host. His boyish love of clandestine organisations endeared him even to OSS, who had discovered that some American commanders held a less indulgent view of secret service. Richard Heppner, the senior OSS officer in Kandy, remarked in January 1945: 'It is fortunate that we have a Supreme Commander and a Chief of Staff who are truly appreciative of the value of clandestine activity and enthusiastic about its use.'[22] The importance Mountbatten attached to unorthodox warfare was underlined in early 1944 by his grave dismay at the death of the Chindit leader, Orde Wingate, when he wrote to Roosevelt of the blow he had felt at this 'shattering news'.[23]

Mountbatten's enthusiasm for secret service activities and special warfare was initially shared by some senior advisers. During early 1944 a team led by the perceptive Brigadier John Lethbridge was despatched to investigate the experience of fighting the Japanese that had been gained in neighbouring theatres, notably under MacArthur in the South West Pacific Area. His brief was wide, requiring him to examine everything from tactics and weaponry to overall strategy and command issues. Lethbridge was 'greatly impressed by the part played by irregular forces' and achieved a sophisticated under-

9 Mountbatten tours the OSS Headquarters at SEAC in Ceylon; behind him, left to right, are Major Moscrip, Colonel Heppner and Commander Taylor

standing of their advantages and potential problems. In particular he emphasised that they were 'at their best when they are allowed to wage war after their own manner, that is in an irregular way'. Conversely, attempts to impose regulations and restrictions upon their mode of operation were usually 'fatal'. Mountbatten took his advice to heart within SEAC.[24]

OSS arrived in Mountbatten's SEAC as OSS Detachment 404 and was eventually placed under the command of Richard Heppner.[25] OSS Detachment 404 was given the cover name 'US Experimental Branch' and located in a large bungalow three miles outside the main town, next to St Peter's College. OSS also enjoyed facilities for maritime training at Galle and jungle training facilities at Dambulla and Clodagh.[26] Alongside these military activities, OSS in SEAC was also gathering political material on Allied wartime and post-war intentions.

OSS spread its net wide, examining the attitudes of the imperial business community in Asia, of civil affairs officers, of the military, and when possible, those at the centre of the policy-making process. An excellent example of this is an OSS report to Abbot Low Moffat, Director of the newly formed Division of South East Asian Affairs within the State Department. This was made by Mani Sanasen, a Thai diplomat and member of the OSS-sponsored Free Thai organisation in Washington. He visited those Thais working for the SOE and SIS in India and Ceylon on a liaison and 'morale boosting visit' in the summer of 1944 and was asked to also try to gain a sense of British post-war intentions in Asia.[27]

On 27 July 1944 he returned to Washington carrying a grim picture. Among the British business community in India, he reported, diverse schemes for post-war South East Asia were already under discussion. He stated that one group of British businessmen wished to see a confederation or regional organisation which would bring Burma, Thailand, Indochina and Malaya somehow under the aegis of the British. Meanwhile:

Another group of British businessmen would favour a free Thailand after the war but greatly reduced geographically – in particular this group would include peninsular Thailand south of Petchaburi with either Malaya or Burma, thus putting all of the rubber and tin areas into the hands of British businessmen. Other British interests, he says, think in terms of a revival of Thailand's absolute monarchy and would like to elevate a member of the royal family to the throne who would be so dependent on British support that Thailand would virtually become a British protectorate.

More importantly, Mani Sanasen secured an interview with Sir Reginald Dorman-Smith, Governor Designate of Burma at Simla, in order to discuss British post-war planning. Dorman-Smith frankly informed Mani Sanasen that recently he 'had proposed to Mr Churchill, in London, that Burma be promised independence in the post-war period'. He added that 'Mr Churchill had accused him of being one of those who would like to break up the empire and then had added that in his opinion what the Burmese and other orientals needed was not independence but the lash.' Mani Sanasen observed with understatement that 'this attitude, if truly Mr Churchill's, might make the future of small nations in Southeastern Asia difficult'. At a time when Churchill and Roosevelt were not articulating their views on this subject directly, such tangential insights were of real interest.[28]

Sanasen's opportunity to associate with the Thai programmes of both the SOE and OSS had allowed him to form a sceptical assessment of these matters. Referring to his discussions with both Major Edmund Grut of SOE and Major Herman Scholtz of OSS, he observed that 'many men were representing their own, rather than their government's interests with respect to Thailand, particularly men who had formerly been in business in Thailand'. He added that the terms of the peace and sort of government established in post-war Thailand 'would probably be determined more by business interests than by ideological concepts'.[29] These observations were shared by others. In 1945 Bickham Sweet-Escott, an SOE staff officer from London, gained much the same impression when visiting SOE's forward headquarters at Calcutta. The principal officers there, he noted, 'were drawn for the British business houses operating in the Far East, such as Butterfield and Swire'.[30]

Significantly, many such political reports by SIS, SOE and OSS were summarised by their chiefs and reached high-level policy-makers in London and Washington. Typically, on 27 October 1944, Donovan wrote to Roosevelt about SEAC warning that:

There can be no doubt that the British and Dutch have arrived at an agreement with regard to the future of Southeast Asia, and now it would appear that the French are being brought into the picture. Recently, it has become known that a French Military Mission will arrive at SEAC shortly. At first they are to have a strictly unofficial status and will be quartered at hotels. Gradually, their mission will be transformed into an official one . . . meanwhile, this mission will participate in secret discussion and will have made available to them all of the data on hand.

The strategy of the British, he asserted, was to recover control of South East Asia 'making the fullest use possible of American resources, but foreclosing the Americans from any voice in policy matters'.[31] The catalyst was clearly the 'unofficial' arrival in SEAC of a French Military Mission under General Blaizot which was quietly accommodated by SOE away from the main SEAC HQ. Roosevelt had blocked French participation for over a year, but with de Gaulle installed in Paris Churchill had finally approved this move unilaterally.[32]

Roosevelt was clearly animated by these reports. On 16 November 1944 Roosevelt wrote to the United States Ambassador at Chungking, Patrick J. Hurley, seeking independent confirmation of the activities of the French and Dutch missions that had joined Mountbatten's SEAC headquarters to work with SOE. Roosevelt now suspected a co-ordinated European effort to recover colonies in South East Asia. Hurley confirmed this and added that:

In addition to the organisations of the three Imperial Governments at Mountbatten's headquarters there has now been set up an organisation at Kunming, China, known as the South East Asia Confederacy which is headed by the British. There are no reports in this embassy on this organisation. None of our diplomatic agencies know its purpose. There are twelve separate American so-called intelligence organisations in China. Some of them are elaborately housed and staffed. None of our own organisations have been able to give me any of the basic facts pertaining to the British–French–Dutch operations in South East Asia.[33]

This was unfair to OSS, for they were working closely on this question with American diplomats in Ceylon.[34] Indeed, by the end of 1944, OSS were confident that they were providing the State Department and the White House with most of its political intelligence on SEAC. Senior OSS officers in SEAC such as Richard Heppner and Edmond Taylor liaised with local American diplomats over what to send to the State Department. But privately, they were increasingly concerned that OSS might not be receiving full credit for what was a core activity and suggested some sort of OSS 'by-line' on these reports.[35]

Fears of some sort of Pan-European 'imperial conspiracy' continued to preoccupy Roosevelt in January 1945, and so this was finally taken up by American diplomats in London. Eden advised Halifax that they had denied most strongly the existence of joint British–French–Dutch colonial planning.[36] But this was clearly misleading, for European colonial solidarity was established policy throughout the Foreign Office. Cavendish-Bentinck, chairman of the JIC, asserted as early as the Autumn of 1943: 'If the Dutch, French and ourselves do not stick together as regards the Far East we shall experience great difficulty in getting back our own possessions.'[37] Cadogan similarly emphasised the importance of 'the colonial powers sticking together in the Far East'.[38] It was at the level of SOE and its European partners in SEAC that this solidarity was implemented.[39]

There were other misleading denials. On 12 December 1944 the British Ambassador in China, Sir Horace Seymour, informed London that Hurley had called upon him and insisted that he had information 'that some kind of discussions were going on in Kandy (in Ceylon) about the future of their various imperial interests and also that plans were being made for annexing Siam'. Seymour denied this, and with specific regard to designs on Thailand he replied contemptuously that 'the rumour was a hardy annual here and was complete nonsense'. However, in the Foreign Office, an official noted that Seymour's response on the Thailand rumour was 'hardly correct' for, he asserted, 'we have designs on the Kra Isthmus'.[40]

Meanwhile, British clandestine organisations in SEAC, which were more diverse and fragmented than those of the United States, were busy on the task of gathering intelligence to support the business of imperial recovery. Even before SEAC had been created, the British Chiefs of Staff had tasked Far Eastern commanders with collecting 'civil intelligence' on Malaya, including assessing the extent of damage to the infrastructure of tin and rubber production, to assist in the speediest return of British administration.[41] Nevertheless, during early 1943, prior to the arrival of OSS in India, or the creation of SEAC, attitudes amongst the policy-makers in London to immediate issues of imperial competition were fairly relaxed. In May 1943, Amery, a keen student of American policy, conceded that Americans generally look upon this war as 'an opportunity for opening the door to a new era of American economic imperialism'.[42] Nevertheless, he remained optimistic, focusing on the Sino-centric nature of American policy and hoping for a 'spheres of influence' arrangement, adding 'all might be well and we might mutually support each other'.[43] On 1 June 1943 he discussed the Viceroy's conviction that the United States would intrude into South and South East Asia with Clement Attlee, but was dismissive.[44]

The activities of the secret and semi-secret services did much to undermine this hope of a *modus vivendi*. By 1944, the propaganda staff of PWE in India and Ceylon were spending less time on the war against Japan and more time countering OWI information about the Philippines. They were hard pressed:

Unfortunately this task is one of considerable difficulty ... The Americans are adopting the role of helpful friend towards the orientals; they have not only promised independence to the Filipinos, but they have acted promptly in handing over the administration of the Philippines even before their entire liberation to a government composed of Filipinos: great publicity in the Orient is being given to this by both Americans and Filipinos.

PWE accepted that it was natural that Americans, themselves successfully emancipated colonials, should 'itch to free others from the same imperialist yoke'. But PWE could not accept that this was underpinned only by idealism and warned that the Americans 'mean to derive the utmost capital (at present political but later financial too)' out of the implications of this. PWE were at something of a loss to know how to respond. They hoped to project the message that Britain was 'a mature power ... in harmony with the past' but confessed that they felt unequal to the task of competing with an ally that offered 'an exciting Utopia'. British propagandists feared that they were now cast in the role of 'minor collaborators of the Americans' not only materially, but also ideologically.

OWI, PWE and similar agencies in India and SEAC sharpened the sense of ideological competition between the British and American ways of life. This was picked up and intensified by the political reporting of bodies such as OSS, SIS and SOE. Curiously, both sides perceived themselves as on the defensive, the defeatist tone of British PWE staff echoing that of American officials who felt their record as liberators had been hopelessly sullied by association with the British. The overall result was the displacement of more relaxed ideas about spheres of influence with a more paranoid view: what one senior OSS officer, Edmond Taylor, called 'institutional delusion'.[45] These delusions became greater during 1944 as the secret services shifted from mere reporting to a stronger operational role.

P Division and operational conflict

In 1944 a new wave of special operations into Japanese-occupied South East Asia generated considerable friction. The possibilities for establishing influence with senior political figures in Asian countries and for laying the foundations for the return of colonial rule were obvious to all. Rival political operations were launched by organisations which sat cheek-by-jowl with each other in the green huts dotted around Mountbatten's headquarters. This situation was exacerbated by the Donovan–Gubbins agreement of August 1943, which guaranteed that the greatest number of different organisations could operate into South East Asia, without co-ordination between the several Allied commands on its fringes.

Most political operations achieved relatively little, set against the damage they inflicted upon Anglo-American relations when uncovered. Moreover, they conformed to one of the abiding rules of special operations or 'covert action', namely that they rarely remain covert for very long. A further consequence of this was that the focus of political intelligence gathering itself gradually shifted, from the wider questions of mutual political intentions in 1943, towards the narrower issue of political activities by rival secret services by 1945. As this closed loop became a vicious circle, subject and object became hopelessly confused.

Mountbatten addressed these problems within SEAC earlier and more effectively than any other Allied commander. He was assisted by three factors: first his own experience in Combined Operations, with its high proportion of special forces. Second, the wide-ranging Lethbridge Report. Third, the alarming prior examples of the secret services suffering crossed wires in the Middle East in 1942 and in Burma during 1943, resulting in several near disasters. Wavell had recounted in May 1943 'the case of the American representatives of OSS . . . who had laid delayed action mines on the railway [in Burma] at the very point where it was to be crossed by the British Long Range Penetration Group'.[46]

Mountbatten's system was designed to avoid these sorts of collisions between secret services, whether military or political, and was finalised with the help of Donovan, who paid a long visit to SEAC in December 1943. Together they refined an organisation known as Priorities Division or 'P Division', which allocated priority to operations in SEAC.[47] P Division became a more influential body than anyone had originally envisaged, although its remit did not extend to propaganda.[48] OWI only worked with a SEAC Combined Liaison Committee that was something of a cipher. OWI staunchly asserted its political independence, alluding to its fears of a US Congressional enquiry into OWI activities. Practical restrictions were more important than committees, with Delhi insisting on a veto upon all material broadcast by OWI from India. Accordingly, OWI conducted as much of its work as possible from the West Coast of the United States, from northern Burma and, from 1944, from the Philippines.[49]

Mountbatten tried to assert his authority over secret service at the outset in a clear three-point directive issued on 18 December 1943. First, British and American 'quasi-military operations' and irregular forces within SEAC 'will not operate without my authority'. Second, no operation could take place without clearance by P Division, to whom all written reports on current activities and future plans had to be submitted. Third, and most significantly, Mountbatten insisted that the 'highest authorities' had agreed that secret services would not operate into South East Asia from other areas without his prior authority as Supreme Commander. Conversely, this restriction applied to operations from SEAC into 'a neighbouring theatre'.

Mountbatten's sensible directive begged many questions. It directly contradicted many other established procedures and agreements. OSS, SOE and SIS did not consider themselves military organisations and expected only to 'co-ordinate' with theatre commanders, looking instead to separate chains of command originating in London and Washington. Moreover, the secret services tended to disregard Mountbatten's injunction about neighbouring theatres, and followed the OSS–SOE agreement of the summer of 1943 which declared much of South East Asia to be a 'no-man's land', inviting an operational free for all.[50] Mountbatten could make a reasonable effort at co-ordinating activities launched from SEAC into South East Asia, but not those launched from China.[51]

The high priority that Mountbatten gave to these issues from the outset is underlined by his visit to Chiang Kai-shek in Chungking in November 1943 and the so called 'Gentleman's Agreement' that resulted. At this conference, which was also attended by the American General Somervell, Chiang initially pressed for both Thailand and Indochina to be placed within his sphere to boost Chinese morale, adding that this would prevent the Japanese from making propagandistic claims about a predatory British imperialism. He also proposed that all secret service activities launched into this area be co-ordinated by a British-American-Chinese committee based at Chungking. Although such a multi-national committee co-ordinating clandestine operations across several *theatres* was undoubtedly needed, the British suspected a Chinese ploy and declined the offer.[52]

In London the Foreign Office saw Chiang's proposals as a Chinese plan to control post-war Thailand, installing a 'puppet' Chinese government in Bangkok that would then cast its eyes upon Malaya, with its large ethnically Chinese population. They also saw Chiang's proposal as purpose-designed 'to prevent pre-operational activity by Allied SO, SI and PWE in Siam and Indochina, and to secure political ascendancy for China in these areas'. London declared it to be 'quite unacceptable' and insisted that any clandestine co-ordination committee for South East Asia was going to be located at SEAC.[53] Chiang's proposal, although abortive, together with Roosevelt's worries about French missions, underline the extent to which the struggle for supremacy in pre-occupational activity was anything but bilateral.[54]

On 9 November 1943, Chiang and Mountbatten reached a nebulous verbal 'Gentleman's Agreement' over clandestine operations into Thailand and Indochina, agreeing that both could operate into the area as opportunity allowed. The draft written form of this agreement also included Chiang's proposals for a co-ordination committee based in China and so remained unsigned. Subsequently, Mountbatten would claim that all his subsequent operations into Indochina drew their authority from this verbal 'Gentleman's Agreement', a focus of much theological disputation by all parties.[55] Moreover, it has not been appreciated that there were several sequential versions of this agreement, developed by Mountbatten and Chiang during a tête-à-tête at the Cairo Conference on 25–26 November 1943, with both Gubbins and Donovan on hand.[56] On 30 November they both visited Stilwell's base at Ramgarh. Here Mountbatten had spent eight hours with Generalissimo and Madame Chiang Kai-shek to clear up outstanding points, 'at least it definitely seemed so this time', but again little was committed to paper.[57]

Mountbatten's P Division was therefore immersed in vexed issues from the outset. It was cheerfully directed by the 'bluff and hearty' Captain G. A. Garnons-Williams, RN, with Lt Commander Edmond Taylor of OSS as deputy, presiding over an Anglo-American staff.[58] OSS were delighted with the approach of P Division, which aimed to co-ordinate the activities of separate secret services, rather than trying to integrate these services. This contrasted with Eisenhower's Allied Forces HQ in Algiers, where Taylor had witnessed the creation of a joint Anglo-American Psychological Warfare Board within which all were supposed to submerge their previous identities, resulting in the 'complete swallowing up' of some OSS sections. The idea of merger would periodically appear on the SEAC agenda, but it was not championed by Garnons-Williams or by P Division.[59]

OSS recognised that P Division would be fundamental to facilitating its activities in a British-dominated command, and worked from the outset to enhance its powers. Cawthorn, the Director of Military Intelligence in India and an opponent of OSS, also recognised this and did the reverse. In October 1943, he attempted to set up an additional SEAC clandestine 'co-ordinating' committee, with wider membership, including the Dutch, and chaired by himself. OSS stood its ground, insisting on recognising P Division only, and citing the Allied directive on SEAC structure, drafted by Churchill.[60] Pownall, Mountbatten's Chief of Staff, who regarded Cawthorn as an incompetent, rolled up his committee.[61]

Colonel Richard Heppner, the OSS Chief in SEAC, did not take long to identify his friends and opponents. Cawthorn and Mackenzie, who were both close to the Viceroy, quickly revealed themselves as hostile. In contrast, much of SEAC, including SIS, managed to convey an air of benign neutrality. Heppner explained to Donovan in Washington:

In all our dealings with SEAC we have been faced with an invariable hostile attitude on the part of SOE whose chief, Mr Mackenzie, is a thoroughly unscrupulous behind-the-scenes manipulator. It would be well to keep this in mind in connection with any proposals that might be made directly by you to Baker Street. Our relations with SIS, on the other hand, are characterised by frankness and friendliness, and we seem to be operating to our mutual benefit.[62]

The approach of SIS was perhaps dictated by its small size. In the autumn of 1943, newly arrived officers from the OSS SI branch in Delhi visited Colonel Leo Steveni, head of SIS in the Far East. He read out to them the firm instructions he had received from Commander Gibbs in Broadway Buildings exhorting him to work with OSS 'to the n'th degree'. Nevertheless, as in Europe, OSS found the 'constant problem that the British wished to control all SI activities'.[63]

All three secret services were, however, mutually agreed on the desirability of their own independence. This revealed itself in the important matter of communications in SEAC. From 1940, SOE had been forced to rely on the SIS communications network, prior to the development of its own facilities. London now proposed to extend this sharing, with all messages from OSS, SOE and SIS in SEAC to their head offices in London and Washington passing over 'the SIS Delhi–London circuit'. OSS reported that Brigadier Gambier-Parry, the SIS communications chief, was extremely reluctant to relinquish this SIS privilege, while SOE predictably were 'no more enthusiastic about this proposal than we were'.[64] By 1944, OSS, SIS and SOE had all insisted on operating their own separate communication systems, resulting in extravagant duplication of effort and resources.[65] It was only in 1945 that P Division persuaded Mountbatten to press a shared system on the three secret services.[66]

In the immediate wake of Donovan's visit of December 1943, P Division continued to work well for OSS. On 20 January 1944, its new chief, Garnons-Williams, arrived and stayed for a few days with Mountbatten, at the house lent to him by the Raja of Faridkot, 'the last word in millionaire luxury', getting to know his immediate circle.[67] Garnons-Williams was genuinely committed to allied co-operation, which he felt was encapsulated in Donovan's phrase 'intelligent self-interest', and had a natural liking for American officers, finding them 'easy to work with'.[68] He ran P Division as a commission rather than a committee. Although P Division 'met' as a formal committee, this forum dealt largely with small administrative issues, such as the worrying surplus of carrier pigeons for clandestine communications accumulated by mid-1944.[69] Key decisions were taken by P Division chiefs after innumerable liaison meetings with other sections of SEAC. His American deputy, Edmond Taylor, was enthusiastic and explained to Donovan in July 1944:

Garnons-Williams is pro-American and particularly pro-OSS. He has been much more than fair to us and actually OSS has more freedom of action and enjoys more high level military support in this purely British theater than in any theater in the world . . . As a result, Dick Heppner's unit [OSS SEAC] is organising an American intelligence service and bringing American influence in many ways into the toughest stronghold of British imperialism.

In contrast to many other theatre commanders, Mountbatten believed in the military potential of secret services and allocated them scarce resources. OSS in SEAC, claimed Taylor, were 'doing so much better' while he claimed other OSS centres, such as those in the Mediterranean and the Middle East, were 'jealous and suspicious' of their results.

Predictably, SOE disliked P Division and offered 'a great deal of sabotage and passive resistance'. Edmond Taylor noted that 'the quiet and unassuming Garnons-Williams is a much more ambitious man than he seems' and so the remit of P Division was constantly expanding. SOE seemed to wish to remove him and OSS support helped to reinforce his position. Taylor continued:

It is a very pretty game, but a very tricky one. If Garnons-Williams loses his fight with Baker Street [SOE], we need have no illusions: our day in Southeast Asia will be over, at least as far as working in or from British imperial territory is concerned . . . Baker Street and Broadway [SIS] will proceed to squeeze us out of this part of the world.

SOE was not the only problem on the horizon for OSS in SEAC. The so called 'John Davies–CBI crowd' was pressing for an overall OSS controller covering both SEAC and Stilwell's CBI, threatening a hostile takeover of Heppner's OSS SEAC organisation. In this world of cross-cutting political rivalries, curious alliances were emerging. In July 1944, when Garnons-Williams embarked on a liaison visit to London and Washington, OSS officers in SEAC asked Donovan to offer him 'the red carpet on a grand scale'.[70]

P Division's key task was to act as traffic policeman for proposed clandestine operations. It also ensured that the resources available to the growing numbers of secret and semi-secret organisations were shared out evenly, including very limited air and sea transport. From January 1944, P Division began to allocate scarce sorties provided by the newly arrived 357 Special Duties Squadron. In the previous year the transport situation had been desperate and an astonished RAF liaison officer recalled the hair-raising OSS remedy: 'The few airborne operations that they have carried out have been done by ordinary bomber or transport aircraft. The personnel had no practical training before they "jumped" '.[71] These problems were endemic, since SOE, SIS and PWE shared only four aircraft for all their needs in the Middle East and the Eastern Mediterranean.[72]

OSS, SIS and SOE also found that regular commanders wished to use their aircraft and submarines for 'straight' military operations, and not as taxis for the secret services. Admiral Somerville was beset by the heads of the various secret services urging special treatment for their operations. During 1943 he regularly turned down entreaties by Colonel Niall Rankin, the SIS operations officer, for access to long-range Catalina flying boats for delivering agents, as they were all required to counter Japanese submarines. He was equally resistant to the entreaties of Commander Slocum of SOE.[73] Somerville's irritation was understandable, for in the first week of January 1944 signals intelligence provided Somerville with news of the movements of a Japanese cruiser squadron based at Singapore. But the pre-occupation of his submarines with landing secret service parties prevented an attack. A furious Somerville told Mountbatten that 'it is quite clear now that some of these are not justified and designed to give the various MEW, SOE etc. parties something to do . . . a number of these people are in Ceylon kicking their heels and have had no work for some time'. Accordingly, Somerville welcomed the advent of P Division which, by February 1944, provided one rationalised channel for such requests. Like many others, Somerville found dealings with Garnons-Williams 'refreshingly simple and direct'.[74]

Air and sea transport was not the only common resource problem for OSS, SOE and SIS in SEAC. They also competed for indigenous agents, resulting in an undignified 'scramble for native personnel'. The problem of finding high-quality agents with up-to-date local knowledge and background for operations in specific areas was formidable. By 1944 an exhaustive search in India and Ceylon was under way, but even when good potential agents were found, their knowledge was often out of date. P Division now encouraged active collaboration in schemes to resolve the overall problem. Eventually SIS, SOE and OSS, evolved an innovative 'large-scale program – seemingly fantastic but actually quite successful – of recruitment in enemy territory'. All operations had a secondary objective of recruiting and exfiltrating new personnel. In areas where there was already a well-organised underground, such as Thailand, this was straightforward and eventually there were even secret jungle airfields where planes could land in relative safety. In Burma, agents were sometimes recruited immediately on the liberation of a village and sent back behind enemy lines, resulting in operations that were high in volume, but low on security. But for Malaya and Indonesia 'rather desperate methods were used . . . initial recruitment was usually made at the point of a gun'.[75] In the summer of 1944, Heppner outlined this novel recruitment scheme more fully to Donovan:

We have, however, evolved a new technique which should prove more fruitful . . . What this amounts to is nothing less than piracy on the high seas off the coast and in the harbours of the East Indies. On each submarine mission undertaken, our conducting officers have the subsidiary task of boarding junks and country craft and capturing passengers and members of the crews. In one operation we gathered 16 Indonesians in our net. Of these at least five are potential agent material. Moreover the intelligence we have gotten from them through exhaustive interrogation has been, in some cases spectacular and I feel we are really beginning to pierce the veil of silence . . . We plan to expand this sort of activity.[76]

En route to Ceylon the prisoners were treated to 'glowing accounts' of the life of a clandestine agent, 'promised big pay' and confronted with the brutal alternative of spending the rest of the war in an internment camp.[77] The unfortunates who disappeared from junks in this manner found themselves interned in Ceylon at the Mahara Examination Center, a purpose-built camp about 8 miles from Colombo which served as a 'holding tank' for potential agent material. When such prisoners accepted employment as agents they were listed on a SEAC roster and shared out by P Division. The size of Mahara continued to grow, receiving over 100 prisoners in a few weeks during the summer of 1944, and eventually being divided into Japanese and non-Japanese wings.[78] Inevitably there was competition for these fresh bodies.[79]

Mahara came under the South East Asia Translation and Interrogation Centre (SEATIC), while the work-a-day administration of Mahara was supervised by Commander Lushington RN and five other naval officers. The guard was provided by the Indian Army.[80] The treatment of those scooped up and interned at Mahara was not always good and there were reports of some subjects being drugged or beaten. In April 1945, an OSS officer, Dwight Bulkey interviewed Ma Hem, one of fifteen Thai fishermen picked up near Phuket, who offered a detailed picture of life at Mahara. Ma Hem stated that all fifteen had been beaten by the guards. 'He himself was hit on four occasions by a British soldier because he did not walk fast enough.' All were being used as labourers and he dwelled on his general feeling of homesickness and low morale.

Notwithstanding their summary removal and subsequent ill-treatment, many remained keen to work for Allied organisations against Japan. In some cases this was because their treatment at the hands of the Japanese had been far worse:

Ma Hem personally witnessed the hanging of a Thai woman captured among a group of twenty by the Japanese, and who were apprehended because of their attempts to steal metal from the three large steel ships sunk off the harbor of Phuket. He heard that ten had been hanged of the twenty . . . the Thais hate the Japanese. He himself was robbed of fish while peddling in Phuket, his fish being taken by the Japanese without payment.

. . . he would be willing to *die* for us in eliminating the Japanese, and to speed up the war . . . His offer to die was made very simply and sincerely. His manner is calm and stoic.[81]

But in most cases, and as with Indian agents employed by the Japanese, agent work was primarily attractive because it offered the opportunity to escape internment and return whence they had been summarily plucked.[82]

Understandably, this new source of interrogation and recruitment for the clandestine services was controversial and SOE, one of its main customers, became so worried during July 1944 that it recommended closure. John Keswick, previously a senior SOE officer, insisted that 'the practice of taking these prisoners should be discontinued, in view of the political implications'.[83] But from the operational point of view Mahara was simply too valuable to be dispensed with and instead its activities expanded. In 1944 its programme included experimental attempts by SOE at what they described as the 'reconditioning' of Japanese prisoners, prior to putting them through the SOE training school on Ceylon.[84]

Mahara was the most important joint facility shared by OSS, SIS and SOE under the auspices of P Division, but OSS were wary of participation in others. In July 1944, they were invited to make use of a British scientific laboratory 'for the turning out of secret inks, secret photography, fake passports and finishing documents'. The laboratory was set up in Calcutta by SIS and run by Dr Higgins, an eminent scientist, previously a Fellow of Corpus Christi College, Cambridge. However, OSS chose not to participate. Stanley P. Lovell, Director of the OSS Research and Development Branch in Washington, was suspicious because OSS were asked to contribute neither personnel nor finance. In his opinion it was merely 'another aspect of the repeated attempt by SIS to catalog OSS personnel'.[85] Instead the facility continued under SIS and opened its services to SOE in late 1944.[86]

Conclusion

Mountbatten was not possessed of a military mind, but arguably, his qualities as a charismatic leader and as a diplomat equipped him superbly for a curious command like SEAC where, arguably, political considerations were often paramount. Military operations like *Zipper*, scheduled for the recapture of Malaya in the winter of 1945/6, were never executed; meanwhile the preparatory activities were more political. In June 1944, after lengthy talks on SEAC, Brooke complained: 'My God how difficult it is to run a war and keep military considerations clear of all the vested interests and political fooling attached to it.' But it was precisely in these areas that Mountbatten excelled.[87]

By 1944 twelve secret and semi-secret organisations had arrived in SEAC. Word had passed around that Mountbatten was sympathetic to 'funnies' and in 1945 he was politely declining offers from SAS teams in Italy. This multiplicity rendered some conflict inevitable and the acronym SEAC, it was sometimes muttered, stood for 'Supreme Example of Allied Confusion'.[88] Notwithstanding this, Garnons-Williams was widely regarded as intelligent and fair-minded. He stamped a measure of SEAC authority on an elusive area, a remarkable achievement given that P Division had no place in the elaborate global treaties drawn up by OSS and SOE in the summer of 1943. Mountbatten knew he was far ahead of his peers in addressing this problem. As he observed to Donovan, he was one of the few supreme commanders not troubled on a daily basis by matters of adjudication between the secret services. Both Donovan and Gubbins urged Mountbatten to keep Garnons-Williams at his post and to give him more authority.[89]

P Division knew its own limitations, the most important of which corresponded to command boundaries. In the summer of 1944, Garnons-Williams set off for London and Washington, armed with a rational solution, 'some sort of super-P Division under the Combined Chiefs of Staff to coordinate American and British clandestine activities in the Far East'. OSS in SEAC were enthusiastic, hoping that such an organisation would at last permit OSS full entry in the hitherto hostile commands of Nimitz and MacArthur. However they followed his progress with more hope than expectation, believing the plan would be 'knocked on the head' in London. They were correct and nothing more was heard of 'super-P Division'.[90]

Donovan viewed the effective workings of P Division as a matter of the first importance. It allowed OSS a strong position in SEAC and allowed Donovan, like Mountbatten, to ignore some of the frequent local squabbles which were the work-a-day business of secret service in every theatre. Therefore, in early September 1944, Donovan was alarmed when Edmond Taylor reported what he saw as attempts by the Head of SOE in the Far East to end P Division. He suspected 'a systematic effort by the British to sabotage our organisation in SEAC . . . headed by the SOE', adding 'it is obviously directed at amalgamation along Balkan lines'. Taylor warned of a repeat of the Anglo-American confrontation over clandestine operations in the Balkans in late 1943, which had caused sharp disagreements between Roosevelt and Churchill.[91] This energised Donovan and he assured Gubbins in London and Stephenson in New York that such a crisis would have to be aired with Roosevelt and the US Joint Chiefs of Staff. With this wide support, Garnons-Williams continued as SEAC's secret service umpire into 1945.[92]

> I have pointed out . . . what we tell the British – that is, all tactical intelli-
> gence, they know all about the supplies we drop, where we drop them, when
> we drop them; they know the personnel we put in, where we put them in
> and when we put them in. We do not give them political or economic
> information . . . we co-ordinate but we never integrate. I am sure that is our
> policy at the highest level and that is our policy here.
>
> Colonel Coughlin (OSS) to Heppner, June 1945.[1]

Malaya and the Netherlands East Indies

As in so many South East Asian countries, resistance in Malaya was not
controlled by SOE or OSS, but by indigenous organisations. At the outset,
colonial officials had opposed SOE's idea of arming the indigenous population, and especially the ethnically Chinese Malayan Communist Party. However, in December 1941 these reservations were overcome and the MCP were
asked to retreat into the jungle, harass the Japanese and await the return of
the British. They were joined by a handful of hastily prepared SOE and SIS
stay-behind parties of Europeans. Only a few of the latter survived or avoided
capture for any length of time.[2]

The aftermath of the Malayan Campaign had been traumatic for all parties
and the British had to confront the fact that some Malay nationalist organisations worked with the Japanese. However, resistance was dangerous, for the
Japanese Kempei Tai (Military Police) had launched Operation *Clean-up* or
'sook ching' designed to round up stay-behinds, former civil servants and
members of both the KMT and the MCP. Interned in five concentration
camps, they were then 'screened' by hooded informers and many of the
70,000 detainees were executed.[3] Unsurprisingly, the surviving MCP guerrillas quickly developed a vigorous anti-informer apparatus. London viewed
continued contacts between SOE and the MCP resistance as a way of gathering intelligence to assist in planning for re-occupation, and as an opportunity
to keep an eye on potentially troublesome allies. The initial meetings in
December 1941 between SOE and the MCP were held at Singapore Special
Branch Headquarters. The SOE Malaya section contained a high proportion

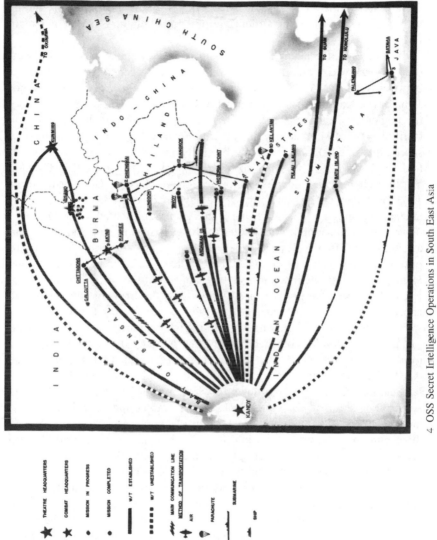

4 OSS Secret Intelligence Operations in South East Asia

of former Malayan policemen and Malayan Civil Service officials, while the Colonial Office offered SOE further Malayan Civil Service personnel.[4] By contrast, in 1942, SOE urged the support of MCP guerrillas, who adopted the name 'Anti-Japanese United Front' (AJUF), on military grounds. They asserted that they would 'be of vital use' in any pre-occupational activities, such as capturing airfields, prior to an amphibious attack by a main force.[5]

Even in 1943, the planned Allied re-invasion of Malaya, known as Operation *Zipper*, was years away and operations proceeded slowly. Contact between SOE and AJUF was not achieved until August 1943 when Major John Davis, leading a series of operations codenamed *Gustavus*, achieved a meeting with Chin Peng, a key guerrilla leader in Perak. It was only on Christmas Day 1943 that they met up with Spencer Chapman, one of the few successful 'stay-behinds', who had been training guerrillas for two years. It took until April 1944 to establish full radio links between SOE in Calcutta and the AJUF, which now extended throughout Malaya.[6] On 29 November 1943, on Mountbatten's authority, John Davis had concluded a purely military agreement with 'Chang Hung', an AJUF representative. It promised money, arms and supplies but asked for the guerrillas to stay their hand and await a major offensive by the Allies. Both sides agreed that no questions of post-war policy would be discussed. SOE officers failed to recognise 'Chang Hung' as Lai Tek, the pre-war Secretary General of the MCP. The mercurial Lai Tek had been put in place as an informer by the British in the 1930s and appears to have had some contact with the Japanese during the war.[7]

SOE liaison officers serving with the AJUF admired their 'magnificent morale and discipline', but spent much time pressing the AJUF to allow its local commanders more autonomy. Spencer Chapman characterised the AJUF as a strict 'pyramid organisation'. The control of AJUF HQ was 'absolute and all embracing', even down to whether an individual guerrilla could smoke. For security, the system was highly compartmentalised, with each unit remaining separate, even to the point of operational paralysis. 'Everything must be referred above, and the answer, if it ever comes at all, will take several months.' The AJUF were clearly aware that the British were present partly to observe them and never allowed SOE to visit AJUF Central HQ in Perak. In August 1943 the leader of the Pahang district told SOE 'in darkest confidence' that this was located in the jungle east of Kuala Lumpur. Most of the AJUF there had a good enough cover to spend part of their time in the towns. There was also a 'university' for training military and political leaders who would ultimately hold office in the future 'republic'. SOE also encountered several internal affairs units or 'traitor killing camps', which claimed to have accounted for over 500 informers.[8] SOE personnel in Malaya personally felt the immense weight of the task of imperial restoration. Spencer Chapman recorded that it was 'very embarrassing' living among people who had lost 'every shred' of faith in the British and questioned not only their military competence but also their integrity and courage. SOE were berated for not having the courage and imagination to start arming and training Asiatics sooner. He recorded that 'though I could not tell them so, I had to concur with their verdict' and the obstacles to British rehabilitation seemed, to him, insurmountable.[9]

London took a different view. By 1943, Edward Gent, Head of the Eastern Department of the Colonial Office, had drawn up 'A Programme of Detailed Projects for SOE' with a view to eventual re-occupation. This included 'counter-scorch', which envisaged the use of SOE parties in the weeks before re-occupation to prevent retreating Japan from destroying valuable industrial plant and mining facilities.[10] SOE and the Colonial Office also held a series of higher level meetings in 1943 and 1944 on broad aspects of policy. SOE was represented by George Taylor, who was now the SOE Chief of Staff in London, together with Egerton Mott, the London officer superintending SOE Far East, and Leslie Sheridan. The Colonial Office were represented by Gent and Paskin. The Colonial Office expressed its fears about OSS and stressed that 'the Colonial Office wish to co-operate as closely as possible' with SOE, enhancing established machinery for lending Colonial Office staff to SOE.[11] At a lower level, there were joint working parties on specific countries and subjects. In February 1944 when the Colonial Office established an informal inter-departmental planning staff for Malaya they included members of SOE and MEW. SOE's relations with the Colonial Office were thus very different in texture to their relations with the Foreign Office.[12]

OSS were taking an interest in Malaya by 1944, while SOE, encouraged by the Colonial Office, were seeking to limit this. By May 1944, OSS in SEAC had acquired an officer with considerable pre-war experience of Malaya who hoped to exploit contacts with the 'burgers', a group of old Dutch and Portuguese resident families with strong Singhalese and Malayan family connections. OSS hoped to use them to develop a coast-watching intelligence project on islands in the Malaya–Sumatra area. They were also hopeful of obtaining captured Malay sailors from Mahara.[13]

Somewhat less realistic were plans for OSS Operation *Jukebox* in the summer of 1944, which aimed to stimulate Malay resistance in the northern Malay state of Kelantan, now under Thai control. Thai, rather than Japanese, occupation was an awkward problem for the Americans, given the close OSS relations with the Free Thais, and the result was an improbable approach. The Thai–Malay issue on the peninsula was dodged and instead OSS set off on an improbable track:

Rather than exploit the historical antipathy of the Malays for the Thai, we should take advantage of the pro-United Nations orientation of Thailand, the Free Thai movements, and consolidate it with that of Malaya. Therefore, our material should emphasise the common objectives of the pro-United Nations underground in Thailand with that of Malaya.

Equally improbably, they envisaged the Sultan of Kelantan, Ismail Ibin Sultan Mohamad IV, or the Prime Minister Dato' Perdana Mentri, as excellent potential leaders of this pro-Thai resistance movement. British officials in SEAC were perhaps justified in their scepticism about such proposals.[14]

In December 1943, Colonel Richard Heppner, the local Head of OSS in Kandy, told Donovan that he had persuaded SEAC to accept his 'very far-reaching programs'.[15] But by the summer of 1944 they were encountering detailed resistance. In August 1944, Edmond Taylor, Deputy Head of P Division, was cataloguing attempts to block OSS operations into Malaya, and believed that lurking beneath this was a comprehensive SOE master plan which aimed at 'eliminating, discrediting, or weakening' P Division, and then absorbing OSS 'into the SOE organization'. He saw SOE's Lt Colonel Guise as the key figure in this initiative. But, just as with reciprocal London worries over OSS plans, he had suspicions, but 'no proof'.

Operation *Jukebox* was a *cause célèbre* for OSS. SOE initially tried to persuade P Division to forbid this on the grounds that it might compromise their own proximate Operation *Carpenter*, but Garnons-Williams refused. OSS was finally persuaded to cancel when the East Indies Fleet claimed to have discovered hitherto unsuspected minefields in the area. Taylor suspected the intervention of 'Mr Ross', who had previously worked for SOE and was now responsible for SOE liaison with Admiral Layton, C. in C. Ceylon. Layton had repeatedly refused OSS requests for assistance with naval transport. Ross had also raised security questions about the OSS Malaya expert in Kandy, John Meade, prompting an investigation by Lt Colonel Airy, the local MI5 officer, although the charges proved to be groundless.[16] Air transport was another important conduit of control. Both SOE and SIS were more fully represented at weekly RAF Special Duties Operations committee meetings, compared to OSS.[17] This seemed to allow some evasion of P Division rulings.[18]

This general climate of resistance extended to a high level. In December 1944 Dening learnt for the first time that OSS were committed to operations in Malaya and urged that this only be permitted with formal Colonial Office approval.[19] Heppner also felt *Jukebox* to be a landmark episode and complained to Donovan:

Relations with SOE continue on the familiar pattern. While everything is very friendly on the surface, we are the target for constant sub rosa attacks by this organisation. One of the most notable occurred this week when SOE tried to prevent us from landing Operation Jukebox II [into Malaya], claiming they had a better and similar operation. It is significant to note that their operation was filed with P Division a full month after ours and after they had been fully advised of the details of our operation.

[The British] continue to follow the line they took in the Middle East and the Balkans, that is to claim the right to make first contacts with any group inside the country, following which they will permit us to enter on their terms.[20]

P Division finally insisted that OSS combine *Jukebox* II operation with SOE's *Oatmeal* operation, using the same submarine transport and with equal representation. 'Just a few hours prior to the takeoff' the SOE party declared that they would not work with the OSS party.[21] Eventually *Jukebox* II was cancelled and SOE's hastily prepared *Oatmeal* went ahead, only to be captured immediately by the Japanese on the coast of Malaya.[22] SOE countered that the US Navy in MacArthur's SWPA were under instructions from Washington not to facilitate SOE operations into Malaya from Australia.[23]

In the Netherlands East Indies the situation was similar. Early in 1942 the Dutch government in exile in London was granted permission to establish a Netherlands Special Operations Executive in Ceylon, which became the 'Korps Insulinde', a commando unit working alongside a further Anglo-Dutch section within SOE at SEAC by early 1944.[24] Meanwhile the Dutch Admiral Helfrich, Commander Allied Naval Forces in the South-West Pacific, worked to block OSS operations into the Netherlands East Indies, as in Malaya.[25] OSS observed that 'SOE has the Dutch sewed up completely'.[26] Indeed the Dutch Colonial Minister, Van Mook, and the Dutch Admiral Helfrich, had only agreed to meet OSS under circumstances of some duress. Heppner reported:

As a result of my plea to 'P' Division, Captain Garnons Williams got Van Mook and Helfrich together on the mat in the presence of Pownall [SEAC COS] and Wedemeyer [SEAC Deputy COS] and got their verbal assurance that they would release to 'P' Division, for use by the three clandestine organisations, any trained Indonesians suitable for work in Sumatra now in Australia.

But these promises were of no avail and the Dutch returned to their accustomed evasiveness.[27]

Operations from SEAC into the Netherlands East Indies were, in any case, limited by the fact that only the island of Sumatra came within SEAC's boundary during the war, and the terrain was difficult. In early 1944, P Division had attempted the wisdom of Solomon and had sectioned Sumatra into three areas for OSS, SOE and SIS. In May 1944, OSS launched *Sugarloaf* II, an extremely hazardous week-long reconnaissance of landing-strips on the Japanese occupied island of Simalur off the west coast of Sumatra. The OSS party of seven was delivered by a British submarine, HMS *Truculent*, and were lucky to return.[28] No permanent clandestine parties were introduced into Sumatra until June 1945.[29]

The growing atmosphere of political cynicism that surrounded clandestine operations into colonial territories was occasionally lightened by naive individuals. In September 1944, a young OSS officer of Dutch extraction, Amry Vandenbosch, was assigned to liaise with the Dutch in SEAC. Vandenbosch wrote indignantly to Heppner, complaining that a fellow OSS officer had assured him that they were in SEAC to 'keep an eye on the British' and to win the friendship of native peoples. Developing an analogy that would have brought joy to the British Colonial Office, he continued: 'It would be as if Great Britain should send agents into the United States to stir up the negroes, or send a representative to Puerto Rico to express British sympathy for Puerto Rican aspirations. I am sure that Americans would not view any such act with tolerance.'[30] Senior OSS officers in SEAC were amused, but 'not greatly impressed', with his protestations and 'inept' analogies.[31]

On 30 January 1945, difficulties over clandestine operations into Malaya were finally resolved at a major meeting of the heads of the clandestine services in SEAC, with Donovan, George Taylor and also Commander J. P. Gibbs of SIS London. Donovan conceded that the British should handle all guerrilla movements in Malaya and that OSS would have absolutely no dealings with them except through the British.[32] Donovan now recommended that his officers try to reach 'informal understandings' with SOE directly before they went to P Division.[33] Magnanimous in victory, SOE increasingly attached token OSS and SIS officers to the growing numbers of parties that they inserted into Malaya.[34] Everyone now looked to the planned amphibious invasion of Malaya – Operation *Zipper* – scheduled for November 1945.[35]

Thailand (Siam)

More than any territory in South East Asia, Thailand served to draw out the nuances of complex regional disagreements between London and Washington. Arguably, for this reason, it was here that the work of OSS and SOE assumed practical importance. American anxieties were accentuated by London's clear failure to articulate a clearly defined British policy for the whole region, resulting in what they conceded was 'ignorance of our intentions'. In the summer of 1944, the Foreign Office precisely identified this problem, but explained that they were 'by no means the Department solely, or even chiefly concerned, in the formulation of British Far Eastern policy'. The Colonial Office, the India Office and a host of military and economic departments were in disagreement on Thailand and indeed on most other issues. Only a Cabinet-level Far Eastern Committee could resolve such complex questions decisively, but the Cabinet Secretary, Sir Edward Bridges, was resisting proposals for the revival of this defunct committee. While those in London stalled, opportunities were taken to make policy by men on the spot.[36]

SOE operations into Thailand gathered pace in 1943, encouraged by agents of the Thai resistance exfiltrated into China. These agents were representatives of Luang Pridi, the pre-war Finance Minister, who had subsequently been 'kicked upstairs' to become Regent by the more pro-Japanese Premier, Luang Phibul. Although the resistance mission to Chungking eventually met with an unhappy fate, it succeeded in persuading SOE, and indeed OSS, that there was a substantial resistance movement in Bangkok and that Pridi might be brought out to help form a free government in exile. A series of operations was now launched by aircraft and submarines from India. The agents on these missions were mostly young Thais from influential families who had been undertaking university education in Britain in 1941.[37] Some, like Prince Subha Svasti, had experienced public school education in Britain or had served in the British Army, and their consequent mannerisms prompted SOE to dub them the 'old school Thais'.[38]

Similar figures found employment with SIS and with the PWE broadcasting organisation in Delhi called the Far Eastern Bureau (FEB). In October 1944, Herbert Deignan of OSS passed through Delhi and visited Lt Colonel Edward Van Millingen, head of the SIS Thai section and also Alec Adams, formally a British Consul in Thailand and now controller of the FEB Thai section. He met the Thais working for Adams and noted his impressions:

Of the five men I then met, all wore the uniforms of British lieutenants and were on the whole more English than the English, down to the last Oxford mannerism. This slavish imitation went beyond speech and manner, since the lot of them argue with fervor the British point of view on the future of Thailand (which is very distinct for the Free Thai view) . . . I was thoroughly disgusted with what I found here and made no further effort to meet or talk with any one of them.[39]

SOE attempts to contact Pridi with their plans for extraction proceeded at a constabulary pace. In December 1943, a submarine-based mission led by Major Phuey Ungphakorn failed to make contact with the landing party. In March 1944, the same party tried again by parachute, only to land in police captivity, and to endure a long and painful journey to a Bangkok gaol. Despite being interrogated by the Japanese, they succeeded in conveying a letter from Mountbatten to Pridi. A further SOE team descended into police custody in April 1944. They were soon joined in gaol by OSS agents making their way in overland from China. By June 1944, with the tide of the war obviously turning, Luang Adul, the Chief of Police, allowed his captives to begin to communicate with SOE in India. Although London had, as yet, conspicuously failed to produce the declaration of British policy on Thailand that SOE had requested, SOE ignored this and handed to the Thais a message, which far exceeded London's wishes, addressing the possibility of Thailand switching sides to join the allies.[40]

August 1944 saw the collapse of the strongly pro-Japanese Phibul government and a new regime which, although outwardly compliant to Japan, was neutral. Mountbatten and officers in SOE's Thai country section now envisaged major resistance operations against Japan and pressed London harder for a favourable declaration on Thailand's future to encourage the resistance. But influential figures in London, including Churchill, blocked any declaration that might restrict Britain's post-war freedom of action in Thailand. Endless papers circulated but little progress was achieved, prompting Eden to observe 'this silly business becomes an increasing bore'.[41] After months of effort, a vaguely benign 'declaration' emerged, only to be inexplicably killed off in Cabinet by SOE's own Minister, Lord Selborne, who declared the belaboured text to be of little help. SOE were 'considerably distressed' by the behaviour of their own minister and sought 'to save what they can from the wreckage'.[42]

By the summer of 1944 tensions were developing between SOE and Mountbatten on the one hand and sceptical Foreign Office officials on the other, including Mountbatten's political adviser Esler Dening. Denied a benign 'declaration' by London, SOE were reduced to drafting further sympathetic letters from Mountbatten to Pridi to accompany their next mission. But this practice was uncovered and scotched by Dening. Nevertheless, Mountbatten felt the new government in Bangkok would allow SOE to 'get on much faster' and told Eden that he was 'definitely anxious' that SOE should 'push on strenuously with the infiltration of parties . . . there is a real urgency about the execution of their present plans'. Mountbatten knew military arguments carried the greatest weight and emphasised the 'strategic value of some of their targets' and the value of work in Thailand as a deception to cover the main effort against Malaya. But Eden found this very hard to accept: 'I don't pretend that I understand Far Eastern affairs. But here we are having dealings with a Government or creature that collaborates with the Japanese as head of their Government.' Mountbatten had, however, played the military-necessity card, which could not be trumped, and clearance for further SOE operations into Thailand was confirmed by the War Cabinet in September 1944, with the caveat that they should not indulge in political activity.[43]

At the end of September 1944 SOE dropped two further Thai agents, bearing neutered letters from Mountbatten, at the seaside resort of Hua Hin, from whence they travelled to Bangkok. But the lukewarm British message contributed little to mutual confidence and there followed three months of indecisive arguments with the British. SOE wished to exfiltrate Pridi or a senior colleague to India, while Pridi wished SOE to send in a high-powered delegation to Bangkok. Pridi finally consented to send a senior diplomatic figure to SEAC in the form of Direk Jayanama, the former Thai Foreign Minister, and a senior General, bringing substantial intelligence on Japanese dispositions in Thailand. This Thai mission, codenamed Operation *Sequence*, arrived in early 1945, but they were not permitted to meet Mountbatten for fear that this might raise undue hopes about Thailand changing sides. Instead they met Dening, who stuck closely to a cold London brief emphasising that Thailand was still an enemy state who would have to 'work her passage home'.[44]

American attitudes to Thailand were very different. As the historian E. Bruce Reynolds has observed, OSS and the State Department saw clandestine operations there not only as part of an effort to defeat Japan but also as 'the opening wedge for post-war American economic and political influence in Southeast Asia'. The American idea of Thailand as an attractive foothold, uncomplicated by colonial links, was strikingly similar to the Japanese view of Thailand in the 1930s, when Tokyo was seeking to expand in a region dominated by European empires.[45] This was underlined when a Thai delegation's visit to Ceylon in January 1945 coincided with Donovan's arrival in SEAC.[46] After talking with Dening then Donovan, its leader subsequently chose to be escorted back to Washington by the latter, carrying plans for a government in exile.[47] This underlined Donovan's personal interest in Thailand. As early as November 1941 he had recruited the former American Foreign Affairs Adviser to the Thai government, Frederick Dolbeare, to prepare resistance plans for Thailand, perhaps the earliest American planning of this sort for any Asian country.[48] Donovan's interest was now heightened because during 1944 the post-war fate of Thailand was becoming an issue of symbolic importance for American policy in Asia. OSS pointed out that if Britain were allowed to impose extensive post-war economic or political controls upon independent Thailand, or to annex territory, this would increase Asiatic distrust of the Western powers in general. Imperial recovery was distasteful to OSS, but imperial expansion seemed intolerable, and consequently Thailand represented a line in the sand. OSS put this succinctly: 'To America a strong democratic Thailand would be a support for peace and self-government in Asia. To Great Britain a strong independent Thailand might be a challenge to the colonial system in Asia.'[49]

When Edmond Taylor undertook a liaison visit to Washington in September 1944 he explained that, like Indochina, Thailand had recently served as a catalyst for deteriorating OSS–SOE relations. Initially, OSS and SOE had both sought the exfiltration of Pridi to head a Free government in exile. But trouble arose over who would mind the Thai representatives and competing operations were launched. SOE had tried to end the scheme in

August, insisting that the plan was 'blown', but Edmond Taylor suspected this was because the British were pro-royalist and did not really want Pridi to be extracted. Heppner, he noted, had vetoed contact with some Thai emissaries in SEAC, whom he considered to have 'developed acute anglophilia'.[50]

Although these political difficulties had their origin in London and Washington, they were worsened by deliberate efforts by OSS, SIS and SOE to evade co-ordination by P Division. In October 1944, for example, an investigation was launched into the unauthorised Operation *Bramble*, which SIS had launched with the help of the unsuspecting US Air Force and which RAF Special Duty Squadron officers in P Division only discovered a month later.[51] OSS had resorted to similar tactics for operations into Thailand in 1944. Heppner asserted that he perceived British and American objectives in Thailand as 'completely opposed' and stressed the close co-ordination between OSS and the State Department: 'We were working with the State Department and the State Department was anxious that the first important contact [with Thai resistance leaders] be American.' He added: 'I think, of all places in the world, curiously enough, Thailand is one of the few where the United States has a firm foreign policy.'[52]

OSS therefore took steps to ensure that the first important political contacts in Thailand were American. Heppner explained that during Mountbatten's absence at a conference in London, in September 1944, General Stilwell, then the American Commander in CBI, exercised his right as Mountbatten's Deputy Commander of SEAC to come and sit in Mountbatten's chair in Ceylon for three weeks. This presented OSS with opportunities. Heppner recalled:

COL HEPPNER: . . . this is where the fun commences. . . . General Stilwell, Supreme Allied Commander [CBI] came to Ceylon to be Supreme Commander [South East Asia] and lived with us at the OSS Bungalow. I told General Stilwell the whole situation and asked him to furnish us American planes without British knowledge and told him I proposed, although it might cost us our entire position, to drop these two [OSS agents] Ben and Wyman, into Thailand with the object of making their way to Bangkok and contact Ruth [Pridi, leader of the Thai resistance].
MR WARNER: . . . I think that decision took an enormous amount of courage.
COL HEPPNER: It had to be done, we thought. I don't know whether it should go on the record because it compromises General Stilwell . . . I went to him on a personal basis; whatever they say about the old man he is acute politically, because some of these American generals couldn't see the utility of our being in Thailand, but Stilwell sees these hookups immediately.
. . . during all this time we had very close contact with the State Department, and of course the US have never gone to war with Thailand and the British have and American interests in Thailand have always been fairly substantial.
MR WARNER: Ten million dollars' worth of trade with Thailand.[53]

The two OSS agents were 'smuggled' out of the OSS base at Mountbatten's headquarters in Ceylon and taken to an OSS bungalow 150 miles from Calcutta near an American Air Force Bombing field. Stilwell had issued orders to General Stratemeyer, the Commander of the US Strategic Air Force, to facilitate the mission. After three attempts they were successfully dropped near Bangkok and made contact with Pridi.[54]

By early January 1945, Dening was conscious of the growing political role of OSS and SOE, and also of Britain's weakening position regarding Thailand. Dening attempted to clear the air by talking directly to OSS, and specifically trying to disabuse them of the idea that Britain had 'ulterior motives on the Kra Isthmus'. His arguments that British qualifications about the sovereignty of this location merely reflected its strategic status, akin to the Dardanelles Straits, needing some international security guarantee, did not convince OSS.[55] Meanwhile OSS now regarded themselves as being engaged in a straight race with SOE for Pridi's affections. On 18 January three senior OSS officers dealing with Thailand met with Moffat and Landon of the State Department. Colonel Hutchinson explained that:

OSS has an official group, including an American, going into Thailand in about two weeks to talk with the Regent. He said that he had learned that the British SOE is sending in a similar group, including white officer, to Thailand with the hope that they can talk to the Regent first and get him to agree to deal chiefly with them . . .
Colonel Hutchinson asked if the Department could give him any informal statements which their officials might transmit to the Regent which would encourage him to co-operate further with the United States.[56]

OSS were clearly nudging ahead in their race for political contact with the Thai resistance. Britain was ahead in the military race, being still in a state of war with Thailand and scheduled to occupy that country on Japan's surrender. Meanwhile the Thais hoped to benefit from playing the two allies off against each other.

As the pressure for sympathetic policy statements on Thailand built up in both London and Washington, Dening had some incisive observations to make on SOE's 'special pleading'. To assist SOE in its quest for a sympathetic British policy declaration, in competition with OSS, would be, he insisted, a 'psychological error', allowing Bangkok to 'put a price on their willingness to assist us in the ejection of the Japanese'. He remained sceptical of the Thai plan to set up a Free Thai government outside the country. Dening saw this merely as a ruse to liquidate the increasingly inconvenient state of war.[57] In February 1945, John Coughlin, who had recently replaced an exhausted Heppner as Head of OSS in SEAC, had a somewhat guarded conversation with Mackenzie, Head of SOE in SEAC. Coughlin too was unsure about Pridi and reported: 'I have a feeling we are in a stronger position with respect to the Thais but they [SOE] are not exactly in the cold and get much the same information as we do . . . It could easily be that the Thais are playing us one off against the other.'[58] Allied realisation that the Thai resistance was neither pro-American, nor pro-British, but instead pro-Thai, was gradually dawning.

Burma

On 19 December 1941, shortly after Pearl Harbor, Donovan addressed Roosevelt on the colonial aspects of the war in Burma. His report was based largely on interviews with the Burmese leader, U Saw, obtained by W. Norman Brown and Conyers Read of his British Empire section. He attributed the 'profoundly resentful' anti-British attitude of the population to a constitutional settlement in 1937 which offered them less local autonomy than the Indians. He dwelt on the inequalities of colonial life and on the rebellion of 1930–1, driven by 'one motive and one object – hatred of the British Government and intention to destroy it'. U Saw had forecast a campaign of non-co-operation and sabotage by the Burmese people, who might well join the Japanese in fighting the British.[59] But Japanese occupation had a transformative effect on the indigenous population, for less than a year later Donovan was forwarding material to the White House explaining that Japan's 'bestial' behaviour had destroyed their reputation as liberators. Much of the Burmese population was now convinced that the defeat of Japan was the first step to independence. OSS reported that some Burmese nationalists had escaped from the Japanese to Delhi and were now working with a will for the British PWE radio organisation there, the Far Eastern Bureau.

Initial collaboration with Japan had been led by Aung San, leader of the Thakin Party, who had joined the Japanese in return for promises of independence. Aung San organised a small Burma Independence Army with weapons supplied by Japan even before the war, swelling to 30,000 at the outbreak of war. But by mid-1942, their attitude had changed from 'admiration of Japan and hopefulness, to one of despair, disillusionment and preparation to oppose Japan at the first opportunity'. The Burmese, having been promised immediate independence, found that Japan now took a line similar to the British in India, insisting that freedom must wait until after the war. The key factor was the appalling ill-discipline of the Japanese army and the catalogue of atrocities inflicted on the Burmese population. Rape and murder were commonplace. Theft and looting, not only of valuables but of everyday objects, 'even slippers and furniture', was uniform practice. 'Their hopes', reported one Thakin, 'had crumbled to pieces, reduced to particles of sand and dust.' Donovan's message was clear. A firm British promise of post-war independence, but not 'vague assurance' of the 'Amery type', would win Burmese support against Japan.[60]

The main PWE radio effort at Delhi was focused on Burma. When Mountbatten toured their headquarters in late 1943 he found them 'an odd looking bunch', but was eventually convinced of the value of their work. As PWE noted in their final report, it was almost impossible to gauge the effect of propaganda. But a great deal of their effort was directed at Aung San's forces, now styled the Burmese National Army (BNA), who surrendered in droves in late 1944 and early 1945. They claimed, probably rightly, that their key achievement was to dispel the carefully inspired Japanese myth that all captured BNA and INA would be shot by the British.[61] In February 1945, when Mountbatten visited one of their broadcast units at Calcutta, he was amazed to find groups of Japanese POWs also 'hard at work helping us to convince their colleagues how wrong they were to continue the struggle'.[62] Despite the hostility of most lowland Burmese groups to the British, SOE were eventually rewarded in mid-1944 when the BNA was a secret signatory to an alliance of anti-Japanese elements in Burma, the Anti-Fascist Organisations (AFO). Nevertheless the large geographical obstacles of this region made for slow progress.[63]

Precisely because the majority of the lowland Burmese were initially neutral or hostile to Britain, SOE operations in Burma from early 1942 had concentrated on collaborative minorities such as the Karens and Kachins, who had formed large components of the inter-war police and army. The Karen operation was commanded by Lt Colonel Stevenson and fought with distinction, delaying the Japanese advance by a crucial period, permitting an orderly evacuation.[64] During the latter stages of the Japanese advance, SOE's 'gallant and almost saint-like figure', Major Seagrim, had remained behind in the Karenni areas, training a guerrilla force in that area and building an intelligence network that ran throughout Burma.[65] OSS gradually took over Kachin areas to the north, while SOE fought to maintain its monopoly of Karens.[66] In January 1944 the Japanese Kempei Tai caught some SOE personnel in the Karen area. By torturing local villagers they persuaded Major Seagrim and others to surrender, whereupon they were executed. Nevertheless, the value of the Karens as a willing resistance force had been established and plans for expansion were afoot.

Relations with the Americans in Burma were dominated by the presence of the American CBI to the north under 'Vinegar Joe' Stilwell. This position obtained until November 1944, when CBI was split into the China Theater under Wedemeyer, and the IBT under General Sultan. Stilwell was simultaneously Commander of the American forces in Burma, senior military adviser to Chiang Kai-shek and also Deputy Supreme Commander in SEAC. His anti-diplomacy towards both the Chinese and the British has been well catalogued, but this hostility even extended towards American commanders in SEAC, whom he regarded as guilty of displaying a spirit of Allied cooperation. Admiral Somerville noted: 'Vinegar Joe has always given me a pain in the neck and continues to do so. Joe has been systematically offensive, in my opinion, to Wheeler and Wedemeyer, and it seems quite fantastic that we should be burdened with him as Deputy.'[67] Strategy was the key source of tension. The Americans demanded a land campaign in northern Burma to open up supply routes to China, while Churchill complained that fighting the Japanese in the north would be like 'munching a porcupine quill by quill', and so pressed for amphibious operations to the south, directed at Rangoon, and eventually Singapore.[68]

OSS first arrived in Burma in the form of Carl Eifler's Detachment 101, which had been developed by Donovan at the request of Stilwell, responding to Japan's own fifth-column operations.[69] Like SOE, OSS found the minority hill tribes like the Kachins to be staunchly pro-Allied, in contrast to the lowland Burmese. The tough Kachins were a match even for the prickly Stilwell. On meeting one of the headmen, or Duwa, of a Kachin tribe, Stilwell expressed scepticism about the numbers of Japanese they claimed to have killed. The Duwa took a bamboo tube off his shoulder and dumped its contents in a pile on the table. It was a pile of ears secured from the corpses of Japanese soldiers. 'Count them', suggested the Duwa, 'and divide by two.'[70] In Burma, the area of most intense military conflict in mainland Asia, political problems and dilemmas of authority confronted the secret services at every level. Both OSS and SOE officers serving with the Karens and the Kachins had considerable difficulty adapting themselves to the norms of these societies, especially to their indigenous practices of war. This was highlighted by the problem of dealing with informers:

To the Kachins, torture was the normal way to treat a captured enemy, quite apart from the need to acquire intelligence . . . Americans who tried to stop their men from torturing quislings quickly came to understand that they ran the risk of losing their authority and having the men turn on them as well. The result was that Americans either turned their backs on the torture or themselves participated. The result was sense of guilt, sometimes severe.

Where cases were clear cut, OSS commanders at least tried to conduct a proper trial 'very short, but proper' before approving a firing squad. But the process had only a dubious legality.[71]

Eifler's Mission was one of Donovan's most important assets in Asia. Although 'indiscreet' and eccentric, his sheer commitment to the war against the Japanese in Burma won him friends on all sides. He enjoyed particularly good relations with British field commanders and with the Government of Burma. OSS noted with pride that 'the British 4th Corps call upon him for jobs which they will not trust to the MEW [SOE]'.[72] Dorman-Smith, the Governor-General designate of Burma was quite intoxicated by Eifler, and wrote long letters to Amery in London recounting his exploits in blowing up the Myitkyina railway in eighteen places. Because many of Eifler's personnel

10 Kachin guerrillas execute a pro-Japanese traitor

were British, Anglo-Burmese or Burmese, he viewed this as a supreme example of Anglo–American co-operation in action:

One lad, an Anglo-Burman, appears to have been discovered at work on a railway bridge and it [is] thought that he blew himself up with the bridge. Anyway the bridge was destroyed and he has not been heard of since. Very nearly VC job, but I doubt whether we will ever get the full story.

Dorman-Smith was amused at the reaction of SOE, who were 'quite angry' that the British Army should prefer OSS for such tasks. 'But there it is', he enthused, 'Eifler, who is a professional "G" man, does produce results.'[73]

Colin Mackenzie was indeed unhappy and, almost from the moment of his arrival in India, pressed for the implementation of the London OSS–SOE agreements of 1942 which would have brought Eifler under his control. Eifler, however, claimed to be under Stilwell's authority and used his considerable personal charm to slip past SOE in India. Mackenzie observed wistfully that: 'Major Eifler, while genuinely co-operative, is, even for an American, difficult to control. He has no conception of higher policy, but ... immense energy and considerable common sense.' Already in December 1942, an approximate geographical separation between SOE and Eifler's Detachment 101 was emerging, based on the Karen and Kachin tribes respectively.[74] By late 1943, although still 'outstanding' as a 'lusty killer and saboteur', Eifler had suffered a head wound and was beginning to display a 'lack of mental and emotional stability'. He was soon replaced by Colonel Ray Peers on the recommendation of John Paton Davies.[75]

By the end of 1944 SOE had established itself more fully and in the words of the head of SOE's Burma country section 'could deal with Det. 101 on more equal terms', leading to more genuine co-operation.[76] On 6 November they collaborated on Operation *Natterjack* which concerned 'the planting of doctored ammunition on the Japanese'. SOE specialists were designing the ammunition while Detachment 101 undertook its distribution in Burma.[77] The prosecution of a large-scale ground war against the Japanese was not the only factor which promoted good relations between OSS and their British hosts in Burma. OSS had quickly fallen foul of command politics in CBI, despite the fact that Donovan had carefully chosen Eifler as a former Stilwell protégé. Eifler's mission had eventually been forced to find shelter with the British in Assam. In part this reflected the growing alignment of OSS with General Chennault of the 14th Air Force, who advocated a rival 'air strategy', instead of the land war in northern Burma. This 'air strategy', which involved the Chinese in less fighting, had the backing of Chiang Kai-shek. Chennault viewed Donovan as an important channel to the White House in his campaign to denigrate Stilwell.[78]

Stilwell's growing hostility to Detachment 101, together with efforts to achieve a single OSS commander for both CBI and SEAC, underlines the manner in which OSS attitudes to their allies in SEAC were framed by an awareness of the hostility to OSS displayed by American commanders in neighbouring theatres. OSS encountered similar problems with MacArthur and Nimitz, but less so with Wedemeyer's new China theatre during 1945. This was not just a Far Eastern phenomenon. Colonel David Bruce of OSS London complained to Donovan that Eisenhower, the American Supreme Commander in Europe, 'insisted on going to British colleagues for their opinion as to our functions . . . in view of which it is remarkable that we enjoy any independence whatsoever'.[79]

French Indochina

French Indochina, like Thailand, occupied a unique political position in South East Asia, and so attained a prominence greater than its military significance. Roosevelt's strong personal interest in the fate of the colony earmarked it for the concerted attention of the secret services. Britain, France, Japan, the United States and China all had their rival schemes for the future of this colony, each informed by their own regional ambitions and a limited understanding of Indochina and its history.[80] In April 1942, Sumner Welles, the American Assistant Secretary of State, had offered the French Ambassador in Washington explicit assurances that France would remain sovereign in Indochina.[81]

Numerous historians have struggled to explain why, despite these assurances, and having backed away from interference in the British and Dutch empires, Roosevelt rounded on the French in Indochina. There were at least three reasons. Firstly, the pragmatic form of Roosevelt's idealism, which noted that the transparently moral bankruptcy of 'Vichy' in Indochina seemed to offer a golden opportunity. At Teheran, Stalin told Roosevelt that here 'the French must be made to pay for their criminal collaboration' and Roosevelt responded that 'he was in 100% agreement'.[82] Secondly, the proximity of China, to whom the United States wished to emphasise its alternative and anti-imperialist credentials. Thirdly, Roosevelt's intense dislike of de Gaulle. Roosevelt simply regarded de Gaulle as a fascist, a view initially supported by OSS. MI5 in London and elements of OSS and the FBI in Washington initially believed that de Gaulle's intelligence chief, Passy, practised torture on suspected traitors at his London headquarters.[83] Although the R&A Branch of OSS resisted the Washington caricature of de Gaulle as a potential dictator, it was not until a few days before Roosevelt's death, on 6 April 1945, that OSS completed a lengthy investigation of Passy, acquitting him of 'black interrogations', and identifying de Gaulle's left-wing opponents as the source of the malicious rumours.[84]

Neither is it immediately apparent why the British, being in receipt of growing American assurances about non-interference in India and Malaya, were so concerned about Indochina. French behaviour in the region during 1940–1 had not inspired confidence, while British strategic post-war planners concluded that it was American, rather than French, support that would be essential to the post-war defence of mainland South East Asia.[85] For British policy-makers in London, including Churchill, motivation probably lay in a desire to rehabilitate France in Europe, both economically and psychologically.[86] Indochina also raised a matter of principle. British officials saw a clear 'danger' in the idea that the future depended on 'the United Nations (or rather the United States) satisfying themselves that the French record in Indo-China justifies the restoration of French authority'.[87] In Asia, British officials were concerned to achieve European colonial solidarity and, as elsewhere, British anxiety to assist French restoration was first implemented through SOE.

Uniquely in Indochina, SOE tended to avoid indigenous agents. This reflected a number of factors: the perceived hostility of the local population to European rule, the inability to 'body-snatch' potential agents from its distant seaboard, and the fact that under a Vichy Government a European population was at large alongside the Japanese presence, rendering the use of European agents possible in that country. Most importantly, SOE in the Far East were inclined to 'contract out' such operations through its French and Dutch country sections that were all but small independent foreign services in their own right.[88] SOE's Indochina 'section' had been in existence since 1941 under François de Langlade, a confidant of de Gaulle, but had been almost eliminated in 1942. The French were quick to send further representatives, including Commander Coudrais, whom de Gaulle hoped to attach to the British in China in order to work into Indochina. Having secured SOE's approval, his party arrived in Delhi bound for China just as Chiang Kai-shek was engaged in throwing a British SOE group out of China. Their timing was hardly auspicious, but with persistence the French joined the increasingly complex network of organisations in Chungking.[89]

In the organisation that SOE constructed in India in 1943, the Indochina section was simply the local action branch of the French secret service, Lt Colonel Jean Boucher de Crèvecoeur's Service d'action (SA), which sought to link up with the Gaullist resistance under General Eugène Mordant inside Indochina. Intelligence operations into Indochina from 1942 were run by the newly established Free French intelligence service, the Service de reseignements (SR) which also attached itself to SOE. These bodies referred to themselves collectively as Service Liaison Français d'Extrême Orient (SLFEO). All were subsumed into a new Gaullist secret service, the DGER, by 1945. Although internecine rivalries between the various French organisations in the Far East were bitter, they were agreed on protecting French control over Indochina against all comers.[90]

SOE control over their French element was limited. As Mackenzie later recalled, they were a self-contained unit 'and we left them pretty much to their own devices'.[91] The same pattern was emerging with SOE's pro-Gaullist activity in North Africa.[92] However, this was not a universal pattern, for in areas of the Middle East, such as Syria, Anglo-French intelligence relations were poor.[93] From early 1944, SOE in SEAC consistently pressed for the transfer of a 1,200 strong SAS/Ranger type unit, the Corps Léger d'Intervention (CLI), from North Africa, under French command, as 'the best means' of strengthening the resistance in Indochina. The French, Mountbatten noted, had applied pressure to SOE, with thinly veiled threats to decamp to China if they did not achieve prominence in SEAC.[94] Indeed, as the historian Martin Thomas has shown, Britain's codebreaking efforts against the communications of her Free French (and other) allies, revealed extensive talks to this end between the French Military Missions in Chungking and the Chinese in August 1944. The French offered substantial economic concessions in return for support in re-establishing sovereignty and help in suppressing the Viet Minh in southern China. Similarly, Eden wished to retain the French section of SEAC's Political Warfare Division, where he felt, 'we can control what the French say'.[95]

Roosevelt, however, blocked the transfer of CLI and Churchill came under unwelcome pressure from Selborne, Eden and Mountbatten to persuade the White House to lift this veto. Churchill consistently refused to confront the President on awkward questions like Indochina. Writing to Eden on 21 May he re-affirmed his view that Indochina was a subject that could wait: 'It is erroneous to suppose that one must always be doing something. The greatest service that SOE can render is to select with great discrimination their areas and occasions of intervention.' Churchill's reticence was reinforced by troublesome dealings with the Free French in the Middle East.[96]

The CLI issue would drag on for many months. But in SEAC, SOE and the French SA refused to bide their time. The French were anxious not only to have pre-occupational elements in place, but also to be seen to have fought the Japanese. Accusations about French collaboration with Japan were at the centre of Roosevelt's arguments for trusteeship status, and this stain could only be wiped clean with French blood. Significant SOE activities in Indochina began with the controversial *Belief* programme of operations. *Belief I* took place during May 1944, *Belief II* on 13 July 1944 and *Belief III* during the autumn of 1944.[97] *Belief I* was abortive, but *Belief II* put François de Langlade and two other French officers into Indochina. The official plan emphasised the organisation of local resistance, including logistics reception and W/T communications. But messages carried from de Gaulle to General Eugène Mordant, head of the Vichy French military in Indochina, set American alarm bells ringing. In the words of Edmond Taylor: 'Evidently this SO operation was a really big political thing – not just operational, but part of a big political operation. The question of good faith was involved. I insisted that SOE put their cards on the table and there was a hell of a row.'[98] The mood of OSS was not improved when they discovered that P Division had not been informed of this political aspect. Nor indeed had SOE bothered to inform the Foreign Office or Dening. SOE claimed innocence, insisting that the letters were merely personal credentials without political content, but the choice of de Langlade to head the mission suggested otherwise.[99]

Initially OSS in SEAC employed this issue in a creative way to try and improve the position of their own local station. On 25 July, Edmond Taylor informed Donovan that he was being 'sorely pressed' to grant approval to the British plans for Indochina without telling the proper US Military officials 'the whole story'. Taylor suggested to Donovan that he agree to this in return for a concerted British effort to keep SOE 'off our backs' in SEAC.[100] Nothing came of this horse-trading and instead, by August 1944, the full story of *Belief* had emerged. Edmond Taylor now complained to Donovan that the episode constituted 'a unique combination of duplicity and arrogance'.[101]

Operation *Belief* offers a good example of the manner in which low-level clandestine operations could resonate at the highest level. In Washington, OSS now informed the State Department and the matter was taken up by Joseph Grew with Stettinius, the new Secretary of State. Grew explained that they had known for some time that SOE were training French officers in India. Now the British had 'dropped a de Gaullist agent in Indochina' utilising American airfield facilities in China for the purpose while 'making efforts to prevent General Chennault from learning the exact nature of the operation'. He continued:

At a recent staff meeting of SEAC, presided over by Lord Mountbatten, it was decided to proceed with two additional operations proposed by the British S.O.E. to drop de Gaullist agents in Indochina by parachute, one of whom is said to carry a holographic letter from de Gaulle. The American staff officer responsible for coordination of S.O.E. and O.S.S. was not present having been told the meeting was cancelled.

In view of Roosevelt's position, expressed on 17 February 1944, that there was to be no American aid to the French in liberating Indochina, Grew suggested a ruling that American facilities be denied to the British SOE and to the Free French. The US Joint Chiefs of Staff now raised the matter with the White House. Although there is no record of Roosevelt's response, Wedemeyer's subsequent withdrawal of SOE air-staging rights through Kunming probably originated in Washington at a high level, perhaps with Roosevelt himself.[102]

The direct result was the so-called 'Mountbatten–Wedemeyer dispute' regarding rights over clandestine operations into Indochina.[103] The immediate practical effect was to prevent the easy extraction of de Langlade and his team. The long-term consequences were more serious. Wedemeyer had been Mountbatten's Deputy Chief of Staff in SEAC until October 1944 and their relations had been good, but under the pressure of this volatile issue, they deteriorated badly.[104] The Mountbatten–Wedemeyer dispute has been discussed largely in the context of a clandestine conflict over French Indochina. However, this dispute was more complex and also reflected the sentiments of military staffs imbued with both a genuine spirit of Anglo-American cooperation and a desire to fight Japan, who were thus increasingly irked by secret political operations of any hue. Wedemeyer betrayed this attitude, although he was clearly in receipt of political directions from Washington.[105]

Mountbatten had negotiated a 'Gentleman's Agreement' with Chiang in November 1943, but was obviously uncomfortable with its unwritten status.[106] The disagreements over Operation *Belief* broadly coincided with the division of Stilwell's CBI Command in October 1944, after which Wedemeyer was given China and Sultan was allocated India–Burma. Against the background of controversy over *Belief*, Wedemeyer now denied all knowledge of the 'Gentleman's Agreement' and insisted, correctly, that Indochina lay formally within his command, facilitating his right of veto over Mountbatten's clandestine operations there. There were testy exchanges between Mountbatten and Wedemeyer in which the British denied any political facet to these missions, while in reality they knew little about de Langlade's real activities in Indochina.[107] In October 1944 the British Chiefs of Staff requested Churchill's intervention, who passed the matter to Eden, knowing him to be absent.[108]

Bitter exchanges between Mountbatten and Wedemeyer had reached crisis point by January 1945, and a despairing Foreign Office finally persuaded Halifax to approach Roosevelt on the matter. Roosevelt reached a private *modus vivendi* with Halifax on 10 January. Roosevelt stated that with regard to clandestine operations into Indochina:

If we felt it was important, we had better tell Mountbatten to do it and ask no questions. He did not want to appear in any way committed to anything that would seem to prejudice the political decision about Indochina in a sense favourable to the French status quo ante.

But this seemingly generous concession from Roosevelt was of little use in quelling the Mountbatten–Wedemeyer dispute; Halifax pointed out that, in a typically Rooseveltian fashion, his remark, 'should not be quoted in the ordinary sense, since the President clearly did not want to recognise himself as committed by it, and was liable to disown it without having any legitimate grievance'. Halifax added that 'if Mountbatten is already doing all he wants to do, without challenge from the Americans, I should be inclined to let sleeping dogs lie'.[109] But Wedemeyer continued his ban on British special duties flights staging through American airfields at Kunming and continued his vigorous attempts to impose a veto on Indochina, probably at Washington's behest. As Dening remarked mournfully: 'The dogs have failed to remain asleep.'[110]

Dening now prepared a hard-nosed brief for Mountbatten on a range of secret service issues, foreshadowing the arrival of Donovan for major discussions with British representatives in SEAC on 19 January 1945. He emphasised that they involved 'political considerations of the highest importance' and so urged Mountbatten to stand firm on the boundary dispute over Indochina and on the issue of Thailand, adding that unless Donovan came round to the British point of view 'there is obviously no basis for discussion'.[111] The clandestine services provided a chain of irritation by which separate issues were now linked together, including suspicions that Wedemeyer was intending to pushing SOE out of China.[112] At this potentially explosive meeting, Donovan showed his intelligence and discretion, recognising privately that many of these issues could only be resolved at the highest level, and professing, diplomatically but improbably, his confidence that they could be resolved by reasoned 'conversation' between Mountbatten and Wedemeyer.[113]

Disaster now followed. Denied access to the staging airfields at Kunming in southern China, SOE had asked the RAF's Special Duties squadrons to maintain supplies to the resistance in Indochina by flying especially long and hazardous missions from Burma. Moreover because of the boundary dispute, SOE had ceased to inform Wedemeyer's command of these operations, risking unannounced night-time intrusions into the American air defence network. On the night of 22/23 January, eleven Liberator aircraft of 375 Squadron left Digri in Burma on Operation *Bazaar*, to drop supplies over Langson and Hanoi. Chennault informed Britain's General Carton de Wiart that two of the three British Liberators that were lost on the operation were probably destroyed by P-61 Black Widow fighters of the 14th Air Force.[114]

At the time, the British authorities looked into the matter and seemed in no doubt about the nature of this event. Air Vice-Marshal Harcourt Smith wrote a month later:

It now seems certain that two of the Liberators missing from No. 358 Squadron on the night of January 22/23 were destroyed by American fighters over Northern F.I.C. or en route to Kunming. The ban on informing the Americans was called off on 25th Jan. I am convinced that it will be in the best interests of all concerned if we adopt sealed lips on these incidents and drop all ideas of any investigation.[115]

This incident has generated some historical controversy. Predictably perhaps, the British official history of SOE in the Far East makes no mention of it. Some accounts have sought to confirm this story, pointing to the generally high rate of American aircraft losses due to similar friendly fire incidents. By this phase of the war, many of the 14th Air Force's night-time kills turned out to be Allied aircraft.[116] Others, including Colin Mackenzie, have suggested that, like so many Special Duties aircraft, they were probably lost due to the appalling weather in the region, which could literally tear aircraft apart.[117] The reality of the event is perhaps less important than the manner in which Wedemeyer employed it to deter further British incursions into Indochina. If intended as a deterrent it was not effective, for during the first eight weeks of 1945 seventy-one successful sorties were flown by RAF Special Duties aircraft to northern French Indochina.[118]

At Yalta in January 1945, Roosevelt re-affirmed Washington's opposition to the despatch of the 1,200 strong CLI unit to SEAC. Rather than arguing with Roosevelt, Churchill simply disregarded this objection and gave SEAC his unilateral approval.[119] SOE's momentum now increased and Mountbatten took a growing interest, visiting the French officers personally at SOE's Group A Headquarters at Barrackpore, but finding it 'rather a strain making separate conversations in French with each of them'.[120] By February 1945 approximately one hundred personnel had been inserted into Indochina with three hundred more under training in India. Large quantities of weapons, explosives and more than a million rounds of ammunition had been dropped. But SOE's plans had become unrealistic and these groups could not be sustained under military pressure by airdrops alone.[121]

In February 1945, Churchill again evaded an attempt by Eden to persuade him to broach these controversial matters with Roosevelt.[122] Accordingly, in March 1945 the British Chiefs of Staff handed the matter to Field Marshal Wilson, the capable Head of the British Joint Staff Mission in Washington, urging him to have 'a frank discussion with Marshall'.[123] But when Wilson and Marshall met with Wedemeyer during March they found him uncompromising and listened to him denouncing the SOE-backed resistance in Indochina as 'rotten to the core'.[124] Exasperated, they confessed the problem to be beyond their combined powers of resolution: 'What it boils down to is we feel on our side that until a common political policy has been evolved, there is little hope of a permanent solution.'[125] London had already concluded that they would not get 'a satisfactory solution, except through the personal intervention of the Prime Minister with the President'.[126]

On 19 March Lord Selborne, the Minister responsible for SOE, took his turn to press Churchill to speak to Roosevelt.[127] Churchill procrastinated and finally assented to a personal telegram to Roosevelt, albeit apologetically worded, during late March. But before Roosevelt could respond he had been overtaken by a stroke and was dead. Finally, Truman replied, giving his full support to the 'Gentleman's Agreement'.[128] Wedemeyer visited Mountbatten's command during April and he too now appeared to acknowledge the 'Gentleman's Agreement'. But relief was premature, for the dispute rumbled on until the Combined Chiefs of Staff divided Indochina in two at the Potsdam Conference in July 1945.[129]

Conclusion

By the end of 1944, secret service rivalry in SEAC was accelerating. P Division had its work cut out acting as a referee and providing basic guarantees of equal access to key resources. These included aircraft sorties and the unfortunate abductees who passed through the Mahara Examination Center outside Colombo. In October 1944, the OSS liaison officer at Mahara told his superiors that he felt the British were now getting priority over 'bodies':

In discussing the disposition of various bodies at the Mahara Camp . . . I have regularly been impressed by their attitude that we will never get any body in whom any other of ten agencies is interested. For example . . . an English-speaking Chinese has disappeared to an unnamed British colonel; and I am informed that our lengthy flirtations with three Burmese cannot be consummated until it is learned whether 'Delhi' would not rather have them. They are by far the best specimens that have been here in the past month, and its obvious that unless this policy is modified, we will only draw the lame, the halt and the blind.[130]

But this report reflected a degree of paranoia. In the previous month twenty-seven Chinese had arrived at Mahara and, after some argument, OSS had successfully indented for all of them.[131] If OSS had any problems at Mahara, they were of a different sort. Mahara was now superintended by the SEATIC organisation under Colonel Blunda of the US Army. Blunda was sceptical of the value of OSS, frankly pointing out 'the fact that MacArthur's command was getting along quite well without our assistance'.[132]

As Edmond Taylor has observed, the British and the American 'cloak-and-dagger agencies' resorted more and more in their bureaucratic duels to 'the conspiratorial trickery that was after all their reason for being, though it was officially supposed to be reserved for outdoor use against the common enemy'. Nevertheless, bureaucratic skulduggery had its own etiquette, which P Division managed to reinforce, and which kept conflict within certain bounds: 'each side cheated to about the same degree . . . and usually with a certain amount of gentlemanly restraint'. When an OSS group was discovered where it was not supposed to be, the opportunity was seized on by its British rivals to 'surface' some equally unsanctified activity of its own, and the end result was that no reprimands were issued, while both illicit missions received the belated blessing of SEAC.[133]

These operations were often the concrete manifestations of political tensions at the very highest level; thus, it was remarkable that Mountbatten's P Division machinery remained intact and continued to regulate clandestine operations, albeit imperfectly and sometimes retrospectively. This was no small achievement. Even as Donovan and Mountbatten negotiated the format of P Division in late 1943, OSS–SOE relations were coming apart in the Balkans. In November 1943, Churchill had refused Roosevelt's request that Donovan be allowed to coordinate all Balkan clandestine operations. Donovan had then flown out to the Mediterranean to announce that OSS would henceforth run their own separate missions to the various resistance groups in this area. Repeated reference by those in SEAC to calamitous developments in the Balkans and the Middle East, suggests the existence of at least a shallow learning curve.[134]

12 The British Secret Intelligence Service (MI6) in the Far East

> SIS in that part of the world is a rather sleepy organisation.
>
> Lt Commander Edmond Taylor, Deputy Head of P-Division[1]

SIS after the fall of Singapore

If the Far Eastern War remains the missing dimension of our understanding of intelligence during the wider Second World War, then the role of the British Secret Intelligence Service (SIS) or MI6 remains the darkest corner of this generally neglected area.[2] Remarkably little attempt has been made to investigate intelligence in Asia, and almost nothing has been written on SIS during the war against Japan.[3] There are several reasons for this. Most importantly, there is the decision by the official historians not to extend their work to Asian theatres on the grounds that this subject would require an Anglo-American approach that ran beyond their official remit. Meanwhile, a proportion of the unofficial historians who have turned their hand to the war against Japan have become unduly fascinated by the Pearl Harbor controversy, and have not been able to move beyond that intractable historical quagmire. Others have presumed that there is not enough primary material, believing that all the relevant archives remain closed to public inspection.[4] On the last point they have been wrong. In reality the wartime files of the three armed services teem with material generated by the Secret Intelligence Service (SIS). One explanation for this might be that the cover name adopted by the Secret Intelligence Service in Asia after 1942, the Inter-Service Liaison Department, seems to have confused the departmental 'weeders' who prepare files for release more than it confused the enemy. As a result, entire files dealing with SIS have sat in the Public Record Office since the late 1970s. Furthermore, in the 1990s the Waldegrave Initiative on Open Government led to a decision to begin the process of releasing approximately 10,000 files generated by SOE. The material dealing with SOE in the Far East, released in 1993, contains a surprising amount of material on relations between SOE and SIS. Taken together with equally dramatic releases in the United States, it is now possible for the first time for unofficial historians to make an assessment of the nature of Britain's SIS in Asia during the 1930s and 1940s. Accordingly, this chapter seeks to shed some light on a hitherto unexplored subject, the troubled Asiatic branch of SIS during the wartime period.[5]

That SIS was not an impressive organisation in any part of the world during the inter-war years is already well understood. Under-funded and moribund, SIS as a whole deteriorated through the 1920s and a decade later was entirely unprepared for war.[6] SIS in Asia was the 'Cinderella branch' of a broadly impoverished service. This can partly be explained by the primarily colonial interpretation of intelligence requirements East of Suez during this period, which ensured that, while police intelligence was active, SIS was almost non-existent in this region. As we have already seen, although by mid-1941 belated efforts were made to 'ginger it up', the apparatus for the collection of secret intelligence was not something that could be rushed. Good networks took months, if not years, to construct and so the opportunity for remedying the situation had already passed.

It appears that the general problems that beset SIS during the 1930s were supposed to be addressed by late 1939 with the arrival of a new SIS chief, Sir Stewart Menzies, at its London headquarters at Broadway Buildings close to Pall Mall. In 1940, anxious to speed expected improvements, the Foreign Office, to which SIS was subordinate, appointed a diplomat, Patrick Reilly, as Personal Assistant to Menzies, with the intention of keeping a closer eye on SIS.[7] Having lost many of its networks in Europe during 1940, SIS had the opportunity to start afresh, working in new areas such as deception. It also gave more attention to counter intelligence in foreign territories (which lay outside the remit of MI5). These efforts against Axis secret services, such as the German *Abwehr*, were undertaken by Section V of SIS and were greatly assisted by the ability of GC&CS to read *Abwehr* communications. But SIS, who controlled signals intelligence, increasingly basked in the reflected glory of the codebreakers at Bletchley Park. In theory this gave SIS a breathing space to transform itself into a more modern service, but in practice these reforms made almost no impact.[8]

The experience of SIS in Asia after 1941 was rather different in character. Unlike SIS in London, it encountered new problems that became more awkward and intractable as the war progressed. In Japanese-occupied Asian countries it laboured under a number of special disadvantages. In particular, it was hard to find high-grade oriental agents and it was difficult for European agents to move or operate in remote Japanese-controlled areas without the knowledge and co-operation of significant numbers of the local population. As a result a different British clandestine service, the newly constituted SOE, which was busy arming and training resistance groups and developing contact with leading indigenous figures, discovered that it enjoyed a far larger intelligence net. SIS was quickly outstripped by the amateur saboteurs of the new SOE. Indeed by 1945, in areas such as Thailand, agents independently inserted by SIS were more likely to be picked up and detained by the ubiquitous resistance than by the Japanese security police. The result was a long period of poor relations between SIS and SOE, punctuated by moments when SIS was increasingly inclined to concede defeat to its sister service.[9]

These operational problems, peculiar to Asia, were compounded by serious mistakes committed at a higher level, notably by the regional head of SIS, Lt Colonel Leo Steveni, during the period 1942-4. His unduly close relationship with the Indian Army and GHQ India led to pressure to deploy SIS agents in and just behind the battle area for the purpose of operational, even tactical, intelligence. This was a perverse development given that the traditional role of SIS was, in fact, long-range political, economic and strategic intelligence. The willingness of SIS to subordinate itself to local demands proved a serious mistake. Yet the pressures of local commanders in Asia were fierce and unrelenting and those organisations that did not respond risked being eclipsed by one of the many other clandestine services.

SIS in wartime Asia was thus beleaguered by two separate types of difficulties. Firstly, operational problems that were unique to that part of the world. Secondly, managerial problems mostly related to the complexities of an organisation responsible to its 'Head Office' in London, yet working in co-operation with region or 'theatre' commands. These bureaucratic problems were widespread during the Second World War, but they were exacerbated by the distance between London and the centres of command in Asia. As a result, by 1945, SIS in Asia had deteriorated badly and was only saved from *de facto* extinction in Asia by the intervention of Mountbatten and his far-sighted clandestine operations supremo, Garnons-Williams. Their decision was a radical one. They urged the withdrawal of SIS from the war against Japan altogether, suggesting that it concentrate resources on developing long-range projects focused on the post-war period, to which SIS was temperamentally better suited.[10]

Following the fall of Singapore, SIS decamped to India. This move coincided with the arrival of Lt Colonel Leo Steveni as the new Director of SIS in Asia.[11] Steveni, who remained until March 1944, was a crucial factor in the depressed fortunes of SIS in this region for the remainder of the war. In order to understand Steveni's contribution we must explore his background. Steveni had served in the British Army during the Russian Civil War acting as liaison with Admiral Kolchak's forces. Steveni was a military intelligence officer and during the late 1920s and early 1930s he had served in Persia at Meshed where he was required to watch Soviet activity. During the 1930s he returned periodically to London and was offered employment by both MI5 and SIS but the prospective pay was meagre. Instead he opted for a commercial career in the timber trade in Northern Europe. He maintained contact with Menzies, estimating whether his stock was rising or falling on the basis of whether he was lunched at White's Club or the Travellers' Club.[12] Steveni may have worked informally for SIS at this time, gathering information through timber-trading operations in the Baltic for he was 'intimate' with many Soviet officials, particularly those based at the Soviet Exports Department in London.[13] In 1939, he joined SIS at a time when there were growing worries about the Soviet threat to India and SIS attached him to the War Staff at the India Office as a Soviet specialist. Here, in an organisation that consisted of officers from the Indian Army, he commented on appreciations and examined the possibility of agent penetration into southern Russia with Afghan help.[14]

From mid-1940 and through to early 1941 he remained in London but was now given SIS responsibility for military intelligence relating to the Far East and he spent much of his time liaising with MI2c, the relevant section of the Directorate of Military Intelligence.[15] By June 1941 he had been promoted to Lieutenant Colonel and was clearly heading for more senior responsibilities within SIS. An experienced career officer with a comprehensive and current knowledge of Asia, he was the obvious candidate to succeed Denham as Regional Director of SIS.[16] Steveni secured permission to take personnel from his timber firm with him, including Hugh Lenanton, who became his deputy. Meanwhile Denham returned to London and, in March 1943, was still kicking his heels looking for an appropriate role at Broadway Buildings.[17]

At New Delhi, Steveni exercised overall control with the assistance of his deputy, now Colonel Lenanton, and third in command Major L. G. Hunt.[18] More or less contemporaneous with Steveni's arrival in mid-1942, SIS in the Far East adopted the same cover-name employed at GHQ Middle East, namely the Inter-Service Liaison Department (ISLD). For the rest of the war the terms 'SIS' and 'ISLD' were used interchangeably in Asia.[19] SIS had two main stations in India. Its principal station appears to have been Baroda House in New Delhi, which dealt with policy, staffing and administrative matters along with most of the correspondence with London. As the war developed SIS also established a forward station at Belvedere House in Calcutta, where it received most of its radio reports from the field and which was conveniently close to the headquarters of one of its main customers, the 14th Army at Barrackpore.[20]

Given that Steveni had already worked with senior Indian Army officers on the War Staff of the India Office in London it was natural that, from mid-1942, SIS should have co-operated closely with the Military Intelligence sections of GHQ India. Steveni already knew Cawthorn, the DMI whom he met in Petrograd in 1915.[21] As a result, when Mountbatten's new SEAC moved to Ceylon in early 1944, SIS was reluctant to leave its established home in India for the anonymous sea of huts that constituted his headquarters at Kandy on Ceylon. There were other reasons for Steveni's reluctance to move to Kandy. Steveni was not held in high regard by Mountbatten or SEAC, and from mid-1943 Broadway began a long and unproductive search for a replacement. SIS only shifted the balance of its headquarters work to Kandy with the eventual arrival of a successor to Steveni, Brigadier P. Bowden-Smith, in mid-1944.[22]

In India, Steveni was continually hampered by a scarcity of transport and agents, factors which tended to compound the general mistake of tasking SIS with battle intelligence duties. From 1942, SIS and SOE in the Far East were in continual competition for scarce air transport to allow the insertion of their agents and also to re-supply them. This reflected similar arguments under way in London which eventually percolated up to the level of Churchill and the Cabinet Defence Committee.[23] However, in Asia these problems were exacerbated by the fact that aircraft often found it impossible to locate a dropping zone by night over the jungle and many missions were therefore aborted, returning with their full complement of agents or stores. Nor would SIS and SOE share aircraft for missions in contiguous areas.

As in other theatres, all aircraft were in demand for 'straight' military operations and both Mountbatten and the RAF were initially reluctant to divert them to special duties.[24] It was only in the summer of 1943 that a special RAF unit, Flight 1576, was allocated to SOE and SIS for the purpose of agent insertion. Although the unit was small, Steveni and his newly appointed operations officer, Lieutenant Colonel Rankin, believed that their problems were now over and the formation of this unit would open a new chapter in their operations.[25] This was far from being the case for, during 1942 and 1943 combined, SIS dropped only seven parties of agents by aircraft, all of them into nearby Burma. There were several reasons for this. The new Special Duties flight initially consisted of a few Hudsons, an aircraft of limited range that could not reach areas beyond western Burma. The RAF were also inclined to divert Special Duties aircraft for other purposes at the last minute, to the abiding fury of SIS. In December 1943 Steveni wrote to the RAF commander responsible advancing the argument that: 'as Intelligence must always precede Operations our claims for extra aircraft should be given pre-operational priority.' But all such arguments fell on deaf ears.[26]

SIS were only granted limited access to the long-range Catalina flying boat in January 1944, while the long-range Liberator aircraft became available in March of the same year. SIS seized this double opportunity to mount its first airborne operation into Thailand, codenamed Operation *Sun*, although the RAF report records laconically that the five agents 'were captured soon after landing'. Even after these longer-range aircraft came on stream SIS continued

11 Mountbatten inspects a training centre for clandestine operations; note the special forces canoe (SUL)

to focus its airborne effort on providing operational intelligence for the war in Burma. During the first half of 1944, about 90 per cent of its thirty-three airborne missions went to Burma, with only a handful of personnel despatched further afield into Thailand or Indochina.[27]

Aircraft were not the only form of transport available. The alternative was transport via submarine and then inflatable boat. However, this was a hazardous method of launching an operation. By January 1945 a statistical survey of accounts of agents being captured revealed that 'in 90% of cases the hunt was started due to the discovery of a boat on the beach'.[28] Air transport by night over the jungle in appalling weather conditions was also hazardous and the numbers of agents lost in transit was surprisingly high.[29]

Air transport was not the only resource problem faced by SIS. The growing number of clandestine organisations in the Far East also competed for indigenous agents. The problem of finding high-quality agents with the right local knowledge and background for operations into specific areas was formidable. By 1944 an 'exhaustive search in India and Ceylon for desirable prospects' was under way. But even when potential agents were found, their local knowledge was often sadly out of date. Eventually SIS, SOE and the equivalent American organisation, the Office of Secret Services (OSS), decided to collaborate on a scheme to solve the problem. This was the innovative and piratical Mahara scheme for the capture of indigenous civilians off the coasts of Malaya and Indonesia, described above.[30] SIS seems to have secured a sizeable percentage of these agents while Mahara was in operation, fending off the competing claims of SOE, OSS and other organisations.[31] Even so Mahara could not meet the growing appetite of SIS for indigenous agents, so by March 1945 SIS had persuaded SEAC's coastal raiding organisation, the Small Operations Group (which consisted largely of Marines), to ferry its personnel on operations 'to try snatches for bodies'. But this new practice proved too dangerous and SIS eventually decided that the operations should be halted.[32]

SIS and Slim's 14th Army

SIS would probably have been content to co-exist with SOE and other clandestine bodies, frequently refereed by P Division, until the end of the war. Friction with parallel organisations such as SOE was present in most theatres and was only to be expected. What SIS had not counted on was a forceful and dramatic takeover bid by an overt organisation, Slim's 14th Army in Burma. At the outset of the war against Japan, the function of SIS had initially been defined as intelligence in the 'strategic role' and for this reason the Army was initially happy to accept that, 'though subject to local co-ordination' SIS was 'responsible directly to its own head office in London'.[33] However, in practice, as we have seen, SIS found itself quickly drawn into the task of gathering operational intelligence in the Japanese rear area in Burma, and even in the battle area itself. As a result, the 14th Army took a growing interest in its activities.

Slim had been complaining about the inadequacies of the intelligence in Burma since the end of 1943, insisting that 'it was far from being as complete or accurate as in other theatres' and that he was offered almost no information about Japanese reserves.[33] Confronted with the very serious problem that signals intelligence was not offering him sufficient information about enemy reserves or enemy intentions, he had turned to the various secret services that ran human agents, primarily OSS, SIS and SOE. He had also pinned some hopes on the various long-range patrol reconnaissance organisations, code-named 'V' Force and 'Z' Force. In July 1944 various reforms had been attempted in the hope of placing 20 'Z' Force patrols behind enemy lines. But by October 1944 only two such patrols had been sent out. The innumerable organisations doing this sort of work continued to squabble over the admittedly scarce supplies of manpower and transport. P Division contained the acrimony generated by these problems, but could not resolve them. By late 1944 an increasingly frustrated Slim turned his attention to the reform of

OSS, SIS and SOE activities in Burma in a continued attempt to offset some of the limitations of signals intelligence.[35]

However, his relations with SIS only began to deteriorate badly during October 1944, as SIS moved more of its activities to Mountbatten's Ceylon HQ and had less contact with HQ 14th Army at Barrackpore. Perhaps this belated move was a deliberate attempt by SIS to achieve distance, for Slim's 14th Army was increasingly inclined to vet SIS plans, attempting to veto some operations and slimming down their personnel requirements wherever possible.[36] By November 1944 Slim was ready for a showdown. 'The Chief expressed himself as exceedingly dissatisfied with I [Intelligence]', developing these criticisms into a case for Army control over the allocation of tasks to SIS and a reorganisation of intelligence gathering throughout Burma.[37]

All this came to a head on 4 January 1945 during a highly charged conference on operational intelligence in SEAC, held at the 14th Army's rear area HQ at Barrackpore just outside Calcutta. Here, Slim's staff officers advanced a number of proposals so radical that their shock waves reverberated all the way to London. Slim's Chief of Staff, Major-General Walsh, opened the conference with a provocative suggestion. He remarked that the Americans operated one unified secret service in Burma called OSS which 'was giving excellent service'. Why not amalgamate all the British secret services operating into Burma, including SIS and SOE, and then subordinate this British body to the better organised and more efficient OSS? Walsh must have known privately that the idea was unacceptable to both Mountbatten and his superiors in London, but he enjoyed making it all the same.

Garnons-Williams acted as the spokesman for the various secret services in SEAC and he quietly rejected this proposal as 'unsound'. But Slim's officers pressed home their attack on a new front. Brigadier Gwyn, Slim's senior intelligence officer, complained that all operational intelligence collected by both SIS and SOE had first to be collated and sifted by SIS in Delhi before it was belatedly passed on to the 14th Army. By this time it was usually stale. Gwyn insisted that he would rather have the intelligence delivered direct, albeit in its raw form. The 14th Army would do its own collation and analysis, cutting out SIS from this activity.

This was a valid point and Garnons-Williams now began to give some ground. He warned that they were now treading on matters of high policy that would have to be referred to Sir Stewart Menzies, the Chief of SIS in London. Nevertheless, he admitted that he had raised the central problem of SIS doing unsuitable tactical work with Menzies during his visit home in July 1944. Menzies had agreed that this was undesirable, expressing a wish to get out of battle-area work in Burma, leaving it to anyone who cared to fill the gap. Slim's staff officers did not grasp the sensitivity of the ground upon which they were treading. Major-General Walsh took all this as an admission of defeat and retorted: 'There you are! why should not Force 136 [SOE] take over ISLD [SIS]'? Walsh's iconoclastic suggestion was wholly ser-ious. Other officers explained that, as the Burma campaign was entering its final stage there was less need for SOE to conduct sabotage and in practice SOE and its guerrilla bands were increasingly employed to conduct armed reconnais-sance, fulfilling a 'strong arm intelligence role'. The inescapable facts were that, on the ground, SIS and SOE in Burma were now doing the same job. The Army came back to the example of the American OSS with one easily con-trolled organisation, which was doing the work of twelve poorly co-ordinated British clandestine and semi-clandestine bodies in Burma.

It fell to Garnons-Williams to sum up and to make constructive proposals that both accommodated the sensitive politics of rival secret service organisa-tions based in London and took full account of the situation on the ground in Burma. As a short-term measure all operational intelligence would go direct to forward headquarters, including that of Slim's 14th Army, without SIS collation or analysis. In future, P Division would allocate whatever clan-destine service was best placed to collect intelligence in each area, regardless of its formal role. In the long term, SEAC would seek to absorb all opera-tional intelligence gathering under the control of one service in Burma. This was likely to be SOE, who would also absorb local reconnaissance army groups like 'Z' and 'V' Force. Moreover, in Burma, operational intelligence, not sabotage, would now be SOE's first priority until Mountbatten told them otherwise.

The proposals put forward by Garnons-Williams were certainly radical. They suited Slim's 14th Army in Burma, but they cut across the accepted functional divisions between the secret services as agreed in London. Accord-ingly, Garnons-Williams warned that they would have to be cleared again with Menzies in London 'as it involves British S.I.S policy'.[38] SIS had no more trouble from Slim and the 14th Army, for two months later the curious decision had been taken to remove him as its commander.[39] Nevertheless, SIS were now in a tight corner. From the start of the war they had taken a wrong turning and concentrated on operational intelligence in Burma, an area in which SOE had quickly overtaken them. Various *ad hoc* agreements had already pointed the way to the decisions of the Barrackpore Conference in January 1945. Indeed, as early as October 1944, OSS reported to Washington that recent SIS operations had 'been almost universally crowned with failure due to the very nature of their operations'. Accordingly, SIS had begun to merge with SOE parties. Mackenzie had gleefully informed OSS that this was 'a triumph for SOE, and that they were probably going to succeed in swallowing SIS up in this Theater'. Conversely, Bowden-Smith insisted that SIS could now blame SOE for any operational failures on such joint ven-tures.[40] Slim's demands now acted as a catalyst. After Barrackpore, an

12 An intelligence group of Slim's 14th Army in Burma (SUL)

increasingly confident SOE tried to establish control over all operational intelligence gathering by agents throughout Mountbatten's command.

Mountbatten, SIS and SOE

The precise nature of the operational problems that had been plaguing SIS on the ground in Burma during 1944, and which allowed SOE to steal a march upon them, can be thrown into relief by examining the fate of an individual SIS party, Operation *Barnowl*, launched in September 1944. This operation illustrates the typical problems confronted in Burma when operating independently and without the assistance of the local resistance organisations. Operation *Barnowl* involved sending an SIS party by submarine to Mergui, an island off the coast of southern Burma, from where they were to report on shipping and Japanese movements by radio. This part of the operation was successful, but they were soon embarrassed by encountering five persons from the local indigenous population whom they captured to maintain the security of their position. In the words of the report: 'They were presented with the alternative of bumping them off or having them taken away by aircraft.' The *Barnowl* party explained their predicament by radio and senior SIS officers approached the RAF with a view to mounting some sort of extraction. The RAF were impressed by their arguments noting 'we should make every effort to save this ISLD [SIS] party from the extremely unpleasant duty of committing murder in cold blood' and agreed to send in a Catalina aircraft. They also noted the additional practical argument that these were 'five valuable prisoners' worthy of interrogation at the very least. But at this point radio contact with the party was lost. Attempts were made to conduct air reconnaissance but bad weather prevented any further progress. There is no further record regarding the fate of Operation *Barnowl* or its prisoners who were presumed captured or killed.[41]

The major problem was simply an operational one: SIS was at a significant disadvantage compared to SOE with its powerful resistance organisation on the ground. But this was exacerbated by administrative problems throughout 1943 and 1944. SIS headquarters in Broadway in London knew that Leo Steveni left much to be desired as a the regional head of SIS. Brigadier Beddington, one of the Deputy Directors of SIS in London and who superintended Asian activities, had been engaged in an ineffective search for a replacement through much of 1943.[42] The role was regarded as immensely unattractive. One possible candidate for the post, Gerald Wilkinson, having declined, then observed in his diary that this was 'an area where our organization [*sic*] is so ineffective, the obstacles so difficult and the future requirements so great . . . a vigorous new administration is what is required'. Wilkinson asked Beddington why he did not go himself, but he pleaded old age and ill-health. Instead an ineffective 'compromise patchwork' of improved training was put in place to little effect and Steveni remained by default.[43]

Broadway was only propelled into action by a complete collapse of Mountbatten's confidence in SIS leadership in April 1944. Steveni was now 'a complete laughing stock at the Supreme Commander's meetings'. Beddington himself had been sent out to examine matters in India and Ceylon, but had made no better impression on Mountbatten. During one conversation towards the end of his visit, Mountbatten rounded on Beddington and asked him bluntly: 'Are you a knave or a fool?' Beddington lamely replied that he must be a fool. Radical change was now unavoidable. In Broadway, Menzies decided that Beddington should no longer superintend Asian matters and this task was passed to Commander John Gibbs. Steveni was removed in July and shunted on to the Political Intelligence Centre in Cairo, but still no career SIS officer was willing to replace Steveni 'in an area where everything remains to be done'. All knew that the problem was less one of individual competence and more one of being asked to put to rights problems that arose from years of neglect. In the end, Menzies' choice fell upon someone from outside SIS, a cavalry officer called Brigadier P. Bowden-Smith. This officer was regarded as 'a nice chap and had a sound record', but as Colonel Wilkinson remarked, he 'does not know the first thing about our work and it is doubtful if he sees the crying need for complete revamping and energizing of the whole organisation'. Despite the arrival of this new regional director, matters did not improve much during the latter part of 1944.[44]

The remarkable way in which Steveni's successor, Bowden-Smith, was secured is worth recounting, because it confirms the suspicions of some historians, for example Harrison, that Menzies managed to evade the serious reforms suggested for SIS in 1939-40, and indeed throughout the war. Beddington's last task as overall London supervisor for SIS in the Far East was to try and find Steveni's successor. Beddington records that 'I could not see one in our organisation', but it seems more likely that this was a duty that everyone in SIS was anxious to avoid, knowing that the task of building up from very little was formidable, and the chances of real success slim. SIS therefore resorted to its traditional inter-war recruiting pattern. Beddington records:

In the Club I met Brigadier Bowden-Smith (Bogey), whom I had known for years and who commanded the 16th Lancers between the wars, looking very depressed and worried. He told me that he had just been told that he was considered too old to take his Tank Brigade on Active Service, and that he was soon going to be out of a job. I made him walk back with me towards my office and outlined the work of our head man in India, and asked him to think it over and tell me the next day if he would like it, provided I could get him the appointment. I told my Chief [Menzies] what I had done and that I thought Bogey would say 'yes' if he had the offer. So the next afternoon I took Bogey over to see him and it was agreed . . .

All parties were quite aware that it was 'work he had never done before' but after a two-month course he was despatched to SEAC to replace Steveni.[45] It was against this background of dire SIS operational and management problems that the struggle for control of intelligence collection within SEAC accelerated as the war entered its final stages. By the spring of 1945, Garnons-Williams decided that persistent problems required that the whole issue of intelligence be confronted again. On 16 April he wrote to Colin Mackenzie, the Head of SOE in Asia, and also to Bowden-Smith of SIS calling for a meeting 'to iron the matter out'. He warned that if a sensible agreement could not be reached, then Mountbatten would intervene and settle the issue for them.

He also took the opportunity to offer his preliminary views. Intelligence gathering had suffered from initial confusion for a variety of reasons, the most important of which had been 'ill-direction' by previous regional directors of SIS. In SEAC intelligence was belatedly evolving into two main target groups: (i) long-range intelligence on political, economic and social targets, and (ii) operational military targets. This, he added, was how 'it should have been from the beginning'. For unavoidable practical reasons, the second category, operational intelligence, was increasingly dominated by SOE. But he also warned that the intrusion of SOE into wartime intelligence gathering should not to be regarded as a precedent. 'It is important that we preserve a long range view in which the British Secret Intelligence Service shall (a) carry out its proper function and (b) have an eye to the future.' The time would come when military operations ceased and the methods used by SOE to gather intelligence would no longer be applicable. Therefore, despite all its shortcomings, Garnons-Williams was determined to defend SIS from further erosion. He warned:

The greatest danger in the past . . . has been interference by the Military and other Organisations with the British Secret Intelligence Service and continued steps are being taken, with the fullest support of the C.O.S and S.A.C. [Mountbatten] himself to undo the harm which has been done in the last two or three years. It is not the concern of anybody what the British Secret Intelligence Service does and any inquisitiveness on the part of unauthorised persons tends to compromise one of our main British weapons.[46]

But his exhortations for a dispassionate approach which would focus on future requirements fell on deaf ears.

On 19 April Mackenzie replied to Garnons-Williams, claiming that in reality the gathering of operational intelligence by human agents throughout SEAC was now dominated by SOE. In Europe, he explained, operational intelligence had largely been collected by civilian agents in the same way as long-term intelligence. But in SEAC he insisted, 'conditions are entirely different', adding that there were three main reasons why this was so. First, many local inhabitants had neither the patriotic motive nor the level of education to provide adequate agents. Second, the alternative, European agents, could not mingle unnoticed with the local population, as they could in Europe. Third, a much larger proportion of the local population in which they had to move was 'neutral or even hostile'. He felt confident that any analysis of intelligence produced by oriental agents without European leadership 'has been relatively small'. In short, he argued that while in Europe it was desirable to keep SIS and SOE separate, 'this distinction is neither possible nor desirable in this theatre'. SOE should become the dominant intelligence collector in all of SEAC while SIS would be relegated to the 'collation, interpretation and distribution of intelligence'.[47]

How convincing were Mackenzie's claims? Documents produced later that year by SOE provide some fairly precise answers (although they are hardly an impartial source). During the period April–August 1945 SOE claimed to have undertaken a careful statistical analysis of the source of all intelligence reports issued by SIS concerning Malaya, Siam and French Indochina. In all cases SOE were providing over 70 per cent of the material. There were no figures for Burma because intelligence was now passed straight to formations in the field, but SOE guesstimated that they were producing 90 per cent of this Burma material.[48] At the same time SOE also conceded that this was an analysis of quantity not quality. Moreover, there were some subjects in which SOE showed little interest. Typically, all intelligence from human agents on enemy technical and scientific developments such as radar and chemical warfare seems to have emanated from SIS rather than SOE sources.[49]

Bowden-Smith responded by pointing out that Mackenzie's 'whole argument' was based on the contention that the achievements of oriental agents were relatively small. This, he flatly stated 'is not true'. He also insisted that a European could still operate in charge of a small party behind Japanese lines, unattached to any guerrilla band. This, he conceded, was difficult 'but not impossible'. Nor did he accept Mackenzie's ever-expanding definition of operational intelligence which seemed to include all things military whether they were inside or outside the battle area. Instead he insisted that, in enemy rear areas, troop movements and order of battle information was best acquired by single static agents. He was willing to attach SIS officers to some SOE parties. Nevertheless, he warned, 'they should not be regarded as the only way' of gathering intelligence.[50]

SIS offered some impressive figures in support of their contentions which focused on the independent assessment of their intelligence by the Services. Over a two-year period to the end of August 1944 they had assessed 3,233 SIS reports as either 'of value' or 'of considerable value'. Without extensive research they could not give a precise figure on the proportion of these results obtained from oriental agents penetrating deep into occupied territory beyond the direction of European officers in the field. But their conservative estimate was a proportion of 75 per cent. They also offered concrete examples of their work in eastern Burma and southern Thailand prior to March 1944, when these areas were out of range of photographic reconnaissance. Oriental agents working for SIS had also stolen invaluable documents from Japanese naval vessels. Nevertheless, SIS figures deliberately ignored the period after August 1944, which had witnessed 'the rapid growth' of SOE parties in the field.[51]

SIS and SOE had clearly selected different criteria and different time-periods in order to present the best possible figures and there is little point in comparing them. However, what could not be disputed was that by the end of the war SOE had grown much bigger than SIS in the Far East and the presence of the forces it controlled on the ground in Japanese-occupied Asia was almost ubiquitous. This was reflected in their authorised staff levels, for in January 1945 the Joint Intelligence Committee reported that in contrast with SOE's permitted Far Eastern ceiling of 1,250 men, SIS was permitted only 175. The actual figures for establishment also reveal an even starker contrast, for on 1 December 1944 numbers for SOE personnel were 1,122, while SIS could muster only 86 personnel in Asia.[52]

At the end of April, Garnons-Williams, having received a variety of submissions, offered his final judgement. Demonstrating his own considerable capabilities, it was Garnons-Williams, not Bowden-Smith, who advanced the most persuasive case for protecting SIS. He began by noting that in London things had reached such a state that SOE and SIS would not presently speak to each other so it fell to him to impose a local arrangement. Reviewing the past, he tactfully placed the blame for previous problems that originated with the under-funding of the inter-war years. He also observed that while the personnel of clandestine services always seemed to display the characteristics of 'jealousy' and 'scoop mindedness', nevertheless the activities of the two services were, in his mind, more complementary than most people recognised.

Turning to the present and the future, he chose first to remind them of the inherent and long-standing principle that SIS was 'not amenable to control by anyone except the British Prime Minister'. He then explained that his judgement was driven by the fact that the end of the war was in sight. 'The danger we are faced with', he warned, is of the large SOE organisation 'upsetting the small Service of S.I.S., which by long-range standards is infinitely the most important'. They needed to look to the future when SIS would return to its peacetime role of gathering long-range 'political, social and economic intelligence, its true role'. Accordingly, he suggested that all wartime agent work directed against military targets be handed to SOE or OSS, allowing SIS to focus on the future.

This radical proposal was buttressed by two further factors. Firstly, SIS would have its work cut out adjusting to peacetime operations. He observed caustically that 'no single member of ISLD (SIS) in this Theatre will be of the slightest use after the war because he is completely and absolutely ''blown'' already and the organisation will have to be built anew'. Secondly, and more importantly, there was the crucial but unspoken factor of signals intelligence 'which fortunately is unknown to all except 5 officers' in SEAC. Garnons-Williams observed that, if one took into account that SIS was also in control of signals intelligence, then agents accounted for less than 8 per cent of the whole contribution they made. The future clearly belonged to this crucial and extremely secret source. Nothing should be allowed to damage or interfere with the organisation that controlled it, however inept the direction of its human activities might have been during the war in Burma.[53]

SIS did not like the upshot of this decision, which gave SOE increasing control of wartime intelligence from agents in SEAC. Nevertheless, in areas where SOE primacy was accepted, such as Malaya, relations between

Bowden-Smith and Mackenzie now quickly improved. As early as 11 May 1945, in a new round of discussions, Bowden-Smith freely conceded that much of his activities in the Malaya area 'could not be described as S.I.S. as they were concerned in the collection of operational intelligence'. Moreover, in Malaya, the bulk of information clearly came from the communist AJUF forces through SOE channels. With the caveat that SIS should be free to develop its own separate KMT network in Malaya, they reached a detailed agreement whereby all SOE parties would have single SIS officers attached to them.[54] They all agreed to redeploy two officers responsible for much previous inter-service bickering over Malaya. SOE then imported an Australian officer, Lt Colonel Wylie, who had previously been a police officer in Malaya and who knew many of the AJUF personalities, to preside over the new combined effort. Only SOE would deal directly with the AJUF. All operational and strategic intelligence would be passed over the SIS link to their station in Calcutta, with the proviso that they would have to indicate whether SOE agreed with the view expressed. There was also a complex complaints procedure.[55] The relationship between SIS and SOE in Malaya, although complex, was an effective one, which recognised the importance of preserving their key asset, good relations with the AJUF on the ground.

The recommendations of Garnons-Williams were sensible, but arguably he had little choice, given the overwhelming SOE presence in Japanese-occupied territories. SOE dominance extended even to the more complex situation that obtained in French Indochina. By May 1945 Mackenzie was confirming his *de facto* control of all the French secret services in the Far East. This control extended not only to the French equivalent of SOE, the sabotage body, SA, but also the French intelligence body, SR, who were the equivalent to SIS. Mackenzie pointed out that SOE had always enjoyed closer relations with SR for historical reasons. During 1942 and 1943 the main SR centre in Asia had been the main French Gaullist Military Mission Headquarters in China under General Pechkoff. SOE had developed 'informal' contacts there at a time when SIS 'were forbidden by their London office to have any contact with General Pechkoff'. Mackenzie reached a deal with Pechkoff whereby he secured 100 per cent co-operation from both SA and SR in return for an SOE promise to inform the French of all their activities in outline. SIS could not persuade their London office to sanction a similar agreement. During 1944, as SR expanded its operations, it turned primarily to SOE for its logistical support. In December 1944 Mackenzie wrote to Commander Gibbs of SIS, asking whether he would consider a closer working relationship with SR, reporting to the SIS station in Calcutta. But Gibbs was unable to obtain a clear directive from London and both SA and SR personnel arriving in India continued to be sponsored by SOE.

Now, in the early summer of 1945, Mackenzie asked SEAC for a ruling that formalised SOE's dominant position. He argued persuasively that, given the close integration of French SA and SR activities, it would be 'simpler and more effective' for all French organisations to be sponsored by one British organisation. Moreover, Colonel Dewavarin (Passy), the French intelligence chief in London, had given SR orders to concentrate on operational intelligence, which required close co-operation with both SA and SOE. Most importantly he insisted that SIS were not in a position to offer SR the required radio provision in Indochina and Mackenzie warned that if 'SR find that their demands are not met, they will inevitably turn to the Americans'. This latter point was unanswerable.[56]

The new SEAC machinery for the control of the French clandestine services, agreed in May 1945, reflected the predominance of SOE.[57] All French operations in Indochina would be planned collectively to avoid any crossed wires. It was also agreed that not only in SR operations but also in SA operations 'more stress should be laid on intelligence and reconnaissance'. Yet while intelligence had become the central concern of all these organisations, and while Indochina could hardly be considered a 'battle area', nevertheless it was Mackenzie of SOE who chaired joint meetings between the four services, including SIS. Detailed planning of both SA and SR operations was handled by SOE. It was Mackenzie who dictated a strategy of first laying down a more effective SR radio network. He also instructed SR on the appropriate size of groups to be inserted for intelligence work.[58] Mackenzie did not hesitate to place draconian limits on the activities of the French, extracting from them a categorical assurance that they would not put a clandestine station of any sort into China.[59]

That these arguments were arrived at locally underlines the fact that SOE and SIS in London had no interest in resolving such disputes peacefully. In May 1945, Dening found it necessary to write back to Cavendish-Bentinck, Chairman of the JIC, to complain about the attitude of London-based staff officers. Colonel Taylor of SOE and Commander Gibbs of SIS had recently been to SEAC, but they had refused to co-operate and 'one rather despairs of them working together at all'. Their presence was undermining the recent agreements. He offered Thailand as a classic example of somewhere they were now supposed to work on 'a fifty-fifty basis' with SIS collating and distributing the intelligence collected by SOE. But SIS claimed that SOE had never passed anything to them and refused to acquaint them with some of their missions in the country. Dening asked for heads to be knocked together at a higher level, but he was clearly ignorant of the state of impasse that existed in Whitehall regarding SOE–SIS relations, a situation to which even Churchill had resigned himself.[60]

Nevertheless, the experience of SIS officers working into Thailand confirmed the wisdom of joint operations with SOE. As late as July 1945, SIS was still trying to mount its own independent clandestine operations into this country, but without success. At this point SOE had fourteen different groups operating under the auspices of the Thai resistance organisation including Brigadier Jacques, who was regarded as Mountbatten's personal representative in the country. The resistance were greatly confused by the arrival of parties 'of a second British organisation' and this was creating suspicion at a time when Mountbatten was most anxious to keep the resistance there sweet. SIS had recently put three parties of Chinese agents into Thailand, two with the active co-operation of the resistance and a third independently. The latter 'were completely compromised' within two days. The lesson was clear. The officer in charge of Thai operations conceded that SIS 'cannot establish a network with Siamese agents without help of resistance movement' adding 'the chance of survival of Chinese parties infiltrated by clandestine means is extremely remote'. Instead he suggested putting in more trained intelligence observers to work with SOE to 'improve both quality and volume of the intelligence emanating from the resistance movement'. In short, even hundreds of miles beyond the battle area, SIS increasingly found it necessary to work with SOE networks when collecting intelligence.[61]

Conclusions

The nature of the British Secret Intelligence Service in Asia before and during the Second World War is best summed up by Edmond Taylor, the Deputy Head of P Division, who remarked that it was a rather 'sleepy' organisation.[62] It had been rendered drowsy by under-resourcing in the period prior to 1940 that was even worse than that which afflicted the Europe branches of the service. During 1940 and 1941 the attention of SIS headquarters in London was elsewhere and there was little improvement. It deteriorated yet further once the war with Japan began because its new Director, who was too close to GHQ India, allowed it to be used for an unsuitable purpose. Thus by 1945, surrounded by unsatisfied customers, and eclipsed by signals intelligence and a vigorous SOE, SIS in the Far East seemed on the verge of being put to sleep forever. It was saved in the short term by the foresight of P Division in SEAC and then by the turn of events in London at the end of the war, in which SIS took over the remnants of SOE.[63]

The problems of SIS in Asia can be explained in two different ways. Firstly, in Asia, there were clearly special factors at both the operational and administrative level that debilitated SIS prior to 1945. But we can also observe a second kind of problem that was generic to most secret services working in most wartime theatres. SIS, like most centrally controlled services, encountered problems in making transitions from peace to war. Wartime Asia was now dominated by theatres within which commanders were anxious to subordinate everything to their control. SIS suffered partly because it allowed itself to be subordinated to GHQ India at an early stage of the war and Slim wished to take this process to its logical conclusion. Yet if SIS had entirely ignored regional structures they would have risked being further eclipsed by other clandestine organisations. Similar problems recurred in the context of the Korean War resulting in furious exchanges between MacArthur and American agencies in Washington DC.[64]

Moreover, regulations concerning security which were laid down by SIS Headquarters in London, while making sense in Europe, prevented a weak SIS from developing a collaborative relationship with the French or with OSS at an early stage that could have helped to mask their own inadequacy in Asia.[65] SIS refused to operate under joint Anglo-American direction and was more insistent than SOE on subordinating all its activities directly to 'head office' in London. This problem arose in the context of SIS–OSS relations in a number of theatres. Typically, in January 1945 Eisenhower's SHAEF Command in Europe had proposed subordinating SIS operations to a joint Anglo-American clandestine planning committee. However, SIS observed that 'it would not be practicable for SIS to operate under an Anglo-American command. SIS insisted that whatever unit carried out their operations should be entirely under British command for policy.' A similar line was taken by SIS in the Middle East.[66]

It is only now that one of the underlying reasons for this stand-offishness is becoming clear. The tasks of SIS included distributing highly sensitive signals intelligence decrypts, including the traffic of neutral and even allied countries. The British were breaking some American diplomatic communications at least until December 1941 and Bletchley Park took a great interest in the communications of Chiang Kai-shek's nationalist government throughout the war. They were also routinely breaking Free French traffic through the war and examples include exchanges between French diplomats in the Middle East and de Gaulle in Paris as late as May 1945. This subject is alluded to in retrospective reports prepared at the end of the war by NID 12, an Admiralty section dealing with signals intelligence, which recorded: 'What we called "*THE ALLIES MAY NOT SEE*" were a number of CX's containing reports of our having which "C" did not wish our Allies to become aware. These we circulated (so that they would not be in the files of our Sections where our Allies might work) and had no further responsibility.' This subject remains sensitive and the documents relating to this subject, released in 1994, were nevertheless sanitised by the removal of some paragraphs.[67]

Against the background of these awkward problems, Garnons-Williams and P Division made a major contribution to the management of clandestine organisations in SEAC generally, and to the protection of SIS as a service specifically in the Far East. His presence underlines one of the crucial lessons of intelligence management during the war, tinkering with the system to achieve the right bureaucratic apparatus was at times important, but more often the determining factor was the quality of personnel. Garnons-Williams was universally regarded as bright and 'very charming'. Sadly for SEAC, his health deteriorated towards the end of the war.[68]

Finally, it should be emphasised that any verdict on SIS operations in the Far East must be a tentative one. SOE may look more effective partly because most of what remains of its records are now open to public inspection. The available SIS material is much less. It is also clear that in the case of certain types of SIS operations, no written record was kept.[69] Nevertheless, the emerging picture of SIS during the 1930s and 1940s is not a flattering one. In the summer of 1943, Colonel Gerald Wilkinson returned to London for a spell and held discussions with a wide range of senior figures across Whitehall and Westminster. He then recorded in his diary 'Far East Intelligence from C's organisation has now dwindled to a trickle from a few Chinese coolies.'[70] When the full SIS archives are finally opened to public inspection, perhaps in the not too distant future, they are unlikely to suggest a different verdict.

13   Centre and region: the politics of signals intelligence

> Cracked cipher material was, indeed, as things turned out, the staple product of MI6, and provided the basis for most of its activities. The old procedures, like the setting up of agents, the suborning of informants, the sending of messages written in invisible ink, the masquerading, the dressing up, the secret transmitters, and the examining of the contents of waste-paper baskets, all turned out to be largely a cover for this other source: as one might keep some old-established business in rare books going in order to be able, under the cover of it, to do a thriving trade in pornography and erotica.
>
> Malcolm Muggeridge, SIS, 1939–45.[1]

Intelligence for war

The politics of British and American signals intelligence during the Far Eastern War was markedly different in nature to that of the organisations that ran human agents. Signals intelligence, or 'sigint', organisations were gathering as much as 80 per cent of the work-a-day intelligence which informed the strategy and operations of major formations in the war against Japan. Thus, their sights were primarily fixed on the prosecution of the war, rather than the vagaries of the post-war settlement. While it is clear that both British and American sigint organisations devoted a proportion of their work to neutral and even allied communications traffic (the Free French were a favourite target), this remained a sideline compared to their main work against the Axis.[2] In a broader sense, the sigint organisations were the essential facilitators of the intra-allied espionage that preoccupied the human agent services to a greater degree. Arguably, the intelligence revolution provided by modern cryptanalysis lifted a major burden from the shoulders of services like OSS, SIS and SOE, giving them spare capacity for longer-range political activities.[3]

Nevertheless, sigint was politically highly charged in other respects. There were severe tensions both within and between the British and American organisations and these took three main forms. First, and most importantly, there was the tension between centre and region. The main American sigint

234

centres were located in Washington, with any number of personnel working at smaller outstations in locations such as Honolulu and Melbourne. Washington was anxious to retain control of the analysis of material, employing its outstations as mere collection points. Conversely the outstations were determined to develop their own analytical capability. The same was true of relations between British outstations and Bletchley Park.

This tension was more visible from early 1942, when the tough and dynamic Sir Edward Travis took over from Commander Denniston at Bletchley Park. Although Denniston had presided over the construction of Bletchley Park, the main GC&CS centre, he was nevertheless a codebreaker of a previous era, unsuited to the management of machine cryptanalysis and large organisations. Denniston moved on to run the smaller diplomatic and commercial codebreaking wing of GC&CS in London at Berkeley Street. Denniston and Travis had shared a background in First World War sigint, known as 'Room 40', but only the stocky bespectacled Travis, now in his mid-40s, had the managerial talents to preside over intelligence collection on an industrial scale. Travis was determined to maintain the central position enjoyed by Bletchley or 'BP' and proved a tough customer for the outstations to deal with.[4]

The second form of tension was that existing between Bletchley and Washington. Bletchley was clearly ahead in terms of work on German and Italian systems in Europe, but had not the spare capacity from 1942 to make headway against Japanese communications. In contrast Washington was well-resourced by 1942 and quickly became the main centre of work against Japan, which arguably was even more demanding. Each guarded their achievements jealously and it was only in 1944, in the wake of the negotiation of further Anglo-American sigint treaties, the so-called BRUSA (Britain–USA) agreement, that information began to circulate in an efficient way. As late as 1945, the US Army Air Force in Europe complained to Washington about its dependence on the British for material on Germany. Although this material was freely given, they remained uncomfortable with dependency.

Within the American system in particular, there was also a third tension in the form of marked inter-service rivalry, which has already been touched on in a previous chapter. These problems persisted beyond 1945 to plague American efforts during the Korean War, eventually triggering the creation of a single centralised sigint body, the National Security Agency. Indeed, fragmentation was very much a characteristic of the American system. Even within the US Army, the collectors and cryptanalysts of the Signals Intelligence Service based at a new location, a former private school for girls called Arlington Hall to the west of Washington and across the Potomac in the Virginia suburbs, had almost no contact with their customers, the Special Branch of the Military Intelligence Service. The Navy had similar problems following its expansion to the ivy-clad Mount Vernon Academy on Nebraska Avenue on the outskirts of Washington.[5]

Kilindini, 1942

On 5 January 1942, a month after the outbreak of the war against Japan, British sigint units were evacuated from Singapore in a state of disarray. There was some dispute as to whether they should go to East Africa, India or Ceylon and in the short term most settled on the Indian Ocean Naval Headquarters at Colombo on Ceylon. Others, including FECB's lower level 'Y' interception units under Commander Sandwith, stayed longer and eventually joined the ill-fated ABDA Command in Java.

On Ceylon the main FECB sigint unit moved into a school building five miles away from Naval Headquarters at Colombo. For the first time those responsible for interception and collection, and those responsible for cryptanalysis found themselves conveniently in the same building. Nevertheless, conditions were primitive with receiving aerials hung from palm trees where passing motor traffic interfered with reception. Then, in April 1942, Ceylon was attacked by Vice-Admiral Nagumo's highly effective Japanese Carrier Task Force. These were the darkest days of the Far Eastern War, with forces in Burma still in headlong retreat and with SOE stay-behind parties ready for Japanese landings on the east coast of India. Captain Lammers, the United States Naval Liaison Officer at Colombo, recalled:

The Easter Sunday raid on 5 April, 1942, on Colombo and other ports of Ceylon had left the British more unsure of themselves than ever . . . The members of the British Far Eastern Intelligence Unit at Colombo consisted mostly of Supply Corps officers of the Royal Navy, and a large number of WRENS, who were quartered in a girls' school called the 'LOONEY BIN' on the outskirts of the city of Colombo, and were very discouraged and over pessimistic.[6]

Admiral James Somerville, the new Commander of the East Indies Fleet, now decided to evacuate his base and a demoralised FECB to Kilindini on the East African coast.

Decamping in two stages to ensure there was no break in its work, they were relocated at Alidina, a requisitioned local school and placed under the command of Commander Bruce Keith who had recently come out from Bletchley. The East African period was a miserable one, battling against poor facilities and bad reception from their targets on the other side of the Indian Ocean. Nevertheless, there were recent triumphs to celebrate. They recalled that they had given 'ample warning' that Japan was going to war in December 1941. They had learned that the HMS *Prince of Wales* and the HMS *Repulse* had been spotted and would be attacked from the air four hours before the attack was launched, although the attack had begun by the time the information reached Admiral Tom Phillips. A new Japanese naval code, JN40, introduced during early 1942, was broken while the unit was at Colombo and then in transit to Kilindini. Moreover the evacuation of themselves and much merchant shipping from the vicinity of Ceylon ahead of the Nagumo raid was in itself a sigint achievement.

FECB also made mistakes. During the attack on Ceylon in April 1942, they claimed that the Japanese carriers were only escorted by cruisers. But Somerville, who 'was not receptive to Special Intelligence', preferred to believe aerial reconnaissance, which eventually proved right. The air observers realised the elaborate superstructures were not Mogami class cruisers but a battleship squadron. As a result the formation was considered too strong and was not attacked. Thereafter the Japanese sank two cruisers and the aircraft carrier HMS *Hermes*. Somerville, like Brooke-Popham, had preferred the old-fashioned eye-ball to the new science of sigint. In this instance his scepticism allowed him to avoid a potentially disastrous clash with a much stronger force.[7]

Only a month later, FECB helped to secure a revenge. Allied cryptography against naval codes was now making rapid progress and in early May Americans at Pearl Harbor and also FECB intercepted a long operational order from Yamamoto to the Japanese fleet. The target for the Japanese attack was not clear, but on 22 May FECB voiced its suspicion that it might be Midway Island. Further work confirmed this, paving the way for American success at the Battle of Midway, the turning point of the Pacific War.[8] Success was accompanied by the problem of hiding sources. Japanese codes that had been penetrated because of the capture of a complete codebook from a submarine at Guadacanal were now revised. This may have been the result of an extraordinary American press story in June, stressing that the victory was owed to the fact that the US Navy knew the precise nature and timing of Japanese actions in advance. This seemed to confirm British suspicions about American insecurity with sigint voiced earlier in the war, but Britain too was losing material. On 10 May the merchantman SS *Nankin* was boarded by a German raider and secret mail from a sigint station in New Zealand was captured.[9]

By the summer of 1942 Somerville was not only convinced of the virtues of sigint, he also suspected that he was receiving a raw deal over sigint. The conditions that FECB were working under at Kilindini could have not contrasted more dramatically with the 700 staff working on similar problems at Washington DC 'with every possible advantage and facility'. Somerville now pressed for all investigation and research into unbroken Japanese ciphers to be concentrated in one place, Washington, Honolulu or Melbourne. The other places would then be stripped of those doing research work, leaving only the operational staffs doing interception, deciphering and interpretation of intelligence derived from Japanese traffic that was already understood. In August 1942, Somerville despatched Lt Commander Burnett, an experienced cryptanalyst who had served in Hong Kong and Singapore, to London to make his case to the DNI, and to GC&CS.[10]

Burnett knew that the main attack on the frequently changing Japanese naval ciphers was being conducted primarily by the Americans. As well as Washington, there were also a large US Navy and a smaller US Army station at Hawaii, together with a combined American–Australian naval cryptanalytical station in Melbourne, utilising a Purple machine recovered from the Philippines. In June 1942, the US Army despatched one of its top cryptanalysts, Colonel Abraham Sinkov, to command this station which, together with the Central Bureau at Brisbane, would become the focus of MacArthur's wholly independent signals intelligence effort in the South West Pacific Area.[11] In September 1942, a further American interception station opened at Chungking in China. In the summer of 1942 the American made the first breaks into the Japanese Army Attaché's code. But Bletchley had no intention of allowing its regional outstations like Kilindini to deal directly with the Americans over this sort of material.[12]

Accordingly, Burnett's reception in London in the summer of 1942 was not auspicious. The Director of Naval Intelligence refused to receive him and he was told to attend a meeting at Bletchley the following week. Here assembled were senior staff from NID and senior administrators from GC&CS including Travis; also the head of the Army section, Colonel Tiltman, together with Frank Birch and Nigel de Gray. Hugh Foss, the senior Japanese cryptanalyst at Bletchley was also present. Burnett was told firmly that he could not have a direct link to Washington, explaining that the Americans would not supply Kilindini with the necessary cipher machine for the link. Burnett was also told that Bletchley would soon take over research work on the Japanese Naval General Cipher, JN25. Travis and Birch were about to depart for Washington to negotiate a new agreement with the Americans regarding work on Japanese ciphers and he was told to 'await the outcome of their visit'.[13]

The Anglo-American meetings in Washington during September and October 1942 were of the first importance. The British delegation, which included Travis, Birch and Tiltman met with senior American naval representatives to hammer out the first comprehensive, albeit cautious, agreements on the exchange of naval signals intelligence. Ultra and the war in the Atlantic was covered by the so-called Holden agreement. However, they also achieved an important, but little-known consensus on co-operation against the complex Japanese naval operational ciphers.[14]

Under the Holden agreement, Washington would remain the main centre for work on the latest version of the demanding Japanese naval operational cipher JN25d. Recovered 'keys' would then be sent to Bletchley for forwarding to Kilindini. Similarly any finished intelligence relevant to the Indian Ocean area would be forwarded by the Americans to the Admiralty in London for eventual transfer to Somerville. Meanwhile Bletchley would take over work on the Japanese General Naval Cipher which hitherto had been studied at Kilindini. Burnett looked on this new agreement with suspicion. He believed there would be severe delays for the consumers, and that GC&CS and NID would not pass on all that they received from the Americans. Kilindini, he insisted, needed a direct teletype link with Washington.[15] Bletchley allowed Kilindini to develop direct relations with the small independent unit under MacArthur at Melbourne, which was a joint British–Australian–American operation under American control. But Bletchley feared that Kilindini would become an outstation of Washington.

Burnett then travelled to Washington to liaise with Commander Wenger, the American Navy's top communications and cryptanalytical expert, but was warned by GC&CS against subverting the recent Birch/Travis agreement. Burnett's sojourn in Washington during November and December 1942 only increased his desire for Kilindini to defect from Bletchley, and to join Melbourne and Honolulu on Washington's direct circuit, which was codenamed *Tuna*. His irritation with GC&CS intensified:

Washington . . . is a large and most efficiently run organisation, and they were very easy, helpful and pleasant to work with. I was given access to everything I wanted to see, including their twice daily produced summary of Japanese translations and derived intelligence, a copy of which was said to be sent to the Admiralty (but could be traced neither there nor at B.P. [Bletchley] when I raised the point after return to the U.K.).

He also claimed that the Americans could not understand why Bletchley, which was overburdened with European work, and had little Japanese experience, wished to begin work on the Japanese Naval General Cipher, but even so had been willing to 'accommodate us'.

Denied his direct teletype link to Washington, Burnett was nevertheless persistent in searching out other links with Washington. In December 1942, Colonel Tiltman arrived in Washington from Bletchley. Tiltman, head of the GC&CS Army section, was an impressive figure, tall with a clipped moustache and renowned for his distinctive tartan regimental trousers. Rather improbably, Burnett suggested to him that an air courier service might be set up between Washington and Kilindini. He also pointed out that the current British liaison officer for Japanese materials, Major Stevens was preoccupied with Army ciphers and so he himself should stay on in Washington to provide better naval liaison. Tiltman was sympathetic, but emphasised that Commander Travis would only allow Kilindini to communicate with Washington via Bletchley.

An irate Burnett returned to Bletchley to write his report. He claimed that the 'Japanese Naval Section there [at BP] is snowed under with raw material supplied to them by Washington, and can only raise enough staff to sort it and file it away.' Moreover, he complained that Bletchley 'only forwards to Kilindini those records which arrive from Washington in duplicate'. 'Kilindini', he complained, 'will suffer from malnutrition, while B.P. grows fat on the pick of the food'.[16] Officers with Naval Intelligence in London (NID) read this report and were drawn into 'the swearing match' between Bletchley and Burnett. Although tactful, they clearly found Burnett's reasoning, based on Somerville's urgent operational requirements, compelling. Somerville would indeed be best served, they argued, by a direct link 'to what is the main source – the American network'. By contrast, they found the line taken by Bletchley 'difficult to follow'. This was a long-term problem that would not go away.[17]

NID were convinced that Somerville was receiving a raw deal in other respects prior to 1944. A key section of NID was the Operational Intelligence Centre which kept track of all Axis shipping movements, using a great variety of sources, including sigint, but its Far Eastern section, known as 8J, was only created in March 1942. Hitherto this region had been dealt with by the Mediterranean section in their spare moments. In 1943 and 1944, 8J consisted of two officers who only received part-time clerical assistance as the war in the Atlantic faded away. 8J remarked that until mid-1943 all their information came from 'overseas originators'. Mountbatten complained about this in 1944.[18]

The root of Bletchley's miserly attitude was political, stemming from the delicate balance of sigint relations between the British and the Americans during 1942. Both countries remained suspicious of each other's security arrangements, and the British were somewhat reluctant to allow the US Army to have access to all Ultra material, for example withholding some German Order of Battle material even as the Americans entered North Africa. This was partly as the result of the 'Fellers Affair', in which the ciphers of an American military attaché had become compromised, resulting in a serious haemorrhage of information about British operations in Western Desert. The British had also been unnerved by American newspaper discussion of intelligence success at the Battle of Midway. US Naval Intelligence had wanted to prosecute those responsible but London urged that this would only result in further unfortunate publicity. The upshot of all this was that the various Anglo-American agreements in 1942–3 placed a strong emphasis on security procedure.

Bletchley believed that too much direct British access by Somerville and operational units in the Indian Ocean to American sigint material on Japan might prompt unwelcome American requests for reciprocation. These concerns were complicated by Bletchley's desire to obtain the high-speed computing equipment, known as 'Bombes', that the Americans were beginning to produce quickly and in large numbers in later 1942 and early 1943. These important considerations underpinned the important Holden agreement in October 1942. But this high-level Anglo-American bartering was not the sort of thing that Burnett or indeed Somerville were likely to be privy to.[19]

Bletchley therefore had reasons for its obstinacy which related to the high politics of Anglo-American sigint co-operation. In October 1942, when the Holden agreement was reached with the Americans, and even in the spring of 1943, co-operation was still uneasy and Travis was required to consider British long-term interests. However hard-pressed Bletchley might be with European work, was it wise to surrender all work on Japan to the Americans? There was as yet no guarantee that co-operation would continue beyond the end of the war. These types of concerns were still present after the BRUSA agreement of 1943.[20]

This study does not extend to the complex politics of intelligence that prevailed under Nimitz or MacArthur in the Pacific.[21] However, it is worth contrasting Somerville's anxiety to link up with other centres with cryptanalytical concerns in MacArthur's SWPA, which were quite different and typified the latter's hostile attitude to intelligence liaison generally. In SWPA, Australian cryptanalyst units of long-standing were joined by an American naval team evacuated from the Philippines, and a handful of British fleeing from ABDA, in February 1942. In April 1942 MacArthur formed his own unit known as the Central Bureau, commanded by Dr Abram Sinkov, which, surprisingly, received only limited Allied cryptanalytical material directly from other commands for the most of the Pacific War.[22]

Central Bureau was closely attached to MacArthur's HQ and so moved to Brisbane in August 1942, then to Hollandia in the late summer of 1944, to Leyte in October 1944, to San Miguel in the Philippines in May 1945 and finally to Tokyo in September 1945, before being deactivated in November 1945. Its isolation was increased by its concentration on low-level tactical codes. Naval work and 'Purple' traffic was handled by an entirely separate unit called 'Belconnen' which employed 75 personnel evacuated from the Philippines. The Army–Navy friction in Washington was mirrored by these two local organisations.[23]

Unlike Somerville, who was initially sceptical of sigint but became a convert, Brigadier General Charles Willoughby, MacArthur's intelligence chief, remained a doubter to the end. The cost of this scepticism was sometimes heavy. In 1945, the landings at Leyte Gulf, which incurred heavy casualties, reflected poor use of both signals intelligence and ground intelligence provided by the guerrillas.[24] As MacArthur observed in 1944, with some under-statement: 'There are only three great [Intelligence Officers] in history and mine is not amongst them.'[25] But these calamities also underlined the fact that MacArthur himself was capable of ignoring sigint completely when it threatened to contradict his own strategic purposes.[26]

The BRUSA Agreement, 1943

Joint Anglo-American operations in North Africa during late 1942 provided much of the impetus towards the more wide-ranging agreements on sigint collaboration concluded in mid-1943, given the collective name BRUSA. This was partly driven by embarrassing disparities. Eisenhower found himself privy to a vastly greater range of material than Washington and by early 1943, the US Army were increasingly aware that they were getting less Ultra material from the British than from the US Navy, who had profited from the agreement in 1942.[27] During 1943 this manifested itself in nasty exchanges over the German 'Order of Battle' (O of B).[28] The US Army now began to make a case for an independent American effort against Enigma employing the large resources coming on stream. American pressure on the British to provide not only volumes of intercepts of German Enigma traffic but also Soviet signals traffic mounted in early 1943. However, while Bletchley would allow operational American headquarters in Europe greater access to Ultra, they would not countenance an American centre for its exploitation.[29]

The Far Eastern War also generated pressure for fuller cryptanalytic exchange. The US Navy, MacArthur's Central Bureau and British code-breakers in Delhi had all made significant inroads against high-grade Japanese cipher systems and were sharing the fruits of their labours very effectively. Meanwhile, just to the north of London, at St Albans, two coun-ter-intelligence sections – Section V of SIS and X-2 of OSS – had been busily sharing German *Abwehr* agent material. It was only now that Wash-ington began to appreciate the full scale of the work of Bletchley's 5,000 personnel. The pressure of operations drove the globalisation of allied sigint co-operation, overcoming the conservatism of 'old guard' figures at Bletch-ley, such as Nigel de Gray (now Deputy Director), and pointed the way to a more comprehensive agreement. Bletchley despatched a negotiating team to Washington for this purpose in April 1943.[30]

On 17 May 1943, Britain's Captain Hastings and the American General Strong concluded BRUSA, a short document of no more than twenty-four paragraphs. This agreement, which was of the first importance and which remains in existence in a modified form, concentrated on the sharing of fin-ished intelligence rather than raw intercepts. Strict security procedures were the key facilitator to wider circulation of high-grade material.[31] This focused on the rigid application of the need-to-know principle with the phrase 'Burn After Reading' at the start of each paragraph. Subsequently, it was agreed that the United States would continue to focus on Japan while the British would work primarily on the Germans. Bletchley had successfully blocked the extensive exploitation of ULTRA outside the United Kingdom.[32] BRUSA was paralleled by equally important efforts to rationalise the flow of finished intelligence of all types on the Far Eastern War between the large service intelligence headquarters which had mushroomed in London and Washington (especially G-2) since early 1942. Typically, in September 1943, Washington was designated the main Allied centre for the study of the Japanese Air Force.[33]

This new agreement had unforeseen results, especially in the United States, where the US Army and the US Navy were propelled towards better mutual relations.[34] Alfred McCormack, one of the three senior American signals intelligence officers who began to negotiate BRUSA in the summer of 1943, remarked at length on this:

There is one aspect of our relations with the British in intelligence matters that has struck me very forcefully. Our intelligence agencies in Washington appear to spend a lot of their time keeping information secret from one another, in competing for credit and in beating one another into print. All of them have some liaison or other with the British intelligence agencies; and for some reasons they are freer in giving information to the British than to one another. The British do not keep their information in watertight compartments, nor do their various agencies seem to care who gets the credit. They are so set up that their intelligence is put together and evaluated; and the job is done promptly. This gives them a great advantage over us in intelligence matters.

Some might have quarrelled with this idealistic picture of the British system, but Bletchley's relatively centralised machine made a firm impression upon the Americans. Conversely, visiting British liaison officers were stupefied by the level of resource available to their American colleagues.[35] BRUSA initiated reorganisation in Britain as well as in the United States. Travis brought the various service sections under more central control. This was underlined by changing the name Government Code and Cipher School (GC&CS) to Government Communications Headquarters (GCHQ), although the terms 'BP' and 'GC&CS' remained in common usage until the end of the war.[36]

BRUSA created a more elaborate system for disseminating sigint to regional commands. Inzer Wyatt took charge of the system for distribution across Asia and the Pacific from early 1944. Wyatt studied the elaborate system operating in the Mediterranean before heading out to Delhi to meet Wing Commander John Stripe who ran the Special Liaison Unit distributing sigint to GHQ India, and now SEAC. Wyatt and his thirty-five staff also supervised similar arrangements for Stilwell and Chennault, then Wedemeyer and Sultan. MacArthur proved to be Wyatt's most ticklish customer and direct orders from Marshall in Washington were required to secure his obedience.[37] Wyatt's duties allowed him a clear insight into the recurrent problem of poor Army–Navy co-operation. Although overseeing the distribution of decrypted Japanese Army and Air Force material to Chennault's 14th Air Force headquarters in China, he could not persuade the Navy in Washington to offer Chennault Japanese naval material. This had the effect of denying information on Japanese convoys to Chennault's well-placed bomber squadrons. The convoluted solution was to ensure that all Japanese naval traffic was sent from Washington to London then to SEAC, whence the SLU commander John Stripe passed it to Wyatt who finally made it available to Chennault in China. Eventually, Chennault enjoyed great success against Japanese coastal convoys. Such Byzantine arrangements abounded in all commands.[38]

HMS Anderson: sigint in SEAC, 1943–1944

By mid-1943, with the creation of Mountbatten's SEAC underway, Somerville was convinced of the need for a sigint unit closely linked into the command of military operations in South East Asia. With the tide of war turning in New Guinea and the Solomon Islands, eyes now turned to Ceylon. FECB staff at Kilindini returned to Ceylon in September 1943 and the ever-expanding SEAC headquarters began to arrive soon after. There, a new sigint station, known initially as HMS *Anderson* W/T station, was the first purpose-built sigint facility in the Far East and was conceived on a huge scale. Its key purpose was to work on JN-25, the main Japanese naval operational code and by March 1944 it was handling up to 200 messages a day.[39]

Anderson, a sprawl of single-storey huts, was located in a somewhat unhealthy situation on the south east fringe of Colombo, about a mile from the sea. Clerical work was now undertaken by Wrens rather than casual civilian staff. During 1944 it boasted 1,280 staff with plans to expand to 1,704. Even the small liaison office that Anderson maintained at the nearby Naval Headquarters for the purpose of helping to interpret its output numbered forty-three staff. Such expansion led to fierce global competition for communications personnel. There was also a shortage of Japanese language specialists to fulfil Bletchley's undertaking to the US Navy of continued research work on Japanese naval materials, and, from Bletchley's point of view, 'to avoid being in the hands of the Americans for this sphere of intelligence'. This problem crystallised in September 1943, when the Americans offered Anderson the equipment for two teletype channels between Anderson and Honolulu via Guam, to make US sigint material from those locations available without delay. Somerville was very keen, for all British sources together at that time could only give him 15 per cent of the totality of Japanese material. However, with D-Day taking first priority, London refused him the further 200 operating personnel required. Somerville was forced to find staff by stripping other local requirements to the bone.

Somerville and his new sigint adviser, Commander Malcolm Saunders, also continued Lt Commander Burnett's struggle against Bletchley's block on free communication with Washington. Neither the Americans nor Bletchley would allow this. Somerville suspected that in 'their anxiety to keep control in their own hands' Bletchley was 'concealing from the Admiralty' the true nature of the situation. He also refused to believe that Bletchley was capable of framing an appropriate policy for an operational centre geographically so far distant.[40] Somerville's requests were also rejected by the DNI in London who insisted that 'this short-circuiting of G.C. & C.S. was wanted neither by the Americans nor by the Admiralty'. Both London and Washington understood each other's desire to maintain direct authority and control over their respective outstations. Nevertheless, during 1944, the situation softened a little, with a special communications service between Bletchley, Honolulu, Melbourne and Anderson which permitted rapid intelligence exchange and cryptographic 'back-chat'. Thus while GC&CS remained in control for matters of policy, work-a-day problems were now a matter of free discussion.[41]

The rapid growth of Anderson propelled Somerville into continual confrontations with Bletchley and the Admiralty. On 24 November 1943, Somerville requested Hollerith punch-card machinery for Anderson to assist with the rapid processing of material, but Bletchley insisted that it was not available, adding that it was 'not the practice to equip "outstations" with such machinery'. Somerville's answer was always to play the operational card: 'The delay of a few hours' he insisted 'may spell the difference between success and failure' in battle.[42]

In early December 1943, Somerville received considerable comfort from the visit of Commander Holtwick, a senior American naval officer liaising with the cryptanalytical centre at Pearl Harbor in Hawaii. Holtwick suggested that Anderson should be expanded up to the capacity of the large station at Pearl Harbor, allowing Washington and Bletchley to confine themselves to technical research, leaving 'all the exploitation to Anderson and Pearl'. Holtwick also noted 'with some amusement that the attitude as between B.P. and Anderson was almost exactly reflected between Washington and Pearl'. But there were also differences. Holtwick was astonished at the poor promotion prospects of British naval officers engaged on cryptanalytical duties.[43]

Other visits by British and American liaison officers had confirmed Somerville's view that Anderson, and also its sister station, the Wireless Experimental Centre at Delhi, were being kept on a thin diet. Accordingly, few days

13 Admiral Somerville, who struggled with Bletchley Park over sigint in Asia

after Holtwick's visit, Somerville convened a meeting with the Director of Intelligence at GHQ India, Major General Cawthorn together with senior sigint personnel – including Saunders and Tuffnel – to discuss relations with Bletchley. They agreed on a direct appeal to the British Chiefs of Staff, stressing 'the urgent need to build up exploitation at these [regional] centres as much as possible and confine B.P. to technical research'. Somerville confided in his diary:

It seems quite clear to me that it is very largely a matter of prestige and not principle which is preventing these exploitation centres from being properly equipped. B.P. was admirably situated geographically for exploitation of German matter and Italian matter, and is obviously reluctant to give up this exploitation and the immediate prestige which results in producing very hot news of a most secret nature. I sincerely trust that they will be brought to their senses and since our joint signal was addressed to the Chiefs of Staff one can only hope there will be no short circuiting.

But Somerville was quite unaware of the longer-term issues which preoccupied Bletchley and the Chiefs of Staff in this area. Accordingly, while Anderson would continue to expand incrementally, the fanciful idea of Bletchley being relegated to a technical research centre would not be countenanced by London for even a moment.[44] On 17 March 1944, Saunders reported back to Somerville following conversations with the DNI and Bletchley. Many of Anderson's technical requests had been conceded but Somerville refused to accept the assurances of Bletchley that 'they never had any intention of starving Anderson'.[45]

Somerville's interminable arguments with Bletchley were not his only intelligence concern during 1943 and 1944. He was also engaged in a protracted struggle with OSS, SIS and SIS to prevent them from drawing his submarines away from naval operations to serve as a taxi service for clandestine parties. Nothing disturbed Somerville more than the experience of receiving 'special intelligence' from Anderson about Japanese naval movements, but then finding himself powerless because his submarine assets were on loan. On 2 January 1944, 'special intelligence' indicated that part of a Japanese cruiser squadron stationed at Singapore was proceeding up the Malacca Straits. He had no less than three submarines in the vicinity, but because they were all engaged on special operations they would 'not be in a position to intercept'. Four days later an exasperated Somerville recorded, '3 recent submarine clandestine operations have failed to establish connect with their agents'.[46] He took the issue to Mountbatten, insisting that he had clear evidence that some of these operations were not justified and seemed to have no obvious military purpose or much chance of success.[47]

Once again Mountbatten's P Division showed its worth. Mountbatten recommended a conference with Garnons-Williams and the SEAC Director of Intelligence, General Lamplough. P Division accepted that it would be impossible to exploit the growing dividends of Anderson without at least two flotillas of submarines available for conventional operations. But Somerville was also impressed by the P Division presentation, understanding for the first time 'that clandestine operations are essential' to obtain the very specific types of intelligence, such as beach gradients, required in preparing a re-occupation of Malaya and the Netherlands East Indies.[48]

The problem of Chinese insecurity

Although sigint in SEAC continued to be denied direct access to Washington, nevertheless the BRUSA agreement had accelerated mutual Anglo-American confidence in security and cryptanalytic co-operation against Japan. In 1943 and 1944 there were two major Anglo-American–Commonwealth conferences on the Japanese Army and air order of battle, drawing largely on sigint. In March 1944 a particularly important meeting at Arlington Hall, the American Army sigint centre, redistributed the responsibilities for breaking Japanese Army and Air Force ciphers. However, as late as October 1944, rivalry between the two American armed services ensured that the United States was compelled to resist British requests for a new over-arching BRUSA-type agreement covering all cryptanalytic activities in Asia and the Pacific. Both armed services continued to find it easier to deal with the British than with each other.

Sideways co-operation with and between neighbouring cryptanalytic centres at the theatre level was also problematic. MacArthur's Central Bureau in the Pacific had grown to constitute an impressive American–Australian entity, but communication facilities were never good enough to make more than half this material available to Washington. Meanwhile, material that reached MacArthur from other commands was rarely passed on to his own Central Bureau. British officers from Colombo quickly became aware that the American sigint effort in CBI was hermetically sealed and did not communicate with them. Throughout 1944 the efforts of Anderson to develop further links with the Americans were continually slapped down, partly for fear that Anderson would become 'a complete subsidiary of Washington'.[49]

But the most troublesome liaison issue of the Far Eastern War for sigint personnel was co-operation with the Chinese. The KMT enjoyed a large and secretive cryptanalytical bureau, but as with so much KMT activity, it was focused on Chiang Kai-shek's domestic enemies, and had little time for the war against Japan.[50] As early as January 1942, the British had concluded that they dare not exchange intelligence material with the Chinese because of leaks. These leaks occurred not only because of Japanese espionage, but because the Japanese were reading Chinese communications.[51] Even before the fall of Singapore, London had ordered that the Chinese representative to Brooke-Popham be shown almost nothing, while sigint material was out of the question. In March 1942, the British Ambassador in China broached this awkward issue with Chiang Kai-shek. Chiang seemed very understanding and asked for a cipher expert to be sent out from India to help China improve her communications security. New machinery and cipher tables were despatched from both London and Washington, but matters did not improve, rendering sigint co-operation with the Chinese all but impossible for the duration of the war.[52]

Theatre commanders had reason to be personally anxious about these issues. Just prior to Mountbatten's visit to Chiang Kai-shek in October 1943 (during which he negotiated the ill-fated Gentleman's Agreement), the Chinese Foreign Minster warned him that news of his impending visit had probably leaked. Mountbatten therefore changed the date of his departure and flew by night. On the day he had originally planned to fly the Japanese 'put on a terrific fighter sweep . . . for the first time for many months and shot down three wretched transport aircraft'. Mountbatten had only narrowly avoided the fate of Japan's Admiral Yamamoto, who had perished at the hands of the Americans in a similar pre-planned air interception in April of the same year.[53]

The Chinese security problem became worse during 1944, for it was clear that Chungking was attempting to improve its liaison with both British and American intelligence centres. In June Mountbatten expressed concern when the Chinese appointed a Naval Liaison officer to the staff of General Carton de Wiart, Churchill's special representative in Chungking. De Wiart, like Gordon Grimsdale, had additional intelligence duties. Mountbatten was suspicious and observed pointedly that, as the Japanese happened to occupy the entire seaboard of China, the Chungking government had no Navy and so it was difficult to see how naval liaison could legitimately occupy this person's time. One of Mountbatten's senior commanders commented on 'the entire lack of security at Chungking which is notorious; any items of information of real importance sent to Chungking appear to be invariably passed on to the Japanese'.[54] The visit of the Chinese Director of Military Intelligence, General Cheng Kai-min, to Delhi in August 1944 was an especially awkward business. Escorted by Lt Colonel Harmon, the senior SIS representative in Chungking, his time was spun out with routine tours of POW interrogation and letter censorship. Further offers of help with security training were pointedly made.[55] The Chinese problem was nothing less than global in scale. In April 1944, as the preparations for D-Day placed Britain under a tight cloak of security, the Chinese Embassy in London was summarily deprived of its cipher and diplomatic bag privileges, resulting in vigorous protests. Eden assured Churchill that in the circumstances they had no choice.[56] Eden could not tell the Chinese Ambassador that the Americans had intercepted a Japanese message of 9 March 1944, discussing the fact that Japan had, in turn, decoded a message from the Chinese Ambassador in London to Chungking, recounting his latest conversation with Eden.[57]

Both Bletchley and Arlington had themselves been intercepting and breaking Chinese material since before the outbreak of the Pacific War, and so were painfully conscious of the insecurity of Chinese communications. Similar worries applied to the security of Free French ciphers in the Far East, based on British and American work on Free French traffic that continued throughout the Second World War.[58] The material passed to Chungking was continually reduced. By 1945 Op-20-G, the US Navy sigint centre had prevailed on the British to cease passing MEW intelligence summaries to Chungking because they contained Ultra material, albeit in a heavily diluted form. In March 1945 the British Military Attaché at Chungking took the extraordinary step of asking to be taken off the Ultra circulation list because security in China was so poor.[59]

As the European War drew to a close in April 1945 the situation had still not improved. The British and American JICs had wrestled with this embarrassing subject for years, but still: 'No United States–British agreement has been reached as to how to stop this leakage which continues at an alarming rate.' Despite all the measures that they had taken, the British Chiefs of Staff complained that 'a great deal of useful intelligence is leaking to the Japanese'. London felt that they had narrowed the main problem down to the ciphers used by Chinese service attachés serving abroad, but no solution was found.[60] This concern was overtaken by news of the compromise of a British–American cipher system, used by American naval personnel in China.[61]

The Wireless Experimental Centre at Delhi

Interception work had been carried out in India since the arrival of the wireless telegraph and was certainly well developed by the advent of the First World War. However, the scale of this activity remained small even after the outbreak of the war in Europe. It was only in September 1941, with the acceleration of the war in the Middle East, in which the Indian Army was heavily involved, that General Wavell, the newly arrived C. in C. India, pressed London for an expansion of his cryptanalytical capabilities. Wavell requested four special wireless sets and eight cryptanalysts to compete with the Germans in the Baghdad area and received the usual reply from London, that the necessary personnel and VHF equipment was in short supply.[62] Wavell was amongst a minority of senior officers who had always given a high priority to intelligence and his recent experience in the Middle East confirmed the wisdom of this.[63]

By October 1941, Wavell had pushed through a programme entitled the 'Expansion of "Y" Service in India'. The JIC noted that 'India has a small "Y" organisation which deals with material from Russian, Persian and Afghan sources', but conceded that the threat to India from Germany in the west, and from Japan in the east, now rendered a large Indian organisation essential. This firm assertion that Russian traffic was still being worked in October 1941 is interesting.[64] German traffic in central Asia could not be intercepted from the UK and so the intention was to create an inter-service cryptanalytical centre in Iraq and India, somewhat similar to the Combined Bureau Middle East, though in practice it would be Army-dominated.[65]

The most awkward questions of policy and principle again concerned the relationship between centre and region. Hitherto Britain had maintained the line that the 'solution of High Grade Ciphers is undertaken at B.P. only', but relaying the estimated 50,000 groups of locally intercepted German cipher traffic to the UK for processing would have placed an impossible strain on the cable networks. Many interception sites, such as Abbotabad, in North West India were 1,000 miles from the cable network. 'The conclusion would appear to be that arrangements must be put in hand to enable the solution of

High Grade Ciphers to be undertaken in India.' Delhi could have been for-
given for thinking Bletchley unhelpful for, once it was plain that they were
to be cut out of this arrangement, Bletchley declared their staff engaged on
High Grade Ciphers too small to provide even a skeletal staff for the new
Indian organisation. An entirely new organisation would now be raised in
India, recruiting research scientists and mathematicians in the UK and in
India. Tiltman, together with Colonel Nicholls of MI8, was despatched to
India to advise on the initial stages of this project which was expected to
take at least a year to construct.[66]

Even in the last months of 1941, the emphasis in India was upon the
interception of German traffic, especially that of the Luftwaffe, whose
Enigma keys had been some of the first to fall. As late as 9 December 1941,
India's requests for Japanese-speaking personnel were rebuffed on the
grounds that they were all busily engaged at FECB Singapore. But within
weeks they were deluged with cryptanalytical refugees from Singapore. The
senior Army cryptanalyst evacuated from Singapore, Edward Marr-Johnston,
was installed as head of the newly expanded Indian organisation in Delhi,
entitled the Wireless Experimental Centre (WEC).[67]

By 23 March 1942, the liquidation of ABDA Command had prompted
Wavell to ask Sir Stewart Menzies, Chief of SIS, to reorganise the signals
intelligence system in Asia. In May, acting in his capacity as Chairman of
the Y Committee in London, Menzies produced a detailed plan. Menzies
observed that while most of FECB had been evacuated to Ceylon, this was
primarily a centre of naval operations. Land and air operations were instead
being directed from India. Henceforth, these naval cryptanalysts would serve
mainly as Combined Operations Intelligence Centre designed for the Navy.
The overall combined intelligence picture for Supreme Commanders would
instead be assembled in Delhi with the help of WEC, who would concentrate
on Army and Air Force Traffic. The two centres would have to liaise
closely.[68]

Menzies took the opportunity to re-emphasise that the Chiefs of Staff had
designated Bletchley and Washington as the main cryptanalytical centres as
a matter of policy, while outstations abroad should confine themselves to
'low-grade cryptography'. Their purpose, he lectured, 'was not to weaken the
work of the Government Code and Cypher School by the dissipation of its
skilled and limited staff to stations abroad'. But Menzies now accepted that
circumstances required that this directive be modified. Although he recommended that WEC Delhi and its various substations should continue to try to
relay high-grade German and Italian traffic back to Bletchley, it could not
send all of it. Moreover, WEC was to develop a substantial independent
capacity for high-grade work against Japanese ciphers. Although long-term
research into Japanese ciphers would be done by Bletchley, 'the whole of the

Japanese Cryptographic work should be done in India'. This was a major departure from previous policy.[69]

WEC therefore expanded fast using GHQ India as its cover, hence its designation GHQ(x). It occupied the buildings of Ramjas College which had been a former part of Delhi University, a few miles outside the city. This organisation, with over 1,000 staff, had none of the professorial eccentricities and informality that characterised Bletchley. Its commander, Colonel Marr-Johnston, ran it not only with strict security but also with military formality, although many of the intercept operators were Indian civilians.[70] WEC also maintained three outstations, the Wireless Experimental Depot at Abbotabad near the Afghan frontier, the Western Wireless Sub-centre in southern India on the northern outskirts of Bangalore and the Eastern Wireless Sub-centre at Barrackpore near Calcutta and close to Slim's rear area HQ. The daily product from the outstations was taken by safe hand to WEC.[71] Adjacent to WEC there was also an 'enormous' American sigint station at Delhi with the laconic title 'US 8' which worked closely with WEC and its sub-stations, routinely sharing out intercept tasks. There were also a host of mobile field units working on low-level tactical traffic.[72]

As well as trying to 'break' Japanese cryptographic systems convention-ally, WEC also interrogated captured Japanese cryptographers. These rare and important POWs were flown back to CSDIC HQ at the Red Fort at Delhi and subjected to cheerful and considerate treatment. They were remarkably forthcoming. WEC personnel like Alan Stripp chose to treat them as fellow professionals and engaged them in conversation on the technicalities of Japanese procedure, whereupon the Japanese would confirm or politely cor-rect the contentions put to them. Later on, personnel from WEC were attached to Intelligence Assault Units with the less fruitful task of attempting to recover cryptographic archives from the retreating Japanese.[73]

WEC achieved the first piecemeal penetration of the high-level Army cipher systems in March 1943, with the first readings of the Japanese Army 'water transport code'. This provided clues to a variety of other systems and new advances in Washington and across the Pacific followed. In August 1943 the solving of the 'address code' used in messages released an avalanche of information about the Japanese Army O of B. By the end of the year the chief administrative code of the Japanese Army had also been penetrated. Two months later, with the capture of a complete copy of this code and some of the mechanical cryptographic devices associated with it, Japanese Army communications were largely compromised.[74]

Yet this picture of an increasingly generous flow of sigint on the Japanese Army after March 1943 presents a major historical problem. It is difficult to reconcile with Slim's own account of the Burma War which repeatedly suggests the opposite, emphasising a severe shortage of intelligence to underpin his operations:

Improving as our intelligence was since 1942, it was far from being as complete or accurate as that in other theatres. We never made up for the lack of methodically collected intelligence, or the intelligence organisation which should have been available to us when the war began. We knew something of Japanese intentions, but little of the disposition of their reserves, and practically nothing about one of the most important factors that a general has to consider – the character of the opposing commanders.

Alan Stripp, in his own invaluable WEC memoir, has attempted to reconcile the evidence. He points out that Slim was writing almost twenty years before the Ultra secret made its way into the public domain. Accordingly Stripp argues that Slim's well-known complaints about intelligence for the 14th Army may have applied mainly to SIS, rather than sigint, which Slim could not refer to at his time of writing. As we have seen, Slim's unhappiness with the many human agent organisations, especially SIS, had prompted his ferocious attack at Barrackpore in late 1944.[75] This interpretation is supported by the memoir of Frederick Winterbotham, a sigint distribution specialist, who visited SEAC in 1944. Slim reportedly spoke to him of his satisfaction with the material he was receiving. Winterbotham visited Slim at his forward headquarters located in a large and beautiful house with spacious gardens at Comilla. The sort of material that Slim was receiving here concerned operational and movement orders, strengths, locations and other OB material. The most crucial material gave indications of shortages of rations and equipment. During the desperate battles of Imphal and Kohima this revealed that the Japanese supply position was hopeless and so the Japanese objective had been to capture supply depots. This gave Slim's staff the confidence to stand their ground in a battle that proved to be the turning point in the Burma War.[76]

Yet more recent documentary evidence demonstrates that, despite Slim's praise for the specific achievements of sigint, which were substantial, nevertheless Slim believed that he was being short-changed compared to other theatres. Nor was Slim alone in his concerns about sigint, for in the spring of 1943 Wavell too had complained to London about the poor quality of intelligence about the Japanese Air Force. London had admitted that material was 'scanty' and that improvements in the sigint network across the whole region were required.[77]

There were three reasons for this deficiency. First, Japanese commanders did not communicate with their senior commanders and with the Japanese rear area headquarters in Indochina frequently or in much detail. So there were few indicators of intention. Second, some Japanese cipher systems remained unbroken. On 1 October 1944 the combined effect of these problems was bluntly summarised by Lamplough, SEAC's Director of Intelligence, in a personal letter to Victor Cavendish-Bentinck of the JIC in London:

> What we know and what we don't know. We *know* the total strength of the Japanese Army, Air Force, and Navy in S.E.A.C. We also *know* the composition of these forces in sufficient detail. We also *know* the location of the more important H.Q.'s, down to Adv. Div. H.Q.'s in most cases. We can usually say if and when reinforcements are likely to come into S.E.A.C. All the above is from SIGINT. We do not know Japanese intentions and can only guess what they may be in the light of the known facts mentioned above.

It was these limitations on the quality of sigint that had propelled Slim in his attempts to control SIS in 1944, in an effort to improve his human agent sources. Lamplough also identified a third problem which ensured that sigint was not being used to its greatest effect. In SEAC the local JIC system for assimilating intelligence and feeding it into current operational planning left much to be desired. It looked good in theory but 'in practice here it does not work'. Indeed in the twelve months in which SEAC had existed the three service directors of intelligence who constituted the core local JIC membership had never met together once.[78]

To make matters worse, related deception measures that had worked well in Europe and the Middle East had much less effect in Burma. Deception had not worked well because Japanese commanders had poor intelligence and did not always take much notice when it was available. D Division, SEAC's deception planners, lamented that in March 1944 the Japanese commander in Burma had set out with three divisions to conquer a subcontinent which Tokyo had assured him was garrisoned with more than fifty British divisions.[79] In the spring of 1945 London had developed schemes designed to draw Japanese forces away from Malaya, but these were never operationalised.[80] Extra deception resources sent out by London did not arrive until July 1945. Radio deception was employed to try to cover a number of strategic moves, but the results were unknown, other than for a single operation to hide the real location at which the 14th Army would cross the Irrawady River, which 'achieved its object most effectively'.[81] In the war against Japan, for a variety of reasons, some beyond British control, commanders in the Far East did not receive the level of support from sigint or deception that was enjoyed elsewhere.

SEAC, sigint and the end of the war, 1944–1945

By mid-1944 the higher direction of the war in Burma and throughout South East Asia had completely passed to SEAC, along with the subordinate service headquarters, and they now constituted the main consumers of sigint in the region. Locally, intercepted material was turned into a digestible form by the SEAC Signals Intelligence Directorate. The separate Service headquarters were the ultimate authorities on OB questions, while SEAC itself handled strategic material for Mountbatten and also intelligence policy. Lengthy reports were largely avoided and so-called 'hot' items were relayed immediately to forward commanders. Each afternoon, after due consultation about the subjects of current interest, key items were annotated and clipped to a single board, which was then quickly circulated to a limited number of officers.

Yet this new command contained some strange and disturbing anachronisms. When an American liaison officer visited SEAC in March 1945 he found that the officers supplying sigint on the Japanese air OB were preoccupied with 'selling' their material to high-ranking RAF officers who were unfamiliar with sigint and were 'still reluctant to believe the stuff is really accurate and reliable'. Even more remarkably, at Mountbatten's well-appointed and generously staffed SEAC headquarters, proper provision for the secure handling of sigint had not yet been made. He reported:

Major Lane's small [Ultra OB] section was housed in one room of a basha shared with other intelligence outfits not briefed for Ultra, under conditions obviously unsuitable from the point of view of security. The physical arrangements were such that all sorts of odd characters, all legitimately within the headquarters area but thoroughly unsanitary from our point of view, could and did wander in and out of Major Lane's office more or less at will.

All this was somewhat reminiscent of Hong Kong in 1938 and reflected the fact that Britain continued to give Europe priority for staff until the end of the war against Germany.[82]

Efforts to place sigint on an efficient basis in SEAC only appear to have begun at the end of 1944 as Mountbatten began to contemplate large offensive amphibious operations. This was helped by the completion of the BRUSA Circuit which linked Bletchley, Colombo, Melbourne, Honolulu and Washington at speed by means of automatic teleprinter.[83] Mountbatten's large sigint station at Anderson was alone in not enjoying these automatic systems and this continued to cause problems. In late July 1944 the US Naval Liaison officer at Anderson, Commander Fabian, complained to Somerville that he was not being shown all the reports that concerned the Americans and he thought 'these were being deliberately held back'. Although Somerville conceded that the Anderson staff had been rather lax, he rightly pointed out that such suspicions were bound to arise where all the product was not automatically shared. Somerville added that: 'As is well known, all officers engaged in this special class of work are a bit odd and peculiar, and tend to become very short tempered.'[84]

Tempers continued to flare at Anderson during 1944. Although the work was vital it was also extremely monotonous 'and in this climate especially tends to breed discontent'. Somerville tried to counter this by giving 'off the record' talks to the Anderson staff, showing the important part they were playing in recent operations against the Japanese. On 2 June 1944 he spoke of their crucial contribution to the destruction of a large Japanese naval force off Sourabaya.[85] Sigint from Anderson also gave advanced warning of the Japanese withdrawal from the Andoman and Nicobar Islands, resulting in the destruction of the convoy and the Japanese cruiser *Haguro*. In mid-July 1945 Mountbatten told the staff that in operational terms they were worth 'ten divisions'.[86]

Disputes between Somerville and Bletchley over specific technical issues at Anderson inevitably transmuted themselves into general issues of authority. These problems became so acute that the Admiralty had to despatch an investigative team, which included Commander Ian Fleming of NID 17. They ruled in Somerville's favour and recommended that Anderson be controlled by Somerville's Chief Intelligence Officer as the local representative of the London Signals Intelligence Board who was even given a say in BRUSA policy decisions. This was indicative of the way in which operational pressures resulted in a general diminution of the central power during the war. In the late spring of 1945 London fought back with a new 'charter' making regional units more responsible to the London Signals Intelligence Board. But by the summer of 1945 the Japanese Navy had all but vanished from the Indian Ocean, while the British Pacific Fleet was supplied with sigint from Honolulu.[87]

Somerville never achieved the long-desired link with Washington that would have cut out Bletchley. It may have been his persistence in seeking this that ensured his transfer in mid-1944 to become head of the British Admiralty Delegation in Washington. His new post allowed him to visit the main US Navy sigint operation at the Op-20-G Communication Annex in late 1944 where he was received by the commander, Captain Wenger. Somerville was stunned by the vast scale of the operation which had 'been built up apparently regardless of cost and is extremely well equipped and organised'. Perhaps Somerville now began to appreciate Bletchley's reservations about the possible defection of their Asian outstations to this larger American organism. American post-war predominance in the resource-hungry field of cryptanalysis was already emerging.

Somerville was also impressed by American candour about some of their security failures which seemed to compete with Britain's spectacular loss of a 'Purple' analogue as the Japanese advanced on Singapore in 1942. He was shown some 'interesting' diagrams concerning the effect on Japanese ciphers of stories by a US war correspondent after Midway concerning the ability of the Americans to read Japanese messages. 'This produced immediate reaction in the shape of cypher changes which had been a continual headache to the establishment ever since.' There had been equally alarming mishaps in Europe:

I was also informed that a US Army cypher machine had been loaded onto a lorry in France for transfer to a Divisional HQ and that while the driver was either having a meal or was asleep the lorry had been stolen and there was no trace of the Machine. As a result of this appalling negligence some 60,000 wheels used in this machine will have to be rewired and the cypher is technically compromised until this has been done.[88]

Somerville also heard tell of the bitter infighting over sigint between the two American Services. A joint co-ordinating committee set up in June 1944 had made no progress. In February 1945 Marshall and King, the two service chiefs, had to put their personal weight behind a higher-level Army–Navy Communications Intelligence Board. However these problems persisted into the 1950s.[89]

Other aspects of post-war sigint were prefigured in the Far Eastern War, including the rise of an important new sub-field known as electronic intelligence. During 1944 a small band of British and American officers at SEAC began to operate special 'ferret' aircraft to monitor Japanese radar developments. By early 1945 this had developed into a substantial organisation, the SEAC 'Noise Investigation Bureau', under Dr Fareday, which worked closely with similar units under MacArthur. Most of their work was carried out by elaborately modified Halifaxes and Liberators belonging to the Special Radar Investigation Flights of 159 and 160 Squadrons. Some Japanese radar stations on the Andaman Islands were also physically inspected during a remarkable operation by OSS.[90] By the end of the war specialist Radio Counter-Measures Intelligence Parties were searching for abandoned equipment as troops entered Rangoon and other major centres.[91]

As the Far Eastern War drew to a close, interest in the diplomatic material being exchanged between Tokyo and its ambassadors in Berlin and Moscow became intense. In August 1944, the Japanese instructed Oshima in Berlin to urge the Germans to make a separate peace with Russia, to facilitate concentration against Britain and the United States. By late March 1945 they had won over Ribbentrop, but not Hitler. In May 1945, Moscow denounced her neutrality pact with Japan, pre-figuring her advance into Manchuria. By 11 July, sigint revealed 'frantic attempts' by Tokyo to secure Russian assistance as mediator for peace between Japan and the West, prior to Molotov's departure for the Potsdam Conference. But Moscow was clearly quite uninterested.[92]

Conclusion

From the point of view of the efficient conduct of the war against Japan, Bletchley's decisions to stay in the business of breaking high-level Japanese codes, and to obstruct direct links between its Far Eastern outstations and the vast American sigint operations on the outskirts of Washington made little sense. The resources that Bletchley's Hut 7 and Block B under Hugh Foss could devote to Japanese cryptography were paltry. As one contemporary from Bletchley has observed: 'All in all the value of this work seen in retrospect was highly questionable. The American effort was much larger than ours and their coverage was more extensive.' But this was to ignore the importance of politics of intelligence. Bletchley was also required to defend national assets and areas of advantage against a partner whose vast technological resources were already apparent even in 1943. This was, after all, the 'crown jewels' of Britain's intelligence apparatus, and efforts to maintain at least some sort of foothold appeared only prudent.[93]

Remarkably, as early as September 1944, managers at Bletchley were recommending that efforts to get themselves in shape for the post-war period 'should take priority over the part played by G.C.&C.S. in Signals Intelligence for the Japanese war'. British work on Japanese ciphers at Bletchley was to be continued, but primarily because this area was intellectually the most demanding, and so to drop out of this area of business was to risk losing cryptanalytical skills. The real war against the Japanese in the jungles of Burma, and the command problems of Slim, did not loom large in the minds of the senior British cryptanalysts. Instead, by late 1944 the managers at Bletchley were acutely focused on the fate of their organisation in the post-war period.[94]

But the realpolitik required to manage intricate intelligence alliances, together with the need to consider Britain's future place amongst other leading intelligence powers, only explains part of the picture. Throughout the Far Eastern War, Wavell, Somerville, Slim and Mountbatten all complained independently of being 'starved' of sigint, just as they were starved of other types of war materials. The provisions made for the creation of WEC in India, which was largely constructed with local resources, and the lack of automation at Anderson, were only two examples of the shameful under-resourcing of the sigint effort in Asia, compared to other theatres. In September 1944, loud complaints by Mountbatten led to a major conference in London, which recommended a package of reforms designed to improve sigint for SEAC. But at the end of February 1945, Mountbatten penned an irate personal letter to Menzies asking why the London Signals Intelligence Board had still not implemented these measures. Menzies' reply is not on file.[95]

Part 4

Rivalry or rivalries? China, 1942–1945

14   American struggles in China: OSS and Naval Group

> I deplored the fragmentation of the American presence in China under the military and wartime agencies that left it a multiheaded monster incapable of a unified policy.
>
> John King Fairbank, OSS in China, 1942[1]

America and China

The importance of China within the overall conception of American policy in Asia during the Second World War cannot be overstated. For Roosevelt, China offered many possibilities, but above all it constituted an important long-term element in his attempt to re-shape the world according to the internationalist principles of freedom and democracy. In November 1943 Roosevelt wrote privately to Mountbatten, who had just arrived in SEAC, to explain that, while China was currently weak, nevertheless: 'I really feel it is a triumph to have got the four hundred and twenty five million Chinese on the Allied side. This will be very useful twenty five or fifty years hence, even though China cannot contribute much military or naval support for the moment.'[2] China, it seemed could provide a buffer between American and Soviet spheres in the Pacific and, because of her hostility to the treaty port system, sided with the United States on dismantling the colonial empires.[3]

But Roosevelt's vision, although prescient, often ignored the immediate practicalities of dealing with Chiang Kai-shek's Koumintang (KMT) regime, which consisted of a fragile coalition of landlords, tycoons and independently minded generals. The KMT had reacted to the Japanese invasion in 1937 by trading space for time and retreating into the hinterland, establishing a new capital at Chungking. After December 1941, Chiang Kai-shek was content to pursue a phoney war with the Japanese, who were now over-extended, while waiting for the war to be won elsewhere. Meanwhile they hoarded American supplies, awaiting a coming civil war against the Chinese Communists. The KMT were painfully aware of the speed with which the Communists were using wartime conditions to help them expand their territorial base.

Moreover, disappointed by previous attempts to secure alliances with the Soviet Union and Germany in the inter-war period, all foreign assistance, although necessary, was a matter for legitimate KMT suspicion.[4]

American policy was not improved by the improbable nature of the American military, civilian and intelligence organisations operating in China, which at times seemed no less absorbed in Byzantine struggles than the KMT. The contest between the two main American clandestine organisations in China, OSS and Naval Group China, which also embroiled their British and Chinese counterparts, holds a significance that extends beyond the politics of secret service into the wider currents of international history. As the historian Michael Schaller has pointed out, the opposing elements of OSS and Naval Group China also stand symbolically for paths chosen, and paths not chosen, in Washington's East Asia policy. OSS, through its part in the famous Dixie Mission to the Communists in Yenan, and because of its independent lines of communication to the White House, probably offered the United States the best opportunity of objectively reassessing its commitment to the KMT regime.

In contrast, Naval Group China worked intimately with, supplied and trained the KMT's fearsome secret police, the euphemistically named 'Bureau of Information and Statistics' under General Tai Li.[5] Naval Group constituted the American organisation closest to the inner circles of the KMT and most firmly committed to counter-revolution.[6] Naval Group achieved its unique co-operation with the KMT by abandoning the mainstream American policy of reconciliation with the Communists, and of urging an anti-Japanese coalition upon the Chungking government. Naval Group's line endeared it to the inner circles of the KMT. This, in turn, served the interests of the US Navy who resented the dominance of Stilwell and the US Army in China.[7] Both OSS and Naval Group played a role in shaping Sino-American mutual perceptions that belied their relatively small size.[8]

Naval Group and OSS arrive in China

When representatives of Tai Li proposed the establishment of Naval Group China in the summer of 1941 during discussions with the US Army and US Navy in Washington, neither showed much interest. But after Pearl Harbor intelligence from the Western Pacific took on a new urgency for the Navy, meanwhile, their long-standing intelligence officer in Chungking, the US Naval Attaché, James McHugh, had fallen under a cloud because of his close relations with the British. Tai Li's proposal now received the support of Admiral King, who chose Lt Commander Milton Miles, who had served in China in the 1920s, to lead a naval mission.[9] Miles was given the broadest of remits: to gather intelligence, to harass the Japanese and to test some experimental sabotage weapons. Arriving in April 1942, he was attached to the American Embassy as 'Naval Observer'.[10]

Tai Li, his main collaborator, was perhaps the single most powerful figure in Nationalist China aside from Chiang himself, personally commanding a secret police force estimated at about 40,000. Tai Li was also a member of a powerful Army clique. His principal duty was regime security both inside and outside nationalist China, together with guerrilla operations against the Communists. Chou En-lai, the Communist representative in Chungking, asserted that he was also *de facto* controller of most of the KMT's military communications, finances and some aspects of its foreign policy. Chiang's approach to controlling the KMT, which emphasised an equilibrium of forces, meant that Tai Li was balanced by one of the other four KMT secret service groups, the 'party police'. Nevertheless, American officials noted that Tai's position was special, symbolising the underlying texture of the regime, viewing him as 'the personification of the latter day repressive tendencies of the Koumintang'.[11]

Miles was fully cogniscent of the activities of Tai Li's BIS organisation, which had liquidated thousands of Chiang's opponents and earned him the soubriquet the 'Chinese Himmler'.[12] But in a China that was fantastically obstructive, chaotic and corrupt, Miles nevertheless found Tai Li to be reliable, efficient and superbly orderly, joking that at least he had 'never had anyone shot without proper authorization'. Miles quickly agreed to work under Tai Li's direction in return for real intelligence co operation.[13]

Miles began his work with a formidable three-month tour of China, partly behind Japanese lines, during which his party was bombed and Miles was seriously burned. On this eventful tour Tai Li offered him the opportunity to train a Chinese force of 50,000 guerrillas, which was quickly accepted. Miles was impressed by the unaccustomed freedom with which he was able to move around China with Tai Li's support and the corresponding intelligence opportunities from networks that reached all the way to the eastern seaboard. By the end of 1942, 6,000 guerrillas had been trained, intelligence and sabotage activities had commenced, all on the basis of an informal agreement with Tai Li. Naval Group was already far ahead of any other Allied secret service in China.[14]

Miles' uncritical relationship with Tai Li ensured that he did not enjoy good relations with General Stilwell, whose efforts to persuade the KMT to reform their military system and commit to the war with Japan were as abrasive as they were ineffective. Stilwell took an immediate dislike to Miles, who responded by supporting General Claire Chennault, Commander of the 14th Air Force in China and an advocate of winning the war in China through air power. Together with the US Naval Attaché in China he campaigned for Stilwell's recall in favour of Chennault. In their reports, which reached

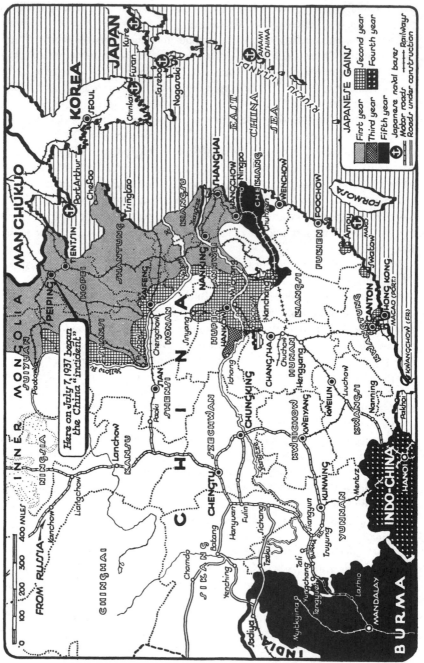

5 The China Theater

Roosevelt, they also campaigned for an end to Stilwell's efforts to press military reforms upon Chiang, advocating instead an unrestricted flow of aid, tied to post-war trade opportunities.[15]

Miles and Naval Group suffered poor relations not only with Stilwell, but with anyone else who adopted a critical perspective on the KMT, including OSS, with whom Naval Group began to work in 1942. This relationship began quite accidentally in April as Miles made his way out to Chungking via Calcutta. Here, quite by chance, he met A. R. Lusey of Donovan's organisation, and later extended to him an invitation to join his introductory tour of China with Tai Li. Like Miles, Lusey was quick to appreciate the vast intelligence opportunities offered by the developing Miles–Tai Li relationship. Lusey worked with Miles and Tai Li on a number of projects, including propaganda broadcasts into India and Afghanistan, and also 'a very comprehensive intercept station'. Tai Li's only inflexible condition for co-operating fully with both Miles and Lusey was that there should be no contact with the British. Nevertheless, Lusey was under no illusions: 'the inner circle of Tai Li's organisation were 'a bunch of cutthroats' and 'utterly ruthless'.[16]

Returning to Washington, Lusey discovered that OSS had just received its charter and that Donovan was now anxious to make up for lost time by co-opting any available network. This attitude was partly driven by the fact that Donovan's previous attempts to get into Asia had met with repeated failure. His first China initiative had been overtaken by the Japanese attack in December 1941, and the second, the 'Esson Gale Mission' of January 1942 had produced an unworkable scheme that was quickly dropped.[17] Even Donovan's carefully crafted Eifler Mission to Stilwell's CBI had found itself in semi-exile in Assam, while a separate mission to CBI under Joseph Hayden had come to nothing. Therefore by the summer of 1942 Donovan was desperate to establish OSS in China and so opened talks with the US Navy. On 19 September 1942 they agreed that Miles should also be designated head of OSS in China, informing Miles of his newly extended responsibilities in a letter that travelled slowly by 'safe hand'.[18]

Accordingly, because of the tardy progress of this letter, the omniscient Tai Li learned of this appointment from a number of sources even before Miles, such as OSS elements arriving in Burma under the auspices of Stilwell.[19] When asked about this new title by Tai Li, Miles, in good faith, firmly denied being in charge of OSS. The KMT knew otherwise and were immensely sensitive to unauthorised foreign activities, and so their relations cooled. Meanwhile Miles suspected Stilwell of embarking on the construction of some rival apparatus in parallel to Naval Group. The confusion was not resolved until Lusey reappeared in China with Washington's documents, explaining the joint OSS–Navy decision.[20]

Considerable damage had been inflicted on Miles by this OSS link. Tai Li was immensely suspicious of anyone who enjoyed close relations with the British, including the embryonic OSS and also the Anglophile US Naval Attaché in China, James McHugh. The first OSS officers arriving in China had associated with SOE at a time when the British were least popular, with their commando training staff being ejected from China.[21] Although Tai Li's relationship with Miles was restored, questions continued to be asked about the OSS presence. While Tai Li and Miles could not prove it, they rightly suspected that OSS officers sent to China to work with Miles as instructors in sabotage had a deeper secondary role as collectors of intelligence. Meanwhile Donovan was creating an entirely separate secret intelligence apparatus through the American Embassy, using representatives like John King Fairbank. The noisy OSS Hayden mission passed through Chungking at the end of 1942 and there were also a number of independent China projects being developed with Britain's SIS.[22]

Uncontrolled foreign operations in China were completely unacceptable to the KMT and so Chiang now insisted that Sino-American intelligence co-operation be codified with a formal agreement that dealt with rights and permissions. Tai Li politely explained that he wanted to avoid the misunderstandings that had bedevilled British efforts to train commando troops with SOE in China in 1942. A further important reason was logistics. Japanese gains in Burma had resulted in a deteriorating supply situation into China and Tai Li was adamant that the new agreement should ensure American proper supplies, independent of the US Army and the temperamental Stilwell. Tai Li was to be director of this new apparatus with Miles as his deputy. Predictably, many US officials, including Donovan, henceforth regarded Miles as nothing more than a tame 'procurement office' for Tai Li.[23]

In common with the many secret service agreements that had begun to appear in 1942, negotiations for what was to become known as the Sino-American Co-operative Organisation (SACO) dragged on. They were slow partly because the Chinese sought an agreement that would bind both OSS and Miles 'hand and foot' in terms of their activities in China.[24] Finally, on 31 December 1942, a conference was held at the home of T.V. Soong, the Chinese Foreign Minister, which also included Miles, Tai Li and Lusey of OSS. Soong stated that Chiang had given the organisation his blessing, but he required Roosevelt's signature on the SACO agreement.[25] Further tortuous negotiations followed in Washington during which Marshall attempted to subordinate SACO to Stilwell. But Miles and Tai Li stood their ground and made it abundantly clear that Chinese participation was dependent upon a Chinese Director of SACO.[26] The US Joint Chiefs of Staff gave their approval in February 1943, providing it with six invaluable transport planes which rendered it independent of Stilwell's supply system. Donovan remained unhappy about the degree of control accorded to the Chinese, but by 1 April

Miles had persuaded King, Marshall and Roosevelt to approve the agreement. Finally, on 15 April, Frank Knox, Secretary of the Navy, signed on Roosevelt's behalf.[27]

OSS and SACO part company

The SACO organisation, with its privileged independent supplies, expanded rapidly. By the end of the war more than fifty thousand troops were under their command, including twelve thousand guerrillas who had passed through ten training centres around China, mostly staffed by US Marine instructors, some of which were technically behind Japanese lines. By 1944, Miles title of 'Naval Observer' at the American Embassy was clearly absurd and he became commander of the re-styled Naval Group China.[28] Despite these achievements, Donovan had remained extremely unhappy with the command arrangements for SACO and, even as the agreement was signed, OSS had begun to part company. This was partly the result of pressure from the US Army, who made it very clear in October 1943 that Donovan 'should take full responsibility for Miles and his attitude of insurgency towards General Stilwell'.[29]

Donovan's determination to press forward independently in China was also informed by the fact that during the summer of 1943, Tai Li had found his own power trimmed by Chiang after a litany of disasters. In early 1942 an espionage ring, run by the formidably effective Khan Sheng, Head of Communist intelligence, was uncovered at the heart of Tai Li's organisation. A few months later his successful ouster of an SOE commando training operation from China brought him into conflict with T.V. Soong.[30] Reports varied as to the reason for his continued troubles in 1943. Some suggested Madame Chiang had picked up on the general impression in Washington that Tai Li, rather than Chiang, actually controlled China through his 'ruthless utilization of Nazi and Japanese political police methods'.[31] Others suggested that it was a result of a confrontation with the powerful interests of the Kung family and the 'rough handling of Kung proteges'. But once open criticism had begun, his enemies, 'who are legion', joined the fray. Tai Li's power was diminished and Mao Chin-hsiang, Chiang's brother-in-law by his first marriage, was brought in to head the rival KMT party police.[32] More broadly, Donovan, who always took care to acquaint himself with the latest White House thinking, knew Roosevelt was becoming frustrated with Chiang's inaction against the Japanese. Donovan could therefore afford to be abrasive.

Relations within SACO reached a crisis in November 1943 when Donovan tried to replace Navy officers and Chinese officers with OSS personnel, while simultaneously trying to integrate SACO into the OSS chain of command. Donovan displayed his unhappiness in remarkably blunt exchanges with

Chiang and Tai Li during his visit to Chungking in the first week of December 1943. On the last day of his visit Chiang treated Donovan to a stern lecture on Chinese sovereignty and emphasised that all OSS operations in China must be avowed to the Chinese. But Donovan, adopting an manner of which Stilwell would have been proud, announced his intention of with-drawing from SACO, while appointing one of Eifler's officers, Colonel John Coughlin, as Head of a separate OSS presence in China. Then, with Tai Li present, he proceeded to bait Chiang openly by taking him to task about Tai Li's activities and reputation. Miles was not at this meeting, but the inter-preter, 'a personal friend of Miles', later informed him that Donovan had enjoyed informing Chiang that:

he was requested by his President to place agents in China, and he would follow his directive accordingly. Also that if these agents were killed by General Tai Li's guards, that he, General Donovan, would replace those agents. No matter how many times these agents were wiped out they would replace these agents with other ones.

Donovan himself recounted this exchange in almost exactly the same words when visiting Mountbatten a few days later. Whatever the exact wording of Donovan's exchanges with Chiang, Tai Li and Miles, they were clearly nasty and served to underline the starkly contrasting philosophies of Donovan and Miles. Donovan was convinced that nothing could be achieved while working under the Chinese. Miles was convinced of the exact reverse and later insisted that 'every man in O.S.S. . . . in China had a complete dossier on file in the BIS, and his exact movements were kept at all times'. OSS dependence on the Chinese for agents, clerical staff and servants certainly made them rather vulnerable.[33] Yet both men had a measure of the truth, for whether through SACO, or outside SACO, the KMT were determined to keep the firmest grip on American activities. Donovan continued his campaign against Miles in Washington, but the US Joint Chiefs of Staff stepped in to affirm Miles' independence.[34]

Miles also sought to represent these conflicts with Donovan, Stilwell and later with Stilwell's successor, General Al Wedemeyer, as more than mere local theatre command politics, or traditional Army–Navy rivalry. Instead he insisted that the US Army and OSS, like the British, were guilty of an imperi-alist 'old China hand' attitude which could not tolerate a Chinese controlling interest. For Miles, as for General Hurley, the American Ambassador in Chungking, support for Chinese nationalism and opposition to both Commun-ism and foreign imperialism, were the quintessential ingredients for any suc-cessful relationship with the KMT.[35]

Roosevelt's disillusionment with Chiang had, in part, been triggered by Britain's recent refusal to assent to a northern strategy focused on the Burma Road into China. On 6 December 1943, during an interlude at the Cairo

Conference, a frustrated Roosevelt held a meandering conversation with Stilwell, John Paton Davies and Elliot Roosevelt. Roosevelt asked how long Chiang would last if the Burma route into China was not opened. Stilwell asserted that Chiang would soon be in serious difficulty. Roosevelt then replied: 'Well, then we should look for some other man, or group of men, to carry on.' Roosevelt's meaning was clear to Stilwell:

The Big boy is fed up with Chiang and with his tantrums and said so. In fact, he told me in that Olympian manner of his: 'If you can't replace him, get rid of him once and for all. You know what I mean. Put someone in you can manage'.

The tone of these discussions would certainly have confirmed all Miles' suspicions about the prevalence of the 'Old China hand' mentality.[36]

Underneath the confrontation between Miles and Donovan over control of SACO in November–December 1943 there lurked a more important and complex political conflict. Roosevelt was looking for alternatives to Chiang and as early as October 1943, Roosevelt had specifically directed Donovan to gather intelligence on Communist-controlled areas. Donovan's eventful visit to China in December 1943 was therefore not merely an attempt to control Miles and browbeat Chiang; it was also intended to arrange an intelligence mission to Communist forces in Yenan, led by himself. Miles and Tai Li were adamant in their refusal. Donovan, preoccupied with his troubled relations with Naval Group, eventually delegated the Yenan mission to another OSS officer, Brooke Dolan, who had recently contacted the Dalai Lama in Tibet. The consequent delays ensured that a joint US Army–State Department 'Dixie Mission', also launched with Roosevelt's approval, and masterminded by John Paton Davies, reached Yenan first.[37]

After a series of convoluted arguments, OSS had succeeded in attaching a team of five people to the 'Dixie Mission', whose primary purpose was to co-operate with the Communists on intelligence work, not least in investigating the KMT's armed forces, whose real fighting capability remained unknown to CBI. Real surprises awaited OSS in Yenan, where they discovered the vast intelligence potential of the Communist network. Considerable attention was given to improving the Communist radio network which proved to be supported by a British 'radio expert', Professor Michael Lindsay, who had been despatched by Colonel Harmon, the head of SIS in Chungking in December 1941. Lindsay provided a most detailed report on Communist communications to the Dixie Mission which formed the basis of OSS plans for major communications assistance to the Communists.[38]

Throughout early 1944, Roosevelt appears to have become increasingly dependent upon OSS for clear intelligence about the situation in China as he pressured Chiang to fight the Japanese. OSS intelligence on Sino-Soviet border incidents in Sinkiang and Mongolia were especially important, suggesting that Chiang had provoked the Soviets and was becoming increasingly anti-Russian. OSS suggested that uncritical support for Chiang would look like backing for internal anti-communism and therefore threaten Soviet–American relations.[39]

But, spectacularly, Miles and Tai Li succeeded in blocking any further attempts at American rapprochement with the Communists in 1944. In late 1944, in parallel to stagnating KMT–Communist discussions sponsored by Ambassador Hurley, Colonel David Barrett, leader of the Dixie Mission, remained in Yenan while an attached OSS officer, Lt Colonel Willis R. Bird, the Deputy Head of OSS China, secretly discussed plans for a large scale OSS-backed Communist offensive against the Japanese in north China. Yenan clearly thought the tide of American policy was turning and so suggested that Mao Tse-tung and Chou En-lai visit Roosevelt in Washington, hoping to escape the fruitless talks with Hurley and the KMT. This dramatic bid by the Communists also reflected their alarm at the removal of Stilwell and Hurley's gradual purging of elements critical of Chiang from the American presence in China.

American opponents of contact with the Communists, including Hurley, Joseph Grew and the new commander of the China Theater, Al Wedemeyer, first learned of this planned visit to the United States through Naval Group China. Hurley concluded that this, together with the proposed American military assistance to the Communists, represented some sort of scheme to destroy the KMT. Angry messages were fired off to Roosevelt. However, because Donovan had cultivated good personal relations with Hurley the accusations were kept vague, speaking only of 'military' plans. It was John Paton Davies, the originator of the Dixie Mission, along with its chief, Colonel Barrett, who were ejected from the theatre while OSS escaped the wrath of the ensuing enquiry.[40]

One of the most critical, but yet often unremarked, contributions made by both Naval Group and OSS, whether in China, Thailand or elsewhere, was their ability to provide their contacts with back-channels of communication with Washington. As Michael Schaller points out, Naval Group provided Hurley with a secure communications link with Washington, separate from main State Department channels that Hurley considered to be contaminated with pro-Communist sentiment. Much of the discussion concerning Stilwell's ignominious recall and replacement by Wedemeyer during September and October 1944 was sent via this channel. Naval Group was a crucial facilitator, helping to manipulate the flow of information between Chungking and Washington to press a strong pro-KMT policy.[41] In any case, by the end of January 1945, the hopes and plans of a disparate range of American elements in China for collaboration with the Communists, the most effective anti-Japanese force in China, were neutralised.

Naval Group activities

The so-called 'Dixie Mission' to the Communists in Yenan, in common with OSS 'Deer Mission' to Ho Chi Minh in Vietnam in 1945, has generated deep controversy. During the Korean War some of the architects of 'Dixie', such as John Service, were hounded as fellow travellers. John Paton Davies, whose incisive writings are quoted in this study, and whose glittering career took him on to the Policy Planning Staff in the late 1940s, was expelled by the same purge. By the 1960s Davies found himself an exiled furniture maker in Peru. A decade later, when President Richard Nixon 'rediscovered' China, the same figures were hailed as purveyors of a missed opportunity that could have saved the United States from the hottest episodes of the early Cold War. But as recent, and more balanced, historical enquiry has demonstrated, the 'Dixie Mission' was a fragmented group whose activities gradually shifted away from action towards intelligence gathering and weather reporting. The possibility of dramatic political initiatives was always somewhat remote.[42]

While the significance of the 'Dixie Mission' has tended to be exaggerated, the political dimensions of Naval Group intervention in China have probably been underplayed. During 1943 and 1944, Miles had developed a vast training and supply programme for KMT guerrillas. These were probably employed more regularly against the Communists than the Japanese, something which Miles viewed as recompense for the treasonous presence of Americans in Yenan. Other Naval Group sponsored units, especially in the north, were saving their strength for the post-war conflict with the Communists yet to come.[43] One of Miles' most important projects was the creation of a police training centre which delivered 'FBI school instruction' to Tai Li's security personnel. An unlikely collection of fifty former FBI, Narcotics Bureau, Secret Service, Treasury and New York bomb squad officers were engaged on this training programme located in Chungking from the summer of 1943. Miles viewed this programme as a key contribution to China's post-war future, confiding that it 'has a political involvement that cannot be put on paper'. During 1944, the relationship between some of Tai Li's more unsavoury repressive activities and this training school prompted Stilwell, the Army and the American Embassy to protest to Washington, but to no avail.[44]

This controversial internal security programme was directed by Commander Charles Johnson and four assistants under the title 'Unit Nine'. The first class of 110 security police assembled at Chungking in July 1943 and a second class arrived in September. Tai Li conceived of this as a pilot scheme. The same training was soon offered to larger numbers of cadets at an expanded Police School in Chungking and at Tai Li's other main training centre at Sihfeng in Kweichow Province. By January 1945, the Chungking programme boasted a camp of fifty buildings with a photographic wing, forensic identification laboratories and demolition training areas.

Growing protests that Naval Group were assisting in the creation of a police state forced cosmetic changes. The title of the Chungking centre was changed from 'Police and Investigators School' to 'Intelligence and Counter-Espionage Unit', in order to lend it a spurious wartime focus.[45] Early accounts of Naval Group attempted to dismiss the 'frightening mythology' around Tai Li, claiming that 'most of the tales were untrue'.[46] However, the contradictory evidence is overwhelming, and the reputation for torture and execution only too well founded. John Paton Davies, Stilwell's shrewd political adviser, wrote to Donovan warning him that its 'scientific police methods' were used 'primarily against other Chinese and only secondarily – if at all – against the enemy'.[47] In September 1944, Stilwell despatched Davies to Washington for private discussions with Roosevelt's trusted emissary, Harry Hopkins, and offered a lengthy catalogue of Miles' more distasteful activities. Hopkins conceded they were bad enough to have 'endangered American interests'. But Roosevelt's removal of Stilwell during that month threw the complaint into disarray.[48]

Yet Miles' claim that results in China could only be obtained by working wholeheartedly with the KMT were supported by the scale of its intelligence activities against Japan. Miles was a key intelligence distributor in the theatre, feeding material from Chinese sources and SACO coast-watching nets to American formations. He also served as the main interface between Chennault's 14th Air Force and the Pacific Fleet. In early 1944 Naval Group presided over its own large photo-interpretation unit and was responsible for training all American bomber crews in recognition for maritime reconnaissance. By June 1944 Miles had also established a naval operational intelligence headquarters at Kunming, which was later commended for locating a hitherto undetected Japanese carrier force. Naval Group moved seamlessly to take charge of the aerial mining of the China coast and the Yangtze River, implemented by the 14th Air Force. The reluctance of the US Navy in Washington to give their sigint to Chennault made Miles all the more valuable.[49]

Wedemeyer's search for control

With Roosevelt's approval, OSS circumvented the restrictions of the SACO agreement by seeking out powerful allies in China in the shape of Chennault's 14th Air Force, and later General Al Wedemeyer, the commander of the new China Theater, who arrived in October 1944. The former possibility had in fact been explored as early as 1942.[50] By December 1943, when Donovan appointed Colonel John Coughlin to replace Miles as the Head of OSS in China, Chennault looked an increasingly attractive sponsor, seeming to offer some escape from Army–Navy controversies. Outwardly OSS maintained some links with SACO at Chungking, but increasingly sought to divert them with dull research and analysis projects.[51]

In July 1944, Donovan explained to Roosevelt how much of OSS in China had merged with A-2, the intelligence staff of the 14th Air Force, to form the 'Air and Ground Forces Resource and Technical Staff', with its deliberately unpronounceable AGFRTS, hidden in a sprawling network of airfields at Kunming.[52] Kunming was located in the southern province of Yunnan, where Chiang's power was weak. The OSS relationship with AGFRTS had followed 'a great deal of discussion with theatre officers' and was backed by John Paton Davies. To facilitate this new system Chennault had transferred '14 of his key officers to OSS'.[53] OSS also pervaded other American organisations in China such as the Air–Ground Aid Service (AGAS), officially for the recovery of downed pilots. OSS achieved their more significant accomplishments in China under these covers.[54]

While operationally successful, these covers brought their own problems, inspiring jealousy from Army G-2 officers in CBI and, more importantly, raising the spectre of OSS in China being swallowed by Chennault. John Coughlin articulated such fears as early as April 1944.[55] Fears of being gobbled up by Chennault's 14th Air Force were articulated even more strongly by Coughlin's replacement, Richard Heppner, when the two OSS chiefs in SEAC and China effectively swopped appointments in November 1944. Wedemeyer, the commander of the new China Theater had previously served as Mountbatten's Deputy Chief of Staff in SEAC and had specifically asked to bring Heppner with him from SEAC as his new OSS chief. Heppner's good personal relationship with Wedemeyer at last offered the chance to put OSS on a proper footing in China.[56]

Accordingly, OSS only finalised its relationship to the newly constituted theatre commander and with Chennault in November 1944. Lt Commander Turner H. McBaine, the Head of OSS SI in the Far East, had taken the opportunity to review the future of OSS in China for the rest of the war, identifying three options. The first option was to work within the 'preclusive' SACO agreement under which OSS could legally do very little. 'We have, of course, worked outside of SACO and are carrying on a precarious extra-legal existence through respectable organisations such as the 14th Air Force, Theatre G-2, and others, which for a substantial consideration, have offered us shelter.' But this informal arrangement, he maintained, could not go on. In any confrontations with the Chinese over this they were outside the protection of Wedemeyer. But, more alarmingly, OSS were being forced 'to sell our birthright' as an intelligence organisation, to their hosts. Intelligence produced by OSS in China was not being distributed as OSS intelligence and so they gained no credit, moreover they did not control the distribution list. For example, with the 14th Air Force:

The price we pay for AGFRTS and for the magic of Chennault's name is the intelligence we produce. A-2 [Chief of Air Force Intelligence] naturally takes the position that he acquires title to what is produced by those in his employ. It is a master–servant relationship, not a partnership.

This was equally true of the relationship with AGAS, with the Dixie Mission in Yenan, and of many other cover organisations employed in China.

A second option was an entirely independent OSS organisation in China, of the sort that existed in Europe and the Mediterranean. But this was clearly 'impossible' because such a stand-alone body would be obstructed by Tai Li. Moreover, at present, the arrangements with Chennault and others were simply working too well to be abandoned: 'Our defense is to awe him [Tai Li] with strong patrons and to confuse him with a multiplicity of covers. We need as many as we can find or create.' McBaine therefore recommended a third way, a unique organisation for OSS, tailored to the peculiar politics of the China Theater. This third option involved a top organisation or 'holding company' under the theatre commander, headed by a senior OSS officer who would be the theatre Strategic Services Officer. But below would be a network of 'operating subsidiaries'. This would allow OSS to take some credit for its work, would extend some protection from the theatre commander, and yet cover organisations would be exploited. Moreover, there would be no need for a violent confrontation with SACO and Tai Li, with whom token relations would be maintained.[57]

Donovan accepted these recommendations, but remained acutely conscious of the potential for OSS to be damaged in major political confrontations over China, which never seemed far away. He therefore worked hard to keep Roosevelt informed of the OSS–Miles situation. In November 1944, he wrote to the President at length, further justifying his decision to work outside SACO:

For eight months after SACO we tried to abide faithfully by its terms and to carry out our functions within the limitations it imposed. But the position was an impossible one. So far as OSS is concerned, no intelligence or operations of any consequence have come out of SACO since its inception . . . the essential reason is that we were placed under the operational control of men determined that we should not carry out our principal function, i.e. to produce intelligence.

OSS, he explained, having teemed up with Chennault and some 'independents', was moving from strength to strength.[58] With the approval of Roosevelt, and of the theatre command in China, McBaine's template became the way ahead for OSS during the last year of the war in China. However the

14 General Wedemeyer, Commander Milton Miles of Naval Group and Chiang Kai-shek

transition was not as smooth as McBaine had hoped. The opportunities offered by Stilwell's recall were temporarily overshadowed by the infamous 'Miller Incident'. In mid-October 1944 a senior OSS officer, General L. H. Miller, used a dinner with Tai Li to launch into a vitriolic two-hour attack upon Chiang Kai-shek and all things Chinese, with much recourse to mule-drivers' language. The shock-waves reached as far as Washington and marred the beginning of a new chapter in China for OSS.[59]

The arrival of Wedemeyer in China, and of Sultan in the small India–Burma theatre, in the autumn of 1944 did not signal an end to confrontations over secret service. It did, however, usher in a new phase in which OSS, for the first time, enjoyed a proper footing, with Heppner's OSS headquarters located close to Wedemeyer's office in Chungking. The well-known diffi-culties between OSS and Naval Group, together with an accelerating dispute with Mountbatten over Indochina and the 'Gentleman's Agreement', alerted Wedemeyer to the problems in this area. Wedemeyer was therefore deter-mined to ensure that at least in China there was nothing ambiguous about his control of secret service activity, whether by American, British or French organisations.

Most problematic for Wedemeyer was Naval Group. Wedemeyer was deeply worried about a public outcry in the United States about American support for Tai Li's more distasteful activities, or that they would provoke a wider civil war before the end of the conflict with Japan. His growing distaste for Miles pushed him closer to OSS. During December 1944 and January 1945, Wedemeyer held a series of meetings with Donovan and Miles in which he tried to subordinate SACO to OSS, in clear violation of the original SACO agreement. Miles viewed this as a pro-Communist initiative and persuaded Admiral King in Washington to intervene. In practice Wedemeyer was overtly sympathetic neither to the Communists nor to Miles' fiercely pro-KMT position, although he did join with Hurley to purge pro-Communists elements from administrative staffs.[60]

By the end of 1944 Miles was regarded with almost universal distaste. On 26 June 1944 Mountbatten had written to Donovan to explain that he 'had to have one of Miles's officers removed from Ceylon' for unacceptable behaviour.[61] When Wedemeyer began his major re-organisation of secret service organisations in China during late 1944, Mountbatten asked Menzies in London whether he would accept a scheme for more co-ordination of OSS and SIS activities in China. Menzies attached only one stringent condition: 'You should state definitely that this offer of co-ordination is entirely dependent on the complete removal of MILES and his organisation. Without this I see no possibility of the scheme working.' Mountbatten agreed and passed on Menzies' views to Wedemeyer.[62] By January 1945, as we shall see, Wedemeyer and Miles were in open confrontation, with the latter inevitably claiming that his authority and directives came from Admiral King in Washington. After weeks of evasion, Wedemeyer finally took Miles back to Washington for a heated debate with the US Joint Chiefs of Staff. In April 1945 Wedemeyer won his struggle, subordinating not only the OSS, but also the Naval Group component of SACO, to his command. However, the war was almost over.[63]

Conclusions

By the spring of 1945, the United States had simultaneously explored both modes of liaison with its Chinese allies: the avowed under Naval Group and the unavowed under OSS. It is difficult to conjure up a balanced appreciation of the work of Naval Group in China. Its achievements against both the Japanese and the Communists were significant. But its most impressive aspect was the genuinely close relationship of mutual respect and trust with one of the most powerful KMT organisations. Miles could claim an instinctive, if not an analytically clear, understanding of the Chinese, their customs and the limitations of their governmental system. Moreover, he fully embraced the xenophobic nationalism of the right wing of the KMT. His officers 'slept, played and fought with the Chinese ... even celebrated each other's holidays ... Miles demanded good relations even above success, but success followed easily.'[64] Yet the price of this special relationship with the KMT was high.

The unavowed route taken by OSS in China was not only different, but needs to be considered comparatively, for, unlike Naval Group, OSS was a global organisation. Despite the indignity of being forced to operate under cover in an American-dominated theatre, OSS fared better in China than in neighbouring American commands by 1945. Despite the strenuous efforts of Donovan, neither Admiral Nimitz in the Pacific nor General MacArthur in SWPA would allow proper OSS organisations to enter their territory.[65]

This book does not extend to MacArthur's SWPA or Nimitz's Pacific Ocean Area (POA), which have been thoroughly analysed elsewhere. Nevertheless, some understanding of the misfortunes of OSS there is essential to place the OSS China predicament in perspective. General MacArthur and SWPA presented Donovan with a formidable opponent. In June 1943 in Washington, Donovan developed plans to send Joseph Hayden as his emissary to SWPA, hoping to build up MacArthur's confidence in OSS. But Hayden, who had endured the hostility of Stilwell on a similar mission to CBI in 1942, and who knew all about MacArthur and his staff, expressed 'reluctance to going'.[66] By the beginning of 1945 Donovan had managed to second thirteen personnel to MacArthur for guerrilla work in the Philippines, but they did not function as an OSS unit.[67] MacArthur was proud that he had managed to keep SWPA free of OSS and on 23 May 1945 declared that: 'The OSS has not up to the present time operated within this area, I know little of its methods, have no control of its agencies, and consequently have no plans for its future employment.'[68]

OSS did not fare much better in Nimitz's POA. A handful of R&A staff were attached to service intelligence branches at Honolulu and Fort Shafter to study psychological warfare as early March 1942. But further expansion was blocked. It was only in April 1944 that Donovan persuaded Nimitz to tolerate one single theatre Strategic Services Officer, Dr Lovell, at his HQ.[69] Donovan continued to court Nimitz assiduously. In July 1944, seeking to advertise his services, Donovan sent Nimitz a gift of a special pistol with a silencer. Nimitz and his aide were amused and immediately tested it outside, scoring 81 and 95 respectively in a stiff breeze. But they were not won over.[70] In October 1944, OSS put up a plan to make available to POA intelligence on Japan gathered in China, but this would clearly have involved vast duplication with existing bodies.[71] Nimitz's refusals were polite but firm, insisting on US Joint Chiefs of Staff clearance, which never came.[72] As in SWPA, only a handful of specialist OSS personnel ever made their way to Hawaii.[73] Only a single OSS liaison officer accompanied Lt General S. B. Buckner of the 10th Army during the invasion of Okinawa.[74] The British were conscious of the irony of the harsh treatment of OSS in American-controlled theatres. Indeed, they enjoyed reminding Donovan of this, offering him expanded facilities for OSS in SEAC in return for his arranging reciprocal expanded rights for the British in SWPA where, as they knew full well, Donovan's organisation cut no ice at all.[75]

It is hardly surprising, then, that OSS were schizophrenic about their presence in SEAC. Under Mountbatten they may have had to tolerate the attentions of a diverse range of unsympathetic organisations, from SOE to the vast security apparatus of IB and GHQ India. But at least they enjoyed a large open presence and, from the outset, were conducting a substantial range of operations under a commander who was wholly convinced of their utility. Curiously, of all the theatres in Asia and Pacific, it was probably within SEAC that OSS was least fettered. Commander Edmond Taylor wrote from SEAC in July 1944, that in spite of their political differences, 'actually OSS has more freedom of action and enjoys more high level military support in this purely British theatre than in any theatre in the world'.[76] Colonel Richard Heppner was of the same opinion and pointed out to Donovan in June 1944 that 'our presence in South East Asia is of great significance to long-term United States policy since we are able to operate with more liberty into Thailand and Indochina [from SEAC] than from any other theater'.[77] Heppner's successor in SEAC, Colonel John G. Coughlin, shared this view.[78] For OSS, perhaps more than any other wartime secret service, co-operation with the organisations of Allies was perceived through the prism of its own vexed relations with other American organisations. The large OSS component in SEAC then, no less than the vast OSS station in London, which had reached 2,000 staff by the end of the war, offered a refuge from serious intra-American problems.

15   Britain and her allies in China

To what extent are we prepared to force the Chinese to comply with our wishes, now that the 'gunboat policy' of former days is démodé? Are we going to remember that the Chinese are a race that 'yields everything to force and nothing to reason', or are we going to continue, as we have done for so long now, to take a back seat accepting loss of face and even insults, without making any serious protest at all?

Major General Gordon Grimsdale, China, 1 July 1943[1]

SOE is 'ejected' from China

Although China was the weakest of the four major wartime allies, her wartime ambitions were nevertheless accorded importance by London, Moscow and Washington. Roosevelt periodically made efforts to accommodate Chungking's desire to reshape the international order in Asia, although his public observations were somewhat ambiguous. Roosevelt's ambiguity in the face of Chinese policy is partly explained by what has been aptly described as the absolute nationalism and confrontational style of the Chinese approach to post-war Asia, which contrasted with the international system he himself envisaged, and not infrequently shaded over into overt anti-Americanism.[2] These concerns were even more marked for the British who feared an intense Chinese interest in neighbouring territories from Tibet, through Burma and Thailand to Indochina. For London this threat in the East seemed no less real than growing concerns about Soviet ambitions in the West.[3] As soon as Chinese troops appeared in Burma to assist the Allies against the Japanese, the Indian Government responded with the Chinese Intelligence Wing, an agency wholly dedicated to watching Chinese and Sino-American ambitions in the region.[4]

The scale of British investment in East Asia, especially the Japanese-occupied territory of Hong Kong, prompted the British secret services to shift from merely observing to intervening. SOE's effective integration with extensive British banking and commercial interests in Hong Kong, through the appointment of John Keswick of Jardine Matheson and Company to superintend its work in China, seemed to place SOE on a firm footing. Mean-

15 Major General Claire Chennault of the US 14th Air Force and Major
General Gordon Grimsdale (IWM)

while the arrival of new SIS personnel in the region in 1941 seemed to
promise an improvement in intelligence activity.

Britain's extensive pre-war presence on the east coast of China ensured a
long-standing relationship with both KMT and Communist intelligence. As
early as 1937 the British had permitted the KMT to set up a signals interception station in the New Territories area of Hong Kong, run by Tai Li's BIS.[5]
SIS also seems to have been close to some Europeans working for KMT
intelligence.[6] In October 1940 this collaboration had gathered pace. Major
Boxer, the senior Army intelligence officer in Hong Kong, had travelled to
Chungking to seek co-operation on the performance of the Japanese Army.
The KMT allowed British W/T stations to be secreted into Canton, Bocca

Tigris and Hainan, providing considerable information about troop movements prior to December 1941.[7]

British SOE-type activities were also quick off the mark. Indeed, even as the European War broke out in mid-September 1939, one of SOE's predecessors, known as MI(R), planned to send a party to China to explore in 'an entirely non-committal way' how they could help China against the Japanese. This party was to consist of the adventurer Peter Fleming, the academic Michael Lindsay and John Keswick. They were to travel under a Ministry of Information cover, carrying credentials that would only be shown to Chiang Kai-shek. This initiative was blocked by Cadogan, who saw the potential dangers of such provocative action against Japan as 'incalculable'.[8] However, by 1940, they had secured permission, and these figures began to appear under a variety of covers: Michael Lindsay, for example, materialised as a press attaché at the British Embassy in Chungking.

The KMT welcomed this demonstration of support and by mid-1941 Britain was running guerrilla and commando training operations for the Chinese, both in China and in Burma. The overall programme was superintended by the new British Military Attaché, Major General Gordon Grimsdale, who had been Deputy Head of FECB Singapore. The first phase was carried out by a group of British-recruited Danes, led by Erik Nyholm, thus avoiding using British nationals against Japan before the outbreak of war. In September 1941, the American Military Attaché visited their facilities and reviewed 400 students undergoing training at the South Western Guerrilla Training School at Nanchang. He considered it 'very well organised' with a 'general atmosphere of alertness that one does not normally associate with Chinese institutions'.[9]

SOE enjoyed a fragmented existence in China. Alongside John Keswick's SOE 'commando' training mission, a parallel and semi-overt enterprise was set up entitled 204 Military Mission, with the same purpose of training Chinese guerrillas. It began life just over the border in Burma, moving into China as war began between Britain and Japan in January 1942. Commanded by General Dennys, there was an experienced training staff, comprising figures such as Colonel Munro-Faure, who liaised with the Chinese through General Li Mo-An. This mission had a large SOE element buried within it and included figures such as Colonel Michael Calvert of MI(R).[10]

Training guerrillas was not SOE's primary purpose. SOE sought, in the short term, to 'show the flag' to Chinese forces, thus raising Britain's battered prestige. In the long term, SOE hoped to prepare the ground for a British return to Hong Kong. SOE were thus prepared to co-operate with anyone who would help them to establish a foothold in the adjacent southeastern region of China. This included elements that alarmed Chiang: the forces of errant local warlords and also Communist guerrillas. As a result, John Keswick and the commando training mission were dramatically banished by Tai Li in mid-1942 for improper dealings with provincials. The exact nature of these dealings is unclear but one report stated that they involved a furore in customs over 'two tons of silk and lipstick'.[11] On 9 May, Keswick was told that he was coming under more direct Chinese control and to hand over all his stores and equipment. He refused and a confrontation ensued which ended with his departure. This was a serious matter for, as we have seen, it triggered off a major confrontation between Tai Li and Keswick's close friend, the cosmopolitan KMT Foreign Minister, T.V. Soong, the reverberations of which were felt for some time to come.[12]

Tai Li's decision revealed not only an accurate appreciation of the real reasons underpinning the presence of SOE in China, but also reflected the fact that Tai Li had previously been arrested by British security elements in Hong Kong. The arrest had occurred in the summer of 1941 when Tai Li had arrived with a Chinese delegation at Kai Tak airfield. The local police had been adamant that he was 'wanted' and marched him off to jail, where he sat bereft of belt and shoelaces. The next day the British Chief of Police arrived to rescue him and, as a gesture of apology, escorted him back to Chungking. When no-one seemed willing to name the specific crime of which Tai Li had been suspected, Madame Sun Yat-sen, who had followed the story with obvious interest, explained to an American diplomat: 'Don't you know? He's the biggest assassin in China.'[13]

Keswick, who had been SOE's key figure in China, was now at a loose end, holding a variety of diplomatic posts in London, Washington and SEAC, including Mountbatten's adviser on China, but remained pre-occupied with a mixture of SOE and economic business.[14] SOE now chose Findlay Andrew to carry its work forward inside China. Andrew was a respected pre-war denizen of China, who arrived in a 'semi-diplomatic capacity' as an MEW representative, rather than with any para-military paraphernalia, and who searched delicately for an alternative basis to work in China. In a manner similar to Miles and Naval Group, SOE now had to seek a viable Chinese partner. Andrew's attention fell upon one of China's five rival intelligence organisations, run by General Wang Ping-sheng, a close confidant of Chiang Kai-shek.

The KMT secret services were, inevitably perhaps, quite fragmented, with General Wang Ping-sheng running intelligence and propaganda for occupied China. Andrew and his staff were taken on as 'advisers' on propaganda and out of this grew Wang's new propaganda and intelligence organisation, the Institute for International Studies (IIS), with the British sub-section entitled the Resources Investigation Institute (RII). This collaboration went from strength to strength, with SOE enjoying considerable confidence, partly because, like Miles and SACO, they treated the organisation as Chinese, and partly because SOE provided one-third of the budget. This gave them access to a large network of agents extending into occupied China, Mongolia and Korea, and also to a propaganda organisation which had contact with many subversive organisations including Vietnamese nationalist groups.

Almost by accident, with the ejection of an SOE guerrilla training mission in 1942, SOE in China lost its sabotage function and became one of the more important British intelligence organisations. In May 1942, John Keswick had remained just long enough to open a separate liaison office that handled SOE external relations with groups as diverse as the burgeoning Free French missions, the NKVD, OSS, and various British organisations sent by India Command. This liaison office allowed SOE to keep its identity very separate from IIS/RII, reflecting its anxiety to keep the latter free of interference by either OSS or by Naval Group and Tai Li. With Donovan still struggling with SACO in 1943, SOE considered that the time was 'not yet ripe' to inform OSS about its Chinese friends. SOE were not impressed by Donovan's decision to join SACO and complained in May 1943 that OSS was 'very much under the control of this Chinese Himmler'.[15] SOE's decision to remain silent about its IIS/RII activities enjoyed the support of Chiang Kai-shek, who clearly considered compartmentalisation a virtue. In his own words, Wang Ping-sheng was the brains, and Tai Li was the hands, of his secret services. In practice the divisions were more complex. The former concentrated on intelligence and propaganda into occupied China, as well as dealing with the British, while the latter concentrated on police and security activities in Free China, as well as maintaining a large network of agents overseas and working with the Americans.[16]

However, by July 1943, Donovan was increasingly aware of the outlines of the IIS/RII operation and considered that it broke the terms of previous OSS–SOE agreements designating China as area of American primacy.[17] SOE knew they had little chance of convincing Donovan that SOE was 'not guilty', despite their protestations that IIS/RII was a purely Chinese, rather than a Sino-British, activity. London gave John Keswick the delicate task of negotiating with OSS in Washington on this matter and expected Donovan to demand participation, if not total control. The strong commercial background of many in SOE (no less than the legal expertise of many in OSS), made for tough negotiations. SOE in London suggested to Keswick that:

the argument could proceed on the hard-headed business lines which a large company would adopt when selling its subsidiary company in China to powerful American and Chinese interests, aiming at the same time, to obtain a working third party interest. How this could be done you will know better than I . . . If G.50,000 [Donovan] should prove intransigent, and insists on displacing S.O.E. for O.S.S. in R.I.I., we should have to make him pay as big a price as possible, should we sell out.

But by repeatedly invoking Chiang Kai-shek's desire for demarcation and separation, SOE overcame Donovan's objections and succeeded in main-taining its IIS/RII relationship.[18]

OSS were not the only potential objectors to SOE's joint intelligence ven-ture with the Chinese. As we have seen elsewhere, the ambitions of Macken-zie and SOE in the Far East were without limit, and Britain's SIS was being squeezed as the main agent-based intelligence collector. However in China, SIS recognised the peculiar circumstances and were also more confident of their own achievements there, so they were content to allow IIS/RII to develop. SOE's product was transferred to SIS once outside China for distri-bution in London; in other words SIS eventually claimed title to the product.[19] All this was facilitated by old SIS China hands in London, such as Charles Drage and Harry Steptoe, who appreciated the local complexities.[20]

SOE struggles on in China

Although 204 Military Mission continued its guerrilla training activities, in contrast to the ejected SOE school, it too was engaged in an uphill battle. The Chinese troops earmarked for training were certainly not 'special troops' and lacked the calibre required for this sort of warfare; moreover the facilities afforded by the Chinese were extremely basic. Relations with the Chinese Army deteriorated and they received a further blow when their charismatic leader, General Dennys, was killed in a plane crash in March 1942. Capable SOE officers working within the Mission, such as Lt Colonel Gill-Davies and Captain Ananand, quickly realised that their energetic spirit constituted a direct threat to Chinese hopes for an informal *modus vivendi* with the Japanese, under which both sides did as little fighting as possible. Indeed, they were so dejected about their prospects that in May they recommended a reduction in the scale of their own operation, leaving a small team under Munro-Faure. London initially refused; however, by September 1942 their general condition had become so bad that this reduction was implemented.[21]

During 1943, 204 Military Mission came under the direct control of the tough British Military Attaché, Gordon Grimsdale, who re-negotiated its lease with General Li Mo-An. In February it was agreed that new demolition schools would be set up at Pihu and that Munro-Faure's highly successful team would remain at Chiki, concentrating on officer training.[22] But this improvement did not last and, by May 1943, 204 Military Mission were suffering further indignities. Tai Li had now established firmer links with Naval Group who were willing to provide preferred American Marine train-ing teams. Americans were therefore called in by the Chinese to take over some British locations. This was a rude shock to those who had spent two years building up guerrilla training camps under the most difficult conditions. One officer reported:

16 A Chinese guerrilla undergoing British training at Pihu (IWM)

Have just learned from Munro-Faure that party of American demolition experts,
accompanied by mobile trucks of stores and supplies, have arrived Chiki school, and
states that they have been engaged to teach Chinese guerrilla forces previously receiving [British] instructions Chiki School. This is the first news I have had of this . . .
Did you know anything about this? . . . Apart from the double-crossing aspect on part

of both Americans and Chinese, I am afraid sudden arrival of American and departure of British from this part of third War Zone will look as if we have been kicked out and result in loss of British face.[23]

This was Tai Li's intention. But the diversity of British organisations in China always permitted another alternative. Therefore, Lt Colonel Munro-Faure, the most successful 'tutor' of guerrillas in China, was sent to the southern city of Kunming to be 'Military Liaison Officer' and to run operations on the China–Burma border. Britain's guerrilla school at Pihu continued effectively into 1944, by which time Mountbatten was pressing once more for its expansion, with plans for further artillery and weapon schools, although this was wrong-footed by a new Japanese offensive. The 204 Military Mission continued with this concertina existence into early 1945.[24]

SOE's multiple identities made it hard for the Chinese authorities to squeeze out. A further example of this was its China Coast Section, working under the cover of the POW escape organisation, the British Army Aid Group (BAAG) near Hong Kong. BAAG had been set up by Dr Lindsay Ride following his own escape from a POW camp in Hong Kong, initially with a view to assisting other escapers and downed pilots from the 14th Air Force. Inevitably, and akin to most British entities in China, it was gradually co-opted for intelligence gathering and quiet preparations for the restoration of British rule; indeed BAAG were given some of the staff supposedly 'expelled' with SOE's commando school in May 1942.[25]

SOE's multiple identity in China was sustainable because only a minority of its activities were para-military. SOE's most successful activities in China, perhaps in all of Asia, were financial and therefore notably low profile, code-named Operations *Remorse* and *Waldorf*. From the outset SOE's operations in China had exploited banking and business contacts, a natural reflection of an organisation whose first London chiefs were drawn from the City. SOE's largest activities in China addressed foreign exchange and balance of payments. In 1943 these operations received the approval of the Minister of Production in London, Oliver Lyttelton, and were placed under the command of Walter Fletcher, described as 'a thug with good commercial contacts'. Fletcher's initial plans aimed to exploit Chinese black-market networks to smuggle rubber out of occupied Malaya and then Indochina, but proved fruitless. Colin Mackenzie, however, recognised that this could serve as a cover for the exploitation of the currency black market in China. This provided the Chinese Nationalist dollars required for the various British establishments in China at a fraction of the official rate of exchange and the savings for the Exchequer were vast. SOE eventually provided the foreign exchange for private, as well as public, organisations including the Red Cross, ICI Ltd and Reuters. Official transactions through the Chinese Central Bank were phased out. Inevitably perhaps, Tai Li's organisation received one-fifteenth of the profits. Fletcher's staff eventually dealt in everything from sterling and rupees to machinery and diamonds, exchanging for black-market Chinese dollars at approximately ten times the official rate. The overall profit ran to over £70 million.[26]

Even with this 'unofficial support', British representatives in China themselves found life hard, enduring a market that had been thrown into chaos by a large supply of Allied money, set against a restricted supply of goods coming into China 'over the hump'. Cecil Beaton, who visited SOE in China as an official MOI photographer, escorted by Gordon Grimsdale, and whose work is reproduced in this volume, was astounded:

Baffling were the prices they quoted: the official rate of exchange here is eighty dollars to the pound, but on the black market the pound is worth 1,200 dollars. A candle costs twenty shillings, a pound of boiled sweets thirty shillings, or, in dollars, pork costs seventy dollars a pound, a bottle of ink 200 and a gallon of petrol 900 dollars.

The British Ambassador, Sir Horace Seymour, 'a lanky overgrown schoolboy with witty eyes and a tired but benevolent smile', explained the misery this inflicted on his staff, who rarely had a proper meal and were just 'picnicking'. Seymour confessed that he received, via the King's Messenger, a pound of butter and a pot of marmalade every month, and almost everything else had to be bought on the black market.[27]

By 1945, SOE's black-market operations had diversified to exploit this artificial economic climate. Their business now included quinine, the supply of which was concentrated in Japanese-occupied China, and which was essential for Allied troops. They even secured a resupply of Chinese silkworms, after a plague had killed their rival silkworms in Kashmir. SOE probably constitutes one of the few wartime fighting organisations that ran at an overall profit, not a loss.[28] More broadly, these operations underline the general character and purpose of SOE in China, which had a decidedly unparamilitary character.[29]

SIS in China

SIS represented a further British success in China and an important achievement for a service whose performance elsewhere in Asia was lacklustre. Most SIS resources in Asia were unsuitably deployed in the war in Burma. However, SIS was also active in the China and in MacArthur's SWPA. Against the background of the phoney war in China, SIS was able to concentrate on long-term political and economic reporting which reflected their traditional strengths. Indeed, the absence of real war was the factor that continually impressed itself even upon SIS officers whose visits to China were of short duration. When Brigadier Beddington of SIS London passed through in 1943 Menzies requested an independent assessment of the Chinese war effort. One of the first senior officers he spoke to was an American colonel running an artillery training school, who explained that he needed little ammunition because there was almost no fighting. What was delivered was largely 'stolen by the Chinese' and hidden in preparation for the coming war with the Communists. Meanwhile, Beddington noted, the fact that 'much trading was going on between the Chinese and Japanese through the front lines, and very little fighting, and that by arrangement, soon convinced me of what was going on'. In Chungking, he was the guest of honour at a vast banquet in the Army Chief of the General Staff's main operations planning room, a venue which, he observed tartly, saw plenty of banquets, but few operations.[30]

In late 1943, when Mountbatten visited Chungking, he secured the personal agreement of Chiang Kai-shek 'to SIS operating freely in China, especially in coastal areas'. Subsequently the senior SIS representative, Lt Colonel Gordon Harmon, based in Chungking under the cover of the 'General Liaison Office', met only limited bureaucratic obstruction.[31] By the end of December 1943, SIS operated five radio stations across nationalist China, with permission to open three more.[32] SIS in China enjoyed a devolved structure, with Harmon taking responsibility for North China, as well as nominally superintending the rest of the country. Harmon's staff in Chungking was a motley crew of old China hands, including the former Peking Reuters correspondent, a Scandinavian explorer and a Shanghai jailor. In 1944 they ran half a dozen offices across China with radio nets without being molested by the Chinese. This even included an outpost in North China under Major Drake, reportedly operating into Korea with Korean agents.[33] In China, unlike SEAC, SIS remained in full control of intelligence, a fact officially confirmed by the JIC in September 1944.[34]

SIS scored some notable achievements in the area of political intelligence. Remarkably, Harmon had managed to attach Michael Lindsay, a British academic, to the Communists in Yenan as their principal radio adviser. It seems likely that he enjoyed access to much of their incoming traffic and also enjoyed direct radio communications with SIS in China.[35] The work of Lindsay, who was highly sympathetic to the Communists, has yet to be thoroughly assessed, but London was notably well informed about events in Communist areas throughout the war.[36] SOE also had plans for a mission to Yenan in 1944, to be led by Julian Amery, the son of Leo Amery, fresh from his dealings with Tito. However, this proposal was vetoed by Wedemeyer.[37] During 1944 and 1945 SIS were able to give a precise picture of the stalled negotiations between the Communist delegation in Chungking, the Nationalists and Hurley. SIS were clear that these talks had ended in failure long before this became publicly apparent and were even able to summarise the letters sent by Chou En-lai back to Yenan.[38] SIS assessed the struggle against the Japanese in Communist-held areas and took a particular interest in the attitude of the Communists to the United Nations Conference at San Francisco in 1945, to which they had sent a delegate.[39] Much of this came from Chou En-lai himself who was 'in close personal touch' with Harmon in Chungking, as were the military representatives in the Communist delegation.[40]

Despite these successes, both SIS and SOE nevertheless remained extremely wary of Tai Li. In July 1943, John Keswick voiced his fears to Gerald Wilkinson of SIS, depicting him as 'uncultured, unscrupulous, cunning and capable. Would never hesitate to bump off anybody . . . a real blower-upper'. Keswick also rated him as ruthlessly effective, suggesting that the only intelligence activities in China not known to Tai Li in 1943 were some joint SIS–OSS intelligence activities run through the organisations of C. V. Starr, a newspaper magnate. But Keswick conceded that it was only a matter of time before they too were uncovered by Tai Li.[41]

China, like her Allies, used the ploy of integration in its efforts to keep track of British activities. In June 1944, following a meeting between Chiang Kai-shek and Mountbatten, the Chinese DMI surprised and embarrassed the British by proposing the creation of a new Sino-British Intelligence organisation, jointly staffed and with a wide remit, including signals intelligence and deception. Grimsdale, whose duties then included the general supervision of secret service in China, advised London that it would be wise to play along, as the Chinese were increasingly suspicious of the many British organisations, some of whom, he conceded, 'have acted in a highly irresponsible manner'. Such a joint body could not hope to resolve all the complex Allied infighting. 'The Americans', he added, 'have many organisations here which are if possible even less co-ordinated than our own and certainly display greater internecine jealousies.'[42]

In London, Cavendish-Bentinck of the JIC wavered between turning the proposals down flat, and thereby giving the Chinese a grievance, 'which I suspect they would have enjoyed', or accepting and so annoying the Americans. Others in London were convinced that the Chinese were 'really after sigint' and would lose interest once they realised that this choice item was off the menu.[43] After a great deal of consultation about security with the American DMI, General Bissell, London decided to gently turn the Chinese offer down.[44]

Anglo-American co-operation in Tibet

Britain's complex triangular relationship with American, Chinese and other Allied secret services in China spilled beyond its borders into contiguous territories. Given the emerging pattern of Anglo-American frictions in India by 1943, the British decision to support an OSS mission to the Dalai Lama in the sensitive region of Tibet appears, at first glance, somewhat puzzling. Some have suggested that this OSS mission was an attempt to provoke the perennially over-sensitive Government of India.[45] However, it is clear that this mission had full British support. Instead, Delhi probably hoped to use OSS to bolster Tibetan independence against Chinese claims in the region, perhaps by trading assurances of Tibetan independence for a flow of supplies through Tibet.[46] Some British elements probably saw an opportunity for creating friction between OSS and the Chinese in this sensitive area. For whatever reason, in July 1942, Donovan was able to assure Cordell Hull that he had the complete support of 'certain British authorities' and that the project could be discussed with London in the 'fullest confidence'.[47]

With Hull's blessing, and also encouragement from the US Army who wanted alternative supply routes, OSS chose Ilia Tolstoy, the exiled grandson of the Russian novelist, to lead the expedition, accompanied by the professional explorer, Brooke Dolan.[48] The OSS mission arrived in Tibet in December 1942 and Tolstoy handed over a letter from Roosevelt along with Roosevelt's signed photograph. There were elaborate ceremonies of reception followed by a long conversation with the Dalai Lama, facilitated by a senior monk called Ringang who acted as interpreter, having been educated at Rugby public school in England before the war.[49] The Tibetan Government's main concern was its inability to communicate efficiently with the outside world, and they asked OSS to facilitate some W/T equipment. But the State Department now became worried about offending the Chinese, who had territorial claims upon Tibet, noting that they had recently refused to supply this 'potent equipment' to Chungking. OSS were therefore told to cancel the project.[50] However, Donovan persuaded the diplomats to look the other way, with Adolf Berle agreeing to raise no objections if W/T equipment came as 'military supplies' from the US Army. By April 1943, OSS Delhi, together with the Government of India, had arranged for the delivery of three transmitters each with a 1,200 miles range.[51] However, it was only at the end of 1944 that the transmitters had been installed and suitable Tibetan operators trained.[52]

No alternative supply routes into China were established, but the Chinese were provoked. The following month, both the British Agent in Tibet and Tolstoy, who were collaborating closely, reported that Chinese troops were massing on the Tibetan border.[53] By the end of 1943 the Chinese were making wild claims, suggesting that the Tibetans 'aided by Japanese arms and planes' were planning offensive action against Chinese border provinces. Washington saw this as an excuse for some impending military adventure into Tibet.[54] Hull instructed American representatives to give the Chinese a stern warning that any such action 'could not fail' to affect American support for the Chinese war effort.[55]

Tolstoy's Mission were charmed by the Tibetans and were committed to bolstering their independence. They departed in the spring of 1943, confident that they were 'leaving all negotiations in such a shape that they can be carried on by the British'.[56] Tolstoy and Dolan took five months to trek from Tibet to Chungking where they discovered that the Chinese were complaining vigorously about American support for Tibetan independence.[57] OSS became concerned that Tolstoy and Dolan themselves might meet with an unfortunate 'accident' in Chungking. Tolstoy was therefore returned to the United States via Stilwell's headquarters, while Brooke Dolan was sent out of harm's way as an OSS representative to the Communists.[58] In April 1944, Donovan finally conceded to Hull that the Tibetan route into China 'could be of little material assistance to the armed forces of the China theatre'.[59] Exactly what Donovan had hoped to achieve in Tibet remains unclear.[60]

Springboards into Indochina and Thailand

Allied secret service relations in China were given an additional complex twist by operations launched into Indochina and Thailand. Since the North African landings of 1942, SOE had supported Gaullist secret services, while OSS had favoured Giraudist elements within the Free French movement. Attempts to merge the myriad secret services of these factions had been under way since October 1943, with limited success.[61] These schisms transferred themselves effortlessly to Chungking, where the Free French Missions of General Pechkoff and Colonel Emblanc were resolutely Gaullist and intimate with the British SIS, while the rival Meynier Mission was Giraudist and worked with OSS/Navy Group China.[62]

American hopes for the Giraudist Meynier Mission had been high because Colonel Meynier's wife belonged to a leading political and religious family with a vast retinue in Indochina. Miles had travelled to Algiers to preside over her covert extraction by means of a commando raid on a French internment camp which cost the lives of three British and seven French agents. Miles boasted to Donovan that with the assistance of the Meynier family network they would 'have 200,000 to 300,000 agents working for us in a very few months'.[63] Meynier certainly had some success in contacting anti-Gaullist elements in the Decoux's Vichy Indochina regime, but the results remain a matter of dispute.[64] Meanwhile Tai Li made life increasingly difficult for the Gaullist missions, viewing them as an extension of British efforts in China. Some of their agents perished in mysterious circumstances at Mon Cai in July 1943 and by early 1944 Tai Li had ordered them to close their radio links with Indochina.[65]

All the French missions were considered amateurish and constituting a security risk. By late 1943, OSS had catalogued a long list of problems at the Emblanc Mission. They noted that the registry of the Emblanc Mission was run by a Mrs Dean and all was not well in this section: 'Mrs Dean . . . sees even Confidential and Secret correspondence, and sees the Service Records and files of all the officers of the Mission. This woman has a marked inclination for liquor (she has been dubbed ''Mrs Whiskey'') . . . important documents have disappeared.' This was not the sort of organisation that OSS wished to have extended dealings with.[66] Despite these reservations, in December 1943, when OSS withdrew from SACO, they made an unsuccessful attempt to take the Meynier Mission with them, reflecting the fact that their dislike of Miles was greater than their worries about the French.[67]

French elements in China, more than any other, initiated the bitter conflicts between the various secret services over operations into Indochina during 1943 and 1944, while the British and the Americans preserved a somewhat more pragmatic and flexible attitude. In September 1944, following de Gaulle's arrival in Paris, an American liaison officer, Robert P. Larson, was despatched to open conversations with M. Gilbert in the Asian section of the Quai d'Orsay in Paris. But the reception was hostile and Larson recorded:

He disgusted me. He was one of these men who have formulated a distinctly Gaullist opinion . . . He is firmly convinced that the Americans are already trying to carry on an economic penetration of Indochina with the intention of making the country at least a post war economic sphere of the US. He also shares the belief that it is very likely that the US is going to give active support to the Annamese [Vietnamese] in their efforts for a completely independent country after the war. He states that French have proof . . . I was quite surprised to see how violent was his dislike for OSS.[68]

By contrast, prior to the onset of the Mountbatten–Wedemeyer boundary dispute in late 1944, OSS–SIS–SOE relations over Indochina were relaxed. Chennault and the 14th Air Force had facilitated RAF Special Duties flights into Indochina via Kunming. Moreover, in 1943, SIS had set up a successful intelligence network run by Laurence Gordon, a Canadian employee of the Cal-Texaco Oil Company, together with his associates Harry Bernard and Frank Tan (hence its acronym – GBT). During 1944 the GBT group was willingly transferred by SIS to OSS, whereupon it was run by a British-born OSS officer, Charles Fenn. This co-operative venture provided a wealth of target intelligence, as well as assisting with downed pilots.[69] OSS valued GBT because Roosevelt had 'categorically' prohibited intelligence or resistance work with the Free French, re-affirming this ban on 16 October 1944.[70]

Contrary to French claims, links between Ho Chi Minh and the OSS were not established until the spring of 1944, and then at the behest of Ho. Prior to this, Ho had been of primary interest to OWI, who had toyed with the remarkable idea of using him as a broadcaster for one of their West Coast radio stations, run by Owen Lattimore. But nothing had come of this. The European section of the State Department had backed away, noting that Ho was 'in the black books of the French' and insisting that 'OWI should not be allowed to hire Ho' unless the French approved. OWI and Moffat's section in the State Department attempted to reverse this decision, pointing out that OWI had already hired nationalistic Indonesians who were 'persona non grata' to the Dutch Government. However the Secretary of State, Edward Stettinius, seems to have turned the appeal down.[71] The main anxiety on the part of OSS appears to have been simply to discover what was going on in Indochina, where the situation was now complicated by a minor civil war, the 'White Terror', underway in the northern provinces between the Viet Minh and the Vichy French.[72] The nature of Ho's own motivation in opening relations with American officials has been widely debated.[73]

Ho Chi Minh was only able to begin serious guerrilla activity in August 1944, and then at the behest of the local KMT commander in southern China, General Chang Fa-kwei, who released him from semi-captivity. In part this was driven by Chang's troubled relations with Chungking, since Ho's communist background assured Chang that he was independent of the growing KMT intelligence net penetrating Indochina under the auspices of Tai Li.[74] Meanwhile, it is important to emphasise that OSS only turned their attention to Ho, and away from co-operation with British and French networks, such as GBT and Meynier, in early 1945, probably steered by higher authorities and it was from Wedemeyer specifically that one such directive came. OSS in China reported to Washington that:

General Wedemeyer has also expressed his desire to make plans for extensive OSS operations in French Indo-china. He does not trust the GBT Group and on our explaining our relations with them, told us that we did not know the half of it and that he had it from sure sources that this group was deliberately forwarding British aims in Indochina. We are beginning to hold back . . . thinking in terms of our own outfit Indochina.[75]

Repeatedly forbidden to work with the French by Roosevelt during 1944 and now urged not to work with the GBT Group by Wedemeyer, OSS were propelled towards the Viet Minh as one of the few remaining options for intelligence in Indochina. The subsequent eradication of the GBT network by the Japanese coup against the Vichy regime in Indochina in March 1945 only served to reinforce this. With no other options, Charles Fenn, the OSS officer formerly superintending GBT, now began to cultivate Ho.[76]

Both SOE and OSS encountered similar problems in attempting to use China as a springboard into, or indeed out of, Thailand during 1943 and 1944. Thai activity was plagued not only by American–British–Chinese rivalry for control of the Free Thai movement, but also by internal factionalism amongst the Thais. The leader of the OSS-sponsored Free Thai in the United States,

Seni Pramoj, was engaged in a bitter feud against its senior military figure, Colonel Karb Kunjara, gradually 'creating such a cloud of doubt about him', that no American organisation dared to have contact with him. Seni's list of accusations included secret dealings with Luang Phibul, the key pro-Japanese figure in Bangkok and dealings with Tai Li, as well as financial improprieties. Kunjara had been a key figure in OSS attempts to launch operations from China and so the result of this was that 'the OSS Thai unit in China was held inactive for a whole year while Kunjara was being investigated'. Seni Pramoj was remorseless in his attacks, accusing all the Thais attached to OSS in China of 'being mercenaries who were in the war for the money'. Partly because of this paralysis, a second OSS Thai unit had been created in SEAC.[77]

The seriousness of these issues became clear in the autumn of 1943, when several representatives of the Free Thai movement in Bangkok managed to exfiltrate themselves to Chungking. One of these representatives, the short-lived Chamkad Balankura, carried plans for a Free Thai government based in India, while the other two representatives suggested a similar organisation based in China.[78] Karb Kunjara, on his arrival in Chungking, held meetings with these three representatives and also with Tai Li's organisation. Soon afterwards Balankura died 'in circumstances which await clarification'. Seni Pramoj who was 'very upset' at the death of Balankura, suggested that Tai Li and Kunjara, working in collaboration, had 'poisoned him'. Donovan, accompanied by the Head of the OSS Thai section in Washington, Major Carl Hoffman, travelled personally to Chungking to investigate, but the evidence was inconclusive. Although Hoffman believed that Kunjara 'had had no opportunity to cause the death of Balankura' and viewed Kunjara as essential as a leader of the Thai group, nevertheless confidence had been destroyed and paralysis continued.[79]

A full twelve months later, during September 1944, Colonel John Coughlin, the senior OSS officer in CBI, was still expending considerable time investigating the nature of links between Kunjara and the Chinese. After an eight-hour conference with Tai Li he was still no closer to a definitive answer and confessed to Donovan that his feelings on Kunjara remained 'mixed':

I, however, doubt that he can be trusted, certainly not in China. I feel he will make deals with Tai Li of which I will not be informed and that he will likewise make deals with Miles . . . I am at a loss to figure out Tai Li's extreme interest in him, unless there is some agreement between them that I know nothing about.

Major Nicol Smith, perhaps the most experienced OSS SI officer with responsibilities for Thailand, was probably correct when he speculated that Kunjara and the OSS Thais based in China had been used by Tai Li as 'guinea pigs' to develop new agent routes. Meeting Kunjara personally in Karachi in August 1944, Coughlin certainly detected a sense that he felt 'let down' by Tai Li.[80] Simultaneously the British had intercepted letters from Kunjara to the Chinese offering to lead a pro-Chinese Free Thai Group at Chungking.[81] By November 1944, OSS in Chungking had confirmed that Kunjara had been in receipt of 'lavish gifts' and a bank loan from the Chinese. Hoffman now considered it imperative to keep Kunjara out of China and instead sought to tie him up in Washington by setting him to work interpreting intelligence reports.[82]

The story repeated itself in December 1944, when the Thai resistance succeeded in despatching a further mission to Chungking led by Thavil Udon. They were received by BIS and, in the words of OSS, were soon 'completely under Tai Li's wing'. The official purpose of this mission was to consult with Chiang Kai-shek and to encourage him to join Britain and the United States in liberating Thailand. 'What they are really after', reported OSS, 'is to induce Chinese to bring pressure on Britain regarding Thailand's territorial integrity.'[83] The overall effect of these activities was that Tai Li successfully closed down OSS Thai activities based in China.

British interest was also stirred by the arrival of the Balankura Mission in China in 1943. Although Balankura was kept under virtual house arrest by the Chinese, Findlay Andrew of SOE had secured a meeting, accompanied by Prince Subhas Svasti from SOE's Thailand section. In December 1943, SOE's Major Grut also met with the surviving members of Balankura's party. The British drew mixed conclusions from these conversations. The Foreign Office in London were unimpressed by SOE's insistence that Pridi, the resistance leader in Bangkok, should be brought out to set up a provisional government outside Thailand, reinforced by warnings that 'he was in danger of being liquidated'. In London, Eden and his officials saw this as a Thai political manoeuvre to try and nullify the state of war with Britain and to slip onto the winning side. One official noted dryly that he could not lead a provisional government. 'As to his being liquidated, that would admittedly, be a pity, but if he was really in danger my guess would be that he would come out Government or no Government'. This assessment, though harsh, was probably accurate.[84]

In contrast, SOE considered that the Balankura Mission represented exciting evidence of a substantial resistance movement within Thailand. Having been slow to re-establish themselves in the Far East in 1942, SOE were anxious to co-opt any existing indigenous organisation in preference to building from scratch, not only in Thailand but also in Malaya and Burma. Mackenzie urged Wavell to recognise that the Balankura Mission proved that: 'There is no doubt that a Movement does exist in Siam which has active support from important men and wide sympathy among the population.' It was also clear, he insisted, that the leaders would prefer to work with the British rather than the Chinese or the Americans, all things being equal.

Mackenzie chose to emphasise inter-allied competition, warning that 'the Chinese have offered Balankura very considerable sums' in return for establishing the Free Thai movement in China, adding that a reluctant Balankura was stalling. Meanwhile, he stressed, OSS were 'pressing Balankura to fly to America'. But before Wavell could respond to Mackenzie's call for action, the unfortunate Balankura had met his demise and was denied the opportunity to fly anywhere.[85] SOE were highly suspicious and despatched an SOE officer, Major McMulen, masquerading as a doctor, complete with stethoscope, who successfully arranged for him to be transferred from a Chinese to a Canadian hospital. There, a British doctor diagnosed that he had in fact died naturally of cancer, but SOE were hard to convince.[86]

Conclusions

China represented a complex and dangerous arena for Allied secret services. On the one hand the KMT were determined to control all overseas secret service activities in China, no less than the Viceroy had been in British India, propelled by a deep sense of violated sovereignty. This was reinforced by a correct assessment that some would give the war against Japan little more priority than the KMT itself. But, on the other hand, the pressure for the Allied secret services to move into China while evading Chinese control was intense. This was driven by the factionalised and Sinocentric nature of Washington's East Asia policy, and also by the potential springboard that China offered into many neighbouring territories, from Tibet to Korea.

Some of the ensuing conflicts had their origin at the highest level, in unacknowledgeable exhortations from Roosevelt and Churchill. But they were equally capable of occurring spontaneously at the lowest level. Even in the mess halls of the individual secret service outstations in China – where various country sections sat for months at a time, awaiting approval from distant co-ordinators for their operations – internecine strife continually threatened to rear its head. American officers reported that they had to keep each group physically separate because of intense local enmities. Thai groups and French groups, for example, could not be permitted adjacent tables because of the border conflict fought between the two countries in late 1940. Guns had to be checked in at the door in Wild West style, and American nationals interspersed between the two groups, for fear that 'the border war would break out again'.[87]

The principal beneficiaries of this fragmentation were the Chinese, who were often able to practise divide and rule. In November 1943, shortly before his departure as America's Ambassador in Chungking, Clarence Gauss reported that there were at least fifteen known Allied intelligence organisations operating in China (5 British, 4 American, 4 Russian, 1 Dutch and 1 Free French). 'These organisations', he continued', compete among themselves, do not pool their information except through London or Washington, and are completely unco-ordinated to the delight of the Chinese . . . We ourselves are to blame for the facilities we offer for being swindled through lack of co-operation among ourselves.' But the various Chinese secret services were no advertisement for harmony. Most Allied groups had made their way in China by linking with different Chinese secret services, themselves preoccupied with internal political power struggles which foreigners often perceived only dimly.[88] It was with this extraordinarily fissile array of clandestine organisations that the Allies now began to feel their way towards a settlement at the end of the Far Eastern War.

Part 5

The end of the war in Asia, 1945–1946

16   Anti-colonialism, anti-communism and plans for post-war Asia

> General Donovan while in London, insisted upon seeing many American officers, both of OSS and the regular Army, but did not desire to see 'any damned British' . . . there is some friction between him and the British Intelligence Service.
>
> American Embassy London to FBI, 12 July 1945[1]

'The war will go on for a long time'

Churchill has been attacked by more than one historian for his wartime refusal to honestly confront the problems of ebbing British power, and for his failure to articulate any clear conception of Britain's future world role other than growing dependence upon the United States. This, it has been argued, stands in contrast to Eden, who struggled unsuccessfully to persuade Whitehall to reach a frank accommodation with Washington which would have dispelled the miasma of mutual suspicions. As we have seen, instead of negotiation, Churchill preferred a *modus vivendi* based on sullen silence, not only on India, but also on Indochina, Thailand and a host of other sensitive territories.[2] But such criticisms of Churchill are misplaced. Churchill's mind was pre-occupied with post-war questions and his anxiety to postpone any confrontation on empire questions denoted a considered strategy. His approach to these questions was revealed in his response to concerted pressure to speak to Roosevelt about Indochina. Churchill replied: 'the war will go on for a long time'.

One of Churchill's central operating principles was careful timing. Along with the detailed insights that Churchill seemed to gain from his almost insatiable appetite for 'real time' intelligence provided by sigint, came a wider sense of the world as a place in which the balance of power was constantly shifting, sometimes with startling speed. When attending Allied conferences, such as Cairo and Teheran, nothing annoyed him more than difficulties in maintaining his supply of intercepts and SIS reports, specially selected for him by Menzies. This material informed his wider approach to inter-Allied relations, no less than to the Axis.[3] Accordingly, Churchill demanded control over timing above all other things. When, in 1942, Churchill discovered that diplomats had begun to talk to the Soviets about the post-war settlement without his permission, he was seized with almost uncontrollable anger and 'emitted several vicious screams of rage'. But in October 1944, well informed about Soviet progress in the war, Churchill decided that the moment was right to fly to Moscow and propose a 'Percentages Deal' on the Balkans to Stalin.[4]

When absolutely necessary, he would confront Roosevelt forcefully about detailed points of empire, as with India in 1942, but a general reckoning was to be avoided at all costs. In 1942 and 1943, with the idealist–internationalist alignment of Roosevelt, Wallace, Welles and Berle dominating American foreign policy, and with Churchill seemingly alone in a world governed by four powers – as at Cairo and Teheran – he rightly chose to bide his time. Churchill did not have to wait too long. By late 1944, anti-colonialism was losing momentum. London took quiet satisfaction in the way in which China, America's firm ally on matters anti-colonial, had been fatally revealed as a fraudulent fourth power. Meanwhile, Roosevelt had no choice but to receive the detested de Gaulle in Washington as the leader of a new France. The allocation to France of a zone in Germany, and later a seat on the UN Security Council, confirmed the rising status of a figure even more anxious than Churchill to sabotage ideas of UN trusteeship for colonies.

Roosevelt's anti-colonialism was also suffering corrosion from forces inside the United States. In 1943, the US Joint Chiefs of Staff had drawn up a long list of overseas bases they wished to control after the war. Their thinking on areas like Indochina was subtly different to that of Roosevelt. A War Department policy adviser told the British Embassy:

One thing is certain, the status of Indo-China will not remain unchanged at the end of this war. The American General Staff depended on France to defend Indo-China . . . as far as the Americans are concerned, France did not defend Indo-China and they don't want to see that happen again. They want to be sure that Indo-China will be defended and they intend to take part in that defense. They have got to make sure that their flanks are protected. . . . This point of view is strongly shared both by the Naval and by the Military Staffs. They constantly express it . . .

The American military were not far from the view that weak colonial powers needed to be buttressed, rather than removed.[5] Moreover, plans to place dependent areas under UN trusteeship jeopardised hopes for American bases in Pacific islands won at such very high cost.

Roosevelt, who set the tone at the top, was failing by the end of 1944 and by January 1945 it was his turn to be evasive. The Foreign Office noted on the vexed Indochina issue: 'The President refuses to discuss it with anyone save the PM and when he meets the PM he does not mention it.'[6] In April

1945, Roosevelt was swept away by a stroke and succeeded by a Vice-President who had previously been confined to domestic affairs. Publicly he vowed that he would continue Roosevelt's policies, but privately he was not certain what these policies were. The disarray was multiplied by the rapid rotation of American Secretaries of State, no less than three in as many years. By early 1945, in Washington at least, anti-colonialism was largely a spent force.

While the death of Roosevelt in April 1945 certainly accelerated Washington's retreat from anti-colonialism, it also marked a devolution and to some degree a fragmentation. Truman's main areas of interest were in any case Europe and China, leaving India and South East Asia to the State Department. This was an important development and helps to explain the ability of some, like Abbot Low Moffat, to perpetuate aspects of Roosevelt's policies on South East Asia into 1946.[7] Meanwhile anti-communism, while important, was probably not the key factor eroding anti-colonialism, although Truman later adjusted the chronology of his early policy on the Soviets for political reasons.[8]

But Truman was not the only figure who sought to adjust history. Churchill inflicted his delaying tactics not only on his contemporaries, but also on historians, by excising deep wartime controversies over Asia from his own massively influential six-volume history of the war, which was edited in consultation with leading figures on both sides of the Atlantic. This, together with Chester Wilmott's equally path-breaking study *The Struggle for Europe*, disguised the depth and importance of Allied political controversies, especially over Asia, for decades.[9] These powerful distortions continue to reverberate even in recent literature.[10]

London, Washington and emerging anti-communism

In both London and Washington, the military planners constituted the leading edge of growing concern about Soviet power. The complex dynamics of this cannot be explored here, but it is sufficient to observe that, by April 1944, London boasted long-term strategic planning committees advocating the rebuilding of Germany and Japan against the Soviet Union.[11] Word began to leak out and by the autumn a worried Foreign Office warned that: 'It is already becoming known that our soldiers are thinking of a possible war against Russia.'[12] Similar ideas were in circulation amongst the military in Washington and during early 1945 these two streams had begun to meet. Britain's Director of Naval Intelligence returned from a tour of commands in the Pacific in March and April 1945 to report that he had managed to get hold of 'the substance of one of these high level super secret appreciations containing some fantastic remarks such as U.S. and British were negotiating now on terms for Japan and with a view to building up Japan as a bulwark against Russia, with whom U.S. would be at war this generation or next.'[13]

Although the Foreign Office was less pessimistic, nevertheless, by early 1944 the Soviet Union had begun to impinge on its long-term planning for Asia. In February, Dening scanned the post-war horizon from his position in SEAC and warned London of two separate future dangers. First, that the 'ham-fisted' Americans would find themselves in 'a head on collision with Russia if they are not careful', adding: 'We do not want to be dragged into a collision with Russia and the United States.' Secondly, that there was a need 'to convince the United States that it is not in their interests to undermine the stability of the British Empire' and to counter 'American imperialism', repeating his now familiar complaints about 'a smearing campaign' against British policy.[14] Tired and harassed by local events, Dening was unable to take the wider view and failed to connect these two problems. But more senior officials in London could not fail to spot the link. Reading Dening's report, some immediately identified the first problem as the answer to the second. It would be a good idea, they asserted, to allow the Soviets to press forward a little in Asia, just to remind the Americans of the containing value of empire. Historical analogy was rolled out to reinforce the argument, 'just as the Russian and Afghan bogey has often succeeded in keeping India in a reasonable frame of mind, so the same Russian bogey may have the same effect on the Chinese and their self-appointed protectors'.[15]

Senior OSS officers in Washington, having moved closer to the US Joint Chiefs of Staff in 1943, were cogniscent of these subterranean shifts. It seems unlikely that OSS contributed greatly to growing worries about future Soviet power in Asia in 1944, but by early 1945 they had detected them amongst their military colleagues, and were responding to them. A much-discussed example of this began to circulate in early May, just before the UN's San Francisco Conference, when Donovan sent the newly installed President Truman a wide-ranging review entitled 'Problems and Objectives of US Policy'. This had a spheres-of-influence tone and warned that: 'Russia will emerge from the present conflict as by far the strongest nation in Europe and Asia – strong enough, if the United States should stand aside, to dominate Europe and at the same time establish her hegemony in Asia.' It was a very short step from this analysis to a radical revision of declared American policy on the subject of the European empires. The review continued:

In this connection the United States should realize also its interest in the maintenance of the British, French and Dutch colonial empires. We should encourage liberalization of colonial regimes in order the better to maintain them, and to check Soviet influence in the stimulation of colonial revolt. We have at present no interest in weakening or liquidating these empires or championing schemes of international trusteeship which may provoke unrest and result in colonial disintegration, and may at the same time alienate from us the European states whose help we need to balance the Soviet power.

This prescient document took full account of the hopes of the US Joint Chiefs of Staff, speaking of a possible American 'empire' in the Pacific. Here, the United States was 'in a position comparable to that of Russia in Eastern Europe' and so it followed that: 'What we hold, we can retain, if we are so minded.'[16] This represented a complete about-face for senior OSS officers, especially for Donovan. Yet it was not entirely a new trend in Washington, for there were those in European sections of OSS (as in the Eurocentric corners of the State Department) who had long been unsympathetic to anti-colonialism. Archimedes Patti, an OSS officer serving in Indochina at the end of the war, would later complain that OSS in Europe was assisting SOE in finding French personnel for its operations into Indochina.[17]

This policy review, sent by Donovan to the White House, reveals him as an astute and dedicated first-hand observer of trends in American policy. When James Dunn, the Assistant Under-Secretary of State, offered him the opportunity to attend the UN Conference at San Francisco, it was seized with relish. Donovan initially wished to send over 100 observers, including all the Branch chiefs of R&A; however, this raised the issue of cover. Within OSS, Colonel Buxton and Dr Langer led a vexed discussion of the problem, noting that this domestic appearance might fuel the recent bad newspaper publicity about the post-war future of OSS which, they lamented, had included suggestions that it would become 'an American Gestapo at work on its friends'. Rival American organisations were 'attempting to uncover everything possible about OSS' and so they could not risk a 'conspicuous or extravagant' presence. Worries focused on what to tell the local FBI chief in San Francisco about such a large OSS contingent. In the event, OSS did not list many of their staff as OSS, exploiting the fact that many had originated with the State Department. Buxton emphasised that their presence was to be informal and that 'OSS shall not in any circumstances be spoken of as "attending" the conference'.[18] But Donovan could not help himself and over-stepped the mark when he suggested to Stettinius that OSS might do some 'spying' on the other delegations. In fact the United States was gathering most of the intelligence it required for this conference by reading the communications traffic of friendly states such as France and the Latin American states.[19] Nevertheless, OSS were present in force at this crucial conference. It was here that Dunn, together with the Secretary of State, Stettinius, assured the French about the unchanged future colonial status of Indochina.

But OSS as a whole organisation had not yet turned a complete somersault on the issues of colonialism and communism, and instead were fragmented.

17 Donovan watches the launch of an OSS operation in SEAC

In Europe and Washington, OSS moved fairly effortlessly towards anti-communism linking this to some explicit pro-colonialism, by May 1945. The following month, Charles S. Cheston, Acting Director of OSS, was commending the continued presence of OSS X-2 counter-intelligence units in India to the US Joint Chiefs of Staff to strengthen the British Empire, explaining that the approaching political upheavals marked India out as 'a fertile field for Russian propaganda and clandestine activity'.[20] Yet there remained anachronistic bastions of Rooseveltian sentiment. Two linked examples were Abbot Low Moffat's South East Asian Division in the State Department and also OSS in South and South East Asia. To comprehend these complexities we must move away from London and Washington to the crucial level of theatres of command.[21]

OSS and SSU in Asia

The atomic end of the war in Asia in August 1945 took almost everyone by surprise. The general consensus was that the conflict would last until December 1946 and even those few privy to the secret of atomic weapons were unsure whether they would work until its test in June 1945. 'Let me know', Churchill asked Truman before the test in New Mexico, 'if its a flop or a plop'. On 15 July the reply came back: 'It's a plop. Truman.'[22] Churchill told Mountbatten at the Potsdam Conference on 24 July. After dinner they moved into Churchill's study and closed the doors: 'After looking round in a conspiratorial manner', he explained that it would be dropped on 5 August and that the Japanese would surrender on 15 August. Mountbatten could tell a few of his immediate circle in SEAC that the war would end on 15 August, but could not tell them how or why. A vast body of staff in SEAC HQ, including all those in OSS, SIS and SOE, continued 'very unreal' planning for the final assault on Japan.[23] Potsdam held other surprises for Mountbatten. To his dismay, SEAC's domain was now vastly expanded into the Pacific to incorporate areas such as the Netherlands East Indies and all of Indochina south of the 16th parallel. SEAC now stretched from Karachi to New Guinea, extending over 6,000 miles and containing half a million surrendered Japanese, together with 200,000 Allied POWs and internees. Mountbatten quickly realised that these new operations of recovery and rescue would require an effective intelligence screen, no less than those in wartime.

Although OSS were taken unawares by the abrupt end of the Far Eastern War, they had already begun concentrated planning for their own post-war existence in Asia, in common with most Allied secret services. Donovan first turned his attention to an intelligence organisation that would serve post-war American interests in dependent areas as early as June 1944. These thoughts were triggered by interest in the Arab Gulf states and his desire to build up 'some very much under cover intelligence' in Saudi Arabia, perhaps under the pretence of some large archaeological mission. Major Carleton S. Coon was given the job of investigating the long-term possibilities in this region, with the brief that this long-term project might not even begin until 1945.[24]

Coon was a brilliant academic and Arabist. He had been Professor of Anthropology at Harvard before the war and had worked extensively amongst the tribes of North Africa and the Middle East. An extremely tough-minded individual, he had joined OSS and in 1942 he had run the training camp near Algiers through which the French assassin of Admiral Darlan had passed.[25] By September 1944, Coon had toured the region again and presented his findings to Donovan on the future of 'intelligence work in Arab countries'. His central argument was that Saudi Arabia was not a self-contained unit. Its leader, Ibn Saud, was nothing less than the greatest figure in the world of Islam, and so the issue of intelligence in Saudi Arabia naturally begged questions about the future of this sort of work throughout the whole Muslim world which stretched in a broad band between 'points as far distant as Morocco and Japan'. Such a project, he argued, would work only if it attempted to capture intelligence 'from the Moslem world as a whole'.

These vast Muslim areas, which included much of India and what would shortly be Indonesia, were fast becoming a region of conflict among the surviving world powers. Coon argued that partly because of nationalist fervour associated with the Atlantic Charter, in the future wars were bound to rise in these 'areas of primary disturbance'. The 'struggle for spheres of interests has not only begun but has already . . . taken a critical form'. All this had to be meshed with American interests, which, he argued, flowed from two basic assumptions:

(1) Experience has taught us that the United States cannot stay out of World Wars.

(2) The United States has several material interests at stake.

(a) Oil, (b) Airbases, (c) Future Markets.

These core interests required sound intelligence if they were to be protected. For example, he argued American oil interests were dependent on the continuation of the Ibn Saud dynasty and so their rivals, the Rashidi clan, 'must be the object of special attention'. Growing Turkish, and now Russian, influence in the region also had to be watched carefully.

There were important opportunities here. The primary world airline routes to and from Asia, he asserted, 'go directly through Moslem territory'. Because the British and the Dutch operated competing airlines, American companies would not be given airfields by the European colonial powers, but they could cultivate the independent and semi-independent Muslim countries 'with a view to securing special concessions from them'. Meanwhile, the demand of Muslim countries for Western merchandise was growing fast and, with the post-war reconversion of American industry, it was 'essential', he argued, that 'new outlets be found and developed'. Here again, an intelligence service could 'furnish leads of great value to our manufacturing and exporting interests'. Coon stressed that this work would be comparable to that of Britain's SIS, which had in the past 'performed a similar service with great success for British commercial interests'.

But there were also severe obstacles in the way of effective intelligence in Muslim areas. The largest was what Coon termed 'the security problem':

This means in particular security from our present allies, almost all of whom have fingers in the Moslem pie and who have shown themselves particularly anxious to keep us out. The sensitiveness of the French in Morocco, who consider it a major crisis if an American speaks to a native of any prominence, is well known . . . We may count on the French to do all in their power to thwart any program we may start.

The same went for the British, Dutch, Chinese and indeed the Russians whom, he noted, all had significant colonial problems with subject Muslim populations. Accordingly, the level of security required for this programme could not possibly be achieved under the sort of organisational scheme used by wartime OSS, which was in any case full of other nationals, including many British, French and Dutch, which OSS had recruited in their headlong rush for expansion. It was increasingly clear that some of these individuals reported on OSS activities to their home countries:

In Algiers ... we have few secrets from the French Government, and as a result of this penetration, I and several others are on the French black list. The interest that SIS has taken in our affairs from the beginning would be, if possible, increased if they had reason to believe that we were interested in Moslem problems ... they would soon find it out with all the Britishers in our buildings, and all the dates between SIS women and OSS men in other theaters.

Proper security, he concluded, would only be maintained by completely sealing off the 'Islam show' from the rest of OSS. This project would need its own buildings, communication services and technical facilities and 'must report to the top only'. Nevertheless, he remained optimistic, for he insisted that there were, within OSS and Army Counter-Intelligence Corps, enough academic Arabic specialists and American-born Syro-Lebanese, to form the nucleus of this sort of deep cover organisation. Coon concluded by proposing nothing less than a unique 'long-range program ... detached for the Washington offices of OSS and run completely under cover'. He suggested that, on completion of his immediate tasks, he should overtly leave OSS and return to his academic position at Harvard. This would allow him to get this special branch moving 'under an academic cover'.[26]

There is no indication whether Donovan acted on this proposal. But these detailed discussions indicate the conceptions of the future American intelligence in colonial regions that were developing around Donovan in 1944. By November 1944 Donovan was giving some time to this issue, discussing it at length with William Stephenson of BSC and triggering a wave of more detailed planning in Asia.[27] There is no indication that Donovan ordered regional OSS chiefs to undertake such studies, but no such instruction was necessary. By February 1945, it was clear from leaks in the press that a major debate on the future of intelligence was under way in Washington.[28]

Dillon Ripley, the senior SI officer in SEAC, set out his thoughts on 'long-range intelligence in the Far East', including China, for Donovan in March 1945. In common with Coon, the emphasis was not yet on the threat from the Soviet Union, but instead on a wide range of commercial, industrial and political developments in Asia that he regarded as so important that they might 'sway the course of America's history in the next twenty to thirty years'. Ripley set out nothing less than a proto-argument for the 'Pacific Century', arguing that in the post-war years this was likely to be the region of fastest development. It seemed to him inconceivable that such a phenomenon should not be watched closely by a future American intelligence agency.

But his overall analysis was not an optimistic one. Reflecting on the experiences of OSS in both India and China, he joined Coon in identifying security as a key problem. In most countries 'every American, every European for that matter is a marked man', for his contacts and associates become immediately known to the security authorities and natives alike. There were few plausible occupations, perhaps with the exception of academics and missionaries, that allowed freedom of movement. Any interest in political affairs immediately gave the game away. Yet, to Ripley's mind, the employment of native personnel was also 'virtually impossible for long-range intelligence work' as any payment made to such agents resulted in a visible change of status for these agents which could not be concealed. Ripley therefore advocated a system based on casual American visitors, developing short-term contacts with unpaid and unwitting informants.[29]

Perversely, OSS X-2 in India, immersed in the world of IB and the Indian police, took a more optimistic view. Contemporaneously they prepared proposals for a 'Program of Political and Economic Intelligence for India and Burma' based on indigenous agents. The tone of this proposal was more urgent, for with the imminent recapture of Rangoon the military pretext of the OSS presence in India would be gone in three months. Thereafter the British 'may naturally be assumed to take a dim view toward intelligence activities directed at these areas'. X-2 urged Washington to negotiate some residual 'observer' status within India and Burma which would facilitate a transitional phase to some fully fledged post-war intelligence organisation. To support this they stressed the direct relevance of their political reporting to the imminent UN San Francisco Conference.[30]

X-2, like Coon, saw the political and commercial concerns of British intelligence as a model. Although this transitional 'observer' mission OSS would retain the wartime OSS 'branch' structure, its targets would change. R&A branch would now place 'particular emphasis upon economic reporting such as analysis of Anglo-Indian management trusts, cartels, capital structure etc.'. X-2 branch would be engaged in studies showing the structure and organisation of the Intelligence services of India and Burma including: 'The maintenance of biographical files on Intelligence personalities. The maintenance of photographic files on Intelligence personalities. Reporting upon possible infiltration of our own intelligence activities, OSS recommended the establishment of post-war stations at Bombay, Calcutta, Colombo, Kabul, Kandy, Karachi, Madras, New Delhi, Rangoon and Simla.[31]

OSS officers already at these various OSS outstations scattered across India were also busy identifying specific post-war projects. One such scheme was 'Intelligence Project Bingo', again outlined in April 1945, which sought to examine the use which Indian financiers and industrialists in Bombay might make of the large Sterling credit balance that India had accumulated during the war. OSS noted, quite correctly, that this balance was enormous and, moreover, its use was a vital issue of the moment. A powerful group of industrialists and financiers based in Bombay was one the foremost bodies competing for control of this credit, proposing to employ it for a programme of large-scale industrial development entitled the 'Bombay Plan'. OSS detected a potential problem here, recalling the effective way in which cheap Japanese piece-goods had captured pre-war markets:

In particular, it would be interesting to determine whether and how the Indian indus-trial group will undertake to capture the markets of India, China, South East Asia and the Indies which formerly belonged to the Japanese . . . the Bombay group may well attempt to expand their production and capture the Japanese textile markets . . . Information concerning these developments affecting the former Japanese market would be of the greatest interest to the United States, not only so far as its own foreign trade is concerned but so far as it affects the political and economic interests of the United States in China.

Here, as with so many American officials in Asia, the views of OSS were partly informed by the centrality of her ambitions in China.[32]

Meanwhile current American intelligence collection continued to shift quite naturally towards political and economic subjects. In India, R&A ana-lysts initially despatched to India to work on strategic issues were dropping their study of Japanese in favour of Hindi, and becoming immersed in Indian culture and politics.[33] OSS in India and South East Asia seemed almost obli-vious to the growing military concerns about the Soviets and the early phases of the Cold War. Occasionally, contact with personnel from other services offered them a glimpse of this. In July 1945, Ripley passed through Bombay. Here he was introduced to Major Coulter Huyler, a US Army Military Obser-ver from Delhi, previously of the US Army Counter-Intelligence Corps. Ripley was alarmed to discover that Huyler was investigating OSS work with the Burma Patriotic Front (BPF) and the Indian Communist Party (ICP). Huyler reported to Washington that 'OSS in May 1945 served as an agent of the Communist Party in getting eight Burmese Communists into Burma from India'. Ripley protested that OSS co-operation had been purely tactical, but nevertheless realised that Washington might conclude that OSS was 'conspir-ing to import red-hot Communists into British territory'.[34] Ripley's concerns were not misplaced, for by the end of 1945 G-2 increasingly sought to portray OSS as a hotbed of fellow travellers and left-liberals.[35]

OSS succeeded in achieving their desired 'Observer' status within SEAC and India. It was not until 1 October 1945 that Mountbatten issued an order directing that, apart from X-2 units working on war crimes, OSS should cease to function within SEAC.[36] Mountbatten's directive was already technically irrelevant, for OSS had been formally abolished by Truman on 10 September 1945 and had entered a strange post-war half-life. OSS R&A was incorporated within the State Department, while 750 OSS field operatives formed a small intelligence organisation renamed the Strategic Services Unit (SSU) under the War Department. Donovan retired from OSS, though not from intelligence work, and passed these SSU remnants to General Magruder and then General Quinn. The survival of OSS in the field as SSU now owed much to pressure from Moffat and State Department officials concerned with South East Asia, who valued its work.[37]

During September and October 1945, OSS officials in Asia continued to plan for the fully fledged post-war intelligence organisation which they presumed would succeed them. For McCarthy, the Head of X-2 in India, the main problem continued to be British security.[38] Current plans called for American businessmen and industrialists to operate in India under their 'perfectly legitimate cover', controlled by senior intelligence officials in the guise of American Foreign Service officers. He dismissed this as hopeless:

I feel confident that an uneducated or ill-trained person, who makes it his business to go about enquiring for political or economic or industrial or social intelligence will have a short life in this work, for the reason that I am convinced his activity will be reported to the British Intelligence immediately. I have had evidence of this in our past experiences in India.

McCarthy explained that he was already investigating what he considered to be a 'priceless' alternative. He pointed out that there were Indians in many different occupations who welcomed an opportunity to funnel information directly into the State Department through OSS. He continued: 'We have in Delhi selected, as an experiment, two such Indians who are Nationalists.' They had known these men for a year and 'their hatred for British rule'. So far these two agents had performed well, but McCarthy was ever cautious of the activities of the British police. Accordingly, his alternative blueprint called for a system of intelligence 'cells' consisting of no more than ten men. During October two Indian nationalists that they had recruited completed 'an intensive period of indoctrination in the methods of gathering intelligence' and were activated, together with several other trusted informants who had been working on a paid basis for over a year. But Washington appeared to express no interest. By late October 1945, reduced to four officers in Delhi, McCarthy confessed that X-2 were in a state of 'confusion and uncertainty'.[39]

In November there was a volte-face as State Department advocacy began to take effect. The few remaining SSU personnel were informed that their recent work on the political situation in India, and on preparing the way for a permanent intelligence organisation, had 'completely eradicated earlier doubts as to the value of SSU services in the India–Burma Theater' and that 'SSU filled a vital gap for the State Department'. Moreover, they were told that now 'key U.S. officials were becoming conscious of the need for continuing this type of intelligence activity'. As a result SSU was taken fully under the wing of the remaining US Army elements in the India–Burma Theatre and given Army channels of communication. They were told that once Britain requested the final withdrawal of SSU, they would nevertheless remain in the region under 'military cover'.[40]

Details were finalised at a meeting between the State Department and the new head of SSU on 29 November 1945. They agreed to tell Mountbatten that most SSU personnel would be gone by March 1946 and that a complete withdrawal would be completed by 1 April. Meanwhile they would request permission to resume the military attaché system in areas that had been returned to civilian rule. The State Department were anxious to maintain an unbroken flow of material from SSU:

In order to retain the benefits of SSU political reporting . . . Magruder offered to allow selected SSU personnel to be released from the armed services and remain temporarily attached to our officers at Rangoon, Singapore, Bangkok, Batavia and, when they are reestablished, Saigon and Medan. These persons would retain SSU cryptographic channels and would continue to report to and be paid by SSU, but would be administratively under the principal [Foreign Service] officer at each post and would co-operate with him in the political reporting and intelligence fields, making available to him all material gathered or produced by them. General Magruder said that these arrangements were similar to those in effect at many posts in Europe where SSU X-2 officers are stationed.[41]

This arrangement was a crucial step, allowing the SSU organisation to live on under diplomatic cover, and preserving a degree of local infrastructure until the arrival of the CIA in the summer of 1947. The extent of this local continuity from OSS through SSU and CIG to CIA has probably been underestimated.

US Army G-2 officers in South East Asia were anxious to see OSS evaporate, in much the same way that SIS was anxious to retire their sister service, SOE. In January 1946 Brigadier General Thomas S. Timberman, the senior American officer in the area, decided to restrict remaining SSU personnel to his own headquarters at Singapore, a decision reversed by Washington so that 'certain intelligence activities would continue' in India. With this firm support from Washington, SSU still had 112 personnel in the theatre in February 1946 in Delhi, Calcutta and throughout South East Asia.[42]

SSU officers in Singapore were not yet interested in communism and instead were reporting on British attempts to play down the American role in the defeat of Japan. In February 1946 they noted that: 'Most Malays, Chinese, and Indians in Malaya know little about the United States', and voiced suspicions that imports of American goods were being 'obstructed'.[43] In Washington, the focus of SSU was quite different. As one senior SSU officer wrote in March 1946: 'To indicate that coverage of the Soviet Union should have top priority is almost redundant. But it needs to be repeated again and again.'[44] It was only with encouragement from Washington that SSU in Asia began taking more interest in communism. SSU in India now began to report on the prospects for communism on the sub-continent as well as covering the increasingly important activities of Jinnah and the Muslim League.[45] In March 1946 the State Department asked SSU to look at the role of the Indian Communist Party (ICP) in the strikes and disturbances of that month and also on the loyalty of the Indian police and military during any emergency withdrawal by the British.[46] SSU continually illuminated the Indian scene, sometimes with priceless anecdotes. During the August 1946 riots in Calcutta they reported that the Muslim police were responsible for 60 per cent of the looting and that the 'Chief of the Calcutta police received valuable gifts of loot'.[47]

By April 1946 SSU busied itself with 'an interim intelligence reporting program under the aegis of the State Department'. As American consulates opened, SSU recorded 'persons to be discharged from the military service to work for the State Department'. Regular Foreign Service officers were 'fully advised as to details concerning the duties . . . of these persons'. In Rangoon, Major Harry Hunter, Head of the SSU Mission, delayed his departure until 20 April 1946, giving him enough time to welcome the new Vice-Consul, Richard Usher, 'formerly with OSS', and to brief him on the current situation.[48] In November 1946 the reports of SSU began to circulate as the reports of the Central Intelligence Group.[49] By the summer of 1947, this had become the CIA. The same transitions were under way right across Asia. In April 1946, Don Garden was reporting from Saigon as an SSU officer.[50] By April 1947 he was with the transitional CIG developing a relationship with the Emperor Bao Dai.[51]

Much valuable expertise was lost in the period between 1945 and 1947, but one far-sighted decision offset this problem. In the spring of 1945, with large-scale liquidation of OSS in Europe already beginning, OSS set up the 'Continuity Project'. This was a detailed record of 'key OSS personnel' whose future careers placed them in 'strategically advantageous positions for intelligence work' and who were willing to help in the future. The project continued into 1946 on a wholly unofficial basis under SSU officer Peter Karlow. In 1947 this was turned over to Rolfe Kingsley, an operations officer with the Office of Special Operations at the newly formed CIA, and was used as 'a selected personnel procurement guide'.[52] In Asia the considerable number of OSS and SSU personnel that remained in Asia after their demobilisation to set up businesses proved an invaluable asset. In December 1947, Willis R. Bird, former Deputy Head of OSS China, and one of many who stayed on in Thailand, wrote to Donovan offering his services as local politics became more turbulent. By 1949 Bird was employed by the CIA-owned Civil Air Transport Company.[53]

SOE survives in SEAC

In London, as in Washington, the endless political wrangling of the secret services took its toll of the patience of senior policy-makers during the last phase of the war. Confronted with regional secret service controversies in the Mediterranean and in South East Asia, together with a litany of embarrassing incidents in neutral countries, Eden pressed for action declaring, perhaps for the fourth or fifth time in the course of the war, that he had had enough. On 23 November 1944, he proposed to Churchill that he should take over SOE. He argued that SIS, PWE and MI5 were already effectively under his control and it would only be logical to extend this further. The Chiefs of Staff were similarly fatigued by clandestine wrangles and agreed, albeit as 'a temporary measure only'. However, Churchill decided to leave arrangements unchanged.[54]

Like Donovan's OSS, both SIS and SOE had begun to think about their own post-war existence in a concentrated way by 1944. Many in South East Asia could have been forgiven for thinking that SOE would emerge as the dominant regional service, occluding a weak SIS altogether. Garnons-Williams was not the only person worried about this. Even in 1943, William Stephenson of BSC had observed that: 'S.I.S. is old and rather obsolete compared with S.O.E. and that S.O.E. is likely to survive after the war because of its younger and abler organisation; that it may in fact, alternatively take over S.I.S.'[55] But in the four months between October 1945 and January 1946, the reverse process took place. In London the decision was taken to disband most of SOE, while SIS survived, and incorporated a small remnant of SOE, renamed the Special Operations and Political Action Section. This is not the place to recount the associated complex manoeuvring. But this was clearly a hostile takeover rather than a merger. Robert Cecil, who was working closely with Menzies at this time, captured its nature when he remarked: 'SOE was liquidated with almost indecent haste. If relations with SIS had been more cordial, one first-class organization could have been created out of the best of two elements but the chance was missed.'[56]

Although SOE suffered an abrupt termination in London, the story was very different in Asia. Whitehall was already beginning to wind down SOE in London in April 1945 and the needs of the Far Eastern War seem by then to have been almost an irritation to the Chiefs of Staff, who complained that SOE in India and SEAC appeared to be 'very large'. They complained of the tendency of theatre commanders 'to thrust tasks upon SOE which were outside their province'.[57] Nevertheless, in mid-June Mountbatten persuaded the

Chiefs of Staff in London to allow him keep an SOE force of not less than 2,500.[58] This SOE component formed the first wave of British re-occupation right across Asia and supported the restoration of administration in a dozen different countries. On 23 November 1945 the Chiefs of Staff, under pressure to demobilise quickly, urged Mountbatten that SOE 'should be completely liquidated at the earliest possible moment and that it should not continue its activities in territories in your command which you are now occupying'.[59] But this was quite unacceptable to Mountbatten. Plagued by difficult administrative duties in volatile new areas over which SEAC had only just been given administrative control, such as Indochina and the Netherlands East Indies, and responsible for large number of guerrillas in Malaya, Mountbatten found SOE indispensable.[60]

Mountbatten retained some 549 SOE personnel, renamed Allied Land Forces Para-Military Operations (ALFPMO) or G.Ops.4, and placed under the control of Lt Colonel R.V. Johnston-Smith.[61] The operations of ALFPMO were undertaken 'primarily for the purposes of obtaining political intelligence' and continued until 1947.[62] These numbers are startling when we consider that, at any point in the war, SIS never had much more than 100 staff in the region. The post-war duties of ALFPMO included disarming and controlling guerrillas in Malaya, assisting the French secret services against the Viet Minh in Indochina, augmenting a crucial intelligence screen in volatile areas of Thailand and Indonesia and continuing SOE's wartime currency operations in China. Mackenzie retired and returned to London to talk to Bevin about the future of clandestine activities in the region, leaving Brigadier Anstey to liquidate the SOE sections that were not to be preserved. At this point, and rather disingenuously, Browning, Mountbatten's Chief of Staff, told SSU that SOE was being 'inactivated in November' but SSU found Browning's assertion implausible.[63]

Changes in internal security were complex. British security organisations across the region were preparing not only for short term re-occupation, but also for medium-term withdrawal, as the accession of a Labour Government in London confirmed that independence across South Asia was not far away. In Ceylon, remaining OSS X-2 officers claimed that the British 'do not trust the native set-up and are quietly building up MI5 in this area', with a view to its remaining separate from the indigenous police organisation after the war.[64] But British officials were also anxious to ensure the stability of these post-war regimes by handing over to them much of the security apparatus enjoyed by the former colonial state. In India, the main security organisation, IB, passed seamlessly into the hands of the new Indian administration in the summer of 1947.[65]

In August 1945 the sigint work of Anderson diminished rather than ceased. Anderson continued to operate beyond Ceylonese independence in 1948 on into the 1960s, although the Ceylonese administration was ignorant of its true nature.[66] Meanwhile staff from WEC in Delhi were redeployed to meet the early Cold War challenges of the Azerbaijan crisis in Iran. In late 1945 Alan Stripp of WEC moved to Abbotabad near Rawalpindi in the North West Frontier Province. This was a small outpost with a history of interception stretching back to at least 1914 and probably before. Here they were able to break Iranian, Afghan, but not Soviet traffic for the duration of the crisis.[67]

MacArthur was now presiding over the occupation of Japan. Britain's intelligence presence here was an exact reflection of her military presence, a token existence. Nevertheless, Britain had important issues to pursue here, including access to Japanese technology. Britain had wanted a system in Japan modelled on the multinational Combined Intelligence Objectives Committee which was operating successful in Germany. But Japan was not like Germany, with its separate occupation zones. Throughout the Far East, intelligence target exploitation of the enemy was to be effected by the commander in each theatre, although London was assured of free access to targets under MacArthur.[68]

But in practice access proved difficult. By September 1946, a confrontation had developed over the sensitive issue of the exploitation of Japanese atomic research. The British delivered an ultimatum to Washington, declaring that 'unless full and comprehensive information in the field is furnished' they would despatch their own independent British scientific investigation mission.[69] British indignation had been triggered by the discovery that the United States had identified centres of atomic research in Japan and had destroyed the equipment, including cyclotrons and other elaborate machinery, before British teams could inspect them. Occurring shortly after the United States Congress had decided to cease Allied atomic co-operation this destruction did not seem accidental. London reminded Washington of past assurances about access to 'all available information on Japanese scientific research, without qualification as to its potential application'.[70] Washington conceded, fearing that controversy might trigger further embarrassing requests from smaller allies.[71]

Conclusions

MacArthur and his intelligence chief, General Willoughby, were untypical in their early Cold War concerns. In most other Far Eastern theatres, commanders were preoccupied with the practical difficulties of re-occupation, of war crimes, of awkward nationalist movements and with colonial reconstruction. Even in China, where the continued progress made by the Communists and the Soviet incursion into Manchuria impinged very directly on American policy, the focus of intelligence seems to shift slowly. Wedemeyer was

commander here and the only extended discussion of intelligence in his memoirs during this transitional period refers, not to communism, but instead to
the fraught issue of whether post-war China would decide to drive on the
right or the left. Wedemeyer had persuaded Chiang to move over to the
American traffic system, because of the increasing predominance of American vehicles. But the British, he asserted, realising this would 'destroy the
market for British cars', orchestrated a subterranean campaign through the
newspapers to undermine this. This activity was, in turn, uncovered by Wedemeyer's 'secret service' officers whom he had set on the case. The British
counter-campaign was unsuccessful and at the stroke of midnight on New
Year's Eve 1945, Wedemeyer had the 'thrilling experience' of standing on
the balcony of the Cathay Hotel in Shanghai and watching the traffic switching over.[72]

In London too, during 1945 and 1946, the danger posed by Soviet ambitions in Asia, in contrast to Europe, was considered low. Asia seemed geographically remote from the Soviet Union, with even India protected by the
ancient physical barrier of the Himalayas and the JIC gazetted this region the
lowest of Stalin's priorities. Even communist activity in Malaya was dismissed by many as an isolated act of 'dacoity', before the opening of the Malayan
Emergency in 1948.[73] The approach taken in Washington was rather different.
There, by the end of 1945, worries about the Soviet Union were having their
impact on colonial issues in unexpected ways, and not only in areas where
the local nationalists revealed a communistic taint. This was revealed most
starkly in the growing American interest in airbases on the fringes of the
Soviet Union.[74] From this point of view, India's rapid acceleration towards
independence now looked rather inconvenient. In November 1945, James
Byrnes, Truman's new Secretary of State, approached Bevin privately with a
request to keep control of some American strategic airbases located in India.
Later the Americans handed to the British Embassy in Washington a full list
'for Mr Bevin's eyes alone' of such airbases. Byrnes urged that this request
was 'of the highest secrecy' and the material be 'given only the most
restricted and top level circulation'.[75] But Bevin had already indicated to
Byrnes that Indian independence would not be of a qualified sort. Delhi
would have to make up its own mind about the possibility of permitting
American bomber bases, for India, he insisted, was already 'virtually a sovereign state . . . and I really could not handle India in the way suggested'.[76] The
reality of decolonisation and its potential negative impact upon containment
was becoming clear.

17   Resisting the resistance: Thailand, Malaya and Burma

> Thailand can become an 'incubator of Americanism' in the Far East . . .
> Thailand can become an excellent beachhead for American Far Eastern
> policy.
>
> Don Garden, OSS SEAC, 13 April 1945[1]

Thailand

By late 1944 the strain of war was telling on key figures in South East Asia.
Steveni, the displaced Head of SIS had already gone to the Middle East. On
16 October, Colonel Richard Heppner, Head of OSS in SEAC, informed
Donovan that he had been ill for some months and had lost his customary
drive. With the final push against Japan looming, he asked to be relieved.[2]
By December 1944 he had swapped chairs with John Coughlin, Head of OSS
in the China Theater. Garnons-Williams, Head of P Division, submitted his
resignation on medical grounds on 6 March 1945. Having broken his back in
an air crash in January 1943, returning from the Casablanca Conference, he
suffered an 'increasing terror of the air'. Now, his 'flying morale had finally
cracked' and he could no longer visit commanders in the field.[3] But on 9
May 1945 Mountbatten told Donovan that he had failed to find a replacement
and, with the pace of operations mounting, he had pressed Garnons-Williams
to stay on in a desk-bound form, which met with Donovan's approval.[4] Inevitably, perhaps, rumours circulated about the underlying reasons for Garnons-
Williams' resignation. Whatever the reason, by July 1945 he was barely functioning.[5] Meanwhile Edmond Taylor had persuaded Donovan to relieve him
of his work as Deputy Head of P Division. Of all the secret service supremos,
only Colin Mackenzie endured to the end of the war.

In early 1945 the rapid liberation of occupied territory on mainland Asia
began and the political dimension now seemed stronger than ever. On 1 January, Don Garden, the senior OSS SI officer responsible for Thailand, who
had worked on the *Bangkok Daily Mail* before the war, reviewed the year
ahead with concern. With liberation almost upon them, all the Americans

were publicly known for in Thailand was the heavy casualties from their bombing: 'Temples and hospitals have been destroyed, thousands of homes have been wrecked. Instinctive resentment will linger.' By contrast, because Thailand was in SEAC, the British would enjoy the kudos of being the liberators and would run the occupational government. There would be a key role, he warned, for figures such as Major Grut of SOE, while Alec Adams of PWE would 'continue his propaganda role'.

Garden urged a vigorous information counter-offensive, stressing Thai–American co-operation in resisting the Japanese: 'We Americans must be ready and equipped to tell our story, both before and after Thailand is liberated. This by force of circumstances becomes chiefly an OSS job. Members of our organisations or our agents will be the first ''Americans'' in the country.' He suggested a man specially briefed and prepared to give out the American story and to 'keep hammering away at it from every angle, of which there are many'. The story of OSS and the Free Thai Movement was, he insisted, just the thing, including the 'thrills and excitement' of operations. This would make a pleasing contrast to the British, who would put out the sort of 'dreary' stuff that 'makes the Thais yawn'.[6] This made sense and from August 1945 substantial publicity efforts raised the profile of both OSS and the Free Thai movement.[7]

In SEAC, British officers enjoyed spreading rumours about the British occupation of Thailand for the benefit of their American colleagues, but may have been unaware that this gossipy material reached a higher level. The State Department's review of Thailand's post-war status warned that the British planned a 'special arrangement for the Kra Isthmus (the peninsula part of Thailand rich in rubber and tin separating Burma from Malaya)' which would 'effect Thai sovereignty' in the peninsula. They continued:

It is understood that the British propose to appoint Colonel Evelyn Van Milligen, formerly manager of the Bombay–Burmah Trading Corporation, as chief of military government in Thailand. Colonel Van Milligen has expressed the personal view that the southern provinces of Thailand should be attached to British Malaya and that he could see no reason why the Thai should object.

Colonel Van Milligen was the SIS officer running the Thai country section. He had enjoyed winding up his OSS colleagues, but he had not expected his remarks to be given a starring role in the State Department's policy papers, while moderate statements by Eden on the subject were relegated to 'Annex B' of the same document.[8]

The State Department saw Thailand's wider importance for the American policy in the region: 'With our interest in expanding export markets after the war, an independent Thailand may be of particular importance to the United States as the only market in Southeast Asia not complicated by colonial relationships.' More importantly, recalling the problems of colonial commodity cartels which had inflated inter-war prices, they noted that Thailand might be the only independent Eastern source of rubber and tin. Politically, Thailand's continued independence would be a high-profile indicator that 'we are not imperialistic'.[9]

Periodic glimpses of British colonial opinion from open sources seemed to confirm the picture offered in OSS reports. In May 1945, an article in the journal *British Malaya*, which represented the former British residents, looked forward gleefully to the extension of British borders 'to include the Kra' and noted Australian government backing.[10] In the same month a sister journal, the *Crown Colonist*, asserted that this acquisition was nothing less than 'essential' due to the 'craven capitulation' of the Thais.[11] Moffat's Division in the State Department received streams of such material during 1945.[12] Washington had the depth of expertise to evaluate these reports carefully and OSS officers such as Frederic Dolbeare, while identifying the Kra as a serious issue, dismissed reports of an SOE-sponsored Royalist Plot as 'nonsense'.[13]

This was a correct assessment. While Colonel A. C. Pointon of SOE had indeed held discussions with Van Milligen about the potential benefits of contacting the young Thai King, then in Europe, they foresaw unwelcome complications.[14] In early 1945, Alec Adams of PWE had given extended consideration to the issue of 'the Siamese Monarchy and Political Warfare', but had similarly concluded that this sensitive area was unattractive.[15] In contrast, British hopes for something on the Kra Isthmus still remained firm. In March 1945 the British Chiefs of Staff reviewed post-war strategic requirements. The Royal Navy asserted that 'since we were at war with Siam and the US were not, we should be in a position to insist that our special claims were satisfied'. Rather than crude territorial absorption, they hoped for a treaty similar to the existing one governing the Suez Canal. They sought various defence rights in time of war, 'control of the training and equipping of the Siamese armed forces' and supervision of Siamese defence policy.[16]

By early 1945 these conflicting British and American ambitions were increasingly manifesting themselves at the operational level. The Thai case is significant, since here, perhaps more than in any other country, secret service activities had a material bearing on the shape of the post-war settlement. Mountbatten certainly sensed the mounting tension and urged Donovan to visit him in January 1945 in the hope of resolving these issues 'which I am not prepared to delegate authority to my staff to discuss'.[17] As we have seen, Donovan arrived in SEAC in late January 1945 to attend a series of secret service conferences, which also attracted George Taylor of SOE and John Gibbs of SIS from London. Mackenzie and Taylor tried to re-launch the tired concept of amalgamation, suggesting it was desirable to tell the resistance in Thailand 'that the British and Americans were working together', despite the fact that SOE and OSS had separate missions with Pridi, the Thai Regent in Bangkok. Taylor suggested merging the missions, but Donovan refused. He did however offer the assurance that all OSS Thai operations would now be launched from SEAC and not from China.[18] Just before the conference, Donovan cabled Roosevelt explaining that Pridi wished to exfiltrate a prominent Thai diplomat to help set up a provisional government in exile that might eventually be recognised by the United Nations, hoping that 'post-war Thai independence would thus be assured'. On 25 January a Thai diplomat, Konthi Suphamongkon, bearing the appropriate letter of authority, was extracted.[19] Konthi eventually travelled back to Washington with Donovan, who continued to keep the ailing Roosevelt informed of developments.[20]

Field officers from both OSS and SOE were more interested in military issues and were increasingly anxious to facilitate Thailand's transfer to the side of the Allies, regardless of the political consequences. But such field officers were increasingly aware that the Thais would need to be encouraged by sympathetic statements. This issue came to a head when SOE despatched a further mission, Operation *Panicle*, in April 1945, led by Brigadier Victor Jacques, formerly a commercial lawyer in pre-war Bangkok. Before his departure Dening told him firmly that there could be absolutely no political commitment to Thailand. Jacques asked how he should deal with seemingly innocent questions such as whether Britain stood by the Atlantic Charter, but Dening instructed him to reply 'no comment'. When Jacques observed that this was bound to excite suspicion, Dening responded that London had ordered this. Jacques arrived by flying boat and later moved fairly freely, if discreetly, around the city of Bangkok. But his refusal to be drawn on Thailand's future status was an obvious irritation.

Attention now turned to the build-up of a large guerrilla army in northern Thailand, against the moment when the Allies invaded. Pridi's Thai resistance movement was clearly the way ahead. Mountbatten believed there was significant military potential in unleashing Thai guerrillas once the Japanese retreated from Burma, but two dangers confronted him. First, unless the guerrilla build-up was undertaken with extreme secrecy, Japan would take direct control in a coup and crush the resistance, as they did in Indochina on 9 March 1945. Second, the Thai resistance might self-detonate, attacking the Japanese prematurely for political reasons, hoping to escape the charge of being 'eleventh hour allies'. Despite these worries, both SOE and OSS built up very substantial arms stocks to increase guerrilla training areas in remote districts. By July 1945 remote airfields were receiving supply flights every two days.[21] But in July Mountbatten was told that the war would terminate abruptly, and so the Thais would not be permitted to prove themselves against the Japanese. Dening told the Thais that they must 'work their passage home', but they had been ordered into military inaction by Mountbatten.[22]

On 8 August 1945, SOE's Victor Jacques in Bangkok and Dening reviewed the situation. Thai leaders in Bangkok were very anxious to reach an understanding with London and were exasperated by the way in which resistance had been undercut by the early end to the war. They now viewed earlier British requests not to attack the Japanese as 'a card for future policy'. As a result, Jacques warned, the Thais now looked increasingly to the more sympathetic Americans, reporting that 'each principal leader in Bangkok is protected by OSS weapons'. Dening shared these misgivings about London's hard line on the post-war settlement. Even if London kept silent, OSS, he argued, would publicise the fact that Pridi and his resistance movement had 'shown the maximum degree of co-operation and have furnished valuable military intelligence'. Moreover, Washington was quite aware that it was 'only the restraint imposed by us' that prevented Bangkok from openly siding with the Allies. 'Major General Donovan', Dening continued, 'made it clear in a recent visit here that he is determined that pressure upon us about Siam shall continue . . . American suspicions about our intentions are in no way allayed.' Donovan was as good as his word.[23]

Mountbatten had restrained the Thai resistance against the wishes of the guerrilla leaders in Bangkok, and also against the advice of Mackenzie and SOE. In May and June, Mackenzie had persistently argued (but wrongly) that the Japanese were perilously close to action against leaders of the resistance, and would certainly strike during the British invasion of Malaya. Better, SOE argued, to launch the guerrilla campaign now, facilitating British deception plans which attempted to stress Thailand, rather than Malaya, as the next major target. But Mountbatten had refused on purely military grounds, for his logistics could not sustain such an uprising; instead he had insisted that the resistance stay its hand.[24]

OSS intervenes

By August 1945, Dening was negotiating a peace settlement in Ceylon with a delegation from the newly formed Thai Provisional Government. The State Department viewed these talks with the deepest suspicion. The terms had already been softened as a result of exchanges between London and Washington and, most significantly, Churchill's desire to overtly annex southern Thailand had been dropped. But there was still talk of British bases in southern Thailand, harsh currency arrangements and rice reparations to solve the growing food crisis in Malaya. Accordingly, when OSS reported in early September that Dening had persuaded the Thai delegation in Ceylon to sign a treaty, Abbot Low Moffat and Dean Acheson in the State Department attempted to forestall it. Telephoning John G. Winant, the American Ambassador in London, at 8.25 pm on 6 September 1945, they instructed him to seek out Bevin or Attlee and to appeal for a postponement of the Anglo-Thai treaty. Winant understood the urgency and replied: 'If I can't get Bevin tonight, then I'll go to Attlee.'[25] Meanwhile OSS in SEAC advised the Thai delegation on how to stall Dening by raising the technical issue of 'credentials'.[26]

Late at night on 6 September there was an informal discussion at No. 10 Downing Street between Attlee, Winant and the Head of the Foreign Office Far Eastern Department, Sterndale Bennett. The proposed Anglo-Thai Treaty came in two parts, the first dealing with short-term practical issues related to the British occupation, the second dealing with longer-term political issues. All agreed that they did not like the look of the second part and the result was its suspension. Winant declared himself 'satisfied'.[27] But at Mountbatten's headquarters, Dening was shocked at London's abrupt order to halt and complained bitterly that American intervention in bilateral negotiations was unprecedented. He added: 'I am inclined to think that [the] American attitude has been largely influenced by reports of OSS.' It quickly transpired that most of the State Department's information on the negotiations had indeed come from OSS.[28] When OSS explained the matter to Truman they added that, on the afternoon of 7 September, an OSS officer had also seen Pridi alone in Bangkok to discuss the treaty. Pridi said that he had received the text of the two-part treaty on the morning of the 6 September 'with a strongly worded warning to the effect that the sooner Thailand signed the agreement, the better'. Pridi had initially thought that the text had been jointly agreed by London and Washington, but now fully understood that the proposed text did not have American support.[29]

Revelations about the OSS role created an uproar within SEAC, for it contradicted previous direct orders to OSS. Back in April 1945, Mountbatten, together with General Sultan from the IB Theater and their staffs, had all confessed themselves tired of political activity by OSS. A complete ban had been placed on OSS political reporting. Furthermore, General Sultan, who disliked OSS, had insisted on vetting all their messages:

To date the Theater Commander [General Sultan] has not been advised of nor has he approved political and economic reporting within the Theatre by OSS . . . A directive was recently issued by General Timberman, the Theater Commander's [Sultan's] representative in S.E.A.C. that copies of all communications between Washington and Kandy, and Kandy and Washington must be sent to him.

But OSS had concluded that because of the 'extreme delicacy' of political and economic reporting 'it will be impossible to conform with General Timberman's directive'. OSS were resourceful and had successfully evaded the moratorium. They recommended to Washington that in future OSS should send political intelligence via local American diplomatic missions, thereby circumventing SEAC and IBT channels.[30] OSS political intelligence had therefore continued to flow from SEAC into the State Department thereafter.[31]

These worries intensified in August. Max Bishop, IB Theater's political adviser, complained directly to James Byrnes in Washington that both OSS and OWI were 'carried away by their enthusiasm' and were 'more pro-Thai than the Thais themselves'. Bishop explained that this was creating a climate of mistrust and asked if OSS were supported by elements in the State Department. Further prohibitions were piled upon OSS. In August, General 'Speck' Wheeler, who had just replaced Sultan as IB Theater Commander, wrote to Coughlin expressly forbidding OSS to give 'political advice' to the recently arrived Thai delegation in Ceylon.[32]

But after the American démarche to Attlee on the night of 6 September, it was clear to Dening that these multiple injunctions against OSS had been quite ineffective. As State Department and White House records show, OSS were clearly working with the Thai delegation to thwart Dening. On 4 September 1945 the full texts of the agreements had been presented to the Thai Military Mission and that night they were sent by OSS through the American Consulate at Kandy to OSS Washington, who urged the State Department to give the matter 'urgent attention'.[33] Simultaneously Donovan had passed this material to Truman.[34] On 7 September, with discussions halted, Mountbatten chose to confront Coughlin with evidence of political reporting from SEAC. Coughlin spoke frankly to Mountbatten of the continued political dimension of his activities, voicing his suspicion that American officials were being deliberately kept in the dark.[35]

The following day offered a most curious sequel. Dening had been told that Seni Pramoj would be stopping in Ceylon on 8 September on his way from Washington to Bangkok. Seni Pramoj had been the Head of the OSS-sponsored Free Thai Movement in the United States and Thai Ambassador in Washington, and was now Thai Prime Minister designate. Dening hoped to use the visit to calm Thai fears and to emphasise the benign aspects of British policy. Yet, to his dismay, Dening was required to accompany Mountbatten to the surrender ceremony of Japanese forces in newly liberated Singapore and could not be present to greet Seni Pramoj on his arrival in Ceylon. Accordingly, Dening left instructions for an appropriate reception, arranging for him to be accommodated at the King's Pavilion in Ceylon.[36]

Horror awaited Dening on his return. His staff confessed that 'Seni was lost and no-one knew what his movements were'. SOE, together with the local Field Security Section, mounted an investigation and some information was obtained from Denys Page, a young cryptanalyst who happened to have travelled from Washington on the same aircraft. It transpired that a quite unbelievable reception had awaited Seni Pramoj at Ratmalana airfield in Ceylon on 8 September. As if to confirm the worst suspicions of Britain's colonial mentality, the Security Control Section at the airport had recorded Seni as a Burmese, 'thinking Bangkok was in Burma'. The Special Branch at Colombo had then listed him as a citizen of French Indochina. Doubly gazetted a colonial subject, the Prime Minister designate of Thailand found no reception party and forlornly made his own way to the Galle Face Hotel. Unable to find any accommodation reserved for him, he attempted to telephone both the Chief Secretary and his deputy at SEAC headquarters. Both, he was informed, were at a garden party.[37]

OSS responded differently to Seni Pramoj's arrival. Within half an hour of Seni's arrival at the Galle Face Hotel 'an American consulate car drew up and a letter was delivered to the subject'. Seni Pramoj made no further attempts to contact SEAC headquarters and, for the duration of his visit, 'had a lot to do with the American consulate'.[38] By the time this was reported to Dening, Seni Pramoj had left Ceylon for India, *en route* to Bangkok, and was installed in the OSS mess in Calcutta.[39] In London this was seen as confirmation of Dening's worries about OSS. Alec Adams, who had left PWE and was now on the Thai desk in the Foreign Office, observed: 'The OSS have on at least one earlier occasion "kidnapped" important Siamese who were supposed to be looked after by British organisations. The episode smells.'[40] I.A. Wilson Young, who was soon to head a newly formed South East Asia Department, blamed SEAC for 'shocking inefficiency' which had 'enabled the Americans to score off us badly'. Sterndale Bennett wrote: 'No action. But what a mess'.[41]

Victor Jacques reported that once Seni Pramoj arrived in Bangkok in mid-September, the attitude of the Thai delegation in Ceylon had changed markedly. Dening complained that they had come within a whisker of getting the treaty accepted at the start of the month, as 'the Regent [Pridi] first succumbed to 21 demands', but the chance had gone with the arrival of the 'Americophil' Seni.[42] Dening was correct. A further Thai delegation left Bangkok for Ceylon on 21 September. Before departing they explained to Coughlin that their strategy was to delay, meanwhile hoping for further American pressure to soften the terms, although eventually, they warned, they would have to sign.[43]

During October, Jacques continued to chart the changing demeanour of Thai leaders. They no longer had the appearance of a defeated nation, he complained, and instead 'are puffed up their own conceit', believing that they had 'virtually liquidated the state of war'. He saw little chance of Britain achieving her desiderata, for 'they can count on the Americans to back them against us' while the French were 'little inclined to do anything about anything'.[44] In London, the Chiefs of Staff had now learned of the impediments to their plans for the Kra Isthmus. Cunningham, the Chief of the Naval Staff, was incensed:

Why should the State Department feel called upon to criticise so narrowly our interest in our own post war security, when they had not hesitated themselves to seek security arrangements with Iceland, and proposed to do the same in the Azores?[45]

But Thailand's foot-dragging tactics were highly effective. They continually requested 'clarifications' and Dening's patience was slowly exhausted. On 10 December he informed London that if the Thai delegation refused to sign he would simply 'leave them here to rot' until they indicate a change of heart.[46] Dening vented his anger by rubbishing the resistance in Thailand to the press, portraying it as 'ineffectual' and 'not involving loss of life and sacrifice'.[47] But privately Dening knew he was fighting a losing battle while Washington reaped diplomatic rewards. On 24 December, at a private dinner given for senior American officers in Bangkok, the King, Pridi and Seni 'repeatedly expressed gratitude for action of US in ameliorating British terms'.[48]

General Timberman, now head of the US Liaison Section at SEAC Headquarters in Singapore, was less pleased. Having previously made genuine attempts to halt the political work of OSS, he felt he was likely to be the person brought to book by Mountbatten. He now learned 'unofficially' that Dening was preparing a report setting out why OSS, now called SSU, should be 'ejected' from SEAC:

He says in this memo that in the first place the SSU has as its objective collecting intelligence on British imperial interests in South East Asia, and that our alleged purpose for SSU Operations (War Crimes etc.) is no more than a subterfuge. He says secondly that SSU has constantly blocked his efforts to reach an agreement with the Thais; that by undercover activities in Siam, SSU has stiffened the attitude of the Thais towards Britain; and that finally, he can prove these statements . . . As you know, these allegations by Denning [sic] are true, and probably can be proved. Taylor says he has no doubt Denning can prove such charges . . . This will be most serious.

Timberman feared that Dening would now uncover the further role of SSU in more recent delays, 'and the fact that instructions not to sign reached them through SSU channels'. He expected to be called immediately by Mountbatten and to have Dening's charges 'hurled at me'. The situation was going to get 'pretty hot' and he urged American officials to decide what could, and could not, be plausibly denied.[49] However, Timberman was never subjected to an inquisition. Instead the Chiefs of Staff in London advised Mountbatten not to throw SSU out of SEAC, for its formal presence at least allowed SEAC to keep this 'organisation under some control'. Meanwhile Dening and Mountbatten became distracted by a bitter personal argument over events in the Netherlands East Indies.[50]

In the spring of 1946 an Anglo-Thai treaty was signed which was a pale shadow of Britain's wartime ambitions in that country. The final form of this treaty, concluded a full year after Roosevelt's death, and bearing on a country which had never been a formal colony, was nevertheless a concrete testament to the commitment of American officials, working under both Donovan and Moffat, to Rooseveltian ideals. By April 1946, the Colonial Office in London had accepted defeat on the Kra Isthmus issue, concluding that 'the time for action is past'. They noted: 'Had we wished to eject the Siamese from Pattani . . . we should have done so when Siam was still under British Military Occupation . . . we certainly cannot reverse it now.'[51] Instead, the Anglo-Thai Treaty drew a line under wartime issues, to the relief of everyone in Bangkok, not least the new British Ambassador, Geoffrey Thompson. On 2 May 1946, Charles Yost, who had opened the new American Embassy, reported that the British had realised that the 'table-pounding' tactics of Dening, had been 'a disastrous error'. Thompson had confided to him that British behaviour had been 'mistaken and inexcusable' and they had now 'abandoned' attempts to pursue policy 'by force or threat of force'.[52]

SOE's successor, ALFPMO, had also been active in Thailand, but with a different focus. On 5 February 1946 the Headquarters of British Troops Siam under General Geoffrey Evans, reported that they had five groups of ALFPMO in field areas. One of these groups was at Battambang watching the disputed provinces on the border of Cambodia. Two other missions were located on the border with Malaya at Songkhla and Yala, watching 'all kinds of subversive activities'. On 6 March 1946 five more ALFPMO stations were opened and expected to remain until July 1946, but their main focus of activity was not in Thailand, but across the border into Indochina.[53]

In the summer of 1946 the hopes of all sides to escape wartime instability and mutual paranoia in favour of normality was overshadowed by the death of the young King of Thailand, Ananda Mahidol. The King was found shot in his palace in Bangkok in circumstances that were difficult to explain, and which have attracted half a century of speculation. It was inevitable that this event, which may well have been a tragic accident, would nevertheless become connected with all sorts of intrigue. Drew Pearson, the Washington columnist, led the way, offering the implausible assertion that the King was murdered by a 'French agent in co-operation with a palace guard traitor', because the young King had 'stood in the way of French Imperialistic penetration of Thailand from Indochina'.[54] More than two years later American officials were still trying to uncover the real story. They paid more attention to the version of events offered by the Thai Military Attaché in Washington in November 1948. Addressing a meeting of CIA and State Department officials, he explained that King Ananda had regarded the Thai Government as 'riddled with corruption' and had intended to deal with the situation by bringing in large numbers of British and American advisers: 'It was to forestall this action that Pridi's group killed Ananda.'[55]

Other competing explanations entered circulation, but in the public mind, many now associated Pridi, the wartime resistance leader, with the death of the King, casting doubt on the whole Free Thai Movement. Against this background, military factions, led by the wartime dictator, Phibul, gradually restored their influence while Pridi developed relations with the ascendant Chinese Communists to the north during 1947. A new alignment between Thai internal factions and external Cold War pressures was emerging.[56] On 9 November 1947 a military coup directed by Phibul displaced the moderate government and restored the wartime leader to power. Ten days later the new regime moved against Pridi and the Free Thais, arresting the so-called 'King's assassins', seizing Free Thai arms caches and increasing surveillance on Chinese Communist elements in Thailand.[57] In London, Bevin, the Foreign Secretary, warned: 'We must go slowly and with great care or there will be a long period of civil war.'[58] Former OSS officers still in Bangkok were distressed and reported to Donovan that their old wartime associates were now being purged with many thrown into jail on 'absurd charges'.[59] There was particular irritation in Washington, given that Truman had expressly told Bangkok on 23 April 1947 that Phibul was an unacceptable figure.[60] With Free Thai elements being rounded up, and in some cases executed, the issue for British and American officials had, once again, become the exfiltration of Pridi from Bangkok.

Early on the morning of 19 November 1947, Pridi arrived at the house of the British Naval Attaché, Captain Dennis, 'disguised in naval uniform, wearing thick glasses and a new moustache and missing his upper dental plate'. Then, Dennis and his American colleague, Commander Gardes, used an American naval launch to rendezvous with a Shell tanker which took him to Malaya. In Dennis' house, Pridi discarded two or three machine guns, several other weapons and two hand grenades. Ambassador Thompson did not like the 'dangerous melodrama' but felt that they had 'discharged our humanitarian obligation' to the wartime Resistance leader.[61] The authorities in Malaya over-reacted somewhat and were relieved when Pridi departed for China.[62]

Pridi's hurried departure did not quite close the chapter of wartime issues for Ambassador Thompson and Captain Dennis. Although London had now renounced ambitions towards southern Thailand, these ideas persisted at a subliminal level. In October 1948, with the advent of the Emergency in Malaya, Thompson sent Dennis, his former Naval Attaché, to the area to become the new British Consul at Songkhla on the Kra Isthmus. On his arrival Dennis found that the Emergency had provided a cover for the revival of old ambitions. He discovered that a Malay Civil Service official, who had been employed in the British Consulate at Songhkla, 'had made approaches to certain Malayan officials which envisaged the occupation of the four southern provinces by Malayan troops'. Thompson sent an urgent message to Bevin requesting immediate measures to 'discipline' this individual with his 'wild suggestions'.[63] Yet ambitions in the south remained an essential component of British thinking. In 1950, British contingency plans for defence of Malaya in the event of a crisis to the north were simply a revival of the pre-war Operation *Matador*, to occupy the Kra Isthmus at Songhkla with a division of Ghurkas. Two years later this time-honoured concept had been incorporated without comment into the American National Security Council's strategic concept for South East Asia and by 1953 this contingency plan had been renamed Operation *Irony*.[64]

Malaya and Singapore

Britain had long been planning a major, and perhaps costly, amphibious offensive to retake Malaya and Singapore. 'Here', Churchill insisted in September 1944, 'is the Supreme British objective in the whole of the Indian and Far Eastern Theater. It is the only price that will restore British prestige in this region.'[65] Although the atomic attack on Japan intervened in August 1945, British officials could not allow this to interfere with a symbolic event that was the culmination of Britain's Far Eastern War. SEAC insisted that the first elements of the British re-occupation in Malaya should nevertheless arrive as a proper amphibious operation, albeit tardily. SSU reported that one of its officers had accompanied this 'first wave' in September 1945:

Captain Smith went ashore in Malaya with one of the first British landing parties on 12 September 1945. A full-dress assault landing was made through the surf, and he spoke feelingly of the experience of wading ashore with rifle in hand before an admiring audience of Malays dressed in their holiday best and applauding eagerly.

This, he noted, underlined a general British anxiety to emphasise their military contribution to the defeat of Japan in Asia.[66]

In early 1945, as planning for the return to Malaya and Singapore had accelerated, SOE had found itself at the centre of an animated debate over policy towards the AJUF resistance forces. As in Thailand and Burma, SOE formed the leading edge of British contact with indigenous forces that were at once important and ambiguous. In all cases, British policy-makers at a high level were now searching for ways of neutralising these various movements, viewing them as, at best, an unwelcome complication and at worst, a destabilising element. But there were many levels to British policy and SOE, anxious to play a prominent part in the last phase of the war, argued persuasively that only by working with the guerrillas could they be controlled. This argument secured the support of Mountbatten, partly on grounds of practicality and partly on political grounds. SEAC's Supreme Commander was increasingly anxious to lend a flavour of reconciliation and inclusiveness to the post-war settlement.

In Malaya, the AJUF were at least fiercely anti-Japanese throughout the war, but fundamentally they were inimical to the return of British rule. Now armed with the example of effective guerrilla operations against the Japanese underway in Burma, SOE were able to make a strong case for the continued support of the AJUF.[67] During May 1945 Mackenzie stressed an SOE assistance agreement negotiated with the AJUF three months earlier by Major Hannah, arguing that if this were reneged on SOE and SIS operations must stop altogether. In any case, they pointed out, if SOE withdrew the guerrillas would simply obtain their arms from the retreating Japanese.

Only by attaching officers to the AJUF, he argued, would the British get to 'know the whole of its organisation and policy', emphasising the danger that the AJUF might well try to seize power after the war. Mackenzie pointed to other potential benefits. SOE had already considered the problem of the Chinese community in Malaya claiming all the credit for opposing the Japanese and for 'this reason in particular' had organised a small but separate ethnic Malay resistance to 'give the Malays the greatest possible share' in the expulsion of the Japanese and thus pre-empt communal tensions.[68] SOE had anticipated requests from London. On 7 June 1945 the Chiefs of Staff explained: 'In particular, we are anxious that Malay resistance should be encouraged as much as possible in order to avoid giving the impression that we are supporting the Chinese alone.'[69] London judiciously authorised as much assistance to the AJUF as was necessary to achieve control. Building up continued, but its central purpose was retardation.[70]

It was probably Mountbatten's own arguments for the support of the AJUF, which were more sophisticated and more persuasive than those of SOE, that won London over. He had freely conceded that the potential dangers of support included lending the AJUF an enhanced status, which would translate into high political expectations after the surrender. But he insisted that this could be countered by making Britain's constitutional plans transparent at an early stage.[71] Meanwhile, as Chean Boon Kheng has argued, Mountbatten saw an invaluable publicity opportunity. Writing to the Colonial Secretary, Oliver Stanley, he explained:

I very much hope that the War Cabinet will see their way to agreeing with my new proposals. The question of Resistance Movements within the British Empire is in a special category. Presumably we have not previously found Colonial Subjects rising to fight on our behalf when we were about to occupy their territory, and the fact that they are doing so today seems to me a wonderful opportunity for propaganda to the world in general, and to the Americans in particular, at a time when we are being accused of reconquering colonial peoples in order to re-subjugate them.

Mountbatten accepted that many of the AJUF were anti-British but, ever the optimist, he hoped that many of them could be won over by a revised constitution.[72]

The near-complete absence of the Japanese Air Force allowed substantial deliveries of stores by RAF Special Duties aircraft to the six main guerilla groups, three of which hosted SOE missions.[73] These missions continued to grow and by 15 August 1945 there were at least 308 SOE personnel, five Gurkha Support Groups and 46 W/T sets in the field, permitting detailed liaison with SEAC. Nevertheless, efforts to control the AJUF were only partly successful. At the end of the war the total strength of the guerrillas was thought by SEAC to be between 3,000 and 4,000. But during demobilisation this figure crept up to 6,000 to 7,000. The appearance of so many guerrillas of which SOE had no knowledge raised suspicions that they were part of an MCP 'secret army' formed in April 1945, using the new weapons.[74]

Intense confusion reigned in Malaya between the atomic attacks on Japan and the arrival of British occupation forces in mid-September. Many Japanese handed their weapons to the AJUF, in preference to the British and some even tried to contact the MCP leadership hoping to strike an agreement to fight together as Asians against the returning British. In 1977, reports of the remnants of the AJUF guerrilla force, hiding out on the Thai–Malaya border, suggested that two Japanese soldiers were still with them. In Singapore, large INA units were attacked by ebullient AJUF formations and the Japanese responded by supplying their Indian allies with tanks. In this confused period there was a considerable settling of scores. On 11 August SEAC told SOE liaison officers that they should do everything possible to persuade guerrilla forces to stay in their camps and to 'prevent AJUF from seizing power'. This was certainly an option which the AJUF had contemplated, but the predominant faction, including Lai Tek, believed some sort of bargain could be struck with the new British administration.[75]

SEAC's hopes that the AJUF would remain inactive were unrealistic. On 19 August, Colonel John Davis, the senior SOE officer in Malaya, explained that the guerrillas needed to be kept busy. If they were active, well equipped and rationed, then there was every possibility that the guerilla groups not yet under SOE control would join them. The alternative, he noted presciently, was disintegration and a guerrilla problem that 'may take decades to eradicate'. Opinion in SEAC was divided, with Mackenzie arguing for an expanded guerrilla role, but Slim insisting that this was an unwelcome complication. By 24 August, Mackenzie, who had become extremely concerned about guerrillas who were slipping from his control, urged Mountbatten to disclose details of the planned post-war settlement, reassuring them that various grievances would be addressed.[76] SOE had exaggerated their control and in early September, just prior to the arrival of a British fleet, AJUF forces took control in Singapore, raiding army stores, attacking isolated Japanese and liquidating those suspected of collaboration.[77]

OSS had been largely excluded from independent operations into Malaya during 1944, and in January 1945 Donovan declared a lack of interest in the area. Thereafter, OSS had been allowed to insert observer missions. By June 1945, two OSS missions were at Pulai and a third was attached to the British *Cairngorm I* mission. Moving amongst the MCP guerillas at the end of the war, they returned detailed first-hand reports of developments in Malaya.[78] Further missions followed. OSS Operation *Young* was parachuted into northern Jahore on 9 August 1945 to collect intelligence and to assist SOE parties working with the AJUF 3rd Regimental Group Area. They noted that the local AJUF were completely 'red', giving over eight hours a day to political instruction, while remaining poor shots.[79] In September 1945, these OSS missions became SSU and formed Washington's only source of information on much of Malaya.[80] In May 1946, Washington noted that a Captain Mysbergh 'had been assigned to the American Legation since his discharge from SSU' and remained their only source on up-country areas.[81]

SSU considered that the British had behaved 'very astutely' towards the AJUF, neither making martyrs out of them, nor taking them into the government, as the AJUF had demanded. Mountbatten's simple answer was that the interim military administration was not competent to make such a decision. The AJUF were therefore left waiting on the sidelines until the civil administration returned in 1946. By this time they had lost much of their momentum and the civil government then felt confident enough to exile ten key Communists. In 1946 SSU also charted the growing disappointment with the United States, who the majority of the population had clearly expected to provide independence and consumer goods in plentiful amounts. Curious stories had begun to circulate and SSU Singapore reported that belief was widespread in Indonesia that Roosevelt 'was assassinated by elements opposed to granting freedom to colonial peoples and that Truman is afraid of espousing that cause because he fears he would meet the same end'.[82]

Final demobilisation of the guerrillas proved difficult. Colonel John Davis of SOE conducted the negotiations at the headquarters of the AJUF. Hoping to draw in even those forces without SOE liaison officers, a sum of $350 was offered on disbandment, with a further payment later. The target date was 1 December 1945, but the core forces and the best weapons stayed in the jungle.[83] Nevertheless, Mountbatten kept the process rolling with characteristic style and marked disbandment with an AJUF victory parade through Singapore in January 1946, complete with bands from the Royal Marines and Cameronians. Mountbatten decorated the leaders and 'took the whole party up for cocktails at Government House'. Those decorated included Chin Peng, the principal guerrilla leader during the subsequent Malayan Emergency, and the ceremonial photographs taken on this occasion became reference material for the security forces.[84] Mountbatten continued to exercise a liberalising influence, but once he departed in March 1946 the civil government took a harder line.

The uneasy peace that characterised the winter of 1945–6 also denoted a struggle between the MCP leadership of the AJUF, who advocated a semi-constitutional path, and the younger militants. The MCP leadership was gradually giving way and the course was set for a conflagration.[85] Long-term rice shortages and labour troubles offered ready issues for the militants to exploit.[86] Lai Tek had also been a restraining voice but by March 1947 other MCP leaders had uncovered his wartime contacts with the Japanese and he slipped away into Thailand.[87] In mid-1948, as the Malayan Emergency erupted with full force, the authorities reacted by creating six 'ferret force' groups, special units with a high proportion of ex-SOE personnel from Malaya and Burma 'with intimate knowledge of both the country and the enemy'. The remnants of SOE were now engaged on both sides of this new conflict.[88]

Burma

Although the political issues confronting the Allied secret services and the indigenous resistance groups in Burma bore some similarities to those in Thailand and Malaya, the context was different. Burma was the sole area of concentrated fighting in mainland Asia, and this lent all decisions a more military texture. By late 1944 the morale of Japanese forces in Burma was low and, from March 1945, it collapsed quickly.[89] This owed something to the almost total absence of intelligence for mid-level Japanese operational commanders. In July 1945, the Chief of Staff of the 29th Army surrendered and explained that he had no confidence in the material supplied by Singapore, whose staff were 'secretive' and in any case depended on Allied civilian broadcasts. He expressed 'scorn for the antiquated Japanese system, but had little practical idea of how it could be bettered'.[90]

The most controversial issue was, as elsewhere, the handling of resistance forces. From the autumn of 1944 the forces of the Burmese BNA and other AFOs deserted to the British in droves. SOE readily recruited them behind Japanese lines, while in liberated areas the officers of Civil Affairs Service (Burma (CAS B)), supported by large Field Security contingents, sought their arrest as collaborators. Uneasy truces between officials of SOE and CAS (B) had to be negotiated locally by senior army commanders.[91] In November 1944, Mackenzie had decided to go ahead with the arming of BNA without consulting CAS (B) who he knew would object strenuously. But controversy loomed for, as in Yugoslavia, Greece and Malaya, SOE was arming groups inimical to Britain's post-war policy.[92]

CAS (B) only uncovered the SOE decision in February 1945 and a major controversy erupted. They denounced BNA and other AFOs as communist terrorists and on 15 February secured a ban on arming them by the commander of Allied Land Forces in South East Asia, Lt General Oliver Leese. Senior officers, such as Brigadier Prescott, Deputy Head of CAS (B), had advanced the strongest objections to SOE activities in Burma on grounds of long-term civil order. In Europe, he explained, the worst of these problems had to be solved by the returning governments of the country concerned but, 'in Burma, if our clandestine organisations leave awkward legacies, *they leave them for ourselves*'. CAS (B) were particularly anxious about plans to distribute 3,000 further weapons to Karens in the Delta region, which had always been 'a criminal area'. This, they argued would result in a wave of serious crime, the suppression of which 'will be in the nature of a minor military operation'. Moreover, many of the Karen had been massacred by the Burmese in 1942 and, if armed, the temptation to 'pay off old scores' would be overwhelming. Arming guerrillas, he argued, would only result in their expecting large political favours from the post-war settlement. They were not, he argued like the Maquis in France, but were instead 'disgruntled elements who have backed the wrong horse, and who are endeavouring to cover their bets'.[93]

Mackenzie had to work hard to counter these powerful arguments. He stressed expediency, pointing out that the AFOs had rebelled against their Japanese masters and sought contacts with the British of their own accord, thus 'it would be politically most unwise to refuse this offer of co-operation'. The AFOs would arm themselves anyway with materials discarded by the retreating Japanese, but would bear a grudge, knowing that the British had already armed the hill tribes, thus 'sowing the seeds of post war communal grievance'. Moreover, he warned of press revelations of 'the Drew Pearson type' about the reactionary British refusing to co-operate with these antifascist forces of the left.[94] In the event Mackenzie joined up with Coughlin of OSS to persuade Mountbatten to countermand the order, warning that OSS and SOE operations, now with a strengthened intelligence-gathering emphasis for the drive into Burma, might grind to a halt.[95]

But their victory on the issue of arming *disaffected* pockets of guerrillas was now over-shadowed by a much larger question: whether SOE should enter in a formal alliance with Aung San. Both Slim and Mountbatten were favourably inclined.[96] Mountbatten stressed that he was starved of military resources and any help that would speed his drive south towards Rangoon was, as he told the British Chiefs of Staff during March, 'a welcome bonus'. They would be doing no more than the Allies had done for Italy. Most importantly, he insisted, when figures such as the resistance leader, Aung San, became national heroes as they 'are bound to become', they would have achieved this with the British, rather than against them. Mountbatten's Public Relations Division now gave wide publicity to Aung San as an 'example of patriotic resistance within the British Empire'.[97]

SOE were acutely aware of the political problems but insisted that previous experience in Europe and the Mediterranean had shown that the key was 'a positive policy'. During April they argued that the problem in Burma fell naturally into two parts. First, in the staunchly anti-Japanese hill tribes areas, the Kachin and Karen would give little trouble. All that was required here was 'a clear promise from H.M.G. that their special status will be preserved and their undoubted and unwavering loyalty recognised' – a simple request that remained tragically unfulfilled. Second, in the lowland Burmese areas, the main group, Aung San's BNA, was increasingly anti-Japanese and had SOE liaison teams at work, but control was clearly going to be difficult. Having been both communistic and pro-Japanese, they were mostly now very disaffected. Nevertheless, SOE insisted that control 'is possible', especially if its liaison officers were gradually transferred into CAS (B), to ensure continuity.[98] As Mountbatten had observed as early as February 1944, there were few indigenous groups in South East Asia who had not treated with the Japanese in some way.[99]

These arguments reverberated at a high level. In the War Cabinet, during May, Eden warned of the difficulties that most SOE-backed groups eventually caused, adding: 'Surely we must not boost these people too so much. They will give us great trouble hereafter.' Churchill agreed. However, Mountbatten skilfully couched his appeal in military terms and achieved some leeway. The Chiefs of Staff consented to a purely military agreement in which Aung San's forces were to 'work their passage home', a phrase that appeared with increasing frequency. But London cautioned against any degree of encouragement 'beyond what is strictly necessary for operational reasons'. Mountbatten secured these permissions just in time, for the BNA were turning on the Japanese and he barely retained a semblance of control.[100] Dissidents in SEAC had to be restrained, including Air Vice-Marshal Joubert, Deputy Chief of Staff for Information and Civil Affairs, who had to be forbidden by Mountbatten to communicate with the Governor of Burma.[101] By June 1945, Mackenzie was reporting that AFO groups were much larger than they had suspected, and action against them would have been, in his opinion, almost impossible.[102]

During early 1945, despite these awkward political problems, SOE in Burma carried out its most spectacularly successful military operations of the war. Their main focus was a series of operations codenamed *Nation* and *Character*. The guerrillas now scented victory and were hard to restrain as the Japanese attempted to flee southward down the river valleys towards the coast. Guerrilla intelligence also multiplied the effect of Allied air attacks.

Japanese casualties in Operation *Nation* were estimated at between 3,582 and 4,650, while Allied casualties were estimated at between sixty-three and eighty-eight.[103] Operation *Character*, conducted in the Karen area, met with even greater success and consisted of three main groups under Lt Colonel Tulloch, Lt Colonel Peacock and Major Turral. By 13 April 1945, Tulloch's Northern Group commanded a local force of 2,000. As the Japanese 15th Division tried to move south through the Karen areas in a race with the British for the key town of Toungoo, they were repeatedly ambushed. Extended fighting developed with a force of 50,000 Japanese troops which continued into July. On 21 July 1945, General Stopford, Commander of the British 33rd Corps, conceded that SOE's Karen forces had inflicted more casualties in the last month than the regular Army.[104]

Conclusions

Although Mountbatten usually couched his arguments in military terms, both OSS and SOE found Mountbatten broadly sympathetic to arguments for guerrilla support because he privately viewed inclusiveness as the road to political reconciliation. In lowland Burmese areas Mountbatten went out of his way to achieve reconciliation. In June 1945, goose-stepping units of Aung San's BNA were encouraged to join in the victory parades through Rangoon, while Aung San himself, who had so narrowly avoided arrest, was made Deputy Inspector General of the regular Burma Army with the rank of Brigadier. Mountbatten felt he had done nothing less than initiate a new phase of Anglo-Burmese relations and was clearly irked by those who detracted from these achievements. On 15 June he held a cocktail party at Government House in Rangoon for the press, including seventeen American editors touring the Far Eastern War fronts. He noted in his diary that they kept on expressing surprise, 'rather rudely I thought', at his assurance that they had not come in 'to start political persecution, curfews, banning of meetings, political censorship and generally to screw down the Burmese'. He was dismayed that the American and Indian press evidently still regarded the British as merely 'Imperial monsters' and 'little better than Fascists'.

But not all British officers returning to Burma were as liberal as Mountbatten. Only the following day, after addressing officers of CAS (B), he was openly criticised by Brigadier Chettle, the Chief of Police in Burma, who insisted that it was 'a great mistake handling the Burmese too softly' as it would make the British Administration of Burma 'difficult for years to come'. Mountbatten shot back that British rule would soon be gone.[105] Mountbatten then mused on the fate of Aung San, noting that Joubert had 'spent most of his time trying to persuade me to shoot him as a traitor' and wondered what would have happened if Britain had tried to shoot Botha and Smuts after the South African War.[106]

OSS elements accompanied regular British forces as they moved back into Burma during 1945 and charted British attitudes at a lower level. Although the local population found British rule preferable to the 'barbarities' of the Japanese and welcomed the improved economic conditions, political relations were hostile: 'In the opinion of the average British officer, all the natives indiscriminately are "wogs" and most of them are "bloody traitors".'[107] By the end of the war the remaining OSS presence was largely X-2 officers concerned with war crimes and collaborators. However, they thought it best to try and distance themselves from a plan 'for the "snatching" of Chandra Bose' on grounds of both practicality and political sensitivity.[108]

Despite the efforts of Mountbatten and SOE to control Aung San by drawing his forces onto the 'winning side' in Burma, his fate was even less happy than that which overtook wartime resistance leaders in neighbouring Thailand and Malaya. Aung San was assassinated by stolen British weapons during bitter faction-fighting in 1947. Mountbatten's efforts at reconciliation also failed to keep Burma within the Commonwealth and instead U Nu's socialist republic pursued a separate path after independence in 1948. SOE had particular grounds for grave disappointment. Although SOE had won the wartime argument with CAS (B) over policy towards Aung San's forces, they were bitter about the nature of the post-war settlement in Burma. The transfer of power in 1948 created a single centralised state, dominated by the lowland Burmese, within which the staunch allies of SOE, the fiercely anti-Japanese Karen minorities, received no protection.[109]

Across Thailand, Malaya and Burma, the contacts of the various wartime secret services with indigenous groups left a trail of unfinished business that could not be terminated neatly in 1945. Remarkably, in 1948, a renegade group of British officers, led by Lt Colonel Tulloch of SOE, returned to Burma to arrange clandestine supplies and training for the Karens, who found themselves engaged in a developing civil war with the central government in Rangoon. They found ready backing from a range of senior private figures who felt that Britain owed a debt to its most loyal Asian subjects.[110] Meanwhile the Attlee administration in London continued to support the central government in Rangoon through a military mission which helped to keep the Burmese Air Force flying against the rebels. In the Foreign Office, this issue landed on the desk of Esler Dening, now superintending all of Britain's Asia policy, who was uniquely qualified to appreciate the situation. SOE people, he observed stoically, were 'a law unto themselves' and so it was 'not surprising' that they should be working against British policy. In March 1949, when the Karens appeared to be about to take control, one of Dening's subordinates asked: 'I wonder what Tulloch is up to now. His friends may soon be the official Government . . . Do we start to curry favour with him?' However, U Nu clung to power by a whisker and the British Government quietly arranged for Tulloch's removal from the scene.[111]

In Burma and Malaya especially, a conflict involving an ethnically distinct group, initially armed and trained in subversive warfare by an Allied secret service, proved to be remarkably protracted. The Karen National Liberation Army fought on until 1995, still venerating the names of its original wartime SOE leaders. It is difficult to avoid the conclusion that the training of local populations in insurgency, together with the very substantial arms supplies, contributed something to the erosion of civil society in South East Asia and began a process that was easier to initiate than it was to arrest.[112]

18   Special operations in liberated areas: Indochina and the Netherlands East Indies, 1944–1946

> Mr Sheldon called on his own initiative in order to obtain information on the possibilities of trade between the United States and Viet Nam (he wishes to engage in such trade himself) . . . he appeared to have some kind of a chip on his shoulder. This may been the result of a feeling that the United States was assuming too passive and indifferent a role in Indochina.
>
> Conversation with George Sheldon of SSU, 30 August 1946[1]

The coup of the 9 March

In the summer of 1944 American policy towards Indochina had begun to change. De Gaulle established his Provisional Government in Paris and in the State Department those with European responsibilities increasingly favoured the return of her colonies.[2] By the autumn of 1944, Roosevelt's dislike of de Gaulle had softened, perhaps because of evaporating fears that he would use his security police 'for the establishment of a dictatorship'.[3] Roosevelt's physical abilities were ebbing fast, but although the balance of forces was shifting against him, he was increasingly aware that practical dispositions on the ground at the end of the war would be as critical as any high-level settlement. In early 1945, Roosevelt may have identified an opportunity to impede the French restoration in Indochina at this lower level.

In late 1944 signals intelligence revealed the increasingly nervous attitude of Japanese commanders in Indochina, reflecting the possibility of an Allied amphibious landing in southern China or indeed in Indochina, reinforced by the growing volume of Allied clandestine activity.[4] Allied pressure made Japanese *coups de main* more likely right across Asia, with BNA in Burma changing sides and with Phibul's pro-Japanese regime in Bangkok supplanted by a more neutral administration. Everyone knew which way the wind was blowing and as early as June 1944 SOE noted that progress in Burma and the Philippines increased the chance of the Japanese removing the Vichy regime in Indochina.[5]

The historian Stein Tonneson has advanced the hypothesis that Roosevelt

340

may have deliberately sought to increase Japanese fears, perhaps by using the well-developed Allied deception apparatus, to suggest a forthcoming American amphibious landing, in order to trigger Japanese action to remove the French. There is no doubt that OWI worked hard to suggest an imminent American amphibious landing in Indochina, and press stories appeared asserting that Indochina was the gateway to the Allied reconquest of mainland Asia.[6] In October 1944 Roosevelt had asked the US Joint Chiefs of Staff to investigate the possibility of an attack through Indochina, partly as an alternative supply route to China, but they were unenthusiastic.[7]

This hypothesis, though not proven, has attracted support. David Marr has commented: 'Indeed, it is possible that Roosevelt viewed . . . air assaults, together with various covert deception efforts under way, as a device to trigger Japanese elimination of the French in Indochina.'[8] Moreover something very sensitive was being discussed by Roosevelt, Wedemeyer and Admiral Halsey in the early weeks of 1945. Further tangential evidence is offered by an appreciation of Roosevelt's attention to intercepted Gaullist communications traffic regarding Indochina.[9] But intention does not prove effect. Japanese intelligence was poor and D Division officers in SEAC doubted that Japan would respond to elaborate deceptions. When Japan carried out her coup against the French in Indochina on 9 March, it was probably a reaction to French activity, especially the growing volume of SOE-backed flights by the French secret service from India. This coup ended the continuity of French administration and inflicted a blow which Vichy had successfully avoided for five years.

There are many contending explanations for the coup of 9 March. Major Archimedes Patti, who had been organising OSS assistance to Viet Minh military groups to the west of Hanoi in April 1945, believed the main cause was a famine which peaked in February 1945 with at least one million dead. Crucially the Vietnamese were unable to obtain rice 'which had been stored by the French and which was going bad'. The resulting unrest, and Japan's conviction that the French would not be able to control it, was in Patti's opinion 'one of the main reasons for the coup of March 9'. Subsequently, the Japanese opened up the rice stores and doled out food without cost.[10]

The coup of 9 March was of some symbolic importance. After five years of uneasy co-existence, fighting had finally begun in earnest and all groups in Indochina now wished to be seen to oppose the Japanese, hoping to validate their claims to control over Indochina at the end of the war.[11] De Gaulle stated his own view plainly: 'French blood shed on the soil of Indochina would constitute an impressive claim.'[12] But the sight of Vichy and Gaullist elements joining battle with the Japanese so late in the war did little for their stature. Meanwhile, the practical problems of French colonial recovery now became vastly more difficult with the destruction of French administration and the acceleration of nationalist expectations in Indochina. Therefore, even as Roosevelt lost his grip on high policy, events at ground level had now turned markedly in his favour.[13]

Chennault's 14th Air Force immediately tried to offer air support to several groups of French forces retreating into China, but the situation was confused and there were few clear targets. Meanwhile OSS, the China Theater and Washington discussed the wisdom of dropping supplies to the Vichy French.[14] SOE began dropping supplies from SEAC immediately, while the SOE black-market currency operation in southern China, Operation *Remorse*, was also used to aid French refugees. The numerous SOE/SA teams, built up rather hastily in early 1945, although commanding more than 1,000 guerrillas could not stand up to concerted Japanese military pressure. Characterised by over-optimism and poor security, they collapsed rapidly. By the end of March most clandestine W/T stations were silent and their agent networks had been rolled up.[15]

Although the situation in the China Theater remained confused, there was some immediate American assistance to the French. On 20 March, Wedemeyer's acting Chief of Staff, General Melvin Gross, ordered OSS to provide material support to any anti-Japanese forces on purely military criteria. The 14th Air Force, now attacking Field Marshal Terauchi's rear headquarters area, badly needed target intelligence to replace the flow from groups like GBT, which had been disrupted by the coup. They urged OSS to reconstruct their networks in Indochina regardless of political considerations.[16] Much of the confusion emanated from a high level. At one point Roosevelt gave Wedemeyer clear orders not to assist the French troops conducting their fighting retreat into southern China, but the French believed that they had persuaded Roosevelt and General Marshall to reverse this decision as early as 19 March. In reality much of the uncertainty was about volume of supply from a theatre where everything was scarce.[17] Churchill was reluctant to intervene, but was struck by the parallels with the Warsaw rising. On 11 April, he finally urged Roosevelt to render more assistance, but the fighting was nearly over and two days later Roosevelt was dead.[18] Most clandestine networks were now ruptured and OSS reported:

With the Japanese takeover of all French installations in FIC on 10 March and in the few days thereafter without exception every intelligence net in the country was completely disrupted. Not only was the G.B.T. net knocked out, but we have it on unimpeachable authority that all C[hinese] C[ombat] C[ommand] nets and sources of information were disrupted, that the French system was completely destroyed, and last but not least that the Tai Li setup in FIC has been knocked out lock, stock and barrel. The net result has been that FIC is almost completely uncovered.[19]

By default the most promising networks that remained were those provided by Ho Chi Minh.

In Washington, Roosevelt's death in April 1945 heralded a period of drift. In May 1945 Patrick Hurley in China bluntly asked Truman if policy towards Indochina had changed, and he replied, somewhat delphically, that there had been no change; but Truman was probably unaware of shifting State Department policy and the reassurances offered to the French at San Francisco. Significantly, Truman's response asserting no change was shown to Richard Heppner, the OSS Chief in China, in June 1945 and helps to explain why OSS was now somewhat out of step with metropolitan policy-makers.[20]

OSS had established a training team with Ho Chi Minh and his immediate circle by February 1945, and had supplied arms and aid. The reasons for this were largely practical. The French Missions in Indochina had never been impressive. Although the new French metropolitan government's secret service, the DGER, had despatched an energetic figure, Major Jean Sainteny, to Kunming, he was not prepared to accept the authority of Wedemeyer. Ho Chi Minh now appeared to be the most attractive of few remaining options for penetration of Indochina, although his communist associations troubled some members of OSS. Nevertheless, Ho's anti-Japanese credentials were excellent, and certainly markedly better than those of the KMT or the French.[21]

Meanwhile French officials seemed bent on a confrontation with the Americans. At the end of March, Colonel Passy, the Head of DGER, arrived in China on a liaison visit. He unilaterally repudiated local agreements between OSS and the French Missions and insisted that Paris wanted no Americans trespassing into French Indochina. However, OSS felt confident that Passy was not aware of their links with the Viet Minh at that point.[22] OSS tried to improve their relations with the French by working through AGAS, in whom the French had more confidence.[23]

Despite Passy's extremely abrupt manner, and despite the many injunctions from Washington against working with French groups, OSS were determined to achieve at least a reasonable working relationship with the French. Heppner finally reported in May 1945 that:

An agreement was reached with Colonel Passy's representative, and we are now working in partnership with his group in obtaining intelligence from French Indochina. Another agreement has been made with General Sabattier's people ... for important sabotage operations. Passy's people and Sabattier's people are at loggerheads, and it would appear that we are fishing in troubled waters. Every care is being taken to keep our relationship correct.[24]

But with the French situation so unpredictable, Ho Chi Minh was an increasingly attractive alternative.

By May 1945, Viet Minh groups inside Indochina had received considerable shipments of automatic weapons, medical assistance and radio training from an OSS operation known as the 'Deer Mission'. Further parachute drops were followed by the creation of an airstrip to receive visits by American light aircraft. A week before the Japanese surrender on 15 August 1945, the Deer Mission was putting large groups of Viet Minh through a weapons training course north of Hanoi. The sensitivity of this activity was clearly recognised and they were not initially permitted by their superiors to receive Japanese surrenders, or to proceed to Hanoi. Meanwhile, Ho was probing OSS officers, with little success, for clearer indications about future American policy on Indochina.[25] Intentionally or otherwise, the association of OSS with the Viet Minh was clearly of political benefit in building Ho's status in northern Indochina in the summer of 1945 and was exploited to the full. OSS appeared to be visibly supporting the Viet Minh in the eyes of the local population, set against the background of omnipresent American air power.

When the French DGER in India heard of the OSS–Viet Minh associations they assumed that Ho had promised OSS future American economic privileges in Indochina in return for immediate support, or perhaps a naval base at Cam Ranh Bay.[26] But their own efforts were hampered by internal dissension. From April 1945, DGER, commanded by Passy, was aggressively demanding control of all secret service activity, including SOE's French Indochina section, but had met resistance from local military commanders such as Blaizot.[27] DGER now took its orders from the ministerial committee presided over by the former head of the SOE Indochina country section, Baron François de Langlade.[28]

Other familiar disputes rumbled on in the background. By May 1945 the British Chiefs of Staff were lining up with increasing firmness behind Mountbatten in his dispute with Wedemeyer over clandestine operations into Indochina.[29] The Head of BJSM, Field Marshal 'Jumbo' Wilson, observed that this was 'a clash of personalities which is fast becoming irreconcilable'. He added that the nature of the French clandestine apparatus in the Far East made this dispute far worse, noting that there were 'five equal French authorities working into Indochina, either for SEAC or Chungking. Each claims equal rights and refers back to Paris.' Wilson identified the only realistic solution, noting that a command area needed firm boundaries. He suggested dividing the country in half. Wilson's idea was soon to be implemented at Potsdam, giving the occupation south of the 16th parallel to SEAC and the north to China.[30]

Occupation

French diplomats skilfully applied pressure in Washington on the Indochina question during late April. In early May, at the opening of the UN San Francisco Conference, Stettinius went out of his way to reassure his French counterpart that Washington had never 'officially' questioned French sovereignty in Indochina.[31] The European sections of the State Department had long har-

boured reservations about many of Roosevelt's policies, prompting his preference for personal envoys whom he could trust to do his bidding. In early
1945 Roosevelt complained that 'the men in the State Department have tried
to conceal messages from me, delay them, hold them up somehow . . . They
should be working for Winston. As a matter of fact a lot of them are.'[32] But
with Roosevelt gone there was no longer any need to dissemble. Many
viewed this as a victory by the European sections of the State Department
over their colleagues in Asiatic sections.[33]

Major Sainteny was one of de Gaulle's key emissaries *en route* from Paris
to assist with the restoration of French authority in Indochina. In July 1945
he had encountered transport difficulties and found himself stranded in
Athens. He was offered a lift by none other then General Donovan, who was
on his way to meet Mountbatten.[34] But once in Kunming he found that local
OSS were less accommodating. Only on 22 August, after repeated refusals,
did Sainteny finally managed to accompany an OSS team headed by Patti to
Hanoi. As they moved into the city, they encountered thousands of Viet Minh
flags, as well as banners proclaiming 'Welcome to the Allies' and 'Death to
French Imperialism'. A violent crowd, barely contained by the Japanese,
made it clear that the French were less than welcome. Sainteny demanded
reinforcements from the French Mission in Kunming, while Patti insisted that
OSS block them for fear of further provocation.[35]

DGER in Calcutta was also trying to enter the field, but their efforts were
marked by incompetence. Several parachute teams were despatched by RAF
Special Duties aircraft to the administrative centres of Indochina. On 22
August, a team led by Pierre Messmer, designated Commissioner for the
Republic of Tonkin, arrived north of Hanoi and were promptly imprisoned
by the Viet Minh. Jean Cédile similarly materialised north of Saigon as Commissioner for the Republic of Cochin China and was placed under house
arrest by the Japanese. They were fortunate compared to a further team of
six who arrived at Hue in Annam, of whom four were killed and two
imprisoned. The fact that three governors-designate were pushed out of aircraft into the violent confusion that was Indochina in August 1945, armed
only with letters of authority from de Gaulle, typified the hopeless unreality
of much French secret service activity.[36]

Meanwhile, in Hanoi, Patti, whose mission had been general reconnaissance and speedy location of Allied POWs, was now hailed as the senior
Allied representative and found himself out of his depth. Patti considered the
Viet Minh administration in Hanoi to be 'rather incompetent' but had the
'highest opinion of Ho'. However, it was his encounter with an anti-French
demonstration on 23 August, which he estimated at a million persons, which
impressed the realities upon him. Thereafter Sainteny and the French officers
who had accompanied him were 'all practically quarantined in the Governor's

Palace'. Meanwhile the Japanese were busy turning over whole truckloads of weapons 'including some mortars and small cannon' to the Viet Minh.[37]

Relations between Patti, the Japanese and the Viet Minh, who had assumed control of Hanoi, were amicable, but all were nervous of the locust-like Chinese occupation troops now flooding in from the north. Ho continued to skilfully exploit the OSS presence, presenting its purpose publicly as the American support for national liberation. Patti's role has been much discussed. It has been suggested that Patti might have wanted to make his mark before the general officers arrived: 'Enjoying his role as amateur plenipotentiary, Patti said too much . . . his Vietnamese listeners, desperately eager for American recognition, heard even more than Patti uttered.'[38] But this situation did not last for long. By 30 August, Patti was out of his depth, receiving a harsh reprimand from OSS headquarters in Kunming for not offering fuller assistance to Sainteny's team and their efforts to re-assert French authority. Meanwhile Ho and his circle probed him for hours at a time about policy-developments in Washington of which he knew nothing.[39] By 31 August, Sainteny had been allowed out to meet with Viet Minh representatives and 'began to dictate terms' to Ho's representatives.[40] In September Patti was recalled and replaced.[41]

The interest in Patti's role in Hanoi during August 1945 has been so great that historiographical waves of interpretation can now be charted. Initially, before the archives were opened, some saw OSS as the first to warn of the communist danger represented by the Viet Minh. Thereafter, various historians have asserted that naive OSS officers were used by Ho. But OSS were hardly eulogistic about the disorderly Viet Minh government in the north or the south.[42] Indeed throughout the period from March to September 1945, OSS activities here were characterised by caution and restraint, compared to other territories, uneasily conscious of a vacuum where American policy was supposed to be. Beyond humanitarian relief to POWs and internees, they tried to restrict their activities to reporting, and to conversations, rather than dramatic action. Yet in Saigon there were reports of French groups dressing in American uniforms, pretending to be OSS and acting as 'provocateurs'.[43] OSS were symbolic of everything that the French feared about what they saw as American ambition in South East Asia.[44] OSS were no less sceptical about the French, predicting that recent promises of liberalisation would be 'throttled' by the institution which they saw as the *eminence grise* behind the colony, the Banque d'Indochine.[45] This uneasy situation prevailed in the north until the negotiated return of the French in 1946.

South of the 16th parallel, the French enjoyed a faster ride back to power on the coat-tails of Mountbatten's SEAC. An Allied Control Commission was established in Saigon, effectively an augmented version of General Gracey's crack 20th Indian Division, which began to arrive on 6 September to displace the Viet Minh Provisional Government, in power for only a few days. Gracey's anxiety to transfer civil affairs back to the French inspired him to release and re-arm 1,400 interned French colonial troops. Although assured of their restraint by Jean Cédile, the now liberated senior French representative, a dreadful orgy of French reprisals followed. Gracey quickly disarmed the troops, but this episode triggered a full-scale guerrilla war with the Viet Minh, whose control over their forces was also poor. By late September, British, Indian, French and re-armed Japanese troops were increasingly called on to fight the Viet Minh around Saigon in a conflict that generated a thousand casualties before the British departure in January 1946.[46]

As in Hanoi, Gracey's arrival in Saigon had been preceded by a vanguard of secret service groups. On 2 September a four-man OSS observer mission had arrived from SEAC, charged with locating POWs and internees, and had set up an OSS headquarters in the Continental Hotel. Further OSS groups arrived and soon there were fifty American intelligence officers, together with their various support staffs, located around Saigon.[47] A key objective for all intelligence teams was the immediate arrest of war criminals and 'suspect categories' including:

(a) Kempei Tai (Japanese Gestapo)
(b) Tokumu Kikan (Japanese Intelligence Organisation)
(c) Hikari Kikan (Japanese/Indian Intelligence Organisation)
(d) General Staff Intelligence Personnnel
(e) Japanese Intelligence agencies . . .
(f) War criminals
(g) Guard of Prisoner of War and Allied Internee Camps.[48]

However in the short term the Kempei Tai had to be re-armed to maintain civil order.[49]

In September 1945, OSS and SIS counter-intelligence officers were working closely together on these targets and had located themselves in a suburban area of Saigon near the golf course on the road to the airport, occupying buildings across the street from the other. The SIS team was led by Colonel Rogers. Major D. B. Graham, the local MI5 officer, headed a Special Counter-Intelligence Unit working closely with Captain R. P. Leonard of X-2. But the location had been criticised by Colonel Bill Cass, the senior British intelligence officer in Saigon, as isolated and vulnerable. The SIS building did not even have the Japanese armed guard deployed by OSS, but allowed the interference-free operation of W/T equipment.[50]

The senior OSS officer in Saigon was an SI officer named Colonel Peter Dewey, whose main brief was political intelligence. Gracey had taken exception to the large OSS presence and, on 20 September, had ordered Dewey to cease some of his activities. But Dewey, who had been delegated consular powers, continued.[51] On 26 August, Dewey had visited Gracey's HQ and then went to the airfield. Returning to the OSS building at 1230, they slowed at a chicane-type road block and a machine gun opened up at point blank range killing Dewey instantly. Major Bluechel, who had been travelling with him was thrown clear and managed to reach the OSS building 600 yards away. For the next two and a half hours the OSS building, which was flying the American flag, was besieged and subjected to 'indiscriminate firing'.[52]

That local guerrillas were deliberately shooting at Americans was confirmed by the fact that Dewey had just learned that one of his staff, Captain Joseph Coolidge of R&A, had been shot in the neck in an ambush the previous day. However, Bluechel, who had accompanied Dewey, made much of the fact that the British had banned American insignia and that Dewey's jeep 'carried no American flag'. Ironically, this order may have been issued at American request, to prevent the appearance of American markings on Lend-Lease equipment used in Indochina.[53] During a lull in the fighting OSS tried to negotiate for the recovery of the body, but proceedings were interrupted by the arrival of a Gurkha unit who engaged the guerrillas.[54] Gracey made considerable efforts in meetings with the Viet Minh to recover Dewey's body, a process which took some time.[55] Mountbatten later reported that the Viet Minh 'confess that they are unable effectively to control their own forces' and that their last meeting with Gracey had been broken up prematurely, so that they could go out to halt further unauthorised attacks by their forces.[56]

Truman explained, in a letter to Dewey's family, that he had been sent to Saigon 'particularly for the benefit of the State Department' which had asked OSS to expand intelligence activity in Indochina.[57] By October 1945 the most senior SSU observer in Indochina was Colonel Austin Glass, whose knowledge of the country was unrivalled, having been a representative of the Standard Oil Company in Indochina for thirty years. Glass expressed concern that the US should be neglecting its interests in the area, and in consequence permitting the French and the British and Chinese 'to further their own interest at our expense. America it appears is the only country not voicing its story to the peoples of Indochina.' Together with other SSU officers in a dozen other locations across Asia, he complained that American prestige had suffered a marked deterioration since V-J Day.[58]

Gracey's troops now found themselves engaged in a protracted guerrilla war which was still in progress when they handed over to the French in early 1946. By the end of September 1945, Gracey was hard pressed to contain the situation and at this point the SOE liaison team at his headquarters in Saigon, headed by Major A. W. Fielding, offered him their assistance in a new role.[59] Originally attached to ensure a full flow of intelligence from various SOE/DGER teams across Indochina, they were now concentrated together in Saigon and were 'at a loose end'. All personnel, Fielding noted, had been through SOE schools in Britain or North Africa and had 'trained in tough tactics'. Fielding now proposed to use them as a crack counter-insurgency unit to carry out tasks such as 'fighting reconnaissance', 'diversions', 'intelligence', even 'assassinations and abduction'. A list of likely targets had already been drawn up, including Viet Minh arms dumps.[60]

The use of such special units is a characteristic sign of forces under pressure from insurgency and terrorist-type activity. Gracey had certainly lost his patience and was soon embarking on a strategy of reprisal. By 13 October, after a series of alarming forays by the guerrillas, Gracey despatched a message to Slim complaining that his troops were suffering from attacks which amounted to 'crimes against the laws and usages of war'. In this 'present emergency' he considered it 'most essential for morale of own troops and French for me to be able in flagrant cases to authorise subordinate comds. [commanders] to try these criminals and if necessary bump them off'. He proposed to 'empower the senior officer on the spot' to deal with such offenders. These sentences 'to be carried out on the spot immediately after confirmation'.[61] Exactly how Gracey's approach materialised on the ground is unclear, for documentation on this sort of subject is rarely complete.

SIS in Hanoi

By late 1945 SIS were following the advice of Garnons-Williams and deploying more experienced officers in the more traditional SIS role of long-range political intelligence gathering, which had little bearing on current developments. This was exemplified by the arrival of Lt Colonel Arthur Trevor-Wilson in Hanoi under the guise of head of the British Military Mission to the occupying Chinese forces. Trevor Wilson was well-suited to a Francophone environment, having been a pre-war bank manager in France. From 1942 he headed an SIS counter-intelligence section in Algiers.[62] By 1944, together with Lord Rothschild and Malcolm Muggeridge, he was amongst the first SIS officers into liberated Paris. The latter regarded him as simply 'the ablest Intelligence officer I met in the war' and as having 'an instinctive flair for the work'. Muggeridge sketched his character:

A cigarette was, as usual, more or less permanently attached to his lower lip, and occasionally smouldering, making his always indistinct speech more so than ever. He was the perfect companion for a Liberation . . . He would, I knew, combine his seemingly surrealist manner with a magical cunning in procuring food and shelter, and in finding his way to exactly the right places at the right time.

Hailed by his colleagues as 'always master of a difficult situation', Trevor-Wilson was ideal for the complex scenario developing in Hanoi at the end of the war.[63]

During September and October 1945, the Chinese General Lu Han, accompanied by an American adviser, Brigadier General Philip Gallagher, had moved in his forces in strength into northern Indochina and received the formal Japanese surrender on 28 September. These remained until the return of French forces to the north in March 1946.[64] Although Trevor-Wilson was technically head of a mission to Lu Han, the Viet Minh were still in control of the civilian administration, and so his key task was to liaise with Ho Chi Minh.[65] Amongst the morass of confused reports generated by the many different agencies operating in Indochina at this time, Trevor-Wilson's material stands out as perceptive. He proved capable of following the convoluted differences between the dominant Viet Minh and the other competing nationalist parties, such as the Dong Minh Hoi. He also discerned the essential difference between the north, where the population was already experiencing unpleasant Viet Minh rule, and the south where they were still idealised. By December 1945, he noted, they had shown their true colours: the administration was 'completely disorganised', the Treasury had been 'completely emptied' and government was carried on 'by terrorist tactics' and arbitrary arrest. This, he stressed, was an independent manifestation of the Viet Minh, for he could see no evidence of contact with Moscow.[66]

Trevor-Wilson remained in Hanoi throughout 1946 and achieved a good relationship with Ho.[67] Remarkably, Trevor-Wilson persuaded Ho to lend his security units for the purpose of arresting Major General A. C. Chatterjee, Deputy Commander of the INA, and Chandra Bose's Foreign Minister, together with some other 'Cabinet Minsters' and senior officers then residing in Hanoi and spending their time writing propaganda against the British and the French. They were then removed to India by aircraft and incarcerated in the Red Fort in Delhi. Trevor-Wilson had also been looking for Chandra Bose, but reported that he had perished in an air crash at Taihokual while trying to flee to Manchuria.[68]

Little documentation remains for the British Military Mission in Hanoi, but former associates attribute to him other curious feats. In late 1945 the Viet Minh had apparently captured a minor pro-French member of the Cambodian Royal Family. The Cambodian royalty had long ruled with French support and Trevor-Wilson was informed that Ho thought it might be useful to have him executed as an example to other collaborators. He was reportedly dissuaded because Trevor-Wilson decided to let him into the 'secret' of what he called the 'Trade Union of Kings', the Secretary-General of which was Great Britain's own George V. If the Cambodian prince was executed, he explained, it would have terrible consequences for Vietnam's future relations with any state with a monarchy, especially Britain. Ho reportedly thought it a tactical mistake to offend Britain at this point, and so relented.[69]

Such anecdotes are quite unverifiable. However, it is clear that Ho valued good relations with British representatives during early 1946. In April he had approached Trevor-Wilson asking that London extend recognition to his government in the north as a 'Free State', but London replied that this was an improper request, given the newly negotiated position of 6 March establishing Vietnam as a free state within the French federation.[70] Despite this disappointment, personal relations remained good and Trevor-Wilson was able to accompany Ho to Paris during his abortive negotiations with the French of May–June 1946. He returned as British Consul in Hanoi and remained for several years, enjoying the confidence of both the Viet Minh and the French.[71] Later he moved into information work, in Malaya in the 1950s, and in Laos in the 1960s, maintaining only an informal relationship with SIS.[72]

Laos and Cambodia

The Japanese coup of 9 March had extended right across Indochina, including Laos and Cambodia and here too it accelerated the pace of nationalism. On 12 March, three days after the coup, with some Japanese prompting, King Norodom Sihanouk declared Cambodia to have become independent of France as 'Kampuchea'. There was only limited French resistance and Sihanouk appointed a Cabinet of former senior officials, but with no Premier. In May, Son Ngoc Thanh, Cambodia's most radical nationalist, returned from a long sojourn in Japan, to become Foreign Affairs Minister. In its last days Japan was deliberately encouraging a legacy of Pan-Asian nationalism, facilitating a public visit by Chatterjee of Chandra Bose's disintegrating Free India government. Finally, on 10 August 1945, with Japanese encouragement, the local militia stormed the royal palace and forced Sihanouk to declare a new government with Son Ngoc Thanh as premier.[73]

On 22 August an Allied aircraft from SEAC dropped propaganda material announcing the imminent return of the French. SOE/DGER operations into rural areas of Cambodia had been under way for some time, and had been well received, despite Viet Minh efforts to extend their influence here. On 29 August, an eight man DGER group approached Phnom Penh, but bided their time, 'playing up' to the Son Ngoc Thanh regime while a 'referendum' on independence was held.[74] General Gracey noted in his report that shortly before his own arrival in Saigon in mid-September, 'British special intelligence forces' and medical relief teams had arrived in Cambodia and reported that law and order were deteriorating. On 8 October, with Gracey established in Saigon, Colonel E. D. Murray was despatched as British Commander in Phnom Penh. Murray, accompanied by Cass, Gracey's senior intelligence officer, soon flew back to Saigon to insist that the quick arrest of Son Ngoc Thanh was 'essential if Cambodia was not to be embroiled in serious political disturbances, or worse'.[75] Murray obtained permission and returned to Phnom

Penh on the morning of 15 October and the war diaries of his HQ record the political changes on that busy day:

1030 PM invited this HQ for an interview on invitation of Commander.
1115 General Leclerc, representative of France ... arrived at this HQ to conduct PM to Saigon. Was rec'd at airfield by Commander.
1130 PM left this HQ under escort with Gen Leclerc for the airfield en route for Saigon.
1730 Defence Minster and Minster of Justice visited this HQ. The latter asked the reason for the sudden disappearance of the PM and was then informed the arrest had been made by General Leclerc who should know his own reasons best.
1830 H. P. Prince Monireth Lord Privy Councillor and His Excellency the Governor of Phnom Penh arrived this HQ to discuss the latest political developments and the future moves. It was decided that the Cambodian Police and Surete would come under direct command of ALFPP [Allied Land Forces Phnom Phenh] and that all anti-French chiefs and agents in Phnom Penh would be arrested.
1930 ... New Cabinet of Ministers formed with Prince Monireth as PM.[76]

A few days later Dening reported that the former Premier 'has been condemned to death' by the French, but the British suggested this would be impolitic, and so he was incarcerated in Saigon Central Prison.[77] In January 1946 the 24-year-old King Norodom Sihanouk was confirmed as head of state under French protection.[78]

French fortunes were more uneven in Laos, much of which was north of 16 degrees and so fell under Chinese control. By December 1944, DGER had raised a force of 700 local guerrillas in Laos, a network that remained largely intact after the coup of March 1945 and by June 1945 they had twelve separate W/T stations.[79] On 29 August, Colonel Imfeld, the senior French officer, felt confident enough to declare himself French Commissioner in Luang Prabang.[80] But the situation now began to deteriorate, with a rise in attacks by nationalist Lao Issara guerrillas working with the Viet Minh against the return of the French. Chinese troops and OSS were also in evidence.

French DGER teams in Cambodia and Laos were greatly assisted by British ALFPMO, based in Eastern Thailand. In late September 1945, ALFPMO officers at Ubon in North East Thailand had asked for permission to hand over all surrendered Japanese weapons to the French groups across the border, who were being attacked by local guerrillas. Senior officers at ALFSEA smelt trouble and referred this request up to Mountbatten, warning:

Staff view here is that it is most dangerous to embark on a policy of arming French guerrillas who are not under our control and are likely to operate in the immediate vicinity of, if not north of, 16 degrees. Furthermore we have reason to believe that the Annamites [Vietnamese] against who these weapons may be used have American backing.[81]

18 ALFPMO under fire from guerrillas on the Mekong (IWM)

Even as this issue was being considered, the inevitable happened. On 28 September a fatal altercation occurred between an Anglo-French party and an OSS–Viet Minh group on the banks of the Mekong. Colin Mackenzie reported that Major Peter Kemp and Lt Klotz of ALFPMO had been moving supplies across the river intended for the French. The Viet Minh confronted them and demanded that they surrender Klotz, who was a French national, as they were 'now at war with France'. Kemp attempted to shepherd Klotz back to the boat while the accompanying OSS officers withdrew, declaring themselves 'neutral'. The Viet Minh then killed Klotz, whose body was eventually ferried across the river by Kemp. Mackenzie was anxious to blame OSS, insisting that the actions and words of OSS in this area 'which have been consistently anti-French must be considered largely responsible for encouraging the Annamites to commit this murder'.[82] Mountbatten reacted by urging ALFPMO to arrest those responsible.[83] However, Mackenzie's report to Mountbatten was inaccurate, suggesting that Kemp's party were merely moving 'medicines' across the Mekong, when its real purpose was to move up weapons, especially heavy mortars, for the French.[84] Despite a continued ALFPMO supply operation, the French situation deteriorated further during November. They were now fighting a Viet Minh force that had grown to approximately 2,000 and the DGER chief reported that two of his officers had been caught, beheaded 'and their heads exposed in Vientiane'.[85]

SOE, and its post-war remnant, ALFPMO, was a diverse body and the attitudes of its officers defy generalisation. But clearly some of its officers were deeply committed to the work of imperial restoration, seeing it as the context of a global retreat from empire, which they resented. When the British Ambassador in Thailand, Geoffrey Thompson visited them in October 1946, he expressed his concern:

I have seen Major Beaumont-Nesbitt [of ALFPMO] . . . at least one member of the French mission is in a very excited frame of mind and talking in a dramatic way of his readiness to make any sacrifices. Major Beaumont-Nesbitt himself says he is prepared to face any risks . . . and that he does not like the way in which in Egypt and elsewhere we British are on . . . the retreat.

Thompson gave the officer a stern lecture, insisting that the British were not there 'to pick up the white man's burden' in Laos and Cambodia, and adding that the French were trying to drag the British into confrontations from which they would rather keep their distance.[86] In December 1946 the last ALFPMO officers were still there, merging with the Mixed Commission dealing with the contested Franco-Thai border.[87]

The Netherlands East Indies

OSS, SIS and SOE played a smaller role in the Netherlands East Indies, subsequently Indonesia, an area transferred from MacArthur's SWPA to SEAC at the end of the war. In September 1945, Mountbatten despatched a representative of P Division, Group Captain Cliff, to Australia, to investigate what sort of preliminary intelligence screen was available. Here Cliff encountered the local SIS organisation, known as Secret Intelligence Australia or SIA and a Dutch intelligence organisation known as NEFIS. Both had worked for a prolonged period within the SWPA.[88]

MacArthur had now departed for Japan and the Australian commander, General Blamey, had decided on the rapid liquidation of all clandestine groups, including SIA. But Cliff now requested the reversal of this decision, handing over a message from Mountbatten: 'I have no Secret Intelligence resources which I can put into these islands . . . The first and most important item is to get NEFIS into Java with its headquarters at Batavia . . . The matter is so urgent and time is so short.'[89] Blamey agreed and fifty-two Australian clandestine personnel in Borneo remained until they could be replaced by SEAC. Wing Commander Pitt-Hardacre led a party of thirteen SIA personnel (a mixture of British and New Zealanders) attached to a further group from NEFIS to establish a joint station at Batavia. There were already four other SIA parties in Java and a further one in Batavia. But before Cliff departed he was given a stern warning by the officers at the SIA station in Brisbane.

They told him that a civil war was likely between the Indonesian nationalist leader, Soekarno, and the Dutch, as soon as the interlude of British administration drew to a close.[90]

OSS had only small numbers of staff in the Netherlands East Indies, but like SIA, they assessed the situation clearly. Jane Foster, a pre-war resident familiar with the language, was in Batavia and during September and October 1945 she mixed freely with members of Soekarno's Cabinet. Foster correctly assessed the Dutch as completely unprepared for the situation, 'highly emotional' and 'chaotic'. Dutch prestige, she noted, had collapsed quickly when the British commander used Japanese troops in preference to excitable Dutch troops to maintain order.[91] The SSU team contrasted the well-equipped paramilitary forces of the nationalists, with the frightened, trigger-happy Dutch colonial troops, and noted that the British administration were anxious to leave.[92] SSU were still in Batavia in March 1946.[93]

SOE encountered severe problems in the Netherlands East Indies which reflected the fact that, as with their Indochina country section, their Anglo-Dutch Country Section was merely a co-opted Dutch organisation. In September 1945, four groups from the separate SOE-backed Dutch Korps Insulinde were inserted to collect intelligence and assist POWs. But by early October no Dutchman could move safely outside the main towns and Mountbatten ordered that no further Dutch personnel should be used.[94] SOE conceded that some Dutch SOE personnel had 'adopted a hostile attitude towards the inhabitants'.[95] Thereafter only British ALFPMO groups were despatched, although they remained hopeful that Dutch parties would again be permitted.[96]

SOE were very anxious to assist Dutch restoration. Even in December 1945, with fighting out of control across Java and Sumatra, optimistic SOE officers suggested that neighbouring British Borneo be employed as a springboard for SOE-backed Dutch missions into Java:

The 'expeditions' would have the objective of converting the Indonesians from their anti-Dutch attitude to one favourable to the Dutch, and to one ready to accept the Dutch back again. The weapons sued would be a) propaganda and political organization, b) money, c) consumption goods such as cotton piece goods and other necessities which are now in very short supply.

Initially no Dutch officers would be used, but as the scheme developed, they would be slipped in.[97] These proposals reflected a view that could not have been further removed from the more realistic picture offered by OSS, or indeed by the SIA officers encountered by Cliff in Brisbane.

The volatile situation in the Netherlands East Indies had stretched SEAC to breaking point, not only administratively but also politically. Relations between the erratic and liberal-minded Mountbatten, and the efficient and conservative-minded Dening, had deteriorated fast. At the end of November 1945 Mountbatten had asked Bevin to remove Dening because of his political interference.[98] But before London could find a replacement, Dening telegraphed his resignation to Bevin, giving full vent to his emotions:

Supreme Commander through his open advocacy of Indonesian cause (of which he could necessarily have no first hand knowledge) and his harmful utterances against the Dutch has been in very large measure responsible for the position in which we find ourselves to-day . . . I could not possibly in the circumstances continue as his political adviser.

Dening went on to deride Mountbatten's own messages to London as a 'mixture of fiction and malice'.[99] But Bevin curtly ordered Dening to withdraw his comments, to apologise and to resume work under Mountbatten.[100]

Dening's contention that Mountbatten was ill informed about the situation on the ground offers a clue to the immediate cause of this explosion. Mountbatten and many of his staff saw the leading Dutch officers and administrators in Java as guilty of muddling ineptitude, while Dening placed more faith in the Dutch. This difference of perspective rested on conflicting reports and a tendency to rely on different sources. General Christison, the British Commander in Batavia, later told the Australian representative in SEAC that 'when he checked the Dutch military intelligence reports he found that nine out of ten were misleading or false'. Christison added that in his view: 'The Dutch remedy is force and still more force, to teach the "natives" a lesson.' Meanwhile it was thought that Dening's dispute with Mountbatten had arisen partly because Dening 'relies mainly on the Dutch for his political intelligence'.[101]

Conclusion

Across most of South East Asia during 1945 and 1946, the various Allied secret services reported more often than they intervened. This is notably true of OSS in Indochina, where support for Ho was limited and driven by a desire to penetrate Indochina for intelligence purposes at a time when most alternative vehicles had been eliminated. Patti's activities were much less directed or purposeful than Paris believed them to be. Meanwhile the coup in Indochina itself, the real body-blow to French rule during 1945, although probably desired, even encouraged, by Roosevelt, was most likely the perverse outcome of ham-fisted efforts by the French secret services, working under SOE in India, to prepare the path for the restoration of French rule.

Although these different agencies were mostly reporting rather than intervening, their reports offered a disconcerting range of advice. Confronted with fighting in the volatile territories of his European Allies, Mountbatten had sent Colonel Chapman Walker, a senior military intelligence officer, on a long tour of Indochina to make an independent assessment of the situation. He returned to inform Mountbatten about the depth of nationalist feeling and the need for a rapid and sensitive transition to indigenous rule, if tragedies were to be avoided.[102] But the intelligence reports funnelled upwards by the Dutch and French officers that SOE had co-opted could not have been more different. On 4 September 1945, Commandant Fabre, the senior DGER officer in Vientianne, struck a quite different note, urging concerted action to suppress the nationalists by all the European powers in Asia: 'The only reasonable policy for the whites to follow is to unite in defence of their respective positions. Every attack against one of them weakens all the others. Unfortunately it does not appear that everyone understands that.'[103]

19   Hong Kong and the future of China

The British are very quiet in China. The men they have are hand-picked and all top people. They spend an enormous amount of money in bribing certain Chinese people who can help them throughout China, and they have an excellent intelligence organisation in China.

Major Nicol Smith, OSS, 21 April 1945[1]

SOE and the recovery of Hong Kong

SOE's main focus of interest in China was the coastal region around Hong Kong, and during 1944 four separate schemes had been mooted for operations in this area. The most promising became Operation *Oblivion* which sought to train groups of Canadian-Chinese as guerrilla parties for action in this area. After intensive training, advanced parties were transferred to Australia and India for final despatch in December 1944. However, at this point the operation, and four further variants were vetoed by Wedemeyer and so SOE's Canadian-Chinese were sent to Malaya in April and May 1945.

Accordingly, SOE's only successful operation in the area around Hong Kong remained the British Army Aid Group (BAAG), directed by Dr Lindsay Ride. BAAG had found the supply of escaped POWs from Hong Kong, its original *raison d'être*, to be drying up by 1943, but had then joined up with the 14th Air Force, to whom it supplied intelligence. During the rapid Japanese advance of late 1944, BAAG was pushed further away from Hong Kong and worked with OSS in conducting road demolitions to slow the Japanese advance. At the end of 1944, with BAAG having fallen back on Kunming, SOE reviewed its plans for the forthcoming year. Ambitious plans were now launched for a Chinese guerrilla army under British direction, to assist in the recapture of Hong Kong. The focus of this was to be a reformed SOE 'Group C' at Kunming under Lt Colonel Gill-Davies. Although Mountbatten correctly dismissed the plan as militarily impractical and politically transparent, nevertheless this scheme preoccupied the JIC and other Cabinet committees during late 1944 and 1945.[2]

In November 1944, when the JIC in London reviewed the purpose and role of SOE, BAAG and 204 Military Mission in China, they concluded that their main value was long-term and political. To the Chinese, they argued, these activities represented the entirety of the British war effort in China. They agreed with the Foreign Office and GHQ India that their withdrawal or reduction 'would have a very bad effect' on relations with China and on Britain's long-term interests. 'The officers of these organisations', the JIC concluded, to some extent replaced, in the areas in which they operated 'the influence formerly exercised by our consuls and the leaders of our trading communities'. The JIC continued:

The Colonial Office also attach great importance to the maintenance of B.A.A.G. It not only provides them with intelligence necessary for their planning, but through it they are organising the recruitment of former Chinese members of the Hong Kong police and other departments whose services will be required when a British military administration is set up in Hong Kong. In addition, in collaboration with the War Office, the Colonial Office are planning an Emergency Civil Affairs Administration for Hong Kong should Hong Kong be retaken by Chinese forces before the main Civil Affairs Unit is able to reach the area. The personnel of B.A.A.G. and other British organisations in China would be indispensable for the organisation of this Emergency Unit.[3]

Meanwhile BAAG was reviled by the Chinese, who were clear about its principal purpose: 'solely to re-establish British prestige in the Hong Kong area and South China'. By the end of 1944, OSS reported that the Chinese were putting BAAG under extreme pressure. Both officially and unofficially every obstacle had been put in their way 'including murdered agents and attempts to interfere with BAAG radio'.[4]

On 29 March 1945, the JIC informed Sir Horace Seymour, the British Ambassador in Chungking, that it now considered that the best way for SOE to retain a place within Wedemeyer's China Theater was to combine with the British Military Mission and BAAG.[5] De Wiart, Churchill's personal representative to Chiang Kai-shek, replaced Grimsdale as overall superintendent of British secret services in China. The main focus of this new group would now be guerrilla training against the Japanese. Superficially, the declared aim of this organisation within Wedemeyer's China Theater would be to train, equip and direct the operations of some 30,000 Chinese guerrillas in the Kwangsi-Kwangtung area including Hong Kong, thereby disrupting Japanese communications. However, the JIC had stated that: 'The ulterior aim would be to facilitate, at the appropriate moment, the re-establishment of British administration in Hong Kong.' Furthermore, the JIC were convinced that such activities would only meet with the assent of Wedemeyer, and indeed Chiang, if their real objective was not known.[6]

Seymour was stupefied by the JIC's proposal. He insisted that Chiang would immediately rumble the purpose of this British-controlled force poised on the outskirts of a British imperial territory and insisted that Chiang would withdraw permission 'when the purpose of establishing ourselves in Hong Kong becomes obvious'. Instead he advised that it was 'better to come clean on this rather than try and conceal anything so obvious'. Local SOE personnel also considered the plan as 'too risky' and pleaded for London to come up with something 'less obvious'.[7] In the event SOE put up a plan for a broader range of guerrilla activity in the area southeast of Kunming at Poseh, which received Wedemeyer's approval at the end of April. The revised command arrangements, designed to smooth relations with Wedemeyer, were clearly working well and de Wiart reported a 'radical improvement' in relations between BAAG and the Americans.[8] Nevertheless, de Wiart had his work cut out as clandestine co-ordinator. To his amazement he was continually uncovering new clandestine sections hidden behind almost every British overt activity in China.[9]

In May 1945, attempts to hide the real purpose of the BAAG and SOE guerrilla build-up continued and Grimsdale reported that he had fully integrated the Hong Kong Civil Affairs Unit into BAAG's platoons.[10] But there was also renewed nervousness about the Americans, since they discovered that AGAS were 'already infiltrating into BAAG area'.[11] By June both AGAS and OSS knew that BAAG was being used as 'a screen for extensive intelligence and political operations' which were most intense around Hong Kong, and so 'friction' was developing between BAAG officers and American and Chinese personnel.[12] But by July, BAAG were more confident, having identified the connections between OSS and the Communists in China. They explained to Gubbins in London that:

If he says that it is being done without General Wedemeyer's agreement it puts us in a very strong position in relation to O.S.S. If, on the other hand, he says that General Wedemeyer has agreed to it, it puts us in a very strong position with General Wedemeyer.

BAAG's observations were tinged with jealousy, since it had 'for years wanted to work with the Reds round Hong Kong' but had been prevented from doing so for fear of Chiang's reactions. BAAG now wished to use this information to resist the American tendency to attach AGAS teams to BAAG parties near Hong Kong.[13] Senior British officers continued to advise SOE to try and work with OSS rather than against it.

Colonial Office interest in the role of BAAG reached its height in July 1945, when it seemed increasingly likely that the Japanese might retreat unilaterally, making an unopposed Chinese occupation of Hong Kong a distinct possibility. Ride was uneasy about the use of BAAG as a temporary Civil Affairs unit for Hong Kong, arguing that it would confirm the worst suspicions of the Chinese. But this cut no ice in London. Sir Edward Gent of

19 British Army Aid Group, the SOE and POW escape operation near
Hong Kong. Ride stands in front of the door (IWM)

the Colonial Office asserted that 'the first duty of the BAAG as a British
organisation . . . must be the effective recovery of Hong Kong'. Gent was
firmly supported by the Foreign Office. The debate continued through July
as to whether the Union Jack over Hong Kong should be raised by a covert
mission from BAAG, or an overt mission from outside China, despatched by
sea or air. On 23 July the conclusion was still that SOE should be used and
the Chinese should not be told.[14] In the event SOE's BAAG were the first
back into Hong Kong, under the watchful eye of accompanying OSS officers
working under the cover of the 14th Air Force.[15] BAAG had in fact pre-
empted its own joint party by sending agents ahead to contact Franklin
Gimson, the captive Colonial Secretary in Hong Kong.[16]

    The key role played by SOE was ensuring the neutrality of local KMT and
Communist forces. In July 1945, SOE planners had confronted the fact that
any military forces put into the area by BAAG could not compete with those
of the Chinese. They therefore turned to what was arguably SOE's most
successful operation in China, its black-market trading activities, Operations
Remorse and *Waldorf*, to lend support. SOE argued for the 'use of money
and bribery'. A *de facto* Chinese government would almost certainly mat-

erialise in Hong Kong and the only way of 'moving it out', they insisted, 'will be by purchase'. They then reinforced this by expounding more widely on the nature of the SOE experience in wartime China:

The lessons of REMORSE over two years, culminating in WALDORF, are surely clear by now. Money talks in China with a louder voice than anything except arms, planes and other munitions. We have not got the arms, planes or munitions. The only voice we have, or can have is the financial one. It is possible, even with the dice loaded against us, to succeed where others cannot do so, if the right inducement has been offered to the right people ... The Americans have not done this ... I think the right way to handle this difficult-as-possible operation is for Ride to carry on with the organisation of getting European personnel right into Hong Kong, but for REMORSE to be put fully in the picture to know who to bribe in the new Chinese Government, and to put one of their men into Hong Kong with the necessary induce-ments as soon as possible, so that the good work of corruption and bribery can start at once.[17]

This extraordinary suggestion by Walter Fletcher, perhaps the most effective figure in SOE China, not only illuminates the purpose of SOE during the Far Eastern War; it also sheds light on the value attached to these activities by high-level policy-makers in London. SOE, plausibly or otherwise, at times appeared to offer a magical solution to those 'difficult-as-possible' problems. By discreetly depressing the right lever at the right moment, the unfavourable shift in the balance of world forces could momentarily be reversed, and seem-ingly impossible constraints escaped.

It is peculiar that the Colonial Office, charged with the recovery of assets that Churchill considered valuable, were not given some inkling of that the end of the Far Eastern War was likely to be abrupt. Nevertheless, they were taken by surprise in August and thus confronted the problem of organising a an administration for Hong Kong overnight. SOE were busy putting small parties into Hong Kong and supporting Franklin Gimson, but the closest regular British unit happened to be Shield Force, embarked on the *Empress of Australia* under the command of Group Captain James Barker. On 21 August he received an unexpected message from the Air Ministry:

Background is that it is essential to get a British Force into Hong Kong at earliest possible date to re-establish British Administration, disarm Japanese, release prisoners, etc. Australians unable to provide a force. SEAC have detailed a Force and will despatch as soon as it can be got through the Straits of Malacca, but this date is uncertain and cannot be before the end of the first week of September.
... make such improved arrangements as are possible ...
We have every confidence that you will interpret this policy in the light of circum-stances in Hong Kong and that your force will give a good account of itself.[18]

In this improvised fashion, the British administration returned to Hong Kong. Admiral Harcourt, the first British post-war Governor, arrived two weeks after the end of the war to take the surrender of Japanese forces. As de Wiart observes, the Chinese were only a few weeks away from capturing Hong Kong from the Japanese by their own efforts and had they done so there would have been 'most serious trouble'. How far SOE's largesse had played a part in slowing the Chinese advance on Hong Kong remains unknown.[19]

Wedemeyer and 'rationalisation' in China

Running in parallel with barely disguised British plans for the recovery of Hong Kong was a process of rationalisation of the secret services in the China Theater, initiated by Wedemeyer on his arrival in October 1944. His initial efforts in this regard were preoccupied with lengthy negotiations over the position of OSS and an unscheduled confrontation with Hurley and Washington over the Dixie Mission. But by 1945 he was ready to turn his attention to the generic issue of secret service control in China, perhaps hoping to achieve a system not unlike that presided over by Mountbatten in SEAC.

Wedemeyer's 'rationalisation' had consequences for the Mountbatten–Wedemeyer dispute over Indochina, and also SOE's worries about Hong Kong operations. This is underlined by Dening's brief for Mountbatten on 30 December 1944 in preparation for the arrival of Donovan for a major secret service conference in SEAC in January 1945. Notably, Dening, like his diplomatic colleagues in London, had ceased to regard these issues as subordinate or low level, and now recognised that they involved 'political considerations of the highest importance'. He urged Mountbatten to stand firm on the boundary dispute, and recommended that on this subject, unless Donovan came round to the British point of view, 'there is obviously no basis for discussion'. He advised Mountbatten to get tough about the prospect of OSS operating into Malaya, observing, 'I gravely doubt whether the Colonial Office would approve'.[20] More importantly, he also held out the possibility of some sort of deal across command boundaries, prompted by rumours that Wedemeyer was intending to push British secret services out of China. Dening explained:

It is clear that the operations of Force 136 [SOE Far East] in China will depend, not only on the goodwill of the generalissimo [Chiang Kai-shek], but also on that of Generals Wedemeyer and Donovan. For this reason I understand that Force 136 are willing to make concessions to General Donovan, possibly in this theatre.

From his own personal perspective, the intrusion of secret services, of whatever hue, into delicate political issues was unwelcome. Dening was therefore not only 'averse from granting concessions to OSS in this theatre', he was also equally averse to a deal to further SOE activities in China 'which', he noted, 'is not our concern'. Dening warned Mountbatten that: 'Considerable

political complications may result from Force 136 [SOE] activities in China.'
But Dening was swimming against the tide, for although he had personally
given SOE 'strict instructions not to become involved in politics', they were
getting the opposite message from many quarters in London.[21]

British fears about secret service in China were exaggerated. On 30
December 1944, the same day that Dening was preparing his briefing for
Mountbatten, Wedemeyer had a 'most friendly' discussion with Grimsdale
on the wide-ranging problems of all their 'private armies' in China. Wedemeyer made clear that he believed that Chiang was trying to encourage Anglo-
American dissent by denying that he had ever given permissions to British
organisations such as BAAG. But Wedemeyer had concluded that Chiang
'was deliberately lying'. Although Wedemeyer was clearly wary of British
activities, his *bête noire* was clearly Naval Group and Miles. Grimsdale
reported that Wedemeyer

told me he is worried about the 'private army' of Commodore Miles which is under
Tai Li and not the theatre commander and stated that he already has General Marshall
working on the US Navy Department to clean this up, and is determined to get his
own way. The impression I got was that he is working to achieve really adequate
coordination, if not either control or disbandment of similar British 'private armies'.
He knew for instance of Force 136 [SOE Far East] plans to arm 30,000 Chinese
bandits . . .

Although Wedemeyer was sometimes in receipt of higher-level political directives on this subject, for example Indochina, his own views were primarily
those of a theatre commander who wished to command: 'There is no doubt
that Wedemeyer regards this as his military kingdom', and, reported
Grimsdale 'he intends eventually to be King'.[22]

Wedemeyer called his various 'private armies' to order at a key meeting
on 24 January 1945. The attendance list was impressive. Donovan was present, having recently visited Mountbatten in SEAC to negotiate a *modus
vivendi* over operations in Malaya and elsewhere. Accompanying Donovan
from SEAC, Mountbatten sent the new Director of the SIS in the Far East,
Brigadier P. G. Bowden-Smith, and also Colin Mackenzie for SOE. Colonel
George F. Taylor of SOE London was in attendance, accompanied by Air
Commodore Blandy, a senior SIS officer.[23] The Chinese contingent included
Tai Li, Commodore Milton Miles and the Chinese Chief of Staff and Cheng
Kai-min, the Director of Military Intelligence.

Wedemeyer read the riot act and gave instructions that in future all clandestine activities would first be co-ordinated and approved both by him and the
Chinese Chief of Staff. In particular Wedemeyer stressed: 'He is not repeti-
tion not in any way interested in any political activities of British or American
organisations.' The reaction of his audience confirmed his worst expectations.

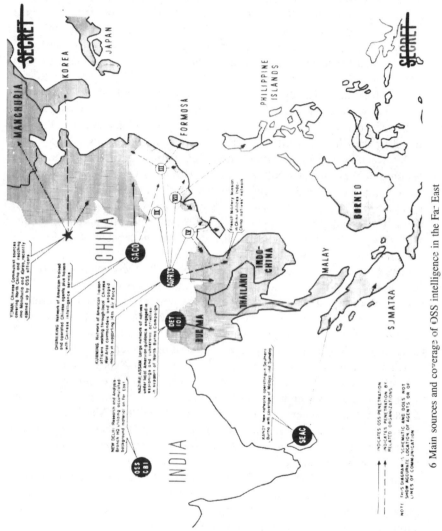

6 Main sources and coverage of OSS intelligence in the Far East

'Miles asked for definition of clandestine. Having got this, he said none repe-
tition none of his activities came under this definition and in any case he was
only the deputy of Tai Li.' The British proved to be equally slippery. Air
Commodore Blandy of SIS lamented to Wedemeyer the difficulty of submit-
ting regular reports of SIS activities in China, 'since', he insisted, 'there is at
present no-one in China who knows all that ISLD [SIS] are doing'. The
assembled group were given 'a strict warning . . . on behalf of the generalissimo [Chiang] that clandestine organisations should have no dealings with
such elements as the Communists, Independent Warlords or Provincial Gov-
ernors'. But these dealings were already universal, indeed obligatory, for
those who wished to operate beyond the immediate vicinity of Chungking.[24]
SOE noted that the Wedemeyer was 'extremely suspicious' and saw them as
'invading the China Theatre to work for certain British interests'.[25]

One week later, Mountbatten chaired a conference at SEAC to consider a
response to Wedemeyer's policy in China. Brigadier George F. Taylor made
the running in this meeting, shrewdly observing that Wedemeyer valued simplicity and coherence, and so British organisations were unlikely to be allocated any substantial role in China unless they integrated themselves, at least
outwardly, 'constituting a single British organisation capable of all forms of
irregular activity . . . as OSS'. If the British did so willingly, then, he
observed, Wedemeyer was likely to incorporate them comprehensively into
his plans for the theatre. Taylor's clear-sighted observation determined the
British response and it was at this point that Churchill's personal representative to Chiang Kai-shek, Major General Adrian Carton de Wiart, was designated overlord of this new grouping in China, with his assistant, Lt Colonel
Cartwright specifically looking after clandestine matters. Their main task
would be to build a good relationship with Lt Colonel Agnew, Wedemeyer's
staff officer co-ordinating clandestine matters.[26] Thus one outcome of the
Wedemeyer rationalisation was the creation of 'British Troops China' commanded by Major General Hayes, absorbing 204 Military Mission in China,
BAAG and the GBT intelligence network.[27] Taylor's scheme was broadly
accepted but not with equanimity. Words such as 'consolidation', and 'integration' conjured up all sort of terrors. By April 1945, SIS in the Far East
together with senior officers in SEAC, including Garnons-Williams and also
Mountbatten's Assistant Chief of Staff superintending secret service activities, Air Vice-Marshal Whitworth Jones, were concerned about the predatory
ambitions of SOE. Whitworth Jones complained that, as a result, SOE was
'swallowing all other organisations' with a view to strengthening their hand
and surviving as an organisation into the post-war period.[28]

On the ground OSS–SOE relations continued in their familiar vein. OSS
were now increasingly worried about deliberate British operations to penetrate the OSS organisation elsewhere in China. In April 1945 OSS considered

that they had finally obtained proof of such operations. Heppner informed Donovan:

During the past month a document has come into our hands which we believe to be authentic, and which proves that one of the British Missions in the China Theater is here to penetrate, for counter-espionage purposes, OSS and American Army and Air force Units. During the month we have uncovered 2 or 3 instances of British attempts to plant employees upon us. Attached is a letter setting forth the pertinent parts of the document referred to.[29]

The letter referred to currently remains closed to public inspection; however, circumstantial evidence suggests that it referred to the intelligence section of the British Military Mission at Chungking, which had already made less than subtle attempts to penetrate OSS compounds in China running operations into Korea.[30]

Wedemeyer's rationalisation had important outcomes for American organisations, slowly tipping the balance in favour of OSS. On 12 March 1945 Wedemeyer moved against Miles, issuing an order that henceforth he controlled all personnel and material of military, quasi-military and clandestine organisations in the theatre, including all the American personnel in SACO. But Miles continued to insist he was only answerable to King in Washington.[31] After a bitter confrontation involving the US Joint Chiefs of Staff, Naval Group was finally placed under Wedemeyer on 5 April 1945. He then ordered Miles to cease all activities that were not directly related to anti-Japanese intelligence gathering, but Miles ignored Wedemeyer.[32]

With the backing of the Chinese and Admiral King in Washington Miles was hard to restrain. In May 1945, Miles informed John T. Whitaker, the senior OSS SI officer in China, that he intended to expel the last token OSS liaison personnel from Naval Group HQ and wished to inform Donovan that 'the further apart OSS and Naval Group get, the better for all concerned'. Whitaker recognised that Naval Group, enjoying the inside track with the KMT, constituted a 'formidable rival' in the field of secret intelligence or 'SI', not least on a simple numerical basis. He warned Donovan:

Of the total 800-odd [OSS] personnel now in the theater only 75 are SI . . . But the ceiling placed on Navy Group is 1,800. The vast majority of this 1,800 will be engaged, not in SO [special operations] etc., but intelligence activities of the sort we plan to undertake with a mere 100-odd officers.[33]

Naval Group reached 2,500 personnel by July 1945 and, together with their force of 60,000 SACO guerrillas, they remained a formidable organisation.[34] However, by the summer of 1945, Tai Li was distracted by internal security issues. When Whitaker met with Tai Li on 21 June he was about to depart for two months of hard work in the field: 'Tai Li is being accompanied by some 120 agents and their mission is to purge the Chinese Army of any officers or men who are pro-Communist or engaged in dangerous thinking.' By July 1945, OSS operations were suffering little harassment at the hands of Tai Li.[35] Donovan now presided over the determined expansion of OSS into northern areas, such as Xian, casting their eyes towards Manchuria, and developing large networks with local KMT generals and with local Catholic leaders. In the closing stages of the war they had finally made their mark on the China Theater.[36]

SACO guerrillas played a key role in the end of the war in China; racing towards China's major cities, they outpaced the Communists and captured Nanking, Peiping, Canton, Shanghai, Hanchow and Swatow.[37] In September, Miles moved the SACO headquarters to Shanghai and the US Navy landed 50,000 American marines in North China to seize strategic ports and airfields. At this point, however, Miles' health collapsed. Suffering from malaria and a nervous breakdown, he returned to the United States in September 1945. This, together with Tai Li's death in an aircraft accident on 15 April 1946, sealed the fate of SACO.[38]

War criminals

A growing dislike of Miles and Tai Li had often provided a rare point of unity amongst most Allied secret services in Asia during the latter stages of the Far Eastern War. Another key unifying element was the intense anxiety to apprehend Allied collaborators and also Japanese war criminals. Chinese areas, and especially cities like Shanghai, were a rich source of collaboration, stemming from their cosmopolitan nature. In Shanghai the Japanese had permitted many of the international staff of the settlement, including police officers of British nationality, to serve on in their posts until as late as 1943. A smaller number crossed the boundary from this uncomfortable semi-captivity to active collaboration.

The German and Japanese propaganda effort in the Far East was heavily dependent upon such individuals. In December 1941 the Japanese took over the *Shanghai Times*, the main English-language newspaper. Although run from the Japanese Embassy, the British proprietor, E. A. Nottingham, remained in place, working with a Japanese editor. Interestingly, one of its tasks was to accuse the British authorities in India of maltreating Japanese POWs. Some of those involved in broadcasting were already alienated figures and had fled to the Far East to avoid prison, as in the case of the American Don Chisolm, son of a dean at Johns Hopkins University. Frank Johnston, a British national with a long criminal record worked for the XMHA station controlled by the Japanese Navy. His varied Axis broadcasting career occasionally involved him in sketches where he played President Roosevelt. Robert Lamb, a retired Indian Army officer, worked for the information offices of the large Nazi organisation in Shanghai, before moving into radio work.[39]

OSS X-2, then SSU, found their hands full as they moved into Shanghai. Here they encountered not only Japanese suspects, but also the thriving Nazi organisation. Most of the Nazi archives had been destroyed, because of fear that the Japanese would seize them as relations deteriorated after the German surrender in May 1945. But SSU captured Klaus Kuether, Ortagruppenleiter of the Party in the city and were able to piece together a history of its activities, including details of collaborators.[40] Gestapo officers in Shanghai and Hong Kong had made use of their excellent relations with the KMT in the 1930s. German members of the French Foreign Legion had been able to penetrate the Free French in the Far East.[41] British security teams went on to arrest five British nationals, including an Army sergeant, who had been broadcasting for a German radio station in Shanghai.[42]

The nature and concept of war crime, and of atrocity, is a heavily contested one and in 1945 the search for major Japanese war criminals proceeded against the background of routine behaviour by many Japanese troops in the field that Western conventions would have deemed criminal.[43] Thus the search for war criminals throughout Asia, led by the intelligence and security elements of Allied secret services, focused upon particularly notorious cases. These cases were accorded a very high priority by theatre commanders who had repeatedly encountered examples of the miserable treatment meted out to their own forces. The secret services had suffered disproportionately, due to their work behind enemy lines, and so had their own scores to settle. Official histories have not always drawn out the extent to which senior commanders, both British and American, were deeply affected by some Japanese actions. Admiral Somerville's diary for 31 March 1944 offers but one example:

I heard with grave concern the shocking atrocities committed by the Japanese submarine on the crew of the Dutch ship TJISALAK, sunk on the 26 of March to the North East of Chagos; after the survivors had taken to the [life] boats the latter were ordered alongside [the submarine] and the Captain and an American Red Cross nurse were ordered below and not seen again. The boats were then cast off and the crew were ordered to fall in before and aft the conning tower with strict instructions that they were not to look towards the conning tower or they would be shot.

The Japanese then began to tie the men together in pairs; on realising what this meant, one of the Dutchman's crew resisted and was promptly shot; this was a signal for a general massacre and the unfortunate crew were killed with tommy guns, axes, swords, crowbars and hammers. The mate, one Lascar and two other Europeans fell overboard wounded, and after swimming 5 miles, regained the boats from which they were subsequently picked up.[44]

Accordingly, by 1945, security units followed hard on the heels of advancing troops in all theatres, armed with long lists of suspects. When a similar fate befell twenty-three soldiers from the West Yorkshire Regiment in April 1944, Mountbatten noted that it 'makes me sick', and expressed his fervent wish to put some of the culprits on trial.[45]

Counter-espionage and security activities thus proved to be an area of intense Allied co-operation. Security teams were also attempting to locate and capture intelligence archives, Japanese cryptanalytical centres and their staff, and to exploit Japanese technical developments.[46] Much attention was given to rounding up 'fanatical stay-behind agents'. In April 1945 SEAC created the Counter-Intelligence Combined Board (CICB) for this purpose under Colonel C. E. Dixon and his deputy Courtney Young, two career MI5 officers.[47] Dixon's CICB represented a very diverse body with staff from MI5, SIS Section V (counter-intelligence), OSS X-2 and SEAC Intelligence Division's own ID 7 counter-intelligence staff. In late 1945, when many elements were being demobilised, security work was a growth industry.[48] CICB was the brains of this operation, while the hands were the Special Counter-intelligence Units (SCIUs), Intelligence Assault Units and Field Security Sections.[49] Some organisations viewed war crimes work as a convenient cover for continuing political activities beyond the end of the war, but this did not render it any less genuine.

Despite the systematic attempts of the Japanese, Germans and others to destroy archives, these field security teams had some notable successes in apprehending suspects and in securing material evidence, especially in Singapore (see plate 20). Mountbatten noted in his diary on 13 September 1945 that security services had captured a set of the 'most revolting pictures' showing the fate of some of the Indians who refused to join with Chandra Bose and the INA: 'The first photo shows two dozen Indian soldiers kneeling upright in front of the graves they had dug, with their eyes bandaged . . . in the last photo one can see the Japanese soldiers finishing off the living with a bayonet.' The next day Mountbatten spoke to Leonard Wilson, Bishop of Singapore, who had endured a period detained by the Kempei Tai or Japanese Military Police. Throughout his seven and a half months he could not recall any period when the jail was not 'ringing with the cries and screams of the inmates as they were taken up in turn to be tortured'. Thus, in late November 1945, Mountbatten took immense satisfaction in viewing 270 Kempei Tai that British Field Security had managed to round up at Terauchi's headquarters, *en route* to the French jail in Saigon.[50]

Obliquely, this security work against Japan also pointed the way towards the Cold War, for Japanese security organisations, such as the Kempetei Tei, had long taken a hostile interest in Asian communism. X-2 had particular success at the Japanese Embassy in Rangoon, securing a mass of documentation on 'the Kempei Tai, Jap political intelligence organisations and spy

20 Captured Indian troops who refused to join the INA are executed by the Japanese

schools, the Jap military police, the Hachure Kikan, and the Minami Kikan'. This included detailed reports of Japanese surveillance of the local communists, now a matter of increasing interest. X-2 noted that their staff in Burma then 'followed up leads on the identification of local Communists reportedly in contact with Russia during Jap occupation of Burma'.[51] In both Europe and Asia, some Allied security bodies now found themselves taking up the burden of anti-communist security work where Axis organisations had ceased.

Secret service in post-war China

The transition from war to peace for British secret services in China was a relatively smooth one. BAAG had outlived their usefulness and were wound up, while little remained of the GBT network in Indochina. Other elements of SOE in China, however, remained valuable. Sino-British Intelligence relations had been compartmentalised, with SIS handling relations with Tai Li's organisation, and SOE dealing with the Chinese DMI through IIS/RII, an organisation that the Chinese specifically asked to remain in place. The British Chiefs of Staff delicately referred to the immense value of an SOE organisation 'which handles financial transactions' and decreed that this too was to remain, and thus Walter Fletcher's black-market empire traded on beyond 1945. The SIS station in China, they reported, was presently 'fully employed' and was not to be disturbed by any changes.[52] With the gradual disbandment of SOE, all activities were transferred to SIS at the end of 1945 including IIS/RII. At this time the currency operation was then delivering 'a saving, as compared with the cost at the official rate, of nearly £20,000,000 a month', a remarkable sum.[53]

The transition from OSS to CIA in China was less even, partly because of bureaucratic succession in Washington, and partly because of confrontations with the Communists. The latter could perhaps be attributed to Donovan's anxiety to make up for lost time by pushing into north China in the last year of the war. This began with Donovan's aggressive northward development of operations in Xian in May 1945. OSS had despatched a team codenamed *Spaniel* with the hope of contacting Communist guerrillas to develop joint operations against the Japanese. However, this mission, and the general momentum of OSS activity in the area, appeared to threaten local collaboration between the Communists and Chinese puppet troops, neither of whom wished to fight the Japanese. The result was that the OSS *Spaniel* team, led by Captain Coolidge, was detained and deprived of communications for months. It emerged in October 1945 to tell its tale of the exaggeration of Communist efforts against the Japanese in that region, but by then the war was long over. The reverberations of this destabilised the efforts of OSS officers to pursue a joint communication project with the Communists which was terminated in June 1945, amid a welter of suspicions.[54]

The infamous death of Major John Birch of OSS at the hands of Communist troops, even more than that of Peter Dewey in Indochina, was eventually taken up by the American political right and transformed into a *cause célèbre*. However, the extant materials suggest that the activities of Birch's group were risky. American investigators later interviewed Lt Tung Fu-Kuan, who had accompanied Birch's thirteen-strong party and who had lost a leg in the same shooting. Tung recalled that they had already encountered three other groups of Communist troops: 'Tung again says that after the first encounter he cautioned Birch against being belligerent towards these armed groups of men' but Birch would not listen. Birch treated an escorting Communist orderly abruptly and, in the company of twenty armed Communist troops, he 'saw Birch shake the orderly by the collar and orally abuse him, using the word "bandits" . . . if he had remained "calm" nothing would have happened'. These sorts of encounters were bound to lead to trouble.[55]

Studies of American intelligence, particularly those focused upon Europe, have often remarked that between October 1945, when OSS was formally closed down, and July 1947, when the CIA was created, the United States had no real secret service.[56] This is misleading. As with SOE in South East

Asia, the volatile situation in China ensured that OSS elements continued their work, albeit with periodic changes of nomenclature, and marched with unbroken step out of the Second World War into the Cold War. In China, as elsewhere, OSS had become SSU by the end of 1945, with its headquarters shifting to Shanghai, adjacent to Wedemeyer's new HQ, and remained an integral part of the China Theater under Colonel Robert Delaney. There SSU marked time until the arrival of the CIA.

The issue of SSU's survival was re-opened in April 1946, as Wedemeyer's China Theater HQ in Shanghai was being wound up, threatening to demobilise the integral SSU station. In Washington, Colonel Quinn, the head of SSU, lobbied US Army planners, pointing out that SSU was their main source of information on China. General Marshall sought Wedemeyer's opinion, who also suggested that SSU should continue independently.[57] Accordingly, in mid-1946 SSU adopted the cover name Economic Survey Detachment/Group 44 (ESD 44) which was maintained and resourced by the US 7th Fleet on behalf of the Central Intelligence Group in Washington. In the summer of 1947 remnants of this were passed to the CIA. But these changes of name meant less to those on the ground in far-flung destinations such as Mudken, where OSS personnel continued their work.

ESD 44, commanded by Lt Colonel Amos D. Moscrip from OSS in SEAC, were employed on a great variety of tasks, including providing intelligence support for the Marshall Mission during 1946. SSU were used to conduct very private discussions with the Communists about possible arrangements for trade relations between the United States and Communist areas of China, if peace was established. Marshall did not want these exploratory talks to be associated in any way with his mission.[58] By August 1946, with the 7th Fleet taking over the support of ESD 44, its emphasis became more strategic and extended beyond China.[59] In April 1947, for example, Major Alexander B. Griswold was holding discussions in China with the Viet Nam National Union Front, a party opposed to both Ho Chi Minh and Bao Dai.[60]

Harassment by rival agencies, a quintessential element of the OSS story, remained. In July 1946, Moscrip and the senior Army intelligence officer in China, Colonel Lewis Leavel, travelled together to Mudken to investigate trouble between the American Military Attaché's Office under Major Robert Rigg and the local SSU detachment under Captain J. K. Singlaub, working under cover as the 'American Army Liaison Group'. Both SSU and the local Chinese regarded the Army too close to local Soviet elements to be trusted, and would furnish sensitive material to SSU only on condition that it was not shared with Rigg.[61]

By 1947 similar tensions were developing between what was now a proto-CIA station and local American diplomats. On 18 April 1947, DeBardeleben, Chief of the Operations Branch of the CIG, met with State Department officials in Washington to emphasise that ESD 44 was under the direction of the National Intelligence Authority only 'and that its activities could not be revealed to anyone'. The diplomats disagreed, asserting that the activities of ESD 44 were 'ill-advised' and needed 'proper co-ordination with the Embassy', adding that the Chief of Mission there was 'directly responsible for all United States Government activities in that country'. They proceeded to brandish a new presidential directive on China which confirmed the State Department's over-arching authority. By October 1947 'a workable compromise' over the new CIA station had been achieved.[62]

The new term 'CIA' was accompanied by old frictions. In December 1947, Ringwalt of the State Department met with Lloyd George of the CIA to discuss 'authentic information' of continued bitterness and friction between CIA, Foreign Service and military personnel. The State Department claimed that CIA directives had been issued 'to the effect that allegedly hostile Foreign Service personnel be watched carefully and that a record be kept of their activities of a discreditable nature, assumably for use in in-fighting at an appropriate time'. George noted that much of the trouble had arisen from the constant changes of organisations, staff and institutional identity in the period 1945–7, developing a sense of turbulence and uncertainty. But by 1947 a permanent American apparatus for the clandestine Cold War had begun to take shape.[63]

20   Conclusion: the hidden hand and the fancy foot

> SOE can lend valuable aid to top-hatted administrators by unacknow-
> ledgeable methods. Lord Killearn in Egypt and Sir Reader Bullard in Persia
> have already employed SOE to important effect in nobbling personalities
> who can make themselves inconvenient to HMG. A 'loan' here, a dir-
> ectorship there, pay dividends out of all proportions, and may save
> battalions ... this can be done in conformity with Foreign Office policy,
> but it can only be done by those who understand the technique, potentialit-
> ies, and limitations of subterranean work.
> Selborne to Churchill, 27 April 1944.[1]

Two views of secret service

It was with the above words that Lord Selborne, the minister responsible for
SOE, wrote to Churchill in April 1944, seeking to prolong the life of his
organisation beyond the end of the war. The texture of this message is highly
revealing. Ignoring the looming problem of the Soviets, which many in
Whitehall and Washington were already preoccupied by, he focused instead
upon the greatest enemy of all, Britain's imperial decline and her troubled
status as a world power, and elaborated on the stratagems that Britain had
employed to try to evade this. Selborne's statement is perhaps as precise an
indication as one could wish for of the relationship between the 'hidden hand'
of secret service, and what has been termed the 'fancy footwork' of Britain's
long retreat from empire. Secret service was especially complementary to the
new forms of empire with which Britain was experimenting in the middle of
the twentieth century – informal empire and indirect rule, systems in which
advisers, residual base agreements and privileged commercial arrangements
replaced the full panoply of colonial administration.[2]

Over and beyond its specific subject, this book seeks to draw a distinction
between two different views of Anglo-American secret service relations in
the twentieth century. The first offers a conventional picture of the wartime
construction of a comprehensive intelligence alliance against the Axis by the
English-speaking powers. Joined after 1945 by some continental European
adherents and eventually constituting the 'Western intelligence community',

this network achieved an unparalleled degree of international co-operation on sensitive subjects. This image represents itself, above all, as an 'enemy-led' process, deriving from struggles with the Axis, followed by the Soviet Union and Communist China. This is the image endorsed by official history, by much memoir material immediately after the war, and which appeared to be confirmed by the vast documentary outflow of the 1970s. It has been bolstered by the greater willingness of governments to declassify intelligence materials dealing with wartime enemies than with other issues.

The second picture, of which this book is an example, emphasises Allied secret services that were, both in war and peace, very sensitive to matters of long-term national interest. It identifies British, and later American, secret services, as giving considerable attention to economic and commercial intelligence, and to watching the activities of neutrals and allies in the wider context of relative world power. This perspective stems partly from a somewhat different archival approach, or methodology, one that is more sceptical of archives, which are, after all, laundered by the very subject that one is attempting to study. The numbers of preserved papers from the first half of the twentieth century not yet open to public inspection are now, admittedly, very few. But the proportion of papers that were not chosen for preservation in the first place was very large. Accordingly, this second, alternative, picture of Allied secret service relations is inevitably more fragmentary, and admittedly, dependent upon an interpretative framework for its coherence.

Yet the evidence of co-ordination between the hidden hand and the fancy foot throughout the twentieth century remains compelling. In 1929, Hugh Dalton, a reader in commerce and economics at the University of London, found himself catapulted into British government as Parliamentary under Secretary at the Foreign Office, dealing with the typical subjects delegated to junior ministers. Dalton was trying to have visas abolished for people travelling between Britain and the United States. The main problem was that the Britain's Passport Control Offices were then used in most countries as cover for SIS. Significantly, the main objectors to the abolition of this cover for secret service work in the United States were not the Foreign Office but the Treasury. Sir George Mounsey, an Assistant Under-Secretary in the Foreign Office, who had long service in the Treasury, reluctantly explained to Dalton the importance that the Treasury attached to these things. Dalton recorded in his diary:

Mounsey can hardly bring himself to say 'Secret Service'. It is like an old lady trying not to say 'W.C.'. He calls it, in a hushed voice, 'certain arrangements'. He had, he says, always been taught, while he was in the Treasury Department, to regard the maintenance of these 'arrangements' as his first duty, to which everything should be subordinated.[3]

We are relatively uninformed about economic and commercial intelligence in this period, but the Treasury clearly placed a high premium upon it.

If we accept that the priorities of British secret service were as much about imperial, financial and commercial power, as about specific military enemies, the landscape changes. For example, taking into account this different sense of priorities, the 'batting average' of the British secret service improves markedly. Its pathetic showing against Nazi Germany in the inter-war years becomes less important, while the highly successful penetration of anti-colonial groups of nationalists, communists and 'agitators' in imperial territories, or the probable interception of the cable traffic of American oil companies in the Middle East, becomes more significant.

But as this book seeks to show, these matters did not enjoy a uniform development throughout the twentieth century. The Second World War marks a mid-century 'intelligence revolution' in several senses. By 1940, sigint in particular was moving into a new era of machine cryptanalysis, with codebreaking increasingly conducted by computer, rather than by hand. This heralded the dawn of a new age, with intelligence gathering on an industrial scale and in 'real time'. It was sigint, primarily, that drove Allied military strategy and military operations, and indeed, even the diplomatic and counter-espionage effort against the Axis during the Second World War.

The vast new power of sigint also had its side-effects. The pressure on the human agent-based services to produce war-winning intelligence was reduced to some degree. Nevertheless, the traditional human services expanded fast in wartime, drawing their higher echelon personnel from the worlds of law, the media, industry and finance. This spare capacity was absorbed with watching and managing innumerable troublesome neutrals and allies, not just the Americans and British, but also the Free French and many others.

A further major change wrought by the Second World War was the vast expansion of American secret service, similarly drawing in 'amateurs' from banks, businesses and the media. Britain played a remarkable part in this expansion and secured the co-operation Americans, not only of Donovan's embryonic OSS, but also of the FBI, in hounding isolationists. Edmond Taylor, who figures more than once in this book, began his secret service career as an 'apprentice scoundrel' to the British. One of Taylor's first ideas was an Anglo-American project to set up something which appeared to be a German underground radio station and to use its broadcasts to America to smear isolationists with the Nazi cause. But close association between the British and American secret services was bound to lead to trouble.[4] OSS officers like Taylor were adept students and by 1943 were increasingly aware of how much secret service effort London was devoting to 'long-range', rather than wartime issues. Moreover, OSS was very much an organisation created at the behest of Roosevelt and his immediate lieutenants, and so naturally attuned itself to Roosevelt's anti-colonialism. OSS boasted 13,000 staff by 1944 and also had spare capacity for 'long-range' issues. Accordingly OSS in Asia became the operational arm of 'anti-colonialist fundamentalism'. This was encouraged by Washington and conducted in accordance with the 'strict, though sometimes unavowed, aims of national policy' and 'under high-level, if left-handed, official supervision'.[5]

Although the rapidly expanding American secret services constituted an important asset in the war against the Axis, in the long term they also made life harder for British policy-makers trying to understand and influence American policy. In the period before 1942, Washington was already a bewilderingly complex government system, with bureaucratic processes more fragmented than those in London. The expansion of American secret service made the business of tracking American foreign policies much harder. Above all, it accentuated those mercurial characteristics which British officials already found annoying: an America that was energetic, idealistic, fluid and yet strangely without centre. In short, OSS seemed the vanguard of an America whose activities in the world were increasingly energetic and corporatist. After all, from 1942 it was through OSS, OWI and their successors that the American government often physically connected with those other important elements of American policy overseas: the public foundations, the mass media and large corporations.

This important shift was identified by officials at an early stage. In 1943 there had been plenty of senior figures who, like Stanley Hornbeck, wished to believe that secret service matters were the stuff of 'gumshoe level' and could be safely ignored. But by the end of 1944 no-one believed this any more. Esler Dening, the senior Foreign Office representative in SEAC caught the significance of these issues succinctly. It was not so much that secret services could change the course of events dramatically (though they were not slow to advance this claim). It was more that their activities appeared to reveal the inner trend at a time when Churchill and Roosevelt steadfastly refused to articulate their disagreements about the future of large areas of the world's surface. In this vein, in December 1944, Dening sent a missive to London that was half warning, half reflection:

It becomes increasingly clear, whatever the policy may be in Washington – if there is one – American imperialists in the armed forces, backed by ubiquitous businessmen in uniform, are determined to do what they please in the Far East, both during and after the war, without regard to any other interest concerned. By voicing their suspicions of British Imperialism they have put us on the defensive, and in the absence of any clearly defined policy of our own, our defence is not a very good one. On our side there is a sense of frustration and resentment, and on the American a spirit of ruthless go-getting, coupled with a conviction of our Far Eastern bankruptcy ... the situation is not a healthy one.[6]

For Dening, the cutting edge of this phenomenon in Asia was what he called 'the ever-sinister activities of OSS'.[7]

Somewhat later, Edmond Taylor, of SEAC's P Division, came to similar conclusions. He reflected that the behaviour of secret services was capable of revealing 'to a certain degree the unavowed values, not only of states, but of the societies on behalf of whom it is conducted. Sometimes it may express the unconscious purposes of peoples themselves.'[8] Whether we accept Taylor's observations as accurate is perhaps not the point. What matters is that British, American and indeed French, Dutch and Chinese secret services had come to believe this by 1943, and accordingly, watched each other as intently as they watched the enemy, in the closing stages of the Far Eastern War.

Levels of analysis

That secret services were more conscious of Allied rivalries than other bureaucratic elements goes only some way to explaining the Byzantine complexity of the politics of secret service during this conflict. Although it is increasingly clear that they were directly encouraged in their 'long-range' interests by Roosevelt, Churchill and others, they also served as catalysts, accelerating existing tensions at different levels. This owed much to the unstable nature of secret services themselves during the war, expanding rapidly with uncertain lines of bureaucratic demarcation, and attracting into their service those who did not have much regard for protocol and enjoyed subterfuge for its own sake. Sir Adrian Carton de Wiart, placed in charge of a curious amalgam of British activities in China towards the end of the war, lamented that 'most of these clandestine fellows get into the state of preferring to make 2/6d dishonestly, to making £1 honestly.'[9]

The problem of different levels was most apparent at the intermediate location of theatres of command, with their temperamental 'Supremos'. Particularly for OSS and OWI, the greatest obstacle in the Far Eastern War was unsympathetic Americans at this intermediate level. OWI discovered this, to their dismay, when attempting to expand their operations (in a race with OSS MO Branch) across the Pacific, from their existing foothold, a large broadcasting operation at San Francisco under the direction of Owen Lattimore.[10] In March 1943, the Director of OWI, Elmer Davis, despatched one of his subordinates, Lt Colonel Ben Stern on an investigative tour. His visit to the only 'purely' American command, namely Nimitz's POA, based at Honolulu, proved to be the most disappointing. Nimitz's reputation went before him and Stern found him 'a blue-eyed, cold-blooded, keen individual

21 Lt Commander Edmond Taylor, Deputy Head of P Division

who knows that he is boss'. He had surrounded himself with similar characters who were especially hostile to OWI and had 'a phobia for "hot air"
artists'. Stern was subjected to an aggressive 'inquisition' for over an hour
by Nimitz and his assembled staff, confessing afterwards that he had 'felt
like Jesus before the Sanhedrin'. OWI made slow progress in POA, and that
only by means of appointing former naval officers. The way ahead here was
treacherous, reported Stern, for 'the Navy is in complete control ... it is
jealous of its prerogatives'. Such autocratic theatre commanders were the key
factor for Americans in the politics of intelligence.[11]

The frustrations for OSS and OWI in American-dominated theatres was
increased by seemingly subordinate allies who generated major problems.
This was certainly the case in China and also in SWPA. MacArthur had not
been happy to hear of OWI's Stern Mission in 1943, and had protested to
Stimson, the Secretary for War. But this protest did not reflect mere obstruc-
tionism on MacArthur's part, instead his main concern was Australian sensit-
ivities, advising that: 'Extreme caution is necessary'.[12] Stern's five-week
sojourn showed MacArthur to be entirely correct. Stern discovered a nightmare situation of multiple jealousies and suspicions which, as in China, were

generated by the presence of a large American military organism in the territory of a weaker ally who was 'jealous of our position in the world'. John de la Valette, the Head of the local British PWE Mission, echoed the need for 'extreme caution' in Canberra. OWI already had a small liaison mission in Canberra, but its existence was precarious: 'Every contact, every friendship, which OWI men make is scrutinized carefully to determine what, if any, political implications may exist.' By 1943 this small OWI mission was supplying 80 per cent of the war photographs appearing in Australian newspapers, but it dared not launch its own monthly bulletin: 'It would look like a piece of American Imperialism. This is the one cry constantly heard . . . American Imperialism.'[13] It was these indignities and exclusions, suffered by OSS and OWI in *American-led* commands, that made their existence under Mountbatten in SEAC seem relatively trouble-free.

The inter-action of wartime politics with secret service is also perhaps most elusive at the intermediate level of the theatre command. The contradictory figure of Mountbatten presents the historian with especially troublesome problems. Mountbatten continually urged the importance of supporting SOE operations in SEAC, pressing the case vigorously over Indochina. Yet the supporting arguments he presented were mostly military, stressing that vital Japanese communications offered ideal targets for irregular warfare. Philip Ziegler, his official biographer, has argued that Mountbatten was first and foremost influenced in his judgements by basic military and administrative issues. Starved of resources for much of the war, SEAC was certainly a command that badly needed a victory.[14]

But underpinning this was a clear personal commitment to self-government for colonies, sooner rather than later, which enhanced his anxiety to work with indigenous forces of any political persuasion in Thailand, Malaya and Burma. Indeed Mountbatten's personal political adviser on Indochina, Peter Murphy, was distinctly left-leaning and was a member of the British Communist Party. While under clear instructions from London to apply himself to the recovery of empire, his personal anxiety was to give it away as soon as possible, while hoping to charm these countries into the Commonwealth. One historian has called him the 'imperial undertaker who never wore black'.[15] In 1946 his political adviser, Dening, resigned in a row over his over-sympathetic approach to the Indonesian nationalists. It is difficult indeed to square these aspects of Mountbatten with the activities of some of the secret services within SEAC. Perhaps stressing practical military and administrative problems was the only approach that allowed him to reconcile these issues.[16]

One further important phenomenon that makes only a limited appearance in this book, but which increasingly pervaded at all 'levels', was the ubiquitous nature of domestic security surveillance. No less fascinating than the high-level strategic work of Ultra, is the simple matter of wartime letter censorship, which provided a huge, almost indigestible, flow of low-level intelligence to the authorities, not only about security matters, but about the morale, the political opinions and indeed social attitudes of their own subjects. This vast activity has been lost to us through the remorseless elite-orientated weeding of our surviving records and only diaries preserve it. Regular security reports, based on the mail of the East Indies Fleet berthed at Colombo, provided its Commander, Admiral James Somerville, with a detailed picture of the morale and opinions of the average deck-hand. It is difficult to avoid drawing comparisons with Soviet monitoring of the mail of soldiers in the Red Army for exactly the same purpose.[17] No-one was safe from this all-embracing net of mass surveillance. In 1942, the political machinations of Mountbatten, then superintending Combined Operations in London, were revealed to the authorities by the same means. Eden's private secretary noted in his diary: 'Mountbatten caught in censorship intriguing against [Major General] Dobbie [the Governor of Malta]' and as a result Churchill was reported to be 'furious'.[18]

Impact

In 1942, the first year of the Anglo-American war against Japan, the impact of secret services co-operation upon Allied relations seemed to be entirely positive. Secret services themselves seemed anxious to deploy their resources, where possible, to improve relations. In November 1942, a remarkable Anglo-American conference was held at the British Embassy in Washington on the subject of 'Anti-British Feeling in the United States and Anti-American Feeling in England', which sought to exploit the dividends of mass surveillance. This conference was the brainchild of R. Keith Kane, Head of OWI's Bureau of Intelligence, and sought to develop a shared analysis on 'points of friction' between the British and American populations and how they might be mollified. 'There was complete frankness on both sides.' British officials suggested a continual exchange of data on popular anti-British and anti-American friction in their respective countries, based on 'intelligence sources' such as routine mail censorship. Armed with this detailed information, both qualitative and quantitative, their ultimate goal was the creation of 'a parallel friction chart', showing where similar friction patterns existed in both countries, as a basis for future ameliorative action through their propaganda work.[19] But after 1942 nothing more was heard of this interesting blend of surveillance and social science.

At the elite level, it is quite clear that Roosevelt, Churchill and their immediate circle were adversely influenced by 'long-range' intelligence reports of each other's objectives. The anxieties that these reports then caused prompted senior officials to privately condone elements of brinkmanship by special operations elements. What is not clear is how far these matters reverberated beyond 1945, with Roosevelt and Churchill removed from the stage and the issue of anti-colonialism occluded by Cold War. For Dening, who was annoyed in equal amounts by the activities of SOE and OSS, this was a formative experience that rendered him hostile to secret services for the rest of his career.[20] In 1946 he returned to London to superintend British policy across all of Asia while Moffat continued to preside over the South East Asia at the State Department. Donovan formed strong opinions during the Thai episode, becoming legal adviser to the Thai delegation at the UN in August 1946 and then Ambassador in Bangkok during the early 1950s.[21] By 1947 Colin Mackenzie was still raising the issue of Thailand, but now as a businessman in meetings with the Treasury and the Board of Trade.[22]

While secret service reports were instrumental in shaping the views of many in London and Washington, their belief that their intervention could make a physical impact on the settlement in Asia was largely misplaced. John Paton Davies had urged OWI to define a separate American identity in Asia as early as 1943, in the hope of countering what he saw as a 'growing belief in China and India that we are now acquiescing in British colonial ambitions'.[23] OSS worked to convey this message to nationalists at the elite level. Yet this may have been counter-productive, because of the high expectations created. In November 1945, John S. Holliday, a missionary for thirteen years at Chiang Mai in northern Thailand and now working for OSS reported to Moffat on the Lao situation, observing that 'it is surprising how much the average Laos, even the peasant, knows'. He added that they had all heard of the decolonisation of the Philippines and so 'have been hoping that the United States would similarly aid them to attain their independence'.[24]

In October 1945, Nehru offered a lengthy exposition to the press on his disillusionment with the United States and its claim to be the champion of freedom. He pointed to American-made weapons deployed in Indonesia and Indochina against the nationalists, on which Washington had merely requested that the American insignia be painted out. Only now, Nehru added, did India realise that 'we cannot rely on any foreign power'. During November, when crowds demonstrating against the trial of INA officers rioted, they turned on British and American military installations alike.[25] In December 1945 SSU held discussions with several prominent Indian politicians and found that they saw no difference between British and American policy, observing: 'Both express beautiful sentiments, both imperialist in action'.[26]

The remnants of OSS R&A British Empire Section diagnosed self-inflicted injury through the creation of this 'high expectation'. Many nationalists saw the United States as a 'tacit partner' in imperial revival, and hence 'US prestige has suffered'. In an Asia which has been 'made race-conscious' by the Japanese, OSS warned that 'disillusionment concerning the moral principles of these democracies might engender a hate towards the white man's world and turn against the white man himself'. OSS had presciently identified the emerging North–South divide, a new form of struggle in which Colonel Peter Dewey was perhaps one of the first casualties. Thailand was the exception. Here a popular appreciation that Washington had interceded in the negotiations with London to thwart colonialism had resulted in the 'all-time high point of American prestige in the country'.[27]

In Britain, too, it was possible to detect a growing awareness that the possibility of unconventional warfare materially effecting Asia's teeming millions seemed remote, perhaps even silly. Prior to joining SIS, Malcolm Muggeridge spent some time doing propaganda work amongst a distinguished group, including Graham Greene and R. H. S. Crossman. He recalls his own sense of declining conviction in the power of radio broadcasts, even at the time, observing that: 'the counterfeit words with which I was required to juggle – like "freedom", "democracy", self-determination" – had died on me . . . an uninspiring task'. Under the auspices of the BBC, George Orwell was similarly engaged as a broadcaster. Reflecting his pre-war experience as a Burma policeman, the special territory allocated to Orwell was India and South East Asia. Muggeridge prompted Orwell to consider the possible impact of this work, the radio-projection of Britain and its values out into Asia:

From a studio deep under Oxford Street, he beamed at listeners in Cawnpore, Kuala Lumpur and Rangoon – assuming of course, that there were any – *Areopagitica*, *The Wasteland* read by the author in person, and other gems of Western culture, with a view to enthusing them for the Allied cause. When I delicately suggested that this may well have failed to hit its target, the absurdity of the enterprise struck him anew and he began to chuckle . . .[28]

Archives and bonfires: a note on methodology

> I have just had a frightful morning burning all the high grade stuff in the
> safe and am quite worn out . . . I am preparing a destruction certificate.
>
> Ensign Price, Signals Intelligence Centre, Ceylon, 21 November 1945[1]

It remains a commonplace assumption that the work of modern secret service
is an impermeable subject, and that their more important internal records are
largely unobtainable. This is not always the case. Secret services exist, as
their name implies, to provide a 'service' to other departments, usually
policy-makers and operational planners, and so, at a high level, records of
the impact of their more important work are inseparably bound up with the
higher direction of foreign policy and strategy. Meanwhile, at the lower level
secret services are dependent on other services, such as air forces, to provide
work-a-day essentials such as transport and here, too, records intermingle. In
Britain, where the destruction of secret service papers has been considerable,
this lateral approach to research has been used extensively. Destruction in
the United States has been less severe. The culture of secret services tends
towards some automatic destruction of documents, once they have served
their purpose, with the intention of ensuring lifelong anonymity for agents,
and protecting methods. Moreover, any historian must confront the possibility
that the limited materials that are extant may constitute a deliberate deception
inflicted by one department upon another, or an inter-departmental exercise
in black humour.

Serious distortions and confusions are inevitable. In the mid-1990s, more
than half a century after the end of the war, some SOE files were finally
trickling into the PRO (beginning conveniently with those for the Far East).
But many of these SOE files were created in the Baker Street headquarters,
and in any case they might represent less than 10 per cent of the original
material.[2] Less survives of the regional archives maintained by the secret
services in Asia and numerous memoirs and documents testify to their routine
destruction. Captain W. Petro of SOE recalls that in the autumn 1945: 'On
my return to Kandy I faced complete absence of work and was offered a

385

flight to Calcutta to witness the destruction of the intelligence records of [SOE] Force 136.'[3]

Secret service records in Asia suffered no less than four catastrophic waves of destruction. The first occurred in 1941 as Japan swept south into European colonial territories, prompting the officials of many countries to burn their records to avoid their capture. Indeed, at this time, the burning of official documents by means of bonfires in embassy gardens was so synonymous with imminent invasion that, in 1941, when Japan wished to coerce French Indochina with the *possibility* of their invasion, they burned their own consular archives in Hanoi as part of the exercise in brinkmanship. The second wave occurred in mid-1945, when Axis officials were able to conduct a somewhat more leisurely programme of destruction as Allied armies closed in, assisted by incendiary attacks on Tokyo.

The third wave followed soon after, as Allied secret services chose to incinerate most of their own records, before departing the region. Alan Stripp, despatched by GCHQ in 1944 to join WEC Delhi, recalls the second and third waves. As the war drew to a close, colleagues were attached to Special Intelligence Assault Units seeking enemy intelligence archives in Japanese command centres, such as General Terauchi's main rear-area headquarters in Saigon, but most cryptographic material had been carefully burnt.[4] Thereafter at WEC, Alan Stripp himself was engaged on the same sort of business. There were millions of British signals intelligence decrypts and rough translations of Japanese messages, 'expendable in the official view'. Stripp recalls:

I became WEC Burning Officer . . . I coolly presided over a warmish Sergeant and a gang of really hot young men who shovelled whole truck-loads of paper into a poorly-designed and hastily-built incinerator, from the chimney of which, as we watched, Top Secret documents wafted, half-burnt, over the astonished western suburbs of New Delhi.[5]

The fourth wave was triggered by the end of the British Raj. A vast quantity of security intelligence records relating to nationalists was destroyed during the transfer of power to the successor states in India, Pakistan, Burma and Ceylon during 1947–8. When Britain prepared to depart from India, the security service, known as the IB, set about the destruction of files on the incoming nationalists, and the agents who had kept them under surveillance across a whole sub-continent. Political surveillance was an open kind of secret in India, and Lord Wavell joked with Nehru about it in September 1946, as they prepared in earnest for the handover: 'I asked how he was getting on with the D.I.B.: he said, "Quite all right, they have destroyed all the compromising papers." I said, "Yes, I told them to make sure of that", and he laughed.'[6] At the Red Fort in Delhi, where both the CSDIC and IB registries were located, bearers with wheel-barrows fed a bonfire in the main courtyard that burned night and day for three weeks.[7]

The destruction of documents alarms historians, yet modern intelligence history to some degree may depend upon such destruction. In the middle of the twentieth century, secret services moved from the era of individual handicraft to the era of intelligence gathering on an industrial scale. Fifty years later, historians too are making the transition to the study of an era characterised by stupendous mountains of papers and one wonders how they will cope. In the case of this particular book, it has to be conceded that if even 10 per cent of the original records had been extant and open to public inspection, it could not have been written. Perhaps historians of secret service will eventually come to appreciate a good bonfire.

Notes

1 INTRODUCTION: INTELLIGENCE AND EMPIRE

1. Churchill minute to Eden, quoted in a Colville minute to Hollis (COS), 18 April 1945, CAB 120/827, PRO.
2. Cf. pp. 95–9.
3. On Donovan's role, 1940–1, see B. F. Smith, *Shadow Warriors*, 84–94. On the growth of Anglo-American intelligence see Andrew, 'The Growth of Intelligence Collaboration'.
4. D. Reynolds, 'A "Special Relationship"', 11.
5. Minute by Selborne to Churchill, 15 March 1945, CAB 120/827, PRO.
6. Minute by Stanley to Churchill, 21 March 1945, ibid.
7. Stafford, *Churchill*, 5.
8. The term 'empire' is used throughout this study in its widest sense, encompassing both formal and informal empire.
9. Louis, 'American Anti-colonialism and the British Empire', 405, n. 26; Watt, *Succeeding John Bull*, 209, n. 59; B. F. Smith, *Shadow Warriors*, 319–20.
10. Exceptionally, Scott Bills has effectively woven OSS into his intriguing study, *Empire and Cold War*.
11. Xiaoyuan Liu, *A Partnership for Disorder;* Schaller, *The U.S. Crusade in China*.
12. Charmley, *Churchill's Grand Alliance*; Sainsbury, *Churchill and Roosevelt at War*.
13. Lamb, *Churchill as War Leader*. The issue is very well brought out in Stafford, *Churchill*.
14. Thorne, *Allies of a Kind*; and also *The Issue of War*.
15. Cruickshank, *SOE*. This historian requested the closure of files in the PRO and also at the IWM.
16. Foot, *SOE in France*; Hinsley, Thomas, Ransom and Knight, *British Intelligence*.
17. For an example see Patrick Beesly's review of Layton, with Pinneau, and Costello, *And I Was There*, in *Intelligence and National Security*, 1, 3 (1986), 484.
18. British secret service in Asia for the period before 1941 is gradually being unravelled, see Elphick, *Far Eastern File*, which deals mostly with 1931–41, and in Best, *British Intelligence and the Approach of War with Japan* (forthcoming). The significance of intelligence in the coming of war is not universally accepted; see for example, Tarling, *Britain, Southeast Asia and the Onset of the Pacific War*, from which intelligence matters are largely absent.

19. See three notable studies: Drea, *MacArthur's Ultra*; Powell, *War by Stealth*; Prados, *Combined Fleet Decoded*.
20. For general accounts of OSS see B. F. Smith, *Shadow Warriors*; and also R. H. Smith, *OSS*. For a detailed treatment of Indochina see Spector, 'Allied Intelligence in Indochina', 23–51.
21. The balance is beginning to be redressed with the appearance of important new work, see: Carter, *Mission to Yenan*; E. B. Reynolds, 'The Opening Wedge', 328–53; Maochun Yu, *OSS in China*.
22. But see M. Thomas, 'Free France, the British Government and the Future of French Indo-China'.
23. Minute by Churchill, 11 March 1944, F1176/66/61, FO 371/41723, PRO; see also COS to Mountbatten, COSSEA 113, 12 June 1944, AIR 23/2132, PRO.
24. Halifax to Eden, 18 January 1944, F360/66/61, FO 371/41723, PRO; Churchill quoted in Peterson to Ismay, 13 March 1944, F1294/9/61, FO 371/41719, PRO.
25. On the failure of Washington to keep theatre commanders abreast of the changing political situation see Spector, *Advice and Support*, 37–76.
26. Memorandum by Davies, 'Anglo-American Cooperation in East Asia', 15 November 1943, File 317, Box 49, Entry 99, RG 226, USNA. Many versions of this were widely circulated, see for example 'British Intimations of the Future' in Merrell (New Delhi) to Hull, 26 October 1943, *FRUS*, China, 1943, 878–80.
27. Ibid.
28. Denham is discussed in DD(1), 1 June 1942, 'Dispatch on the Far East', by Brooke-Popham, CAB 120/518, PRO. Commercial influence in OSS tended to be at a lower level. Major Herman F. Scholtz of OSS Delhi was an American businessman in pre-war and post-war Asia, memorandum of a conversation between Moffat and Scholtz, 24 March 1947, 892.00/3–2447, RG 59, USNA. Interview with Brigadier Sir John Anstey (Deputy Director of SOE Far East), Southwell, 25 May 1999.
29. In 1941 Eden penned the following furious minute with regard to SOE: 'I have had more than enough . . . I must know about this organisation that . . . vitiates my policy, and they must come under direct Foreign Office control.' Minute by Eden, 5 November 1941, F11629/210/40, FO 371/28126, PRO.
30. Stenton, 'British Propaganda and Political Warfare', PhD, 60.
31. Memorandum by Peterson of a conversation with Mackenzie, 10 August 1944, F3770/100/23, FO 371/41798, PRO.
32. Sweet-Escott, *Baker Street Irregular*, 155.
33. Dening to Mountbatten, 30 March 1945, C84, Mountbatten papers, SUL.
34. Memorandum by Sterndale Bennett of a conversation with Taylor, 5 September 1944, F4226/100/23, ibid. Taylor subsequently wrote to the strategic planners on the subject, see Taylor to Read (JPS) 29 September 1944, F5563/100/23. The JPS paper finally emerged as JP(44) 243 (Final), 'Boundaries of SEAC–SEACOS 231', 9 October 1944, CAB 84/66, PRO.
35. Ibid.
36. Cf. p. 191; E. D. R. Harrison, 'British Subversion', 396.
37. Robin Butler, quoted in Heclo and Wildavsky, *The Private Government of Public Money*, xiv–xv.
38. *The Foreign Office List* (London, HMSO, 1941–3). On the politics of British and

American intelligence in Europe and the Middle East, Jakub's excellent study, *Spies and Saboteurs*, is required reading.

39. Ford, *Donovan of OSS*, 121–4; Rifkind, 'OSS and Franco-American Relations', PhD, 13; Greene, 'Men at Work', in *Twenty-One Stories*, 63.
40. Entry for 6 October 1939, Dilks (ed.), *Cadogan Diary*.
41. Entry for 25 May 1940, ibid. On the bankrupt state of SIS see E. D. R. Harrison, 'More Thoughts', also Roskill, *Hankey: Man of Secrets*, 447–8; Stenton, 'British Propaganda', PhD, 36–7.
42. MacPherson, 'Kings and Desperate Men', PhD, 22–3.
43. Stafford, *Churchill*, 164, 173.
44. B. F. Smith, *Shadow Warriors*, 159–70.
45. Clive, *A Greek Experience*, 21.
46. E. E. Thomas, 'The Evolution of the JIC System up to and During World War II', 219–34; Geyer, 'National Socialist Germany: The Politics of Information', 310–17; Marder, *Old Friends*, 291.
47. Eden to Churchill, PM 42/64, 7 April 1942, AP20/9/64, Avon Papers, BUL.
48. Israel (ed.), *The War Diary of Breckinridge Long*, 257.
49. The only substantial treatment of 'liaison' is Bradford Westerfield, 'America and the World of Liaison', 523–61.
50. Aldrich (ed.), *Espionage, Security and Intelligence in Britain*, 202–4.
51. E. Taylor, *Richer by Asia*, 82–3.

2 WING COMMANDER WIGGLESWORTH FLIES EAST: THE LAMENTABLE STATE OF INTELLIGENCE, 1937–1939

1. Wing Commander Wigglesworth (AI2), Notes on the tour of RAF and Combined Service Intelligence Organisations in the Far East', 30 June 1938, AIR 20/374, PRO (hereafter 'Intelligence Organisations in the Far East', AIR 20/374, PRO.)
2. Dockrill (ed.), *From Pearl Harbor to Hiroshima*, 2–3.
3. This was partly the result of favourable television coverage, e.g. BBC Timewatch, *Pearl Harbor*, 1994.
4. For example, Peter Elphick's well-researched study, *The Far Eastern File*, nevertheless devotes seventeen chapters to the descent to 1941, and two to the war itself.
5. Willmott, *Empires in the Balance*, 332–3.
6. IPI shared MI5's 'Box 500' address.
7. French, *Liberty or Death*, xix. For the most detailed account see Popplewell, *Intelligence and Imperial Defence*.
8. E.g. Siam Communist Youth to Malayan Communist Youth Central, 21 January 1933, forwarded by Singapore CID, F1738/42/40, FO 371/17174, PRO.
9. Duncanson, 'Ho Chi Minh in Hong Kong', 84–101.
10. Major (MI2c) to MI1c (SIS), 18 August 1931, WO 208/506A, PRO.
11. Crosby to FO No.108, 12 March 1936, enclosing Annual Report for 1935, 15, F2194/2194/40, FO 371/20302, PRO.
12. On Lai Tek see Short, *Communist Insurrection in Malaya*, 34. Private information.
13. French, *Liberty or Death*, 98–101, 339–40.
14. For example, Sir Basil Thompson, Head of the inter-war Special Branch; Sir

David Petrie, the wartime Head of MI5; Valentine Vivian, the wartime Head of the SIS counter-espionage department, Section V.

15. 'Note of the work of Sir Eric Holt-Wilson in the Creation and Development of the IMPERIAL SECURITY SERVICE, 1912 to 1940', enclosed in Johnson to Dunn, 16 October 1940, 841.00N/14, RG 59, USNA, quoted in Troy, *Wild Bill*, 141.

16. Onraet, *Singapore: A Police Background*; Aldrich, *Key to the South*, 14, 57, 103, 113–14, 132. On French security intelligence work against communists, see Chonchirdsin, 'The Indochinese Communist Party', PhD.

17. On British security liaison with the FBI in Asia see for example Maune (Batavia) to Ronald (FO), 29 January 1938, F867/10/61, FO 371/22165, PRO.

18. On the First World War see Andrew, 'Intelligence Collaboration between Britain and the United States During The Second World War', 112.

19. For two examples see the minute 'Copy informally to Mr Hoover' on the British report 'The League Against Imperialism', enclosed in US Embassy London to DS, 26 February 1929, 800.00B, Box 7148, RG 59, USNA; Captain J. Maine (SIS), British Passport Control Office, New York to SD, 15 December 1928, 800.00B, Box 7149A, ibid.

20. Best, 'Constructing an Image', 404, 407.

21. 'Intelligence Organisations in the Far East', AIR 20/374, PRO.

22. Ibid. Part II: Singapore.

23. NID Vol. 40, 'Far East and the Pacific, I, History', by A. Hillgarth and R. T. Barrett, 'British Intelligence in the Far East', ADM 223/297, PRO.

24. 'Intelligence Organisations in the Far East', AIR 20/374, PRO, Part IV: Hong Kong.

25. Sarngson (MI1c) to MI2c CX 28037/57, 28 July 1938, WO 208/254, PRO; MI1c to MI2c, CX 28037/802–803, 26 July 1939, ibid. See also the opaque autobiography of Charles Drage, *The Amiable Prussian*.

26. 'Intelligence Organisations in the Far East', AIR 20/374, PRO, Part IV: Hong Kong.

27. Best, 'Constructing an Image', 405.

28. N.I.D. Vol. 42, 'Far East and Pacific', III, Special, 'H.M.S. Anderson and Special Intelligence in the Far East', ADM 223/297, PRO.

29. 'Intelligence Organisations in the Far East', AIR 20/374, PRO, Part IV: Hong Kong.

30. 'Intelligence Organisations in the Far East', AIR 20/374, PRO, Part V: Shanghai.

31. NID Vol. 40, 'Far East and the Pacific, I, History', by A. Hillgarth and R. T. Barrett, 'British Intelligence in the Far East', ADM 223/297, PRO.

32. 'Intelligence Organisations in the Far East', AIR 20/374, PRO, Part IV: Hong Kong.

33. NID History, Vol. 40, n.d. 'British Intelligence in the Far East', ADM 223/297, PRO; NID History, Vol. 42, n.d. 'HMS Anderson and Special Intelligence in the Far East', ibid.

34. 'Intelligence Organisations in the Far East', AIR 20/374, PRO, Part IV: Hong Kong. On Italian inquisitiveness see also Rusbridger and Nave, *Betrayal at Pearl Harbor*, 75–7.

35. Layton, Pineau and Costello, *I Was There*, pp. 80–1; NID History Vol. 42, 'Japanese Cyphers Notes', 18 July 1942, ADM 223/297, PRO.

36. Ibid., Part V: Shanghai.
37. Minutes of the Co-ordination of Interception Committee, 8 July 1936, WO 106/5392, PRO.
38. 'Intelligence Organisations in the Far East', Part IV: Hong Kong, AIR 20/374, PRO.
39. Wigglesworth Report, ibid., Part V: Shanghai; Best, 'Constructing an Image', 403.
40. Ibid., Part V: Shanghai; Drysdale, 'British Intelligence Service in China', G-2 Report No. 8704, 6 December 1933, 9944-A-190, RG 165, USNA. For a glimpse of Steptoe during the 1920s see Wasserstein, *The Secret Lives of Trebitsch Lincoln*, 233–4, 244–5, 248–9.
41. Private information, 12 December 1994.
42. Muggeridge, *Chronicles of Wasted Time*, Vol. II, 170–1.
43. Philby, *My Silent War*, 77. On Philby's memoirs see E. D. R. Harrison, 'More Thoughts on Kim Philby's *My Silent War*', 514–25.
44. 'Intelligence Organisations in the Far East', AIR 20/374, PRO, Part V: Shanghai.
45. Ibid.; Wark, 'In Search of a Suitable Japan', pp. 189–212. Holt-Wilson recommended the exploitation of links with the small Moslem community in Japan for intelligence gathering, Varsity minute, 26 July 1938, WO 106/5394, PRO.
46. Piggott to Haining (MI2c), 29 June 1936, WO 208/1214, PRO. On his career see Piggott, *Broken Thread*.
47. On oppressive surveillance in Japan see Tipton, *The Japanese Police State*.
48. The files on Peacocke have been heavily weeded, see FO 371/23563 and WO 106/5821, PRO. Chapman, *The Price of Admiralty*, Vol. I, 170–2; Elphick, *Far Eastern File*, 249.
49. Ibid., Part II: Singapore.
50. Crosby to FO, 28 December 1938, F206/204/40, FO 371/23589, PRO.
51. Ibid.. Part II: Singapore; Robertson, *The Japanese File*, 16–37.
52. Thomas to CO, 22 December 1937, F532/532/61, FO 371/22173, PRO; minutes of a meeting at the Foreign Office, 11 February, 1938, ibid.
53. Reynolds, *The Creation of the Anglo-American Alliance*, 60.
54. Mahnken, 'Gazing at the Sun', 424–41.
55. Ibid., 426, 429, 431.
56. Prados, *Combined Fleet*, 21–3, 32.
57. Ibid., 103.
58. Ibid., 46, 75; Wasserstein, *Secret War*, 201, 266.
59. L. F. Safford, 'A Brief History of Communications Intelligence in the United States', SRH–149, RG 457, USNA.
60. Drea, *MacArthur's Ultra*, 10–11.
61. Entry for 5 June 1941, Leutze, *The London Observer*, 304.
62. 'Intelligence Organisations in the Far East', AIR 20/374, PRO, Part II: Singapore; Aldrich, *Key to the South*, 103, 223, 295.
63. Interview with Sir Julian Ridsdale, formerly a language officer in Japan and also of MI2c, 25 August 1994. See also Ferris, '''Worthy of Some Better Enemy?''', 223–56.
64. 'Intelligence Organisations in the Far East', AIR 20/374, PRO.

3 INSECURITY AND THE FALL OF SINGAPORE

1. Grimsdale (FECB) to Ismay, 8 March 1942, Ismay/IV/Gri/1a, Ismay Papers, LHCMA.
2. Brooke-Popham to Street (Air Ministry), DO/RBP/1, 15 January 1941, V/2/3, Brooke-Popham Papers, LHCMA.
3 Brooke-Popham to Ismay, DO/ISMAY/12, 10 October 1941, ibid.; *PWTM*, Vol.VII/G, MISC, 97.
4. NID Vol. 42, 'Far East and Pacific', III, Special, 'H.M.S. Anderson and Special Intelligence in the Far East', ADM 223/297, PRO.
5. Marder, *Old Friends*, 357–9.
6. C. in C. FE to COS, 6 June 1941, WO 193/920, PRO.
7. C. in C. FE to COS No. 13672, 17 June 1941, WO 193/920, PRO. See also (Hist) (DD), 'Dispatch on the Far East by Brooke-Popham', 1 June 1942, CAB 120/518, PRO. Denham was a director of Anglo-Dutch Plantations Ltd, a rubber concern in Java.
8. WO to C. in C. FE No.70866, 7 June 1941, WO 193/607, PRO.
9. Brooke-Popham to FECB, 21 August 1941, AIR 23/1865, PRO. See also (Hist) (DD), 'Dispatch on the Far East by Brooke-Popham', 1 June 1942, CAB 120/518, PRO.
10. MI6 Political Report No. 111, 'A Statement of Japanese Policy. French Information from Shanghai', WO 208/895, PRO.
11. Steveni (MI6) to MI2c and MI3a, 17 April 1941, CX.37400/I/818 (untranslated), WO 208/1219A, PRO; Winterborn (MI2c) minute 28.12.40 on MI6 CX.37502/991, 21 December 1940, ibid.
12. Gough, *SOE Singapore*, 68–89: Cross, *Red Jungle*, 16–20.
13. B. F. Smith, *Ultra–Magic Deals*, 38, 40, Benson, *History*, 20–1.
14. All British material in the G-2 Far East records appears to have been removed, however the registers give testimony to the quantity of FECB material logged by the G-2 officers, sometimes amounting to a third of the total, G-2 logs for Philippines and Singapore, July 1941, RG 165, USNA.
15. Crosby to FO, 5 June 1939, F7135/246/40, FO 371/23592, PRO.
16. Toland, *But Not in Shame*, 165–6.
17. Aldrich, *Key to the South*, 185–6.
18. Elphick and Smith, *Odd Man Out*, 136–7.
19. Intercept of Japanese Consul General, Singapore, to Tokyo, 9 January 1935, WO 106/5504, PRO. This sort of material was routinely circulated to MI5 in London, Colonel G. S. (MI2) minute, n.d., ibid. See also 'Inquest on Japanese Merchant', *Morning Post*, 17 December 1934.
20. Minute by Varsity, 26 July 1938, WO 106/5394, PRO.
21. Elphick, *Far Eastern File*, 137.
22. Major (MI2c) to Gault (MI1x), 22 December 1939, WO 208/2049A, PRO.
23. GSO1 Int, Singapore to WO, 11 June 1941, WO 193/920, PRO; GSO1 Int, Singapore to WO, 20 May 1941, WO 208/2049A, PRO.
24. GSO1 Int FE Singapore to WO, 19 May 1941, WO 106/2476, PRO.
25. FO to Kabul, 11 April 1941, 2279/2279/G, L/P&S/12/530, IOLR.
26. C. in C. Far East to WO, 3 April 1941, WO 208/2049A, PRO; Grimsdale, Deputy Director FECB to MI2c, 28 August 1941, ibid.

27. Singapore also worried that higher-grade intelligence was being sent back to Tokyo in other cipher systems that they could not read, and that their present sources 'may for technical reasons dry up at any moment', C. in C. China to Admiralty, 14 June 1941, WO 193/920, PRO.

28. JIC (41) 24th mtg (1), 8 August 1941, in FE (41) 174, 'Withdrawal of Facilities from Japanese Consulates in India and Burma', CAB 96/4, PRO; FE (41) 41, 'Restriction of Japanese Activities', 12 February 1941, CAB 96/3, PRO.

29. Brooke-Popham to Ismay, ISMAY/2, 5 December 1940, *PWTM*, Vol.VII/G, MISC, 86; C. A. Vlieland, 'Disaster in the Far East', 12 October 1945, 47, Vlieland Papers, LHCMA.

30. Grimsdale (FECB) to Ismay, 8 March 1942, Ismay/IV/Gri/1a, Ismay Papers, LHCMA. On reluctance over internment see WP (40) 320, 'Treatment of Japanese in Malaya', memorandum by the Secretary of State for the Colonies, 19 August 1940, F3942/2251/61, FO 371/24715, PRO.

31. Extract from Malaya Combined Intelligence Summary, 8/39, 1 August 1939–30 September 1939, 'Activities Among Indian Troops', WO 208/1221, PRO.

32. Captain of Intelligence Staff (Singapore) to DNI, 23 January 1941, WO 208/892, PRO.

33. COIS Singapore to DNI, 21 May 1941, summarising intercepted Japanese Consular Special Intelligence Report, 14 May 1941, WO 193/913, PRO.

34. Ong Chit Chung, 'Operation Matador', PhD, 405.

35. Hauner, *India in Axis Strategy*, 409–10.

36. DNI to COIS, Singapore, 3 October 1941, WO 208/1899, PRO.

37. The classic account of this organisation is Iwaichi Fujiwara, *F Kikan*. See also Lebra, *Jungle Alliance*, 3–26; Gordon, *Brothers Against the Raj*, 495–9.

38. Elphick and Smith, *Odd Man Out*, 163–9.

39. COS Australia to WO, 3 April 1942, CAB 120/615, PRO.

40. Account by Seabridge, 28 February 1942, in DNI records, ADM 199/1472, PRO.

41. On the Japanese system and its Axis contacts see Chapman, 'Japanese Intelligence, 1919–1945'.

42. Report of the Anglo-French Naval, Military and Air Conference at Singapore, 22–27 June 1939, AIR 2/4128, PRO.

43. The interception was Japanese consular Y (wireless traffic) for 29 June 1939 summarised in Captain on Staff, HMS Tamar to C-in-C China and DNI London, 5 July 1939, ADM 1/10227, PRO; Godfrey (DNI) to First Sea Lord, 6 July 1939, ibid.

44. Lee (CO) to Edelsten (ADM), CO 7264/39, 6 July 1939, ADM 1/10227, PRO.

45. Brooke-Popham to Ismay, DO/Ismay/4, 3 February 1941, V/1/5, Brooke-Popham Papers, LHCMA.

46. Crosby to FO No. 45, 21 January 1941, WO 208/1901, PRO; Governor Straits Settlements (Singapore) to CO, 19 January, 1941, F306/5/40, FO 371/28108, PRO.

47. Governor Straits Settlements to CO No. 85, 28 February 1941, F1490/5/40, FO 371/28110, PRO. See also 'Security Measures in Malaya', 15 March 1941, WO 193/913, PRO; WO to GSO1, Singapore No.62477, 20 April 1941, ibid.

48. Elphick and Smith, *Odd Man Out*, 14–17, 73–5, 134–9, 217.

49. Best, 'This Probably Over-Valued Military Power', 72.

50. Entry for 12 December 1940, Chapman (ed.), *The Price of Admiralty*, Vol. I. See also Rusbridger, 'The Sinking of the *Automedon*'.
51. J. W. M. Chapman, 'Japanese Intelligence', 160–2. The India Office had already ceased to send CX [SIS] reports to India by sea mail for fear of this eventuality, Peel to Caroe, 9 March 1940, L/P&S/12/352, IOLR.
52. Wiles to Brooke-Popham, 15 July 1948, V/9/30, Brooke-Popham Papers, LHCMA.
53. The intercept was a high-grade 'BJ' intercept rather than low-grade consular traffic. Japanese Chargé d'Affaires, London to Foreign Ministry, Tokyo, 13 September 1941, Intercept No. 095426, AP 20/8/548, Avon Papers, BUL; Churchill minute, No. 627, 13 September 1941, ibid.
54. Churchill to Eden, Minute M909/1, 20 September 1941, AP 20/8/682, Avon Papers, BUL. The fifth name was the retired former British Military Attaché in Tokyo, Major-General Piggott.
55. Eden to Churchill, PM 41/128, 3 October 1941, AP 20/8/566, ibid.; 'Telephone Check on Sloane 1838', AP 20/8/834A, ibid.
56. Marder, *Old Friends*, Vol. I, 343–6; Elphick, *Far Eastern File*, 230.
57. MO2 memorandum, 'Japan as an Ally', April 1940, WO 106/2436, PRO.
58. Entry for 7 May 1940, Colville, *Fringes of Power*.
59. The Link was kept under Surveillance by Maxwell's B5b section of MI5. Costello, *Ten Days to Destiny*, 63; Thurlow, *Fascism in Britain*, 165, 175, 180; A. Jeffrey, *This Present Emergency*, 35, 41–2, 46.
60. Ismay to Churchill, 21 April 1944, CAB 120/518, PRO.
61. FECB to Air Ministry WX 2021, 12 January 1942, AIR 20/2160, PRO. Although this was the authorised aircraft strength, in practice numbers remained at approximately 133, see AIR 23/1865, PRO *passim*.
62. Hinsley and Simkins, *British Intelligence*, Vol. IV, 112–77.
63. Eden to Churchill, 12 September 1941, F9615/1299/23, FO 371/27981, PRO.

4 SURPRISE DESPITE WARNING: INTELLIGENCE AND THE FALL OF SINGAPORE

1. Entry for 24 December 1941, Pownall diary, LHCMA.
2. (Hist) (DD), 'Dispatch on the Far East by Brooke-Popham', CAB 120/518, PRO.
3. Best, 'This Probably Over-Valued Military Power', 90–1.
4. FECB Intelligence Survey No.1822, 'Warning of Attack by Japan', 9 December 1940, WO 208/888, PRO. These rather antiquated views were shared by senior MI2 officers. Brigadier Leonard Field remarked earlier that year that '"Y" has marked limitations and cannot be used for warning', adding that SIS and attaché work should be expanded, Field (MI2) minute, May 1940, WO 208/871, PRO.
5. This point is made with impressive force in Ferris, 'Worthy of Some Better Enemy?', 224–46. See also Kirby, *Singapore*, 74–6.
6. Elphick and Smith, *Odd Man Out*, 132–57.
7. Hinsley, Thomas, Ranson and Knight, *British Intelligence*, Vol. I, 36–43, 513–14.
8. JIC (41) 11, 'Scale of Attack on Malaya', 1 January 1941, CAB 84/, PRO; JIC (41) 150, 'Future Japanese Strategy', 17 April 1941, ibid.; JIC (41) 160, 'Reported Intention to Attack Malaya', 20 April 1941, ibid. These reports are discussed in 'Comment on DMI's Minute', 3/4 January 1942, WO 208/871, PRO.

396   Notes to pages 53–9

In this retrospective review the DMI was broadly fair. Nevertheless, it ignored JIC (41) 55, 'Japanese Intentions', 5 February 1941, WO 106/5703A, PRO.

9. JIC (40) 335, 'Period of Warning of an attack on Singapore', 23 October 1940, CAB 81/98, PRO.

10. APS (41) 5 (Draft), 'Future Strategy of Japan', CAB 81/101, PRO.

11. JIC (41) 175, 'Future Strategy of Japan', 1 May 1941, CAB 79/11, PRO. Discussed in 'Comment on DMI's Minute, 3/4 January 1942, WO 208/871, PRO.

12. JIC (41) 309, 'Japan's Next Move', 2 August 1941, CAB 79/13, PRO. See also JIC (41) 439 (final), 'Japanese Intentions', 18 November 1941, CAB 79/15, PRO.

13. WO to FECB, 3 August 1941, WO 193/912, PRO; FECB to WO, 4 August 1941, ibid.

14. JIC (41) 320, 'Japan', 11 August 1941, CAB 79/13, PRO. Discussed in 'Comment on DMI's Minute', 3/4 January 1942, WO 208/871, PRO.

15. Entry for 7 August 1941, Barnes and Nicholson (eds.), *Leo Amery Diaries*.

16. Ong Chit Chung, 'Operation Matador', PhD, 377–93.

17. Entry for 16 October 1941, Oliver Harvey diary, MSS 56398, BL. See also Eden to Churchill, 16 October 1941, CAB 69/3, PRO.

18. Ong Chit Chung, 'Operation Matador', PhD, 380, 385–7, 391.

19. Ibid., 404–5.

20. Grimsdale (FECB) to WO, 14 November 1941, WO 208/874, PRO.

21. JIC (41) 439, 'Japan's Intentions', 18 November 1941, CAB 79/15, PRO; 'Comment on DMI's Minute', 3/4 January 1942, WO 208/871, PRO.

22. NID memorandum, 'JIC Appreciations in 1941 of Japanese Intentions', ADM 223/494, PRO.

23. Ike, *Japan's Decision for War*, 50–1. This constitutes the surviving Army record of discussions only.

24. Ike, *Japan's Decision for War*, 180–2, 223–4; E. B. Reynolds, *Thailand and Japan's Southern Advance*, 73–103; Stowe, *Siam becomes Thailand*, 210–21.

25. Herman, *Intelligence Power*, 103–4.

26. Vice Admiral P. W. Wennecker, quoted in Marder, *Old Friends*, 291.

27. For an alternative interpretation see Best, 'This Probably Over-Valued Military Power', 89–91.

28. Special Intelligence No. 380, 28 October 1941, ADM 223/321, PRO; also HW 1/303 *passim*, PRO.

29. DNI to FECB, 20 November 1941, WO 208/1899, PRO; Robertson, *The Japanese File*, 116–26; Cheah Boon Kheng, *Red Star Over Malaya*, 19, 102.

30. Naval Intelligence report, 1945, HW 4/25, PRO.

31. Ong Chit Chung, 'Operation Matador', PhD, 409; Aldrich, *Key to the South*, 337–56.

32. Hist (DD), 'Dispatch on the Far East by Brooke-Popham', 1 June 1942, CAB 120/518, PRO; JIC (41) 449 (Final), 'Possible Japanese Action', 28 November 1941, CAB 81/105, PRO.

33. Halifax to FO No.5519, 1 December 1941, F13114/83/23, FO 371/27913, PRO; DNI to COIS Singapore, 3 December 1941, WO 208/1898, PRO; Aldrich, *Key to the South*, 361–2.

34. Aldrich, *Key to the South*, 367–8; Brooke-Popham to WO No.406/9, 7 December 1941, *PWTM*, Vol. IV, p. 6.

35. Crosby to FO No.46, 4 February 1935 (49/10/35), WO 106/5627, PRO; 29

January 1935, *Bangkok Daily Herald*; Ishimaru Tota, *Japan Must Fight Britain*, 255–8 (the Japanese edition appeared in 1935).

36. Callahan, *Churchill*, 121.
37. Callahan, *Churchill*, 138–9, quoting Kennedy, *Business of War*, 104–10.
38. 'D.M.I.'s paper dated 3rd January', WO 208/871, PRO. See also Davidson (DMI) to Cavendish-Bentinck (JIC), 3 January 1942, ibid.
39. JIC (41) 11, 'Scale of Attack on Malaya', 10 January 1941, discussed in 'Comment on DMI's Minute', 3/4 January 1942, WO 208/871, PRO; JIC (41) 223, 'Petroleum Situation in Japan', 25 May 1941, ibid. These forecasts had been fairly constant, cf JIC (40) 205, 'Appreciation for Future Policy of Conduct of the War', CAB 81/98, PRO.
40. JIC (41) 327, 'Scale of Air Attack on Malaya', 13 August 1941, CAB 79/13, PRO; JIC (41) 362, 'Japan's Intentions', 13 September 1941, discussed in 'Comment on DMI's Minute', 3/4 January 1942, WO 208/871, PRO.
41. JIC (41) 449, 'Possible Japanese Action', 28 November 1941, CAB 81/105, PRO and discussed in 'Comment on DMI's Minute', 3/4 January 1942, WO 208/871, PRO.
42. Interview with Sir Julian Ridsdale MP, formerly of MI2c, 25 August 1994.
43. For a superb analysis see, Ferris, 'Worthy of Some Better Enemy?', 225.
44. Thorne, *Allies of a Kind*, 55. Pownall arrived on 25 December 1941.
45. Ferris, 'Worthy of Some Better Enemy', 223–40, 251.
46. Ibid., pp. 240–51. On dissemination see, JIC (41) 15th mtg (1) and Annex I and II, 6 June 1941, CAB 81/88, PRO.
47. Grimsdale (FECB) to Ismay, 8 March 1942, Ismay/IV/Gri/1a, Ismay Papers, LHCMA.
48. Marder, *Old Friends*, 357, n. 37.
49. Pamphlet on Japanese Army, March 1941, L/MIL/17/20/24, IOLR, discussed in Elphick, *Far Eastern File*, 158.
50. Ferris, 'Worthy of Some Better Enemy?', 232; Eden to Churchill, 17 September 1941, PM 41/110, AP20/8/548A, Avon Papers, BUL.
51. Mahnken, 'Gazing at the Sun', 429–32. See also Best, 'Constructing an Image', 410; Marder, *Old Friends*, 332–56.
52. Churchill to DNI, 11 February 1940, ADM 116/5757, PRO.
53. Richard and Saunders, *The Royal Air Force*, Vol. II, 10–11. See also Ferris, 'Worthy of Some Better Enemy', 247; Marder, *Old Friends*, 308;
54. Elphick, *Far Eastern File*, 167.
55. Prados, *Combined Fleet*, 219; Aldrich, *Key to the South*, 96.
56. FECB Singapore to Air Ministry, 10 December 1941, *PWTM*, Vol. IV, 18.
57. Entry for 28 October 1940, Dilks (ed.), Cadogan Diary. On British stereotypes of the Japanese see Thorne, *Allies of a Kind*, 3–19; and *The Issue of War*, 18–19, 27–32.
58. COS (41) 230, 11 April 1941, CAB 80/27, PRO; JIC (41) 175 Revise, 'Future Strategy of Japan', 1 May 1941, CAB 79/11, PRO. See also JIC (41) 327, 'Probable Scale of Japanese Air Attack on Malaya', 13 August 1941, CAB 79/13, PRO.
59. Marder, *Old Friends*, Vol. I, 346; Wark, 'In Search of a Suitable Japan', 194–6, 216; Best, 'Constructing an Image', 413.
60. Marder, *Old Friends*, Vol. I, 345.

61. Thorne, *The Issue of War*, 18–19, 27–32, 169–72.
62. Marder, *Old Friends*, Vol. I, 354–5. See also Mahnken, 'Gazing at the Sun', 433.
63. Prados, *Combined Fleet*, 32, 39, 55. A near complete Zero was captured in China in May 1941.
64. D. Reynolds, *Britannia Overruled*, 5, citing Frankel, *International Relations*, 101.
65. Ferris, 'Worthy of Some Better Enemy?', 237. On Russo-Japanese confrontation see Coox, *Nomohan*.
66. Andrew, *President's Eyes Only*, 145–8: Aldrich, *Espionage, Security and Intelligence in Britain*, 1–2.
66. Bond (ed.), *Chief of Staff*, 99.

5 CONSPIRACY OR CONFUSION? CHURCHILL, ROOSEVELT AND PEARL HARBOR

1. FitzGibbon, *Secret Intelligence*, 255.
2. See for example Toland, *Infamy*.
3. For recent orthodox studies see: Heinrichs, *Threshold of War*; Marks, *Wind Over Sand*; D. Reynolds, *The Creation of the Anglo-American Alliance*.
4. See for example the BBC *Timewatch* documentary on Pearl Harbor transmitted in 1992.
5. The war in the Far East 'was so much the concern of the United States, it is not possible to provide an adequate account on the basis of the British archives alone', Hinsley, Thomas, Ransom and Knight, *British Intelligence*, Vol. I, ix–x.
6. Kirby, *The War Against Japan*; Howard, *Grand Strategy*; Woodward, *British Foreign Policy*; Cruickshank, *SOE*.
7. Beesly, review of Layton with Pinneau and Costello, *And I Was There*, in *Intelligence and National Security*, 1, 3 (1986): 482–5.
8. Horner, *High Command*. The arguments therein concerning Pearl Harbor, based on the testimony of Eric Nave, were reviewed in detail in Chapman, 'Pearl Harbor', 451–61. See also Ferris, 'Broadway House to Bletchley Park'.
9. James Rusbridger was also the author of *The Intelligence Game*, a trenchantly revisionist analysis. On his demise see, James Adams, 'Sidelined by history, the fantasy is over for the spy who never was', *Sunday Times*, 20 February 1994.
10. Ibid., *Betrayal at Pearl Harbor*, 28.
11. Ibid., 12, 23, 161. Contrast this with Hinsley's accurate picture of FECB in *British Intelligence*, Vol. I, 40. I am grateful to Andrew Gordon for guidance on the career of William Mortimer.
12. Rusbridger and Nave, *Betrayal at Pearl Harbour*, 137.
13. Kahn, 'The Intelligence Failure of Pearl Harbor', 144. I am grateful to Andrew Gordon for permitting me to see a copy of an NSA official statement issued at the anniversary historical conference held in Hawaii, NSA OSSW 123–2, 'JN-25 Before Pearl Harbor', 3 December 1991.
14. Hinsley, Thomas, Ransom and Knight, *British Intelligence*, Vol. I, 24, 52.
15. Ibid., 52 and footnote (my italics).
16. Rusbridger and Nave, *Betrayal at Pearl Harbor*, 177.
17. 'Not a single message escaped the listening post at Hong Kong', Rusbridger and Nave, *Betrayal at Pearl Harbor*, 77.
18. The summaries on Europe and the Middle East were voluminous, while the Far

Eastern material for 1940 and 1941 amounts to a few pages, Dir/C Archive, HD 1, PRO.

19. Chapman, 'Pearl Harbor', 457; NSA OSSW 123–2, 'JN-25 Before Pearl Harbor', 3 December 1991; Kahn, 'Pearl Harbor', 147–8.

20. William F. Friedman, 'A Brief History of the Signal Intelligence Service', 29 June 1942, SRH 029, RG 457, USNA.

21. Andrew, *President's Eyes Only*, 106–7; 216–20.

22. Mahnken, 'Gazing at the Sun', 435–8.

23. On unwarnability see Kahn, 'The Intelligence Failure of Pearl Harbor', *passim*; on blocking see Prados, *Combined Fleet Decoded*, 166–7, 172.

24. William F. Friedman, 'Expansion of the Signals Intelligence Service From 1940 to 7 December 1941', 4 December 1945, SRH 134, RG 457, USNA.

25. Evidence of Brigadier General Hayes A. Kroner, 13 December 1944, SRH 115, quoted in Gilbert and Finnegan (eds.), *U.S. Army Signals Intelligence*, 41–3.

26. The most incisive discussion of this is given in Andrew, *President's Eyes Only*, 120–1.

27. Parker, 'The Unsolved Messages', 295–313.

28. Ibid., p. 296; Erskine, 'Churchill', 64; 'Undeciphered Pearl Harbor warnings laid to lack of funds', *Japan Times*, 28 November 1991.

29. For examples of D/F and traffic analysis at Singapore see: COIS Singapore to DNI, 17 January 1941, WO 208/871, PRO; COIS Singapore to DNI, 24 January 1941, WO 208/892, PRO.

30. Consular Y Darwin, 22 August 1940 and Field to MI2, 25 August 1940, WO 208/873, PRO; Aldrich, *Key to the South*, 265–6.

31. FO to COIS No. 58, 15 December 1940, F5566/116/40, FO 371/24752, PRO; FO to COIS No. 59, 15 December 1940, ibid.; Aldrich, *Key to the South*, 283–4.

32. Best, 'Constructing an Image', 404 and information from Alan Stripp.

33. For example 'Japanese–Italian Anti-Comintern Pact 3 January 1939', No. 07348, 21 January 1939, and 'Anti-Comintern Pact: Translation of German Draft of Supplementary Protocol', No. 073426, 10 December 1938, WO 208/859, PRO. See also the excellent study by Best, *Britain, Japan and Pearl Harbor*, 27–8, 45, 65.

34. JIC (41) 55, 'Japanese Intentions', 5 February 1941, WO 106/5703A, PRO; JIC (41) 61, 'Possible Action Against Japan', annexed to COS (41) 46th mtg (4), CAB 79/9, PRO; JP (41) 95, 'Measures to Avert War with Japan', 5 February 1941, CAB 84/27, PRO. On the war scare see, Marder, *Old Friends*, Vol. I, 185–7.

35. Entry for 6 February 1941, Dilks (ed.), *Cadogan Diary*.

36. See the full treatment in Best, 'Straws in the Wind', 642–64, also Lowe, *Origins*, 219–25.

37. Bletchley Park (BP) was the main centre for military codebreaking, while diplomatic and commercial traffic was worked on at Berkeley Street in London. Both came under the control of Government Code and Cypher School (GC&CS). This changed its name to Government Communications Headquarters (GCHQ) in 1942, but most referred to 'GC&CS' or 'BP' until 1945.

38. Keiichiro Komatsu, 'Misunderstanding and Mistranslation', PhD. This study represents a rigorous and scholarly examination of earlier and briefer conten-

tions by Japanese scholars, such as Toshikazu Kase and Shinji Sudo, on mis-translations, see ibid., H-17.

39. Erskine, 'When a Purple Machine went Missing', 185–9; Kahn, 'Pearl Harbor and the Inadequacy of Cryptanalysis', 285.
40. JIC (40) 263, 'Exchange of Information with the United States Authorities', 1 September 1941 CAB 81/98, PRO.
41. Erskine, 'Churchill and the Start of the Ultra–Magic Deals', 52–7.
42. Entry for 23 September 1940, Leutze (ed.), *London Observer*.
43. For an orthodox account, see B. F. Smith, *The Ultra–Magic Deals*, 43–5, 53–8, 60–1. For airbrushing see, Hinsley, Thomas, Ransom and Knight, *British Intelligence*, Vol. I, 312–13. For the revisionist view, see Erskine, 'Churchill and the Start of the Ultra–Magic Deals', 57–73.
44. Erskine, 'Churchill and the Start of the Ultra–Magic Deals', 63; Benson, *History*, 18–20.
45. Erskine, 'When a Purple Machine went Missing', 185–9.
46. Hinsley, 'The Counterfactual History of No ULTRA', 319; Steiner, 'Deception and its Dividends', 1,310. The counter-argument is skilfully made in Bennett, *Behind the Battle*, xxii, 201–2.
47. B. F. Smith, *Ultra–Magic Deals*, 102.
48. DNI to C. in C. China, 10 February 1941, ADM 199/1477, PRO.
49. Chapman, 'Short Summary of Recent BJ's on Japan', WO 208/896, PRO; 'Indications of Japanese Collaboration with Germany and Italy, MI2c log, 17 March 1941, WO 208/859; log references to BJ 09585 9 April 1941 and BJ 092510 24 June 1941, ibid.
50. Best, *Britain, Japan and Pearl Harbor*, 160–5.
51. Aldrich, *Key to the South*, 329–30.
52. Ibid., 329–30; entry for 14 July 1941, Dilks (ed.), *Cadogan Diary*.
53. Memorandum entitled, 'B.J. Series of Diplomatic Messages', n.d. (presumed 8 October 1945), ADM 223/298, PRO. On Oshima's importance see Boyd, *Hitler's Japanese Confidant*.
54. Hinsley, 'British Intelligence and Barbarossa', in Erickson and Dilks (eds.), *Barbarossa*, 43–75.
55. ADM 199/1477, PRO, *passim*; NID Vol. 42 'Far East and Pacific', III, Special, HMS Anderson and Special Intelligence in the Far East, ADM 223/297, PRO. On informal liaison with the Americans see also C. in C. China to Admiralty, 5 February 1941, F836/54/61. FO 371/27774, PRO. Benson, *History*, 20–1.
56. Entry for 4 June 1941, Leutze (ed.), *London Observer*.
57. On the origins of the JIC see: Andrew, *Secret Service*, 483–5; Hinsley, Thomas, Ransom and Knight, *British Intelligence*, Vol. I, 36–43, 93–100, 291–9; Wark, *Ultimate Enemy*, 117.
58. JIC (41) 15th mtg (1) and Annex I and II, 6 June 1941, CAB 81/88, PRO.
59. Eden to Halifax No.3244, 12 June 1941, CAB 122/1030, PRO. See also B. F. Smith, *Ultra–Magic Deals*, 73–4.
60. B. F. Smith, *Ultra–Magic Deals*, 84–5.
61. WO to C. in C. Far East, 22 August 1941, WO 208/2049A, PRO.
62. Broad minute, 24 October 1941, F11163/9/61, FO 371/27767, PRO.
63. Entry for 1 July 1941, Leutze (ed.), *London Observer*.

64. JIC (40) 105, 'Relationship with the Netherlands East Indies', 5 June 1940, CAB 81/97, PRO.

65. On co-operation over agitators see Malaya Command Intelligence Notes, 6 December 1928, AIR 5/758, PRO. On cypher co-operation see ADM 199/1477, PRO *passim*. The Dutch were also co-operating on telephone taps, Consul Sourabaya to COIS Singapore, 1 February 1941, WO 208/871, PRO.

66. WO to C. in C. Far East, 27 August 1941, WO 208/2049A, PRO.

67. The Dutch were, for example, intercepting telegrams from the Chinese embassy at Vichy, MI6 Political Report No. 137 to Far Eastern Department (FO), 2 October 1941, WO 208/1219A, PRO.

68. Best, 'Probably Over-valued Military Power', 83–4.

69. Hinsley, Thomas, Ransom and Knight, *British Intelligence*, Vol. II, 55–6.

70. Aldrich, *Key to the South*, 281–4.

71. K. Brown, 'Intelligence and the Decision to Collect It', 449–68; Croft, 'Wartime at Berkeley Street' 133–44. Private information.

72. Entry for 4 June 1941, Leutze (ed.), *London Observer*.

73. Erskine, 'Churchill and the Start of the Ultra–Magic Deals', 59.

74. Churchill minute to Eden, 2 December 1941, M.1078/1, F13114/86/23, FO 371/27913, PRO.

75. Stimson Diary, 25–28 November 1941, frames 00298–302, reel 7, BRO.

76. Aldrich, 'A Question of Expediency', 236–9.

77. Betts, *Surprise Attack*; Kam, *Surprise Attack*; Handel, *War, Strategy and Intelligence*.

78. The classic study is Whaley, *Codeword Barbarossa*.

79. Entries for 31 May and 2 June 1941, Dilks (ed.), *Cadogan Diary*; Hinsley, 'British Intelligence and Barbarossa', in Erickson and Dilks (eds.), *Barbarossa*, 43–75.

80. Section 10. 'Japanese Policy and Intentions', ADM 223/298, PRO.

81. Entry for 8 December 1941, Harvey, *War Diaries*, 71.

82. Entry for 7 December 1941, Brooke Diary, LHCMA.

83. Entries for 6 and 7 December 1941, Kennedy diary. Significant sections of the Kennedy diary are reproduced in Ferris, 'Broadway House to Bletchley Park', 439–40; Chapman, 'Pearl Harbor', 454.

84. Hillgarth and Barrett memorandum, 'History of the Far East and Pacific War, ADM 223/494, PRO, discussed in Michael Smith, 'Churchill Cleared over Pearl Harbor', *The Daily Telegraph*, 1 August 1994.

85. Director of Naval Intelligence to Captain on the Staff (Singapore), 25 November 1941, ADM 199/1477, PRO, quoted and discussed in Best, *Avoiding War*, 182–6.

86. Section 10. 'Japanese Policy and Intentions', ADM 223/298, PRO. See also Rusbridger and Nave, *Betrayal at Pearl Harbor*, 148–50.

87. Fitzgibbon asserts 'I quote him directly', *Secret Intelligence*, 255.

88. Casey, *The Secret War Against Hitler*, 7.

89. JIC (41) 36th mtg, 3 December 1941 and JIC (41) 37th mtg, 9 December 1941, CAB 81/88, PRO. The issue is further discussed in Sissons, 'More on Betrayal at Pearl Harbor', 273–80.

90. See for example Steveni (MI6) to Ridsdale (MI2c), 'Japanese Activities in Indo China', CX.37065/1/186, 12 February 1941, WO 208/895, PRO; Steveni (MI6b)

to MI2c/e, 'Japanese Activities in North Western Thailand', CX.37212/81, 8 October 1941, ibid; Ridsdale (MI2c) to Steveni (MI6), 10 October 1941, ibid.

91. I am most indebted to Sir Julian Ridsdale for sharing his recollections with me.
92. In 1999 I was still pursuing a long quest for the still-closed files of the Foreign Office Services Liaison Department, of which Cavendish-Bentinck was head.
93. Hillgarth and Barrett memorandum, 'History of the Far East and Pacific War', ADM 223/494, PRO.
94. These individuals were family friends of Andrew Gordon, a historian at the Cabinet Office Historical Section. I am most grateful to Andrew Gordon for sharing his recollections.
95. 'D.M.I.'s paper dated 3 January [1942]', WO 208/871, PRO.
96. Sir Andrew Gilchrist, 'Diplomacy and Disaster', 265.
97. Tarling, *Onset of the Pacific War*, 366.
98. Komatsu, 'Misunderstanding and Mistranslation', H-13.
99. Ike, *Japan's Decision for War*, 186–8, 224.
100. Prados, *Combined Fleet*, 142
101. Butow, Tojo, 75. E. B. Reynolds, *Thailand and Japan's Southern Advance*, 49, 57, 73–80.
102. Dallek, *Franklin D. Roosevelt*, 269–316; Komatsu, 'Misunderstanding and Mistranslation', PhD, H-15.
103. Tarling, *Onset of the Pacific War*, 202, 292, 212.
104. Roosevelt to Churchill, 24 November 1941, 711.94/2471, RG 59, NARA.
105. Craigie to Eden, 3 June 1941, FO 371/27893, PRO.
106. Mahl, *Desperate Deception*, 58.
107. APS (41) 5 (Draft), 'Future Strategy of Japan', CAB 81/101, PRO.
108. Andrew, *Secret Service*, 494.

6 IMPERIAL SECURITY SERVICES': THE EMERGENCE OF OSS AND SOE

1. BSC memorandum, 'Functions of Security Co-ordination', 1 October 1941, Ministry of Aviation 38/167, PRO.
2. JIC (41) 15th mtg (1), 6 June 1941, CAB 81/88, PRO.
3. Eden to Halifax, 12 June 1941, CAB 120/1030, PRO.
4. Andrew, *Secret Service*, 471–4: Astley, *Inner Circle*, 36–42; Cloake, *Templer*, 69–70.
5. Stafford, *Churchill*, 176–81.
6. Entry for 26 July 1940, Colville, *Fringes of Power*.
7. Entry for Thursday 19 October 1939, Cadogan Diary, ACAD 1/8, CCC. Later Cadogan noted 'I'm afraid its hopeless, though he may go on for some time', entry for 30 October 1939, ibid.
8. Malcolm Woolcombe, head of the political section of SIS called on Cadogan 'to protest at the idea of anyone being brought in from outside to succeed "C"', diary entries for 4 and 5 November 1939, Cadogan diary, ACAD 1/8, CCC.
9. Entries for 25 May 1940 and 15 March 1941, CCC.
10. Stafford, *Churchill*, 186–8.
11. Churchill to Eden, 23 July 1940, AP20/8/73, Avon Papers, BUL.
12. Churchill to Eden, 8 April 1942, AP20/9/341, Avon Papers, BUL.

13. Eden to Churchill, PM 42/29, 23 February 1942, AP20/9/29, Avon Papers, BUL; Eden to Churchill, PM 42/31, 23 February 1942, AP20/9/31, ibid.
14. Pimlott (ed.), *Political Diary of Hugh Dalton*, 288–379.
15. Jebb had been involved in the initial investigations into SIS in 1939–40 and was shocked by what was found, Stenton, 'British Propaganda', PhD, 37.
16. On negative intelligence see Dorwart, *Conflict of Duty;* Jensen, *Army Surveillance in America.*
17. Andrew, *President's Eyes Only*, 89–90.
18. Troy, *Wild Bill*, 25–6.
19. Cave Brown, *Wild Bill Donovan*, 140–51; Ranelagh, *The Agency*, 37–40.
20. Andrew, *President's Eyes Only*, 93.
21. Mahl, *Desperate Deception*, 9.
22. On this security role see AVIA 38/167 and AVIA 38/464. On American concern at the fifth-column menace to supplies to Britain see entry for 4 October 1940, Israel (ed.), *War Diary of Breckinridge Long.*
23. For two overviews of this complex debate see Troy, *Wild Bill*; Naftali, 'Intrepid's Last Deception', 72–100.
24. Hyde, *The Quiet Canadian*, 151–80; D. Stafford, *Camp X*, xvii. See also McLachlan, *Room 39*, 224–39.
25. Jeffreys-Jones, *Espionage*, 45, 73–4; MacPherson, 'Kings and Desperate Men', 8–9.
26. The earliest versions of this were offered by CIA officers such as Kirkpatrick, *The Real CIA*, 14–17; Ford, *Donovan of OSS*, pp. 107–10; R. H. Smith, *OSS*, 2. Troy, *Donovan and the CIA*. See, by contrast, Ranelagh, *The Agency*, 37, who asserts: 'The Central Intelligence Agency was William Donovan's idea.'
27. Donovan to JCS, 19 June 1944, File 'restricted – Pull', Box 1, J. Russell Forgen Papers, HIWRP.
28. Andrew, *President's Eyes Only*, 94–6; Troy, *Wild Bill*, pp. 57–8. See also the important observations about the qualified nature of Donovan's views on Britain holding out in D. Reynolds, *The Creation of the Anglo-American Alliance*, 331, n.27.
29. Quoted in Troy, *Wild Bill*, 77–8, together with other remarkable PRO material long overlooked by other historians. The best source for the tour is the diary of his guide, Danchev (ed.), *Diaries of Brigadier Vivian Dykes.*
30. 'Visit of William J. Donovan to Belgrade', enclosed in Belgrade to SD, 1 February 1941, 740.0118/European War, RG 59, USNA.
31. Churchill to Roosevelt, 10 March 1941, in Kimball (ed.), *Churchill and Roosevelt*, Vol. I, 145.
32. Troy, *Donovan and the CIA*, 40–2; Troy, *Wild Bill*, 20–22, 70; Andrew, Secret Service, 466. On Donovan's visit to the Middle East see AIR 8/368, PRO, *passim*.
33. B. F. Smith, *Shadow Warriors*, 40–1. Edmond Taylor had however, beaten him to it with his description of Hitler's fifth column, *The Strategy of Terror: Europe's Inner Front*, in 1939.
34. WO to CGS Canada, Australia, South Africa, New Zealand, 26 June 1941, WO 193/605, PRO.
35. B. F. Smith, *Shadow Warriors*, 38–40.
36. On the alternatives to COI see Troy, *Wild Bill*, 111, 119.

37. Hyde's suggestion that SIS had 'intrigued and driven him into the job', looks implausible, *The Quiet Canadian*, 152.
38. Mahl, *Desperate Deception*, 17–18.
39. Best, 'Probably Over-Valued Military Power', 83. See also Wheeler-Bennett, *Special Relationships*, 117–48.
40. Andrew, *President's Eyes Only*, 98–9.
41. Reynolds, *Creation of the Anglo-American Alliance*, 219; Hyde, *The Quiet Canadian*, 140–4; FO to Crosby, 8 October 1941, F10505/114/40, FO 371/28134, PRO. For details of Wendler's supposed activities see FO 371/25792 *passim*.
42. Hyde, *Quiet Canadian*, 135–48.
43. Brewer, *To Win the Peace*, 11–55; Cull, *Selling War*, 168–75; Mahl, *Desperate Deception*, 6, 107–36.
44. Memorandum by Morrell, PWE, SO.1 Organization, 10 July 1941, FO 898/103, quoted in Cull, *Selling War*, 236, n.43.
45. Mahl, *Desperate Deception*, 70, 75.
46. Downes, *The Scarlet Thread*, 59–60. See also Winks, *Cloak and Gown*, 152–86.
47. Andrew, *Secret Service*, 466–7, *President's Eyes Only*, 98–9, and 'Intelligence Collaboration', 113. For Godfrey's report on his return see, B. F. Smith, 'Admiral Godfrey's Mission to America', 441–50.
48. Andrew, *Secret Service*, 376–412; Wark, *The Ultimate Enemy*, 188–241.
49. 'Memorandum of a conversation on the Control of Propagandists, Liaison between British and American Intelligence', 28 January 1942, microfilm of Berle Diary, roll 3, FDRL.
50. Philby, *Silent War*, 20.
51. Stafford, *Camp X*, pp. 1–32, 62–71; Philby, *Silent War*, 20.
52. Stafford, *Camp X*, xvii, 69–70; Philby, *Silent War*, 114.
53. Entries for 13 and 14 February 1942, and 'Memorandum of a Conversation Between Berle and Hoyer Millar', 14 February 1942, microfilm of the Adolf Berle diary, roll 3, FDRL.
54. Entries for 6 January 1942 and 13 February 1942, Adolfe Berle diary, FDRL.
55. Entry for 9 January 1942, and memorandum 'Proposed Conference on British-American Intelligence Work', Adolf Berle diary, FDRL.
56. Troy, *Wild Bill*, 74–5.
57. Entry for 4 February 1942, Adolfe Berle diary, FDRL.
58. Eden had also been asked to serve but refused, D. Reynolds, *The Creation of the Anglo-American Alliance*, 176–7.
59. Entry, 6 May 1941, Cadogan Diary, ACAD 1/10, CCC.
60. K. M. Wilson, 'A venture in the "careers of intrigue"', 312–31; Stafford, *Churchill*, 127–54.
61. Thorne, *Allies of a Kind*, 162–3.
62. Entries for 11 and 12 January 1941, Colville, *Fringes of Power*.
63. Ranelagh, *The Agency*, 58.
64. See n.1 above.
65. *Who's Who, 1954*, 1248, 2146.
66. Cable and diplomatic bag facilities for these missions, and subsequently for Killery, were provided by SIS. WO to C. in C. Far East, 24 January 1941, WO 193/603, PRO; C. in C. India to WO, 29 January 1941, ibid.
67. WO to C. in C. Far East, 17 February 1942, HS 1/110, PRO.

68. Gough, *SOE Singapore*, 20. 'List of Officers of the MEW Far East Mission', 10 April 1941, HS 1/110, PRO.
69. Report on STS 101 training school at Singapore by its commander, Major John Gavin, Gavin papers, LHCMA. Cruickshank, *SOE*, 61–5.
70. Mackenzie to Garnons Williams, G3/10/1/4821, 1 September 1945 enclosing Report (A) 'The AJUF in Malaya' and (B) 'The History of the British Left Behind Parties in Malaya, December 1941–May 1945, Vol. II, Garnons Williams papers, IWM.
71. Gough, *SOE Singapore*, 40–1.
72. Ibid., 68–89.
73. By July, Soviet intelligence began to provide intercepted letters from the German Legation in Kabul to the headquarters of the German Secret Service (Abwehr). These gave details of anti-British activities that were of 'very great interest' to British security. Cripps (Moscow) to London, 2 August 1941, W9445/33/804, and IPI minute, 9 August 1941, L/P&S/12/544, IOLR.
74. C. in C. Far East to WO, 11 September 1941, WO 193/603, PRO.
75. WO to COIS Singapore, 9 December 1941, WO 193/607, PRO.
76. It is not clear whether a planned SOE mission to Vladivostok arrived, C. in C. Far East to WO, 25 December 1941, WO 193/607, PRO.
77. Lowe, *Origins of the Pacific War*, 107–9, 154–6.
78. Aldrich, *Key to the South*, 256–9.
79. Ashley Clarke to IO, 8 April 1940, F2169/23/23, enclosing Craigie to FO, 26 March 1940, and 31 March 1940, L/P&S/12/2368, IOLR; Dibdin (IPI) to Silver (IPI), 14 May 1940, ibid. The India Office noted with amusement that the Foreign Office had only recently offered to co-operate with the Soviets against Japanese activities in Sinkiang, Crombie minute, 10 May 1940, ibid.
80. On the military intelligence exchanges of 1936–8 see F3406, FO 371/24241, PRO.
81. There is a vast literature on this vexed subject, but see D. Reynolds, *The Creation of the Anglo-American Alliance*, 102–8.
82. Entry for 21 March 1940, Cadogan Diary, ACAD 1/9, CCC
83. Consul Haiphong to FO, 7 December 1940, F5509/3429/61, FO 371/24721, PRO.
84. MI2 memorandum, 6 October 1940, WO 208/643, PRO; MI6 report No. 83, 8 July 1940, WO 208/873, PRO.
85. Memorandum by Halifax, 24 June 1940, and Catroux to FO annexed to FCP (40) 2nd mtg, 21 June 1940, CAB 96/1, PRO; FO to Saigon, No.16, 29 June 1940, F7405/7327/17, FO 371/24328, PRO; Catroux, *Deux actes*, 70.
86. Kerr (Washington) to FO No.697, 13 August 1940, F3831/3429/61, FO 371/24719, PRO.
87. JIC (40) 267, 'Probable Effects on Japan of an Extension of Far Eastern Hostilities to Indochina', 5 September 1940, F4164/3429/40, FO 371/24719, PRO. See also JIC (40) 266, 'Situation in the Far East', 4 September 1940, F4164/3429/40, ibid. and MI6 Report No.83, 8 July 1940, WO 208/873, PRO. Aldrich, *Key to the South*, 266–7.
88. Clarke to Lampson, 28 January 1941, F278/8/61, FO 371/27758, PRO. The text of this secret treaty is given in C. in C. China to Admiralty, 20 January 1941, WO 106/4479, PRO.

89. Brizay and Langlade to de Gaulle, 26 February 1941, F1454/1454/17, FO 371/28481, PRO.
90. SOE to Dewing, 15 April 1941, WO 193/603, PRO; WO to C in C Far East, 23 June 1941, ibid. Catroux's sketch maps provided for SIS are attached to NID 4 minute, April 1941, ibid.
91. Crosby was bribing *The Bangkok Times*, the largest English-language newspaper in Thailand. Crosby to Minister of Information, 25 September 1939, 165/125/39, FO 930/53, PRO. Cf. Gilchrist, 'Diplomacy and Disaster', 258.
92. FE (41) 16th mtg, 'Infiltration – Thailand', 13 May 1941, CAB 96/2, PRO; JIC (41) 221, 'Action to Counter Pro-Axis Activities in the Far East', CAB 81/102, PRO.
93. Scott (MO 10) to Sugden (SOE), 19 June 1941, WO 193/915, PRO.
94. Killery to SOE London, 30 July 1941, F7487/246/40, FO 371/28134, PRO. Rumours of an imminent coup were based partly on French interception of Japanese mail between their Legation in Bangkok and Tokyo, see MI2(e) memorandum, 'Possible coup d'état in Thailand', 13 May 1941, WO 106/4474, PRO.
95. Gage minute, 12 August 1941, F7487/246/40, FO 371/28134, PRO; Sterndale Bennett to Jebb, 17 August 1941, ibid.
96. Crosby to FO, 31 October 1941, F11629/210/40, FO 371/28126, PRO. Dalton noted 'Bracken explodes with a complaint about some leaflets pushed under the doorways of the Thais . . . a screaming telegram about it', Entry for 4 November 1941, Pimlott (ed.), *Political Diary of Hugh Dalton*.
97. Eden minute, 5 November 1941, F11629/210/40, FO 371/28126, PRO.
98. MI6 Report No.140, 'The Japanese and Thailand', 8 October 1941, WO 208/895, PRO.
99. Despite the existence of Cabinet documents discussing these schemes, there is no mention of the plans for a coup d'état in the official history, Cruickshank, SOE, 70–2.
100. 'Occupation of Southern Thailand', 10 December 1940, AIR 20/2113, PRO. For a detailed analysis see Ong Chit Chung, 'Operation Matador', PhD, 1985.
101. Joint Planners' comments on memorandum by GOC Malaya, 12 February 1941, AIR 23/1865, PRO.
102. 'Operation Etonian without prior military occupation of Thailand by Japan', 9 May 1941, AIR 23/1865, PRO. Aldrich, Key to the South, 328–39.
103. Memorandum by Colonel Playfair (COS Far East), 'Some Personal Reflections on the Malayan Campaign', July 1941 – January 1942, V/9/28, Vlieland Papers, LHCMA.
104. Scott minute, 1 April 1941, WO 106/4474, PRO; Brooke-Popham to Crosby, 27 October 1941, WO 193/869, PRO; COS (41) 396th mtg. (5), 24 November 1941, CAB 79/15, PRO; Cruickshank, SOE, 70; Aldrich, *Key to the South*, 335–6.
105. C. in C. Far East to WO, 16 August 1941, WO 208/1903, PRO.
106. Gough, *SOE Singapore*, 38–40.
107. Colonial Office Secret Monograph, *Relations between Thailand and the Southern States of the Malay Peninsula*, by Dr W. Lineham, MCS (Singapore, 1941), CO 537/7335, PRO. Only thirty-five copies of this secret reference work were printed. Scott (WO) to Gent (CO), 1 September 1941, WO 106/2502, PRO. Gent to Gayter, 1 June 1943, CO 825/35/55104/9/44, I am indebted to the For-

eign Office for allowing me to see this file which was not in the PRO when this study was being researched.
108. Entry for 29 November 1941, Oliver Harvey Diary, MSS 56398, BL; Bruce to Curtin No.113, 1 December 1941, *DAFP*, V, document 149, 265.
109. Gough, *SOE Singapore*, 54–5; Cruickshank, *SOE*, 72–3.
110. Grimsdale to Ismay, 8 March 1942, Ismay/IV/Gri/la, Ismay Papers, LHCMA. Brooke-Popham's retrospective judgement coincided with that of Crosby, stating that Killery and his staff 'were keen, capable, but they had no experience and very little knowledge of how to set about their work' (Hist) (DD), 'Dispatch on the Far East by Brooke-Popham', 1 June 1942, CAB 120/518, PRO.

7 'DO-GOODERS' AND 'BAD MEN': CHURCHILL, ROOSEVELT AND RIVALRY
OVER EMPIRE

1. Davies to Gauss, 9 March 1943, Box 36, PSF, FDRL.
2. Stoler, 'The "Pacific-first" alternative', 432–52.
3. Thorne, *Allies of a Kind*, 131–2, 135.
4. Buell, *Master of Sea Power*, 170–3.
5. Barnett, 'Anglo-American Strategy', 186. I am grateful to James Gooding for this reference.
6. Louis, *Imperialism at Bay*, 5–6.
7. Thorne, *Allies of a Kind*, 161. See Brinkley and Facey-Crowther (eds.), *The Atlantic Charter*.
8. Howard, *Grand Strategy*, Vol. IV, chapter 1.
9. Thorne, *Allies of a Kind*, 149.
10. Brewer, *To Win the Peace*. This gap would not be filled until the end of 1945, when Bevin set out to project Britain 'positively' as a bastion of social democracy.
11. Thorne, *Allies of a Kind*, 221–3; Louis, *Imperialism at Bay*, 192–3, 196.
12. Entry for 12 April 1940, Colville, *Fringes of Power*.
13. A distinguished cast including: Sir Maurice Petersen and Henry Ashley Clarke (FO), Sir Eric Machtig (DO), Sir Derek Monteath (IO), Sir George Gater and Edward Gent (CO).
14. 'Post-war settlement in the Far East', FO record of an inter-departmental meeting, 10 September 1942, and minute by Coulson, 21 September 1942, in Ashton and Stockwell, *British Documents on the End of Empire*, Series A, Vol. I, Part I (hereafter *BDEE*), 179–84. Minutes of a meeting at the Foreign Office, 16 October 1942, L/P&S/12/4628, IOLR.
15. Louis, *Imperialism at Bay*, 37.
16. Thorne, *Allies of a Kind*, 145.
17. *BDEE*, Series A, Vol. I, Part I, xliii.
18. Minutes of a meeting between Churchill and Stalin (codenamed TOLSTOY), November 1944, FO 800/302, PRO (the original draft of the minutes of this meeting).
19. Entry for 13 July 1942, Dilks (ed.), *Cadogan Diary*; Goldstein, 'The British Official Mind', 76. Cf. T. H. Anderson, *The United States*, 85–6; Louis, *In the Name of God Go!*, 146.
20. Churchill's remarks reported in Martin to Harvey, 12 June 1942, F4097/2878/40,

FO 371/31866, PRO. This issue was brought directly to Churchill's attention as early as 25 November 1941. Amongst the decrypts selected for his personal attention was a message to Tokyo from the Japanese Ambassador in Bangkok. It advised that active Thai co-operation could be bought with the offer of border provinces, No. 098583, Bangkok to Tokyo, 25 November 1941, HW 1/303, PRO.

21. Brief by Ashley Clarke for Cadogan, 'Free Siamese', 22 November 1943, F6582/6582/61, FO 371/35935, PRO.

22. See (monitoring) summary of Bangkok radio broadcast 1230 GMT, 9 July 1943, in Far Eastern Bureau Intelligence Report No.9 17 July 1943, CO825/38/17, PRO.

23. Kamon Pensrinokun, 'Adaption and Appeasement', 151.

24. Maxwell to Gent, 'The Heel of Achilles', 15 March 1943, CO 825/35/55104/9/44. I am indebted to the Foreign Office for allowing me to consult this file which was not in the PRO when this study was being researched.

25. McKenown to Paskins, 25 February 1943, ibid.

26. Doll to Neimeyer, 22 February 1943, OV 65/3, Bank of England (BE).

27. Paskins memorandum on North Malaya policy, 11 May 1943, ibid. Edward Day, British Adviser at Perlis (1939–41) recounted accusations of 'harsh' Thai treatment of Muslims and of underdevelopment, minute, 18 September 1943, ibid.

28. Gent to Gayter, 1 June 1943 and Gayter minute, 5 June 1943, ibid.

29. Ashley Clarke to Paskins, 8 July 1942, ibid. The submission to the strategic planners was CO memorandum to Post Hostilities Planning Sub-Committee, RLM/RT/43/99, 26 November 1943, F29222/40, FO 371/35979, PRO.

30. Petersen minute, 3 December 1943, F6287/169/40, FO 371/35978, PRO.

31. Amery to Attlee, 25 January 1944, enclosed in DPM (44) 3, 9 February, W2166/1534/68, FO 371/42677, PRO.

32. FE (45) 29 Final, 'Policy Towards Siam', 14 July 1845, F4377/296/40, FO 371/46545, PRO.

33. *BDEE*, Series A, Vol. I, Part I, xxxi.

34. Brewer, *To Win the Peace*, 134.

35. Dallek, *Franklin D. Roosevelt*, 434, 511–13, 532–3.

36. Louis, *Imperialism at Bay, 3;* Sbrega, *Anglo-American Relations and Colonialism in East Asia*, 16–31; Bills, *Empire and Cold War*, 6–9.

37. Thorne, *Allies of a Kind*, 207, 217.

38. Drachman, *United States Policy*, 34–56.

39. Thorne, *Allies of a Kind*, 217. See also Welles, *Sumner Welles*.

40. Aldrich, *Key to the South*, 15–36; Hess, *The United States' Emergence as a Southeast Asian Power*, 1–46.

41. Thorne, *Allies of a Kind*, 209, 220.

42. Louis, *The British Empire in the Middle East*, 1–23.

43. Reynolds and Dimbleby, *An Ocean Apart*, 96–115.

44. Louis, Imperialism at Bay, 78–85, 259–73; Sherry, *Preparing for the Next War*, 41–7.

45. Thorne, *Allies of a Kind*, 147.

46. US Army intelligence summary, 26 February 1943, 740.0011 PW/3132 1/2, RG 59, USNA.

47. Buck, *American Foreign Policy in Asia*; Thorne, 'American Political Culture', 316–20.

48. Louis, *Imperialism at Bay*, 225–6.

49. Drachman, *United States Policy*, 58–72.
50. Thorne, *Allies of a Kind*, 217–18, citing OSS RA Report No. 719, 'Strategic Survey of Indochina', 4 March 1942, RG 59, USNA.
51. Louis, *Imperialism at Bay*, 29.
52. Thorne, *Allies of a Kind*, 142; Bills, *Empire and Cold War*, 9–10, 32–4; Dallek, *Franklin D. Roosevelt*, 419–21.
53. Discussion of Edmond Taylor in R. H. Smith, *OSS*, 34.
54. Donovan to Roosevelt, 19 December 1941, enclosing report by the British Empire section of COI, 'Burmese and the War', Donovan Papers (DP).
55. Thorne, *Allies of a Kind*, 158
56. Lauchlin Currie to Donovan, 23 October 1942, DP.
57. Louis, *Imperialism at Bay*, 70, 124, discussing OSS R&A Report No. 1972, 'British and American Views on the Applicability of the Atlantic Charter to Dependent Areas', 30 August 1944, Box 37, Harley Notter Files (State Department/Post-War Planning), RG 59, USNA.
58. OSS R&A Report No. 1972, 'British and American Views on the Applicability of the Atlantic Charter to Dependent Areas', Box 37, Notter Files, SD, cited in Louis, *Imperialism at Bay*, 124. Professor Louis argues that this report was 'an important study'.
59. Bills, *Empire and Cold War*, 32–3.
60. On general friction between OSS and the State Department see B. F. Smith, *Shadow Warriors*, 218–22; R. H. Smith, *OSS*, 25.
61. Conversation between Moffat and Landon (SD) and Hoffmann (OSS), 11 December 1944, 892.01/12–1144, RG 59, USNA; and 26 December 1944, 892.01/12–2644, ibid.; conversation between Holliwell, Scribner and Wilson of OSS; and Ballantine and Landon (DS), 26 January 1944, 892.01/46, ibid.
62. For example Baxter (Deputy Director OSS) to Atcheson (Div FE Affairs), 1 July 1942, 893.00/148671, reel 3, LM 65 RG 59 USNA; Langer (OSS R&A) to Atcheson, 19 January 1943, 893.00/14931, ibid.
63. Much of the Wilkinson diary, open for many years, was closed by the authorities in 1998.
64. 'Major Wilkinson . . . was very interesting', recorded Brooke after one such meeting, entry for 26 May 1942, Brooke Diary, Vol. 5, Brooke Papers, LHCMA.
65. 'Interview with Prime Minister', entry for 15 March 1943, Wilkinson Diary, 1/2, 2, CCC. Sir Charles Portal (CAS) was also present. See also entry for 12 May 1943, ibid.
66. Quoted in Thorne, *Allies of a Kind*, 266.
67. Entries for 16 and 17 May 1943, Wilkinson diary, CCC.
68. Entry for 22 March 1943, Wilkinson Diary, CCC.
69. Entries for 22, 25, 26 March, 8 April and 25 June 1943, Wilkinson Diary, CCC.
70. Wilkinson (London) to Dening (Melbourne), 4 June 1943, Box 1/4, Wilkinson papers, CCC.
71. OSS memorandum from Hughes to Shepardson, 'Colonel Wilkinson (British S.I.S.)', 15 September 1943, Folder 446, Box 46, Entry 106, RG 226, USNA.
72. It is not known why this originated as a Canadian operation but two of the six 'principals' were Norman Robertson and Thomas Stone of the Canadian Department of External Affairs, Wilkinson to Donovan, Shepardson and Stephenson, n.d. [October 1944?], DP. See also B. F. Smith, *Shadow Warriors*, 259.

73. Wilkinson (Room 3606) to OSS, 'Possible Flight of Chinese Capital from U.S. to South America', 15 December 1944, DP.
74. SIS directive to Wilkinson, n.d. (presumed late summer 1943), Box 1/4, Wilkinson Papers, CCC.
75. Wilkinson (BSC) to Sir George Sansom, 28 December 1944, Box 1/4, Wilkinson Papers, CCC.
76. Report by Wilkinson, 'Post War China Trade', 28 December 1944, Box 1/4, Wilkinson Papers, CCC.
77. Reports on China enclosed in Wilkinson to Oglivy (British Embassy), 7 and 9 March 1945, ibid.
78. Ibid.
79. Ibid. See also MI6 Political Report, 'Chinese Economic Policy', 5 July 1945, WO 208/474, PRO.
80. Baxter, 'Britain and the War in China', PhD, 334.
81. Minute by Young of a conversation with Major Guise of SOE London, 29 December 1943, F22/23/40, FO 371/41844, PRO. Taylor, however, was still attending the Foreign Office–SOE liaison meeting in mid-1944, see minutes of 30th FO-SOE meeting 13 June 1944, F2920/23/40, ibid.
82.. Sansom to Ashley Clarke, 19 January 1944, F540/23/40, FO 371/41844, PRO; minutes by Young, 20 January 1944, and Peterson, 21 January 1944, ibid. On the relationship between Hornbeck and Sansom see, Sansom file *passim*, Box 370, Stanley Hornbeck papers, HIWRP.
83. Minute by Peterson, F331/23/G, FO 371/41844, PRO.
84. Thorne, *Allies of a Kind*, 142; Sainsbury, *Churchill and Roosevelt at War*, 160–1.

8 AMERICAN INTELLIGENCE AND THE BRITISH RAJ: OSS AND OWI IN INDIA, 1941–1944

1. Downes, *Scarlet Thread*, 31.
2. Important insights are provided by Windmiller, 'Tumultuous Times', 105–24. See also R. H. Smith, *OSS*, 286–319 and Taylor, *Awakening from History*.
3. See Alexander (ed.), *Knowing Your Friends*.
4. Weinberg, *World at Arms*, 327, 1018 n. 34.
5. Thorne, *Allies of a Kind*, 233–9.
6. Donovan to Roosevelt, 'Memorandum for the President' No. 427, 20 April 1942, Donovan Papers. In 1986 Anthony Cave Brown very kindly allowed me to peruse some copies of Donovan material since deposited at the US Army War College and Churchill College Cambridge. This material was not then catalogued and is denoted hereafter by the abbreviation DP.
7. Donovan to Hull, 18 May 1942, enclosing 'Project to be undertaken by an established American business organization', Donovan-OSS file, Box 166, PSF, FDRL.
8. Welles to Donovan, 9 March 1942, DP. On Tagore's abortive visit to the United States see Hess, *America Encounters India*, 14.
9. Baxter (Deputy COI) to Acheson and Berle, 16 March 1942, 845.00/1310–1/2, RG 59, USNA; Baxter to Parker (Near East Div.), 3 April 1942, enclosing British Empire Section Situation Report No.6, 'Tentative Notes on the British War Cabinet's Proposals for India', 31 March 1942, ibid.

10. OSS RA Report 283, 14 May 1942, RG 59, USNA, and OSS RA Report 740, 27 May 1942, RG 59, USNA, quoted in Thorne, *Allies of a Kind*, 241.

11. Hess, *America Encounters India*, 33–54.

12. Kimball, *Churchill and Roosevelt*, Vol. I, 445, 448; Lamb, *Churchill as War Leader*, 198–201. See also Hess, *America Encounters India*, 51–3.

13. Clymer, 'Franklin D. Roosevelt', 261–84; Hess, *America Encounters India*, 81, 88.

14. On the importance of the press in the origins of the Cripps mission see Low, *Britain and Indian Nationalism*, 305, 330–9.

15. Record of a conversation with Major Rusk, British Empire Section MID, on Internal Security Situation in India, 15 June 1942, 845.20/113 PS/MEL, RG 59, USNA.

16. See for example Langer (OSS) to Jester (Near East Div.), 11 January 1943, 845.00/1768, RG 59, USNA.

17. Memorandum by Solbert for MacLeish (Assistant Director of OWI), 'Observations on the Relations of Anglo-Indian Policy to the Grand Strategy of the War in the Middle East', 22 September 1942, Frames 372–4, Reel 5, Part 1, OWI Microfilm series, BRO. On the State Department see, Hess, *America Encounters India*, 18.

18. MI6 Political Report to Foreign Office North American department, 27 March 1942, WO 208/792. On FIS and OWI see B. F. Smith, *Shadow Warriors*, 69–72, 93–4, and 118–20.

19. MI6 Political report to Foreign Office North American department, 27 March 1942, with attached FIS document, WO 208/792, PRO.

20. Donovan to Roosevelt, No. 242, enclosing a memorandum sent to Dr Conyers Read (OSS British Empire Section) by Dr Krishnalal Shridharani, 11 February 1942, DP.

21. Fischer to MacLeish (Assistant Director, OWI), 14 October 1942, Frame 396–7, Reel 5, Part 1, OWI Microfilm series, BRO. On the deployment of Raman by the British Ministry of Information see Hess, *America Encounters India*, 29–30.

22. Krishnalal Shridharani, *My India, My America*, (1941) and Schuster and Wint, *India and Democracy*, cited in Hess, *America Encounters India*, 29–31, 114, 116–17.

23. Butler (British Embassy) to MacLeish (Assistant Director OWI), 17 August 1942, Frame 337, Reel 5, Part 1, OWI Microfilm series, BRO, MacLeish to Butler, 19 August 1942, Frame 336, ibid.

24. OSS Washington to American Mission, New Delhi, 27 November 1942, 845.00/1736A PS/TL, RG 59, USNA. On R&A see Katz, *Foreign Intelligence*, 23–7.

25. Ranelagh, *The Agency*, 59.

26. Leach (San Francisco) to Chief of OSS MO Branch, 'Report on MO Radio Operations at Present and as Proposed in the Western Pacific', 4 June 1945, obtained from CIA under FOIA.

27. PWE report, 'Political Warfare in the US', FO 371/30725, PRO.

28. Hyde, *The Quiet Canadian*, 181–210.

29. PWE memorandum, 'Proposed Unit to Link American Far Eastern Political Warfare Operations Directed From Advanced Bases Overseas with British Operations Directed from New Delhi', 9 March 1943, enclosed in Oechaner (OSS) to Dono-

van, 31 March 1943, DP. Cf. Leahy to Welles (SD) 18 March 1943, Sansom File, Hornbeck Papers, HIWRP.

30. Memorandum by Coughlin (OSS SEAC), 'The Relation of OSS to the SEAC and India–Burma Theatre', 15 January 1945 (One Copy Only for the Personal Use of General Donovan), DP.

31. Senior officials within SEAC appear to have maintained their own separate registries, later subsumed in SEAC records (WO 203), as with Esler Dening, Mountbatten's Chief Political Adviser (CPA), see for example WO 203/5583 and 5585. CPA files suffered drastic weeding in the 1950s.

32. Entry for 12 December 1944, Colville (ed.), *Fringes of Power*.

33. Donovan to Gale (OSS Chungking), 9 April 1942, 845.01/162A, RG 59, USNA.

34. During Anglo-American–Dutch discussions in May 1941, all parties agreed to co-ordinate 'subversive activities in Japan and Japanese occupied territories' but no spheres were agreed at that time, Claude to Halifax, 13 May 1941, FO 115/3425, PRO.

35. 'Notes on Collaboration between British and United States S.O.E.', n.d. (presumed June 1942), File OSS Memoranda June–July 1942, Box 4, Preston Goodfellow Papers, HIWRP.

36. 'Record of a discussion regarding collaboration between British and American S.O.E.' (No. 2), conversation on Western and Central Europe between Goodfellow (OSS) and Gubbins, Taylor, Keswick and Pleydell-Bouverie (SOE), 19 June 1942, File OSS Memoranda June–July 1942, Box 4, Preston Goodfellow Papers, HIWRP.

37. 'Record of a discussion regarding collaboration between British and American S.O.E.' (No. 1), conversation between Goodfellow (OSS) and Garland Williams, Taylor and Keswick (SOE), 17 June 1942, File OSS Memoranda June–July 1942, Box 4, Preston Goodfellow Papers, HIWRP. OSS and SOE originally agreed on 'direction and instructions from London' and 'direct from Washington', with disputes being resolved in London and Washington rather locally, see 'Notes on Collaboration between British and United States S.O.E.', n.d. (presumed June 1942), ibid.

38. 'Record of a discussion regarding collaboration between British and American S.O.E.' (No. 3), conversation between Goodfellow (OSS) and Taylor, Glenconner, Pleydell-Bouverie and Keswick (SOE), 22 June 1942, File OSS Memoranda June–July 1942, ibid.

39. B. F. Smith, *Shadow Warriors*, 170–3; European Theatre of Operation, Strategic Services Officer War Diary, 'Relations with the British', 1 June 1945, p. 35, File: War Diary, Box 3, Entry 147, RG 226, USNA.

40. A variety of regional re-negotiations took place during early 1943, European Theatre of Operation, Strategic Services Officer War Diary, 'Relations with the British', 1 June 1945, p. 3, File: War Diary, Box 3, Entry 147, RG 226, USNA.

41. Phillips, *Ventures in Diplomacy*, 210–11.

42. In November 1942 he reported on the reception of Eleanor Roosevelt's recent official visit to England, including a summary of the enthusiastic comments of C [Sir Stewart Menzies], Phillips to FDR, 4 November 1942, OSS file, Box 53, PSF, FDRL.

43. Linlithgow to Amery, 17 February 1943, 478–S, WO 193/611, PRO. For an alternative view, that stresses the development of OSS in India as a development

of Stilwell, Davies and CBI politics, rather than Donovan's shadowing of Roosevelt's interests, see Maochun Yu, *OSS in China*, 112–14.

44. Minutes of a meeting held on 23 February 1943, L/WS/1/1346, IOLR.
45. Linlithgow to Amery, 19 March 1943, TH-42-S, ibid.; Linlithgow to Amery, 2 March 1943, L/PS/12/2754, IOLR; Linlithgow to Amery, 26 March 1943, ibid.
46. 'Relations Between US Officials in India and the Population', 21 July 1943, L/P&S/12/2754, IOLR.
47. COS to Washington, COS (W) 551, 2 April 1943, L/WS/1/1346, IOLR.
48. Halifax to London for Political Warfare (Japan) Committee, 4 April 1943, ibid.
49. Memorandum by MI2a, 'American Penetration in India', 3 May 1943, ibid.; minutes of a meeting held on 13 May 1943, ibid.
50. Ibid. On the earlier OSS–SOE agreement governing all theatres of June 1942 see COS (42) 327, 30 June 1942, CAB 80/65; also B. F. Smith, *Shadow Warriors*, 171.
51. Memorandum by Cawthorn, DMI (I), 'Washington Discussions on Anglo-US Intelligence Layout in India and CIB Commands', 3 June 1943, L/WS/1/1346, IOLR.
52. JSM Washington to War Cabinet Office, 5 June 1943, ibid.
53. 'Relations with the British', in Vol. I, Preamble, to 1 January 1943 (Directors' Office), pp. 18–20, File 248, Box 220, Entry 190, RG 226, USNA. See also entry for 16 July 1943, Cadogan diary, ACAD 1/12, CCC.
54. COS (43) 126th mtg (5), 12 August 1943, ibid. The text of the agreement is taken from COS to Washington, COS (W) 762, 12 August 1943, L/WS/1/1346, IOLR.
55. Amery to Linlithgow, 6 August 1943, ibid.
56. Minute by Cadogan, 12 August 1943, F4280/4280/61, FO 371/35931, PRO.
57. Entry for 30 September 1943, Cadogan diary, Cadogan papers, ACAD 1/12, CCC; entry for 12 January 1944, ACAD 1/13, ibid.
58. OSS memorandum, 'FETO Operations', 10 March 1944, File 515, Box 52, Entry 110, RG 226, USNA. See also Windmiller, 'Tumultuous Time', 107–8.
59. Thorne, *Allies of a Kind*, 355–6.
60. Memorandum by Davies, 'Anglo-American Cooperation in East Asia', 15 November 1943, File 317, Box 49, Entry 99, RG 226, USNA.
61. Interview with Ralph Block, General Representative in India for Overseas Operations of OWI, by J. N. Hess, May 1967, Oral History OH-30, HSTL.
62. Memorandum by Davies, 'Anglo-American Cooperation in East Asia', 15 November 1943, File 317, Box 49, Entry 99, RG 226, USNA.
63. Thorne, *Allies of a Kind*, 360.
64. Deignan (OSS Det 404) to Ripley, discussing conversation with Carter of OWI Delhi, 5 October 1944, File 2328, Box 133, Entry 154, RG 226, USNA.
65. Entry for 30 September 1943, P. Moon (ed.), *Wavell*; Thorne, *Allies of a Kind*, 360.
66. Dallek, *Franklin D. Roosevelt*, 419, 421; Hess, *America Encounters India*, 142–3; Thorne, *Allies of a Kind*, 476.
67. Hyde, *The Quiet Canadian*, 208–9.
68. Hull, *The Memoirs of Cordell Hull*, Vol. II, 1494–6.
69. British military intelligence investigated how the story had reached India so quickly despite heavily censored news cables, Donovan (Bombay) to SoS, 19 August 1944, 845.00/2–1944, RG 59, USNA; Van Zee (JICA), to US Military

Observer, 'Mr Phillips' Confidential Letter to the President', 4 September 1944, ibid.

70. Churchill to Eden, M931/4, 6 August 1944, AP20/12/433, Avon Papers, BUL.

71. Windmiller, 'Tumultuous Times', 114.

72. Hyde, *Quiet Canadian*, 208–9; Campbell to Butler (FO) 31 July 1944, AN3060/181/45, FO 371/38611, PRO; Halifax to FO No.5011, 114 September 1944, AN3521/18145, FO 371/38612, PRO.

73. Drew Pearson, *Washington Post*, 18 September 1944, reported in Goore Booth to FO, 22 September 1944, AN3703/181/45, FO 371/38613, PRO.

74. Security report on Major Altaf Qadir enclosed in Halifax to FO, 10 October 1944, AN4070/181/45, FO 371/38613, PRO; Hess, *America Encounters India*, 142–9.

75. 'General Donovan's Notes on India', dictated to Halliwell, 14 December 1943, DP. For a plethora of later OSS reports on the political situation in India see File 413, Box 43, and also Files 475–6, Box 48, Entry 106, RG 226, USNA.

76. Hess, *America Encounters India*, 92.

77. Hull to Roosevelt, 2 June 1944, India file, Box 55, PSF, Franklin D. Roosevelt Library, Hyde Park, New York. See also Merrell to Hull No.357, 19 May 1944, ibid.

78. American Consul, Bombay to SoS, No.1494, 'Interest of British Military Intelligence in the Activities of Foreign Government Representatives', 8 August 1944, 845.00/8–844, RG 59, USNA.

79. Entry for 19 August 1946, P. Moon (ed.), *Wavell*. On the transfer of this secret service see French, *Liberty or Death*, 195, 237, 259.

80. SRH-196, 'Reports on the Activities of Dr Marshall Stone in the China, Burma India Theaters, 19 January 1945–31 March 1945', RG 457, USNA.

81. E. P. MacDonald, *Undercover Girl*, 121.

82. Memorandum of a conversation between Rubenstein (OSS) and Cawthorn (DMI(I)), 'Establishment of an American Counter-Espionage Presence in India Command', 28 February 1944, File 515, Box 52, Entry 110, RG 226, USNA.

83. American Consul, Bombay to SoS, No.1494, 'Interest of British Military Intelligence in the Activities of Foreign Government Representatives', 8 August 1944, 845.00/8–844, RG 59, USNA.

84. Report on American activities in Bombay by O. C. Censor Station, 15 March 1943, and noted by Chief Censor India to DMI, 27 March 1943, WO 208/816, PRO. This extraordinary document ran to 87 pages for the Bombay area.

85. Phillips to SoS, 7 May 1943, 845.711/16, RG 59, USNA.

86. The only surviving material produced by the Chinese Intelligence Wing is contained in the file F3473/3473/10, FO 371/41680, PRO. See for example CIW report G/35/83, 26 April 1944, offering information on currency issues based on 'intercepts', including letters between the Military Liaison Office of the US Naval Attachés Office in Chungking and private addresses in Honolulu, ibid. See also Helliwell (Chief SI, OSS, CT) to Donovan, 'A Study of British Intelligence Organisations in China', 13 February 1945, DP. A later draft is available at File 1573, Box 497, Entry 190, RG 226, USNA.

87. Interview with Ralph Block, General Representative in India for Overseas Operations of OWI, by J. N. Hess, May 1967, Oral History OH-30, HSTL.

88. Major Roger A. Pfaff had been Acting Head of the small X-2 presence in India.

89. Rubenstein had also served with US Army Air Intelligence (A-2), and joined

OSS X-2 at its formation in August 1943, 'Personal Report to William J. Donovan from Lt Colonel Sidney S. Rubenstein, X-2 Branch', 1 September 1944, DP.
90. 'Establishment of American C.E. Personnel in India Command', 28 February 1944, signed by Cawthorn and Rubenstein, Box 52, Entry 110, RG 226, NARA. I am indebted to Timothy Naftali for a copy of this document.
91. The key individuals are not named for legal reasons, memorandum from HH/001 (OSS SEAC) to Saint, 'Possible Penetration of OSS at Calcutta', Report No.14, 6 May 1944, DP. See also 'Personal Report to General William J. Donovan from Lt Colonel Sidney S. Rubenstein', 1 September 1944, DP.
92. X-2's informants included other OSS personnel who worked in the separate and more secure OSS Calcutta communications building, memorandum from HH/001 (OSS SEAC) to Saint, 'Mabel Wong', Report No.15, 6 May 1944, DP.
93. Memorandum from HH/001 (OSS SEAC) to Saint, 'Possible Penetration of OSS at Calcutta', Report No. 14, 6 May 1944, DP.
94. This is a sanitised document, Memorandum for the President, 'Report by Colonel Richard Park on OSS in War', n.d., File OSS/Donovan Feb.–Dec. 1945, Box 15, Rose Conway Files, HSTL. For a discussion of the Park Report see Andrew, *President's Eyes Only*, 156–7.
95. Extract from 'Survey of Foreign Intelligence Activities Directed Against Indian Security', 24 July 1944, L/P&S/12/2324, IOLR.
96. Tharp, *White Chinese*, 473–5. I am indebted to E. Bruce Reynolds for this reference.
97. Windmiller, 'Tumultuous Times', 112; O. J. Caldwell, *Secret War*, 123–30.

9 STRANGE ALLIES: BRITISH INTELLIGENCE AND SECURITY IN INDIA, 1941–1944

1. E. Taylor, *Richer by Asia*, 163.
2. On Ceylon see C. in C. East Indies Fleet to Admiralty, 2 July 1942, PWTM, India, 91–2. On the formation of ABDA see 'Draft Directive to Supreme Commander in ABDA Area', US ABC-4/5, 30 December 1941, American–British JCS File, Box 1, PSF, FDRL.
3. JIC (42) 7 (0), 'General Wavell's Command Intelligence Arrangements', 2 January 1942, attached to COS (42) 3, CAB 79/17, PRO.
4. Entries for 13 January, 6 and 15 February 1942, Bond (ed.), *Chief of Staff*.
5. Wavell to War Office, 21 January 1942, *PWTM*, Vol. II, 122. Field had taken over from Grimsdale as Deputy Head of FECB in late 1941.
6. 'ABDACOM HQ', note in diary of Lt General Pownall, 3 December 1941–7 March 1942, Pownall Papers, LHCMA; 'ABDACOM: An Official Account of Events in the SWPC, January–February 1942', by General Staff India, p. 78, ABCD Folder, Box 1, PSF, FDRL.
7. Note by Sir Frank Nelson (SOE) annexed to COS (42) 82 (0), 'SOE Organisation in the Far East', 31 March 1942, L/WS/1/1296, IOLR.
8. It was while on a reconnaissance to Baghdad that Mackenzie heard Roosevelt's radio speech announcing the Pearl Harbor attack, interview with Colin Mackenzie, London, 31 March 1985.
9. SOE memorandum, 'Formation of the India Mission', 1 December 1945, HS 1/203, PRO.
10. SOE memorandum, 'Foundation of the India Mission', 1 December 1945, HS 1/

203, PRO. On 'G(R)' and 'MIR' activity in the Caucasus and Trans-Caspia, see C. in C. Middle East to WO, 30 June 1941, PWTM, Vol. I, Middle East, 105.

11. Glass, *Changing of Kings*, 184–5; Sweet-Escott, *Baker Street Irregular*, 228. Interview with Brigadier Sir John Anstey (Deputy Director of SOE Far East), Southwell, 25 May 1999.

12. Louis, *In the Name of God Go!*, 126.

13. Interview with Colin Mackenzie, London, 31 March 1985.

14. Viceroy to SoS for India, 28 June 1942, L/WS/1/1296, IOLR; Hambro (SOE) to Watson (WO), 10 June 1942, ibid.

15. Hauner, *India in Axis Strategy*, 120.

16. Thorne, *Allies of a Kind*, 356.

17. Hauner, *India in Axis Strategy*, 244.

18. Louis, *In the Name of God Go!*, 170.

19. Entry for 23 February 1945, Colville (ed.), *Fringes of Power*.

20. SRH-196, 'Reports on the Activities of Dr Marshall Stone in the China, Burma, India Theaters, 19 January 1945–31 March 1945, RG 457, USNA.

21. Wavell to COS, 13 November 1942, *PWTM India*, 1940–3, 42.

22. Memorandum from McDonough (OSS Delhi) to Schofield, 'Delhi Enquiry', 21 July 1944, File 1079, Box 104, Entry 144, RG 226, USNA.

23. Amery to Churchill, 13 July 1942, Mansergh (ed.), *Transfer of Power*, Vol. II, 376.

24. JIC (42) 141, 'Japanese Intentions', 18 April 1942, and JPS (42) 413, 'Indian Ocean – Strategy in Certain Eventualities', 18 April 1942, attached to COS (42) 125, CAB 79/20, PRO. See also Butler, *Grand Strategy*, Vol. III, Pt. 2, 486–8.

25. Hauner, *India in Axis Strategy*, 535–6, 545; Cawthorn (DMI India) memorandum, 'The Future of the Internal Security Situation in India', 31 August 1942, WO 208/805, PRO.

26. OSS Report from India, 'The Present National Crisis', UA-X01030, 13 December 1943, File 476, Box 48, Entry 106, RG 226, USNA.

27. IO to Simpson (DDMO(O)), 20 March 1943, L/WS/1/1337, IOLR. This file offers a clear picture of the security crisis.

28. Hauner's unique work, *India in Axis Strategy*, is inexplicably ignored by French, *Liberty or Death*.

29. Taylor, *Richer by Asia*, 161–6.

30. Wilmott, *Empires in the Balance*, 441–7.

31. SOE memorandum, 'Formation of the India Mission', 1 December 1945, HS 1/203, PRO.

32. Memorandum by Mackenzie, 'Communist Party in India', 26 August 1942, HS 1/212, PRO.

33. Interview with Colin Mackenzie, London, 31 March 1985.

34. See for example memorandum by Wood (SOE), PB.2894, 27 September 1944, HS 1/204, PRO. For an alternative version see Cruickshank, *SOE*, 87.

35. Hauner, *India in Axis Strategy*, 102, 104.

36. Ibid., 410–14, 491; Gordon, *Brothers against the Raj*, 456–62; Singh, *Soldiers' Contribution*, 67–95; Toye, *The Springing Tiger*, 182–8; Lebra, *Jungle Alliance*, 16–32.

37. Lewin, *The Other Ultra*, 216–17; Hauner, *India in Axis Strategy*, 487; Weinberg, *World at Arms*, 1018, n.32.

38. Wavell to WO, 13 December 1942, L/WS/1/897, IOLR. MI8 had already been dispensing advice on illegal transmitters to the Government of Burma, see memorandum of detection of illegal transmitters enclosed in Lambert (MI8) to Burma Office, 4 March 1941, L/WS/1/522, IOLR.

39 Lt Col Russell (Broadway Buildings), to Lockhart, summarising discussions with Colonel Vickery (IPI), 8 March 1943, L/WS/1/897, IOLR.

40. Creedy to Monteath (IO), D 563/24, 19 April 1943, L/WS/1/897, (WS15136), IOLR.

41. Fay, *Forgotten Army*, 294–304; Hauner, *India in Axis Strategy*, 593–4, 609–10; Durrani, *The Sixth Column*, 245–368, Singh, *Soldiers' Contribution*, 182–204. Interview with Colonel Hugh Toye, British Army investigator, INA, Oxford, 3 July 1986.

42. Entry for 13 January 1945, Ziegler (ed.), *Personal Diary*.

43. Durrani, *The Sixth Column*, 245–368. Interview with Colonel Hugh Toye, British Army investigator, INA, Oxford, 3 July 1986.

44. Interrogation Report, 'Japanese Agents', 5 May 1944, File 2357, Box 134, Entry 154, RG 226, USNA.

45. Rees, *The Nazis*, 87.

46. Its *long-term* ideological impact has been more profound, cf. the Indian RSS.

47. The definitive study is Popplewell, *Intelligence and Imperial Defence*. See also T. G. Fraser, 'India in Anglo-Japanese Relations', 366–82.

48. French, *Liberty or Death*, 234; Hauner, *India in Axis Strategy*, 59, 132, 150, 167–8.

49. Hazelton, 'Soviet Foreign Policy during the initial phase of the war', PhD, 1989, 182.

50. Hauner, *India in Axis Strategy*, 316–17, 331.

51. Cripps (Moscow) to London, 5 August 1941, L/P&S/12/1778, IOLR; MI2 memorandum, 2 October 1941, L/P&S/12/1774, IOLR.

52. Cripps (Moscow) to FO, 2 August 1941, L/P&S/12/544, IOLR; note by LD to Silver (IPI), 9 August 1941, ibid.

53. Hauner, *India in Axis Strategy*, 334–8, 420, 481, 555–6; Gordon, *Brothers Against the Raj*, 418, 423–31, 432, 451.

54. Ismay to Gubbins (SOE), 10 November 1943, CAB 120/827, PRO.

55. Anglo-Soviet intelligence co-operation is well chronicled in B. F. Smith, *Sharing Secrets with Stalin* and Kitchen, 'SOE's Man in Moscow', 95–109, but these works are light on the crucial Asian dimension.

56. Fay, *Forgotten Army*, 465–72; Hauner, *India in Axis Strategy*, 587–8. After 1943 one in eight soldiers in the Wehrmacht was a citizen of the Soviet Union.

57. Ba Maw, *Breakthrough in Burma*, 194; Vichit Vadhakarn, *Thailand's Case*, 21–46.

58. Thompson, *Make for the Hills*, 87–91.

59. Foot, *SOE in France*, 129, quoted in Callahan, *Churchill*, 88–9. See also Callahan's commentary, 127.

10 SECRET SERVICE AND MOUNTBATTEN'S SOUTH EAST ASIA COMMAND

1. He added that this was especially true of SIS, Browning to de Wiart, 23 February 1945, WO 203/6451, PRO.

2. Thorne, *Allies of a Kind*, 166.
3. Mountbatten to Wedemeyer, 6 May 1945, F3492/11/61, FO 371/46307, PRO.
4. Memorandum by Dening, 'Political Review of Events in the S.E.A.C. during 1943–44', n.d., WO 203/5624, PRO.
5. Ibid.; entry for 19 October 1943, Ziegler (ed.), *Personal Diary*.
6. Linlithgow to Amery, 1 June 1943, L/WS/1/1274, IOLR.
7. COS (43) 294 (0), memorandum by CIGS, 'Re-organisation of Command in South East Asia', 7 June 1943, ibid.
8. Stafford, *Churchill*, 273.
9. Entry for 6 October 1943, Ziegler (ed.), *Personal Diary*.
10. Winterbotham, *The Ultra Secret*, 170–1.
11. Entry for 28 October 1943, Somerville diary, 2/2, Somerville Papers, CCC.
12. Entry for 11 December 1943, Somerville Diary, File 2/2, Somerville Papers, CCC.
13. Layton to Cunningham (CNS), 7 February 1944, Cunningham Papers, MSS 52571, BL.
14. Entry for 12 November 1943, Ziegler (ed.), *Personal Diary*.
15. Entry for 13 November 1943, Somerville diary, 2/2, Somerville Papers, CCC. See also entry for 12 March 1944, ibid.
16. Postscript to diary written in London, January 1945, Pownall Papers, LHCMA.
17. Pyman to Dempsey, 29 October 1945, 5/1, Pyman papers, LHCMA.
18. Entry for 7 August 1945, Alanbrooke Diary, Vol. I, Alanbrooke Papers, LHCMA.
19. Roberts surveys the critics and then joins them, *Eminent Churchillians*, 55–136. But this attack lacks context; for example, he quotes Brooke's acerbic diary on Mountbatten without mentioning that he was equally critical of Pownall, Giffard and Slim.
20. He continued: 'But, alas, we shall never know what confidential orders his Lordship carries from Mr Churchill designed to inhibit his natural vigour.' Memorandum by Davies, 'Anglo-American Cooperation in East Asia', 15 November 1943, File 317, Box 49, Entry 99, RG 226, USNA.
21. Buell, *Master of Sea Power*, 396–7.
22. Mountbatten's Chief of Staff at this time was General 'Boy' Browning, OSS Det 404, Monthly Report for January 1945, Heppner, File 309, Box 48, Entry 99, RG 226, USNA.
23. Mountbatten to Roosevelt, 28 March 1944, C205, Mountbatten papers, SUL.
24. Report of 220 Military Mission, April 1944, A–7236–1, by Brigadier Lethbridge, Lethbridge papers. See also Annex G 'Notes on Irregular Forces in the Solomon Islands', ibid. I am indebted to Mrs K. Lethbridge for permission to make use of these papers. They are now deposited at LHCMA.
25. OSS memorandum, 'SI Plans for China and South East Asia', 6 October 1943, OSS file, Box 6, PSF, FDRL.
26. Little (Det 404) to Stevens (OSS Washington), 23 February 1944, File 510, Box 51, Entry 110, RG 226, USNA.
27. Memorandum of a conversation between Moffat, Landon and Mani Sanasen, 27 July 1944, 892.01/7–2744, RG 59, USNA.
28. Ibid.
29. Memorandum of conversation between Mani Sanasen and Landon, 21 August 1944, 892.01/8–2144, RG 59, USNA. Mani Sanasen skilfully played all sides.

During his visit to SOE in London in 1943 he had handed over all his copies of minutes of meetings with OSS and OWI, see Mani Sanasen to Guise (SOE), 27 October 1943, HS 1/72, PRO.

30. Sweet-Escott, *Baker Street*, 240.
31. Donovan to Roosevelt, 27 October 1944, October 1944 file, Box 169, PSF, FDRL.
32. Marr, *Vietnam 1945*, 268–9; Thorne, 'Indochina', 90–1; La Feber, 'Roosevelt, Churchill and Indochina', 1291–2.
33. Hurley to Roosevelt, 2 January 1945, China 1945 File, Box 11, Map Room File, FDRL; memorandum from China, President-Hurley 1944–45 File, Box 38, PSF, ibid.
34. Memorandum by Bishop, 'Alleged British Desire for a Federation in South East Asia', 12 June 1944, enclosed in Buell to Hull, 12 June 1944, 846C.00/6–1244, RG 59, USNA.
35. 'Solon' to Donovan, Memo No. 60 'Routing of Political Intelligence', 18 November 1944, File 3473, Box 250, Entry 146, RG 226, USNA.
36. Eden to Halifax, 29 January 1945, F626/127/61, FO 371/46325, PRO.
37. Sbrega, *Anglo-American Relations*, 107.
38. Thorne, 'Indochina', 84–5.
39. For the alternative view asserting that there was no such conspiracy see Dills, *Empire and Cold War*, 73 and also Thorne, *Allies of a Kind*, 604.
40. Seymour to Sterndale Bennett, 12 December 1944, F214/127/61, FO 371/46325; minute by Scott, 13 January 1945, ibid.
41. JIC (43) 118, 'Collection of Civil Intelligence About Malaya', 16 March 1943, attached to COS (42) 70, CAB 79/26, PRO.
42. Amery to Dorman-Smith, 13 May 1943, 215/3, Dorman-Smith Papers, MSS EUR.E215, IOLR.
43. Amery to Dorman-Smith, 7 July 1943, 215/3, ibid.
44. Amery to Attlee, 1 June 1943, L/WS/1/1274, IOLR.
45. PWE London memorandum, 'Introductory Note on Far Eastern Political Warfare' (draft), n.d. [mid 1944], HS 1/210, PRO; Taylor, *Richer by Asia*, 83–5.
46. Minutes of a meeting of the Chiefs of Staff (India), 22nd mtg, 21 May 1943, L/WS/1/1346, IOLR.
47. Note by Jacob discussing a memorandum by Churchill, WP (43) 253 (Revised), 'The Organisation of Command for South East Asia', 1 July 1943, CAB 120/697, PRO.
48. Memorandum of a conversation between Edmond Taylor (OSS SEAC) and Thompson, 18 September 1944, DP.
49. Memorandum by Dening, 'Political Review of Events in the S.E.A.C. during 1943–44', n.d., WO 203/5624, PRO.
50. 'Directive from Supreme Commander to All Quasi-Military and Irregular Forces in the South East Asia Theatre', 18 December 1943, File Donovan memoranda, Vol. IV, Box 1, Entry 180, RG 226, USNA.
51. Shaw (CBI) to OSS (CBI), 373.2, 26 December 1943, DP.
52. Dill (JSM Washington) to War Cabinet, 6 November 1943, F5914/4022/23, FO 371/35968, PRO.
53. Minute by Ashley Clarke, 8 November 1943, F5914/4022/23, FO 371/35968, PRO; Ashley Clarke to Hollis (COS), 10 November 1943, ibid.

54. Mountbatten to COS, 9 November 1943, F5915/4022/23, FO 371/35968, PRO.
55. Memorandum by Dening, 'Political Review of Events in the S.E.A.C. during 1943–44', n.d., WO 203/5624, PRO.
56. Dening to War Cabinet, 6 September 1944, WO 106/4475, PRO. Mountbatten clearly spoke with Gubbins at Cairo, O'Brien, *The Moonlight War*, 124–5. On Donovan's attendance at Cairo and Teheran see Smith, *OSS*, 258–9. Neither Donovan nor Gubbins were captured in the photographs of these conferences.
57. Mountbatten to Wedemeyer, 30 March 1943, Annex B, 'Report to the Combined Chiefs of Staff by the Supreme Allied Commander South East Asia', L/MIL/17/5/4271, IOLR.
58. Sweet-Escott, *Baker Street*, 233.
59. Before the arrival of Garnons-Williams in late December 1943, a pre-P Division was chaired by Esler Denning and had a steering committee of Keswick, Edmond Taylor and an SOE staff officer, Edmond Taylor (SEAC) to Buxton (OSS Washington), 30 November 1943, File 2556, Box 193, Entry 139, RG 226, USNA.
60. Churchill had written: 'Finally I propose that the number of American agencies in India, such as the Office of Strategic Services (OSS), the Office of War Information (OWI), the Federal Communications Board (FCC), and the Bureau of Economic Warfare (BEW), shall be taken into the orbit of the Supreme Commander', memorandum by Churchill, COS (43) 314 (0), 'Organisation of Command in South East Asia', 17 June 1943, L/WS/1/1274, IOLR.
61. Pownall noted that it was inauspicious that Cawthorn had been responsible for the Middle East Intelligence Centre 1939–41, since now in Cairo 'things were in such a state that they recently had to ask for an "expert" to come out from London and tell them what to do', entry for 12 November 1943, diary of Lt General Pownall, Pownall Papers, LHCMA.
62. The directive that OSS employed in these discussions was CCS 319/5, on which see memorandum from Heppner (OSS SEAC) to Donovan, 'Co-ordination of O.S.S. Activities in SEAC', 12 November 1943, File 46, Box 205, Entry 190, RG 226, USNA.
63. OSS New Delhi to 154 (Washington), 16 November 1943, File 3473, Box 250, Entry 146, RG 226, USNA.
64. Memorandum by Armour (OSS SEAC) for Bruce (OSS London), 'Communications Agreement for SEAC', 17 December 1943, DP. See also McBaine (OSS Middle East) to Donovan, 26 November 1943, DP. Separate OSS codes allowed some freedom of expression. The Japanese were codenamed 'Paranoids' or 'Manics', the British were 'Liverish' or 'Gastritis', the French were 'Schizos' and the Dutch 'Squares'. The Americans, however, were 'Hep Cats'. See 'Special Code to be Used in Communication with Heppner and Davies', attached to memorandum by Schofield, 'Informal Report on Detachment 101', 13 March 1944, DP.
65. Lowman (OSS Washington) to Donovan, 3 August 1944, DP.
66. Each retained their own ciphers. Memorandum by Garnons-Williams for OSS, SIS and SOE, 'Wireless Communications', P/1847, 7 November 1944, DP.
67. Entry for 11 October 1943, Ziegler (ed.), *Personal Diary*.
68. Garnons-Williams to Donovan, 7 February 1944, DP.
69. Only the P Division minutes of the 72nd–77th meetings (6 August–10 September

1945) are available in WO 203/1801, while the remainder are closed in WO 203/ 1800. However, the minutes of the 38th–77th meetings are available in AIR 23/ 2137 and 2138. Curiously it is minutes of the 70th–77th meetings that are withheld in Washington, in File 10, Box 20, Entry 110, RG 226, USNA.

70. Edmond Taylor to Donovan, 7 July 1944, Mhe-49, DP.
71. Minute by Jonas (RAF), 29 January 1944, AIR 23/2136, PRO.
72. Middle East Defence Committee to Foreign Secretary, Minister of Economic Warfare and Chiefs of Staff, 21 February 1942, PWTM, Vol. II Middle East, 21.
73. Entries for 15 November 1943 and 3 December 1943, Somerville diary, 2/2, Somerville Papers, CCC.
74. Entries for 2 January 1944, 6 January 1944, 18 January 1944, 24 January 1944, 1 June 1944, Somerville diary, 2/2, Somerville Papers, CCC.
75. OSS SEAC History, Section IV, 'Recruiting and Training', n.d., File 678, Box 49, Entry 146, RG 226, USNA.
76. He continued: 'With this sort of information it will be possible to land OGs [Operational Groups] at selected points with the mission of not only exfiltrating desirable people but also with the additional mission of liquidating others, such as Jap Divisional Commanders and the like.' Heppner, Chief of OSS SEAC, to Donovan, 18 July 1944, File 510, Box 512, Entry 110, RG 226, USNA.
77. OSS SEAC History, Section IV 'Recruiting and Training', n.d., File 678, Box 49, Entry 146, RG 226, USNA.
78. Director of Intelligence (D of I) (SEAC)'s 8th mtg, 10 August 1944, AIR 40/ 2443, PRO.
79. Caldwell (OSS SEAC) to Little, 'Conversation with Colonel Blunda, Director of SEATIC', 22 February 1945, File 1097, Box 104, Entry 144, RG 226, USNA.
80. SEATIC was commanded by the American Colonel Blunda. Japanese POWs who were particularly good sources of information were sent on to the Red Fort in Delhi for further interrogation, along with any captured INA. See memorandum by Deak (OSS Det 404), 'Mahara Examination Center, Ceylon', 18 July 1945, File 2694, Box 159, Entry 154, RG 226, USNA.
81. OSS SEAC Report, 'Interrogation and Assessment of Ma Hem (. . . now interned at Mahara)', by Dwight H. Bulkey, 17 April 1945, File 520, Box 37, Entry 148, RG 226, USNA.
82. A file of Mahara intelligence reports is at File 2694, Box 159, Entry 154, RG 226, USNA.
83. D of I (SEAC)'s 7th mtg, 8 July 1944, AIR 40/2443, PRO.
84. D of I (India) to D of I (SEAC), DMI/6937, 16 August 1944, ibid. Also private information.
85. The facilities were also to be shared by DIB India, 105 to Donovan, No. 16043, 31 July 1944, DP; Lovell (OSS R&D) to Donovan, 2 August 1944, DP.
86. George Taylor (SOE London) to Gibbs (SIS London), 9 August 1944 enclosing 'Directive for Dr Higgins: Joint Scientific Laboratory in Calcutta', HS 1/227, PRO; SOE memorandum, 'Dr Higgins of ISLD', 25 April 1945, ibid.
87. Entry for 1 June 1944, Alanbrooke diary, Vol. 9, Alanbrooke Papers, LHCMA.
88. Bills, *Empire and Cold War*, 71. Also 'Save England's Asiatic Colonies', R. H. Smith, *OSS*, 286.
89. Mountbatten to Donovan, 26 June 1944, C89, Mountbatten papers, SUL; Coughlin to Mountbatten, 11 May 1945, ibid; Mountbatten to Gubbins, 26 June

1944, C112, ibid. Even Mackenzie, who had enjoyed more freedom under GHQ India, conceded that through P Division Mountbatten had really exercised a lot of control and it had worked 'pretty well', interview with Colin Mackenzie, London, 31 March 1985.

90. Edmond Taylor (OSS SEAC) to Donovan, 7 July 1944, MHE-159, DP.
91. Edmond Taylor to Donovan, August 1944, DP.
92. Donovan to Stephenson (BSC), 24 October 1944, and Donovan to Gubbins (SOE), 18 October, enclosing copies of Edmond Taylor (P Division) to Donovan, 30 August 1944, DP.

11 SPECIAL OPERATIONS IN SOUTH EAST ASIA

1. Coughlin (OSS SEAC) to Dick [Heppner] (OSS China), 2 June 1945, File 20, Box 20, Entry 110, RG 226, USNA.
2. Cruickshank, *SOE*, 192–3: Cross, *Red Jungle*, 19–37.
3. Estimates of the numbers executed vary widely from 6,000 to 40,000, Cheah Boon Keng, *Red Star Over Malaya*, 20–23.
4. For correspondence between the Colonial Office and SOE on personnel see HS 1/211, PRO, *passim*. F.S. Chapman, *The Jungle is Neutral*, 27–8.
5. SOE report, 'Oriental Mission Operations in Malaya', 8 May 1942, HS 1/115, PRO.
6. Cheah Boon Kheng, *Red Star Over Malaya*, 73–5; Cruickshank, *SOE*, 195–99. Cruickshank has erroneously rendered Chin Peng as Chen Ping.
7. Memorandum by the Head of the SOE Malaya Country Section, 15 August 1945, WO 203/4403, PRO. Lai Tek was denounced by the British as a Japanese informer in November 1945 and fled to Bangkok taking a large quantity of MCP funds. He was assassinated there by an MCP team in 1947. Private information.
8. Memorandum to Garnons-Williams, 1 September 1945 G3/10/1/4821 enclosing 'The AJUF in Malaya' and 'The History of British Left Behind Parties in Malaya, Dec. 1941–May 1945', Vol. II, Garnons-Williams papers, IWM.
9. Ibid.
10. Memorandum by Gent (CO) to Williams, 'A Programme of Detailed Projects for SOE', 55104/1/43, 19 November 1943, WO 106/4720, PRO.
11. Minutes of a meeting held in the Colonial Office, 13 June 1944, HS 1/115, PRO; B/BT to BB.100, 14 June 1944, HS1/115, PRO. See also minutes of a meeting between Gent and Guise, 9 November 1944, ibid.
12. Note by Colonial Office, 7 February 1944, HS 1/115, PRO.
13. Solon (OSS Det 404) to Lilly, 4 May 1944, File 2713, Box 160, Entry 154, RG 226, USNA.
14. Memorandum by Jane Foster (OSS SEAC) to Scofield, 'Jukebox', 10 October 1944, File 1088, Box 105, Entry 144, RG 226, USNA.
15. Heppner (OSS SEAC) to Donovan enclosing OSS SEAC Progress Report, 28 December 1943, File 300, Box 49, Entry 99, RG 226, USNA.
16. Taylor to Garnons-Williams and Donovan, 30 August 1944, DP. The matter of *Jukebox* and *Oatmeal* is recounted in detail in Scofield to Heppner, 3 November 1944, and Heppner to P Division 26 October 1944, Donovan materials, Vol. XIII, Box 3, Entry 180, RG 226, USNA.
17. Collated records from April 1945 are in AIR 23/2148, PRO.

18. See HQ Strat. AF to HQ ACSEA, 18 September 1944, complaining that SIS had admitted they had no P Division authorization for Operation *Bramble*, AIR 23/2136, PRO.
19. Dening to Loxley and Sterndale Bennett, 30 December 1944, HS 1/211, PRO.
20. Heppner (OSS SEAC) to Donovan, 1 November 1944, enclosing OSS SEAC Report for October 1944, File 306, Box 47, Entry 99, RG 226, USNA.
21. Sigex Kandy to Donovan No. 24273, 30 October 1944, DP.
22. Heppner (OSS SEAC) to Donovan, 1 November 1944, enclosing OSS SEAC Report for October 1944, File 306, Box 47, Entry 99, RG 226, USNA. *Oatmeal* was transformed into a successful deception operation by Colonel Peter Fleming of Deception Division and Brigadier P. G. Bowden-Smith of SIS. See Trenowden, *Operations Most Secret*, 159–62.
23. Summary of a telegram from Chapman Walker (SOE Australia) to SOE London and SOE India, 1 April 1944, F1686/100/23, FO 371/41796, PRO.
24. O.C. Anglo-Dutch Country Section to C. in C. Netherlands Forces Far East, 6 June 1945, HS 1/268, PRO.
25. Heppner (OSS SEAC) to Donovan, 1 August 1944, enclosing OSS SEAC Report for July 1944, File 303, Box 47, Entry 99, RG 226, USNA.
26. Memorandum of a conversation between Edmond Taylor and Read, DP.
27. Solon (Det 404) to Lilly, 4 May 1944, File 2713, Box 160, Entry 154, RG 226, USNA.
28. JCS Memorandum 258, Appendix I, 'OSS Reconnaissance off Sumatra', 29 June 1944, File 1556, Box 494, Entry 190, RG 226, USNA.
29. Heppner to Donovan, OSS SEAC Report for May 1944, File 301, Box 47, Entry 99, RG 226, USNA; Cruickshank, *SOE*, 147–9.
30. Vandenbosch to Ripley, 'Obstacles to Cooperation with Dutch and British', 19 September 1944, File 2728, Box 160, Entry 154, RG 226, USNA.
31. Scofield to Ripley, 'Vandenbosch Memorandum', 21 September 1944, File 2728, Box 160, Entry 154, RG 226, USNA.
32. Minutes of a meeting between George F. Taylor and Donovan, enclosed in Sheridan to Sterndale Bennett, 3 February 1945, F803/738/40, FO 371/46560; minutes of SAC's 3rd mtg, 29 January 1945, and Appendix 1, 'Meeting Between Heads and Representatives of Clandestine Services of GB and USA', 29 January 1945, File 510, Box 51, Entry 110, RG 226, USNA.
33. OSS SEAC report, January 1945, File 309, Box 48, Entry 99, RG 226, USNA.
34. Cf. pp. 228–9.
35. Cruickshank, *SOE*, 204–5.
36. Foreign Office memorandum, 'Anglo-American Relations in the Far East', n.d. [presumed June 1944], WO 203/5606, PRO. This is Dening's key 'demi-official file'.
37. Cruickshank, SOE, 104–5; Gilchrist, *Bangkok Top Secret*, 43–55.
38. Private information.
39. Deignan to Ripley, 'Trip to India', 5 October 1944, File 2328, Box 133, Entry 154, RG 226, USNA.
40. Cruickshank, SOE, 109–10, Puey Ungphakorn, *A Siamese*, 263–5, Reynolds, 'Opening Wedge', 329–31.
41. Eden minute, 2 May 1944, F2156/23/40, FO 371/41844, PRO. The story of SOE's pressure for a declaration is in FO 371/41844–5 *passim*.

42. WC Conclusions 89 (44) 11, 10 July 1944, F3360/23/40, ibid.; Young minute, 21 July 1944, ibid.
43. Mountbatten to Eden (and Gubbins) 21 August 1944, and Eden minute 5 September, F3941/23/40, FO 371/41845, PRO. See also Cruickshank, *SOE*, 109–10.
44. Cruickshank, *SOE*, 112–13.
45. E. B. Reynolds, 'Opening Wedge', 328–50 is the outstanding treatment of OSS and Thailand. On Japanese visions see E. B. Reynolds, *Thailand and Japan's Southern Advance*.
46. OSS SEAC report, January 1945, File 309, Box 48, Entry 99, RG 226, USNA.
47. Ballantine memorandum, 'Thai Provisional Government in Exile', 31 January 1945, 892.01/1–3145, RG 59, USNA.
48. Dolbeare to Donovan, 16 November 1941, 892.51/231 1/2, RG 59, USNA.
49. OSS Situation Report, 'Thailand – Current Developments', 11 December 1944, File 483, Box 49, Entry 106, RG 226, USNA.
50. Interview with Taylor conducted by Conyers Read in Norman Brown's office, 21 September 1944, DP.
51. HQ Strategic Air Force, I-B Theatre to HQ ACSEA, SAF/TS/73/3/1/AIR, 18 September 1944, AIR 23/2136, PRO.
52. Debrief of Heppner (OSS SEAC) by Warner, 23–5, File 515, Box 52, Entry 110, RG 226, USNA.
53. Ibid.
54. Ibid., 27–9. See also minute by Jonas, Chief Intelligence Officer, ACSEA, entitled '357 and 358 (Special Duty) Squadrons Policy', 29 January 1944, minute 17, AIR 23/2136, PRO.
55. Bishop to SoS, 9 January 1945, 892.01/1–945, RG 59, USNA.
56. Memorandum of a conversation between Hutchinson, Deignan and Garden (OSS), and Moffat and Landon, 18 January 1945, 892.01/1–1845, RG 59, USNA.
57. Dening to FO, 28 August 1944, DO 35/1624, PRO.
58. Conversation with Mackenzie reported in Coughlin to Donovan, 21 February 1945, File 20, Box 20, Entry 110, RG 226, USNA.
59. Donovan to Roosevelt, 19 December 1941, enclosing report by the British Empire section of COI, 'Burmese and the War', DP.
60. Donovan to Lauchlin Currie (Administrative Assistant to the President), 21 October 1942, DP.
61. 'Psychological Warfare Division', Annex 7, *Report to the Combined Chiefs of Staff by the Supreme Allies Commander South East Asia*, L/MIL/17/5/4271, IOLR.
62. Entries for 29 November 1944 and 20 February 1945, Ziegler (ed.), *Personal Diary*.
63. Cruickshank, *SOE*, 166–7.
64. Ibid., 71.
65. Sweet-Escott, *Baker Street*, 235.
66. 'SOE Memorandum on Operations in the Rangoon and Bassein Delta', 18 December 1943, DP.
67. Somerville to Cunningham (CNS), 27 October 1943, Somerville Papers, 8/2, CCC.

68. Entry for 22 April 1943, Alanbrooke diary, Vol. 5, Alanbrooke Papers, LHCMA.
69. T. Moon, *Grim and Savage Game*, 40–1, 55, 61.
70. Hilsman, *American Guerrilla*, 120–1, 124.
71. Ibid., 137, 187.
72. Lee (OSS) to Donovan, 20 October 1943, DP.
73. Dorman-Smith to Amery, 25 March 1943, 215/4, Dorman-Smith Papers, MSS EUR.E215, IOLR.
74. Mackenzie to Mason (GHQ India), 18 December 1942, WO 106/6092, PRO.
75. Davies to Donovan, 6 October 1943, File 2548, Box 193, Entry 139, RG 226, USNA.
76. History of Force 136 in Burma, CAB 101/198, PRO.
77. Minutes of P Division, 38th mtg, 6 November 1944, AIR 23/2137, PRO.
78. Information was passed through their mutual friend Joseph Alsop, see Alsop to 'Bill', 5 December 1943, DP.
79. 'Relations with the British and Other Allies', Vol. I Preamble to 1 January 1943, Director's Office, p. 27, File 248, Box 220, Entry 190, RG 226, USNA.
80. Marr, *Vietnam 1945*, 86.
81. Drachman, *United States Policy*, 37–9.
82. Record of the Teheran Conference quoted in Hicks, 'Tension at the High Table and Operational Politics', MA, 18.
83. Hoover (FBI) to Attorney general, 13 December 1944, 'Colonel Andre de Wavrin, alias Colonel Andre Passy', File France 1944–5, Box 42, PSF, FDRL; Stafford, *Churchill*, 206.
84. Donovan to Roosevelt, 6 April 1945, File Donovan-OSS, Box 167, PSF, FDRL. See especially Rifkind, 'OSS and Franco-American Relations', 62–5, 267.
85. Halifax to FO, 18 January 1944, F360/66/61 FO 371/41723, PRO; PHP Committee Report on South East Asia, 24 June 1944, U5911/748/G70, FO 371/40740, PRO.
86. Churchill to Eden, 12 January 1944, F223/66/61, FO 371/41723, PRO
87. Bills, *Empire and Cold War*, 73–4
88. In 1943 SOE tried some Chinese agents loaned by Tai Li, and also some Vietnamese communists, but without success, Marr, *Vietnam 1945*, 305–5, Cruickshank, *SOE*, 12–15, 121–6.
89. de Gaulle to Guiaut, 12 February 1942, F1948/582/61, FO 371/31771, PRO; CFR (42) 3rd mtg 17 April 1942, and Guinness (SOE) to Broad, 17 April 1942, F3075/582/61, ibid; Coudrais to de Gaulle, 12 June 1942, F4454/582/61, ibid; Seymour to FO, 1 July 1942, F4596/582/61, ibid.
90. M. Thomas, 'Free France', 146; Marr, *Vietnam 1945*, 39.
91. Interview with Colin Mackenzie, Special Forces Club, London, 31 March 1985.
92. M. Thomas, 'The Massingham Mission', 696–721.
93. For example Colonel C. D. Roberts (DSO Syria) to Colonel Maunsell (SIME HQ Cairo), 17 March 1943, File 81, Box 19, Entry 120, RG 226, USNA.
94. Sbrega, *Anglo-American Relations*, 105.
95. M. Thomas, 'Free France', 153; M. Thomas, 'Silent Partners', 8.
96. Churchill to Eden, 21 May 1944, quoted in M. Thomas, 'Free France', 151–2.
97. For details see 'Brief History of Clandestine Operations in the SEAC Theatre of War, 1 June 1944–31 May 1945', AIR 23/1950, PRO. Accounts of these

operations are also given in Decoux, *A la barre de l'Indochine*, 306–9, and in Sainteny, *Histoire d'un Paix Manquée*, 73.

98. Interview with Taylor by Conyers Read in Norman Brown's office, 21 September 1944, DP.
99. Guise to D of I, 19 July 1944, HS 1/102, PRO; AD to CD, SOE report on Operation BELIEF, 31 July 1944, HS 1/85, PRO; Taylor to Donovan, 30 August 1944, DP; Patti, *Why Vietnam?*, 29–33.
100. Taylor to Donovan, 25 July 1944, DP.
101. Taylor to Garnons-Williams and Donovan, 30 August 1944, DP.
102. Grew to SoS and attached 'Memorandum for the President', and minutes, 27 July 1944, File: Indochina 13.103 Political. French Participation in Liberation, Box 9, PSA records, RG 59, USNA.
103. The full account in Dunn, *First Vietnam War*, 67–111, is well researched but has a particular slant.
104. Entry for 28 October 1944, Ziegler (ed.), *Personal Diary*.
105. The Mountbatten–Wedemeyer dispute has been discussed at length by Thorne in *Allies of a Kind*, 626–30, and also in Thorne 'Indochina and Anglo-American Relations', 73–96. An alternative analysis is offered by Dunn in *First Vietnam War*, 105–18.
106. Dening to FO, 6 September 1944, WO 106/4475, PRO.
107. La Feber, 'Roosevelt, Churchill and Indochina', 1290–1.
108. Churchill minute, 28 October 1944, F5016/66/61, FO 371/41724, PRO.
109. Halifax to Eden, 10 January 1945, F790/11/61, FO 371/46304, PRO.
110. Dening to FO, 12 January 1945, F586/11/61, ibid.
111. Dening to Mountbatten, 30 December 1944, WO 203/4398, PRO.
112. Ibid.; minutes of SAC's 3rd Misc. Mtg, 29 January 1945, and Appendix 1, 'Meeting Between Heads and Representatives of Clandestine Services of GB and USA', 29 January 1945, File 510, Box 51, Entry 110, RG 226, USNA.
113. Record of a meeting between the Heads and Representatives of the Clandestine Services of GB and USA, 29 January 1945, File 510, Box 51, Entry 110, RG 226, USNA.
114. 'Incidents Involving SD Aircraft', 19 February 1945, AIR 23/3595, PRO.
115. Harcourt Smith to Whitworth-Jones, 22 February 1945, MB1/C42/66/4, Mountbatten papers, SUL.
116. Spector, 'Allied Intelligence', 45–7; Dunn, *First Vietnam War*, 87–8.
117. Short, *The Origins of the Vietnam War*, 58–60; Evans, *The Times*, 29 October 1986; O'Brien, *The Moonlight War*, 106–7.
118. Anstey (SOE), 'Force 136 – short term plan for FIC', 19 March 1945, HS 1/321, PRO.
119. Marr, *Vietnam 1945*, 276.
120. Entry for 20 February 1945, Ziegler (ed.), *Personal Diary*.
121. Cruickshank, *SOE*, 126–31; Dunn, *First Vietnam War*, 86–9.
122. Churchill minute to Eden, 13 February 1945, F989/11/61, ibid.
123. COS (45) 71st mtg (7), 19 March 1945, CAB 79/30, PRO. See also JIC (45) 91 (0), 'French Resistance in Indochina', 18 March 1945, ibid.; and JIC (45) 105 (0) Final, 'French Indochina', 30 March 1945, CAB 79/31, PRO.
124. Wilson to COS, FMW 16, 10 March 1945, WO 106/3579. On the BJSM see Danchev, *Very Special Relationship*.

125. Wilson to COS, 18 March 1945, WO 106/3483, PRO.
126. Secretary COS to FO, 5 March 1945, annexed to COS (45) 59th mtg (3), 5 March 1945, CAB 79/30, PRO.
127. Selborne to Churchill, 19 March 1945, F1702/11/61, FO 371/46305, PRO.
128. Churchill to Roosevelt, 20 March 1945, F1714/11/61, ibid.; US JCS to FO, 8 April 1945, F2358/11/61, ibid.
129. Draft memorandum by Wilson, 'Suggested Solution for Special Operations in Indochina', 5 June 1945, CAB 122/1177, PRO; Dunn, *First Vietnam War*, 104–18.
130. Memorandum by Fleischmann (OSS Det 404) to Ripley, 'Recruitment of Bodies at Mahara', 9 October 1944, File 2706, Box 160, Entry 154, RG 226, USNA.
131. Ten of these were thought suitable for OSS operations, the rest were employed as cooks and camp servants, Meade (OSS SEAC) memorandum, 'Chinese Prisoners at Mahara', 26 September 1944, File 80, Box 5, Entry 168, RG 226, USNA.
132. Memorandum from Caldwell (OSS (MO) SEAC) to Little, 'Conversation with Colonel Blunda, Director of SEATIC', 22 February 1945, File 1097, Box 105, Entry 144, RG 226, USNA.
133. Taylor, *Awakening from History*, 349–51.
134. Stafford, *Churchill*, 274.

12 THE BRITISH SECRET INTELLIGENCE SERVICE (MI6) IN THE FAR EAST

1. Debrief of Edmond S. Taylor by Conyers Read, 21 September 1944, DP.
2. E.g. Z. Steiner, 'Deception and its Dividends', *Times Literary Supplement*, 7 December 1990, 1,310. For a superb synthesis of intelligence and the European War see Bennett, *Behind the Battle*.
3. There are notable exceptions at the level of field operations. On Malaya see Trenowden, *Operations Most Secret*, 123–46. SIS also makes appearances in Terence O'Brien's partly autobiographical *The Moonlight War*.
4. Amongst the official historians of British intelligence the exception is Michael Howard who has included Japan in his volume on deception, *British Intelligence*, Vol. V.
5. This release is described in Atherton, *SOE Operations in the Far East*.
6. The classic account is Andrew, *Secret Service*, 339–447.
7. Ibid., 467.
8. Cecil, 'C's War', 170–89.
9. The classic work on SOE remains Foot, *SOE in France*. On SOE–SIS rivalry see Stafford, *Britain and the European Resistance*, 85–7, 205–6.
10. On Garnons-Williams see Cruickshank, *SOE*, 88, 171.
11. Steveni to Baker, Ops/34, 17 March 1944, AIR 23/7679, PRO.
12. Steveni, 'From Empire to Welfare State', 18/4-5, TSS memoir, Steveni papers.
13. Crombie (IO) to Collier (FO), 4 October 1939, L/P&S/12/308, IOLR; Steveni memorandum, 'Recent Events in Eastern Europe (through Soviet eyes)', 26 September 1939, L/WS/1/99, IOLR. The Soviet Export Department which contained many of Steveni's long-term contacts was based at Melbourne House, Aldwych, London.
14. Comments on the COS appreciation 'Russian Threat to India', 2 October 1939, L/

WS/1/99, IOLR. This file is entitled 'Misc. Reports Prepared by Major Steveni'.

15. Steveni (MI6), CX37065/1/186, to Ridsdale (MI2c), 12 February 1941, WO 208/895, PRO.

16. See for example Lt Colonel Steveni (MI6) to MI2e, CX.65400/349, 25 June 1941, WO 208/1900, PRO; Lt Colonel Steveni (MI6b) to MI2c, CX.37400/577–9, 1 September 1941, WO 208/254, PRO; Lt Colonel Steveni (MI6b) to MI2c, CX.28037/666, 19 October 1941, ibid.

17. Steveni, 'From Empire to Welfare State', 21/12, TSS memoir, Steveni papers. In early 1943 Denham was hoping to be made 'Inspector of our Australian organisation' in view of his good knowledge of Java. SIS Australia was then working into the Netherlands East Indies with Dutch co-operation. Entry for 19 March 1943, Wilkinson diary, 1/2, 2, CCC.

18. The other staff officers working under Steveni at new Delhi included: Lt Colonel Rankin in charge of training, Major Van Millingen in charge of correlation of intelligence, Major Cox in charge of communications and Major Candler who liaised with the services, OSS New Delhi to 154 (Washington) 16 November 1943, File 3473, Box 250, Entry 146, RG 226, USNA.

19. The local cover-names for clandestine organisations proliferated throughout the war. For ease of comprehension the term SIS has been retained throughout this chapter.

20. See for example Beddington, Baroda House, Delhi, to Jones (London) concerning allocation of additional temporary and local ranks to SIS personnel, 6 January 1944, WO 203/6383, PRO.

21. Steveni, 'From Empire to Welfare State', 21/15, TSS memoir, Steveni papers. For example of GHQ-inspired operational intelligence gathering in Burma see memorandum by Steveni to Cawthorn, 'Operation 'Buzzard – No. 40', Ops/40, 26 October 1943, AIR 23/7682, PRO.

22. Entry for 7 and 9 July 1943, Wilkinson diary, 1/2, 2, CCC.

23. See for example the acrimonious discussions between Churchill, Eden, Selborne and the COS at DO (43) 7th mtg, 2 August 1943, AIR 8/1749, PRO.

24. Mountbatten, writing to the COS in December 1943, welcomed the transfer of nine battered Catalinas from West Africa for special duties, but stood firm against the use of Liberator bombers for this sort of work, 22 December 1943, AIR 23/2132, PRO.

25. Steveni to Jonas (RAF), 17 August 1943, AIR 23/7678, PRO. See also Lalaltol (SIS) to Jonas (RAF), 3 June 1943, ibid.

26. Steveni (SIS) to Jonas (RAF), 23 December 1943, AIR 23/7679, PRO.

27. Coleman memorandum, 'Clandestine Air Operations: A Brief History of Operations in South East Asia, 1 June 1942–31 May 1945', AIR 23/1950, PRO.

28. Minutes of P Division, 43rd mtg, 9 January 1945, AIR 23/2137, PRO.

29. See for example the letter concerning the loss of two Special Duties aircraft sent by Steveni to Baker (RAF), 17 March 1944, AIR 23/7679, PRO.

30. He continued: 'With this sort of information it will be possible to land OGs [Operational Groups] at selected points with the mission of not only exfiltrating desirable people but also with the additional mission of liquidating others, such as Jap Divisional Commanders and the like.' Heppner to Donovan, 18 July 1944, File 510, Box 512, Entry 110, RG 226, USNA.

31. See for example the claims made for 3 Mahara detainees by Wing Commander

Perkins of SIS recorded in minutes of P Division 50th mtg, 5 March 1945, AIR 23/2137, PRO.

32. Remarks of Colonel Tollemache (SOG) and Major Ferguson (SIS) in minutes of P Division, 51st mtg, 12 March 1945, AIR 23/2137, PRO.

33. Memorandum by Brigadier Walsh (CGS ALFSEA), 'Clandestine and Special Organisations in ALFSEA', Appendix B ISLD, April 1945, WO 203/55, PRO.

34. Slim, *Defeat Into Victory*, 191–2.

35. Lamplough (D of I SEAC) to Cavendish-Bentinck (JIC London), 1 October 1944, WO 203/5606, PRO.

36. BGS (I) to BGS (O), 23 October 1944, WO 203/367, PRO.

37. Deputy BGS (I) Main HQ to BGS GS (I), 17 November 1944, ibid.

38. Account of meeting held at Barrackpore, 4 January 1945, ibid.

39. While there is no evidence of a connection between this and Barrackpore, this issue had caused irritation at a high level in London. On the sacking of Slim see Lewin, *Slim*, 237–47.

40. These early combined operations in late 1944 included attaching the SIS agent 'Mint' to the SOE party 'Carpenter' detained for Malaya; attaching the 'Buffin' SIS party to the SOE party 'Spiers' in Burma; and combining the SIS party 'Aggressive' with the SOE sponsored Gaullist party 'Belief' in Indochina. On this see OSS SEAC memorandum, 'Comments on SIS–SOE Relationships', 12 October 1944, File 3473, Box 250, Entry 146, RG 226, USNA.

41. Letter of introduction for Commander Skyrme (SIS) from Air Vice-Marshal Whitworth Jones (SEAC) to Air Marshal Sir Guy Garrod (ACSEA), 20 September 1944, AIR 23/7678, PRO. See also 628 SD to Strategic Air Force (BAFSEA) 225 Grp, 3 October 1944, ibid.

42. Beddington also held some responsibilities for liaison between SIS and SOE, Kennedy (DMO) to Menzies, 21 October 1942, WO 193/624, PRO.

43. Wilkinson observed that Beddington did not want to be far removed from the post-war opportunities of Europe when Germany was defeated, while Wilkinson himself was about to escape to Washington DC, entries for 7 and 9 July 1943, Wilkinson diary, 1/2, 1, CCC.

44. Record of a conversation with 'Little Bill' Stephenson of British Security Co-ordination of New York, entry for 4 May 1944, Wilkinson diary, 1/2, 2, CCC. Wilkinson observed privately in his diary: 'How stupid and worthless of Brigadier B. to get himself and our organisation in this useless mess.' See also conversation with Colonel Charles Ellis, entry for 4 April 1944, ibid. Also Steveni, 'From Empire to Welfare State', 21/30, TSS memoir, Steveni papers.

45. Beddington, *My Life*, 286–7, TSS memoir, LHCMA. C.f. Harrison, 'More Thoughts', 514–25.

46. Garnons-Williams to Mackenzie and Bowden-Smith, 16 April 1945, HS 1/304, PRO.

47. Mackenzie to Garnons-Williams, 19 April 1945, HS 1/304, PRO. Mackenzie's superiors in Baker Street were aware of his attempts at aggrandisement and on 21 April he warned them that Bowden-Smith had instructions from his own superiors at Broadway Buildings 'which practically prohibits their collaboration with us on our terms or any sensible terms' adding that this 'will result in them doing nothing', to A.D. Personal from B/B 100, No.256, 21 April 1945, ibid.

48. Memorandum, 'Summary of I.S.L.D. Reports', 8 September 1945, HS 1/210, PRO.
49. See for example the report on a chemical warfare factory in Thailand at CX.37200/65/7859, 25 July 1945 to MI6b, WO 208/2238, PRO.
50. Bowden-Smith to Garnons-Williams, 25 April 1945, HS 1/304, PRO.
51. Appendix 'I.S.L.D. Intelligence Analysis', 24 April 1945, ibid.
52. JIC (45) 17, 'Allocation of Personnel with Knowledge of Far Eastern Languages', 14 January 1945, WO 220/52, PRO.
53. Garnons-Williams to Mackenzie and Bowden-Smith, 28 April 1945, HS 1/304, PRO. For examples of SIS control of signals intelligence see for example S. G. Menzies, Chairman of the Y Board, to Secretary of State for India, 16 May 1942, enclosing 'Reorganization of the ''Y'' Services in India and Ceylon', Broadway SW1, 7 May 1942, L/WS/1/897, IOLR.
54. Meeting on Co-ordination of Clandestine Operations in South East Asia between Mackenzie, Bowden-Smith and Garnons-Williams, 10 May 1945, HS 1/103, PRO.
55. Minutes of a meeting held at HQ Force 136, 24 April 1945, HS 1/103, PRO.
56. Memorandum from Mackenzie to Head of P Division, 'Subject: S.R.', 13 April 1945, HS 1/80, PRO. This document has been sanitised by the removal of one of its thirteen paragraphs.
57. Minutes of a meeting on SA and SR plans and commitments held with Force 136 and ISLD at HQ Force 136, 15 May 1945, File G425/3499, Quai d'Orsay, Paris. I am indebted to John W. Young for permitting me to see a copy of this document.
58. Mackenzie informed SR that its initial plan to insert groups of six agents was wrong and smaller groups were more appropriate for intelligence gathering, minutes of a meeting held at Kandy chaired by Mackenzie, 19 April 1945, to discuss SA and SR plans, File G 123, ibid. I am indebted to John W. Young for permitting me to see a copy of this document.
59. Minutes of a meeting held at ISLD on 8 August 1945 between DGER, Force 136 and ISLD, HS 1/95, PRO.
60. Dening to Cavendish-Bentinck (JIC), 11 May 1945, WO 203/5625, PRO.
61. SIS Calcutta to London, 12 July 1945, WO 203/4472, PRO.
62. Debrief of Edmond S. Taylor (OSS SEAC) by Read, 21 September 1944, DP.
63. By 1945 many had become accustomed to the luxury of signals intelligence which arrived in 'real time'. By contrast, even when SIS secured valuable agent intelligence from Japanese occupied countries, it was often regarded as too tardy to be reliable. In August 1945 Captain Eric Northcott of SIS in London forwarded a recent report on railway destruction in Malaya to MI2, who noted that this material was nearly a month old, adding that if this material had been current it would be of real importance. But now it needed further confirmation. Northcott (MI6b) to MI2, CX 37400/63/331, 3 August 1944 (information dated 18 July 1945), and minute by Mitchell of MI2, 14 August 1945, WO 208/1539, PRO.
64. See for example JCS 1969/33, 'Command Relationship of CINCFE with CIA After Cease Fire and Armistice in Korea', 13 October 1952, 385 (6–446), Sec.49 SC Files, RG 218, USNA.
65. A great deal of ISLD reports were made available to the SI branch of OSS, see Dr Dillon Ripley to Washington, 31 May 1944, File 301, Box 47, Entry 99, RG 226, USNA.

66. Payne (SIS) at a meeting held at the Air Ministry, 4 January 1945, AIR 20/7968, PRO.
67. HW1; NID 12 memorandum entitled 'B.J. Series of Diplomatic Messages', n.d. (presumed c. 8 October 1945), ADM 223/298, PRO; 'Report on S.I. Volume 2904–2930', NID 12, 8 October 1945, ibid.
68. General Penney (D of I SEAC) noted that Garnons-Williams was now so nervy that he 'just can't stand being alone', Penney to Mrs Penney, 28 June 1945, 4/20, Penney papers, LHCMA.
69. See for example the remark: 'Stringent security measures were requested by ISLD which resulted in no official RAF record of this operation being kept', in 'Clandestine Air Operations: A Brief History of Operations in South East Asia, 1 June 1942–31 May 1945', prepared by Squadron Leader Coleman, AIR 23/1950, PRO.
70. One of these officers was Commander Ian Fleming, entry for 13 July 1943, Wilkinson diary, 1/2, 2, CCC.

13 CENTRE AND REGION: THE POLITICS OF SIGNALS INTELLIGENCE

1. Muggeridge, *The Infernal Grove*, 128.
2. See for example K. Brown, 'The Interplay of Information and Mind', 109–32.
3. On this general revolution see Weinberg, *World at Arms*, 544–57.
4. Stripp, *Codebreaker in the Far East*, 14–15; B. F. Smith, *Ultra–Magic Deals*, 98–9. On Denniston and Room 40 see, Beesly, *Room 40*, 43–5.
5. Lewin, *The Other Ultra*, 132–3.
6. 'An Official History of the United States Naval Group, China', unpublished typescript, n.d., File China, US Naval Group, Box 5, Preston Goodfellow Papers, HIWRP.
7. NID Vol. 42, 'Far East and Pacific', III, 'Special, Special and the War with Japan' (by R.T.B.), ADM 223/297, PRO. I am indebted to Ralph Erskine on this issue.
8. SRH-012, 'The Role of Radio Intelligence in the American-Japanese War', RG 457, USNA.
9. Rusbridger, 'The Sinking of the Automedon', 8–15.
10. N.I.D. Vol. 42, 'Far East and Pacific', III, Special, Special and the War with Japan (by R.T.B.), ADM 223/297, PRO. See also Denham, 'Bedford–Bletchley–Kilindini–Colombo', 270–1.
11. Gilbert and Finnegan (eds.), *U.S. Army Signals Intelligence in World War II*, 5–6. See also Naval Intelligence History, HW 4/25, PRO.
12. B. F. Smith, *Ultra–Magic Deals*, 105–8.
13. Report by Burnett, 'Co-operation of British and Radio Intelligence', 7 April 1943, NID Vol. 42, 'Far East and Pacific', II, Special, ADM 223/297, PRO.
14. This important early treaty is sometimes called the Holden Agreement and sometimes the Birch/Travis Agreement. Erskine, 'The Holden Agreement'; B. F. Smith, *Ultra–Magic Deals*, 127; Benson, *History*, 60.
15. Material was exchanged using the secure but time-consuming Typex cipher machine, Denham, 'Bedford–Bletchley–Kilindini–Colombo', 269.
16. Report by Burnett, 'Co-operation of British and Radio Intelligence', 7 April 1943, NID Vol. 42, 'Far East and Pacific', II, Special, ADM 223/297, PRO. On Tiltman see Winterbotham, *The Ultra Secret*, 14.

17. Minute by COS 9 April 1943, on 'Co-operation of British and US Radio intelligence', in Report by Burnett, NID Vol. 42, 'Far East and Pacific', III, Special, ADM 223/297, PRO.
18. 'Special and the War with Japan' (by R.T.B.), ADM 223/297, PRO.
19. B. F. Smith, *Ultra–Magic Deals*, 113–14, 125–6; Gilbert and Finnegan (eds.), *U.S. Army Signals Intelligence in World War II*, 5–8; Lewin, *The Other Ultra*, 112–16.
20. Benson, *History*, 97–122; for the full text of BRUSA see *Cryptologia* 21, 1 (1997), 30.
21. But see Drea, *MacArthur's ULTRA* and Prados, *Combined Fleet Decoded*.
22. Drea, MacArthur's ULTRA, 1–32; Benson, *History*, 85–90.
23. 'Central Bureau (CB)', in SRH 349, RG 457 USNA; Ballard, *On Ultra Active Service*, 144–6; B. F. Smith, *Ultra–Magic Deals*, 107–8; Lewin, *The Other Ultra*, 181–3.
24. Elphick, *Far Eastern File*, 414; Weinberg, *A World at Arms*, 554–5.
25. Powell, *War by Stealth*, 182.
26. Drea, *MacArthur's ULTRA*, 223, 230; Lewin, *The Other Ultra*, 148–51.
27. The US Army Signals Intelligence Service changed its name continually, ending up as the Army Security Agency. Gilbert and Finnegan (eds.), *U.S. Army Signals Intelligence in World War II*, 5–7.
28. The British DMI, General Davidson, offered a fascinating sidelight on the status of university academics in this work. He noted a confrontation with his opposite number, the American G-2, Brigadier General Short, over the German OB. Davidson stuck to his guns, explaining: 'I was confident that our estimates were right, partly because the head of our O of B section was a wizard – Major (later Lt Colonel) Eric Birley OBE. He was Professor of Archaeology in Durham University; but his life hobby had been the study of the O of B of the Roman legions, in which field he had proved himself an absolute master when he joined our excellent German Section just before the war started'. Part 1, 'The History of the "Integration" of USA and UK Intelligence in World War II', Davidson papers, LHCMA.
29. B. F. Smith, *Ultra–Magic Deals*, 140–2.
30. Ibid., 149–52; Taylor, 'Anglo-American signals intelligence co-operation', 71.
31. Memorandum for McCloy, 'Personnel Situation of Special Branch, M.I.D.', 23 October 1943, SRH 141–2, RG 457, NARA.
32. Bamford, *The Puzzle Palace*, 315.
33. 'Draft Agreement for Co-ordination of British and American Intelligence on the Japanese Army and Navy Air Forces', signed by Strong (G-2) and Inglis (ACAS(I)), 30 September 1943, G-2 Intelligence Group Files, 1943–7, RG 165, USNA.
34. Gilbert and Finnegan (eds.), *U.S. Army Signals Intelligence in World War II*, 9–10. B. F. Smith, *Ultra–Magic Deals*, 154–5, 171–3. As Smith shows, BRUSA did not address work against the non-service enemy or of neutral traffic.
35. McCormack, 'Origin, Function and Problems of the Special Branch, M.I.S.', 15 April 1943, SRH 116, RG 457, USNA. McCormack added: 'We have had enough to do with the British to have discovered that there is a considerable amount of intelligence which they withhold from us, not especially by design, but because we do not ask for it.'

36. Bamford, *The Puzzle Palace*, 314–15.
37. Lewin, *Ultra Goes to War*, 254–5.
38. Winterbotham, *The Ultra Secret*, 170–1.
39. A small D/F site had existed near Anderson since July 1942. NID Vol. 40, 'Far East and Pacific, I, History', by Hillgarth and Barrett, ADM 223/297, PRO. For explanations of JN 11, 25 and 40 see Denham, 'Bedford–Bletchley–Kilindini–Colombo', 277–9.
40. NID Vol. 42, 'Far East and Pacific', III, Special, Special and the War with Japan (by R.T.B.), ADM 223/297, PRO. See also Denham, 'Bedford–Bletchley–Kilindini–Colombo', 273–4.
41. NID Vol. 42, 'Far East and Pacific', III, Special, Special and the War with Japan (by R.T.B.), ADM 223/297, PRO.
42. Entry for 24 November 1943, Somerville diary, 2/2, Somerville Papers, CCC.
43. Entry for 8 December 1943, ibid.
44. Entry for 13 December 1943, ibid.
45. Entry for 17 March 1944, ibid.
46. Entries for 2 and 6 January 1944, ibid.
47. Entry for 18 January 1944, ibid.
48. Entry for 2 February 1944, ibid.
49. B. F. Smith, *Ultra–Magic Deals*, 180–6.
50. For an excellent account see Maochun Yu, *OSS in China*, 38–40.
51. On Japanese sigint see Chapman's penetrating articles, 'Signals Intelligence Collaboration', 231–56 and 'Japanese Intelligence', 145–90.
52. FO to Delhi and Clark Kerr, 9 February 1942, L/P&S/12/2316, IOLR; Seymour (Chungking) to FO, 8 March 1942, ibid; FO to Washington (for Codrington), 12 March 1942, ibid.
53. Entry for 15 October 1943, Ziegler (ed.), *Personal Diary*.
54. Entry for 11 June 1944, Somerville diary, 2/2, Somerville papers, CCC.
55. Memorandum by Lamplough (DMI SEAC), 'Visit of Chinese DMI to Delhi', DMI/9215, 16 August 1944, WO 203/291, PRO.
56. Eden to Churchill, PM 44/286, 27 April 1944, AP20/11/285, Avon Papers, BUL.
57. Weinberg, *World at Arms*, 1065, n. 59.
58. Andrew, 'The Making of the Anglo-American SIGINT Alliance', 95–109. Considerable quantities of decrypted French traffic for 1945 survive in the papers of James Byrnes. I am most grateful to Geoffrey Warner for drawing this to my attention.
59. B. F. Smith, *Ultra–Magic Deals*, 189. The sanitised references in SRH-196, 'Reports on the Activities of Dr Marshall Stone in the China Burma India Theaters, 19 January 1945–31 March 1945', RG 457, USNA, probably refer to the interception of Chinese traffic, see for example 019.
60. Memorandum by Cornwall-Jones, British Joint Services Mission (BJSM) to McFarland, 'Security of Chinese Cyphers', No. 503/CJ, 18 April 1945, DP. See also COS (45) 100th mtg (8), 14 April 1945, discussing JIC 45 135(0), Limited Circulation, 'Insecurity of Chinese Cyphers', CAB 79/32, PRO.
61. Coughlin reported that Navy Group China was the culprit and that 'the cost of this compromise runs into millions', Coughlin to Donovan, 2 March 1945, DP.
62. Wavell to WO, 30 September 1941, fol.4, L/WS/1/897, IOLR; memorandum 'IE Cypher Machine' from Nicholls (MI8) to McCoy, ibid.

63. Hinsley, Thomas, Ransom and Knight, *British Intelligence*, Vol. I, 10, 408, 424–5.
64. Memorandum to JIC by DMI, 'Expansion of "Y" Service in India', 20 October 1941, L/WS/1/897, IOLR. This firm assertion by the DMI that Britain was still working on Soviet material at end of October 1941 contradicts the view of the official historian that Britain ceased this following the German attack on the Soviet Union on 22 June 1941, Hinsley, Thomas, Ransom and Knight, *British Intelligence*, Vol. I, 199, fn. For further evidence of 'cryptographic material derived from Slavic nations' see Smith, 'Sharing Ultra in World War II', 68.
65. On CBME see Hinsley, Thomas, Ransom and Knight, *British Intelligence*, Vol. I, 220.
66. Memorandum to JIC by DMI, 'Expansion of "Y" Service in India', 20 October 1941, L/WS/1/897, IOLR. See also Lycett (Wireless Telegraphy Board) to Rawson (Director of Signals, WO), 15 October 1941, ibid.
67. Nicholls (MI8) to Wavell, 9 December 1941, L/WS 1/987, IOLR; CIGS to Wavell, 21 December 1941, ibid; MI8b to MI1x, 5 January 1942, ibid.
68. This was eventually achieved by despatching Captain Harkness, RN, formally head of FECB Singapore, to Delhi, together with other naval officers, to strengthen the naval intelligence component there, C. in C. Ceylon to ARMIN-DIA, 26 March 1942, L/WS/1/897, IOLR.
69. Menzies, Chairman, 'Y' Board, to S of S India, C/9490, 16 May 1942, enclosing 'memorandum by the "Y" Committee on the Proposal from the C. in C. India concerning the Reorganization of the "Y" Services in India and Ceylon', Broadway, SW1, 7 May 1942, L/WS/1/897, IOLR.
70. Stripp, *Codebreaker in the Far East*, 39–41.
71. Ibid., 56–8, 93. For a description of the outstations and field units see SRH-196, 'Reports on the Activities of Dr Marshall Stone in the China Burma India Theaters, 19 January 1945–31 March 1945, RG 457, USNA. I am most indebted to Alan Stripp for drawing this document to my attention.
72. Gilbert and Finnegan (eds.), *U.S. Army Signals Intelligence in World War II*, 10–12.
73. Stripp, 'Japanese Army Air Force Systems', 294.
74. Lewin, *The Other Ultra*, 196–7.
75. Stripp, *Codebreaker in the Far East*, 165–72, discussing Slim, *Defeat into Victory*, 221.
76. Menzies also asked Winterbotham to check up on the SIS posts in India, Ceylon and Australia, Winterbotham, *The Ultra Secret*, 169–70.
77. Wavell to COS, 26 March 1943, *PWTM* Vol. IV, Far East, 56; COS to Wavell, 5 April 1943, ibid., 65.
78. Lamplough (D of I SEAC) to Cavendish-Bentinck, 1 October 1944, WO 203/5606, PRO.
79. Fleming (D Div) to Army Corps, 9 October 1944, WO 203/286, PRO; Howard, *British Intelligence*, Vol.V, 221–3.
80. LCS (53) 3, Restricted Circulation, 'Deception Policy in the Far East – SEACOS 370' discussed in COS (45) 112 mtg (20), 28 April 1945, CAB 79/33, PRO.
81. Section 16: WT Deception and Cover, in 'RAF Signals War History, South East Asia', p. 57, 21 June 1946, AIR 20/6150, PRO.

82. SRH-196, 'Reports on the Activities of Dr Marshall Stone in the China, Burma India Theaters', 19 January 1945 – 31 March 1945, RG 457, USNA.
83. 'Special and the War with Japan', (by R.T.B.), ADM 223/297, PRO.
84. Entry for 17 July 1944, Somerville diary, 2/2, Somerville papers, CCC.
85. Entry for 2 June 1944, ibid.
86. Denham, 'Bedford–Bletchley–Kilindini–Colombo', 275.
87. JIC (45) 280, 'Organisation of Intelligence – HQ SACSEA', 6 October 1945, 5/ 24, Penney papers, LHCMA; NID Vol. 42, 'Far East and Pacific', III, Special, 'Special and the War with Japan' (by R.T.B.), ADM 223/297, PRO.
88. Entry for 28 February 1945, Somerville diary, 2/2, Somerville Papers, CCC. In December 1941 US Army sigint had only 181 staff and access to 13 IBM tabulating machines. By 1945 it had over 7,000 staff and was operating 407 machines, Lewin, The Other Ultra, 132.
89. Bissell memorandum, 'Centralised Control of Signal Intelligence Activities for War Against Japan, 1 June 1945, SRH 169, RG 457, NARA; Gilbert and Finnegan (eds.), U.S. Army Signals Intelligence in World War II, 12–13.
90. This was Operation Racon led by Al Boehl, Progress Report, SI Branch/404, 31 May 1945, File 2259, Box 133, Entry 148, RG 226, USNA.
91. Section 17: Radio Counter-Measures, in 'RAF Signals War History, South East Asia', p. 57, 21 June 1946, AIR 20/6150, PRO; Noise Investigation Bureau Report for May 1945, WO 203/4089, PRO. See also HQ ACSEA to HQ Strategic Air Force No.Air/396, 11 January 1945, AIR 20/8445, PRO. 'Ferret' mission reports are available in file AIR 20/8446, PRO.
92. Memorandum entitled 'B.J. Series of Diplomatic Messages', n.d. [presumed 8 October 1945], ADM 223/298, PRO; Report on S.I. Volume 2904–2930, NID 12, 8 October 1945, ibid.
93. Loewe, 'Japanese Naval Codes', 262. See also Denham, 'Bedford–Bletchley–Kilindini–Colombo', 268–9.
94. 'A Note on the Future of GC&CS', 17 September 1944, in Aldrich (ed.), Espionage, Security and Intelligence in Britain, 34–7.
95. Lumplough to Mountbatten, discussing Mountbatten to 'C', 23 February 1945, WO 203/4400, PRO.

14 AMERICAN STRUGGLES IN CHINA: OSS AND NAVAL GROUP

1. Fairbank, Chinabound, 204.
2. Roosevelt to Mountbatten, 8 November 1943, C205, Mountbatten papers, SUL.
3. The classic account is Schaller, The U.S. Crusade in China.
4. Xiaoyuan Liu, A Partnership for Disorder, 3–9, 17–19.
5. Tai Li had headed BIS since 1937. On Tai Li's early background see Easterman, 'Fascism in Koumintang China', 1–31. For a discussion of the wealth of Chinese language material see Maochun Yu, OSS in China, 31–3 and Meyer and Parssinen, Webs of Smoke, 204–11.
6. Schaller offers a critical account of Naval Group in 'SACO!', 527–54 and in The U.S. Crusade, 231–50. A narrative account is offered by Fitzgerald, 'Naval Group China', MA. Autobiographical accounts are offered in, Miles, A Different Kind of War, and in Miles, 'U.S. Naval Group China,' 921. See also Stratton, SACO, and his 'Navy Guerrillas' 85.

7. Schaller, 'SACO', 531.
8. See Maochun Yu, *OSS in China*, 75–96; Yu Shen, 'SACO', PhD, 34–6.
9. Maochun Yu, *OSS in China*, 54–5; Yu Shen, 'SACO', PhD, 83–6.
10. Miles, *A Different Kind of War*, 18–23.
11. Memorandum, 'Influential Elements in the Koumintang (& National Government)', January 1943, Box 11, Lot 110, Record of the Office of Chinese Affairs, RG 59, USNA.
12. Stratton, 'Navy Guerrillas', 85.
13. Schaller, 'SACO', 533, quoting Miles' own account, *A Different Kind of War*, 56. See also Miles, 'U.S. Naval Group China', 921.
14. Fitzgerald, 'Naval Group China', 7; Stratton, 'Navy Guerrillas', 84.
15. Miles, *A Different Kind of War*, 75–7; Schaller, 'SACO', 534; Miles to Lee, 22 July 1942, Ch. 1, Miles papers, RG 38, USNA.
16. Lusey to Donovan, 23 May 1942, File OSS memoranda April–May 1942, Folder 2, Box 4, Goodfellow papers, HIWRP.
17. B. F. Smith, *Shadow Warriors*, 132–3; Maochun Yu, OSS in China, 18–19.
18. Purnell to Miles, 21 September 1942, Box 2, Miles papers, RG 38, USNA.
19. Donovan to Hayden, 21 September 1942, File 3934, Box 267, Entry 139, RG 226, USNA.
20. Miles to Cominch, 14 November 1942, Box 2, Miles papers, RG 38, USNA. See also Fitzgerald, 'Naval Group', 11–12.
21. Maochun Yu, *OSS in China*, 20–21.
22. Miles to Metzel, 2 December 1942, Box 2, Miles papers, RG 38, USNA. Fairbank's activities are only partly described in *Chinabound*, 201–23.
23. Taylor, *Awakening from History*, 347.
24. B. F. Smith, *Shadow Warriors*, 198.
25. Fitzgerald, 'Naval Group China', 15–26.
26. King to Miles, 16 February 1943, Box 2, Miles papers, RG 38, USNA; Miles to King, 23 February 1943, ibid.
27. Ibid.; Miles, *A Different Kind of War*, 117–19; 'Sino-American Special Technical Co-operation Agreement', 15 April 1943, Box 5, Lot 110, Records of the Office of Chinese Affairs, RG 59, USNA.
28. Some of the troops commanded by SACO were a motley crew and included puppet forces and coastal pirates who had sworn allegiance to SACO. The belated change of title to Naval Group occurred in April 1944, 'Naval Group', 28–56.
29. Lee (OSS) to Donovan, 20 October 1943, DP.
30. Maochun Yu, *OSS in China*, 44–45.
31. Atcheson (Chungking) to SoS No.1671, 10 September 1943, 893.105/96, LM 65, Reel 16, RG 59, USNA.
32. Stilwell to Marshall (Eyes Alone), 11 September 1943, Sunderland and Romanus (eds.), *Stilwell's Personal File*, Vol. III, 1056.
33. The quote is taken from Miles to Central Intelligence Group, 'SSU Organisation in China', 17 May 1946, File 1946–7, Box 3, Miles papers, HIWRP. A similar account, and the quotation on Mountbatten's reaction, is offered in Taylor, *Awakening from History*, 347. The exchange with Chiang is also recorded in Stratton, *Army–Navy Game*, pp. 130–2. For an alternative view see Maochun Yu, *OSS in China*, 133 and 304, n. 87.
34. Schaller, 'SACO', 537–8.

35. Ibid., 537–8.
36. Manser, 'Roosevelt and China: From Cairo to Yalta', PhD, 123–4.
37. Memorandum by General Thomas Handy, 'OSS Plans for Mission to Yenan', 10 August 1944, Operations Plans Division, OPD 210.684, China, RG 165, USNA. See also Schaller, 'SACO', 538; Maochun Yu, OSS in China, 159–60.
38. Carter, Mission to Yenan, 55, 92–7; Maochun Yu, OSS in China, 166–7.
39. Manser, 'Roosevelt and China: From Cairo to Yalta', PhD, 162–4.
40. Davies, Dragon by the Tail, 383; Maochun Yu, OSS in China, 184–97.
41. Romanus and Sunderland, Time Runs Out in CBI, 251–2; Barrett, Dixie Mission, 75–8; Schaller, 'SACO', 538–40.
42. Maochun Yu, OSS in China, xii; Carter, Mission to Yenan, passim.
43. SACO forces also claimed to have accounted for 38,000 Japanese casualties, Fitzgerald, 'Naval Group', 61–70. Even Fitzgerald, who offers the most sympathetic account of Naval Group's operational guerrilla activities, concedes that 'the greatest handicap to guerrilla success was the communist and nationalist rivalry', ibid., 51.
44. Schaller, 'SACO', 540–1; Miles, A Different Kind of War, 192–6; Miles to Metzel, 1 September 1943, Ch. 5, Miles papers, RG 38, USNA.
45. Fitzgerald, 'Naval Group China', 32–3; Yu Shen, 'SACO', PhD, 151–62.
46. Fitzgerald (whose study was screened for 'security' before it was submitted in 1968) is the main apologist for Tai Li, insisting that his work was 'vital to the survival of an independent China', Fitzgerald, 'Naval Group China', 5.
47. Davies to Donovan, 6 October 1943, DP.
48. Schaller, 'SACO', 543.
49. 118 downed American flyers were also rescued by SACO units during the war, Fitzgerald, 'Naval Group China', 70–9, 98.
50. Maochun Yu, OSS in China, 66–7.
51. Ibid., 142–9.
52. Donovan to Roosevelt, 4 July 1944, Box 168, PSF, FDRL. However staff officers rendered it memorable by referring to its members as the 'AG-farts'.
53. Coughlin to FETO O33, 21 May 1944, File 2536, Box 192, Entry 139, RG 226, USNA.
54. Donovan to Roosevelt, 6 November 1944, Box 170, PSF, FDRL; Report of Major Hoffman's tour of the Far East (SACO Report), 22 February 1944, AGFRTS Section p. 72, DP.
55. Coughlin to Donovan, 28 April 1944, File 1167, Box 82, Entry 146, RG 226, USNA.
56. Patti, Why Vietnam?, 27–8, 228–9.
57. McBaine, 'OSS Organisation in China', 20 November 1944, DP.
58. Donovan to Roosevelt, 6 November 1944, File Nov. 1–14 1944, Box 170, PSF, FDRL.
59. Maochun Yu, OSS in China, 172–5.
60. Schaller, 'SACO', 543–5; Miles, A Different Kind of War, 443–9; Romanus and Sunderland, Time Runs Out, 254.
61. Mountbatten to Donovan, 26 June 1944, C89, Mountbatten papers, SUL.
62. To P. [Division] from C.S.S. himself, 14 November 1944, WO 203/6451, PRO; Mountbatten to Wedemeyer 'Eyes Alone' (draft) presumed November 1944, ibid.

63. Maochun Yu, *OSS in China*, 201–3.
64. Fitzgerald, 'Naval Group China', 105.
65. B. F. Smith, *Shadow Warriors*, 254, 311.
66. OSS Planning Group, PG 26 'Basic Military Plan for Psychological warfare in the Southwest Pacific Theater' 9 June 1943, File PG26, Box 12, Entry 144, RG 226, USNA. Hayden knew about politics, having been head of political science at the University of Michigan before the war.
67. Report of a meeting on proposed OSS activities in the Philippines, chaired by Donovan, 6 December 1944, DP.
68. MacArthur to US JCS, 23 May 1945, Box 54, Leahy File, RG 218, USNA.
69. Donovan to Nimitz, 27 April 1944, DP.
70. Nimitz to Donovan, 2 July 1944, DP.
71. OSS Planning Group, 'Over-all and Special Programs for Strategic Services Activities Supporting American Forces in the Pacific Ocean Areas of Operation', PG 93/2, 9 October 1944, DP; POA Program – MO, p. 6, ibid.
72. McFarland (JCS Staff) to Donovan, 10 October 1944, DP.
73. These included an OSS underwater demolition team (UDT #10) in September 1944 and an MO unit that arrived just before V-J Day, memorandum, 'OSS Pacific Ocean Areas', 17 April 1947, DP.
74. Donovan to King, 23 March 1945, DP.
75. CPA (Dening) to SAC (Mountbatten), 30 December 1944, WO 203/4398, PRO.
76. Edmund Taylor (OSS SEAC) to Donovan, 7 July 1944, Mhe-49, DP.
77. Heppner to Donovan, 30 June 1944, OSS SEAC Report for June 1944, File 302, Box 47, Entry 99, RG 226, USNA.
78. Coughlin (OSS SEAC) to Dick [Heppner] (OSS China), 2 June 1945, File 20, Box 20, Entry 110, RG 226, USNA.

15 BRITAIN AND HER ALLIES IN CHINA

1. Grimsdale memorandum, 'Post War Planning in the Far East', 1 July 1943, WO 208/511, PRO.
2. Xiaoyuan Liu, *A Partnership for Disorder*, 3–6.
3. See for example Hudson minute, 19 March 1945, on PHP Report, 'Anglo-American Relations in the Far East', F1334/127/61, FO 371/46325, PRO.
4. Cf. p. 152.
5. Miles, *A Different Kind of War*, 24–5; Yu Shen, 'SACO', PhD, 64–9.
6. Drage, *The Amiable Prussian*, 126–7. On the German dimension see Walsh, 'The German Military Mission', 502–31.
7. Best, 'Straws in the Wind', 642–5.
8. Beaumont-Nesbitt (MI) to Cadogan, 15 September 1939, F10282/4027/61, FO 371/23551, PRO; Cadogan to Beaumont-Nesbitt (MI), 19 September 1939, ibid.; Beaumont-Nesbitt (MI) to Cadogan, 20 September 1939, ibid.
9. Mayer, 'Chinese Guerrilla Training School', 12 September 1941, 893.00/14809, LM 65 Reel 2, RG 59, USNA.
10. Baxter, 'Britain and the War in China, 1937–1945', PhD, 1993, 183–5. This is the definitive account of 204 Mission. See also Rooney, *Mad Mike*, 101–36.
11. Wasserstein, *Secret War in Shanghai*, 200.
12. Cruickshank, *SOE*, 78; Baxter, 'Britain and the War in China', PhD, 197–8.

13. Ward (Hong Kong) to SoS, 18 August 1941, 846.00/57, RG 59, USNA.
14. His papers, and those of Jardine Matheson Ltd, remain closed.
15. OX to AD4 9 May 1943, enclosing 'RII', HS 1/165, PRO. Keswick was replaced by Crawford.
16. 'New brief for negotiations with G50,000 [Donovan]', 26 July 1943, HS 1/165, PRO.
17. 'Summary of Agreement between British SOE and American SO', 16–22 June 1942, ibid.
18. O/X to A/DO, 'Future of RII', 18 July 1943, HS 1/165, PRO. There were complex discussions in London and Washington, see meeting of 27 July 1943 between CD, G, D Plans, AD/O and G50,000, ibid.
19. O/X to A/D4 9 May 1943, enclosing 'RII', ibid.
20. O/X to A/DO, 'Future of RII', 18 July 1943, ibid.; OX to AD4, 'SOE and China – Random Reflections', 22 May 1943, ibid.
21. Baxter, 'Britain and the War in China', PhD, 190–1, 194.
22. Ibid., 205.
23. 204 Military Mission to War Office, 5 March 1943, PWTM India, 1943, 48; Chungking to GIIQ India, 6 May 1943, WO 106/3582A, PRO.
24. Baxter, 'Britain and the War in China', PhD, 220; de Wiart, Happy Odyssey, 199–201.
25. The fullest account, by his son, is Ride, British Army Aid Group.
26. Cruickshank, SOE, 211–21; entry for 9 April 1944, Buckle (ed.), Selected Diaries of Cecil Beaton.
27. Entry for Saturday 9 April, Buckle (ed.), Selected Diaries of Cecil Beaton.
28. See files HS 1/ and Cruickshank, SOE, Chapter 11; Sweet-Escott, Baker Street, 253–4.
29. SIS reportedly used £13,000,000 'liberated' from a bank in occupied France to finance de Gaulle's Free French activities, entry for 7 August 1940, Colville, Fringes of Power.
30. Beddington, My Life, 286–7, T33 memoir, Beddington papers, LIICMA.
31. Gage (Chungking) to Dening (SEAC), 10 November 1943, WO 203/5606, PRO. See also OSS New Delhi to 154 (Washington) 16 November 1943, File 3473, Box 250, Entry 146, RG 226, USNA.
32. Steveni (SIS) to Jonas (RAF), Ops. A112, 23 December 1943, AIR 23/7679, PRO.
33. Heliwell (Chief SI, OSS, CT) to Donovan, 'A Study of British Intelligence Organisations in China', 13 February 1945, DP. This report, though not exhaustive, was accurate.
34. JIC to SACSEA No.92601 (MI 17) 10 November 1944, WO 203/367, PRO.
35. Cf. p. 269. Accounts differ as to Lindsay's precise movements in 1940–1 but see Band and Band, Dragon Fangs.
36. Shi An-Li, 'Britain's China Policy and the Communists', 46–53. Lindsay's writings on the communists as an academic in the United States after 1945 are vast, but see M. Lindsay, The Unknown War.
37. J. Amery, Approach March, 411–27.
38. MI6 Political Report No. 15 to FO, 8 April 1945, WO 208/474, PRO; see also MI6 Political Report No. 13 to FO, 3 April 1945, ibid.

39. MI6 Political Report (CX 28100) 'Chinese Economic Policy', 3 July 1945, WO 208/474, PRO.
40. MI6 Political Report No. 13 to FO, 3 April 1945, WO 208/474, PRO.
41. Entries for 30 and 31 July 1943, Wilkinson Diary, CCC. See also B. F. Smith, *Shadow Warriors*, 134–5.
42. Grismdale to DMI, 25 June 1944, F3077/3077/10, FO 371/41676B, PRO.
43. Cavendish-Bentinck minute, 26 July 1944, F3369/3077/10, FO 371/41676B, PRO; US JIC to British JIC, 18 July 1944, ibid; DDMI to DMI and DMI India, 28 July 1944, ibid.
44. DMI to DMI India and Chungking, 9 August 1944, F3678/3077/10, ibid.
45. B. F. Smith, *Shadow Warriors*, 195.
46. Telegram from the FO to British Embassy, Washington, discussed in Hull to Gauss (China), 3 July 1942, Section XVIII, No. III, in Mehra, *The North-Eastern Frontier*, 126.
47. Donovan to Hull, 2 July 1942, and Hull to Roosevelt, 3 July 1942, Section XVII, No. I–II, in Mehra, *The North-Eastern Frontier*, 125–6.
48. R. H. Smith, *OSS*, 254. Tolstoy ended up as manager of Marineland in Florida.
49. Cab/Tibet to Roosevelt, 29 December 1942, 893.00 Tibet/62, reel 7, LM 65, RG 59, USNA; Goodfellow (OSS) to Hornbeck, 20 March 1943, ibid.; OSS Memorandum, 'Procedure of Reception by Major Tolstoy and Captain Dolan by His Holiness (*sic*) the Dalai Lama of Tibet', 20 December 1942, 893.00 Tibet/77, ibid.
50. Conversation with Goodfellow (OSS) reported in Hiss to Hornbeck, 20 March 1943, and memorandum by Atcheson, 30 March 1943, Section XVIII, Nos. X–XI, in Mehra, *The North-Eastern Frontier*, 134–5.
51. Donovan to Hornbeck, 12 April 1943, 893.01/946 PS/GA, reel 12, LM 65, RG 59, USNA; Berle to Donovan, 23 April 1943, 893.01/946, ibid; Donovan to Hornbeck, 2 April 1943, 893.01/946, ibid. The transmitter was supplied through Stilwell's command, see Ferris (IBT) to Goodfellow (OSS), 7 July 1943, File Ferris, Box 1, Goodfellow Papers, HIWRP.
52. In June 1944 three H.T.9 transmitters were delivered along with generators and six receiving sets, allowing a broadcast station to be set up at Deki Linga. See Tibetan Foreign Office to Tolstoy, 22 November 1944, DP; Richardson (External Affairs, GOI) to Tolstoy (OSS China) DO No.F.156-CA/44, 16 January 1945, DP.
53. Merrell (India) to Hull, 15 May 1943, Section XVIII, No. XVI in Mehra, *The North-Eastern Frontier*, 140–3.
54. Atcheson to Hull, 25 May 1943, Section XVIII, No. XVIII in Mehra, *The North-Eastern Frontier*, 142–3.
55. Hull to Atcheson (China) 21 September 1943, Section XVIII, No. XXIII, Mehra, *The North-Eastern Frontier*, 149–50.
56. Tolstoy (Lasa) to Goodfellow (OSS), 17 March 1943, File Tolstoy, Goodfellow Papers, HIWRP.
57. *FRUS*, 1943, China, 637.
58. R. H. Smith, *OSS*, 255.
59. Donovan to Hull, 14 April 1944, Section XVIII, No. XXVIII, Mehra, *The North-Eastern Frontier*, 153–4.

60. These connections would however be revived in the late 1950s, 'The CIA Tibetan Conspiracy', *Far Eastern Economic Review* 89 (5 September 1975): 30–4.
61. OSS R&A Report No.2553, 'The Organization of the French Intelligence Services', 11 January 1945, RG 59, USNA.
62. 'Summary of the Meynier Group', File 4, Box 36, Miles Papers, RG 38, USNA.
63. Miles (Algiers) to Donovan, 7 May 1943, File 3, Box 35, Miles Papers, RG 38, USNA. See also Lawson to Miles, 'General Pechkoff and Lt Col. Emblanc – Report on activities of', 3 January 1944, File 4, ibid.
64. Patti, *Why Vietnam?*, 36–7; Spector, 'Allied Intelligence', 25–6.
65. Marr, *Vietnam 1945*, 258; Patti, *Why Vietnam?*, 36–7.
66. OSS memorandum, 'The French Situation in China', January 1944, File 248, Box 17, Entry 148, RG 226, USNA.
67. 'Report on the Meynier Situation', December 1943, File 2761, Box 6198, Entry 146, RG 226, USNA.
68. Lawson (Paris) to Miles, 21 September 1944, File 3, Box 35, RG 38, USNA.
69. Patti, *Why Vietnam?*, 45. The fullest account of GBT is given in MacLaren, *Canadians Behind Enemy Lines*.
70. Memorandum, 'Employment by OWI of Ho to broadcast from San Francisco in Annamite [Vietnamese]', 7 November 1944, File: Indochina Personalities/Misc, Box 7, PSA records, RG 59, USNA. The date of the original ban is not clear.
71. Ibid.; Moffat to Stettinius, 7 October 1944, ibid.
72. Tonnesson, *The Vietnamese Revolution*, 168; Hicks, 'Tension at the High Table', MA, 49.
73. Dunn, *The First Vietnam War*, 50; Fenn, *Ho Chi Minh*, 74–6; Patti, *Why Vietnam?*, 43–7.
74. Marr, *Vietnam 1945*, 257.
75. OSS Memorandum, 'Future Plans for SO', 26 December 1944, File 200, Box 65, Entry 99, RG 226, USNA.
76. Fenn, *Ho Chi Minh*, 78–82.
77. Memorandum of a conversation between Ananda Chintakananda, Landon, and two Free Thai Lieutenants attached to OSS in China, 19 March 1945, 892.01/3–1945, RG 59, USNA.
78. Balankura to Vincent (US Embassy), 3 May 1943, CID 36004, RG 226 (old series), USNA.
79. Memorandum of a conversation with Hoffman, 25 October 1943, and attached memorandum, 20 October 1943, 892.01/10–2043, RG 59 USNA. Medical report, 'Mr Chamkad Balankura', signed A. Stewart Alen, FRCS (C), Superintendent Canadian Mission Hospital, 9 October 1943, File 3, Box 36, Miles papers, RG 38, USNA.
80. Coughlin to Donovan, Cheston and Hoffman, 'Kunjara', 19 September 1944, File 660, Box 44, Entry 148, RG 226, USNA.
81. Conversation between Mani Sanasen, Moffat and Landon, 27 July 1944, 892.01/7–2744, RG 59, USNA.
82. Memorandum of a conversation between Hoffmann (OSS) and Landon, 1 November 1944, 892.01/11–144, RG 59, USNA.
83. OSS Chungking to Donovan, No.1077, 1 March 1945, 892.01/3–545, RG 59, USNA.
84. Young minute summarising conversation with Guise (SOE), 29 December 1943,

F23/23/40, FO 371/41844, PRO. Grut was an SIS officer on loan to SOE, see B/ B to AD, 16 November 1943, HS 1/72, PRO.

85. Mackenzie to Wavell, 14 September 1943, HS 1/72, PRO.
86. Cruickshank, *SOE*, 105.
87. Miles TSS, 'Siamese Story', File 4, Box 36, Miles papers, RG 38, USNA.
88. McHugh, 'Notes on General Aspects of Military intelligence in China', enclosed in Gauss to SoS No. 1849, 23 November 1943, 893.20/798, LM 65, Reel 17, RG 59, USNA.

16 ANTI-COLONIALISM, ANTI-COMMUNISM AND PLANS FOR POST-WAR ASIA

1. Lynch (London) to Hoover (FBI), 12 July 1945, DP. However, later that month, when Donovan found that Mountbatten was also in London, they had discussions in his room in Claridges, entry for 26 July 1945, Ziegler (ed.), *Personal Diary*.
2. The most vigorous critique is Charmley, *Churchill's Grand Alliance*, 93–7; 184–90; 252–7.
3. Stafford, *Churchill*, 191–5. On the obsessive care that Churchill took see Gilbert, *Churchill*, Vol. IV, *Finest Hour*.
4. On its long-term legacy see J. W. Young, *Winston Churchill's Last Campaign*. One of his long-serving private secretaries recalled that once he had decided on a course of action he demanded 'action this day', and required matters to be completed 'long before it was humanly possible', Colville, *Fringes of Power*, 124–5.
5. Goore-Booth to FO, 28 August 1944, 3008/1/44, FO 660/240, PRO.
6. Foulds minute, on Washington to London, 2 January 1945, F85/11/61, FO 371/46304, PRO.
7. Hess, *America Encounters India*, 159–60.
8. Truman, *Year of Decisions, 1945*.
9. Callahan, *Churchill*, 279; D. Reynolds, 'Roosevelt, Churchill and the Anglo-American Alliance', 17–43; Wilmott, *The Struggle for Europe*.
10. Ben-Moshe, *Churchill*, has 42 index entries for France but none for India, Burma or China.
11. PHP (44) 27 (Draft), 'Report on Work Done – August 1943 to May 1944', 17 April 1944, CAB 81/42, PRO. See also PHP (44) 13 (O) Final, 'Effect of Soviet Policy on British Strategic Interests', 6 June 1944, CAB 81/45, PRO; and JIC (44) 467 (O), 'Russian Strategic Interests and Intentions from the Point of View of her Security', 18 December 1944, CAB 80/89, PRO.
12. Minute by Sargent, 4 October 1944, U7658/748/70, FO 371/40741B, PRO.
13. Penney to Mountbatten, 2 May 1945, 5/1, Penney papers, LHCMA.
14. Paper by Cawthorn and Dening to FO, 8 February 1944, F711/127/61, FO 371/46325, PRO.
15. Minute by Thyne Henderson, 7 March 1944, F1334/127/61, ibid.
16. Donovan to Truman, 5 May 1945, enclosing OSS memorandum, 'Problems and Objectives of US Policy', 2 April 1945, Box 15, Conway File, HSTL. For further discussion see Bills, *Empire and Cold War*, 20–1.
17. Patti, *Why Vietnam?*, 20.
18. Record of a meeting held in the Projection Room vis San Francisco Conference

presided over by Colonel Buxton, 28 March 1945, File 2794, Box 48, Entry 146, RG 226, USNA.

19. B. F. Smith, *Shadow Warriors*, 461, n.52; Schlesinger, 'Cryptanalysis for Peace-time'.

20. Memorandum by Cheston to US JCS, 'OSS Intelligence Activities in the India–Burma Theatre', 1 June 1945, DP.

21. When Moffat visited London in October 1946 British diplomats spoke of him with respect, if not a little anxiety: 'He is an experienced and canny negotiator. Business can be done with him on a horse-trading or any other hard-boiled basis, but he will give nothing away. His attitude towards the problems of the area for which he is responsible is coloured by the tradition of American sympathy for coloured peoples and an almost Republican training in the methods and objectives of Big Business ... Hence he would prize Siam out of such a grip as we have on it in the hope of delivering it to American capitalism.' Everson (Washington) to FO, 26 September 1946, F14255/946/61, FO 371/54040, PRO.

22. Colville, *Fringes of Power*, 610.

23. Entries for 24 July 1945 and 4 August 1945, Ziegler (ed.), *Personal Diary*.

24. Memorandum from Coon to Donovan, 'Intelligence Work in Arab Countries', 23 September 1944, File Donovan Memoranda, Vol. IV, Box 1, Entry 180, RG 226, USNA.

25. Winks, *Cloak and Gown*, 183–4, 186–7.

26. Coon also warned: 'The British, I have recently learned, have much the same idea as ours ... a man whom I know very well, is in charge.' The section dealing with parallel British efforts, and the section dealing with cover in the field, have been sanitised. Memorandum from Coon to Donovan, 'Intelligence Work in Arab Countries', 23 September 1944, File Donovan Memoranda Vol. VI, Box 1, Entry 180, RG 226, USNA.

27. Stephenson (BSC) to Donovan, 15 November 1944, File 'Restricted – Pull', Box 1, J. Russell Forgen Papers, HIWRP.

28. OSS officers at Casserta in Italy learned of these developments through stories in two newspapers, *The Stars and Stripes* and *The Albany Times-Union*. The head of SIS at Casserta expressed disbelief that such a leak could have occurred. OSS Casserta to Donovan, 22 February 1945, File Donovan Memoranda Vol. IV, Box 1, Entry 180, RG 226, USNA. Somerville was equally incredulous, Entry for 24 February 1945, Somerville diary, Somerville Papers, 2/2, CCC.

29. Memorandum by Ripley for Donovan, 'The Development of Long-Range Intelligence in the Far East', 8 March 1945, File Donovan Memoranda Vol. IV, Box 1, Entry 180, RG 226, USNA.

30. Memorandum by OSS India, 'The Development of a Program of Political and Economic Intelligence for India and Burma', undated, attached to Martin to Coughlin, 21 April 1945, DP.

31. Ibid.

32. Memorandum from Martin to Coughlin, 'Intelligence Project Bingo', 21 April 1945, DP. On these issues see Wainwright, *Inheritance of Empire*, 36–41.

33. Windmiller, 'Tumultuous Times', 115–16.

34. Ripley to Wilson (OSS Washington), 12 July 1945, File 2773, Box 196, Entry 146, RG 226, USNA.

35. Huyler's report, based in part on lengthy interviews with a 'surprisingly frank'

P.C. Joshi, is 'The Burma Communist Party and Burma Patriotic Front', 28 June 1945, enclosed in Bombay to SoS, 13 July 1945, 8450.00/14–457, RG 59, USNA.

36. SAC 24210/INT, 24 October 1944, WO 203/5051, PRO.

37. B. F. Smith, *Shadow Warriors*, 408.

38. McCarthy to Coughlin, 12 September 1945, enclosing memorandum entitled 'Long Range Intelligence', File 67, Box 22, Entry 110, RG 226, USNA. Other copies are available at File 75, Box 24 ibid., and at File 2147, Box 124, Entry 148, RG 226, USNA.

39. X-2 Detachment 303, OSS Monthly Report, 1 September – 1 October 1945, File 1126, Box 94, Entry 168, RG 226, USNA.

40. 'Summary of SSU Activities During November 1945', File 2813, Box 210, Entry 146, RG 226, USNA.

41. Record of a conversation with Magruder, 29 November 1945, File US Mission, 1946–8, Box 1, PSA records, RG 59, USNA.

42. SSU India–Burma Theater, Chief of Mission Report – January 1946, 12 February 1946, Folder 2815, Box 201, Entry 146, RG 226, USNA.

43. OSS R&A Report No. 3494, 'United States Prestige in Southeast Asia', summarising various SSU reports, 7 February 1946, RG 59, USNA.

44. Maddox, Chief of 'P' Branch to Chief of SI (SSU), 'Priority Intelligence Targets' 25 March 1946, File 673, Box 48, Entry 146, RG 226, USNA.

45. SSU Report, 'Information on the Result of Elections', 6 February 1946, 845.00/2–646, RG 59, USNA.

46. ORI India Intelligence Section, 'Research and Intelligence Projects', 27 March 1946, 845.00/3–2746, RG 59, USNA.

47. SSU report, 'Looting in August Calcutta Riots', 25 August 1946, 845.00/8–2546, RG 59, USNA.

48. SSU India–Burma Theater, Progress Report – 3 February to 15 April 1946, 15 April 1946, File 2817, Box 210, Entry 146, RG 226, USNA.

49. CIG Intelligence Report, 'India – Political Personalities – Current Situation', 845.00/8–2546, RG 59, USNA.

50. SSU Report ZT 28 (Garden-Saigon), 4 April 1946, File: Indochina Personalities/Misc, Box 7, PSA records, RG 59, USNA.

51. Conversation between Garden (CIG), Moffat, and others, 'Interview with Bao Dai', 11 April 1947, File: French-Indochina relations, Box 9, PSA records, RG 59, USNA.

52. Penrose to Quinn, 'Termination of Continuity Project', n.d. [presumed late 1947], and Peter Karlow, 'Continuity Report: 1 October 1945 to 1 May 1946', File 1553, Box 494, Entry 190, RG 226, USNA.

53. Bird to Donovan, 20 December 1947, File 680, Box 73A, Donovan papers, USMHI. On the many OSS who maintained Thai links see E. B. Reynolds, 'The Opening Wedge', 342–3.

54. Eden to Churchill, PM/44/716, 23 November 1944, and COS (44) 381st mtg (6) Confidential Annex, 27 November 1944, CAB 79/83, PRO.

55. Entry for 24 February 1943, 1/2, 2, Wilkinson diary, CCC.

56. Cecil, 'C's War', 82.

57. COS (45) 114th mtg (2), CAB 79/33, PRO.

58. COS (45) 156th mtg (2), 19 June 1945, CAB 79/34, PRO.

59. COS to Mountbatten, 23 November 1945, WO 203/1735, PRO.
60. Mountbatten to COS 10 December 1945, F11146/9752/61, FO 371/46423, PRO; minute by Sterndale Bennet, 30 November, ibid.
61. Memorandum by Seymour 'ALFPMO Digest, 15 November 1945–31 March 1946', WO 203/2331, PRO. See also Bangkok in Thompson to Bevin No. 69, 13 June 1946, F11330/10/40, FO 371/54389, PRO.
62. ALFSEA to ALFIC, 10 November 1945, WO 203/1735, PRO. In February 1946, Mountbatten was told by London that ALFPMO must be renamed 'Special Operations', to conform to the new SIS terminology, but the locally the PMO term seemed to stick, SACSEA to WO, 9 February 1946, WO 203/4943, PRO. Pridi's colleague, the ex-Premier Luang Dhamrong, arrived in exile at Penang with 21,878 kilograms of opium, worth $27 million at 1947 prices, H. Wilson, 'Best of Friends', 81.
63. Terry to War Dept, 5 November 1945, File US Mission, 1946–8, Box 1, PSA records, RG 59, USNA.
64. Grey to 109, 'Changes and Developments in MI5 Ceylon', 13 February 1945, DP.
65. French, *Liberty or Death*, 237, 259.
66. In the 1950s the Admiralty developed 'a "cover story" to be used in describing its function to the Ceylonese', Draft opening Statement, 3 December 1956, DEFE 13/230, PRO.
67. Stripp, *Codebreaker in the Far East*, 48–9.
68. JIC 322/1, 'Intelligence for the Control of Japan', 25 September 1945, JCS Microfilm, Far East Reel 3, BRO.
69. State–War–Navy Co-ordinating Committee Report No.216/4, 'Information on Japanese Scientific Research', in JCS 1538/6, 18 September 1946, Far East Reel 3, JCS microfilm, BRO.
70. Sansom (British Embassy) to Hilldring, 17 July 1946, Annex A, ibid.
71. JCS 1538/7, 'Information on Japanese Scientific Research', 25 September 1946, Far East Reel 3, JCS Microfilm, BRO; JCS 1538/9, 'Program for Investigation of Japanese Technology', 26 January 1948, ibid.
72. Wedemeyer, *Wedemeyer Reports*, 353–6.
73. See for example JIC (47) 50 (0), 2nd Revised Draft, 'Reports by the Joint Intelligence Committee (FE)', 12 September 1948, L/WS/1/1050, IOLR; JIC (48) 9 (0) Final, 'Russian Interests, Intentions and Capabilities', 23 July 1948, L/WS/1/1173, IOLR.
74. Aldrich and Coleman, 'The Question of South Asian Airbases, 1945–9', 400–27.
75. Wright to Cornwall-Jones, 21 November 1945, FO 115/4230, PRO.
76. Bevin to Byrnes, 15 November 1945, ibid.

17 RESISTING THE RESISTANCE: THAILAND, MALAYA AND BURMA

1. Garden to Ripley, 'Long-Range Intelligence in Thailand', 13 April 1945, File 3469, Box 250, Entry 146, RG 226, USNA.
2. Heppner to Donovan, 16 October 1944, DP.
3. Garnons-Williams to Pownall, 6 March 1945, DP; Donovan to Coughlin, No. 8314, 19 March 1945, DP. This air crash also killed Brigadier Vivian Dykes of the BJSM in Washington, Sweet-Escott, *Baker Street*, 233.

4. Mountbatten to Donovan, 9 May 1945, and Donovan minute, DP.
5. Ripley to Donovan, 11 May 1945, DP; Penney (D of I), to Mrs Penney, 30 July 1945, 4/20, Penney papers, LHCMA.
6. Garden to Solon, 'U.S. Propaganda in Thailand', 1 January 1945, File 3469, Box 250, Entry 146, RG 226, USNA.
7. E. B. Reynolds, 'Opening Wedge', 341.
8. London memorandum 'Postwar Status of Thailand', 10 January 1945, 892.00/1–1045, RG59, USNA. Major Herman Scholtz, an OSS officer who, like Milligen had been in business in pre-war Thailand, was ejected from SEAC in early 1945 after spreading rumours of 'British protectorate', Leigh-Williams (FEB) to FO, 24 July 1945, F5739/296/40, FO 371/46537, PRO.
9. Landon memorandum, 'Postwar Status of Thailand', 10 January 1945, 892.00/1–1045, RG 59, USNA. See also memorandum of a conversation between Moffat and Landon of the State Department; and Hutchinson, Garden and Deignan of OSS, 10 January 1945, 892.01/8–2445, ibid. I am most indebted to J. A. Stowe for drawing the latter to my attention.
10. *British Malaya*, 20, 1 May 1945, reported in Landon to Moffat and Balantine, 'The Isthmus of Kra', 19 June 1945, File: Political Postwar Policy 14.102 – Malaya, Box 14, PSA records, RG 59, USNA.
11. Extract from the *Crown Colonist*, 'The Kra Isthmus', May 1945, 295, File 3469, Box 250, Entry 146, RG 226, USNA.
12. See for example, Colombo to State Department, 5 September 1945, 741.92/9–545, RG 59. For the comments of the State Department see Moffat to Garden (OSS), 24 September 1945, 741.92/9–2245, ibid.
13. Dolbeare to Hughes, 4 January 1944, Vol. XII, Box 3, Entry 180, RG 226, USNA.
14. Pointon to Mackenzie, 'King of Siam', 24 March 1945, HS 1/74, PRO.
15. FEB to FO, 16 July 1945, enclosing 'Memorandum on the Siamese Monarchy and Political Warfare', F4377/296/40, FO 371/46545, PRO; minutes by Adams and Sterndale Bennett, 28, July 1945, ibid.
16. COS (45) 75th mtg (13), 22nd March 1945, discussing PHP (45) 3 (0) Final, 'The Post War Strategic Importance of Siam', 10 March 1945, CAB 79/30, PRO.
17. Mountbatten to Donovan, 31 December 1944, DP.
18. SAC's (misc) 3rd mtg, 30 January 1945, DP.
19. Donovan to Roosevelt, 22 February 1945, Feb 1945 File, Box 171, PSF, FDRL.
20. Donovan to Roosevelt, 5, 8 and 12 March 1945, File 1–15 March, ibid. E. B. Reynolds 'Opening Wedge', 336–7.
21. Cruickshank, SOE, 114–15, 120–1; D. Reynolds, 'Opening Wedge', 334–6.
22. See Tarling, 'Atonement before Absolution', 22–65; Tarling, 'Rice and Reconciliation', 59–112.
23. Dening to Sterndale Bennett, 8 August 1945, F5337/29/40, FO 371/46546, PRO; Dening to Sterndale Bennett, F5450/296/40, ibid.
24. Mackenzie to Mountbatten, 24 May 1945, WO 203/4340, PRO. Cf. E. B. Reynolds, *Thailand and Japan's Southward Advance*, 206–8.
25. Full record of a telephone conversation between Acheson, Moffat and Winant, 6 September 1945, 741.92/9–645, RG 59, USNA.
26. Stowe, *Siam Becomes Thailand*, 350.

27. COS (45) 218th mtg (7), 7 September 1945, Annex 1, 'Record of a meeting at No 10 Downing Street on 6 September', CAB 79/38, PRO.
28. Dening to FO, 7 September 1945, F6583/269/40, FO 371/46549, PRO.
29. Cheston to Truman, 10 September 1945, File Donovan-Secret, Box 15, Rose Conway Files, HSTL.
30. Memorandum by OSS India, 'The Development of a Program of Political and Economic Intelligence for India and Burma', attached to Martin to Coughlin, 21 April 1945, DP.
31. Sultan to US JCS, 23 May 1945, Box 54, Leahy File, RG 218, USNA.
32. Bishop to SD, 24 August 1945, 892.01/8–2445, RG 59, USNA.
33. Oakes (Colombo) to SoS, 5 September 1945, 741.92/9–545, RG 59, USNA.
34. Donovan to Truman, 6 September 1945, File Donovan-Secret, Box 15, Rose Conway Files, HSTL. See also Cheston to Truman, 10 September 1945, ibid.
35. Dening to FO, 9 September 1944, F6613/298/40, FO 371/46549, PRO.
36. Dening to Sterndale Bennett, 138/5/45, 24 September 1945, enclosing Report from Security Section, SACSEA, 21 September 1945, F7788/296/40, FO 371/46552, PRO.
37. Ibid. See also 608 Field Security Section War Diary, 1–30 September 1945, WO 172/9241, PRO.
38. Ibid.
39. Jacques (SOE Bangkok) to Dening, 16 September 1945, WO 203/5581, PRO.
40. Minutes by Adams, 3 October 1945; Wilson Young, 4 October 1945; and Sterndale Bennett, 6 October 1945, F7788/294/40, FO 371/46552, PRO.
41. Ibid.
42. Dening to FO, 10 December 1945, F11538,296/40, FO 371/46555, PRO.
43. Yost (New Delhi) to SoS, 22 September 1945, 741.92/9–2245, RG 59, USNA.
44. Dening to Sterndale Bennett, quoting 'Hector', 5 October 1945, F9305/1073/61, FO 371/46353, PRO.
45. COS (45) 260th mtg (4), 26 October 1945, CAB 79/40, PRO. Washington expected London to continue to 'exert the utmost pressure' over these military requirements, JIS 161/8, 'Estimate of British Post-War Capabilities and Intentions', Limited Distribution, 26 December 1945, OPD Exec. Files Ex.9, Book 21, RG 165, USNA.
46. Dening to FO, 10 December 1945, WO 203/4340, PRO.
47. Mallon (Singapore), 15 December 1945, 741.92/12–1545, RG 59, USNA. See also *Herald Tribune*, 15 December 1945.
48. Yost to SoS, 24 December 1945, 892.001/12–2445, RG 59, USNA. See also Yost to SoS, 27 December 1945, 741.92/12–2745, ibid.
49. Timberman to Yost, 16 December 1945, 800.Anglo-Siamese, RG 59, original italics, I am most grateful to J. A. Stowe for allowing me to see a copy of this document.
50. COS to Mountbatten, 2 December 1945, WO 203/6449, PRO. Dennis, *Troubled Days of Peace*, 182–5.
51. Minute by Bourdillon, 24 April 1946, CO 953/3/4, PRO.
52. Yost (Bangkok) to SoS, 2 May 1946, 741.92/5–246, RG 59, USNA.
53. BT Siam to ALFSEA, 5 February 1946, WO 203/1735, PRO; 'Special Operations: Locations of Stations in Siam 7 March 1946', WO 203/2389, PRO.

54. Memorandum, 'US Opinion on Siam', 25 May–12 July 1946, 892.00/7–546, RG 59, USNA.
55. Conversation between Captain Nitas Chiraprabati, Andrews (CIA), Watts (CIA) and Ogburn (SD), 12 November 1948, File: Siam Internal Conditions, 1948, Box 20, PSA records, RG 59, USNA.
56. The political background to these events is explored in depth in Stowe, *Siam Becomes Thailand* and in Fineman, *A Special Relationship*.
57. Thompson to FO, 17 November 1947, F15320/1565/40, FO 371/63911, PRO.
58. Bevin minute, n.d. [18 November 1947?], F15182/1565/40, ibid.
59. Bird to Donovan, 20 December 1947, File 680, Box 73A, Donovan papers, USMHI.
60. Thompson to FO, 23 April 1947, F508/1563/40, FO 371/63910, PRO.
61. Thompson to FO, 19 and 20 November 1947, F15371 and F15387/1565/40, FO 371/63911, PRO.
62. Entry for 2 January 1948, Killearn diary, St Antony's College, Oxford.
63. Conversation between Thompson and Stanton, 25 October 1948, File: Malaya–Siam Relations: British Malaya, Box 14, PSA records, RG 59, USNA.
64. COS (50) 307, 'Defence of Malaya', 19 August 1950, CAB 21/1981, PRO; Annex to NSC 124, 'US Objectives and Courses of Action with Respect to Communist Aggression in Southeast Asia', 13 February 1952, RG 341, USNA; FARELF to MoD, 5 May 1953, DEFE 7/367, PRO.
65. PM's Personal minute D(0) 6/4, quoted Gilbert, *Road to Victory*, 955.
66. Conversation with Joseph Smith (SSU), 15 May 1946, 846E.00/5–1546, RG 59, USNA.
67. Mackenzie to Mountbatten, 18 February 1945, WO 203/4403, PRO.
68. Mackenzie, 'Memorandum on the AJUF', 21 May 1945, HS 1/115, PRO. See also memorandum by the Head of the SOE Malaya Country Section, 15 August 1945, WO 203/4403, PRO.
69. COS to Mountbatten, 7 June 1945, WO 203/2771, PRO.
70. Cruickshank, *SOE*, 208–9.
71. Mountbatten to COS, 11 May 1945, WO 203/2967, PRO.
72. Mountbatten to Stanley, 11 May 1945, WO 172/1763, PRO, quoted in Cheah Boon Kheng, *Red Star Over Malaya*, 156.
73. Draft brief for SAC, 'Malaya Resistance Movement', July 1945, WO 203/4404, PRO. See also Cruickshank, *SOE*, 209.
74. Memorandum by the Head of the SOE Malaya Country Section, 15 August 1945, WO 203/4403, PRO; Cheah Boon Kheng, *Red Star Over Malaya*, 62–3, 75.
75. Cheah Boon Kheng, *Red Star Over Malaya*, 131–2, 150–52.
76. Mackenzie to Mountbatten, 24 August 1945, WO 203/4403, PRO. See also David to P Division, 19 August 1945, WO 203/5642, PRO.
77. Garnons-Williams to COS (SEAC), 22 August 1945, WO 203/4403, PRO. See also Cheah Boon Kheng, *Red Star Over Malaya*, 140–2, 146–7.
78. OSS Activities Report for July 1945, vi, DP.
79. 'Operational Report Young', 25 September 1945, File 2971, Box 158, Entry 154, RG 226, USNA.
80. Cheston to SoS, 10 September 1945, File: Indochina – Relations with other countries of South East Asia, 1947–50, Box 10, PSA records, RG 59, USNA.

81. Memorandum of conversation with Barnette (SSU), 1 May 1946, 846E.00/5–146, RG 59, USNA.
82. Conversation with Joseph Smith (SSU), 15 May 1946, 846E.00/5–1546, RG 59, USNA.
83. Cheah Boon Kheng, *Red Star Over Malaya*, 258–9, Miller, *Menace in Malaya*, pp. 60–2; Short, *Communist Insurrection*, 35–7.
84. Entry for 1–8 January 1946, Ziegler (ed.), *Personal Diary*.
85. Cheah Boon Kheng, *Red Star Over Malaya*, 242, 246.
86. JIC SEAC (45) 11, 'The Future Situation in Malaya', 5 January 1946, 846E.00/1–548, RG 59, USNA.
87. Akashi, 'Lai Teck'; Short, *Communist Insurrection*, 39, 62; McLane, *Soviet Strategies in Southeast Asia*, 310–11.
88. 'Report on Operations in Malaya, June 1948–July 1949' by General Sir Neil M. Ritchie, WO 106/5884, PRO.
89. HQ 'A Group' Force 136 to Kandy, 1 September 1944, HS 1/10, PRO.
90. 'A Short Account of Japanese Army Strategic Intelligence as Available to 29 Army', prepared by GSI, 34 Indian Corps, August 1945, 5/32, Penney papers, LHCMA.
91. Cruickshank, *SOE*, 176–7.
92. Sweet-Escott, *Baker Street*, 245.
93. Brigadier Prescott, CAS (B), 'Assistance to ALF Burma by Pro-Allied Burmese Elements', 13 February 1945, HS 1/13, PRO.
94. Mackenzie memorandum, 'Political Factors Affecting Co-operation with Anti-Fascist Organisations in Burma', 31 January 1945, HS 1/16, PRO.
95. Conversation with Mackenzie reported in Coughlin to Donovan, 21 February 1945, File 20, Box 20, Entry 110, RG 226, USNA.
96. Cruickshank, *SOE*, 178; Sweet-Escott, *Baker Street*, 244–46.
97. Mountbatten to COS, 27 March 1945, HS 1/16, PRO. See also Dorman-Smith to Mountbatten, 20 May 1945, ibid.
98. B/B210 to AD4, 'Draft Letter for SO', 18 April 1945, HS 1/13, PRO.
99. Mountbatten to Hone, 4 February 1944, C123, Mountbatten papers, SUL.
100. COS to Mountbatten, 22 May 1945, HS 1/16, PRO.
101. Cruickshank, *SOE*, 180–1.
102. Mackenzie to Mountbatten, 'AFO and "Provisional Government"', 5 June 1945, HS 1/16, PRO.
103. Mountbatten, *Report to the CCS Combined Chiefs of Staff*, 173; Cruickshank, *SOE*, 184–5.
104. Over 10,000 casualties, Cruickshank, *SOE*, 189–90.
105. Entries for 15, 16, 23 June 1945, Ziegler (ed.), *Personal Diary*.
106. Entry for 21 July, Ziegler (ed.), *Personal Diary*.
107. Report No. MBP-1, OSS Arakan Field Unit, 'Notes on First Two Weeks of British Re-occupation of Akyab', 21 January 1945, 8450.00/2–1045, RG 59, USNA.
108. Peers (101), Monthly Report, 29 April 1945, File 400, Box 60, Entry 190, RG 226, USNA. The plan is discussed in P Div to BGS (O) Adv HQ ALFSEA, 20 April 1945, WO 203/54, PRO.
109. Allen, 'Burmese Puzzles' and 'The Escape of Captain Vivian'.
110. The first rumours of 'dropping of secret arms by the British together with rice

from aeroplanes, supposed to be dropped for the Karens', are in Packer (Rangoon) to SoS, 25 January 1947, 8450./00/1–2547, RG 59, USNA.

111. Aldrich, 'Unquiet in Death', 202–5. Glass, *Changing of Kings*, 218–19; BBC Timewatch documentary, 'Forgotten Allies', 1996.

112. B. H. Liddell Hart had reached this conclusion in 1950, criticising the 'amoral effect' of resistance and its erosion of the 'rules of civil morality', *Defence of the West*, 53–9.

18 SPECIAL OPERATIONS IN LIBERATED AREAS: INDOCHINA AND THE NETHERLANDS EAST INDIES

1. Conversation between Ogburn and Sheldon (SSU), 30 August 1946, File: Indochina: French–Indochina Relations, 1945–7, Box 9, PSA records, RG 59, USNA.
2. La Feber, 'Roosevelt, Churchill and Indochina', 1287.
3. OSS R&A Report No. 2553, 'The Organization of the French Intelligence Services', 11 January 1945, RG 59, USNA.
4. Marr, *Vietnam 1945*, 38.
5. 'Memorandum on Forward Planning in FIC', 20 June 1944, HS 1/321, PRO.
6. Marr, *Vietnam 1945*, 44–5.
7. Tonnesson, *Vietnamese Revolution*, 187–200.
8. Marr, *Vietnam 1945*, 269.
9. K. Brown, 'The Interplay of Information and Mind', 109–31.
10. Conversation between Patti (OSS), Garden (OSS), Moffat and Sharp, 5 December 1945, File: Indochina 13.104 – Political Internal Affairs, Box 10, PSA records, RG 59, USNA.
11. JIC (45) 91 (0), 'French Resistance in Indochina', 18 March 1945, CAB 79/30, PRO.
12. De Gaulle, *The Complete War Memoirs*, 855, quoted in Hicks, 'Tension at the High Table', 37.
13. Elphick, *Far Eastern File*, 412.
14. Marr, *Vietnam 1945*, 242.
15. Cruickshank, SOE, 132–6, 210–18; Dunn, *The First Vietnam War*, 94–6; Sabattier, *Le Destin de l'Indochine*, 387–93.
16. Spector, 'Allied Intelligence', 28–30, 50; Thomas, 'Silent Partners', 14.
17. Spector, 'Allied Intelligence', 32; Thomas, 'Free French', 157.
18. Cruickshank, SOE, 125; La Feber, 'Roosevelt, Churchill and Indochina', 1288–94; Thorne, 'Indochina', 90–1; Sabattier, *Le Destin de l'Indochine*, 230–2.
19. SI Chief, China Theater to Strategic Service Officer, China Theater, 29 March 1945, File 3426, Box 202, RG 226, USNA, quoted in Thomas, 'Silent Partners', 17.
20. Marr, *Vietnam 1945*, 8–9, 278–9, 291.
21. Fenn, *Ho Chi Minh*, 76–82; Marr, *Vietnam 1945*, 279–96; Sabattier, *Le Destin de l'Indochine*, 227–31, 257–67.
22. OSS Detachment 202 (Kunming), report for March 1945, File 203, Box 65, Entry 99, RG 226, USNA.
23. Fenn to Heppner, 'Monthly Report GBT group', 25 February 1945, File 213, Box 68, Entry 99, RG 226, USNA.

24. Heppner to Washington, SSO China Report, May 1945, File 205, Box 66, Entry 99, RG 226, USNA.
25. Bills, *Empire and Cold War*, 84–5; Marr, *Vietnam 1945*, 364; Spector, *Advice and Support*, 40–2.
26. Marr, *Vietnam 1945*, 341.
27. COS (45) 116th mtg (6), CAB 79/33, PRO. See also Thomas, 'Silent Partners', 20.
28. Memorandum on DGER, 11 June 1945, CAB 122/1177, PRO.
29. COS (45) 140th mtg (15), CAB 79/34, PRO.
30. Wilson, 'Draft – suggested solution for special operations in Indochina', 5 June 1945, CAB 122/1177, PRO; Haydon to Cornwall Jones, B/1/1, 6 June 1945, ibid.
31. Bills, *Empire and Cold War*, 79–86; Marr, *Vietnam 1945*, p. 270; Herring, 'The Truman Administration', 97–117.
32. Manser, 'Roosevelt and China: From Cairo to Yalta', PhD, 171.
33. Interview with John F. Cady of OSS R&A, subsequently SD, October 1984.
34. Marr, *Vietnam 1945*, 345.
35. Donovan to Truman, 22 August 1945, June–August Chronological File, Box 15, Rose Conway Files, HSTL. See also Marr, *Vietnam 1945*, 482–4; Patti, *Why Vietnam?*, 155–8; Sainteny, *Histoire d'une Paix Manquée*, 74–81.
36. Dunn, *The First Vietnam War*, 38–46; Marr, *Vietnam 1945*, 480–1.
37. Conversation between Patti (OSS), Garden (OSS), Moffat and Sharp, 5 December 1945, File: Indochina 13.104 – Political Internal Affairs, Box 10, PSA records, RG 59, USNA.
38. Marr, *Vietnam 1945*, 486.
39. Patti, *Why Vietnam?*, 198–204, 228–9.
40. Donovan to Truman, 31 August 1945, June–August Chronological File, Box 15, Rose Conway Files, HSTL.
41. Heppner, September Report, 'French Indochina', File 1073, Box 88, Entry 168, RG 226, USNA.
42. Bills, *Empire and Cold War*, 88–9. Bills places Kolko, *The Roots of American Foreign Policy*, 92, in the former category and Dunn, *The First Vietnam War*, 22 in the latter.
43. 'Interim Report of Political and Propaganda Developments Within Indochina', 8 and 15 October 1945, File 2475, Box 186, Entry 139, RG 226, USNA.
44. Sainteny, *Ho Chi Minh and His Vietnam*, 60; Patti, *Why Vietnam?*, 105–13.
45. R&A Report No. 3237, 'Japan's Surrender and the Question of French Indochina', 24 August 1945, RG 59, USNA.
46. Dennis, *Troubled Days of Peace*, 47–66.
47. Meiklereid to FO, 1 November 1945, WO 106/4630, PRO.
48. 'Direction of Clandestine Operations after Japanese Surrender', Appendix A, 29 August 1945, File 37, Gracey papers, LHCMA. See also 'Black and Grey List of Persons', 14 August 1945, File 52, ibid.
49. Saigon Control Commission Report No. 2, 6 October 1945, 2, File 36, Gracey papers, LHCMA.
50. Report by General Gracey, 'Death of Colonel Dewey', 29 September 1945, File 2149, Box 127, Entry 148, RG 226, USNA. See also Suggested List of Docu-

ments in Report of Capt. R. P. Leonard (X-2), 12 April 1946, File: Indochina 13.121 – Reports Misc, Box 10, PSA records, RG 59, USNA.

51. HQ 136 to HPD, Appendix A, 27 September 1945, HS 1/103, PRO; Gracey to Browning, 17 September 1945, WO 203/6449. PRO. Dewey is discussed in a balanced way in Bills, *Empire and Cold War*, pp. 122–4 and in Dennis, *Troubled Days of Peace*, 213. Partisan accounts are offered in Dunn, *The First Vietnam War*, Ch. 9 and Patti, *Why Vietnam?*, 320–3.

52. 'Report on the Death of Lt Colonel Peter Dewey US Army based on Statements made by Major Bluechel US Army, Captain White US Army and Major Wenham 14/13 Frontier Force Rifles', 29 September 1945, File 2149, Box 124, Entry 148, RG 226, USNA.

53. OSS Report from Kandy, 27 September 1945, File: Indochina – Relations with other countries of South East Asia, 1947–50, Box 10, PSA records, RG 59, USNA. For a discerning discussion of Dewey see also Bills, *Empire and Cold War*, 124–6.

54. As n. 52. See also Suggested List of Documents in Report of Capt. R. P. Leonard (X-2), 12 April 1946, File: Indochina 13.121 – Reports Misc, Box 10, PSA records, RG 59, USNA.

55. Extracts from minutes of British–Vietminh meetings, October 1945, File 36, Gracey papers, LHCMA.

56. Mountbatten to COS, SEACOS 513, 12 October 1945, WO 106/4630, PRO.

57. Truman to Dewey, 9 October 1945, Box 20, Leahy File, RG 218, USNA.

58. 'Interim Report of Political and Propaganda Developments Within Indochina', 8 and 15 October 1945, File 2475, Box 186, Entry 139, RG 226, USNA.

59. 'Directive to Major A. W. Fielding, Senior Liaison Officer, Force 136/20th Indian Division', File 43, Gracey papers, LHCMA.

60. Fielding to Cass, 29 September 1945, HS 1/103, PRO.

61. Gracey to Slim, 13 October 1945, WO 203/5563, PRO.

62. Bonnefous to Menzies (SIS), 8 December 1943, 9007–235–4, Trevor-Wilson papers, NAM.

63. Muggeridge, *The Infernal Grove*, 192–4, 210–11, 215–16.

64. Patti, *Why Vietnam?*, 291.

65. Gracey to Trevor-Wilson, 24 November 1945, 9001–235–8–1, Trevor-Wilson papers, NAM.

66. Report by Trevor-Wilson, 28 December 1945, WO 203/5563, PRO.

67. See for example Ho Chi Minh to Trevor-Wilson, 14 March 1946, 9007–235–11/12, Trevor-Wilson papers, NAM.

68. Trevor-Wilson memorandum, 'JIFC Officers in HANOI', 19 November 1945, 9007–235–6, Trevor-Wilson papers, NAM. See also Trevor-Wilson to Saigon Control Commission No. 1, 28 December 1945, WO 203/5563, PRO.

69. Private information; several versions of this story circulate.

70. Reed (Saigon) to SoS, No.92, 13 April 1946, 892.014/4–1346, RG 59, USNA. It remains unclear whether Trevor-Wilson, or SIS, generally knew Ho's real identity. Remarkably, it appears that the French did not. In October 1945 the French told Moffat that there was much speculation in French circles as to who Ho Chi Minh, present Head of the Viet-Minh Government at Hanoi, really is. It has been suggested that he is really Nguyen Ai-Quoc but the French authorities now believe that Ai-Quoc probably died of tuberculosis in a Hong Kong jail.

By others it is thought that he may be Bui Ai, others considered that he might still be a third person. Conversation between Jiff and Moffat, 'Ho Chi Minh', 21 October 1945, File: Indochina Personalities/Misc, Box 7, PSA records, RG 59, USNA.

71. Ho Chi Minh to Trevor-Wilson, 29 July 1947, 9007–235–24, Trevor-Wilson papers, NAM.

72. James Fulton (SIS) to Trevor Wilson, 22 March 1954, 9007–235–45, Trevor-Wilson Papers, NAM. Also private information.

73. Chandler, 'The Kingdom of Kampuchea', 80–6.

74. Ibid., 89.

75. Saigon Control Commission No.1 Report, paras. 22 and 46, File 36, Gracey papers, LHCMA.

76. War Diary of HQ Allied Land Forces Phnom Penh, WO 172/7009, PRO.

77. Dening to FO, 26 October 1945, F8953/11/61, FO 371/46309, PRO.

78. Saigon Control Commission No.1 Report, paras 22 and 46, File 36, Gracey papers, LHCMA; Chandler, 'The Kingdom of Kampuchea', 90–1.

79. Cruickshank, SOE, 134.

80. Gunn, Political Struggles in Laos, 132, 140.

81. Kimmins (ALFSEA) to Browning (SEAC), 27 September 1945, WO 208/3040, PRO.

82. Mackenzie to Dening, 29 September 1945, WO 203/5562, PRO.

83. Mountbatten to ALFSIAM, 10 December 1945, WO 203/5575, PRO.

84. The Klotz incident is recounted from different sides in Bank, From OSS to the Green Berets, 122–4; Kemp, Alms for Oblivion, 50–3; Smiley, Regular Irregular, 174–5. I am indebted to David Smiley and Hugh Tovar for sharing their recollections of Laos in 1945 with me.

85. 'FIC Sitrep for week ending 21.11.45', WO 106/4630, PRO.

86. Thompson to FO, 28 October 1946, F15645, WO 208/3040, PRO.

87. Thompson to FO, 26 November 1946, F14060/10/40, FO 371/54393, PRO; Dening to Bevin, 29 November 1946, F17377/10/40, FO 371/54394, PRO.

88. Wilkinson to Dewing, 15 February 1943, 1/4, Wilkinson papers, CCC. On the wartime role of NEFIS and other Dutch secret service see Dennis, Troubled Days, 76–9.

89. Mountbatten to Blamey, 19 September 1945 and Blamey to Mountbatten, 26 September 1945, C35, Mountbatten papers, SUL.

90. Report of Special Mission to General Blamey, C. in C. AMF, on future of SIA in Australia, NEFIS Organisation in NEI, by G/Cpt W. H. Cliff, 9 October 1945, HS 1/303, PRO.

91. Memorandum of a conversation with Jane Foster (OSS), 12 December 1945, 856E.00/12–1245, RG 59, USNA.

92. Bills, Empire and Cold War, 132–5.

93. The cables from Batavia are at Box 533, Entry 88, RG 226, USNA.

94. Lt Col. Burt (ACDS) to Commander Force 136, 'Operation Officers (Ex-Netherlands) of BBO', 22 November 1945, HS 1/268, PRO.

95. Anstey to D of I (SEAC), 22 October 1945, ibid.

96. Mackenzie to Admiral Helfrich, 12 November 1945, ibid.

97. B/B3 to AD, 4 December 1945, HS 1/269, PRO.

98. Mountbatten to Bevin, 25 November 1945, C30, Mountbatten papers, SUL.

99. Dening to Bevin, 29 January 1946, FO 800/461, PRO.

100. Bevin to Dening (To be decyphered by Mr Dening), 2 February 1946, FO 800/461, PRO; Bevin to Mountbatten, 5 March 1946, C30, Mountbatten papers, SUL.

101. MacMahon Ball to Sec. External Affairs Canberra, 17 December 1945, C212, Mountbatten papers, SUL.

102. Report by Chapman Walker, December 1945, CAB 122/512, PRO; Bills, *Empire and Cold War*, 140–1.

103. French Indochina Situation Report No.14/112 4 September 1945, WO 203/5562, PRO. For an excellent survey of British regional policy in South East Asia after 1945 see Remme, *British Policy*.

19 HONG KONG AND THE FUTURE OF CHINA

1. Interview with Smith by Conyers Read, 21 April 1945, DP.

2. Cruickshank, *SOE*, 159–62.

3. JIC/1452/44, draft report by E. J. King-Salter, 'British Interests in China', 2 November 1944, HS 1/167, PRO. Parts of this report were incorporated into JIC (44) 458 (0).

4. Helliwell (Chief SI, OSS, CT) to Donovan, 'A Study of British Intelligence Organisations in China', 13 February 1945, DP.

5. FO to Chungking, 28 March 1945, WO 106/3483, PRO.

6. FO to Chungking, 28 March 1945, WO 106/3483, PRO. See also HQ Force 136 to ADCOS (A), 'Clandestine Operation in China', 1 March 1945, HS 1/169, PRO.

7. Chungking to FO, 30 March 1945, WO 106/3483, PRO.

8. De Wiart to WO, 21 and 28 April 1945, ibid.

9. De Wiart to WO 21 April 1945, ibid.

10. WO to C. in C. India, 6 May 1945, WO 106/3483, PRO; MA Chungking to C. in C. India, 12 May 1945, ibid.

11. C. in C. India to WO 21 May 1945, ibid.

12. Heppner to Washington, SSO China Report, June 1945, File 206, Box 66, Entry 99, RG 226, USNA.

13. BB.100 to CD, 3 July 1945, HS 1/166, PRO.

14. Meeting at the Colonial Office, 5 July 1945, CO 129.591/9 and FO 371/46252, quoted in Baxter, 'Britain and the War in China', 389–90, 393.

15. Ride, *British Army Aid Group*, 292–305. The accompanying AGAS party was commanded by Lt Charles Fenn, USNR. See also AD.4 to CD, 13 December 1944, HS 1/168, PRO.

16. Baxter, 'Britain and the War in China', PhD, 395–6.

17. WF/435 to London, 12 July 1945, HS 1/184, PRO.

18. Air Ministry to Barker, 21 August 1945, Barker papers, LHCMA.

19. De Wiart, *Happy Odyssey*, 210–11.

20. CPA (Dening) to SAC (Mountbatten), 30 December 1944, WO 203/4398, PRO.

21 Ibid.; minutes of SAC's 3rd Misc. Mtg, 29 January 1945, and Appendix 1, 'Meeting Between Heads and Representatives of Clandestine Services of GB and USA', 29 January 1945, File 510, Box 51, Entry 110, RG 226, USNA.

22. Memorandum by Grimsdale concerning a conversation with Wedemeyer, 30 December 1944, WO 106/3577, PRO.
23. Air Commodore Blandy had previously run the RAF intercept service, Lewin, *Ultra Goes to War*, 76.
24. British Military Mission to Chungking, 24 January 1945, WO 203/291, PRO.
25. SOE to Mountbatten, 3 February 1945, WO 203/5767, PRO.
26. SAC's 3rd misc mtg, 30 January 1945, WO 106/3483, PRO.
27. COS (45) 349 (0), 'Future Role of 204 Military Mission in China', 19 May 1945, CAB 122/775, PRO.
28. AD to CD, 6 April 1945, HS 1/170, PRO.
29. Heppner (OSS China) to Donovan, 1 May 1945, enclosing OSS China Theater Report for April 1945, File 204, Box 65, Entry 99, RG 226, USNA.
30. SOE were obtaining information on OSS from a British national serving in OSS in China, Gill Davies, 'Group C Progress Report', 2 February 1945, HS 1/136, PRO.
31. Memorandum, 'Operational Control – US Navy Group China', 12 March 1945, Box 5, Lot 110 Record of the Office of Chinese Affairs, RG 59, USNA.
32. Schaller, 'SACO', 546–53.
33. Whittaker, Intelligence Officer OSS China, to Intelligence Office OSS Washington, 5 May 1945, File 205, Box 66, Entry 99, RG 226, USNA.
34. Fitzgerald, 'Naval Group China', 104.
35. Whitaker, Monthly IO China report, 25 May–30 June 1945, File 105, Box 14, Entry 148, RG 226, USNA.
36. These views largely accord with Maochun Yu, *OSS in China*, 208, 214–17.
37. Fitzgerald, 'Navy Group China', 68.
38. He was positively identified by his distinctive pistol, MA China to SACSEA Int. Div, 15 April 1946, WO 203/5051, PRO. Miles later served as a US naval attaché in South America.
39. See the extensive work by Wasserstein, *Secret War in Shanghai*, 157–95.
40. X-2/SSU memorandum by Major Holomb, 'Nazi Party in Shanghai', 27 December 1945, Box 11, Lot 110, Record of the Office of Chinese Affairs, RG 59, USNA.
41. Elphick, *Far Eastern File*, 280–1.
42. SoS Colonies to Young (Governor), 3 March 1947, CO 537/1949, PRO. But the key evidence, MOI/PWE monitoring records at Delhi, had already been destroyed.
43. See the case of Private Yashinoa in Elphick, *Far Eastern File*, 93.
44. Entry for 31 March 1944, Somerville diary, Somerville Papers, 2/2, CCC. Somerville's reluctance to authorise sabotage operations against Japanese ships using the midget 'X' craft and 'chariot' submersibles was partly because: 'The habit of the Japanese to torture prisoners in order to extract information makes it necessary that survivors should kill themselves rather than fall into the hands of these brutes.' Entry for 17 July 1944, ibid.
45. Entry for 8 April 1944, Ziegler (ed.), *Personal Diary*.
46. In September 1945, Field Security Units located Admiral Chudoh, the Chief Japanese Signals Intelligence Officer for the southern armies, a rare cryptological prize. Penney minute to SAC, 22 September 1945, WO 203/5051, PRO.

47. McDonough (X-2) to Peers (101), 'CICB', 7 April 1945, File 390, Box 60, Entry 190, RG 226, USNA. The previous the head of CICB was Colonel E. A. Airy.
48. Birn (X-2) to McCarthy (X-2 Washington), 15 December 1945, File 2146, Box 124, Entry 148, RG 226, USNA.
49. SAC (45) 85/1, 'Intelligence Assault Units, 27 June 1945, WO 203/1778, PRO.
50. Entries for 13 and 14 September 1945, 30 November 1945, Ziegler (ed.), *Personal Diary*.
51. OSS Activities Report for July 1945, 66, DP.
52. JP (45) 256 (Final), 'Future of British Troops in China', 2 October 1945, CAB 79/40, PRO; COS (45) 241th mtg (6), 4 October 1945, ibid.
53. Col. GS to Hollis, 15 October 1945, HS 1/170, PRO.
54. Maochun Yu, *OSS in China*, 222–4, 227.
55. 'Summary of Interview with Lt Tung Fu-Kuan [Tung Ching-sheng], Chinese Army', Lt Col. J. J. O'Conner, Deputy Theater Judge Advocate, 25 September 1945, DP.
56. E.g., Sayer and Botting, *America's Secret Army*, 317.
57. Quinn (Director SSU) to Moscrip, 1 May 1946, File 2787, Box 198, Entry 146, RG 226, USNA.
58. Auerbach (SSU) to General Marshall, 1 June 1946, File ESD 44, Box 34, Marshall Mission Records, 1944–8, Lot 54 D 270, RG 59, USNA; Caughey (SSU) to Auerbach, 4 June 1946, ibid.
59. Commander 7th Fleet to MacArthur, 8 November 1946, ibid; Memorandum by Commander 7th Fleet, 'ESG 44 – plan for support', 26 October 1946, ibid.
60. Canton to Nanking, 9 April 1947, File: French–Indochina relations, Box 9, PSA records, RG 59, USNA.
61. Clubb to Marshall, 13 June 1946, ibid; Report by Leavell, 18 July 1946, File ESD 44, Box 34, Marshall Mission Records, 1944–8, Lot 54 D 270, RG 59, USNA.
62. Memorandum of a conversation with DeBardeleben (CIG), 18 April 1947, Box 13, Lot 110, Records of the Office of Chinese Affairs, RG 59, USNA; Ringwalt memorandum to Butterworth, 'CIG Directive', 7 October 1947, ibid.
63. Memorandum of a conversation between George (CIA) and Ringwalt (SD), 11 December 1947, ibid.

20 CONCLUSION: THE HIDDEN HAND AND THE FANCY FOOT

1. Selborne to Churchill, 27 April 1944, 'Armistice and Post-War Committee', SOE main office files. I am most grateful to the SOE Adviser, Duncan Stewart, for providing me with a copy of this document, which is in the process of being released.
2. The 'fancy-footwork school' is rarely defined precisely. However, historians such as John Darwin, Wm Roger Louis, Anthony Stockwell and B. R. Tomlinson are often referred to in the same breath.
3. Entry for 11 December 1929, Pimlott, *The Political Diary of Hugh Dalton*.
4. Taylor, *Awakening from History*, 302–10.
5. Ibid., 352.
6. Dening to FO, 9 December 1944, F5802/955/61, FO 371/41746, PRO.

7. Dening to Sterndale Bennett, 7 September 1945, F6867/296/40, FO 371/46550, PRO.
8. Taylor, *Awakening from History*, 356.
9. De Wiart to Mountbatten, 23 February 1945, C43, Mountbatten papers, SUL.
10. Thacker to Lattimore, 12 August 1943, reel 1/4, OWI microfilm, BRO.
11. Stern to Davis, 20 and 27 March 1943, ibid.
12. Stimson to Davis, 8 March 1943, ibid.
13. Stern to Davis, 7 June 1943, ibid.
14. Ziegler, *Mountbatten*, 313–14.
15. David Canadine, quoted in Roberts, *Eminent Churchillians*, 76.
16. O'Brien, *The Moonlight War*, 124–5; Ziegler, *Mountbatten*, 307, 314, 337. Mountbatten also used Murphy to take correspondence 'by safe hand' to Gubbins in London, Mountbatten to Gubbins, 30 November 1944, C112, Mountbatten papers, SUL.
17. Entry for 25 November 1943, discussing reports from 'Base Censor', Somerville diary, CCC. Cf. Holquist, 'Information is the Alpha and Omega of our work', 415–50.
18. Entry for 25 April 1942, Oliver Harvey diary, Harvey Papers, MSS 56398, BL.
19. Kane to MacLeish, 'British Embassy Conference Concerning Anti-British Feeling in the United States and Anti-American Feeling in England', 3 December 1942, reel 1/5, OWI microfilm, BRO.
20. Colin Mackenzie, Head of SOE Far East, suggested that Dening had compiled such a report when interviewed by the author in London, 31 May 1985. His investigations began in July 1945, Dening to FO, 13 July 1945, F4532/738/40, FO 371/46562, PRO. See also Dening to Bevin, 25 March 1946, enclosing 'Review of Political Events in South East Asia Command, 1945–March 1946', F5093/87/61, FO 371/53995, PRO.
21. ALFSEA Isum, 169, 3 August 1946, CO 537/1669, PRO.
22. Minutes of a meeting in McGregor's room (BoT), 14 March 1947, T236/2366, PRO.
23. Memorandum by Davies, 'Anglo–American Cooperation in East Asia', 15 November 1943, File 317, Box 49, Entry 99, RG 226, USNA.
24. Conversation between Moffat and Holliday (OSS), 20 November 1945, File: Indochina 13.1091 – Political Relations with Thailand, Box 9, PSA records, RG 59, USNA.
25. Hess, *America Encounters India*, 164
26. Windmiller, 'Tumultuous Times', 120.
27. OSS R&A Report No. 3494, 'United States Prestige in Southeast Asia', 7 February 1946, RG 59, USNA.
28. Muggeridge, *The Infernal Grove*, 79–80. See also Glass, *Changing of Kings*, 166.

ARCHIVES AND BONFIRES : A NOTE ON METHODOLOGY

1. Price to Penney (D of I), 21 November 1945, 5/84, Box 5, Penney Papers, LHCMA.
2. I am indebted to Professor M. R. D. Foot for his views on the proportion of SOE documents that have survived.
3. Petro, *Triple Commission*, 246.

4. For example, the Germans at the German Embassy at Bangkok reported proudly to the arriving British that they had burnt their *Sonderakten* or special archive, including all their material on Bose, Maham to Dening, 4 October 1945, WO 203/5577, PRO.
5. Stripp, *Codebreaker in the Far East*, 46–7.
6. Entry for 5 September 1946, P. Moon (ed.), *Wavell*.
7. Colonel Hugh Toye, interview, Oxford, 3 July 1986.

Select bibliography

Unless otherwise stated the place of publication is London

UNPUBLISHED DOCUMENTS

PUBLIC RECORD OFFICE, KEW GARDENS, SURREY, ENGLAND

ADM 1	Admiralty and Secretariat Papers
ADM 223	Naval Intelligence Files
AIR 8	Chief of the Air Staff Files
AIR 20	Air Ministry Registry
AIR 23	RAF Regional Commands
AIR 40	Air Intelligence Files
CAB 79	Chiefs of Staff Minutes
CAB 80	Chiefs of Staff Memoranda
CAB 81	Chiefs of Staff Subcommittees (JIC)
CAB 84	Joint Planning Staff Memoranda
CAB 96	Cabinet Far Eastern Committee
CAB 106	Cabinet Office Historical Section Files
CAB 119	Joint Planning Staff Collation Files
CAB 120	Minister of Defence
CAB 122	Joint Staff Mission (Washington) Files
CO 825	Colonial Office, Eastern Department
DO 35	Dominions Office, Correspondence Files
FO 115	Foreign Office, Washington Embassy Files
FO 371	Foreign Office, Registry Files
FO 850	Foreign Office, Communication Department Files
FO 837	Ministry of Economic Warfare Files
FO 930	Ministry of Information Files
HS 1	Special Operations Executive Records, Far East
HW 1	Churchill's signals intelligence summaries
HW 3	Signals intelligence records from Bletchley Park
HW 4	FECB records
HW 10	Signals intelligence records from HMS Anderson
PREM 3	Prime Minister's Minutes
WO 106	Directorate of Military Operations and Intelligence
WO 193	Directorate of Military Operations
WO 203	South East Asia Command Files
WO 208	Directorate of Military Intelligence
WO 212	Orders of Battle

INDIA OFFICE, BLACKFRIARS ROAD, LONDON

L/P&S/12	Political Department, Annual Files

M/3–5   Burma Office, Political and External Departments
L/WS/1   War Staff

BANK OF ENGLAND, THREADNEEDLE STREET, LONDON

OV 65   Malaya: Country Files

NATIONAL ARCHIVES, WASHINGTON DC

RG 38   Navy Group China Records
RG 59   Decimal Files, Lot Files, OSS RA Reports
RG 165   Joint Chiefs of Staff Records
RG 218   Joint Chiefs of Staff Records and Leahy Files
RG 226   OSS Records
RG 319   US Army Plans and Operations
RG 457   Signals Research Histories

FREEDOM OF INFORMATION ACT REQUESTS

Additional documentation was secured from the Central Intelligence Agency; US Air Force, Intelligence Command; US Army, Intelligence and Security Command.

PRIVATE PAPERS

GREAT BRITAIN

Field Marshal Lord Alanbrooke (LHCMA)
General Auchinleck (JRL)
Lord Avon (PRO and BUL)
Air Vice-Marshal J. Lindsay Baker (LHCMA)
Brigadier Sir Edward Beddington (LHCMA)
Air Chief-Marshal Sir Robert Brooke-Popham (LHCMA)
Sir Alexander Cadogan (CCC)
Admiral of the Fleet, Sir Andrew Cunningham (BL)
Hugh Dalton (BLPES)
General Davidson (LHCMA)
Sir Reginald Dorman-Smith (IOLR)
Captain G. A. Garnons-Williams RN (IWM)
Major-General James Gavin (LHCMA)
Sir Andrew Gilchrist (CCC)
Major-General D. D. Gracey (LHCMA)
Lord Halifax (CCC)
Sir Oliver Harvey (BL)
General Sir Hastings Ismay (LHCMA)
Lord Killearn, St Anthony's College, Oxford
Lt Colonel W. J. Martin (IWM)
Field Marshal Lord Montgomery of Alamein (IWM)

Admiral Lord Louis Mountbatten (SUL)
Major-General Sir William Penney (LHCMA)
Air Chief-Marshal Pirie (LHCMA)
General Sir Henry Pownall (LHCMA)
Brigadier Pyman (LHCMA)
Lord Selborne (OBL)
Admiral Sir James Somerville (CCC)
Lt Colonel Leo Steveni (in private hands)
Air Vice-Marshal John Whitworth Jones (RAFMH)
Lt Colonel Arthur G. Trevor-Wilson (NAM)
Lt Colonel Gerald Wilkinson (CCC)

UNITED STATES

Norwood F. Allman (HIWRP)
Adolf Berle (HSTL)
Russell J. Bowen Collection (LL)
Claire Chennault (HIWRP)
General William J. Donovan (private access, now at CMH and CCC)
Brigadier General Frank Dorn (HIWRP)
J. Russell Forgen (HIWRP)
Preston Goodfellow (HIWRP)
Stanley Hornbeck (HIWRP)
Cordell Hull (microfilm, CUL)
General Douglas MacArthur (MML)
Franklin D. Roosevelt (FDRL)
General Stilwell (HIWRP)
Henry L. Stimson (microfilm, BRO)
Thomas P. Thornton (FDRL)
Harry S. Truman (HSTL)
Major-General Charles A. Willoughby (MML and HIWRP)

PUBLISHED MATERIAL

PUBLISHED DOCUMENTS, DIARIES, MEMOIRS AND AUTOBIOGRAPHY

Amery, J., *Approach March* (Hutchinson, 1973).
Amery, L. S., *My Political Life* Vol. III (Hutchinson, 1955).
Ashton, A. and Stockwell, A. (eds.), *British Documents on the End of Empire*, Series A, Vol. I, Part I (HMSO, 1992).
Astley, J. B., *Inner Circle: A View of War at the Top* (Hutchinson, 1971).
Atherton, L., *SOE Operations in the Far East: An Introductory Guide to the Newly Released Records* (Public Record Office, 1993).
Ballard, G., *On Ultra Active Service: The Story of Australian Signals Intelligence Operations During World War II* (Richmond, Victoria: Spectrum Publications, 1991).
Ba Maw, *Breakthrough in Burma: Memoirs of a Revolution, 1939–1946* (New Haven: Yale University Press, 1968).

Band, C. and Band, W., *Dragon Fangs: Two Years with the Chinese Guerrillas* (Allen and Unwin, 1948).

Bank, A., *From OSS to the Green Berets: The Birth of the Special Forces* (Novato, CA: Presidio, 1986).

Barnes, J. and Nicholson, D. (eds.), *The Empire at Bay: The Leo Amery Diaries, 1929–45* (Hutchinson, 1988).

Beamish, J., *Burma Drop* (Elek Books, 1958).

Beevor, J. G., *SOE: Recollections and Reflections* (Bodley Head, 1981).

Bennett, J. W., Hobbart, W. A. and Spitzer, J. B. (eds.), *Intelligence and Cryptanalytic Activities of the Japanese During World War II* (Laguna Hills, CA: Aegean Park Press, 1986).

Berle, B. and Jacobs, T. (eds.), *Navigating the Rapids: From the Papers of Adolph A. Berle* (New York: Harcourt Brace Jovanovich, 1973).

Bond, B. (ed.), *Chief of Staff: The Diaries of Lt. General Sir Henry Pownall, 1940–1944*, Vol. II (Leo Cooper, 1974).

Boulle, P., *My Own River Kwai* (New York: The Vanguard Press, 1967).

Bowen, J. *Undercover in the Jungle* (William Kimber, 1978).

Bright-Holmes, J. (ed.), *Like It Was: A Selection From the Diaries of Malcolm Muggeridge* (Collins, 1981).

Buckle, R. (ed.), *Self-Portrait with Friends: The Selected Diaries of Cecil Beaton, 1926–1974* (Weidenfeld and Nicolson, 1974).

Cably, M., *Gueirillas au laos* (Paris: Presses de la Cité, 1966).

Caldwell, J. C. and Gayn, M., *American Agent* (New York: Holt, 1947).

Caldwell, O. J., *Secret War: Americans in China, 1944–45* (Carbondale: Southern Illinois University Press, 1972).

Callinan, B. J., *Independent Company: 2/2 and 2/4 Australian Independent Companies in Portuguese Timor, 1941–3* (Heinemann, 1953).

Calvocoressi, P., *Threading My Way* (Duckworth, 1994).

Casey, Lord, *Personal Experience, 1939–1946* (New York: McKay, 1962).

Casey, W., *The Secret War Against Hitler* (Simon Schuster, 1989).

Catroux, G., *Deux actes de drame Indochinois* (Paris: Plon, 1959).

Wan Loy Chan, *Burma: The Untold Story* (Novato, CA: Presidio, 1986).

Chapman, F. S., *The Jungle is Neutral* (Chatto and Windus, 1963).

Chapman, J. W. (ed.), *The Price of Admiralty: The War Diary of the German Naval Attaché in Japan, 1939–1943*, Vol. I (Brighton: Ripes, 1982).

Chennault, C. L., *Way of a Fighter*, (New York: Putnam, 1949).

Churchill, W.S., *The Second World War*, Vols. I–VI (Cassell, 1948–54).

Clague, P., *Bridge House* (Hong Kong: South China Morning Post, 1983).

Clive, N. *A Greek Experience, 1943–1948* (Michael Russell, 1985).

Colville, J., *Fringes of Power* (Hodder & Stoughton, 1985).

Cross, J., *Red Jungle* (Robert Hale, 1957).

    First In and Last Out: An Unconventional British Officer in Indochina, 1945–6 and 1972–6 (Brassey's, 1992).

Danchev, A. (ed.), *The Anglo-American Alliance at War: The Diaries of Brigadier Vivian Dykes* (Brassey's, 1989).

Decoux, J., *A la barre de l'Indochine: Histoire de mon gouvernemente générale, 1940–1945* (Paris: Plon, 1949).

De Wiart, A. Carton, *Happy Odyssey* (Jonathan Cape, 1950).

Dilks, D. (ed.), *The Diaries of Sir Alexander Cadogan, 1938–1945* (Cassell, 1971).

Direk Jayanama, *Siam and World War II* (Bangkok: Social Science Association of Thailand, 1978).

Documents on Australian Foreign Policy, 1937–44 (Canberra: Department of Foreign Affairs, 1976–88).

Downes, D., *The Scarlet Thread: Adventures in Wartime Espionage* (New York: The British Book Centre, 1953).

Drage, C., *The Amiable Prussian* (Blond, 1958).

Dunlop, R., *Behind Japanese Lines, with the OSS in Burma* (Chicago: Rand McNally, 1979).

Durrani, M. K., *The Sixth Column* (Cassell, 1955).

Evan, G., *The Johnnies: Z Force in Burma* (Cassell, 1964).

Fairbank, J. K., *Chinabound: A Fifty-Year Memoir* (New York: Harper and Row, 1982).

Fellowes-Gordon, I., *Amiable Assassins: The Story of Kachin Guerrillas in North Burma* (Robert Hale, 1957).

Fergusson, B., *The Trumpet in the Hall* (Collins, 1970).

Foreign Relations of the United States, 1940–6 (Washington, DC: Government Printing Office, 1952–68).

Fujiwara, Iwaichi, Gen., *F Kikan: Japanese Army Intelligence Operations in World War II* (Hong Kong: Heinemann Asia, 1983).

Gilbert, J. L. and Finnegan, J. P. (eds.), *U.S. Army Signals Intelligence in World War II: A Documentary History* (Washington, DC: Center of Military History, 1993).

Gilchrist, A., *Bangkok Top Secret: Force 136 at War* (Hutchinson, 1970).

  Malaya, 1941 (Robert Hale, 1992).

Gladwyn, Lord, *Memoirs* (London 1972).

Glass, L., *The Changing of Kings: Memoirs of Burma, 1937–49* (Peter Owen, 1988).

Goldstein, D. M. and Dillon, K. V., *Fading Victory: The Diary of Admiral Matome Ugaki, 1941–5* (Pittsburgh: University of Pittsburgh Press, 1991).

Greene, G., 'Men at Work', in *Twenty-One Stories* (Penguin, 1980).

GSI(x) GHQ India, *Intelligence Notes from Burma, 1943–5* (Delhi: GHQ India, October 1945).

Guthrie, D., *Jungle Diary* (Macmillan, 1946).

Harrison, T., *World Within* (Cresset Press, 1959).

Harvey, J. (ed.), *The Diplomatic Diaries of Oliver Harvey, 1937–1940* (Collins, 1970).

  The War Diaries of Oliver Harvey, 1941–1945 (Collins, 1978).

Hilsman, R., *American Guerrilla: My War Behind Japanese Lines* (Washington, DC: Brassey's, 1990).

Holman, D., *Noone of the ULU* (Heinemann, 1958).

  Green Torture (Robert Hale, 1962).

Horton, D., *Ring of Five* (Leo Cooper, 1983).

Hull, C., *The Memoirs of Cordell Hull*, Vol. II (Hodder & Stoughton, 1948).

Hunter, C. C., *Galahad* (Texas: The Naylor Company, 1963).

Hyde, H. M., *The Quiet Canadian* (Hamish Hamilton, 1962).

Ike, N. (ed.), *Japan's Decision for War: Record of the 1941 Policy Conferences* (Stanford: Stanford University Press, 1967).

Ind, A. W., *Allied Intelligence Bureau: Our Secret Weapon in the War Against Japan* (New York: David McKay, 1958).

Irwin, A., *Burmese Outpost: V Force* (Collins, 1945).

Kauffman, R. F., *The Coconut Wireless* (New York: Macmillan, 1948).

Kemp, P., *Arms for Oblivion* (Cassell, 1961).

Kennedy, J., *The Business of War* (Hutchinson, 1957).

Kimball, W. F. (ed.), *Churchill and Roosevelt: The Complete Correspondence*, Vols. I–II, (Princeton: Princeton University Press, 1984).

Kirkpatrick, L., *The Real CIA* (New York: Macmillan, 1968).

Layton, E. T. with Pineau, R. and Costello, J., *And I Was There: Pearl Harbor and Midway – Breaking the Secrets* (New York: William Morrow, 1985).

Leutze, J. (ed.), *London Observer: The Journal of General Raymond E. Lee* (Hutchinson, 1972).

Lifu Ch'en, *The Storm Clouds Clear Over China: The Memoir of Lifu Ch'en, 1900–93* (Stanford: Hoover Institute Press, 1994).

Lindsay, M., *The Unknown War – North China, 1937–1945* (Bergstrom and Boyle, 1975).

Lindsay, O., *At the Going Down of the Sun* (Hamish Hamilton, 1981).

Lucas Phillips, C. E., *The Raiders of the Arakan* (Heinemann, 1971).

McCrae, A., *Tales of Burma* (James Paton of Paisley, 1981).

MacDonald, E. P., *Undercover Girl* (NY: Macmillan, 1947).

McKie, R., *The Heroes* (Angus and Robertson, 1960).

McLachlan, D., *Room 39: Naval Intelligence in Action 1939–45* (Weidenfeld & Nicholson, 1968).

Mains, A., *Field Security: Very Ordinary Intelligence* (Picton Publishing, 1992).

Mains, T., *The Retreat from Burma: An Intelligence Officer's Personal Story* (Foulsham, 1973).

Mansergh, N. (ed.), *The Transfer of Power, 1942–7: Vol. 1, The Cripps Mission* (London, 1970).

Mars, A., *HMS Thule Intercepts* (Elek Books, 1956).

Mehra, P., *The North-Eastern Frontier: A Documentary Study of the Internecine Rivalry between India, Tibet and China. Vol. II, 1914–54* (Delhi: Oxford University Press, 1980).

Miles, M., *A Different Kind of War: The Little Known Story of the Combined Guerrilla Forces Created in China by the U.S. Navy and the Chinese During World War II* (Garden City, NY: Doubleday, 1967).

Moon, P. (ed.), *Wavell: The Viceroy's Journal* (Oxford University Press, 1973).

Moon, T., *This Grim and Savage Game* (New York: Burning Gate Press, 1991).

Moon, T. N. and Eiffler, C. F., *The Deadliest Colonel* (New York: Vantage Press, 1975).

Morrisson, I., *Malayan Postcript* (Faber and Faber, 1942).

  Grandfather Longlegs (Faber and Faber, 1947).

Moss, W. S., *A War of the Shadows* (Boardman, 1958).

Mountbatten, Lord, *Report to the Combined Chiefs of Staff* (HMSO, 1951).

O'Brien, T., *The Moonlight War: The Story of Clandestine Operations in South East Asia, 1944–5* (Collins, 1987).

Paillat, C., *Dossier Secret de l'Indochine* (Paris: Presses de la Cité, 1964).

Patti, A. L. A., *Why Vietnam? Prelude to America's Albatross* (Berkeley: University of California Press, 1980).

Peacock, G., *The Life of a Jungle Wallah* (Ilfracombe, Devon: Arthur Stockwell, 1958).

Peers, W. R. and Brelis, D., *Behind the Burma Road: The Story of America's Most Successful Guerrilla Force* (Boston: Little, Brown, 1963).

Petro, W., *Triple Commission* (John Murray, 1968).

Philby, K., *My Silent War* (MacGibbon and Key, 1968).

Phillips, W., *Venture in Diplomacy* (Boston: The Beacon Press, 1952).

Piggott, F. S. G., *The Broken Thread: An Autobiography* (Aldershot: Gale and Polden, 1950).

Principal War Telegrams and Memoranda (Nedeln: KTO Press, 1976).

Puey Ungphakorn, *A Siamese for All Seasons* (Bangkok: Komol Keemthong Foundation, 1981).

Robertson, E., *The Japanese File: Pre-War Japanese Penetration in World War Two* (Hong Kong: Heinemann Asia, 1979).

Roosevelt, E., *As He Saw It* (New York: Duel, Sloan and Pearce, 1946).

Sabattier, G., *Le Destin de l'Indochine* (Paris:,1953).

Sainteny, J., *Histoire d'une Paix Manquée* (Paris, 1953).

Singh, M., *Soldiers' Contribution to Indian Independence: The Epic of the Indian National Army* (Delhi, 1975).

Singlaub, J. K., *Hazardous Duty: An American Soldier in the Twentieth Century* (New York: Summit Books, 1991).

Sivavam, M., *The Road to Delhi* (Rutland, Vermont: Charles E. Tuttle, 1967).

Slim, W., *Defeat Into Victory* (Cassell, 1956).

Smith, N. and Clarke B., *Into Siam, Underground Kingdom* (Indianapolis: Bobbs-Merrill, 1946).

Stockwell, A., *Malaya, Part 1, The Malayan Union Experiment, 1942–8*, BDEE Series B, Vol. 3 (HMSO, 1995).

Stratton, R. O., *SACO: The Rice Paddy Navy* (Pleasantville, New York: C. S. Palmer, 1950).

   Army–Navy Game (Falmouth: Volta, 1977).

Stripp, A. J., *Codebreaker in the Far East* (Frank Cass, 1989).

Strutton, B. and Pearson, M., *The Secret Invaders: Combined Operations Pilotage Parties in World War II* (Hodder & Stoughton, 1958).

Stuart, G., *Kind Hearted Tiger* (Boston: Little and Brown, 1964).

Sweet-Escott, B., *Baker Street Irregular* (Methuen, 1965).

Taylor, E., *Richer by Asia* (New York: Houghton Mifflin, 1948).

   Awakening From History (Boston: Gambit, 1969).

Te Kang Tang and Li Tsung Jen, *The Memoirs of Li Tsung Jen* (Boulder: Westview, 1979).

Thakin Nu, *Burma Under the Japanese* (Macmillan, 1954).

Tharp, R., *They Called Us White Chinese* (Charlotte, NC: Tharp, 1994).

Thompson, R., *Make for the Hills: Memoirs of Far Eastern Wars* (Leo Cooper, 1989).

Tinker, H. (ed.), *Burma: The Struggle for Independence, 1944–1948*, Vols. I–II (HMSO, 1983–5).

Tota, I., *Japan Must Fight Britain* (New York: Telpress, 1936).

Troy, T. F. (ed.), *Wartime Washington: The Secret OSS Journal of James Grafton*

Rodgers, 1942–1943 (Frederick, MD: University Publications of America, 1987).

van der Poel, J. (ed.), *Selections from the Smuts Papers*, Vol. VI (Cambridge: Cambridge University Press, 1973).

Van Der Post, L., *The Night of the New Moon* (Hogarth, 1960).

Van Der Rhoer, E., *Deadly Magic: A Personal Account of Communications Intelligence in World War II in the Pacific* (New York: Scribner's, 1978).

Wheeler-Bennett, J., *Special Relationships: America in Peace and War* (Macmillan, 1975).

Williamson, Sir Horace, *India and Communism* (Delhi: Government of India, 1935).

Winterbotham, F. W., *The Ultra Secret* (Weidenfeld and Nicolson, 1974).

Young, K., *The Diaries of Sir Robert Bruce Lockhart, 1919–1965*, Vol. II (Macmillan, 1980).

Ziegler, P. (ed.), *Personal Diary of Admiral Lord Louis Mountbatten: Supreme Commander South East Asia, 1943–1946* (Collins, 1988).

SECONDARY WORKS: BOOKS AND THESES

Aldrich, R. J., *The Key to the South: Britain, the United States and Thailand During the Approach of the Pacific War, 1929–42* (Kuala Lumpur: Oxford University Press, 1993).

(ed.), *British Intelligence, Strategy and the Cold War, 1945–51* (Routledge, 1992).

(ed.), *Espionage, Security and Intelligence in Britain, 1945–1970: Documents in Contemporary History* (Manchester: Manchester University Press, 1998).

Aldrich, R. J. and Hopkins, M. F. (eds.), *Intelligence, Defence and Diplomacy: British Policy in the Post War World* (Frank Cass, 1994).

Alexander, M. (ed.), *Knowing Your Friends: Intelligence Inside Alliances from 1914 to the Cold War* (Frank Cass, 1998).

Allen, L., *Singapore, 1941–1942* (Hart-Davis, 1977).

The End of the War in Asia (Hart Davis McGibbon, 1976).

Anderson, T. H., *The United States, Great Britain and the Cold War, 1944–47* (Columbia: University of Missouri Press, 1981).

Andrew, C. M., *Secret Service: The Making of the British Intelligence Community* (Heinemann, 1985).

For the President's Eyes Only: Secret Intelligence and the American Presidency from Washington to Bush (HarperCollins, 1996).

Andrew, C. M., and Dilks, D. N. (eds.), *The Missing Dimension: Governments and Intelligence Communities in the Twentieth Century* (Macmillan, 1984).

Andrew, C. M., and Gordievsky, O., *KGB: The Inside Story* (Hodder & Stoughton, 1991).

Andrew, C. M., and Noakes, J. (eds.), *Intelligence and International Relations, 1900–1945* (Exeter: Exeter University Press, 1987).

Bagby, W. M. *The Eagle–Dragon Alliance: American Relations with China in World War II* (Newark: University of Delaware Press, 1991).

Bamford, J., *The Puzzle Palace: America's National Security Agency and Its Special Relationship with GCHQ* (Sidgwick and Jackson, 1983).

Barker, R., *One Man's Jungle: A Biography of F. Spencer Chapman* (Chatto and Windus, 1975).

Barrett, D., *Dixie Mission: The United States Army Observer Group in Yenan* (Berkeley, CA: Center for Chinese Studies).

Baxter, C. E., 'Britain and the War in China, 1937–45', PhD thesis, University of Wales, Aberystwyth, 1993.

Beesly, P., *Room 40: British Naval Intelligence 1914–18* (Hamish Hamilton, 1982).

Bell, S. W. 'British Political Warfare, 1939–1945', PhD thesis, University of Leeds, 1998.

Ben-Moshe, T., *Churchill, Strategy and History* (Boulder: Lynee Reinner, 1992).

Bennett, R., *Behind the Battle: Intelligence in the War with Germany* (Sinclair Stevenson, 1994).

Benson, R. L., *A History of U.S. Communications Intelligence during World War II: Policy and Administration*, US Cryptologic History, Series 4, World War II, no. 8 (Fort Meade: National Security Agency, 1997).

Best, A., *Britain, Japan and Pearl Harbor: Avoiding War in East Asia, 1936–41* (Routledge, 1995).

Betts, R. K., *Surprise Attack: Lessons for Defence Planning* (Washington: Brookings Institute, 1982).

Bills, S. L., *Empire and Cold War: The Roots of US–Third World Antagonism, 1945–7* (Macmillan, 1990).

Blake, R. and Louis W.R. (eds.), *Churchill* (Oxford: Oxford University Press, 1993).

Blumenthal, H., *Illusion and Reality in Franco-American Diplomacy, 1914–1945* (Louisiana: Louisiana State University Press, 1986).

Boyd, C., *Hitler's Japanese Confidant: General Oshima Hiroshi and MAGIC Intelligence, 1941–5* (Kansas: University of Kansas Press, 1993).

Brailey, N., *Thailand and the Fall of Singapore: A Frustrated Asian Revolution* (Boulder: Westview Press, 1986).

Breur, W. B., *MacArthur's Undercover War* (New York: Wiley Inc, 1995).

Brewer, S. A., *To Win the Peace: British propaganda in the United States during the World War II* (Ithaca: Cornell University Press, 1991).

Brinkley, D. and Facey-Crowther, D.R. (eds.), *The Atlantic Charter* (Macmillan, 1994).

Brown, M. and Zasloff, J. J., *Apprentice Revolutionaries: The Communist Movement in Laos, 1930–1985* (Stanford: Hoover Institution Press, 1986).

Buck, P., *Asia and Democracy* (Macmillan, 1943).

Buell, T. B., *Master of Sea Power: A Biography of Fleet Admiral Ernest J. King* (Boston: Little and Brown, 1980).

Bull, H. and Louis, W. R. (eds.), *The Special Relationship* (Oxford: Oxford University Press, 1986).

Burlingame, R., *Don't Let Them Scare You: The Life and Times of Elmer Davis* (Connecticut: Greenwood, 1961).

Butler, J. R. M., *Grand Strategy*, Vol. III, Part 2 (HMSO, 1964).

Butow, R. J. C., *Tojo and the Coming of the War* (New Jersey: Princeton University Press, 1961).

Cain, P. J. and Hopkins, A. G., *British Imperialism: Crisis and Deconstruction* (Longmans, 1993).

Callahan, R. A., *Churchill: Retreat from Empire* (Wilmington: Scholarly Resources, 1984).

Carter, C. J., *Mission to Yenan: American Liaison with the Chinese Communists, 1944–1947* (Kentucky: The University Press of Kentucky, 1997).

Cave Brown, A., *The Last Hero: Wild Bill Donovan* (New York: Times Books, 1982).

'*C*': *The Secret Life of Sir Stewart Graham Menzies* (NY: Macmillan, 1987).

Chalou, G. C. (ed.), *The Secrets War: The Office of Strategic Services in World War II* (Washington, DC: National Archives and Records Administration, 1992).

Charivat Santaputra, *Thai Foreign Policy, 1932–1946* (Bangkok: Social Science Association of Thailand, 1987).

Charmley, J., *Churchill's Grand Alliance: The Anglo-American Special Relationship, 1940–1957* (New York: Harcourt Brace and Company, 1995).

Chonchirdsin, S., 'The Indochinese Communist Party in Cochin China (1936–1940)', Ph.D thesis, University of London, 1995.

Clausen, H. C., and Lee, B., *Pearl Harbor: Final Judgement.*

Clayton, A., *Forearmed: A History of the Intelligence Corps* (Brassey's, 1993).

Cloake, J., *Templer: Tiger of Malaya* (Harrap, 1985).

Colvin, J., *No Ordinary Heroes* (Brassey's, 1995).

Coox, A. D., *Nomohan: Japan Against Russia, 1939*, 2 vols. (Stanford: Stanford University Press, 1985).

Costello, J., *The Pacific War, 1941–1945* (New York: Quill, 1981).

Ten Days to Destiny: The Secret Story of the Hess Peace Initiative and British Efforts to strike a Deal with Hitler (NY: William Morrow, 1991).

Days of Infamy: MacArthur, Roosevelt, Churchill – The Shocking Truth Revealed (New York: Pocket Books, 1994).

Cruickshank, C., *SOE in the Far East: The Official History* (Oxford: Oxford University Press, 1983).

Cull, N. J., *Selling War: The British Propaganda Campaign Against American 'Neutrality' in World War II* (NY: Oxford UP, 1995).

Dallek, R., *Franklin D. Roosevelt and American Foreign Policy, 1932–1945* (New York: Oxford University Press, 1979).

Danchev, A., *Very Special Relationship: Field Marshal Dill and the Anglo-American Alliance, 1941–44* (Brassey's, 1986).

Davies, P., *Dragon by the Tail: American, British, Japanese and Russian Encounters with China and One Another* (New York: W. W. Norton, 1972).

Davies, P. J., *The British Secret Services: A Bibliography* (Oxford: Clio Press, 1996).

Davis, D. H., *Peter Fleming* (Cape, 1974).

Day, D., *Reluctant Nation: Australia and the Allied Defeat of Japan, 1942–5* (New York: Oxford University Press, 1992).

Dennis, P., *Troubled Days of Peace: Mountbatten and South East Asia, 1945–6* (Manchester: Manchester University Press, 1987).

Dimbleby, D. and Reynolds, D., *An Ocean Apart: The Relationship Between Britain and America in the Twentieth Century* (Hodder & Stoughton, 1988).

Dockrill, S. (ed.), *From Pearl Harbor to Hiroshima: The Second World War in Asia, 1941–5* (Macmillan, 1993).

Donnison, F. S., *British Military Administration in the Far East, 1943–1946* (HMSO, 1956).

Dorwart, J., *Conflict of Duty: US Naval Intelligence, 1919–41* (Annapolis: Naval Institute Press, 1987).
Drachman, E. R., *United States Policy Towards Vietnam, 1940–1945* (Rutherford: Fairleigh Dickinson UP, 1970).
Drea, E. J., *MacArthur's ULTRA* (Kansas: Kansas University Press, 1992).
Dunlop, R., *Donovan, America's Master Spy* (Chicago: Rand McNally, 1982).
Dunn, P. M., *The First Vietnam War* (Hurst, 1985).
Edwards, D. A., *Spy Catchers of the US Army in the War Against Japan* (Gig Harbor, WA: Red Apple Publishing, 1994).
Elphick, P., *Singapore: The Pregnable Fortress* (Hodder & Stoughton, 1995).
  Far Eastern File: The Intelligence War in the Far East, 1930–45 (Hodder and Stoughton, 1997).
Elphick, P. and Smith, M. *Odd Man Out: The Story of the Singapore Traitor* (Hodder & Stoughton, 1993).
Erickson, J. and Dilks, D. (eds.), *Barbarossa: The Axis and the Allies* (Edinburgh: Edinburgh University Press, 1994).
Fay, P. W., *The Forgotten Army: India's Armed Struggle for Independence, 1942–45* (Ann Arbor: University of Michigan Press, 1994).
Fenn, C., *Ho Chi Minh: A Biographical Introduction* (New York: Scribner's, 1973).
Fineman, D., *A Special Relationship: The United States and Military Government in Thailand, 1947–1958* (Honolulu: University of Hawai'i Press, 1997).
Fitzgerald, O. P., 'Naval Group China: A Study of Guerrilla Warfare During World War II', MA thesis, Georgetown University, 1968.
Fitzgibbon, C., *Secret Intelligence in the Twentieth Century* (New York: Stein and Day, 1976).
Foot, M. R. D., *SOE in France* (HMSO, 1966).
  Resistance (Eyre Methuen, 1976)
Foot, M. R. D. and Langley, J. M., *MI-9: The British Secret Service that Fostered Escape and Evasion 1939 1945 and its American Counterpart* (Boston: Little, Brown, 1979).
Ford, C., *Donovan of OSS* (Boston: Little, Brown, 1970).
Frankel, J., *British Foreign Policy, 1945–1973* (Oxford: Oxford University Press/ RIIA, 1975).
French, P., *Liberty or Death: India's Journey to Independence and Division* (HarperCollins, 1997).
Gilbert, M., *Road to Victory: Winston S. Churchill, 1941–1945* (Heinemann, 1986).
Gilmore, A. B., 'In the Wake of Winning Arms: Allied Psychological Warfare Against the Imperial Japanese Army in the South West Pacific Area During World War II', PhD thesis, Ohio State University, 1989.
Goodman, G. K., *Japanese Cultural Policies in Southeast Asia During World War II* (Macmillan, 1991).
Gordon, L. A., *Brothers against the Raj: A Biography of Indian Nationalists, Sarat and Subhas Chandra Bose* (New York, Viking, 1990).
Gough, R., *SOE Singapore, 1941–1942* (William Kimber, 1985).
Gunn, G. C., *Political Struggles in Laos (1930–1954)* (Bangkok: Editions Duang Kamol, 1988).
J. Hamilton-Merritt, *Tragic Mountains: The Hmong, the Americans and the Secret War for Laos, 1942–92* (Indiana: Indiana University Press, 1993).

Handel, M., *War, Strategy and Intelligence* (Frank Cass, 1989).

Hart-Davis, D., *Peter Fleming – A Biography* (Cape, 1981).

Haseman, J. B., *The Thai Resistance Movement during the Second World War* (Illinois: Northern Illinois Center for South East Asian Studies, 1979).

Hathaway, R. M., *Ambiguous Partnership: Britain and America, 1944–7* (New York: Columbia University Press, 1981).

Hauner, M., *India in Axis Strategy: Germany, Japan and Indian Nationalists in the Second World War* (Stuttgart: Klett-Cotta, 1981).

Hazelton, C. S. R, 'Soviet Foreign Policy during the initial phase of the war with Germany, June-December 1941', Ph.D, LSE, 1989.

Heclo, H. and Wildavsky, A., *The Private Government of Public Money: Community and Policy inside Britain* (Macmillan, 1981).

Heinrichs, W., *Threshold of War: Franklin D. Roosevelt and American Entry into World War II* (New York: Oxford University Press, 1988).

Herman, M., *Intelligence Power in Peace and War* (Cambridge: Cambridge University Press, 1996).

Hess, G. R., *America Encounters India* (Baltimore, MD: Johns Hopkins, 1971).

Hicks, N. 'Tension at the High Table and Operational Politics: British, French and American Relations over Indochina, 1942–45', MA thesis, University of Nottingham, 1997.

Hinsley, F. H., Thomas, E. E., Ransom, C. F. G. and Knight, R. C., *British Intelligence in the Second World War*, Vols. I–III (HMSO, 1979–83).

Hinsley F. H. and Stripp, A. (eds.), *Codebreakers: The Inside Story of Bletchley Park* (Oxford: Oxford University Press, 1993).

Horner, D.M., *High Command: Australia and Allied Strategy, 1939–1945* (Sydney, 1982).

Howard, M., *Grand Strategy*, Vol. IV, (HMSO, 1974).

  British Intelligence in the Second World War: Strategic Deception, Vol. V (HMSO, 1990).

Ienaga, S., *Japan's Last War* (New York: Pantheon 1979).

Iriye, A., *The Origins of the Second World War in Asia and the Pacific Region* (Longman, 1989).

Israel, F., *The War Diary of Breckinridge Long: Selections from the Years 1939–1944* (Lincoln, NE: Nebraska University Press, 1996).

Jackson, R., *The Secret Squadrons* (Robson Books, 1983).

Jakub, J., *Spies and Saboteurs: Anglo-American Collaboration and Rivalry in Human Intelligence Collection and Special Operations, 1940–45* (Macmillan, 1999).

Jeffrey, A. *This Present Emergency: Edinburgh, the River Forth and South East Scotland and the Second World War* (Edinburgh: Mainstream, 1992).

Jeffrey, R., *Asia: The Winning of Independence* (Macmillan, 1981).

Jeffreys-Jones, R., *American Espionage: From Secret Service to the CIA* (New York: Free Press, 1977).

  (ed.), *Eagle and Empire: American Opposition to European Imperialism, 1914–82* (Aix en Provenance: Dupuis, 1983).

  The CIA and American Democracy (New Haven: Yale, 1991).

Jeffreys-Jones, R. and Lownie, A., *North American Spies: New Revisionist Essays* (Edinburgh: Edinburgh University Press, 1991).

Jensen, J. M., *Army Surveillance in America, 1775–1980* (New Haven: Yale University Press, 1980).

Jones, M. C., 'Anglo-American Relations in the Mediterranean Theatre of Operations', PhD thesis, University of Oxford, 1992.

Kahn, D., *The Codebreakers* (New York: Scribner, 2nd edn, 1996).

Kam, E., *Surprise Attack: The Victim's Perspective* (Cambridge, MA: Harvard University Press, 1977).

Katz, B. M., *Foreign Intelligence: Research and Analysis on the Office of Strategic Services, 1942–1945* (Cambridge, MA: Harvard University Press, 1989).

Cheah Boon Keng, *Red Star Over Malaya: Resistance and Social Conflict During and After the Japanese Occupation, 1941–6* (Singapore: Singapore University Press, 1987).

Kirby, S. W., *The War Against Japan*, Vols. I–V (HMSO, 1959–69).

Singapore: The Chain of Disaster (Cassell, 1971).

Kolko, G., *The Roots of American Foreign Policy: Of Power and Purpose* (Boston: Beacon, 1969).

Komatsu, Keiichiro, 'Misunderstanding and Mistranslation in the Origins of the Pacific War of 1941–45: The Important of "Magic"', PhD thesis, University of Oxford, 1994.

Kratsuoka, P. H., *The Japanese Occupation of Malaya, 1941–45* (Hurst, 1997).

Lacoutre, J., *Ho Chi Minh* (New York: Random House, 1968).

Lamb, R., *Churchill as War Leader: Right or Wrong?* (Bloomsbury, 1991).

Lane, A. and Temperley, H. (eds.), *The Rise and Fall of the Grand Alliance, 1941–45* (Macmillan, 1995).

Lash, J. P., *Roosevelt and Churchill, 1939–41* (Andre Deutsch, 1977).

Lebra, J. C., *Chandra Bose to Nihon* (Tokyo, 1968).

Japanese-Trained Armies in Southeast Asia: Independence and Volunteer Forces in World War II (NY: Columbia University Press, 1977).

Jungle Alliance: Japan and the Indian National Army (Singapore: Asia Pacific Press, 1971).

Leutze, J. (ed.), *A Different Kind of War* (Annapolis, Naval Institute Press, 1981).

Lewin, R., *Slim: The Standardbearer* (London, 1976).

Ultra Goes to War: The Secret Story (Hutchinson, 1978).

The Other Ultra: Codes, Cyphers and the Defeat of Japan (Hutchinson, 1982).

Lewis, J., *Changing Direction: British Military Planning for Post-War Strategic Defence, 1942– 7* (Sherwood Press, 1988).

Liddell Hart, B. H., *Defence of the West* (Cassell, 1950).

Lohbeck, D., *Patrick J. Hurley* (Chicago: Henry Regnery, 1956).

Louis, W. R., *Imperialism at Bay: The United States and the Decolonisation of the British Empire, 1941–1945* (Oxford: Clarendon Press, 1977).

In the Name of God Go! Leo Amery and the British Empire in the Age of Churchill (New York: Norton, 1992).

The British Empire in the Middle East: Arab Nationalism, the United States and Post-War Imperialism (Oxford: Oxford University Press, 1984).

Low, D. A., *Lion Rampant: Essays in the Study of British Imperialism* (Frank Cass, 1973).

Eclipse of Empire (Cambridge: Cambridge University Press, 1991).

Britain and Indian Nationalism: Imprint of Ambiguity, 1929–42 (Cambridge: Cambridge University Press, 1997).

Lowe, P., *Great Britain and the Origins of the Pacific War* (Oxford: Clarendon Press, 1977).

Britain in the Far East: A Survey from 1819 to the Present (Longman, 1981).

Lunt, J., *A Hell of a Licking* (Collins, 1986).

McCoy, A. W., *South East Asia Under Japanese Occupation* (New Haven: Yale University Press, 1980).

MacDonald, F., *Insidious Foes: The Axis Fifth Column and the American Home Front* (New York: Oxford University Press, 1996).

Mcenery, J. H., *Epilogue in Burma: The Military Dimension of the British Withdrawal* (Tunbridge Wells: Spellmount, 1990).

McLane, R., *Soviet Strategies in Southeast Asia* (Princeton: Princeton University Press, 1966).

MacLaren, R., *Canadians Behind Enemy Lines, 1939–1945* (Vancouver: University of British Columbia Press, 1981).

MacMahon, R. J., *Cold War on the Periphery: The United States, India and Pakistan* (Columbia: Columbia University Press, 1994).

MacPherson, B. N., 'Kings and Desperate Men: The US Office of Strategic Services in London and the Anglo-American Relationship, 1941–1946', PhD thesis, University of Toronto, 1995.

Maguire, G. E., *Anglo-American Policy Towards the Free French* (Macmillan, 1995).

Mahl, T. E., *Desperate Deception: British Covert Operations in the United States, 1939–44* (Washington: Brassey's, 1998).

Manser, R. L., 'Roosevelt and China: From Cairo to Yalta', PhD thesis, Temple University, 1987.

Marder, A. J., *Old Friends, New Enemies: The Royal Navy and the Imperial Japanese Navy, Volume I, 1919–41* (Oxford: Oxford University Press, 1981).

Old Friends, New Enemies: The Royal Navy and the Imperial Japanese Navy, Volume II, The Pacific War, 1942–1945 (Oxford: Clarendon Press, 1990).

Marks, F.W., *Wind Over Sand: The Diplomacy of Franklin D. Roosevelt* (Athens, GA: University of Georgia Press, 1988).

Marr, D., *Vietnam 1945: The Quest for Power* (Berkeley: University of California Press, 1995).

May, E. (ed.), *Knowing One's Enemies: Intelligence Assessment Before the Two World Wars* (Princeton: Princeton University Press, 1984).

Meo, L. D., *Japan's Radio War on Australia* (Carlton, Victoria: Melbourne University Press, 1968).

Meyer, K. and Parssinen, T., *Webs of Smoke: Smugglers, Warlords, Spies and the History of the International Drug Trade* (Lanham: Rowman and Littlefield, 1998).

Miller, H., *Menace in Malaya* (Harrap, 1954).

Montgomery, H. H., *The Quiet Canadian: The Secret Service Story of Sir William Stephenson* (Hamish Hamilton, 1962).

Moore, R. J., *Churchill, Cripps and India* (Cambridge, 1979).

Muggeridge, M., *Chronicles of Wasted Time, Vol. II, The Infernal Grove* (Collins, 1973).

Munroe, E., *Philby of Arabia* (Pitman, 1973).

Nish, I. (ed.), *The Indonesian Experience: The Role of Japan and Britain, 1943–48* (1979).

Nortien, J. J., *Acties in de Archipel de intelligence-operations van NEFIS III in Pacific oorlog* (Franeker: Wever, 1985).

Ong Chit Chung, 'Operation Matador and the Outbreak of the War in the Far East', Ph.D, University of London, 1985.

Onraet, R., *Singapore: A Police Background* (Crisp, 1946).

Perlmutter, A., *FDR and Stalin: The Not So Grand Alliance, 1943–5* (Kansas: University of Missouri Press, 1993).

Pimlott, B. (ed.), *The Political Diary of Hugh Dalton, 1918–60* (Cape: 1986).

Pointon, A. C., *The Bombay-Burmah Trading Company Limited, 1863–1963* (Wallace Brothers, 1964).

Popplewell, R., *Intelligence and Imperial Defence: British Intelligence and the Defence of the Indian Empire, 1904–1924* (Frank Cass, 1995).

Potter, E. B., *Nimitz* (Annapolis, MD: US Naval Institute Press, 1976).

Powell, A., *War By Stealth: Australians and the Allied Intelligence Bureau* (Melbourne: Melbourne University Press, 1996).

Prados, J., *Combined Fleet Decoded: A Secret History of American Intelligence and the Japanese Fleet in World War II* (New York: Random House, 1995).

Probert, H., *The Forgotten Air Force: A History of the Royal Air Force in the War Against Japan* (Brassey's, 1995).

Ranelagh, J., *The Agency: The Rise and Decline of the CIA* (NY: Simon and Schuster, 1986).

Rees, L., *The Nazis: A Warning from History* (BBC Books, 1998).

Remme, T., *British Policy for Co-operation in South East Asia* (Routledge, 1994).

Reynolds, D., *The Creation of the Anglo-American Alliance, 1937–1941: A Study in Competitive Co-operation* (Europa, 1981).
  Britannia Overruled: British Policy and World Power in the 20th Century (Longman, 1991).

Reynolds, D., Kimball, W.F., and Chubarian, A.O., (eds.) *Allies at War: The Soviet, American and British Experience, 1939–1945* (Macmillan, 1994).

Reynolds, E. B., *Thailand and Japan's Southern Advance, 1940–1945* (New York: St Martin's, 1994).

Richard, D. and Saunders, H. St G., *The Royal Air Force, 1939–1945* (HMSO, 1953–4).

Ride, E., *British Army Aid Group: Hong Kong Resistance, 1942–1945* (Hong Kong: Oxford University Press, 1982).

Rifkind, B. D. 'OSS and Franco-American Relations, 1942–1945', PhD thesis, George Washington University, 1983.

Roberts, A., *Eminent Churchillians* (Weidenfeld and Nicolson, 1994).

Romanus, C. and Sunderland, R., *Time Runs Out in CBI* (Washington, DC: Government Printing Office, 1959).

Rooney, D. *Mad Mike: A Biography of Brigadier Michael Calvert* (Leo Cooper, 1997).

Roskill, S., *Hankey: Man of Secrets*, Vol. III (Collins, 1974).

Rusbridger, J., *The Intelligence Game: Illusions and Delusions of International Espionage* (New York: New Amsterdam Press, 1990).

Rusbridger, J. and Nave, E., *Betrayal at Pearl Harbor: How Churchill Lured Roosevelt into War* (Michael O'Mara, 1991).

Sainsbury, K., *Churchill and Roosevelt at War* (Macmillan, 1994).

Sayer, I. and Botting, D., *America's Secret Army: The Untold Story of the American Counter Intelligence Corps* (Grafton, 1989).

Sbrega, J. J., *Anglo-American Relations and Colonialism in East Asia, 1941–1945* (New York: Garland Publishing, 1983).

Schaller, M., *The U.S. Crusade in China, 1938–1945* (New York: Columbia University Press, 1979).

Seagrave, S., *The Soong Dynasty* (New York: Harper and Row, 1985).

Sherry, N., *The Life of Graham Greene*, Vol. II: *1939–1955* (Cape, 1994).

Shipway, M., 'France's "crise colonial" and the breakdown of policy-making in Indochina, 1944–7', PhD thesis, University of Oxford, 1993.

Short, A. *The Communist Insurrection in Malaya, 1948–1960* (Muller, 1975).
  The Origins of the Vietnam War (Longman, 1989).

Smiley, D., *Irregular Regular* (Michael Russell, 1994).

Smith, B. F., *The Shadow Warriors: OSS and the Origins of the CIA* (Andre Deutsch, 1983).
  The Ultra–Magic Deals and the Most Secret Special Relationship, 1940–1946 (Airlife, 1993).
  Sharing Secrets with Stalin: How the Allies Traded Intelligence (Lawrence: UP of Kansas, 1996).

Smith, M. and Elphick, P., *Odd Man Out: The Story of the Singapore Traitor* (Hodder & Stoughton, 1993).

Smith, R. B. and Stockwell, A. J., *British Policy and the Transfer of Power in Asia* (SOAS, 1988).

Smith, R. H., *OSS: The Secret History of America's First Intelligence Agency* (Berkeley: University of California Press, 1972).

Soley, L. C., *Radio Warfare: OSS and CIA Subversive Propaganda* (New York: Praeger, 1989).

Sparagana, E. A., 'The Conduct and Consequences of Psychological Warfare: Operations in the War Against Japan, 1941–1945', PhD thesis, Brandeis University, 1990.

Spector, R. H., *Advice and Support: The Early Years of the United States Army in Vietnam* (Washington, DC: US Army Center for Military History, 1983).
  (ed.), *Listening to the Enemy: Key Documents on the Role of Communications Intelligence in the War with Japan* (Wilmington, DE: Scholarly Resources, 1988).

Stafford, D., *Britain and the European Resistance, 1940–1945: A Survey of the Special Operations Executive, with Documents* (Macmillan, 1980).
  Camp X: SOE and the American Connection (Viking, 1987).
  Churchill and Secret Service (John Murray, 1997).

Stenton, M., 'British Propaganda and Political warfare, 1940–1944: A Study of British Views on How to Address Europe', PhD thesis, University of Cambridge, 1979.

Stockwell, A., *British Policy and Malaya Politics during the Malayan Union Experiment, 1945–8* (Kuala Lumpur: Royal Asiatic Society, 1979).

Stowe, J. A., *Siam Becomes Thailand: A Story of Intrigue* (Hurst, 1991).

Tanner, R., *A Strong Showing: Britain's Struggle for Power and Influence in South East Asia, 1942–50* (Stuttgart: Franz Steiner Verlag, 1994).

Tarling, N., *British Imperialism in South East Asia* (Singapore: Oxford University Press, 1975).

The Fall of Imperial Britain in South East Asia (Kuala Lumpur: Oxford University Press, 1992).

Britain, Southeast Asia and the Onset of the Pacific War (Cambridge: Cambridge University Press, 1996)

Taylor, E., *The Strategy of Terror: Europe's Inner Front* (Boston: Houghton Mifflin, 1939).

Taylor, R. H., *Marxism and Resistance in Burma* (Ohio: Ohio University Press, 1984).

The State in Burma (Hurst, 1988).

Thomas, M., *The French Empire at War, 1942–5* (Manchester: Manchester University Press, 1998).

Thorne, C., *Allies of a Kind: The United States, Britain and the War against Japan, 1941–1945* (Hamish Hamilton, 1978).

The Issue of War: States, Societies and the Far Eastern Conflict of 1941–1945 (Hamish Hamilton, 1985).

Border Crossings (Oxford: Blackwell, 1988).

Thurlow, R., *Fascism in Britain: A History, 1918–85* (Oxford: Blackwell, 1987).

Tipton, E., *The Japanese Police State: The Tokko in Interwar Japan* (Athlone, 1991).

Toland, J., *But Not in Shame: The Six Months After Pearl Harbor* (New York: Random House, 1981).

Infamy: Pearl Harbor and its Aftermath (New York: Berkeley Books, 1983).

Tonnesson, S., *The Vietnamese Revolution of 1945: Roosevelt, Ho Chi Minh and de Gaulle in a World at War* (Berkeley: Sage, 1991).

Toye, H., *The Springing Tiger. Subhas Chandra Bose – A Study of a Revolutionary* (1959).

Trenowden, I., *Operations Most Secret: SOE in the Malayan Theatre* (William Kimber, 1978).

Troy, T.F., *The Co-ordinator of Information and British Intelligence* (Washington, DC: CIA, 1976).

Donovan and the CIA: A History of the Establishment of the Central Intelligence Agency (Frederick, MD: University Publications of America, 1981).

Wild Bill and Intrepid: Donovan, Stephenson and the Origins of the CIA (New Haven: Yale, 1997).

Truman, H. S., *1945: Year of Decisions* (Hodder & Stoughton, 1953).

Tuchman, B., *Sand Against the Wind: Stilwell and the American Experience of China, 1911–45* (New York: Macmillan, 1971).

US Army, *FECOM, A Brief History of the G–2 Section, SWPA and Affiliated Units*, 10 vols., (Tokyo: FECOM, 1948).

Vadhakarn, Vichir, *Thailand's Case* (Bangkok: Thai Commercial Press).

Van Praagh, D., *Alone on the Sharp Edge: The Story of M. R. Seni Pramoj and Thailand's Struggle for Democracy* (Bangkok: Editions Duang Kamol, 1989).

Viorst, M., *Hostile Allies: F.D.R. and Charles de Gaulle* (New York, 1975).

Wainwright, A. M., *Inheritance of Empire: British India and the Balance of Power, 1938–55* (Westport: Greenwood, 1994).

Wakeman, F., *Policing in Shanghai, 1927–27* (Berkeley: California University Press, 1995).
Wark, W., *The Ultimate Enemy: British Intelligence and Nazi Germany* (Oxford: Oxford University Press, 1986).
Wasserstein, B., *The Secret Lives of Trebitsch Lincoln* (New Haven: Yale UP, 1988; Penguin, 1989).
   Secret War In Shanghai (Profile, 1998)
Watt, D. C., *Succeeding John Bull: America in Britain's Place, 1900–1975* (Cambridge: Cambridge University Press, 1984).
Wedemeyer, A., *Wedemeyer Reports* (New York: Henry Holt, 1958).
Weinberg, G.H., *A World at Arms* (Cambridge: Cambridge University Press, 1994).
Welles, B., *Sumner Welles: FDR's Global Strategist* (Macmillan, 1998).
Whaley, B., *Codeword BARBAROSSA* (Cambridge, MA: The MIT Press, 1973).
Wilkinson, P. and Astley, J. B., *Gubbins and SOE* (Leo Cooper, 1993).
Willmott, H. P., *Empires in the Balance: Japanese and Allied Pacific Strategies to April 1942* (Orbis, 1982).
Winkler, A. M., *The Politics of Propaganda: The Office of War Information, 1942–1945* (New Haven: Yale University Press, 1978).
Winks, R.W., *Cloak and Gown: Scholars in the Secret War, 1939–61* (New York: William Morrow, 1987).
Winton, J., *Ultra in the Pacific* (Leo Cooper, 1993).
Woods, R. B., *The Changing of the Guard: Anglo-American Relations, 1941–6* (Chapel Hill: University of North Carolina Press, 1990).
Woodward, Sir E. L., *British Foreign Policy in the Second World War*, Vols. I–V (HMSO, 1970–6).
Xiaoyuan Liu, *A Partnership for Disorder: China, the United States and Their Policies for the Postwar Disposition of the Japanese Empire, 1941–1945* (New York: Cambridge University Press, 1996).
Young, C. F., and McKennna, R.B., *The KMT Movement in British Malaya, 1912–1949* (Singapore: Singapore University Press, 1990).
Young, J. W., *Winston Churchill's Last Campaign: Britain and the Cold War, 1951–1955* (Oxford: Clarendon Press, 1996).
Maochun Yu, *OSS in China: Prelude to the Cold War* (New Haven: Yale, 1997).
Yu Shen, 'SACO: An Ambivalent Experience of Sino-American Co-operation During World War II', PhD dissertation, 1995, University of Illinois at Urbana Champagne.
Ziegler, P., *Mountbatten* (Collins, 1985).

SECONDARY WORKS: ARTICLES AND PAPERS

Akashi, Y., 'Lai Teck, Secretary General of the Communist Party of Malaya, 1939–1947', *Journal of the South Seas Society*, 49, 1 (1994): 87–95.
Aldrich, R. J., 'A Question of Expediency: Britain, the United States and Thailand, 1941–1942', *Journal of Southeast Asian Studies*, 19, 2 (1988): 209–44.
   'Imperial Rivalry: British and American Intelligence in Asia, 1942–46', *INS*, 3, 1 (1988): 5–55.
   'Unquiet in Death: The Survival of the Special Operations Executive, 1945–51', in

Gorst, A., Jonman, L. and Lucas, W. S. (eds.), *Contemporary British History: Politics and the Limits of Policy* (Pinter, 1991), 193–217.

'Never Never Land and Wonderland? British and American Policy on Intelligence Archives', *Contemporary Record*, 8, 1 (1994): 133–52.

'OSS, CIA and European Unity: The American Committee on United Europe, 1948–60', *Diplomacy and Statecraft*, 8, 1 (1997): 184–227.

'Britain's Secret Intelligence Service in Asia During the Second World War', *Modern Asian Studies*, 32, 1 (1998): 179–217.

Aldrich, R. J. and Coleman, M. 'Britain and the Strategic Air Offensive Against the Soviet Union: The Question of South Asian Airbases', *History*, 242 (1989): 200–46.

Allen, L., 'Japanese Intelligence Systems', *Journal of Contemporary History* 22, (1987): 547–62.

'Burmese Puzzles: Two Deaths that Never Were', *INS*, 5, 1 (1990): 193–9.

'The Escape of Captain Vivian: A Footnote to Burmese Independence', *Journal of Imperial and Commonwealth History*, 19, 1 (1991): 65–70.

Anderson, S., ' "With Friends Like These . . ." The OSS and the British in Yugoslavia', *INS*, 8, 2 (1993): 140–72.

Andrew, C. M., 'The Growth of Intelligence Collaboration in the English Speaking World', *Wilson Center Working Paper*, No 83 (November 1987).

'Churchill and Intelligence', *INS*, 3, 3 (1988): 181–94.

'Intelligence Collaboration between Britain and the United States During The Second World War', in Hitchcock, W. T. (ed.), *The Intelligence Revolution: A Historical Perspective* (Washington, DC: US Air Force Academy, 1991), 111–23.

'The Growth of the Australian Intelligence Community and the Anglo-American Connection', *INS*, 4, 2 (1989): 213–57.

Andrew, C. M., 'The Making of the Anglo-American SIGINT Alliance', in Peake, H. B. and Halperin, S., *In the Name of Intelligence* (Washington, DC: NIBC Press, 1994).

Ball, Desmond J., 'Allied Intelligence Co-operation Involving Australia during World War II', *Australian Outlook*, 32 (1978): 299–309.

Barnett, C., 'Anglo-American Strategy in Europe, 1941–5', in Lane and Temperly, (eds.) *The Rise and Fall of the Grand Alliance*, 174–89.

Best, A., 'Straws in the Wind: Britain and the February 1941 War Scare in East Asia', *Diplomacy and Statecraft*, 5, 3 (1994): 642–64.

'Constructing an Image: British Intelligence and Whitehall's Perception of Japan, 1931–1939', *INS*, 11, 3 (1996): 403–23.

' "This Probably Over-Valued Military Power": British Intelligence and Whitehall's Perception of Japan, 1939–41', *INS*, 12, 3 (1997): 67–94.

Brook, R., 'The London Operation: The British View', in Chalou, *The Secrets War*, 69–77.

Brown, K., 'Intelligence and the Decision to Collect It: Churchill's Diplomatic Signals Intelligence' *INS*, 9, 2 (1994): 273–80.

'The Interplay of Information and Mind in Decision-Making: Signals Intelligence and Franklin D. Roosevelt's Policy-shift on Indochina', *INS*, 13, 1 (1998): 109–31.

Carter, C. J., 'Mission to Yenan: The OSS and the Dixie Mission', in Chalou (ed.), *The Secrets War*, 302–18.

Cecil, R., ' "C"'s War', *INS*, 1, 2 (1986): 170–89.

Chandler, D. P., 'The Kingdom of Kampuchea, March-October 1945: Japanese Sponsored Independence in Cambodia in World War II', *Journal of Southeast Asian Studies*, 17, 1 (1986): 80–93.

Chapman, J. W. M., 'Japanese Intelligence, 1919–1945: A Suitable Case for Treatment', in Andrew and Noakes (eds.), *Intelligence and International Relations*, 145–90.

'Pearl Harbor: The Anglo-Australian Dimension', *INS*, 4, 3 (1989): 451–61.

'Signals Intelligence Collaboration (2)', *Japan Forum*, 3, 2 (1991): 231–56.

'Tricycle Recycled: Collaboration among the Secret Intelligence Services of the Axis States, 1940–41', *INS*, 7, 3 (1992): 268–300.

Clymer, K. J., 'The Education of William Phillips: Self-Determination and American Policy Towards India, 1942–5', *Diplomatic History*, 8, 1 (1984): 13–37.

'Franklin D. Roosevelt, Louis Johnson and Anti-Colonialism: Another Look', *Pacific Historical Review*, 57, 2 (1988): 261–84.

Costello, J., 'MacArthur, Magic, Black Jumbos and the Dogs that Didn't Bark: New Intelligence on the Pearl Harbor Attack', in Peake, H. B., and Halpern, S., *In the Name of Intelligence: Essays in Honor of Walter Pforzheimer* (Washington, DC: NIBC Press, 1995), 197–249.

Croft, J., 'Wartime at Berkeley Street', *INS*, 13, 4 (1998): 133–43.

Darwin, J., 'Imperialism in Decline? Tendencies in British Imperial Policy between the Wars', *Historical Journal*, 23, 3 (1980): 657–79.

'British Decolonization since 1945: Pattern or a Puzzle?', *Journal of Imperial and Commonwealth History*, 12, 2 (1984): 187–210.

De Graff, B. 'Hot Intelligence in the Tropics: Dutch Intelligence Operations in the Netherlands East Indies During the Second World War', *Journal of Contemporary History*, 22, 4 (1987): 563– 84.

Denham, H., 'Bedford–Bletchley–Kilindini–Colombo', in Hinsley and Stripp (eds.), *Codebreakers*, 265–81.

Drea, E. J., 'Reading Each Others Mail: Japanese Communications Intelligence, 1920–1941', *Journal of Military History*, 55, 2 (1991): 185–206.

Duncanson, D., 'Ho Chi Minh in Hong Kong, 1931–2', *The China Quarterly*, 57, 1 (1974): 84–101.

Ephron, H.D., 'An American Cryptanalayst in Australia', *Cryptologia*, 9, 4 (1985): 337–40.

Erskine, R., 'When a Purple Machine went Missing: How the Japanese nearly Discovered America's Greatest Secret', *INS* 12, 3 (1997): 185–89.

'Churchill and the Start of the Ultra–Magic Deals', *Cryptologia*, 10, 1 (1997): 57–73.

'The Holden Agreement on Navel Sigint: The First BRUSA', *INS* 14, 2 (1999): 187–97.

Ferris, J., 'From Broadway House to Bletchley Park: The Diary of Captain Malcolm Kennedy, 1934–46', *INS*, 4, 3 (1989): 421–51.

' "Worthy of Some Better Enemy?" The British Estimate of the Imperial Japanese Army 1919–41, and the Fall of Singapore', *Canadian Journal of History*, 28 (1993): 223–56.

Foot, M. R. D., 'Was SOE Any Good?', *Journal of Contemporary History*, 16, 1 (1981): 167–83.

'OSS and SOE: An Equal Partnership?', in Chalou (ed.), *The Secrets War*, 295–301.

Fraser, C., 'Understanding American Policy Towards the Decolonization of European Empires, 1945–64', *Diplomacy and Statecraft*, 3, 1 (1992): 105–26.

Fraser, T. G., 'India in Anglo-Japanese Relations during the First World War', *History*, 63, 209 (1978): 366–82.

Geyer, M., 'National Socialist Germany: The Politics of Information', in May (ed.), *Knowing Ones Enemies*, 310–17.

Gilchrist, A., 'Diplomacy and Disaster: Thailand and the British Empire in 1941', *Asian Affairs*, 13 (Old Series), 69, 3 (1982): 249–65.

Goldstein, E., 'The British Official Mind and the United States, 1919–42', in Otte, T. G., and Pagedas, C. A., *Personalities, War and Diplomacy: Essay in International History* (Frank Cass, 1998), 66–80.

Goulter-Zervoudakis, C., 'The Politicization of Intelligence: The British Experience in Greece, 1941–1944', *INS*, 13, 1 (1998): 163–91.

Gubbins, C., 'SOE and the Co-ordination of Regular and Irregular Warfare', in Elliott-Bateman, M. (ed.), *The Fourth Dimension of Warfare* (Manchester: Manchester University Press, 1970), 83–111.

Handel, M., 'The Politics of Intelligence', *INS*, 2, 4 (1987): 5–47.

Harrison, E. D. R., 'More Thoughts on Kim Philby's *My Silent War*', *INS*, 10, 3 (July 1995): 514–25.

'British Subversion in French East Africa, 1941–42: SOE's Todd Mission', *English Historical Review*, 114, 456 (1999): 339–70.

Herring, G., 'The Truman Administration and the Restoration of French Sovereignty in French Indochina', *Diplomatic History*, 1, 1 (1977): 97–117.

Hinsley, F. H., 'The Counterfactual History of No ULTRA', *Cryptologia* 20, 4 (1996): 319–27.

Hogan, D. W., 'MacArthur, Stilwell and Special Operations in the War Against Japan', *Parameters*, 25, 1 (1995): 104–15.

Holquist, P., 'Information is the Alpha and Omega of our Work: Bolshevik Surveillance in its Pan-European context', *Journal of Modern History*, 69, 3 (1997): 415–50.

Horner, D. M., 'Special Intelligence in the South-West Pacific Area in World War II', *Australian Outlook*, 32 (1978): 310–37.

Kahin, McT. G., 'The United States and the Anti-Colonial Revolutions in South East Asia', in Yonosuke Nagai and Akira Iriye (eds.), *Origins of the Cold War in Asia* (New York: Columbia University Press, 1977), 338–59.

Kahn, D., 'The Intelligence Failure of Pearl Harbor', *Foreign Affairs*, 70, 5 (1991/2): 142–52.

'Pearl Harbor and the Inadequacy of Cryptanalysis', *Cryptologia* 15, 4 (1991): 285.

Kamon Pensrinokun, 'Adaption and Appeasement: Thai Relations with the Allies and Japan in World War II', in Chaiwat Kamchoo and E. B. Reynolds (eds.), *Thai–Japanese Relations in Historical Perspective* (Bangkok: Innomedia, 1988), 125–59.

Kitchen, M., 'SOE's Man in Moscow', *INS*, 12, 3 (1997): 95–109.

Kruh, L., 'British-American Cryptanalaytic Co-operation and an Unprecedented Admission by Winston Churchill', *Cryptologia*, 13, 2 (1989): 123–34.

La Feber, W., 'Roosevelt, Churchill and Indochina', *American Historical Review*, 80, 4 (1975): 1277–95.

Litten, F. S., 'The Noulens Affair', *The China Quarterly*, 138 (1994): 492–512.

Loewe, M., 'Japanese Naval Codes', in Hinsley and Stripp (eds.), *Codebreakers*, 257–63.

Louis, W. R., 'American Anti-colonialism and the Dissolution of the British Empire', *International Affairs*, 61, 3 (1985): 395–420.

Lowe, P., 'Great Britain's Assessment of Japan Before the Outbreak of the Pacific War' in May (ed.), *Knowing One's Enemies*, 456–75.

McMahon, R.J., 'Anglo-American Diplomacy and the reoccupation of the Netherlands East Indies', *Diplomatic History*, 2, 1 (1978): 1–24.

Mahnken, T. G., 'Gazing at the Sun: The Office of Naval Intelligence and Japanese Naval Innovation, 1918–1941', *INS*, 11, 3 (1996): 424–41.

Miles, M., 'U.S. Naval Group China', *US Naval Institute Proceedings*, 72 (1946): 921

Naftali, T., 'Intrepid's Last Deception: Documenting the Career of Sir William Stephenson', *INS*, 8, 3 (1993): 72–100.

Newsinger, J., 'A Forgotten War: British Intervention in Indonesia, 1945–46', *Race and Class*, 30, 1 (1989): 51–66.

Nicholas, S., '"Partners Now": Problems in the Portrayal by the BBC of the Soviet Union and the USA, 1939–45', *Diplomacy and Statecraft*, 3, 2 (1992): 243–72.

Parker, F. D., 'The Unsolved Messages of Pearl Harbor', *Cryptologia*, 15, 4 (1991): 295–313.

Pinck, D., 'Getting to Mrs Nestor's Farm: A Secret Agent in Wartime China', *Encounter*, 71, 2 (1988): 15–21.

Reid, B. H., 'Tensions in the Supreme Command: Anti-Americanism in the British Army, 1939–45', in Reid, B. H. and White, J. (eds.), *American Studies* (Macmillan, 1991), 270–97.

Reynolds, D., 'Competitive Co-operation: Anglo-American Relations in World War II', *Historical Journal*, 23 (1980): 233–45.

'A "Special Relationship"? America, Britain and the International Order since 1945', *International Affairs* 62, 1 (1985/6): 1–20.

'Roosevelt, Churchill and the Anglo-American Alliance, 1939–1945: Towards a New Synthesis', in Louis W. R. and Bull, H. (eds.), *The Special Relationship: Anglo-American Relations Since 1945* (Oxford: Clarendon Press, 1986), 17–43.

'Re-thinking Anglo-American Relations', *International Affairs*, 65, 1 (1989).

Reynolds, E. B., 'Aftermath of Alliance: The Wartime Legacy in Thai-Japanese Relations', *Journal of Southeast Asian Studies*, 21, 1 (1990): 66–88.

'The Opening Wedge: The OSS in Thailand', in Chalou (ed.), *The Secrets War*, 328–53.

'"International Orphans" – The Chinese in Thailand During World War II', *Journal of Southeast Asian Studies*, 28, 2 (1987): 365–88.

Rusbridger, J., 'The Sinking of the Automedon and the Capture of the Nankin', *Encounter*, 64, 5 (May 1985): 8–15.

Sbrega, J., 'Anglo-American Relations and the Selection of Mountbatten as Supreme Allied Commander in South East Asia', *Military Affairs*, 46 (1982): 139–45.

'"First Catch Your Hare"': Anglo-American Perspectives on Indochina during the Second World War', *Journal of Southeast Asian Studies*, 16, 2 (1985): 63–78.

'The Anti-Colonial Policies of FDR: A Reappraisal', *Political Science Quarterly*, 65 (1986): 64–84.

Schaller, M., 'SACO!: The U.S. Navy's Secret War in China', *Pacific Historical Review*, 44, 4 (1975): 527–53.

Schlesinger, S., 'Cryptanalysis for Peacetime and the Birth of the Structure of the United Nations', *Cryptologia*, 19, 2 (1995): 217–35.

Selth, A., 'Race and Resistance in Burma, 1942–1945', *Modern Asian Studies*, 20, 3 (1986): 483–507.

Shi An-li, 'Britain's China Policy and the Communists, 1942–46 – The Role of Ambassador Sir Horace Seymour', *Modern Asian Studies*, 261, (1992): 46–65.

Sissons, D. C. S., 'More on Betrayal at Pearl Harbor', *INS*, 10, 3 (1994): 449–68.

Smith, B. F., 'Admiral Godfrey's Mission to America, June/July 1941', *INS*, 1, 3 (1986): 441–50.

'A Note on the OSS, Ultra and World War II's Intelligence Legacy for America', *Defense Analysis*, 3, 2 (1987) 184–9.

'Sharing Ultra in World War II', *International Journal of Intelligence and Counter-Intelligence*, 2, 1 (1988): 59–72.

Smith, R. B., 'The Japanese Period in Indochina and the Coup d'etat of 9 March 1945', *Journal of Southeast Asian Studies*, 9, 2 (1978): 268–302.

'The Work of the Provisional Government of Vietnam, August–December 1945', *Modern Asian Studies*, 12, 4 (1978): 571–609.

Spector, R. H., 'Allied Intelligence in Indochina, 1943–1945', *Pacific Historical Review*, 51, 1 (1982): 23–50.

Stafford, D., 'Intrepid: Myth and Reality', *Journal of Contemporary History*, 22, 2 (1987), 304–16.

Steiner, Z., 'Deception and its Dividends', *Times Literary Supplement*, 7–13 December 1990, p. 1310.

Stockwell, A. J., 'Colonial Planning During the Second World War: The Case of Malaya', *Journal of Imperial and Commonwealth History*, 2, 3 (1974), 333–51.

Stoler, M. A., 'The "Pacific-First" Alternative in American World War II Strategy', *International History Review*, 2, 2 (1980): 432–52.

'Half a Century of Conflict: Interpretations of US World War II Diplomacy', *Diplomatic History* 13, 3 (1994): 375–403.

Stratton, R., 'Navy Guerrillas', *US Naval Institute Proceedings*, 89 (July 1963): 85.

Stripp, A. J., 'Breaking Japanese Codes', *INS*, 2, 4 (1987): 135–50.

'Japanese Army Air Force Codes at Bletchley Park and Delhi', in Hinsley and Stripp (eds.), *Codebreakers*, 288–99.

Tarling, N., 'Atonement before Absolution: British Policy towards Thailand during World War II', *Journal of the Siam Society*, 66, 1, (1978): 22–65.

'Rice and Reconciliation: The Anglo-Thai Peace Negotiations of 1945', *Journal of the Siam Society*, 66, 2 (1978): 59–112.

Taylor, T., 'Anglo-American Signals Intelligence Co-operation', in Hinsley and Stripp (eds.), *Codebreakers*, 71–3.

Thomas, E. E., 'The Evolution of the JIC System up to and During World War II', in Andrew and Noakes (eds.), *Intelligence and International Relations*, 219–34.

Thomas, M., 'The Massingham Mission: SOE in French North Africa, 1941–1944', *INS*, 11, 4 (1996): 696–721.

'Free France, the British Government and the Future of French Indo-China, 1940–45', *Journal of Southeast Asian Studies*, 28, 1 (1997): 137–60.

'Silent Partners: SOE's French Indo-China Section, 1943–1945', forthcoming *Modern Asian Studies*.

Thorne, C., 'The Indochina Issue between Britain and the United States, 1942–1945', *Pacific Historical Review*, 95, 1 (1976): 73–96.

'MacArthur, Australia and the British, 1942–3: The Secret Journal of MacArthur's British Liaison Officer, Part One', *Australian Outlook*, 29, 1 (1975): 53–67.

'MacArthur, Australia and the British, 1942–3: The Secret Journal of MacArthur's British Liaison Officer, Part Two', *Australian Outlook*, 29, 2 (1975): 197–210.

'American Political Culture and the End of the Cold War', *Journal of American Studies* 26, 4 (1992): 303–31.

Tolstoi, I., 'Across Tibet from India to China', *National Geographic Magazine*, (August 1946): 169–222.

Tonnesson, S., 'Did FDR Provoke the Japanese Coup of March 1945 in French Indochina? Paving the Way for Ho Chi Minh', unpublished paper to the SHAFR Conference, Hyde Park, New York, June 1992.

Troy, T. F., 'Knifing of the OSS', *International Journal of Intelligence and Counter-Intelligence*, 1, 2 (1986): 95–108.

'The British Assault on J. Edgar Hoover: The Tricyle Case', *International Journal of Intelligence and Counter-Intelligence*, 3, 2 (1989): 169–209.

Valmy [pseud.], 'Parachutistes et Partisans dans la Brousse Laotienne', *Indochine-Française*, 28, (1947): 24–9.

Walsh, B. K., 'The German Military Mission in China, 1928–1938', *Journal of Modern History*, 46, 4 (1974): 502–31.

Ward, J. R., 'The Activities of Detachment 101 of the OSS', in Chalou (ed.), *The Secrets War*, 318–28.

Wark, W. K., 'In Search of a Suitable Japan: British Naval Intelligence in the Pacific Before the Second World War', *INS*, 1, 2 (1986): 189–212.

'Great Investigations: The Public Debate on Intelligence in the United States after 1945', *Defense Analysis* 3, 2 (1987): 119–32.

'In Never Never Land? The British Archives on Intelligence', *Historical Journal*, 35, 1 (1992): 196–203.

Wen-Hsin Yeh, 'Dai Li and the Liu Geying Affair: Heroism in the Chinese Secret Service During the War of Resistance', *Journal of Asian Studies*, 48, 3 (1989): 545–63.

Westerfield, H. B., 'America and the World of Intelligence Liaison', *INS* 11, 3 (1996): 523–60.

Wiebes, C. and Zeeman, B., 'United States Big Stick Diplomacy: The Netherlands Between Decolonisation and Alignment, 1945–9', *International History Review*, 14, 1 (1992): 47–51.

Wiles, M., 'Japanese military codes', in Hinsley and Stripp (eds.) *Codebreakers*, 283–305.

Willoughby, C. A., 'Intelligence at War: A Brief History of MacArthur's Intelligence Service, 1941–51', in Willoughby, C. A. (ed.), *The Guerrilla Resistance Movement in the Philippines* (NY: Vantage, 1972): 69–82.

Wilson, H., 'The Best of Friends: Britain, America and Thailand, 1945–48', *Canadian Journal of History*, 25, 1 (1990): 61–83.

Wilson, K. M., 'A venture in the "careers of intrigue": the conspiracy against Lord Curzon and his Foreign Policy, 1922–3', *Historical Research*, 70, 173 (1997): 312–31.

Windmiller, M., 'Tumultous Times: OSS and Army Intelligence in India, 1942–1946', *International Journal of Intelligence and Counter-Intelligence*, 8, 1 (1995): 105–24.

Wylie, N., '"Keeping the Swiss Sweet": Intelligence as a Factor In British Policy Towards Switzerland during the Second World War', *INS*, 11, 3 (1996): 442–67.

Maochun Yu, 'OSS in China – New Information About an Old Role', *International Journal of Intelligence and Counter-Intelligence*, 7, 1 (1994): 75–96.

Index